D1536559

The Last Emperors

A

Philip E. Lilienthal

B O O K

_____

*The Philip E. Lilienthal imprint honors
special books in commemoration of a
man whose work at the University of
California Press from 1954 to 1979 was
marked by dedication to young authors
and to high standards in the field of
Asian Studies. Friends, family, authors,
and foundations have together endowed
the Lilienthal Fund, which enables the
Press to publish under this imprint
selected books in a way that reflects the
taste and judgment of a great and
beloved editor.*

The Last Emperors

A Social History
of Qing Imperial Institutions

EVELYN S. RAWSKI

University of California Press

BERKELEY   LOS ANGELES   LONDON

University of California Press
Berkeley and Los Angeles, California

University of California Press, Ltd.
London, England

© 1998 by
The Regents of the University of California

First Paperback Printing 2001

Library of Congress Cataloging-in-Publication Data

Rawski, Evelyn Sakakida.
  The last emperors : a social history of Qing imperial institutions /
Evelyn S. Rawski.
      p.   cm.
  "Philip E. Lilienthal book."
  Includes bibliographic references and index.
  ISBN 0-520-21289-4 (alk. paper)
        0-520-22837-5 (pbk : alk. paper)
  1. China—History—Ch'ing dynasty, 1644–1912.   2. China—
Kings and rulers.   3. China—Court and courtiers.   4. Rites and cere-
monies—China.   5. Political culture—China.   I. Title.   II. Title: So-
cial history of Qing imperial institutions.
DS754.R38   1998
951'.03—DC21   97-38792
                                                                   CIP

Printed in the United States of America

08 07 06 05 04 03 02 01 00
9 8 7 6 5 4 3 2 1

Contents

Illustrations

Photographs follow page 194

Maps

Charts

Tables

Acknowledgments

Since I began the archival research for this book in the spring of 1987, I have incurred many debts of obligation. My first and greatest debt is to the staff of the First Historical Archives, Beijing, whose materials I used in my annual trips to the archives from 1987 to 1991. Xu Yipu, the director of the First Historical Archives, and Qin Guojing graciously permitted me to use the archives. Mrs. Liu and Mrs. Yin Shu-mei were in charge of the foreign scholars' reading room during those years and helped me obtain the documents I needed. I must also express my gratitude to Prof. Wang Hongchang and Zheng Yuxin of the Institute of Quantitative and Technical Economics, Chinese Academy of Social Sciences, for helping me during these research trips.

My first research trip in 1986 was funded in part by a Research Development Fund grant from the University of Pittsburgh. In subsequent years my research was supported by a Fellowship in Chinese Studies from the Joint Committee on Chinese Studies, American Council of Learned Societies, a Guggenheim Fellowship, and a Senior Fellowship from the University Center for International Studies, University of Pittsburgh. I spent a wonderful year writing draft chapters of this book as a fellow at the Woodrow Wilson International Center in Washington, D.C. Research funds granted by the University Center of International Studies, University of Pittsburgh, helped defray my research expenses.

I also want to thank my colleagues who helped me bring this project to publication. The staff of the East Asian Collection at the University of Pittsburgh, especially Lisa Woo, Agnes Wen, and Sachie Noguchi, have gone out of their way to obtain the xeroxes and interlibrary loans of secondary literature that I requested. I have drawn on the advice and technical assistance of Pamela Crossley, Susan Naquin, Thomas Rawski, Jan Stuart,

Rubie Watson, and Woody Watson. In revising this manuscript I profited enormously from the comments of anonymous readers for the University of California Press and Dru Gladney. I am grateful for the professional support of Sheila Levine, senior editor at the University of California Press, and Laura Driussi. As always, I am solely responsible for the errors and flaws that remain.

MAP 1.   The Qing empire, circa 1820.

Introduction

The modern traveler arriving in Beijing today finds a bustling metropolis in which the physical reminders of the city's historic past are rapidly disappearing. Even though the former imperial residence, the Forbidden City, still stands, virtually everything else has changed. The massive city walls have been leveled to the ground to make way for ring roads and expressways. New high-rises have destroyed the numinous atmosphere of the Altar of Heaven, and ordinary citizens and tourists crowd into the formerly sacred precincts of the state altars. The traveler might assume that the citizens of the People's Republic of China have no need to remember the Qing, the last imperial dynasty that ruled this land from 1644 to 1911. But that would be a mistake.

Many geopolitical issues confronting policymakers in the People's Republic of China derive from the Qing heritage. The Qing (1644–1911) was the last and arguably the most successful dynasty to rule China. It was also the last conquest regime. The rulers came from Northeast Asia and claimed descent from the Jurchen, who had ruled part of North China during the Jin dynasty (1115–1260). In the late sixteenth and early seventeenth centuries, a minor tribal chieftain named Nurgaci (1559–1626) successfully united many of the northeastern tribes. His son Hongtaiji (1592–1643) transformed these diverse peoples into a new solidary group, the Manchus. Although he died before the Manchus entered the Ming capital, scholars identify Hongtaiji as the central figure in the creation of the Qing imperial enterprise.[1]

Manchu banner troops swept south of the Great Wall in 1644. After pacifying the Ming territories, they turned to the consolidation of the Inner Asian frontiers. The late seventeenth and early eighteenth centuries saw the fixing of the border with Russia and the incorporation of the Mongolian steppe, the Tibetan plateau, and the Tarim Basin into the Qing empire. The Qing conquests laid the territorial foundations of the modern Chinese nation-state, but Qing policies also created the ethnic problems that accompanied the growth of nationalism. The Qing conceived of themselves as rulers of a pluralistic, multiethnic empire. They regarded the peoples inhabiting the strategic Inner Asian peripheries as major participants in the imperial enterprise, imperial subjects on equal footing with Han Chinese. Peoples speaking a variety of non-Sinitic languages and adhering to Islam, Tibetan Buddhism, and shamanism were encouraged during the eighteenth century to develop and sustain their separate cultures and belief systems. The issue of how these non-Han peoples were to be accommodated within Chinese nationalism remains unresolved today.

This book explores issues of ethnicity and historical interpretation within Qing history from the perspective of the Manchu rulers. It addresses a major theme in modern histories of the dynasty, the early Manchu rulers' adoption of "a policy of systematic sinicization" as the key to their success.[2] What Pamela Crossley calls the "sinicization model" in Chinese history emerged from debate about how the nation was to be defined after the end of the Qing dynasty in 1912. In the late nineteenth century Chinese intellectuals like Liang Qichao, reacting to social Darwinism, introduced the concepts of "race" and "ethnicity" to a Chinese audience. The term *Hanzu*, or "Han ethnic group," entered the Chinese political vocabulary. With its lineage/descent group (*zongzu*) connotations, *Hanzu* enabled Chinese to "imagine" the nation as a "Han lineage."[3]

Hanzu became conflated with race. Some Chinese thinkers argued that the Han dominated the "yellow race," which, like the white race, could claim a distinguished history of cultural achievement. Manchus, Japanese, and Mongols were at best peripheral and, in the opinions of some writers, did not even belong to the same biological group.[4] Sun Yat-sen, who was subsequently identified as the "father of the Chinese Republic," argued that China's inability to resist European and American aggression stemmed from the foreign origins of its rulers, the Manchus. Because they were not Chinese, not members of the Han ethnic group, the Qing lacked the will to wholeheartedly combat Western imperialism. Sun sought to mobilize the Han people to rise up and overthrow the Manchus, to create a Han nation.

Who belonged to the Han *ethnos*? Sun Yat-sen asserted that the *Hanzu* were a "pure biological entity." Despite the historical evidence that many different peoples had lived in China, he asserted that "for the most part, the Chinese people are of the Han or Chinese race with common blood, common language, common religion, and common customs—a single, pure race."[5] The different peoples who invaded or migrated into China had, over the centuries, blended into the Han Chinese population: they became "sinicized" (*hanhua*). This was one of the primary themes developed by Sun after 1912, when he and other nationalist leaders attempted to form a new Chinese nation from the regions that had been part of the Qing empire. Although Sun occasionally spoke about the need to create a new "national people" out of China's many peoples, he also assumed that eventually the minorities would be assimilated into the Han majority.

As Prasenjit Duara notes, "Historical consciousness in modern society has been overwhelmingly framed by the nation-state."[6] The emergence of Chinese nationalism and a discourse focusing on national identity directly affected Chinese historiography. The task that lay before Chinese scholars, according to Liang Qichao, was to discard the dynastic framework of earlier histories and to write a "history of the nation." The depiction of the non-Han conquest regimes that had ruled over the territory of the modern nation ranked high on the nationalist agenda. Writers like Fu Sinian tried in the 1920s to present Chinese history as a history of the Han race. The history of cultural contact among different peoples in the territory of China was rewritten as the triumph of Chinese culture (whatever that might be). Perhaps conquest dynasties had defeated Chinese ruling houses through sheer brute force, but they all succumbed to the more sophisticated Chinese system and ended up being absorbed by Chinese culture.[7]

An influential example of the "sinicization" interpretation as applied to the Qing house is Mary C. Wright's 1957 work, *The Last Stand of Chinese Conservatism* (critiqued by Pamela Crossley). In answering those historians who blamed the Manchus for the imperialist victories in the nineteenth century—an echo of Sun's revolutionary theme—Wright also rejects the argument that conquest dynasties like the Liao and Qing were not sinicized. She points to the erosion of the cultural barriers that separated the conquest elite from the subjugated population to argue that Qing and Chinese interests were "virtually indistinguishable" by the middle of the nineteenth century. The Tongzhi restoration is for her an example of the working out of Chinese Confucian political ideals, and the failure of the reforms, the failure of Confucianism.[8]

Crossley cites several reasons why Wright's assumptions concerning the assimilation of Manchus into Chinese society were mistaken. Even if, as Wright noted, the Manchu homeland was increasingly infiltrated by Chinese immigrants, and bannermen lost many legal privileges during the late Qing, these developments did not destroy the cultural life of the garrisons. Crossley's monograph on the Suwan Gūwalgiya magnificently documents the distinctive identity of this banner family in late Qing and early Republican times. Proof that Manchus were separate, in their own eyes and in the view of the Han Chinese, is found in the mob actions against Manchus during the Taiping rebellion and the 1911 Revolution. Crossley argues that the Manchus had certainly not disappeared into the Chinese *ethnos* or, in light of the antagonism expressed toward them by Han Chinese, thought of themselves as "Chinese." Moreover, twentieth-century Manchus developed a modern ethnic identity in counteropposition to the growth of a Han nationalist identity.

Mary Wright wrote during a period when the rich archival materials of the Qing dynasty were unavailable for scholarly use. Crossley's study of the garrison culture also relied on other kinds of primary sources. My study, which uses archival materials produced by the Imperial Household Department and housed in the First Historical Archives in Beijing, will show that one of Wright's assumptions, which Crossley did not challenge, is also mistaken. Wright assumed that the Tongzhi court was sinicized. For Crossley, "Knowledge of life at the court sheds no light upon the life of the Manchu people in China. . . . The behavior of the Qing emperors was not intended to serve as a model for the bannermen."[9] What the archival materials now available show is that the Qing rulers kept their Manchu identity. An explanation of why this is so requires a further examination of the issue.

The academic use of sinicization has not been very rigorous. Studies of Manchu-language use at court, for example, almost all conclude that the loss of Manchu as the first language of the rulers and the conquest elite implies their absorption into Chinese culture. As Pamela Crossley and I explain elsewhere, historians who ignore the Manchu-language documents that exist throughout the history of the dynasty do so at their peril.[10] The language did not die but remained alive, not only in the capital but in garrisons in Xinjiang and in the northeast (see chapter 1). Bilingual shop signs and lingering shamanic traditions in the northeast prompted one Manchu scholar to conclude, "In this region, Manchu traditions live together with the traditions of the other Minorities and with those of the Han people, in a compact amalgam where it is not always possible to distinguish the separate elements."[11]

More importantly, Manchu identity is not contingent on whether individuals speak Chinese or Manchu as their "native speech." Nineteenth-century Qing rulers seem to have been more comfortable using Chinese, but that did not mean that they ceased to identify themselves as Manchu. Anyone who assumes that Manchu identity was solely a product of the

Manchu language needs to reflect on the comparable situations of English speakers. The fact that American colonists spoke English did not prevent them from creating a separate identity for themselves and declaring independence from Britain. English did not prevent the Indian nationalist elites from using that language to promote self-rule for India. It is absurd to assume that language and identity are always coterminous.[12]

A growing body of secondary literature demonstrates that the issue of the creation and maintenance of primary identities is complex and historically contingent. Ethnicity is a concept that developed fully with the nineteenth-century emergence of the modern nation-state, first in Europe and then elsewhere.[13] As Crossley points out, applying the term to earlier periods is anachronistic and distorts the historical reality. That does not mean that the Qing rulers did not have concepts concerning their own identities and the identities of other peoples, but the political context and the definitions of self were significantly different. The Qing political model was not the nation-state; the goal of the government was not to create one national identity, but to permit diverse cultures to coexist within the loose framework of a personalistic empire. Ethnicity in its modern sense did not exist, nor did the state seek to create it.

Modern ethnicity implies not only the bonds that create a solidary group but also ones that set off that group from other groups. These social boundaries were very fluid in the Jurchen homeland of Northeast Asia, where three different ecosystems the Mongolian plateau, the densely forested *taiga*, and the fertile Liao River plain—came together and brought pastoralists, hunting and fishing peoples, and sedentary agriculturalists in contact with one another. The seventeenth-century Jurchen were agriculturalists whose close cultural interactions with Mongols were revealed in shared vocabulary words, the Jurchen use of Mongolian in both spoken and written form, and the adoption of Mongol names and titles by some of Nurgaci's kinsmen. Pointing to Mongol sources for the banner organization, David Farquhar shows that many Chinese elements in the early Manchu state were actually filtered through the Mongols.[14]

The Manchus incorporated individuals from many different cultural traditions into the banners and tried to remake these people "like Manchus"—governed by the same laws, dress codes, and social rules. Prior identities were subsumed under a new banner identity, at least until the eighteenth century, when the court moved significantly toward defining identity in terms of descent. Even then, the conquest elite remained explicitly multicultural. New Muslim, Tibetan, and Mongol notables who were incorporated into the Qing ruling group in the eighteenth century ensured that there could not be one single ethnic focus or identity for the conquest elite.[15] Similarly, despite a few "xenophobes" like Wang Fuzhi, most Confucian scholars stressed the universal nature of their doctrines; their primary mission was to "transform" (*jiaohua*) or to "civilize" (*wenhua*), without regard to racial or ethnic categories.[16] In both groups, identity was not fixed and unchanging, but rather the opposite.

Moreover, the attitude of Qing rulers toward issues of culture depended very much on the object of their attentions. As individuals, they were intent on preserving their lineage, the Aisin Gioro, and the conquest elite. As rulers, however, they did not espouse policies that would transform or change the cultures of their subjects. Their status as rulers of multiple peoples instead dictated that they patronize and promote the cultures of their subjects and address each of the different constituencies within the realm. Most Qing rulers, until the end of the dynasty, were multilingual: they studied Mongolian, Manchu, and Chinese. Some rulers, like the Qianlong emperor, took the trouble to go further and to learn Tibetan and Uighur. Hongli himself said:

> In 1743 I first practiced Mongolian. In 1760 after I pacified the Muslims, I acquainted myself with Uighur (Huiyu). In 1776 after the two pacifications of the Jinquan [rebels] I became roughly conversant in Tibetan (Fanyu). In QL 45 [Qianlong 45, or 1780] because the Panchen Lama was coming to visit I also studied Tangut (Tangulayu). Thus when the rota of Mongols, Muslims and Tibetans come every year to the capital for audience I use their own languages and do not rely on an interpreter . . . to express the idea of conquering by kindness.[17]

During the seventeenth-century conquest period, the Shunzhi and Kangxi emperors sought to win over Han Chinese literati by presenting themselves as Confucian monarchs. They studied Chinese, accepted the Confucian canon as the foundation for the civil service examinations, and adopted the civil service examinations as the primary mode of recruitment for the bureaucracy. Manchu emperors patronized Chinese art and literature, issued Confucian decrees, and reformed Manchu marriage and burial practices to conform to Chinese customs. Filiality became an essential prerequisite of rulership. These strategies were successful. Despite the persistence of an underlying tension in their relationship, Manchu patronage gradually eroded Han Chinese resistance and encouraged support of the dynasty.[18]

The Sinitic aspects of Qing rule, and the intense scholarly focus on their governance of the former Ming territories south of the Great Wall, cause many scholars to gloss over the non-Han origins of the rulers, and to emphasize sinicization as the main historical trend during the dynasty. The chapters that follow show that Qing rulers never lost their awareness of their separation from the mass of the Ming population and never shed their Manchu identity. They adopted Chinese customs when it was politically expedient for them to do so and rejected them when it did not help them achieve their political goals. Qing rulers studied Jin history with equal fervor and built on many of the Jin policies. Crossley analyzes the importance of these precedents for Qing rule: "Attempts to use the examinations for the promotion of commoners or for restricting aristocratic access to high office were consistent, in the Jin empire, with aggressive state programs to limit the privilege and influence of the nobility, to centralize the state, and to prepare the dynastic constituency for a very broad role in the maintenance of a civil system. These practices were all forerunners of the bureaucracy of the Qing empire." [19]

Recent studies of the conquest regimes that ruled China's northern and northwestern territories from the tenth to the fourteenth centuries provide a fresh interpretation of the distinctive political style brought to rulership by these non-Han states. The Khitan, Tangut, Jurchen, and Mongol rulers all incorporated Chinese-type bureaucracies into their own polities, but at the same time they adapted the Chinese political model to suit their own circumstances. They focused on how to control an empire with nomadic as well as sedentary subjects that spanned Inner and East Asia. All the conquest regimes created administrations that were differentiated according to region. Different laws applied to different peoples, and officials were recruited from different groups. Moreover, although Han Chinese were employed in government, all four states resisted sinicization. Each created its own national script. All pursued bilingual or multilingual language policies. Each carried out extensive translation projects, seeking legitimacy not only in the Confucian but in the Buddhist realm.[20]

The Qing was neither a replica of the Chinese dynasties nor a simple duplicate of its non-Han predecessors. Representations of the Qing must acknowledge the non-Han origins of the rulers but go beyond that to analyze the innovations of Qing rulership. Rather than cite sinicization as the primary cause of Qing success, this work lays out the case for a very different conclusion: the key to Qing achievement lay in its ability to implement flexible culturally specific policies aimed at the major non-Han peoples inhabiting the Inner Asian peripheries in the empire. Whereas a native ruling house would have to throw off the dominant Confucian ideology to pursue a multicultural policy, the Qing expanded on precedents set by previous conquest regimes. These findings point indirectly to the need to reexamine the historical contributions of earlier Inner Asian states to Chinese history.

The full scope of Qing policies relating to its peripheral regions lies outside the scope of this study, which focuses instead on the Qing imperial court itself. The book is divided into three parts. The first, "The Material Culture of the Qing Court," consists of a chapter on court society and identifies several significant features of Qing rule that link the rulers to their non-Han predecessors. The Qing court and administration moved in seasonal rhythms between multiple capitals, located outside the Great Wall and in the North China plain, in order to maintain important linkages with Inner Asian allies and the Han Chinese population. Like their predecessors, the Qing spatially divided capital cities in order to segregate the conquest elite from the subjugated population. Having created a Manchu identity for the northeastern tribes in the early seventeenth century, the rulers issued regulations governing hairdo, dress, language, and the martial arts, which defined and perpetuated the separate identity of the conquest elite. Although the content of Manchu identity varied over time, it never disappeared. At the same time, Qing rulers created through the arts an image of cosmopolitan rulership to stress the spatial breadth and catholicity of the imperial charisma.

The second part, "The Social Organization of the Qing Court," consists of four chapters. Chapter 2 analyzes the construction of the Qing conquest elite in the early seventeenth century out of multiethnic coalitions formed with Mongols, Manchus, and northeastern "transfrontiersmen." The rulers incorporated these diverse subjects into a military-civilian organization called the banners and created a banner nobility to lead them. The primus inter pares of the banner elites, however, were all imperial kinsmen. The imperial lineage, the Aisin Gioro, claimed descent from the Jurchen Jin who ruled North China and Northeast Asia in the twelfth century and constituted an "inner circle" of support for the throne. In comparison with their predecessors, the Ming, Qing rulers severely limited the number of imperial princes whose titles could be passed on without reduction in rank. The regulations governing hereditary transmission of titles produced a highly stratified imperial lineage. During the eighteenth and nineteenth centuries, as the fiscal cost of subsidies rose, emperors upheld the privileged status of their kinsmen while curbing their claims to employment and special favor.

Chapter 3 examines the internal rivalries among the imperial kinsmen. Manchu rulers had to eliminate the autonomous powers of their brothers and close kinsmen before they could wield centralized authority over the state. The "domestication" of the banner princes, and the concomitant transition from collegial to one-person rule, was accomplished by the 1730s. Although the sibling politics set off by the Qing refusal to adopt the Chinese dynastic principle of eldest son succession continued until the middle of the nineteenth century, imperial princes also reverted to earlier patterns of fraternal solidarity and support. The late Qing prominence of princes Gong and Chun in governance thus paralleled earlier political structures.

Manchu attitudes toward women also contrasted with Han Chinese norms. Chapter 4 argues that the treatment of the emperor's mother, sisters, consorts, and daughters cannot be understood without reference to non-Han models of political rule. Han Chinese regimes barred imperial agnates from governance and used affinal kinsmen as allies in the throne's struggles against the bureaucracy; the Qing strategy focused on maintenance of solidarity within the conquest elite. Marriage policy amounted to political endogamy within the conquest elite. Intermarriage with the subjugated Chinese population and their descendants was prohibited.

Qing marriage policies reduced the political importance of empresses' families and incorporated consorts into the imperial lineage, forcing them to cut their relationships with their natal families. In sharp contrast to Han Chinese ruling houses, Qing empresses dowager consistently formed regencies not with their natal kin but with their husband's brothers. Since imperial princesses did not lose membership in their natal families on marriage, the alliances brought their grooms into the inner circle.

The final chapter (chapter 5) in part 2 focuses on palace servants and analyzes the master-servant relationship in terms of the ruler's political and symbolic agenda. The size and diverse composition of the palace establishment was a corollary of the emperor's preeminence. The very size of the staff, however, created control problems. The Qing resolved the age-old issue of eunuch subversion by employing another subordinated status group, the imperial bondservants, in supervisory roles within a bureaucratized palace administration. Together with inner-court and banner officials, the bondservants formed the Imperial Household Department (Neiwufu) and enabled the emperors to bypass the Han-dominated civil service (the outer-court staff) in many arenas, extending far beyond the rulers' domestic affairs. Palace politics had its own dynamic. The complex hierarchy of servants within the palace was a mirror image of the court's internal structure;

master-servant relations gave favored eunuchs and bondservants informal authority that subverted the normative order. That rulers were keenly aware of these challenges is evident from the vigor with which they attempted to enforce palace regulations and keep servants "in their place."

The third part, "Qing Court Rituals," consists of three chapters, each of which explores a different cultural realm. Rituals were essential in the construction of imperial legitimation. The Qing understood very well that compliance was not merely a matter of coercive force, but rather the result of successful attempts to persuade subjects of the moral and ethical correctness of the dominant political structure. The Qing constructed a personalistic empire, held together at its pinnacle by a charismatic ruler, who was able to speak directly in the cultural vocabularies of each of his major subject peoples. Qing rulers patronized Confucianism for the Han Chinese, shamanism for the northeastern peoples (the Manchus), and Tibetan Buddhism for the Mongols and Tibetans. The rulers also supported Islam, the religion of the Turkic-speaking Muslims of Central Asia, but were much less successful in winning over this group (see chapter 7).

Chapter 6 focuses on the Confucian state ritual arena. Within Confucian political thought there was a basic tension between two principles of legitimation—virtue or heredity—that remained unresolved. Qing emperors sought to raise "rule by virtue" over "rule by heredity," but as analysis of ritual delegation shows, heredity continued to be an element in imperial legitimation. When their legitimacy, as defined by Confucian political theory, was directly challenged by drought, political exigencies demanded that rulers pursue an eclectic policy of religious patronage. Efficacy mattered more than consistency: Confucian virtue could not be the sole arbiter of imperial legitimation.

Chapter 7 turns to the court's patronage of shamanism and Tibetan Buddhism, and thus to the court's pursuit of a multicultural policy directed at different subject peoples in the empire. Shamanism was the avowed traditional belief system of the Manchus but originally focused on the resolution of individual problems. State shamanic rites developed as an alternative and counterpart to the Han Chinese political rituals; then, in the eighteenth century, the court attempted to preserve shamanic rituals through codification. Shamanism provided not only the foundation myths legitimating the Qing ruling house but also a cultural umbrella for integration of northeastern tribal groups. Tibetan Buddhism attracted Manchu rulers because it was the belief system of the Mongols and in the seventeenth century a key to supremacy in Inner Asia. Manchu patronage of the dGe lugs pa sect sustained that order's dominance in Tibet and enabled the

Qing emperors to use the religion as a means of integrating and stabilizing Mongol society.

Chapter 8 examines the religious life of the inner court, in which palace women as well as men participated. Shielded from official scrutiny, the private altars erected in palace residences, as well as the halls in Jingshan, north of the palace compound, were ritual spaces within which private emotion and sentiment could prevail over the strict hierarchical order dictated by dynastic regulations. Tibetan and Chinese Buddhist, Taoist, and shamanic observances commingled in the imperial household's performance of the calendrical rituals common to residents of the capital. The private or domestic rituals of the Qing court were a synthetic, eclectic blend of the many cultural and religious traditions espoused by Qing rulers. As such, these rituals symbolized the final denouement of Qing imperial institutions, which created a fusion of the diverse cultures of the empire.

The foundation for this book's argument is a large body of primary and secondary materials on Qing imperial institutions that became accessible during the 1960s: the Chinese- and Manchu-language palace memorials in Taipei and Beijing, the official records and regulations published along with a flood of works on Qing rulers, the Qing banner system, and the governance of different regions within the Qing empire.[21] To assess the full value of these records and documents for historical analysis, we must understand the context in which they were produced.

Every Qing historian relies on the Collected Regulations ([*Qinding*] *da Qing huidian*) and the accompanying collections of historical precedents (*huidian shili*) for a grasp of the bureaucratic framework that structured official action. Collected regulations were also periodically compiled for each ministry in the central government, as well as for the Imperial Clan Court, Imperial Household Department, and other offices within the palace administration. These specialized regulations record details of historical changes that supplement the archival records.

It is hard for historians to remember that the Veritable Records (*Da Qing shilu*) were not accessible during the Qing itself. We know that emperors read—or said that they read—the Veritable Records of their predecessors. With the partial exception of the Kangxi emperor, most rulers permitted recording officials to be present at imperial audiences in order to compile the Diaries of Rest and Repose (*Da Qing qijuzhu*). Compiled in both Manchu and Chinese, these accounts of the daily activities of the Qing emperor were collected and bound together on a monthly, then yearly, basis.

After an emperor died, his successor would commission a group of scholar-officials to peruse the diaries and relevant official documents from the ministries and the History Office in order to compile the Veritable Records of the reign. As Feng Erkang notes, the diaries and the Veritable Records are therefore not identical. Those with recourse to the archives know that both also omit certain kinds of activities amply documented in the "working papers" housed in the archives.[22]

Even though they were not intended for wide circulation, the Veritable Records were addressed to a future audience of descendants and, eventually, historians. Moreover, the many transcripts of imperial communications with officials included in the Veritable Records show the emperor speaking to the bureaucracy, and representing himself in their ideal discourse. Rhetorical flourishes in Chinese-language imperial edicts were most often couched in Confucian language.

Those who would study the Qing imperial lineage must also consult the genealogical information found in the *Aixin juelo zongpu* (1937). Printed in Mukden during the Manchukuo period, the genealogy seems to be relatively rare. The compilers must have referred to the manuscript genealogy, *Da Qing yudie*, which was periodically revised throughout the course of the dynasty. Produced in Manchu as well as Chinese, and kept in Shengjing (Mukden) and Beijing, the working genealogy provides information on the birth and marriage of daughters (omitted from the printed version) but lacks the brief official biographies outlining the careers of kinsmen found in the printed genealogy.[23]

This book could not have been written without the archival materials that have become available to scholars in the 1980s. The archival materials housed in Taiwan's National Palace Museum and Beijing's First Historical Archives were never intended to be presented to a public readership, as were the Veritable Records and the Diaries of Rest and Repose. They were rather "working documents," such as are found in any large-scale bureaucracy. Their value for historical research has been amply demonstrated by recent monographs on topics as diverse as the evolution of the Grand Council and millenarian uprisings.[24]

This book relies primarily on the archival materials of the Imperial Household Department held in Beijing at the First Historical Archives. In contrast with the high-level documents emanating from the Grand Council, which treat all the major affairs of the Qing state, these are papers of the palace administration, which was in charge of the inner court. Rather than confine itself to the emperor's private and personal affairs, the Imperial Household Department supervised a broad range of activities, which included foreign relations with the newly conquered territories and rituals of the state. Similarly, archival materials of the Imperial Clan Court, which I have read, touch on matters related to the imperial clan outside the normal purview of the Qing bureaucracy. Manchu-language documents, found in the Imperial Household Department files, are often not duplicated in the Chinese language, despite the general bilingual policy.

Qing archival materials include a substantial body of Manchu-language as well as Chinese-language documents. Elsewhere, Pamela Crossley and I argue for the importance of using these Manchu-language documents, which have all too frequently been assumed to be duplicates of those written in the Chinese language. Recent analysis by scholars in China indicates that the Manchu language served as a security language for the early Qing rulers, protecting communications on military activities, relations with Mongolia, Russia, and Tibet, and affairs within the imperial lineage from scrutiny.[25]

In every society, the perspective of the rulers is likely to differ significantly from the perspective of the ruled. The Manchu- and Chinese-language archival documents provide an unrivaled depth of information concerning the life of the inner court and are doubly valuable because they were never intended for public consumption. The Qing period has an additional source in the Jesuit reports that cover activities at the court from the late seventeenth to the eighteenth centuries. Published in Europe, these observations are frequently unique in their perspective, and valuable for that reason.

All the materials cited above, regardless of the language in which they were written, are "insider's views"—produced either for working purposes or as part of the imperial communication with the bureaucracy. When combined with other documentation, they enable us to look at the dynasty from the perspective of its rulers. That this perspective excludes much that is familiar to us from readings of the Chinese-language sources should not be surprising, nor does it in any way reject the importance and relevance of the Chinese view. Nonetheless, in part because that view has dominated our understanding of the Qing dynasty for at least the last seventy years, it is time to change the lenses and reorder the narrative. The result is analyzed in chapters that follow.

Part 1

THE MATERIAL CULTURE
OF THE QING COURT

Chapter 1   The Court Society

A survey of the material culture of the Qing court reveals a great deal about the self-image of the rulers and the politics of rulership. It was no accident that Qing court society was an eclectic blend of several cultural traditions. The Qing empire was founded on multiethnic coalitions, and its rulers sought to perpetuate these alliances by addressing each of the constituent peoples that came under Qing rule in their own cultural vocabularies. While determined to retain their own identity as Manchus, heirs to the ruling tradition of the Jurchen Jin, the Qing rulers projected images of rulership in the cultural patterns of the Han and Inner Asian peoples whom they identified as their primary constituents. Their first and most powerful ties were with the Mongols. They courted Han Chinese literati in the language of Confucianism and cast Manchu rulers as *dharmarāja* in the Tibetan Buddhist tradition for the benefit of Mongols and Tibetans. With the conquest of the Tarim Basin, they patronized Muslim mosques and sought (though unsuccessfully) to pose as protectors of the faith. All these elements were present in the material culture of the Qing court.

The major capital, Peking, was not only the capital of the preceding dynasty, the Ming (1368–1644), but was a capital of the Liao, Jin, and Yuan as well. The Manchus also commemorated Shengjing as a symbol of the Manchu homeland, and Rehe (Chengde after 1824) was an informal summer capital for at least the first half of the dynasty. Like earlier Inner Asian conquest regimes, the Manchus adopted a policy of residential segregation for the conquest elite. In their language, dress, and other cultural policies the rulers strove to perpetuate their own separate identity as a people, continuing a process of self-definition that began in the late sixteenth century. Nurgaci commissioned the creation of a written language. His successor took the name "Manchu" by imperial injunction in 1635, elaborated on the historical origins for the ruling group, and strengthened Manchu identification with a martial tradition. This chapter focuses on the ways in which Qing court society deliberately included many signs of the non-Han cultural origins of its rulers and promoted representation of the regime as cosmopolitan and multiethnic.

MULTIPLE CAPITALS

The Qing system of multiple capitals was modeled after that of the Khitan Liao (907–1115), Jurchen Jin (1115–1234), and Mongol Yuan (1272–1368), the non-Han conquest regimes that dominated North China from the tenth to fourteenth centuries. Herbert Franke summarizes the significance of this pattern: "Unlike a proper Chinese dynasty, which normally had one capital, the Liao had five capitals, as did the Chin. In both cases this can be interpreted as a remnant of the times when even the rulers had no fixed abode, but it was also a remnant of a ritualized system of seasonal sojourns. On a more practical level, the system of multiple capitals also provided the means to establish centralized agencies in more than one locality."[1]

Capitals were moved as geopolitical circumstances changed, to facilitate military advance and to consolidate control over newly acquired lands. These policies are illustrated in the history of the Liao and Jin capitals, which moved southward as their armies pushed into North China. Since the political center of these regimes was wherever the ruler and his troops chose to be, capital designations, which adopted the Chinese vocabulary of the cardinal directions, were subject to changes that must have been bewildering from the Han Chinese perspective. Thus the Jin "northern capital" was first Lindong (1138–50), then Ningcheng (1153–1215); their "central capital" was first Ningcheng (1120–53), then Peking (1153–1215), and finally, after the Mongols took Peking, Loyang (1215–33). Liaoyang, like Ningcheng and Peking a former Liao capital, was at various points the Jin "southern capital" (1132–53) and their "eastern capital" (1117–32, 1153–1212), while Datong, the "western capital" of the Liao, was also the western capital of the Jin.[2]

The desire to be close to the prospective battlefield prompted Nurgaci, the founder of the Manchu regime, to shift his headquarters seven times as he unified the Jurchen tribes by force. Only two of these early political centers were commemorated after 1644. The first, Hetu Ala, was Nurgaci's capital from 1603 until 1619 and the site at which he declared the establishment of the Later Jin state (1616). His successors retained an administrative presence at Hetu Ala (renamed Yenden or Xingjing in 1636) throughout the dynasty. Shenyang, renamed Mukden *hoton* (in Chinese, Shengjing) in 1634, was Nurgaci's last capital city and the capital until 1644. After the Shunzhi emperor (reigned 1644–61) moved to Peking, Shengjing was retained as a secondary capital.[3] Nurgaci and his son Hongtaiji were interred in nearby tombs, so Shengjing was periodically visited by the Qing rulers, and its palaces were renovated through the Qianlong reign (1736–95).

Chengde

If Peking was the primary capital and Shengjing the symbolic "original" capital, the summer capital of Chengde was selected for symbolic and practical reasons. It lay north of the Great Wall, on the boundary between the North China plain and the Mongolian steppe. The Liao, Jin, and Yuan had all had capitals in this area, and the Kangxi emperor consciously followed their precedent when he decided to create a summer capital here. Philippe Forêt argues that the Qing "assumption of simultaneous responsibilities as Emperors of the Han subjects, Khans of the Manchu-Mongol populations and bodhisattva for Lamaist believers led to the elaboration of a system of three capitals, one in Manchuria (Mukden), one in China proper (Peking), and one in Inner Mongolia (Chengde)," with Chengde also serving as "a religious capital for Tibet."[4]

The search for a northern summer retreat began even before the end of the conquest. Dorgon, regent for the infant Shunzhi emperor, cited the precedents set by previous non-Han dynasties of removing from Peking to "escape the heat of summer days" and ordered construction of a small summer retreat in Chengde shortly before his death. Work on the summer villa stopped when he died and did not resume until after the suppression of the Rebellion of the Three Feudatories.[5]

Chengde and Mulan were selected as imperial sites by the Kangxi emperor (r. 1662–1722), who turned his attention to the Russian incursions on the empire's northern border as the pacification of southern China drew to a close. Xuanye liked to inspect the terrain for himself, with an eye to military strategy, and the 1675 revolt by Burni, grandson of the Chahar leader Ligdan Khan, underlined the importance of cultivating his Mongol allies. In 1681, on the second of his northern tours beyond the Great Wall, the emperor ventured into the territory of the Kharachin banner of the Josoto League and hunted on the southeastern edge of the Mongol plateau, in lands occupied by the Khorchin, Aokhan, and Ongnirod Mongols. This site became Mulan, the Qing imperial hunting preserve. Xuanye also visited the military governor's headquarters in Jilin, a garrison created to keep closer tabs on this northeastern frontier. The court built an official road (with postal stations) to expedite official communications between the northeastern garrisons, the office of the Mukden (now Fengtian) governor, and Peking.[6]

The imperial preserve of Mulan was situated 117 kilometers north of Chengde. Its name came from the Manchu word *muran* (to call deer), referring to the Manchu method of hunting deer by imitating the stag's mating call. Historical precedents tied this huge hunting preserve to the Liao-Jin imperial hunting grounds. Mulan was initially managed by Mongol princes, then after 1706 by a grand minister (*zongli dachen*) under the Lifanyuan (court of colonial affairs). The preserve was off-limits to unauthorized persons and was surrounded by a willow palisade. Eight hundred, later fourteen hundred, Manchu and Mongol bannermen were stationed in forty outposts (*karun*) to patrol its perimeter. The hunting grounds within this vast preserve were subdivided into sixty-seven (later seventy-two) hunting sites, each bearing a Mongol name.[7]

The Kangxi emperor hunted at Mulan every autumn from 1681 to the end of his life, with the exception of only two years when he was engaged in major military campaigns. Mongol nobles who were excused from coming to Peking to pay homage because they were vulnerable to smallpox were instead invited in rotation to accompany the emperor in his annual hunts at Mulan: this was the *weiban* or "hunting rotation," as opposed to the *nianban* or "annual rotation" to Peking. During these hunts, which lasted an average of thirty days, the emperor and his retinue would kill deer, pheasants, and tigers. Several different hunting methods were used, but the most distinctive was the Manchu *abalambi,* in which mounted riders would encircle an area then drive the game down from the hills into the valleys, where the emperor and Mongol nobles would shoot them.[8]

Until 1702, the Kangxi emperor and his entourage lived in tents during their travels to and from Chengde. The imperial retinue, which included imperial consorts, sons, and daughters, was gradually accommodated in rest houses. "Temporary palaces" (*xinggong*) were constructed along the official route from Peking through Gubeikou, the pass out of China proper, to Mulan and ranged from simple structures for a brief rest, the drinking of tea (*chagong*), or taking of meals (*jian'gong*) to substantial buildings for the nightly stop (*zhugong*). These buildings probably housed only the imperial family: others still used tents.[9]

Xuanye and his retinue also lived in tents while hunting. The spatial arrangement of the tent cities that sprang up around him echoed those found in his capitals. The emperor's yellow tent (yellow being the imperial color) stood in the very center of the encampment, fenced off by yellow screens. The area outside the screens, but enclosed by another fence, was the "inner city" (*neicheng*), filled with approximately 75 tents. The inner city was surrounded by the "outer city" (*waicheng*), with perhaps 254 tents. The mobile government offices of the Grand Secretariat, Six Boards, Censorate, and general in chief were located in tents on the eastern side of the outer city.[10]

The Yongzheng emperor never went to Mulan, but the autumn hunt was revived by the Qianlong emperor. Hongli spent less time there than his grandfather (an average of twenty days per visit) but still led the autumn hunt some forty times during his reign. He also constructed temporary palaces within the hunting ground beginning in 1755 and developed the preserve to its fullest extent.[11] Although the Jiaqing emperor (r. 1796–1820) led the autumn hunt at Mulan twelve times, he spent even less time there than did his father. Yongyan was the last Qing emperor to stage the autumn hunt. Under his successors the hunting preserve languished, while visits to the imperial complex at Chengde flourished.

Requiring precise coordination and planning of movements, provisions, and shelter, the large hunts of the Kangxi and Qianlong reigns closely resembled military campaigns. The parties of imperial princes, central government ministers, banner officials, and nobles of Mongol, Kazakh, and Uighur origin that hunted with Hongli at Mulan are said on occasion to have numbered thirty thousand persons. The hunt regulations show a formalized and ritualized sequence of events, with displays of imperial archery by the emperor, his sons, and grandsons; mock battles between forces led by Manchu and Mongol nobles; presentation to the emperor of the annual Mongol tribute of the "nine whites" (nine white camels or nine white horses); and reciprocal feasting, with Mongol ballads, dances, horse races, and wrestling as well as the emperor's presentations of silk, silver, and gold to the Mongol nobles.[12]

The building of the imperial complex of Bishu shanzhuang (villa to escape the summer heat) at Chengde began in 1702 and continued until 1792. The Rehe temporary palace, as it was initially called, stood on the southwestern bank of the Wulie River. The walls around this temporary palace enclosed an area that was 5.64 square kilometers, making it larger than the three gardens comprising the Yuanmingyuan, near Peking. Within, a complex system of artificial lakes and islands provided venues for palaces modeled after those in Peking, lakes that imitated Jiangnan gardens; a mountain district; and terrain made to resemble the Mongolian steppe, with sites for banqueting and military displays. The whole has been critically analyzed by Philippe Forêt as an "imperial landscape," in which the walled temporary palace was balanced in a Buddhist-inspired universe by the huge temples constructed on the opposite bank of the river.[13]

The Kangxi and Qianlong emperors also constructed eight (originally twelve) temples outside the Bishu shanzhuang. The first two, the Purensi and the Pushansi, were Tibetan Buddhist temples, part of the court patronage of this religion (see chapter 7). The Qianlong emperor built nine major temples on the surrounding slopes, many of them for specific occasions. The Puningsi was consciously modeled on bSam-yas, the first Tibetan monastery, and constructed in honor of the Qing success against the Zunghars (1755);[14] another, the Anyuanmiao, was patterned after a temple destroyed by the Zunghar leader Amursana during his revolt against the Qing.

Both Forêt and Ning Chia point out that Chengde functioned as a third capital of the Qing empire, even though it did not bear that official designation.[15] The region surrounding the imperial villa was administratively designated as a subprefecture (Rehe *ting*) during the 1720s, then in 1733 made into a department, Chengde *zhou*, under the Zhili lieutenant governor. Reverting to subprefectural status in 1742, it became a prefecture in 1778.[16] Symbolically it was the outer capital, where Mongols, Uighurs, and Tibetans performed court rituals under the jurisdiction of the Lifanyuan. Chia argues that the ritual of submission before the emperor (*chaojin*) was inspired by Muslim pilgrimage traditions and thus bore religious connotations. Although Tibetans were excused from *chaojin*, other Inner Asian nobles were divided into rotas for the annual trip to the Qing court. *Chaojin* was frequently performed at the summer palace at Chengde, just as another court ritual, the imperial hunt (*weilie*), was performed at Mulan. Chia characterizes the imperial hunt, in which Tibetan prelates, Mongol nobles, and Muslim *begs* participated, as a form of ritual activity that derived from Mongol and Manchu customs. The hunt gave lower-ranking members of the Inner Asian elite an opportunity to come in close contact with the emperor while participating in an activity that linked the Manchus to Inner Asia.

Chengde was the scene of lavish spectacles during the Qianlong reign. Celebrations of the emperor's birthday—over forty of them—added to the magnificence of the banquets and entertainments staged here. It was at Bishu shanzhuang that the emperor celebrated the submission of the

Dörböt Mongols (1754) and received the Sixth Panchen lama (1780) and Lord Macartney's embassy (1793).[17]

Imperial Villas

Ming emperors remained within the Forbidden City, whereas Qing rulers escaped Peking and frequently conducted the affairs of government from villas in the suburbs. After taking over personal control of government in 1667, the young Kangxi emperor began to use the parks of the former Ming rulers well outside the Forbidden City. In 1682 he had a temporary palace erected in the Nanyuan, a hunting preserve six miles southwest of Peking. Suppression of the Rebellion of the Three Feudatories in 1683 permitted further construction in the hills northwest of Peking, where he could relax amid scenic vistas. The Changchunyuan (garden of joyful springtime), completed in 1690, occupied a site that had been favored by the Jin, Yuan, and Ming rulers. The Changchunyuan became the Kangxi emperor's favorite residence; because he spent so much time there, all the major central government agencies opened offices at the villa so that government business could go on as usual. The Changchunyuan was the site for Xuanye's public denunciation of Yinreng, his heir apparent in 1712; it was where the ailing emperor was taken in 1722, and where he died. After his death, the villa became the residence of the empress dowager.[18]

In 1709 Yinzhen had received land for a princely garden slightly north of the Changchunyuan. His villa was named the Yuanmingyuan. The Kangxi emperor visited the Peony Terrace in this garden in 1716 and again in 1722. After 1725, as the Yongzheng emperor, Yinzhen expanded the buildings to accommodate the different government offices that moved there when he was in residence. He used this villa extensively and died there in 1735.[19] His successor, the Qianlong emperor, also favored the Yuanmingyuan, which had been his home as a youth (he lived in the Changchun xian'guan during his father's lifetime).[20]

Hongli added more imperial villas: the Jingyiyuan (1745) and the Changchunyuan (garden of lasting springtime, 1749–70), adjoining the Yuanmingyuan on its eastern boundary. Giuseppe Castiglione designed and erected fountains and palaces in the European style in the northern part of this garden. By 1772 the Yuanmingyuan, Changchunyuan, and Qichunyuan (subsequently renamed the Wanshouyuan) sprawled over a vast acreage northwest of the capital. In honor of his mother's sixtieth birthday, the Qianlong emperor dredged this lake, renamed it Lake Kunming, and renovated the Qingyiyuan, a villa on its eastern shore that had been completed in 1749. After its gardens were destroyed by the Allied Expeditionary force in October 1860, the Qingyiyuan was rebuilt, expanded, and renamed the Garden to Nurture Harmony (Yiheyuan) by Empress Dowager Cixi.[21]

PEKING

Major aspects of Peking's spatial structure and its architecture had been set long before the Qing occupation. A capital in the Liao, Jin, Yuan, and Ming dynasties, the city was oriented along a central north-south axis, had very wide streets leading to the massive palace complex at the center, and was divided into a chessboardlike pattern of squares (*fang*) that were further subdivided into smaller alleys or *hutong*. Even the lakes inside the city walls were constructed features that persisted seven centuries later.[22]

What the Qing added to the city, however, was not insignificant. Dai Yi, the distinguished Qing historian, credits the Qianlong emperor with the renovation of Peking. No other Ming or Qing ruler had as great an impact on the capital. The empire was at peace; the surpluses in the imperial treasury were diverted to finance public works. For three decades after 1738, Hongli carried out an ambitious building program. He improved the city's water control system, repaired the city's roads and walls, renovated palaces and villas, and built the Ningshou palace for his retirement.[23] The dilapidated Temple of the Ancestors was reconstructed in 1736; during the 1740s and early 1750s many temples were erected and the major state altars were rebuilt.

The Manchus retained Peking's Confucian symbolism. Peking was a sacred city, the secular equivalent of the capital of the deity Shangdi, the emperor of heaven. Since the two primary functions of a state were sacrifice (i.e., religious worship) and war, the major altars in the state religion were a crucial component of the capital city. Canonical precedent located them in the suburbs, outside the city walls. From the Later Han dynasty (25–220 A.D.), the sacrifice to Heaven at the winter solstice should take place in the southern, the sacrifice to Earth at the summer solstice, in the northern suburbs (map 2). Peking's Altar to Heaven stood in a vast walled park in the extreme south of the Outer City; the Altar to Earth stood north of the Inner City.[24] The Altar of the Sun and the Altar of the Moon, located to the east and west of the Inner City walls, completed imperial worship in the four cardinal directions.

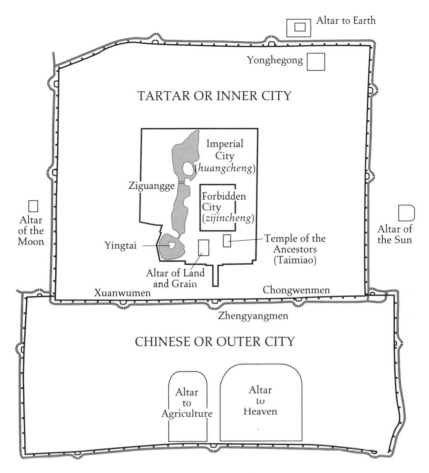

Altar to Earth

Yonghegong

TARTAR OR INNER CITY

Imperial City (*huangcheng*)

Ziguangge

Forbidden City (*zijincheng*)

Altar of the Moon

Yingtai

Altar of the Sun

Temple of the Ancestors (Taimiao)

Altar of Land and Grain

Xuanwumen

Chongwenmen

Zhengyangmen

CHINESE OR OUTER CITY

Altar to Agriculture

Altar to Heaven

MAP 2. Location of major altars and divisions of Qing Peking.

The most important modification made by the Manchus was the division of Peking into an Outer City (*waicheng*) and an Inner City (*neicheng*). This double-city model, which first appeared in Peking with the Liao dynasty, was duplicated in all the pre-1644 Manchu capitals, and even in the spatial arrangement of the tent city created during the emperor's trips north of the Great Wall (see the earlier discussion of Chengde and Mulan).[25] Peking's subdivisions coincided with the political and social divisions of the empire. The rulers and bannermen lived in the Inner City (foreigners referred to it as the "Tartar city"); the conquered Chinese population resided in the Outer City. This residential segregation began four years after the Manchu armies had entered Peking. Earlier, Dorgon had encouraged Chinese acquiescence to Manchu rule by forbidding bannermen from plundering civilians (1644) and proclaiming that "Manchu and Han are one family" (1647). Ethnic strife, however, forced the regent to rule on October 5, 1648, that the two races should be separated so that each could "live in peace." All Chinese were ordered to move to the southern city. The policy of residential segregation was implemented throughout the empire, so that bannermen lived in separate walled quarters within Chinese cities.[26]

The Outer City

The Outer or Chinese city was the commercial heart of the capital and served China's largest consumer market. The busiest shopping streets were at the Xuanwu, Zhengyang, and Chongwen gates between the Inner and Outer Cities. The city may have had 600 or 700 shops in 1744.[27] Merchants from all parts of the empire assembled in Peking to do business, and this southern city was full of *huiguan*, native-place associations patronized by officials and traders to pursue mutual advantage. Liulichang, the book and antiques district, became famous during the 1780s when the "four treasuries" project drew over 160 scholars to the capital. The Chinese city was also the entertainment center for bannermen. With the exception of the *erja*, the little gates on the northern side connecting it with the Inner City, the popular pleasure districts were in the Chinese city. The brothel district developed in the Outer City in the streets between Qianmen and Hepingmen, north of Zhushigou (pearl market street).[28]

Inner City

Approximately sixteen miles in circumference, the Inner City was the center of Qing government. The Six Boards, the Censorate, the Lifanyuan, some agencies of the Imperial Household Department, and banner offices were all located here. It was also the residential quarter for the conquest elite. In the mid-nineteenth century, an estimated one hundred thirty thousand bannermen lived in the Inner City and the suburban district around the imperial villas: they formed the Metropolitan Divisions of the banners and staffed the gendarmerie, a thirty- to forty-thousand-man force who patrolled the residential districts and guarded the sixteen gates of the Inner and Outer Cities.[29] The banners were assigned quarters to live in accordance with the colors assigned to the different compass directions. The troops of the Plain Yellow Banner occupied the city's northwestern sector, the Bordered Yellow the northeastern, the Plain White the eastern, the Bordered White the southeastern, the Plain Blue and the Bordered Blue the southern, the Plain Red Banner the western, and the Bordered Red Banner the southwestern sector. These troops were organized into two wings: the left wing consisted of the Bordered Yellow, Plain and Bordered White, and Plain Blue Banners who lived in the eastern half; the right wing of the Plain Yellow, Plain and Bordered Red, and Bordered Blue Banners. Each of the banners included a Manchu, Mongol, and Hanjun banner unit, headed by a lieutenant general (*dutong*) and two deputy lieutenant generals (*fudutong*).

Because the conquest elite eventually included many different peoples, Peking's Inner City housed a diverse population. There were Russians enrolled in the Bordered Yellow Banner, who had been captured in the Albazin campaign (1685); Russian Orthodox priests, in an ecclesiastical mission established after the Treaty of Kiakhta (1727). From a dozen to fifteen high ministers of Han Chinese background were given houses within the Inner City as a mark of special imperial favor. Europeans serving the Qing court had churches in different parts of the Inner City. Turkic Muslim elites and artisans, brought to the Qing capital after the conquest of the Tarim Basin, were clustered in a Uighur camp located just south of Nanhai. Tibetan artisans were brought to Peking in the 1740s to build stone watchtowers in the Tibetan style for army drills; after Fuheng's victory in the first Jinquan campaign (1749), the emperor had them construct the Tibetan Shishengsi (temple of victory) in the northwestern suburbs. Later, in 1776, the Tibetans were incorporated into a bondservant company of the Plain White Banner under the jurisdiction of the Imperial Household Department.[30]

The emperor was the principal landlord in the Inner City. When Han Chinese civilians moved out of the Inner City in 1648, their houses were assigned to bannermen, who gradually asserted property rights over their residences, as is demonstrated by existing contracts for mortgages, sales, and purchases of houses.[31] In theory these houses continued to belong to the state but in reality became imperial property: much of the land within the Inner City in the nineteenth century was owned by the emperor and managed by the Imperial Household Department, the Neiwufu. The Guanfangzuku (office for collecting rents of official properties) had initially been under the palace's own Department of Works (Yingzaosi) but later became an autonomous agency supervised by a Neiwufu minister.[32]

The Guanfangzuku was in charge of maintaining, renting, and otherwise managing all state property within Peking. That included the mansions given to members of the imperial lineage, the Aisin Gioro, and to banner nobles (see chapter 3). Because the size, structure, and ornamentation of the mansions were governed by sumptuary laws, houses were assigned to princes without regard for their banner affiliation and taken back as the rank of descendants was reduced. Princely residences rarely remained in the same family for generations. Three maps of the Inner City in 1750, 1846, and circa 1911 show only five residences remaining in the same family. Not surprisingly, all five belonged to princely lines with the right of perpetual inheritance (see chapter 2).[33]

Most of the houses handled by the Guanfangzuku were modest in size. In 1800 the Jiaqing emperor gave permission for these houses to be sold to Aisin Gioro. Of the ten such houses and their purchasers listed in an 1803 memorial, half were smaller than 20 *jian*, and only two were larger than 100 *jian*.[34] There is no information on how many nobles availed themselves of the opportunity to buy; judging from a study of the eighteen houses assigned to nobles in less than two weeks at the end of 1855 and early 1856, the Guanfangzuku retained its centrality in this part of Peking's housing market.[35]

Imperial City

Within the inner city and separated from it by a wall six feet thick, fifteen feet high, and eight miles in circumference lay the imperial city. Here were located the horse stables, storehouses, workshops, and offices of the Imperial Household Department and the residences of the imperial family. The imperial city was dominated by three lakes, the Beihai, Zhonghai, and Nanhai, which the Qing rulers ornamented with pavilions, temples, and other buildings. In the years before the Kangxi emperor constructed his villa in the Western Hills he moved to summer quarters on Yingtai, an island constructed in the Nanhai. From 1898–1900 and after the Boxer Uprising, Yingtai was also the residence of the Guangxu emperor (r. 1875–1908). On the western bank of Nanhai stood the Ziguangge, built by the Kangxi emperor, where after 1761 the Mongol affines were feted during the New Year celebrations. Adjoining this hall was a drill ground, where the emperor held archery contests.[36]

Two important altars in the Confucian state rituals were in the imperial city. The Temple of the Ancestors, or Taimiao, was located just southeast of the main entrance into the Forbidden City. The installation of the tablets of Nurgaci, his wife, and the recently dead Hongtaiji was accomplished only eight days after the Manchus entered Peking. The Taimiao housed not only the tablets of imperial ancestors but, in a side hall, tablets of meritorious generals and civil officials. To its west stood another large enclosed compound housing the Altar of Land and Grain (*sheji tan*), a single square altar made of stone, on which five-colored soil was arranged on the day preceding the ritual. Ming and Qing ritual specialists seem to have regarded the *sheji* as fertility gods. In ancient times, enfeoffment rituals involved bestowing a clump of soil from the *sheji* altar to a vassal, so the *sheji* appear to have represented the territory over which a ruler reigned. This old association was symbolically continued when soil from the provinces was deposited on the altar during later dynasties.[37]

The imperial city housed other altars linked to the Qing polity. Chinese Buddhist temples, several erected by Qing emperors, were scattered on the streets and along the lake shores. Several Tibetan shrines and temples also testified to the active patronage of Tibetan Buddhism by the Qing rulers. These included the White Pagoda, erected in 1651 to commemorate the visit of the Dalai lama to Peking; the Mahākāla temple, a historical artifact of the dynasty's affinities with Tibetan Buddhism (see chapter 7) which was located in the southeastern corner; and the Fayuansi near Jingshan, one of the temples built by the Kangxi emperor to house Mongol lamas who translated and printed Tibetan and Mongol liturgical books. Perhaps because the Jesuit missionaries had entered imperial service, there was also a Catholic church in the imperial city from the eighteenth century.[38]

The Forbidden City

This innermost palace was simultaneously the emperor's administrative headquarters, his residence, and the center for a vast array of activities supervised by the Imperial Household Department (see chapter 5). Since palace construction was directed by a hereditary descent line that survived the Ming-Qing transition, the architectural style and construction of palaces remained unchanged despite extensive renovations.[39] Architectural continuity concealed changes in the use of the various halls within the palace that reflect Qing strategies of rule.

Four gates, located in each of the compass directions, provided access into the Forbidden City (map 3). The central gate in the southern wall, the Wumen, was used for rituals and was normally closed. By tradition, with the exception of the three top degree-winners in the palace examinations, only the emperor was entitled to use the Wumen's central gate.[40] Civil officials

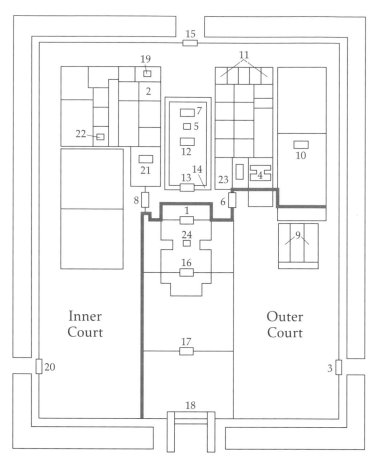

MAP 3.   A simplified plan of the Forbidden City.

1. Baohedian	9. Nansansuo (Agesuo or Sansuo)	17. Taihemen
2. Chuxiugong	10. Ningshougong	18. Wumen
3. Donghuamen	11. Qiandongwusuo	19. Xiersuo
4. Fengxiandian	12. Qianqinggong	20. Xihuamen
5. Jiaotaidian	13. Qianqingmen	21. Yangxindian
6. Jingyunmen	14. Shangshufang	22. Yuhuage
7. Kunninggong	15. Shenwumen	23. Yuqinggong
8. Longzongmen	16. Taihedian	24. Zhonghedian

with business at court were supposed to enter by the east gate (Donghu-amen), their military counterparts by the west gate (Xihuamen). Consorts were obliged to use the back gate (Shenwumen).

The Forbidden City was divided into the outer and inner courts. An in-dividual fortunate enough to obtain admission found himself in a walled courtyard (see map 3), confronting the three public halls arranged on a north-south axis that dominated the "outer court" (*waichao*). The Taihedian (throne hall of supreme harmony) was the primary hall for important state rituals, the Zhonghedian (hall of central harmony) was where the Qing emperor inspected the agricultural tools before the plowing rites and rested before ceremonies in the Taihedian, and the Baohedian (hall of preserving harmony) was where the emperor received ambassadors from vassal states, presided over the palace examinations, and received the degree winners. These halls were erected on a three-tiered marble platform and were completely enclosed by high walls. On ordinary days, when no major ritual was scheduled, the Wumen and Taihemen, the two sets of gates leading to them, would be closed.[41]

The scale and grandeur of the three public halls were designed to awe officials and ambassadors, who were forced to dismount at the Wumen and walk. The immensity of the space must have been especially impressive at dawn, the customary hour for court audiences: "Recall that imperial elephants stood between the tunnel openings through the Wumen, and that they would have been dwarfed by the openings which are six to seven meters high. . . . [The Taihedian courtyard] was the closest the ordinary minister got to the emperor; these were the stones against which he knocked his head. He must have had keen eyesight indeed even to see the emperor on his throne."[42] In earlier dynasties, the outer court was the space within which government business was conducted. What the Qing did was to move a substantial part of government affairs from this area into the emperor's private residence, into the area known as the Great Interior (*danei*).

The Great Interior   The distinction between the public space of the outer court and the private residences of the inner court dates only from 1669, when the young Xuanye, the Kangxi emperor, moved his sleeping quarters from the Qingning palace (later renamed the Baohedian) into the Qianqing palace. He and his father, who had also resided in the Baohedian for eight years, seem to have preferred this hall for its good condition and its grandeur. After renovation of the Qianqing palace in 1669, the separation of public and private space in the Forbidden City became permanent.[43] The inner court was an area barred to all but a handful of selected high officials and princes (the army of eunuchs, maids, and other servants who worked in this area was not, of course, counted). The inner court included not only the residences of the imperial family, but also the offices from which the emperor conducted the daily affairs of state.

If the outer court was the natural home of the Han Chinese literati, the inner court was the bastion of a Manchu-dominated coterie of imperial advisers. Beatrice Bartlett describes how the Kangxi emperor's inner court was dominated by high-level Manchus and Mongols, with Han Chinese largely segregated in the Nanshufang or Southern Study. Using the palace memorial system and ad hoc committees to deliberate on military strategy and other important state matters, the Kangxi emperor sought to bypass the constraints imposed on his prerogative by the bureaucratic culture of the outer court. Although the personnel of the inner court underwent important changes during the Yongzheng and Qianlong reigns, this kind of division continued throughout the dynasty and was characteristic of Manchu rule.[44]

Two gates, the Jingyun to the east and the Longzong to the west, marked the boundary between the outer and the inner courts. These gates opened onto the courtyard behind the Baohedian. Located just inside the Jingyun gate was the outer office of the Chancery of Memorials, where palace memorials that bypassed the routine bureaucratic channels were handed in to be read by the ruler. The chancery, which was headed by a guardsman and supervised by an adjutant general, also had an office staffed by eunuchs, just inside the Qianqing gate on the west side. The chancery played a critical intermediary role: it transmitted oral edicts to outer court bureaucrats to write up in draft form, handled all the tallies that permitted officials and princes an audience with the emperor, managed the daily work shifts at the outer chancery and the Qianqing gate, and received all presents intended for the emperor.[45]

The Qianqing gate led directly into the Qianqinggong. The Qianqing palace was the first of the three central buildings that paralleled the three halls of the outer court. During the Ming era the palaces behind the Qianqing gate had been residences that were used for government business only in emergencies. The Kangxi emperor, however, converted the Qianqing palace into an office for the conduct of routine business, using the buildings located in the eastern and western sections of the Great Interior as residences. With his successor, imperial audiences and conferences with high officials also took place in the Yangxindian, a large building complex in the Great Interior located to the west of the Qianqinggong, which served as the emperor's sleeping quarters.[46]

The second of the three back halls, the Jiaotaidian (hall of fusion and permeation), was where the imperial seals were kept in the Kangxi reign. These seals, which were reengraved in the Qianlong reign, were differentiated according to their use for different state functions, such as the naming of an heir to the throne, the issuing of orders for war, or investiture of nobles. To its north lay the Kunninggong (palace of earthly tranquillity), which had been the residence of the empress during the Ming dynasty. Although the Qing retained the use of this palace as a bridal chamber (see chapter 5), Qing empresses resided elsewhere. Instead, the Kunning palace housed the Office of Shamanism (Shen fang) and the altars at which shamans made daily offerings to the ancestral spirits.[47]

An east and west gate (*neizuo men, neiyou men*) flanked the Qianqing gate and led into narrow alleys with gates to individual courtyards where the empress dowager, empress, and consorts lived. The informality and human scale of these buildings contrasted markedly with the impersonality and massiveness of the public halls. Their arrangement of rooms facing south into interior courtyards reproduced the intimacy of commoner residences. The bifurcation of the Forbidden City into public and private space was thus very different from a European palace or noble's townhouse, which by combining public and private rooms into one building forced the aristocracy to live in drafty large rooms.

During the seventeenth and early eighteenth centuries, compounds to the east and west of the Qianqing palace also served as residences for imperial sons and grandsons. The five residences to the east (Qiandong-wusuo) were separate walled compounds, some with a small front hall as well as a sleeping chamber. All the Daoguang emperor's sons lived here in separate compounds with their staffs of eunuchs, wet nurses, nurses, and maids. A special commissary or tea office was established to prepare meals for them.[48]

During the first part of the Yongzheng reign, Hongli and his wife lived in one of the residences to the west of the Qianqing palace (the Xiersuo). After he became emperor, he converted these residences to other purposes and replaced them with the Nansansuo (southern three residences), located outside the inner court.[49] The Yuqing palace, situated to the southeast of the emperor's Qianqing palace, was the residence of crown prince Yinreng. Kangxi's grandsons Hongli and Hongzhou lived here before Hongli's marriage. Home for many of Hongli's brothers and nephews after they entered the Palace School, the Yuqing palace was also where his successor lived from the age of five to fifteen. Yongyan later reminisced about his life there with his brothers Yongxing and Yonglin: "every day we would hasten to the Shangshufang [palace school] and study together."[50] After he ascended the throne, however, Yongyan decided to discontinue its use as a residence for princes, fearing that residence there implied selection as heir apparent.

The Nansansuo was also known as the Xiefangdian or as the Agesuo (prince's residence) or as the Sansuo (three residences). It stood on the site of a former Ming structure within its own walled enclosure to the east of the main public halls. The young Hongli lived here for a time. Yongyan, the Jiaqing emperor, moved here in 1775, when he was fifteen and apparently remained until he was declared crown prince in 1795. His successor, Minning, was born in the Sansuo and continued to live here after his marriage, along with his elder brother; other cousins also lived within the compound. Abandoned temporarily in 1831 when Yiwei, the Daoguang emperor's eldest son, died there, the Nansansuo was used again by Yizhu, the future Xianfeng emperor (r. 1851–61).[51]

The Qing made important changes in the way the halls of the Forbidden City were used. From the Kangxi reign onward, high-level decision-making moved into the inner court, the private domestic realm of the imperial household. This was the space that in Ming times (and in Han Chinese commoners' households) would have corresponded to the women's quarters. Even in the Qing, admission into the Great Interior was strictly limited to a select circle. The spatial shift reflected the emperor's reliance on an "inner circle," drawn predominantly from the conquest elite that bypassed the Han Chinese bureaucracy.

Another major change made by the Qing was integrally tied to its policies concerning sons and brothers (see chapter 3). Whereas the Ming emperors had designated the heir apparent when he was still a child, removing all other sons to fiefs in the provinces, the Qing made all sons eligible for the throne and required that they remain in Peking. Imperial princes were mobilized for administrative and military duties, and it was therefore in the ruler's interest to strengthen fraternal bonds. The co-residence within the Forbidden City of all the emperor's sons extended the period during which the emperor could evaluate his sons, test their abilities through governmental assignments, and consolidate the fraternal sentiments that were a bulwark of dynastic strength.

SEASONAL SOJOURNING

Like other non-Han rulers, the Qing adhered to a pattern of seasonal sojourning. Emperors spent a great deal of time in their imperial villas in the northwest, outside the city walls. For the first 150 years of the dynasty, they also spent the summer and early autumn on the plateau outside the Great Wall, at Chengde and Mulan.

In the first decades after 1644, the emperors divided their time between the Forbidden City, the three lakes in the imperial city, and the Nanyuan. The Shunzhi emperor fled the capital when outbreaks of smallpox occurred, moving to Nanyuan or even to Zunhua, northeast of the capital (although he died of the disease).[52] After the adoption of variolation in 1681, it was no longer so important to avoid Peking during the winter and spring months for health reasons, but the completion of the conquest (1683) enabled emperors to expand their alternative residences. During 1681, the Kangxi emperor was in residence in Peking for slightly over half the year; he spent August and most of September in Yingtai; in April, May, and October he traveled to the imperial cemetery, Dongling, and to the northeast in what was only his second visit to districts outside China proper. The emperor began to spend more and more time at his villa, the Changchunyuan, and at his new hunting grounds north of Chengde. In 1714, for example, he spent only 18 days in the Forbidden City, 131 days in the Changchunyuan, and 139 days in Chengde and its environs.[53]

Seasonal sojourning also aptly described the movements of the Qianlong emperor. As Father Benoit reported:

> During the year the emperor only lives in Peking about three months. He ordinarily spends some time there before the winter solstice, which must be in the eleventh month of the Chinese year. The spring equinox is always in the second month of the following year . . . before the fifteenth [of the first month] the emperor with his entourage goes to live in his villa at Yuanmingyuan, which is situated five miles northwest of Peking. . . . All the rest of the year, excepting the time he hunts in Tartary, he spends at Yuanmingyuan; whence he goes to Peking when called by ceremony; the ceremony completed, he immediately returns to the Yuanmingyuan.[54]

During 1762, the emperor spent about half of his time in his villa or in the Bishu shanzhuang at Chengde; he resided in the Forbidden City for about one-third of the time and spent the rest of his days on the road.[55]

CULTURAL POLICIES

From the onset of their entry into Peking, the Manchu conquerors assiduously courted the Han Chinese literati while simultaneously enacting policies to perpetuate their separate cultural identity. What this identity was, and how it was created, will be treated in chapter 7; this section focuses on the retention of Manchu language, clothing, archery, and food as symbolic markers for the Qing conquest elite.[56]

Language Policy

The name "Manchu" was adopted in 1635 by Hongtaiji, who proclaimed:

> Our *gurun* (tribe, state) originally had the names Manju, Hada, Ula, Yehe, and Hoifa. Formerly ignorant persons have frequently called [us] *jušen*. The term *jušen* refers to the Sibo and Chaomergen barbarians and has nothing to do with our *gurun*. Our *gurun* establishes the name Manju. Its rule will be long and transmitted over many generations. Henceforth persons should call our *gurun* its original name, Manju, and not use the previous demeaning name.[57]

By this action, Hongtaiji accomplished several goals. He provided a new identity that could superscribe the tribal identities of the Jurchen and other northeastern tribes, many of whom had been subjugated by force. Chapter 7 will describe the policies that inscribed this new identity with an origin myth and transformed shamanic rituals to serve new political goals. This new identity was accompanied by the invention of a Manchu written language.

The invention of a writing system coincided with the emergence of the Qing state. Jurchen belongs to the Tungus group of Altaic languages. Although the Jurchen Jin had devised a written language, the Jianzhou Jurchen ancestors of Nurgaci had abandoned its use in favor of Mongolian. In 1599 Nurgaci ordered two men to create a "national writing system"; they produced an adaptation of the Mongol script called (retroactively) *tongki fuka akū hergen* (script without circles or dots) or "old Manchu."[58] Changes to the script in 1632 produced the *tongki fuka sindaha hergen* (script with circles or dots) used for the rest of the dynasty.

Mongolian continued to be a major language among the banner elite, but the documents were now written in Manchu, and the new offices created by the growing state apparatus were given Manchu names. After 1644 Manchu, which was called "Qing writing" (*Qingwen*) in Chinese, became one of the two official languages. In actuality, since many officials during the Shunzhi reign did not know Chinese, spoken and written Manchu dominated the highest levels of government until the 1670s. Thereafter, Manchu became a security language for the rulers. Manchu officials were required to communicate in Manchu and documents relating to the imperial lineage, banner affairs, and Inner Asian military matters were often written only in Manchu. Numerous studies demonstrate the importance of these Manchu-language archival materials for Qing historians.[59]

Manchu was altered by the conquest. While Jianzhou Jurchen, the spoken language of Nurgaci and his kinsmen, was rendered into writing and became the standard for "classical" Manchu, the growth of the bureaucracy stimulated a rapid increase in the Chinese terms that were directly imported into the language. The Chinese words for "capital city" (*ducheng*), "imperial city" (*huangcheng*), and Forbidden City (*zijincheng*) were among many that found their way into Manchu. Meanwhile, beginning in the 1620s, the Manchu rulers ordered translations of a large number of Chinese-language works on Confucian thought, Chinese law, and history.[60]

The use of Manchu for governance created a demand for dictionaries. Dictionaries answered the needs of Chinese officials who studied Manchu and also served as texts in the new banner schools. The earliest Manchu-Chinese dictionary, completed in 1682, was compiled by a Chinese named Shen Qiliang. His second work, the *daicing gurun-i yooni bithe* (in Chinese, *Da Qing quanshu*), appeared in 1683 and was reprinted in 1713. According to scholars, it preserves many colloquial terms and unstandardized renderings of words found in the Manchu of the Kangxi era, which disappeared after the 1708 publication of the imperially authorized *han-i araha manju gisun-i buleku bithe* (*Yuzhi Qingwenjian*). In its 1772 revision, the *han-i araha nonggime toktobuha manju gisun-i buleku bithe* (*Yuzhi zengding Qingwenjian*) became a standard primer in banner schools. Eventually this work was produced in the five languages of the subject peoples identified by the Qianlong emperor: Manchu, Tibetan, Mongolian, Turkic, and Chinese.[61]

Manchu was purged of much of its Chinese-derived vocabulary during the Qianlong reign. The emperor complained that too many Chinese terms had crept into Manchu-language memorials and ordered a group headed by Grand Secretary Nacin to draw up a list of new Manchu terms that would replace the old loan-words. In 1747 a list was distributed and officials were ordered henceforth to "write in a Manchu manner" (*manjurame ubaliyambuhe bithe*).[62] At this point, capital became *gemun hecen,* the imperial city *dorgi hoton,* and the Forbidden City *dabkuri dorgi hoton* in Manchu. Place-names were also changed. Hongli himself seems to have suggested the Manchu renderings that would differentiate homophones, both pronounced "Jinzhou," in two place-names under the jurisdiction of Shengjing. He ordered that the Chinese renderings of Manchu and Mongol place-names be standardized and written in their entirety, lest errors be made. The project eventually introduced over 1,700 new Manchu words.

The purification of Manchu vocabulary took place in the written language used for official communications and in prayers to shamanic deities. The written or "classical" form of Manchu was preserved until 1911, while spoken Manchu continued to evolve. Phonetic changes in the language spoken by Peking bannermen reflected the influence of other Jurchen dialects, imported into the capital by native speakers in banner units, and were also products of prolonged contact with a Chinese-speaking society.[63] Imperial edicts notwithstanding, classical Manchu became an artifact of the bureaucratic communications that were its primary raison d'être. Its colloquial flavor was lost as the written style influenced Manchu speech. Sentences became longer, and more indirect expressions were used. But Manchu survived as a living language among banner troops garrisoned in the far west and northeast.

During the early seventeenth century the Manchus had subjugated the Mongol- and Tungus-speaking peoples inhabiting Northeast Asia. To counter Russian penetration into the Amur River drainage, the Qing incorporated many of these peoples into the banners as "new Manchus" (ice manju) and stationed them in garrisons constructed in the region.[64] Like the other banner troops, the new Manchus were "Manchuized." Banner schools were established in the garrison towns to teach Manchu and to acculturate groups of hunter-fishers to the bureaucratic routines. The first school was created in 1693 by the military governor of Jilin, and eventually the major northeastern garrisons had schools. The impact of this "Manchuization" on the Daur Mongol language was lasting and has been studied by several scholars.[65]

Linguists classify Manchu into four regional subgroups, of which the standard, Peking speech, is called the western dialect. Shengjing, the pre-1644 capital, is the center of southern Manchu; Ningguta, the center of eastern Manchu; and the speech of persons living along the Sahalian and Nun Rivers is designated as northern Manchu. According to linguists, southern Manchu is the speech closest to the parent language, Jurchen. Ice manju troops were assigned to garrison duty in Shengjing, and others were later sent to Xinjiang, so Manchu-speakers were dispersed from their original homeland and lived in enclaves for much of the dynasty. Xibo communities in Xinjiang and a few Manchu communities in remote parts of Heilongjiang preserved Manchu as a living language through the late nineteenth century. Even today, when virtually everyone in the three northeastern provinces speaks Chinese as their native language, researchers claim to have identified one village in Heilongjiang in which Manchu is still spoken.[66]

Until about 1750, the Qing rulers believed that Manchu was (or should be, for the non-Manchus) the native language of bannermen. Banner education, which had initially focused on training bannermen to govern Chinese-speaking populations, now emphasized training in the traditional martial arts and proficiency in spoken and written Manchu. Although schools were also established for ordinary bannermen's children, the proportion of places to the size of the potential school-going population heavily favored imperial kinsmen. The Imperial Clan Academies (*zongxue*) and their counterparts (*jueloxue*) for descendants of Nurgaci's brothers held periodic examinations among candidates for appointment to office, in the banner administration, palace administration, and civil service.[67]

Manchu Names

Manchus were forbidden to adopt the Han Chinese custom of using a surname and the Manchu equivalent, the clan (*mukûn*) name, was not cited in normal official correspondence. Emperors railed against persons who adopted three-character personal names because the first character of such names, written in Chinese, might be mistaken for a surname. Even more objectionable were attempts to use *man* (as in Manchu) or *juelo* (*gioro*) as names: in 1767, the emperor issued an edict: "Recently the Board of Rites nominated Manjishan, the son of Mamboo. The name Manjishan is really using 'man' as a surname. I have changed Manjishan's name to Jishan. Jishan is a *juelo*, which is very prestigious. But Jishan doesn't honor this, instead he takes 'man' as a surname, like Han people. Where's the principle in this? The Imperial Clan Court ought to pay attention to prevent this kind of thing." [68] During the late eighteenth and nineteenth centuries, emperors ordered the banner officials and the Imperial Clan Court to ensure that imperial kinsmen did not adopt three-character names. Nonetheless, within four generations kinsmen in the main line were taking Chinese names that followed the Han conventions (see chapter 3). In the collateral (*juelo*) line, however, Manchu naming seems to have persisted.[69]

Clothing

In contrast to the "ample, flowing robes and slippers with upturned toes of the sedentary Ming," the Manchus wore the "boots, trousers, and functional riding coats of nomadic horsemen."[70] Manchu clothing resembled the dress of earlier conquest dynasties in its fundamental features. Hoods provided insulation for the head, essential in the cold Northeast Asian win-

ters. Whereas the wide and long-sleeved loose robes of the Han Chinese
encumbered movement, Manchu clothing allowed physical mobility. The
coat was close fitting, and slashed openings on four sides helped the wearer
move freely when on horseback. Its long, tight sleeves ended in cuffs shaped
like a horse's hoof, designed to protect the back of the hands from the wind.
Trousers, worn by both sexes, protected the wearer's legs from the horse's
flanks and the elements. Boots with rigid soles facilitated mounted archery
by allowing riders to stand in the iron stirrups. The stirrup, "perhaps man-
kind's most important technical invention since the bit," made mounting
easy and permitted the rider to stand in the stirrups, thus extending the
distance a horse could cover. Moreover, standing in the stirrups permitted
an archer to shoot with greater force and accuracy.[71]

Manchu dress was made synonymous with martial vigor. Hongtaiji,
who drew up a dress code after 1636, made a direct connection between the
decline of the Liao, Jin, and Yuan dynasties and their adoption of Han Chinese clothing, speech, and the sedentary way of life. In 1636 and again in
1637, he exhorted the banner princes and Manchu officials to "always remember" that the Manchu conquests were founded on riding and archery.
He argued that the "wide robes with broad sleeves" of the Ming were completely unsuited to the Manchu way of life and worried lest his descendants
forget the sources of their greatness and adopt Han Chinese customs.[72]

The Manchu conquerors firmly rejected the adoption of Ming court
dress. Chen Mingxia, an early Ming adherent to the Manchu cause, was
impeached and executed in 1654 for suggesting (among other things) that
the Qing court adopt Ming dress "in order to bring peace to the empire."[73]
This theme was reiterated by the Qianlong emperor, who cited Hongtaiji's
historical analogies and enjoined his descendants to retain the Manchu
clothing. All bannermen, regardless of whether they were in the Manchu,
Mongol, or Hanjun banners, were required to wear Manchu dress.

The Qing also forced the conquered Han Chinese population to adopt
the Manchu hairstyle. From 1645, every Chinese male was ordered to shave
his forehead in the Manchu manner and to wear his hair in a queue (*tifa*)
as a symbol of his acquiescence to Manchu rule. This North Asian hairstyle
contrasted sharply with the Ming custom, in which men combed their long
hair into elaborate arrangements hidden under horsehair caps. Especially
in central and south China, the Manchu regulation of 1645 united educated
men and peasants in outraged resistance.[74]

Qing rulers did not uniformly apply the same regulations to all subjects.
Rather, they followed the Liao and Jin precedents in adapting different regulations for different ethnic subjects. While the Han Chinese population

were governed using the Ming precedents, bannermen were subject to the very different banner laws, shaped outside China proper, just as Mongols, Tibetans, and Uighurs were ruled in accordance with their own traditions. Scholars note that the shaved forehead and queue was not required of Mongols, Tibetans, Uighurs, or the minorities in southwestern China. Even though attempts to assimilate the southwestern minorities were intensified during the Yongzheng reign (1723–35) and after the suppression of the Jinquan rebellions in the 1770s, the *tifa* policy was only nominally applied.[75]

Bannerwomen were forbidden to adopt the Chinese custom of footbinding. They were also barred from wearing Ming-style dresses with wide sleeves, and the Chinese single earring instead of the Manchu custom of wearing three earrings in one ear. From the middle of the eighteenth century, emperors complained that the dress code was being infringed. As the Qianlong emperor stated,

> When I inspected the *xiunü* [marriage draft] this time, there were girls who emulated Han Chinese clothing and jewelry. This is truly not the Manchu custom. If they do this before me, what is willfully worn at home? . . . Although this is a small matter, if we do not speak to correct it, there must gradually be a change in our customs, which are greatly tied to our old Manchu ways. Take this and have the banner high officials proclaim it to the bannermen.[76]

Bannerwomen continued to break the rules. In another inspection of potential brides in 1775, the emperor observed that bondservant daughters were wearing only one pendant earring and not three pierced earrings in one ear. In the 1804 *xiunü* inspection, nineteen young girls in the Bordered Yellow Hanjun showed up with bound feet. An 1839 edict punishing the fathers of young girls who presented themselves for imperial inspection wearing Chinese-style coats with wide sleeves shows that emperors continued to resist these signs of acculturation.[77]

Court Robes Qing officials wore a variant of Manchu dress at court. The Shunzhi emperor responded in 1651 to a censor's request that the Ming imperial robe and crown be adopted: "Each dynasty has its own regulations. A court consists in venerating Heaven and loving the people, and in ruling the empire in peace. Why must it consist of using the robe and crown?"[78] The clothing of the emperor, nobles, and court officials was divided into three categories: court dress (*lifu, chaofu*) for ritual occasions, semiformal dress (*jifu*), and ordinary wear (*changfu, bianfu*). Court dress, the most formal attire, "was the most conservative" in "preserving features distinctive to Manchu national costume worn prior to the conquest."[79] The color and decorative motifs on the clothing of all males and females at court were seasonally regulated to conform to the rank of the wearer. Rank badges (*puzi*), square insignia displayed on the surcourt worn with semiformal dress by civil and military officials, were a Ming practice that was continued by the Qing.

The dragon robes that constituted semiformal attire first appear in Chinese court records in the late seventh century. The dragon was a popular symbol in both Han and non-Han culture. From the Song dynasty, the dragon became the symbol of the emperor and by convention to refer to the emperor's person: his body was the dragon body, his hands the claws, his capital the dragon's pool. The Song, Liao, Jin, and Yuan dynasties forbade subjects to wear robes with dragon patterns. But the dragon symbolism did not simply isolate the emperor from everyone else. There was a hierarchy of nine types of dragons, of which the highest, the five-clawed dragon (*long*), was prominently featured on the emperor's court robes. The four-clawed dragon (*mang*) appeared on the robes of his brothers who held the higher princely ranks. And dragons topped the seals of rank (*bao*) presented to empresses and consorts.[80]

The Jurchen elaborated and modified the Ming ranking system, which classified dragon robes by their color and the type of dragon portrayed. Initially (1636) first-rank princes and the emperor were permitted to wear yellow robes with five-clawed dragons. The 1636 code reflected a collegial political tradition in which the emperor was primus inter pares; as the imperial power increased at the expense of the princes, the clothing hierarchy was altered to reflect the new power configuration. In the dress code of 1759, it was not the five-clawed dragon so much as the twelve symbols that were reserved for the sole use of the emperor and empress. The right to wear robes decorated with nine five-clawed dragons was restricted to the emperor, his sons, and princes in the first and second ranks. Among males, only the emperor could wear bright yellow (*minghuang*) robes; his sons wore other shades of yellow, while other princes and all Aisin Gioro wore blue or blue-black robes.[81]

Court clothing was part of the Qing emperor's gift exchanges with the rulers of Tibet and Mongolia. The privilege of wearing five-clawed dragon robes was extended to the Dalai lama, Panchen lama, and Jebtsundamba khutukhtu of Urga, the three most prominent dignitaries of Tibetan Buddhism. In Tibet dragon robes could be worn only by nobles and high lamas. Dragon robes were presented to Mongol nobles as the Mongol tribes were brought under Qing control: from 1661, the Qing dress code was applied to the Mongol nobility. Mongol nobles and their wives who accepted Aisin Gioro brides for their sons were given court robes as part of the bride's dowry; sons-in-law also received court robes. The use of these robes on special occasions in Mongolia seems to have persisted even after the dynasty ended.[82]

Archery

Although their direct ancestors were sedentary agriculturalists, the Manchus prized horses and the art of mounted archery. They used the Asian reverse or composite bow, which accumulates significantly more force than the European simple bow, yet is short enough for use by warriors on horseback. The arrow used with the Asian bow was also much lighter than its European counterpart, enabling riders to carry up to fifty arrows in a quiver. Accurate to at least three hundred yards, this bow was capable of piercing through armor at a hundred yards.[83]

Archery was of course not confined to the steppe peoples. Archery and riding are cited in the *Zhou li* among the six arts, and the founder of the Ming had himself held archery contests among officials. Skill in archery, particularly mounted archery, was however part of the steppe tradition. The mounted archers of the Manchu banners had the central role in the conquest of Northeast Asia and North China; the banners needed to maintain this skill in order to remain an effective fighting force. "Shooting the willow" (*sheliu*) a popular competition among the bannermen, was itself derived from a Khitan shamanic ritual.[84]

From 1667, each banner was responsible for manufacturing its own bows and arrows, using materials that came from the northeast. Bows were made in specified grades, determined by the "pull"—that is, the force with which the arrow would be released. Bows of the lowest grade, made for ordinary bannermen, had a pull of eight; those made for imperial princes and for the emperor had pulls of up to eighteen. Different kinds of wood were used for different qualities of bows: the emperor's "inspection bow" (*dayue gong*) and his "hunting bow" (*xingwei gong*) were made of mulberry wood, while princes' bows were made of birch and banner officers' bows of elm. Arrows were also differentiated by length and point into twenty-seven types, made out of poplar, willow, and birch. Manufacture of the emperor's own bows and arrows was the responsibility of the Imperial Armory, which was part of the Imperial Household Department.[85]

Qing emperors singled out mounted archery as a vital feature of Manchu identity and exhorted their descendants never to abandon it. As Hongtaiji once boasted, "Because [our soldiers] are skilled at mounted archery, they are victorious in fierce combat. When they attack cities, they take them. The people of the empire say of our soldiers, 'If they stand, they will not waver; if they advance, they will not retreat.' Their reputation is awesome, and nowhere more than in the vanguard." [86] Hongtaiji required bannermen to be put into three classes depending on their ability to hit a target on foot and on horseback. Those who failed to make the three grades were disciplined. If ten or more men in a company failed the test, their captain was stripped of his post; a banner with six hundred or more delinquent troops would have its top officers punished. [87]

The emphasis on archery and horsemanship increased in the eighteenth century. Complaints at the deterioration of the martial spirit actually began in 1636, when Hongtaiji contrasted the spirit of his generation with the lackadaisical attitude of the younger set:

> Nowadays sons are only acquainted with roaming the streets and planning plays and music. In the old days when everyone was poor, we were happy if a hunt were announced. Very few had servants; everyone looked over their horses, cooked food, and saddled up to go. Even with hardship everyone still unceasingly put forth their best effort. . . . Nowadays when there is a hunt, many youngsters say, "My wife or son is sick," or "I'm busy with affairs at home." If they're clinging to wife and babies and don't know how to exert themselves, how can the nation not be weakened? [88]

Precepts about continuing the hunting traditions were reiterated throughout at least the first half of the dynasty. Hongtaiji, Xuanye, and Hongli had chairs made with deer antlers with the ancestral precepts carved on their backs (see figure 1). In 1752 Hongli ordered steles inscribed with Hongtaiji's exhortations erected at the arrow pavilion within the Forbidden City, the viewing platform in Yuanmingyuan, and the drill grounds of the imperial guards and banners "in order that later generations will all know the traditional customs of the Manchus and respectfully follow them, studying mounted archery and familiarizing themselves with the Manchu language, prizing simplicity and eschewing extravagance." [89]

Archery was emphasized in the curriculum at the Palace School. The emperor's sons and some of his daughters were taught to hunt with the bow and arrow. A reminiscence by Yihuan, Prince Chun, discloses that imperial daughters continued to be proficient at archery into the 1850s:

> During the Xianfeng reign, I accompanied eighth brother . . . and ninth brother . . . to reside in the Agesuo. We would be summoned to test our literary and martial skills for glory or shame. One day the emperor . . .

ordered me, followed by fourth elder sister . . . to compete in archery. Eighth brother put four arrows into the cloth target, ninth brother thirteen arrows, and the emperor gave each of them a jade piece. I hit the target three times, but I was not rewarded. Instead, he ordered a tiny pigeon five *cun* in size to be hung and said to me, "If you hit this pigeon, you'll get a reward." At this point fourth sister bent her bow and took her first shot, hitting the target. I then shot and with my second arrow I hit it. I was summoned in front of the emperor and he personally handed me a jade lion.[90]

Skill in martial arts was naturally a prerequisite for rulership. Court painters were commissioned to depict emperors using the bow and arrow during the hunt. The Kangxi emperor proudly recalled the skill of his heir apparent, Yinreng, who brought a tiger down when he was nine. The Qianlong emperor recalled, "Since I was twelve *sui* and waited on my grandfather [the Kangxi emperor], I received great praise whenever I shot."[91] Another anecdote tells how the future Daoguang emperor (r. 1821–50), then nine years old, pleased his grandfather by hitting the target three times.[92]

Archery contests were a regular feature of imperial inspections of the troops. The Kangxi and Qianlong emperors held archery contests for banner and Green Standard troops during their southern tours and personally participated in them. Stories about the archery skills of the Kangxi emperor abound. The emperor could apparently pull the bow with either hand. Xuanye once stated that he could bend a bow with a pull of fifteen *li* and fire a fifty-two-inch arrow.[93] The emperor shot before an assembly of soldiers and officials on many occasions and, according to the Veritable Records, rarely missed the target.

One of the more dramatic of these attempts has been translated by Jonathan Spence.[94] In 1699, the emperor was in Hangzhou. He led his sons and the best archers in shooting from horseback. "After his first arrow had hit the target, he . . . dropped the reins and rode straight toward the target, but just as he was about to shoot the horse shied sharply away to the left; quickly the Emperor changed his grip on the bow and shot, the arrow hitting the target as the horse galloped past." According to the Veritable Records, the assembly knelt and praised the emperor's "godlike" martial skills (*shenwu*). On another occasion in 1684, when the nineteen-year-old emperor displayed his riding and archery skills, the Mongol nobles and high officials witnessing his "superhuman horsemanship and archery" (*qi she chaoshen*) and his "severe military countenance" (*junrong yanzheng*) were all awestruck.[95]

Imperial skill at archery figured in Qing relations with their Mongol allies. The archery contests held every year at the Mulan hunting grounds were intended to impress the Mongol nobles.[96] The Qianlong emperor once wrote,

> The Mongols used to esteem military matters. When in former years I would practice mounted archery or shoot a rifle at Mulan hunting ground, none of the Mongols who had accompanied me for several decades was unaware of the excellence of my martial skills. But since I did not go to the hunting ground this year, Mongol princes may say that I have become lazy . . . so I had deer (driven forth) to test my skills; those that I have recently killed were all killed with one shot. When I had this announced to the Mongol princes, they all submitted themselves with joy.[97]

Food

The palace kitchens had to prepare food for the emperor, his family, and the large number of maids, eunuchs, and other palace staff. Ordinary meals for the court came under the jurisdiction of the Imperial Household Department, in particular the Yuchashanfang (imperial buttery); state banquets were managed by the Guanglusi (court of banqueting), an agency of the Board of Rites. The Imperial Buttery itself was initially composed of several subdepartments specializing in tea, milk tea, and food. Although these were merged into one unit in 1750, the agency was later split into two units serving the inner and outer courts.[98]

When the Manchus entered Peking, they found Shandong chefs running the palace kitchens. The Manchus installed their own cooks, and Manchu taste dominated palace tables during the Shunzhi, Kangxi, and Yongzheng reigns. New food influences were introduced by the Qianlong emperor, who added famous chefs from Suzhou and Hangzhou to the kitchen staff. Zhang Dongguan, a Suzhou cook favored in the 1765–80 period, accompanied the emperor on his travels and received special rewards five times. During the late Qianlong and Jiaqing reigns, the palace employed approximately four hundred chefs. This staff was cut in half during the 1820–50s but expanded again during Empress Dowager Cixi's regencies. Chefs held lifelong tenure and could pass their posts on to a son. They were generally well treated. The best—a very small percentage of all employed—received stipends that were the equivalent of a district magistrate's salary.[99]

Qing imperial cuisine was cosmopolitan. With the exception of dog meat, which was taboo for Manchus, the food at court mirrored the diverse cultures in the empire. Although (see below) Manchu food was served to tributary ambassadors at the formal banquets and at court celebrations, the mingling of chefs representing different cuisines eventually gave rise to a new palace cuisine, with elements borrowed from the northeast, from Shandong, and from the Lower Yangzi, called the "Manchu-Chinese banquet" (*Man Han quanxi*). Never featured in palace banquets, the new eclectic style was described by writers during the 1760s as the fashion in government office kitchens. By the nineteenth century, the Manchu-Chinese cuisine had developed regional variants and could be found in major cities from Canton to Tianjin.[100]

The raw materials for the cuisine were also drawn from across the empire. Although the palace purchased some of its supplies in Peking, many of its grain, meat, fish, vegetables, and fruit came from its own estates. While the palace staff ate yellow, white, and purple "old rice" from the official granaries, the imperial table was supplied with first-grade rice from its own estates in the Yuquan mountains, Fengzeyuan, and Tangquan and some rice from Korea. Butter, milk cakes, and koumiss for the court were produced from cattle pastured outside the Great Wall at Zhangjiakou. Imperial estates sent muskmelons, watermelons, peas, eggplants, cabbages, cucumber, and different types of dried vegetables to Beijing, where they were put into vegetable vaults. The palace also had its own sources of honey, grapes, apricots, peaches, Chinese hawthorns, and other fruits.[101]

A significant part of the imperial diet was also supplied by tributary presentations. The seasonal shipments of local produce were a concrete manifestation of submission to imperial rule, required of subjects and of tributary states. Each winter the military governor stationed at Mukden sent sixty head of young deer to the court. Outer Mongols sent sheep and koumiss. Milk cakes, special kinds of local fish, winter bamboo shoots, deer tails (a delicacy), deer tongues, and a myriad of different foodstuffs were sent in seasonal rotation to Peking. A list of hundreds of such items sent to the court from 1774 to 1778 shows that the northeast ranked first in terms of the frequency, quantity, and types of foodstuffs sent to the court.[102] Father Ripa, residing in Peking during the Kangxi reign, observed: "'During the period of frost,' that is, from October till March, Northern Tartary sends to the capital an enormous quantity of game, consisting chiefly of stags, hares, wild boars, pheasants, and partridges; whilst Southern Tartary furnishes a great abundance of excellent sturgeon and other fish, all of which being frozen, can easily be kept during the whole winter."[103] Fresh lichee was sent by governors and governors-general from Zhejiang, Fujian, and Guangdong.[104] Interest in southern products was dampened during the Daoguang reign—Minning preferred northern dishes—but rose to new heights under Empress Dowager Cixi. Coastal areas submitted sharks' fins, abalone, sea cucumber, prawns, jellyfish, kelp, and other seafoods during the late nineteenth century to satisfy the Guangxu emperor's love of these foods.

The most elaborate palace cuisine was served at banquets. The court distinguished between Manchu banquets, which were subdivided by cost into six grades, and Han Chinese banquets. The first-, second-, and third-class Manchu banquets were prepared for the deceased imperial ancestors. The highest grade of Manchu banquet served to living human beings, grade four (at a cost of 4.43 taels per table), was the food served at the New Year, on imperial birthdays, weddings, and the winter solstice. Korean ambassadors, Mongol sons-in-law, the Dalai lama, and the Panchen lama were feted at grade-five Manchu banquets, other tributary envoys at grade six (2.26 taels per table).[105]

In keeping with their cultural policies, the Qing rulers regarded their traditional cuisine as the primary cuisine of their empire, especially appropriate for their relations with the non-Han peoples. Manchu food was served to tributary missions coming to court and at the birthday, wedding, and major seasonal banquets held for the emperor and his court: the latter included banquets feting Kazakh, Tibetan, Uighur, and Mongol nobles, held in Chengde and Peking; the banquet for Mongol sons-in-law, held every year as part of the New Year festivities; and the banquet for close kinsmen (see chapter 2), which was held annually beginning with the Daoguang reign. Han banquets, which were also classified into six grades, were served to compilers of the Veritable Records, examiners at the metropolitan civil service examination, and civil and military degree-winners at the metropolitan examinations.[106]

Archival documents, which preserve the daily menus and food expenditures for at least part of the Qing dynasty, reveal the eating habits of the imperial family on ordinary days. According to Father Benoit,

> His Majesty always eats alone, being assisted at his meals only by the eunuchs who serve him. The hour of his dining is fixed at 8 A.M. and of his supper at 1 P.M. Outside these two meals, he takes nothing during the day except some drinks, and toward evening some light refreshment. . . . His ordinary drink during meals is tea, which may be simply infused with ordinary water, or mixed with milk, or composed of different types of tea. . . . Despite the quantity and the magnificence of the meals that are served to his Majesty, he never takes more than a quarter of an hour for each repast.[107]

Usually the emperor ate in his residence, sometimes he ate in the palace in which he held audiences and conducted business. The meals were served at his order, in whatever locale he chose. The archival records tell us that on November 2, 1747, the Qianlong emperor had his morning meal, served after 6 A.M., in the Hongdedian. The next day he took his evening meal—normally served after the noon hour, and the major meal of the day—in the Chonghuagong. The emperor might have snacks in between these meals, or a light snack at 6 P.M. These meals tended to be much simpler and featured traditional Manchu specialties such as boiled pork, wild meat, and sweet cakes (*bobo*). Many emperors, including the Kangxi, Qianlong, and Daoguang emperors, preferred plain dishes.[108]

Milk, used in tea and in cakes, was a distinctive feature of the Qing imperial diet. While in residence in Peking, the court was supplied with milk from cows in paddocks in Nanyuan, the hunting preserve south of the capital. When the emperor traveled north to Chengde and the hunting grounds at Mulan, milk cows were moved from imperial estates in the northeast. Palace regulations show that twenty-four milk cows, each supplying two catties of milk a day, were reserved for the empress dowager; one hundred cows for the emperor and empress, and so on down to the two cows designated for a fifth-ranking imperial consort. In the early nineteenth century, these allowances were significantly reduced because of a shortage of milk cows, but the practice continued.[109]

The Language of Rank

The Qing dynasty's special titles were partially derived from non-Han and partially from Ming precedents. The official terminology referred to the emperor with the character *shang* meaning "supreme." References to the emperor were elevated above the text to show respect. The character *zhen* was reserved for the imperial "I" used in edicts, and special verbs (*yi, yu*) were used to describe his movements. Special terms—*zhuanshan* (transmitting food), *jinshan* (presenting food), and *yongshan* (using food)—were used to describe the act of eating by imperial personages.[110]

Imperial ancestors were called by their temple names; prayers addressed to them used their temple and posthumous names. Each ancestor had Manchu and Chinese posthumous names.[111] In Manchu records, Nurgaci, who had been called the *sure beile* (wise prince) in the first part of his life, and, after 1616 *han* (khan), became *dergi hūwangdi*. Since *dergi* signified "upper" or "superior," the title itself was a conflation of the Manchu *dergi ejen* (superior ruler) and the Chinese *Taizu huangdi*, being the title frequently given to the founder of a dynasty. Hongtaiji's name was probably a rendition of the Mongol noble title, Khongtaiji, and many imperial kinsmen in the conquest period had Mongol titles and names.[112] Mongols called the Manchu emperor the Ejen Khaghan (ruler khan of khans) or Bogdo Khaghan (great khan of khans). In the Khalkha Mongol chronicle of the different reincarnations of their highest Tibetan Buddhist prelate, the Jebtsundamba khutukhtu, the Manchu ruler is the "emperor of the Black Kitad," as opposed to the Russian czar, the "emperor of the Yellow Kitad." Echoing the Mongol practice, the Russian embassy of 1653 addressed the emperor as the "Bogdo khan czar."[113]

Officials addressed the emperor as "divine khan" (*enduringge han*) and "divine ruler" (*enduringge ejen*) in their Manchu-language memorials. Until 1723 memorialists referred to themselves as "slaves" (*aha* in Manchu, *nücai* in Chinese); this phrase probably originated in Manchu custom: Ishibashi Takao argues that the Manchu hierarchy created during the seventeenth century and culminating in the Yongzheng reign emphasized the lord-slave (*ejen-aha*) relationship and made the ruler the only *ejen* within the state. Thereafter, the use of *nücai* by high officials was prohibited, but it continued to show up in memorials, even when the memorialists themselves were imperial princes. Examples of such memorials include reports in 1799 on the Qianlong emperor's tomb, written by Prince Zhuang and other imperial agnates.[114]

High officials and princes holding office normally used the term meaning "minister" (*amban* in Manchu, *chen* in Chinese), except in the formulaic memorials giving thanks for imperial grace, when *nücai* remained. The term (*amban*) was also used by the emperor himself when addressing his ancestors.[115] An emperor's references to his parents (in the third person) would also be elevated above the rest of the text to show respect. The Manchu act of respect, putting one knee on the ground, continued to be normative behavior for the social inferior when two bannermen met. The accompanying hand gesture was initially to have the right hand hanging down while kneeling with the right leg. Later the gesture was simplified so that the right leg was deeply bent but not kneeling, while the body was upright with the right hand down. Imperial nobles performed the "double kneeling," kneeling on the right leg while placing both hands on the left knee, which was bent. The superior would acknowledge this greeting by bowing. There were parallel gestures appropriate for bannerwomen.[116]

The court vocabulary extended to birth and death. The birthday of an empress or consort of the first three ranks was "a thousand autumns" (*qianqiu*); the empress dowager's birthday was the "ten thousand years" (*wan shou jie*); and the emperor's birthday, "ten thousand years' sacred fete" (*wan shou sheng jie*). There was a special verb (*beng*) for the death of an emperor or empress; another (*hong*) for the death of a prince, princess, or higher-ranking consort; and yet a third (*ke, keshi*) for the deaths of other court personages. There were at least three different terms for coffins, and two for tombs. References to these matters in Manchu also used special terms.

Qing Rulership in Art

"The early Ch'ing emperors used the arts as tools for the glorification of the state."[117] Nowhere was the multicultural nature of Qing rulership more evident than in the paintings, porcelains, and other objets d'art that were created for palace use and for presentation to officials and embassies. The use of material culture as an expression of the court's cosmopolitan vision is exemplified in the activities of the Qianlong emperor.

Hongli pursued the traditional connoisseurship of Han Chinese literati. He began to collect Chinese paintings and calligraphy while still in his teens, and eventually owned "the finest collection of antique Chinese paintings in history." He acquired inkstones and inscribed inkstones, ink cakes, and brushes for presentation to officials as well as for personal use. He was an avid collector of many things. Throughout his life he kept a staff of assistants busy cataloging his acquisitions and he himself wrote innumerable colophons commenting on individual pieces in his collection. With his various kinds of antiques and *objets d'art*, the Qianlong emperor owned "more than a million objects."[118]

Han Chinese aesthetic pursuits were behind only one part of the imperial collection. The Qing palace also held curiosities from Europe such as the elaborate clocks presented by embassies to the court, which were imitated in the palace workshops with technical assistance from Jesuits (see chapter 5). European enameling techniques entered through trade and through the Jesuits, inspiring production of new kinds of colored enameled porcelain such as *famille rose*. Although many of these porcelains were made for export, very fine porcelains and cloisonné pieces, decorated with European decorative motifs, were also produced for the palace.[119] Hongli prized Hindustan jades, a term that includes jades carved in territories under Ottoman and Mughal rule. The jades were presented as tribute and, especially after the Qing conquest of the Tarim Basin, as trade items. The

Qianlong emperor's poems, which are inscribed on many of the pieces in the imperial collection, extol their delicacy, the thinness of the carving, and the refinement of the decorative designs.[120]

The court lived amongst possessions that came from every part of the globe; and designedly so. The syncretic and eclectic taste displayed in the products of the palace workshops testify to the exposure of the court to the technical and aesthetic accomplishments of both east and west. The paintings commissioned by the Qing emperors for their palaces speak even more directly to their political goals. Sometimes the political motivation was direct and explicit, as in the Qianlong emperor's desire to commemorate the Qing victory over the Zunghars (1755). Hongli ordered Jesuit artists to engrave sixteen prints of decisive battles in this campaign, commissioned portraits of meritorious officials (mostly soldiers), and personally inscribed (in both Manchu and Chinese) the first fifty portraits. Portraits such as the one of Ayusi (see figure 2) were displayed in the Ziguangge, a hall on the shores of Zhonghai within the imperial city, where European ambassadors were received and Mongol in-laws were entertained.[121]

Qing emperors also wished to display the might of their empire in paintings. The political inspiration for handscrolls depicting "Foreign Envoys Bearing Tribute" commissioned by the Qianlong and Jiaqing emperors seems straightforward: artists were to show, as accurately as possible, the vast (290 persons in all) and diverse peoples who had submitted to Qing overlordship.[122] Something of the same interest—showing the diversity of peoples who came to offer tribute—probably prompted the emperor to order Ignace Sichelbart (1708–80) to paint on the upper and middle portions of a screen depictions of the faces (*lianxiang*) of ambassadors from Europe (Xiyang) who visited the court in the Kangxi, Yongzheng, and Qianlong reigns; the faces of the Jesuits Ignace Kögler (1680–1746), Castiglione, and Sichelbart himself were painted on the bottom portion.[123]

Other political messages conveyed through paintings can be ascertained from an inspection of the subject matter. Giuseppe Castiglione's wonderful painting "A Hundred Horses," painted at court during the Yongzheng reign, depicts a herd of horses in a setting reminiscent of the pasturelands of the north. The Qianlong emperor commissioned many paintings of hunts at Mulan and entertainments at Chengde. He inscribed (in Manchu, Mongolian, Chinese, and Uighur) paintings of his favorite horses each with its own name; and paintings of his hunting dogs (in Manchu, Mongolian, and Chinese).[124]

The most interesting and subtle imperial self-images that pertain to

Qing rulership appear in paintings recently analyzed by Wu Hung. Although scholars have commented before on the ideological significance of the *tangkas* representing the Qianlong emperor as Mañjuśrī, the bodhisattva of compassion and wisdom (see chapter 7), it is Wu Hung who in 1995 introduced to a Western audience the fourteen album paintings held by the Palace Museum, Beijing, which depict the Yongzheng emperor in different guises. Although some of the paintings depict Yinzhen in a Han Chinese cultural setting—as a Daoist or a Chinese scholar—others show him as a Tibetan Buddhist monk, a Mongol noble, and even in European wig, vest, and breeches.[125] When Wu Hung notes, "No previous emperors, either Chinese or Manchu, had ever had themselves portrayed in this manner," he must be referring to the explicitly non-Han representations of Yinzhen, since there are many Qing court paintings depicting not only Yinzhen but other Qing emperors dressed in (the forbidden) Han Chinese robes.[126] What should we make of such paintings?

In other writing, Wu Hung rightly stresses the importance of the format of a painting in interpretations of its meaning.[127] Paintings that are mounted on screens are on permanent public display; if they are displayed in halls where audiences or other formal assemblies take place, the emperor must have intended to convey messages through their visual representations. One example of this kind is a set of paintings of twelve Chinese beauties, which were initially mounted in a screen in Yinzhen's study when he was still a prince. Scholars dismiss the notion that the women depicted on the screen were Yinzhen's consorts. The women are idealized figures and belong to a well-known Chinese painting genre. Wu Hung argues that such paintings "gained new significance when they were transported from their original Chinese cultural context into the court of non-Chinese rulers."[128] Among their several meanings is a discourse about the relationship between the Qing and the subjugated Han Chinese. The beauties symbolize "an imaginary south" (China), exquisite but also decadent and weak, which the Qing rulers possessed or conquered. What adds to the interest is that these paintings were displayed in the period before Yinzhen ascended the throne. Wu speculates that placing these idealized beauties in his study is evidence of a "fundamental dualism" in the prince's self-identity—a dualism that disappeared when he became emperor. Yinzhen then altered his villa and had the paintings of the twelve beauties rolled up and put into storage.[129]

Paintings mounted in scrolls could be unrolled and hung on walls—this was the case for the "ancestor portraits" hung in the Shouhuangdian (see chapter 8), the imperial hall lying north of the palace that was used for family rituals in which women, who were banned from the Temple of the Ancestors, could participate. Ancestor portraits were intended for display only on specified ritual occasions. Album paintings, and paintings in a handscroll format, however, can really only be seen by an individual viewer. As such, they are the most private of the different paintings that appear in an imperial collection. The album paintings of Yinzhen in different cultural guises would thus fall into a category of paintings produced not for those admitted to imperial audience but presumably for the emperor himself. The paintings suggest that Yinzhen had already developed the idea that part of being emperor in an empire composed of diverse peoples was to take on the persona of the conquered subject(s). Yinzhen's use of painting to convey symbolic messages foretells the multicultural policies that culminated in the Qianlong reign.

"Spring's Peaceful Message" is a painting by Giuseppe Castiglione that was originally part of a screen in a room holding the Qianlong emperor's most prized Chinese art pieces. Although some date it to the Yongzheng reign, Wu Hung argues that it was commissioned by the Qianlong emperor. The painting has a deep blue background, against which two men, dressed in informal Chinese robes with their hair in topknots, stand facing obliquely toward each other and the center of the painting. The older man holds a branch of flowering prunus; the younger grasps the lower end of the branch with his left hand while his right touches a bamboo stalk. The faces on the men make it clear that the older is Yinzhen and the younger, Hongli. The painting conveys the message that Hongli is his father's chosen successor. Wu's interpretation of the symbolism of this painting suggests that a further advance in the image of rulership has taken place: garbed in Chinese robes, the Yongzheng and Qianlong emperors "have themselves become representatives of Chinese culture; their virtues are manifested through traditional Chinese symbols. . . . The emperors' disguise [in Chinese robes] . . . legitimates their possession and appropriation of the Chinese tradition by denying, however artificially, their image as outsiders who came to own this tradition through seizure."[130]

Taken as a whole, Qing court paintings exemplify the vision of Qing rulership held by the rulers themselves. Produced by court painters from Europe as well as China, the paintings range widely in their subject matter. They depict not just emperors masquerading as Han Chinese literati, but emperors hunting in Mulan, and sitting as manifestations of bodhisattvas in Tibetan Buddhist iconography. The Qing rulers did not present themselves simply as Chinese or Manchu monarchs. Governing diverse peoples, they "took on" different cultural guises and portrayed themselves within different cultural frames. Only thus could they act as the integrating center of the empire.

Part 2

THE SOCIAL ORGANIZATION
OF THE QING COURT

Chapter 2   The Conquest Elite and the Imperial Lineage

The conquest elite evolved during the Qing dynasty as a group that was legally separated from the Han Chinese conquered population. It played a significant role in Qing governance, particularly but not only in the administration of the Northeast and Inner Asian peripheries that were added to the empire. Although they also filled positions in the civil service, these banner nobles were particularly dominant in the inner-court posts and thus advised the emperor. Their activities supplemented and overlapped with those of the Han Chinese literati who dominated the outer-court offices. This political bifurcation was another aspect of the realpolitik of imperial rulership that originated in the politics of conquest.

The first major division in Qing society was between bannermen and the civilian population. As indicated by the Manchu, Mongol, and Hanjun divisions of the banners (see below), the division was not ethnic but political, between conquerors and conquered population. Territorial expansion brought new groups into the conquest elite. Some, like the Khalkha Mongols, were incorporated into the banners and the noble titles of their leaders were confirmed by the throne. Others, including high prelates of the Tibetan Buddhist orders and Muslim *begs*, had their elite status confirmed in exchange for their submission to the Qing. They too joined the conquest elite.

Although the conquest elite persisted as a privileged group throughout the dynasty, shifts in imperial perspective after 1722 prompted shifts in self-identities within their ranks. Previously Manchu rulers had focused their efforts on building multiethnic coalitions in the northeast. Ethnic lines were blurred and flexible in the banners, the primary institutional mechanism for integrating diverse peoples into an efficient military organization. Expediency and battle efficiency were certainly more important than ethnic classifications during this critical period in Manchu state-building. Nurgaci classified "individuals on the basis of their culture," and the Kangxi emperor was willing to move whole tribes from the Mongol or Hanjun registers to the Manchu banners.[1] In the eighteenth century, however, the political circumstances were very different.

The conquest of the Ming territories had been completed; the empire was on a much more stable foundation. Qing rulers substantially revised their priorities. Pamela Crossley describes how hereditary assignment of banner captaincies and other posts stimulated disputes among rival claimants and led first the Yongzheng then the Qianlong emperor to order that genealogies be compiled for all bannermen. She notes that the shift from oral to written charters of descent groups hardened Manchu conceptions of kinship, which were much more fluid in the sixteenth and early seventeenth centuries than they became by the late eighteenth century. Identity within the ruling elite became a matter of genealogical descent. During the Qianlong reign, policies attempting to preserve Manchu identity (see chapter 1) reinforced the emphasis on ethnicity.[2]

Alongside the compilation projects came another development that underlined ethnic divisions within the banners. The Qianlong emperor's reconsideration of *erchen,* individuals who served two ruling houses, along with his rewriting of earlier histories to reflect his "insistence upon absolute loyalty to the dynasty under which one has been nurtured and rewarded," offers telling evidence of the dynasty's new stance. No longer a challenger, the Qing was now the status quo. For the sake of preserving a Confucian "loyalty" to the throne as an abstract value, it sacrificed the memory of the Han Chinese officials who had come over to the Manchu cause. Now it would lay claim to the same kind of loyalty from Han Chinese officials.

The reevaluation of *erchen* was in keeping with the altered imperial attitude toward the Hanjun. In the late eighteenth and nineteenth centuries, those intent on cutting bannermen subsidies gave preference to Manchu bannermen and hit hardest at the Hanjun. Many Hanjun were expelled from the banners and put into the civilian population. In short, the rulers came increasingly to see Hanjun as "Chinese" rather than as members of the conquest elite. The same trend can be seen in policies toward the empire's subject peoples. Hongli's vision of himself as the penultimate and only unifier of the diverse peoples under his rule also advanced the concept of separate cultural identities within the conquest elite. The emperor himself had to be all things to all people but the subjects—Mongols, Tibetans, and Turkic-speaking Muslims—were to remain distinctly different in their religions, languages, and traditions.[3] The policies enacted by the Qianlong emperor enabled leaders of these peoples to voice specifically ethnic goals by late Qing and early republican times. That too was a consequence of the Qing vision of empire in the Qianlong reign.

The Manchus created a multiethnic fighting force, the banners, and rewarded outstanding Manchu, Mongol, and other leaders with noble titles. These banner nobles, an important pillar of Qing rule, were bound to the imperial house by history, imperial favor, and marriage exchanges. The innermost circle within the banner elite consisted of princes who belonged to the Aisin Gioro, the imperial lineage. Imperial princes, banner nobles, and bannermen were carefully separated from the subjugated Ming population and dominated the inner court during most of the dynasty. The throne succeeded in removing the autonomy of imperial princes and subjugating all nobles to the imperial will in the course of the seventeenth and early eighteenth centuries. It was then able to balance the conquest elite against the Han Chinese literati in the governance of the empire.

BANNERMEN

The Qing sociopolitical structure privileged the Manchus, Mongols and the Chinese-martial (*hanjun*) bannermen. All were members of banners, which were the major mechanism for the creation of new identities that were to have lasting historical significance. The banners were large civil-military units created from 1601 on to replace the small hunting groups of Nurgaci's early campaigns.[4] Banners were made up of companies, each composed (at least in theory) of three hundred warrior households. Manchus, Mongols, Chinese and others who joined the forces of Nurgaci and his kinsmen were organized into companies within the banners. The banners became administrative units for registration, conscription, taxation, and mobilization of the tribes and peoples who enlisted in the Manchu cause before 1644. Eight Manchu banners that were organized in 1616 expanded to include eight Mongol banners by 1635 and eight Chinese banners by 1642. The conquest of China was achieved by these combined multiethnic forces.[5]

The banner organization facilitated the creation of a Manchu nation by putting the diverse peoples of the northeast under one regimen. Bannermen's ethnic backgrounds did not always match the ethnic demarcations of the banners. Detailed analysis of pre-1644 documents shows that every pre-1635 banner had a Mongol cavalry. Some of these Mongol units remained in the Manchu banners when the Mongol banners were created in 1635. The Manchu banners also had Korean and Han Chinese companies: the first belonged to the regular forces, the second to the bondservant companies who bore the flags and drums of the banner lords and the *han*. There was even a Russian company in the Bordered Yellow Banner, composed of soldiers captured in various engagements during the late seventeenth century.[6]

Except for a brief period in the 1640s, bannermen, whether in the Manchu, Mongol, or Chinese banners, were sharply differentiated from the conquered Chinese population. They were free men, as distinguished from hereditary bondservants (*booi*), Mongol, Korean, and Chinese prisoners of war who were enslaved and registered in companies under the banners. Bondservants, especially those in the upper three banners (the Bordered Yellow, Plain Yellow, and Plain White) that came under the emperor's personal control in the late seventeenth century, were appointed to important positions within the Imperial Household Department (see chapter 5). Bannermen were subject to separate laws and were forbidden to intermarry with the conquered Chinese population.[7] At least in theory, they were supported by the state, who settled them in garrisons at strategic points throughout the empire, and on agricultural lands in Northeast and North China. Despite gradual acculturation—bannermen living in garrisons in China lost the ability to speak Manchu—bannermen remained a distinctive population in the eyes of Han Chinese.[8]

The relationship of bannermen to banner nobles was shaped by historical tradition and Nurgaci's statebuilding efforts.[9] The status of bannermen or *jušen*, the largest single group in sixteenth-century Jurchen society, declined as the power of their masters, the *beile*, increased. The term *beile* initially denoted chieftains of even fairly small numbers of subordinates. Nurgaci, for example, was one of the five Ningguta *beile* in the early 1580s, when he had at most five hundred men under him.[10] At this early stage in his career, Nurgaci's relations with his followers, his "companions" (*gucu*), was that of a primus inter pares.[11]

This situation changed after Nurgaci consolidated control over the Jianzhou Jurchen in the 1590s and began bringing the Haixi Jurchen under his authority. The term *jušen* acquired servile connotations.[12] After 1600, Nurgaci could punish and even enslave his *jušen*. At the same time, success in battle increased the size of the slave population in Jurchen society, a group that had been minuscule in Nurgaci's youth. Its members would later be enrolled in the bondservant companies of the banners (see chapter 5).

In 1644, on the eve of their entry into China proper, Manchu society was thus highly stratified. There was a small privileged elite whose status was derived from their military achievements, a large subordinated mass of warrior households, and a growing number of enslaved war captives. The population was organized into banner companies (*niru*) that continued to observe the older clan (*mukūn*) designations under which they had been organized. In companies composed of several different kinship groups, the strongest group's leader would frequently be named *niru ejen* (company captain). Companies were the constituent elements of the banners, headed at the top by a *gūsai ejen* (the banner commander), who was a distinguished military leader. Above the *gūsai ejen* were the banner lords (*beile*), who were the sons or other close kinsmen of Hongtaiji. The *beile* and the *amban* (councillors) were the highest decision-making officers in the Manchu state.[13]

In addition to filling hereditary military posts, bannermen became eligible to compete in the civil service examinations under special quotas and to serve in the Qing bureaucracy. Half of the presidencies of the Six Boards in the central government were reserved for bannermen; governors-general tended to be bannermen, while governors were usually Han Chinese. This was a fundamental element of the Qing system of joint rule, which sought to ensure that the administration of the former Ming lands would not be completely dominated by Han Chinese officials. One study shows that twelve out of twenty-one individuals appointed by the Yongzheng emperor as "high officials serving on the Grand Council" were bannermen belonging to the emperor's upper three banners.[14] Together with the imperial kinsmen, bannermen participated actively in Qing governance.

Manchu Nobles

The hereditary banner nobility was composed of men who were not of imperial descent and Aisin Gioro who did not belong to the *zongshi* (see below). Nurgaci heaped rewards on Northeast Asian chieftains who brought their tribesmen over to his side, presenting them with wives, slaves, fine horses, military responsibilities and heritable titles, the most lasting of which were the headships of the banner companies.[15] The creation of the Manchu nobility can be illustrated by tracing the histories of Nurgaci's most prominent nonkin associates, the Five Councillors (*amban*) appointed by 1615: Eidu (1562–1621), named *baturu* (hero) in 1587 after he captured the town of Barda in one of Nurgaci's early campaigns; Fiongdon *jargūci* (lawgiver; 1564–1620), hailed as "Nurgaci's most valuable associate";

Hohori (1561–1624); Hurhan (1576–1623), who "was brought up by Nurgaci as one of his own sons"; and Anfiyanggu (1559–1622).[16]

Several of these men were allied to Nurgaci through marriage. Like other non-Han regimes, the Qing used marriage exchanges to cement Inner Asian alliances while forbidding intermarriage with the subjugated Ming population (see chapter 4). Eidu married Nurgaci's sister; Hohori wed Nurgaci's eldest daughter, Fiongdon his eldest granddaughter. All displayed great bravery in battle and won victories for the Manchus.[17] According to their official biographies, each was a "first-class high official" (*yideng dachen*) but that seems to have been a generic term without specific bureaucratic meaning. In 1620, in conjunction with attempts to systematize the organization of the banners, Nurgaci applied Chinese titles to banner offices. He appointed Eidu as the regional commander (*zongbingguan*) of the left wing; Fiongdon also became a regional commander of the left wing, one of the two major divisions incorporating the individual banners. Fiongdon, Anfiyanggu, and Hohori were appointed *gūsai ejen*, the highest banner post under the banner lord, which was later converted to the post of lieutenant general (*dutong*).

From the beginning the Manchus distinguished between a military rank that was occupied at the pleasure of the ruler and one that was hereditary. Each of the Five Councillors predeceased Nurgaci and passed his military rank to a son. Eidu's son Ebilun inherited the title of first-class "garrison general" (*zongbingguan*); the heirs of Fiongdon, Hohori, and Hurhan were appointed third-class garrison generals; and Anfiyanggu's heir inherited a sixteenth-rank title. In 1634 the military offices created by Nurgaci were translated into Manchu titles of nobility.[18]

During the Shunzhi reign (1644–61), hereditary titles were ordered into eight ranks, with the first six ranks (*gong* [duke], *hou* [marquis], *bo* [earl], *jingkini hafan* [chief officer of a banner], *ashan i hafan* [deputy officer of a banner], and *adaha hafan* [banner commander]) each subdivided into three classes. Changes in 1736 and 1752 produced twenty-seven separate noble ranks. The first fifteen were the most important.[19] Each rank was hereditary for a specified number of generations: the higher the rank, the greater the number of generations in which the title could be passed to an heir. A dukedom was ordinarily inheritable twenty-six times, while the lowest rank (*enqiyu*) was inheritable for only one generation. As the conquest drew to a close, however, these privileges were extended. In 1670 holders of the three highest ranks were given the right of perpetual inheritance. Holders of other high ranks were entitled after 1651 to the lowest rank in perpetuity, to guarantee that their descendants would never become mere commoners.

Nurgaci's successors heaped additional honors on Nurgaci's Five Councillors. When Hongtaiji declared himself emperor (1636), he posthumously honored these men. Eidu became Hongyi duke; Fiongdon had earlier (1631) been granted the title Zhiyi duke. Both men had their ancestral tablets installed in the Aisin Gioro ancestral temple erected in Mukden. But Eidu's heir, his son Ebilun (1618–73), was one of the regents under Oboi for the infant Kangxi emperor and lost his inherited rank (first-class viscount) as a result of the 1669 purge. The Kangxi emperor restored the title to Ebilun's heir in 1713; in 1755 the Qianlong emperor raised the hereditary title to second-class duke.[20]

The branch of the Niohuru clan descended from Eidu's eleven sons, registered in the Bordered Yellow Manchu banner, was one of the leading Manchu noble houses during the first half of the dynasty. During the reigns of Nurgaci, Hongtaiji, and Fulin, Eidu and his sons were generals who helped conquer China. Two grandsons marched against Galdan, the Zunghar Mongol leader, and still other descendants filled top banner and civilian posts in the provinces. During the nine generations covering the first two centuries of Qing rule, each generation renewed marital ties with the Aisin Gioro, with seventy-seven Niohuru males marrying Aisin Gioro daughters, and seventy-two Niohuru women marrying into the imperial family (several became empresses). The Niohuru also intermarried with other prominent Manchu noble houses: the Fuca, Magiya, Suwan Gūwalgiya.[21]

The postconquest policy of raising the noble ranks of conquest heroes like the Five Councillors reinforced the centrality of the conquest experience in the identity of the Qing elite. In 1659 the emperor commemorated Fiongdon's feats by lifting his heritable rank to a third-class dukedom. In 1778, the title was raised to the first class and by 1789 had gone through its eleventh transmission.[22] Hohori's title was elevated to third-class duke in 1628 and its hereditary transmission renewed in 1701. By the late Qianlong reign the title had been passed twelve times.[23]

Neither Anfiyanggu nor Hurhan's descendants fared as well. One of Anfiyanggu's grandsons was made a first-class baron for his own military achievements;[24] but Hurhan's heritable rank was stripped from his descendants because of his son Junta's actions. During the Shunzhi reign, the heritable title of third-class viscount was restored to the line to commemorate Hurhan's feats.[25]

Commemoration of the conquest shaped imperial decisions regarding the formation of new banner companies. The hereditary captaincies of the banner companies transmitted to the descendants of Fiongdon's father, Solgo, included not only the seventh, eighth, and twelfth companies of the second division in the Manchu Bordered Yellow Banner but three new companies, created in 1667, 1684, and 1695. Eidu's descendants held the captaincies of seven companies in the first division of the Manchu Bordered Yellow Banner, four of them created after 1644. One of the three companies in the first division of the Manchu Plain White Banner commanded by Hurhan's descendants, and two of the four in the first division of the Manchu Bordered Blue Banner commanded by Anfiyanggu's, were also post-1644 additions.[26]

Fiongdon's Suwan Gūwalgiya clan, Eidu's Niohuru clan, and Hohori's Donggo clan were among the eight great houses of the Manchu nobility, which included the Sumuru, Nara, Hoifa, Irgen Gioro, and Magiya clans. In all, fifty Manchus were awarded high noble titles before 1644.[27] Rank and family prestige gave the Manchu descendants of these heroes privileged access to military and civil office, beyond the hereditary posts to which they were entitled. With the exception of the Hoifa, these descent lines all enjoyed multiple marriage exchanges with the Aisin Gioro.[28]

Descendants of famous heroes of the conquest period enjoyed favored access to high military and civil positions after 1683. The inheritors of banner titles could also earn new titles through their own achievements. The post-conquest period, especially the eighteenth century, saw the establishment of new noble lines among Manchu bannermen. The Fuca, who gained high office through service under three emperors, are an example (see below).

Mongol Nobles

Mongol princes had intimate ties to the Aisin Gioro lineage that began in the sixteenth and persisted into the early twentieth century. The inclusion of Mongol nobles into the conquest elite parallels the process by which Mongols were incorporated into the Qing empire.

During the seventeenth century Mongols may have occupied about half of present-day Manchuria and all the region later known as Chengde, so winning their support was vital to the Manchu unification of the northeast. Nurgaci and Hongtaiji adopted the same policies of promotion and reward toward Mongol tribal leaders who came over to their cause. Early adherents like Gürbüshi, son of the *beile* of the Khalkha Bayot tribe, were rewarded with high rank, banner companies (Manchu as well as Mongol), gifts, and

Aisin Gioro wives. A total of thirty-seven Mongols held high noble titles before 1644.[29] Throughout the dynasty, rulers recognized and rewarded battle merit and meritorious service in administrative posts. The significance of the Qing creation of a Mongol nobility, however, lay not in its recognition of individual merit but in its direct linkage to the strategic and geopolitical concerns of the throne.

Early Manchu history shows that Nurgaci and Hongtaiji were able to seize opportunities created by intra-Mongol feuds to divide and conquer the Mongols. Although the Khorchin had joined a nine-tribe coalition to attack Nurgaci's forces on 1593, they decided in 1627 and 1628 to ally with Hongtaiji against the Chahar Mongol leader Ligdan Khan. Other tribes followed, and a combined force of Jurchen and eastern Mongols defeated the Chahar, who submitted to Manchu overlordship after Ligdan Khan's death in 1635.

Mongol alliances were usually temporary and ad hoc in nature. The Qing succeeded in changing this state of affairs. They awarded noble titles to their Mongol allies. At first they applied the same tactics to the Chahar Mongol leadership. Although Erke Khongkhor Eje, Ligdan Khan's son, became an imperial son-in-law (and his mother a consort of a Manchu prince, Jirgalang), the uprising of the Chahar prince Burni (1675) underlined the need for better control of the Chahar Mongols, who were moved back to their traditional pastures north of Datong, Kalgan, and Dushikou. After 1675, each Chahar banner was put under the administrative control of a higher administrative officer (*zongguan*) and later (after 1761) of a lieutenant general. The Chahar banners were also diluted with the incorporation of Khalkha, Khorchin, and Ölöd troops.[30]

Rewarding one's allies and punishing one's enemies is a commonplace of political activity. The Qing went further. They reduced the autonomy of the hereditary Mongol nobility by enrolling the tribes into the banner organization. In 1636 the Khorchin, Tümet, Ongnirod, Aokhan, Naiman, Bairin, Aro-Khorchin, and Jarod tribes were incorporated into banners, which were eventually organized into two leagues, the Josoto and the Western or Jo-oda League. The "inner" (*nei*) Mongol banners eventually totaled twenty-four tribes and forty-nine banners.[31] Administrative control of the newly created banner units was taken out of the hands of the nobles. A new office, the *jasagh*, was created to take charge of banner affairs. Although the *jasagh* was selected from the hereditary nobility, the Qing court could and did shift the appointment from one descent line to another for a variety of reasons, including incompetence, old age, and illness.

Jasagh too were put under higher administrative officers. The central organ dealing with personnel matters for the Mongol banners and leagues was the Lifanyuan or Court of Colonial Affairs.

The eastern Mongol tribes had been comparatively weak and divided in the seventeenth century. They were eventually completely incorporated into the Qing system. The Qing rulers next confronted the Khalkha Mongols, who in the late sixteenth and early seventeenth centuries dominated what is now Mongolia. Like the eastern Mongols, the Khalkha were internally divided into three groups. The seven Khalkha banners, in the left wing, were under the leadership of the Jasaghtu khan; succession disputes separated them from the Khalkha of the right wing, led by the Tüshiyetü khan. A third group of Khalkha was under the Setsen (Sechen) khan. Internal disputes among the tribes under each wing weakened Khalkha cohesion and made them vulnerable to attacks from other Mongol tribes.[32]

Although some Khalkha chieftains had presented tribute to the Manchus in 1635–37, relations between the Manchus and the Khalkha were highly volatile through the 1640s and 1650s.[33] Though internally divided, the Khalkha were too formidable a force, spread over too wide a territory, for the Manchu forces. A major turning point in the power balance within the Khalkha territory came in the 1670s with the unification of the western Mongols (Oirat, or Uriad) under a new Zunghar khan, Galdan. The son of Batur Kontaisha, an important Zunghar leader, Galdan had studied in Lhasa to enter a Tibetan Buddhist order. A succession struggle sparked by the death of his father drew Galdan back to secular affairs. He unified the Zunghar tribes during the 1670s, while the Manchu forces were still engaged in consolidating their conquest of China. Galdan received a mandate from the Dalai lama (1678) to negotiate on behalf of the Oirat confederation with the Khalkha Mongols to the east about the Oirat desire to move into some of the Khalkha pasturelands.

When Galdan led the Zunghars against the Khalkha in 1688, the tribes under the Tüshiyetü khan sought protection from the Qing court, while the Jasaghtu khan and his followers allied with Galdan. Eventually all the Khalkha formally submitted to the Kangxi emperor at Dolon Nor in May 1691. Their submission was crucial to what followed. Efforts to negotiate a settlement between the Oirat and the Khalkha having failed, the emperor took to the field and, in a series of campaigns culminating in the battle of Jao Modo (1696), vanquished Galdan. His demise did not mean the end of the Zunghar empire, which was now led by Galdan's estranged nephew Tsereng Araptan, and the Zunghars and their allies continued to drive Qing frontier policy into the eighteenth century. The Qing military effort to stabilize the empire's Inner Asian borders did not end until the conquest of Ili (1756), and the new territories brought into the empire during these campaigns expanded China's borders to an unprecedented extent.[34]

Qing policies toward the Khalkha after 1691 followed the pattern set by their treatment of the eastern Mongols. The khanates (*aimak*) were organized into banners. Although the court confirmed the titles of the Setsen khan, Tüshiyetü khan, and Jasaghtu khan, it gave them only nominal leadership. In 1728, after the Sain Noyon khanate was created out of part of the Tüshiyetü khanate, the *aimak* were converted into four leagues. Both the banners and leagues were governed by *jasagh* appointed by the Lifanyuan.[35] The process of eliminating Khalkha autonomy had taken less than four decades.

The "outer" (*wai*) Mongol banners were administratively quite separate from the "inner" (*nei*) banners and retained a greater degree of autonomy throughout the dynasty.[36] Nonetheless, the throne created a series of administrative posts to oversee Outer Mongol affairs. A governor-general of Mongolia was appointed to oversee Khalkha banner affairs during the middle of the eighteenth century, and he was stationed at Uliasutai. Uliasutai replaced an earlier headquarters at Kobdo, erected in 1718 on the then borders of Khalkha and Zungharia.[37] Kobdo became the site of a new office, with its own *amban* to govern the western Mongol territories (1761). In 1758 an *amban* was stationed at Urga to administer the affairs of the Jebtsundamba khutukhtu. In 1786 the Urga *amban* also took over the administration of the affairs of the Tüshiyetü and Setsen *aimak* in eastern Mongolia.[38]

By the time the Qing had finished, the Outer Mongols were organized into roughly two hundred banners that formed eighteen leagues. The life of the traditional tribal groups changed as transhumance, the free seasonal migration between summer and winter pastures, became limited to movement within territories whose boundaries were drawn by the Qing court. Mongols could no longer move to pastures outside their banner's territory; after 1843, Mongols and lamas wishing to move outside their assigned locales were required to obtain passes.[39] Moreover, under the *pax Mandjurica*, and with Qing encouragement, a rapid expansion of Tibetan Buddhist monasteries in Mongolia took place and had profound impact on Mongolian culture (see chapter 7).

The Mongol noble component of the conquest elite was internally differentiated. Imperial favor was most lavishly bestowed on the inner Mongol nobles, who had enjoyed the longest historical associations with the Manchu rulers. Although the Qing rulers confirmed the traditional Khalkha

khans, they were quite careful to limit the size and rank of the Khalkha nobility. One study shows that half of the Khalkha *jasagh* were first-rank *taiji*
(Mongolian princely title), and more than one-third were *fuguogong*,
whereas three-fifths of *jasagh* in the inner Mongol banners were princes of
the first three ranks. Although there were outstanding exceptions, Khalkha
nobles as well as the Mongols in Qinghai and Xinjiang were less favored as
imperial sons-in-law.[40]

Regardless of their status, all Mongols were subject to bureaucratic regulation from Peking. Their titles had to be confirmed by the Lifanyuan,
which kept noble patents on file and handled succession issues. No one could
inherit a title without its approval.[41] Even though the Qing did punish
them, Mongols were treated with greater leniency than imperial kinsmen.
A survey shows that most Mongol nobles received promotions rather than
demotions, although heritable ranks were reduced with each transmission
unless the holder had been granted perpetual rights of inheritance.[42]

Mongols performed valuable services for the Qing. They staffed many
of the eighty-two frontier posts on the Qing border with Russia and furnished the troops for most of the campaigns against the western Mongols.
Mongol princes served with Manchus in the Lifanyuan. Many Mongols
held office and led armies for the Qing and were rewarded for their service
with noble titles. One such example is Bandi (died 1755), a Borjigit Mongol who belonged to the Mongol Plain Yellow Banner. Bandi entered government service after attending the banner school and advanced through
service in the Lifanyuan, the Board of War, and provincial posts. His work
in 1754–55 in the campaign to suppress the Zunghars won him imperial
approbation and the heritable title of viscount first-class. Bandi was one of
the fifty officials whose portrait, made to hang in the Ziguangge, was personally inscribed by the Qianlong emperor. Although Bandi himself was
promoted to first-class duke (1755), it was the title of viscount that was
passed on to his son Balu after Bandi's death.[43]

The Qing commemorated outstanding Mongol descent groups with
offices and honors, treating them like the illustrious Manchu lines descended from conquest heroes. Sanjaidorji, general of the Tüshiyetü *aimak*,
was a descendant of the younger brother of the Tüshiyetü khan, Chakhun-
dorji. Son of a Qing princess, he was raised in the palace in Peking before
himself marrying a princess. He played a major role in the suppression of
the 1756 rebellion of Chingunjav and served later as the Mongol *amban*
of Urga, as did many other members of his descent group.[44]

Tsereng (d. 1750) is another notable example. A Khalkha noble, Tsereng
was introduced into the Qing court when his tribal leader, the Tüshiyetü

khan, surrendered to the Manchus in the 1680s. The Kangxi emperor invited Tsereng to study in the palace school in 1692. In 1706 he married the emperor's tenth daughter. After her death in 1710, Tsereng led his men to pasturelands northwest of Erdeni Zuu, where he successfully led Qing troops in battles against the Eleuths (1721). In 1723 Tsereng, now a second-degree prince, was assigned to patrol the passes of the Altai mountains. He helped organize his kinsmen into the Sain Noyon khanate, represented the court at the Kiakhta negotiations (1727), and signed the resulting treaty. For battle merit in the campaign against the Eleuths (1731) he was promoted to a first-degree princedom and awarded 10,000 taels of silver. The next year he was given the designation "Chaoyong" in recognition of his role in the Eleuth defeat at Erdeni Zuu. Military governor of Uliasutai and captain general of the Sain Noyon khanate, he was permitted to wear the yellow belt "as though he were a member of the royal family."[45] Tsereng was one of only two Mongols whose spirit tablets were installed for sacrifice in the imperial Temple of the Ancestors. Tsereng's grandson Lhawangdorji married the Qianlong emperor's seventh daughter (see chapter 4). The renewal of affinal ties with the imperial house continued until the end of the dynasty. Prince Nayentu, a seventh-generation descendant, was married to the eldest daughter of Yikuang, Prince Qing. Nayentu accompanied Empress Dowager Cixi when she fled to Xi'an after the Boxer rebellion and translated for her when she had audiences with Mongol nobles.[46]

Hanjun

Not all Hanjun were of Chinese descent, nor were the origins of the *hanjun* designation itself ethnic (as we understand the latter term). Pamela Crossley shows that the term *nikan*, later translated as "Han" or "Chinese," was initially a more general term describing persons who lived "in the Chinese style." The term was applied to individuals of diverse origins, living in Liaodong, who joined the Manchu cause before 1644. The northeasterners who voluntarily joined the Manchus before 1644 were registered in the Hanjun, which were originally organized as artillery divisions to supplement Mongol and Manchu cavalry.[47]

The most famous Han Chinese adherents who joined the Manchu cause were the ill-fated Wu Sangui, Shang Kexi, and Geng Jimao. These Ming generals were rewarded with princely titles and imperial brides but subsequently lost everything in their unsuccessful rebellion (1673–81). Many other less well known figures—twenty-five are recorded with high noble titles before 1644—founded noble lines that persisted through the dynasty.

One of the most famous of these founders is Li Yongfang (d. 1634). Li was a major in the Ming forces guarding Fushun who surrendered the city without a struggle to the Manchus. During Nurgaci's lifetime, Li was registered in the Hanjun Plain Blue Banner and became a third-class *zong-bingguan*. The heritable rank of third-class viscount was transmitted to his descendants, many of whom achieved life peerages of higher rank on their own merit. By the end of the Qianlong reign, Li's title had gone through ten transmissions.[48]

The Kangxi emperor bestowed his ninth daughter on a grandson of Tong Guowei, the emperor's uncle and father-in-law. Tong Guowei was the second generation in his family to serve the Manchus.[49] The Tongs of Fushun were eventually rewarded for their meritorious service by being shifted to registration in the Manchu Bordered Yellow Banner. Five Tongs were generals in the Manchu armies, six were chamberlains of the Imperial Guard; thirteen held the top post of lieutenant general in the banner organization, twelve became provincial governors and governors-general, and several rose to become presidents of central government ministries. Another Tong, Longkodo, was commandant of the Peking gendarmerie during the last years of the Kangxi reign and is sometimes credited with putting Yinzhen on the throne.[50]

There were several other categories of nobles. First were the members of the imperial lineage, discussed below, who were under the jurisdiction of the Imperial Clan Court. Then there were the *waifan* or Outer Mongol nobles, who were under the jurisdiction of the Lifanyuan. All other nobles fell under the jurisdiction of the Board of Personnel. It became customary for rulers to give their fathers-in-law dukedoms, inheritable for three generations, and to award lesser titles to the fathers of consorts. Like their predecessors, the Qing honored the descent line of Confucius by awarding a dukedom to the head of the Kong lineage in Qufu. In 1724 the Yongzheng emperor also made Zhu Zhida, a descendant of the Ming imperial house, a first-class marquis and assigned him to offer the spring and autumn sacrifices at the Ming imperial mausolea. In 1749 the title Yan'en marquis was given to this line.[51]

THE AISIN GIORO

The imperial lineage was created by Nurgaci and his successors. By taking this name (*aisin* means gold in Manchu, and was the name of the Jin dynasty), Nurgaci claimed the legitimacy of the Jurchen Jin and set off his descent group from the other *gioro* or clans.[52] As Tong Wanlun notes, the story of Manchu origins first appeared in 1612 in the *Manwen laodang* and was elaborated in the *Jiu Manzhou dang* in records dated 1635–36. By 1655 the Veritable Records, compiled in Manchu, Mongol, and Chinese after 1635, included accounts of the origins of the Aisin Gioro and the Manchu people. In its completed form, the myth states that the Manchu people came originally from the area of Bulhūri omo, a lake situated at the foot of the Bukuri mountain northeast of Changbaishan (long white mountain), a mountain range at the border between present-day Jilin province and Korea. It was here that three heavenly maidens came to bathe one day. A sacred bird, the magpie, dropped a red fruit. When one maiden, Fekulen, put it into her mouth, it sank into her abdomen and became a fetus. Fekulen could not return to heaven with her sisters. She remained behind and gave birth to the progenitor of the Manchus, Bukuri Yongson. Bukuri obeyed his mother, who commanded him to take a boat and float downstream to a region where three clans were feuding with one another. Bukuri announced to them that heaven had granted him the surname Aisin Gioro and had sent him to mediate among the clans. After he resolved their disputes they accepted him as their lord. Bukuri adopted the name Manju for his state.[53]

The myth of the origins of the Manchus synthesized elements of legends circulating among many Jurchen tribes to claim divine origins for the ancestors of Nurgaci. Bukuri Yongson became the progenitor of the Jurchen-Manchu people. One of his later descendants, Möngke Tëmur, an eastern Jurchen tribal leader living on the border between present-day Jilin and Korea, was the direct sixth-generation ancestor of Nurgaci. Eighteenth-century compilations of Manchu history traced the origins of the Manchus to Changbaishan. After an expedition explored the mountain range in 1677, the emperor entered its mountain spirit into the state registers. Sacrifices were offered each spring and autumn from 1678. In 1682 and 1698, the Kangxi emperor visited Jilin city in order to kowtow to the deity of the mountain from the banks of the Sungari River. Later a temple to the deity was erected at Wendeliang, a mountain east of Jilin city, where the military governor of Jilin lit incense on the first and fifteenth of each month. The Qianlong emperor paid his respects to the Changbaishan deity at this temple in 1754.[54]

While their founding myth affirmed a northeastern identity for the Manchu ruling house, Nurgaci and Hongtaiji simultaneously claimed legitimacy within the Han Chinese cultural realm by establishing an imperial descent line. To do so involved the creation of an ancestral cult. Chinese dynastic founders traditionally honored their direct ancestors for four generations. When Hongtaiji took the Chinese title of emperor (*huangdi*) and the dynastic name of Qing in 1636, he awarded his principal ancestors the title of "king" (*wang*).[55] From 1636 Qing rulers sacrificed to their ancestors in a Chinese-style Temple of the Ancestors (Taimiao), first in Mukden (Shengjing) and subsequently in Peking.[56] In 1648, when the government adopted the Han custom of conferring on these imperial ancestors the temple and posthumous names by which they were known during the Qing dynasty, their titles were upgraded from king to emperor (see appendix 1).

An imperial ancestral cult demanded that graves be constructed with tumuli, stele, sacrificial halls, and walls. Nurgaci first created an imperial-style tomb for his parents and grandparents near Liaoyang, which was renamed Dongjing (eastern capital) after he settled there in 1622. Later, a new mausoleum complex was built outside Xingjing, and in 1657 the ancestors were reinterred there, together with the focal ancestor Möngke Tëmur and his great-grandson. This tumulus was named the Yongling in 1659. It was marked by a trilingual stele bearing Manchu, Mongolian, and Chinese inscriptions. Nurgaci's own grave, northeast of Mukden, was the Fuling; the grave of his successor, Hongtaiji, located in a suburb of Mukden, the Zhaoling. Together these three imperial tumuli (*sanling*) came under the same kind of ritual rules as those later located within China proper.[57]

Hongtaiji was the first to define the membership of the imperial lineage, in an edict issued March 14, 1635: "Taizu's descendants should all be called *age;* the descendants of the Six Ancestors (*liuzu*) should all be called *juelo*. Those who speak of them should use their name and call them X *age* and X *juelo*."[58] *Age* was the Manchu term for "brother." As a result of this edict, *age* came to mean "prince." Hongtaiji's edict used the terms *zongshi* and *juelo* in a very different sense from their subsequent usage. Both *age* and *juelo* were now construed as part of a larger descent group, the *zongshi*. By assigning a special term (*age*), Hongtaiji drew a narrow circle around Nurgaci's descent group and separated them from the descendants of the "Six Ancestors," the sons of Giocangga, Nurgaci's grandfather, who were the *juelo*.[59]

In 1636 the definitions governing membership in the imperial lineage were altered. According to the Kangxi edition of the Collected Regulations, the term *zongshi* now included all the descendants of Nurgaci's father, Taksi, demolishing the previous year's distinction between Nurgaci's descendants and those of his brothers. This definition of *zongshi* persisted through the rest of the dynasty. *Juelo* now became imperial kinsmen who were more distantly related to the imperial house through descent from earlier ancestors.

From 1636 all Aisin Gioro descendants were registered and set apart from the rest of the population. Detailed regulations for the reporting of births, marriages, and deaths began in 1655. The Zongrenfu (imperial clan court), established in 1652, had jurisdiction over all Aisin Gioro, who were organized under "lineage heads" (called *zuzhang* for *zongshi;* and *shouling* for *juelo*) in the Manchu banners. The court required quarterly reports on births and deaths among lineage members to be sent to the Imperial Clan Court, which used these records to compile (once every ten years) updated editions of the imperial genealogy, the *Da Qing yudie,* in the Manchu and Chinese languages. In the course of the dynasty (1644–1911), the imperial genealogy was revised twenty-eight times.[60] Imperial clansmen who were guilty of crimes were stripped of their titles and in extreme cases expelled from the lineage to become commoners.[61]

Membership in the imperial lineage brought sumptuary privileges. Nurgaci's assumption of the title of *han* (khan) in 1612 was marked by a procession in which he was preceded by yellow umbrellas (a sign of imperial rank) and processional music. In 1622 he issued the first of many regulations to specify the number of small banners, umbrellas, horns, and drums that nobles of different ranks could display. Additional orders in 1631, 1632, and 1636 dictated official attire for nobles and their wives when appearing at court. After 1644 these dress codes continued to be modified and to become more and more elaborate.[62]

In accordance with the Chinese custom, every male descendant of the imperial lineage received support from state funds. All Aisin Gioro orphans and adult males (those 18 *sui* and older) were eligible for monthly silver stipends and an annual grain subsidy, and disabled males were to receive additional funds. Subsidies were granted to pay the extraordinary expenses incurred during weddings and funerals. Regulations carefully discriminated in favor of the *zongshi.* Eighteenth-century *zongshi* descendants were distinguished by their yellow, the *juelo* by their red belts. Only *zongshi* descendants were eligible for princely ranks and there were significant differences in the stipends as well. The specific sums to be paid varied over the course of the dynasty. The regulations of 1671, for example, specified that unranked *zongshi* descendants would receive 36 taels of silver a year, and 45 *hu* of grain; *juelo* would get 24 taels of silver and 21.2 *hu* of grain. During the late seventeenth century, *zongshi* descendants were granted 100 taels of silver and *juelo* 20 taels for wedding expenses; *zongshi* descendants received 120 taels, *juelo* only 30 taels to cover funeral costs.[63]

IMPERIAL PRINCES

Evolution of the Rank System

Nurgaci seems to have first used the title *beile* in 1598, when he awarded this rank to his eldest son, Cuyeng. *Beile* was a Jurchen title for tribal chieftains; he also used another title, *taiji*, which was a Mongol title for nobles. Later, when Nurgaci marked the occasion of his accession to the khanate of the Later Jin dynasty (1616) by giving his sons titles, he made four sons *hošoi beile. Hošoi beile* outranked other sons, who were *beile*. The systematization of princely titles came only under the reign of Hongtaiji, who shortly after proclaiming the Qing dynasty established a nine-rank system for the *zongshi*.[64] The rank system achieved its final form in 1748, when each of the three lowest titles was subdivided into three grades, making a total of eighteen ranks.

After 1748 Qing princes of the blood were ranked into eighteen grades (see appendix 2 for specific titles). Princes of the first rank, *hošoi cin wang*, received an annual stipend of 10,000 taels of silver and 5,000 piculs of rice; princes of the lowest rank received 110 taels and 55 piculs of rice a year.[65] Only first- and second-rank princes were given names (*hao*) along with their titles; they were also the only princes to automatically receive posthumous names (*shi*) after they died.[66] The princes of the blood were divided as well by the so-called eight privileges (*bafen*). Those of rank seven and below were denied the eight sumptuary privileges accorded to those of the first six ranks: the right to wear a purple button, a three-eyed peacock feather, an embroidered dragon plaque on court robes; the right to have red-painted spears at the gate of their residences, to attach tassels to their horse's accoutrements, and to use purple bridle reins; the right to have a servant carry a special teapot; and to have a special carpet for seating themselves.[67]

Imperial decisions shaping the imperial lineage after 1644 responded to the new conditions created by the conquest. The throne waged a successful struggle against its most powerful kinsmen, the banner lords, and subordinated them to centralized authority (see chapter 3). In order to perpetuate a distinctive Manchu identity, the emperors glorified the heroes of the conquest generation and ordered that their descent lines be preserved "forever." For similar reasons, the previous emphasis on succession by the Chinese "eldest-son" rule gave way to an insistence that Aisin Gioro nobles personify Manchu culture and values. Finally, in order to reduce the financial burden of supporting a large number of kinsmen, the throne sharply reduced the number of princes holding high ranks and stipends. In partial compensation for the loss of stipend, Aisin Gioro like other bannermen could sit for the examinations, win degrees, and be appointed to civil service posts. The transformation of the Aisin Gioro lineage into a highly stratified social group is described below.

Merit versus Favor: Forms of Hereditary Transmission

Qing policies concerning the transmission of hereditary noble titles evolved with the changing political and military context. In the conquest period, and particularly before 1644, inheritance was not an issue because the rapid expansion of banner forces and the many military campaigns gave imperial kinsmen ample opportunities for promotion. The descendants of Daišan, the second son of Nurgaci, provide a relevant example. Daišan (1583–1648) was one of the *hošoi beile,* an active campaigner who won renown in the conquest of the Ula tribe (1607, 1613) and in subsequent victories at Fushun (1618), Sarhū (1619), and Shenyang (1621). He played a leading role in the early campaigns against the Ming (1629–34) and was prominent in the highest councils throughout his life.[68] In addition to his seventh son, Mandahai, who inherited Daišan's first-degree princedom, Yoto, the eldest, Sahaliyen, the third son, and Wakda, the fourth son, all distinguished themselves on the battlefield and were rewarded with first- or second-rank princedoms of their own.[69] Sahaliyen's son Lekdehun, Yoto, and Daišan all founded princedoms that enjoyed the privilege of perpetual inheritance and were among the "eight great houses" of the imperial lineage.

The privilege of perpetual inheritance became more and more circumscribed over the late seventeenth and eighteenth centuries. An imperial ruling in 1684 limited this privilege to the holders of first- and second-degree princedoms, who could pass the title on to one son. All other sons would be reduced one rank until they reached the lowest noble rank with "eight privileges."[70] If a prince died without sons, the court did not automatically designate an heir to carry on the title and descent line: the imperial genealogy includes numerous examples of lines that were allowed to perish. The emperor could however choose to designate a successor, and occasionally he had his own sons adopted as heirs to other princely lines.[71]

In 1750 a memorial from the Board of Rites seeking imperial guidance on a question of protocol stimulated an investigation that culminated (1751) in new policies concerning hereditary transmission of titles that would prevail for the rest of the dynasty. First, Hongli required all potential heirs to present themselves for imperial audience. Inheritance of a noble title would no longer depend on birth order but on merit, defined as competency in spoken and written Manchu and in mounted archery. This new policy was underlined in 1762, when Dejao, who held Dodo's second-rank princedom, died and the emperor interviewed his sons. He noted with disgust:

> None can speak Manchu. Their ability at drawing the bow is average. . . . Among Dejao's sons, there are individuals who have reached 40 *sui* [in age] but cannot speak Manchu and cannot draw a bow. How can one transmit a princely title to such? All this is Dejao's fault. While he was alive, he did not properly educate his sons. Dejao's princely title should not be passed on, but his ancestor's battle merit was what created the princedom, and I cannot bear to cut off the transmission.[72]

Because Hongli did not wish to cut off the hereditary princedom of Dodo, an imperial kinsman of the conquest era, he reluctantly selected Rusong, "the best" of Dejao's sons, to inherit the princedom. But he added, "Inform all the princes that they must pay attention to the education of their sons. If they cannot speak Manchu, ride, and practice archery at the time of inheriting the title, I must take proper measures."[73]

In 1764 the emperor decreed that the holder of a princedom should be selected for his ability to fulfill its duties, regardless of his mother's status. His decree repudiated the principle, established in the Kangxi reign, and spelled out in the Collected Regulations: "a wife's son should inherit the title. If there is no wife's son, then a concubine's son is permitted to inherit."[74] This regulation was not very different from the Han Chinese succession principle that the heir should be the eldest son of the wife. Furthermore, the age at which sons of princes would receive their own ranks was raised from fifteen to twenty *sui* in 1688: the emperor added that candidates for investiture would be inspected for their skills in literature, riding, and archery.[75] Sons inheriting the title of a deceased father, however, were exempted from the age requirement.

Under Hongli, princely titles based on merit (*gongfeng*) were separated from those based on descent (*enfeng*). *Gongfeng* referred to the merit of the founder of the princedom, in most cases a hero during the conquest period. After 1644, sons of emperors continued to receive princely titles, but they were now conferred by imperial favor (*enfeng*) rather than earned through merit. Most (though not all) sons received a first- or second-degree princedom. Although *enfeng* titles could be transmitted, they were reduced with each transmission. With the rank came a stipend, ownership of banner companies, a residence, furnishings, servants, and bodyguards.

In exchange, emperor's sons were liable for ritual, military, diplomatic, and bureaucratic assignments in the capital and abroad (see chapter 3).

The Qianlong emperor thus discriminated against his closer kinsmen (and his own sons) in order to commemorate Aisin Gioro of the conquest period who would be exemplars for current and future generations of *zongshi*. In 1767 Hongli ordered:

> To determine whether or not a title should be transmitted to the next generation, examine the ancestor's achievements and make distinctions to reward merit. In the cases of Prince Jian [descendant of an imperial kinsman, Jirgalang] and Prince Xin [descendant of Dodo], their ancestors were both present at the foundation of our dynasty and exerted themselves to the utmost, displaying meritorious service. Some had battle achievements, others died for the state. The state has conferred rank to recompense them for their merit; these should be perpetually transmitted.[76]

In 1776 Hongli reiterated his decision to allow titles based on military merit the privilege of perpetual inheritance while reducing titles awarded by imperial favor, protesting that his "favor" toward his own descendants was still markedly greater than that of the Song emperors.[77] Hoping that these new rules would be permanent, he ordered that the edict be circulated among the *zongshi* princes.[78]

The emperor was aware that "these princely achievements happened a long time ago" and were no longer well known. He suggested that biographies recording the achievements of the *zongshi* princes should be written up, published, and distributed to the princes and high officials. The heroes of the conquest must never have their titles reduced in rank, while princes of the first and second ranks with *enfeng* titles should have their titles reduced when they were passed on.[79]

The same motives impelled Hongli to rehabilitate some of the victims of past purges. The founding generation (those ennobled before 1644) experienced heavy political casualties during the seventeenth-century struggles between the emperor and the princes (see chapter 3).[80] In 1778 the Qianlong emperor focused on the problem of perpetuating the imperial tradition in future descendants: "in my spare time I peruse the veritable records of my ancestors. Thus I know the difficulties of establishing the dynasty, of how the kinsmen of that time exerted themselves to the utmost to settle the central plain. . . . Truly from ancient times there has never been anything like it."[81] The descendants of the Aisin Gioro should know about the feats of their ancestors so that they would be inspired to emulate them. But how could this be done when kinsmen like Dorgon, who contributed so greatly to the Manchu victory, were unjustly excised from the genealogical record? Dodo and Ajige, Dorgon's brothers, were also heroes, yet because of their relationship to Dorgon, they too had been wrongly accused of crimes and demoted. Whereas the other Manchu nobles had their titles transmitted without change, the titles of the Aisin Gioro had all been altered, with the result that the continuity between the founders and their descendants was broken: "as the descendants become more distant from the ancestors, they almost forget the sources of their ancestors' investitures." [82]

The emperor ordered that Dorgon be restored to the imperial genealogy. His line, which had been abolished in 1652, was reinstated with the appointment of an heir, who inherited his princely title. The original titles of three of Nurgaci's sons, two of Hongtaiji's sons, and Šurgaci's son Jirgalang, were restored. The original titles of the second-degree princedoms of two sons of Daišan (Nurgaci's second son) were also restored. The emperor granted the descendants of these eight first- and second-degree princedoms the privilege of perpetual inheritance; collectively this select group was called the "iron-capped princes" (*tiemaozi wang*). The privilege of perpetual inheritance was granted in 1775 to the descendants of Yinxiang, Prince Yi, Xuanye's thirteenth son. In the nineteenth century the descendants of Yixin, Prince Gong, and of Yihuan, Prince Chun, obtained this privilege.[83]

Other imperial kinsmen in the founding generation were also commemorated. In 1778 the emperor, noting that only one descendant of Abatai, Prince Raoyou, and his son Yolo, Prince An, held princely rank, granted a sixth-degree princedom to their descendants. He gave a fifth-degree princedom to the descendants of Nikan, Prince Jingjin. To the descendants of Wakda, Prince Qian, Mandahai, Prince Xuan, and Tunji, who held no titles, the emperor granted a ninth-, twelfth-, and fifteenth-degree princedom respectively. All these grants carried the privilege of perpetual inheritance.[84] With these measures the Qianlong emperor symbolically renewed historical links with the warrior heroes of his lineage.

The Qianlong emperor's validation of the Aisin Gioro's martial past was continued by his successors. In 1830 the Daoguang emperor used his grandfather's reasoning to reject transmitting a "favor" title to Yonggao while ordering an investigation of Huaying, who was due to inherit the eighteenth rank. Huaying, said the emperor, obtained the title from his ancestor Fulehe, who was posthumously made a *gong*, then implicated and stripped of his title. Fulehe was the second son of Ajige, Nurgaci's twelfth son, himself the victim of political intrigues. Although Fulehe had been subsequently rehabilitated, many of Ajige's other sons remained outside the Aisin Gioro. The emperor ordered the Imperial Clan Court to investigate Ajige's descendants and select potential heirs.[85]

Examination Titles

From 1688, imperial nobles were subject to periodic evaluations that served as a basis for investiture. The requirement initially applied only to sons who had inherited their titles while minors or adult sons who were excluded from inheriting their father's title: heirs were examined on literary as well as martial skills, unranked sons on Manchu, riding, and archery. In the middle of the eighteenth century, investiture through examination (*kaofeng*) became a systematic way to recruit *zongshi* for employment and to ensure a minimal level of Manchu skills. Imperial kinsmen from the age of ten *sui* were to attend *zongxue* (imperial clan academies) established within the lower five banners and to be periodically evaluated.[86] Applicants who successfully passed tests of translation and of archery from horseback and on foot would receive degrees in accordance with their father's rank and might also receive employment in the Imperial Household Department, banners, Lifanyuan, or the central government. Aisin Gioro who failed might be reduced in rank or might have their stipends stopped for three years. After 1760 individuals were not permitted to retake the examination at some later date.[87]

A SERVICE NOBILITY

Despite their European-sounding titles and unlike their European counterparts, the Qing nobility were firmly subordinated to the throne. Qing peers had no autonomy. Their estates were bureaucratically administered. The same was true of military resources: personal control of a banner company by banner nobles gave way to bureaucratic control in the late seventeenth and early eighteenth centuries (see chapter 3).

The histories of the famous Manchu and other banner houses, as well as of branches within the Aisin Gioro, show that the throne exercised constant surveillance over nobles, rewarding meritorious service and punishing actions the throne deemed against its best interests. If bannermen were the slaves of banner lords, nobles were the slaves of their master, the emperor. The Qing peers constituted a service nobility, whose power derived entirely from the throne.

The Imperial Guard

Studies of the Imperial Guard (*shiwei*) and their place in the structure of the Qing state have been neglected in Western-language analyses of the Qing system, yet recent work in Chinese demonstrates that they offered a channel of upward mobility for the conquest elite. The guards were a visible and prestigious elite unit responsible for the security of the emperor. Their special status was signaled by their clothing. Imperial guardsmen were permitted to don "bright yellow" riding jackets (*minghuang magua*) and wear peacock feathers. During the early Qing, only inner-court officials wore peacock feathers. A 1661 edict permitted these high officials, along with guardsmen and imperial sons-in-law, to wear one-eyed peacock feathers in their hats (the feathers were classified into one-eyed, two-eyed, and three-eyed ranks). Similarly, "bright yellow" was the imperial color that even first-degree princes were not allowed to wear without special permission. Since the guards accompanied the emperor on all his public appearances, their riding jackets and hats set them apart and nurtured their esprit de corps.[88]

The origins of the imperial guards lie in the late sixteenth and early seventeenth centuries, when all high-ranking nobles had personal guards. Nurgaci used bondservants, the younger brothers and sons of important allies, kinsmen, and outstanding warriors as his personal guards. The *hiya kadalara dorgi amban* not only ensured Nurgaci's personal security but also carried his insignia on public occasions, transmitted documents between the khan and troop commanders, and guarded the palace compound.

Under Hongtaiji, the *hiya* gained autonomy and a command structure and were internally ranked into three grades. Hongtaiji favored the descendants of those who had served his father. His guards came from varied social backgrounds and included servile bondservants as well as imperial kinsmen. Those who became "inner-court high officials" (*nei dachen*) were generally Mongol or Manchu heroes and Aisin Gioro. *Nei dachen* were placed in the vanguard in battle, where they carried messages between the commander in chief and the field units or took the place of a fallen commander. Elite guardsmen were also trusted imperial emissaries to Mongol tribal chieftains and to the Ming and Chosôn courts, or escorts for Mongol sons-in-law, imperial princesses, and other important personages. Hongtaiji ruled that the number of guards he employed had to be twice the number employed by the banner *beile*; on an individual level, his guards outranked theirs. The guards' ranks were also incorporated within a larger system of military ranks, so that a *nei dachen* became equivalent to a *meiren janggin*, the top banner post, which later became the lieutenant generalship of a banner.

Recruitment for the imperial guards was expanded after 1644 to include sons of banner officers, but from the 1650s most of the men appointed were bannermen from the upper three banners, banner nobles, or imperial kinsmen. The organization of the guards changed through the late seventeenth century, as the throne's authority increased. The top post, chamberlains of the Imperial Guard (*ling shiwei nei dachen*) was established in 1652 and given a civil service rank of 1A. Normally six persons, two from each of the upper three banners, were personally selected by the emperor to fill this office. The chamberlains were in charge of all military affairs of the guard units of the upper three banners and the imperial guard (*qinjun*). They handled recruitment, training, and promotion or demotion of the 570 guardsmen and determined daily assignments and assignments for imperial tours.

The senior assistant chamberlains (*nei dachen*, rank 1B) and junior assistant chamberlains (*sanzhi dachen*) were important offices under the chamberlains. Eventually there were six senior assistant chamberlains, two from each of the upper three banners. The junior assistant chamberlains tended to be "grace" appointments, bestowed on Mongol sons-in-law, meritorious officials, descendants of conquest heroes, and imperial kinsmen.

To forestall any erosion of the emperor's personal control of this vital security organ amid the guards' increasing bureaucratization, two important high-level guards posts were created during the Kangxi reign. They did not fall under the purview of the chamberlains' office. The first were the adjutant generals (*yuqian dachen*), who were in charge of the guards of the antechamber (*yuqian shiwei*) and the guards at the Qianqing gate (*Qianyingmen shiwei*). The adjutant generals were Manchu and Mongol princes' sons, frequently imperial affines, or imperial kinsmen, who were personally selected by the ruler. These elite guard units handling the security of the inner court were thus organizationally separated from the guard units of the outer-court portions of the Forbidden City.

Adjutant generals—by the late Qing, this post, which originally had no set quota, tended to be filled by four individuals at any one time—waited on the emperor in shifts around the clock. Although their prestige and informal power extended beyond that of the chamberlains because of their attendance on the ruler, the post was not bureaucratically ranked. Similarly, the guards at the Qianqing gate included outstanding bannermen from the upper three banners, princes' sons, and imperial kinsmen. There were two other posts, nominal in nature, which served as stepping stones into the guards at the Qianqing gate or the adjutant generalship: these were the attaché to the emperor's suite (*yuqian xingzou*) and the probationary guards at the Qianqing gate (*Qianqingmen xingzou*). Appointees tended to be kinsmen or banner nobles.[89]

The Forbidden City was subject to the most stringent security regulations. The emperors did not permit one office to control all palace security but instead deliberately created a system of agencies with overlapping jurisdictions. The guards were stationed at the gates leading into and out of the inner court. The guards of the antechamber and guards at the Qianqing gate were the elite of the palace force. Workshops, storerooms, and the sleeping chambers of the imperial consorts were separately guarded by the upper three bondservant divisions. At night, when the gates were locked, a watchman made the rounds to check the major gates in the inner court. The commanders of these units were directly responsible to the emperor. In addition, the chamberlain of the Imperial Guard (*ling shiwei nei dachen*), high officials, and the lieutenant generals of the banners were expected to carry out night patrols and spot checks on the guards. These supervisory functions were reinforced after the 1813 Trigram rebels broke into the palace.[90]

Relatively few officials enjoyed the privilege of entering the Qianqing gate. Princes or civil and military officials entering the inner court for audiences were limited (according to rank) in the size of their entourage. Artisans and servants posed a much greater security problem, and one that periodically caught the imperial eye. All workmen were supposed to wear waist (or belt) tallies, which were changed once every three years. One memorial reported a total of 3,668 belt tallies issued for the various subagencies of the Imperial Household Department for 1773 and requested an additional hundred. Regulations requiring that each workman's entry be recorded and reported to the emperor began in 1777 and were still in force in 1819.[91] Because of the anxiety about theft, the movement of goods in and out of the Forbidden City was also carefully monitored, and a gate list of the items being transferred had to be presented for inspection at the gates.

The work of the guards was gradually diversified. Many guardsmen held concomitant posts in other key palace organs. An adjutant general was normally assigned to supervise the Chancery of Memorials (Zoushichu); senior and junior assistant chamberlains headed the Imperial Armory (Wubeiyuan), the Imperial Stables (Shangsiyuan), and the Bureau of Imperial Gardens and Parks (Fengchenyuan). Because food preparation was directly linked to security, guardsmen were assigned to work under the ministers of the Imperial Household Department in the Imperial Buttery. Guardsmen were also present at ceremonial audiences, routine audiences, state banquets, imperial weddings, and at shamanic rituals in the Kunning palace.

These were their routine duties. Their extraordinary assignments allow us to examine how emperors used the inner-court personnel to supplement the outer-court bureaucracy in the implementation of imperial policies. Inner-court officers were especially likely to be given assignments linked with reconnaissance, intelligence gathering, and military-strategic issues. One example is the exploration of the mountain range of Changbaishan, ordered by the emperor in 1677. Changbaishan, the legendary site of the origin of the Manchu people, had not been mapped and was located in the midst of a thickly forested uninhabited region. The emperor dispatched *nei dachen* Wumona and three guardsmen to "respectfully gaze" (*zhanshi xingli*) at the mountain. A collateral descendant of the imperial house, Wumona had enjoyed a long career in the imperial guards. He left the capital on June 3, 1677, and arrived at the garrison headquarters of the Jilin military governor on the twenty-second. A search for a guide took some time, as did the logistics of arranging that sufficient supplies for the guards and their accompanying military escort would be sent by river.

Sabsu, a Manchu bannerman who was later to achieve fame and promotion in battles against the Russians, was assigned to lead two hundred troops from the Ningguta garrison to support this exploration, which began on July 1. On July 10, the group began to hack a way into the densely forested belt surrounding Changbaishan and reached the foot of the mountain on the sixteenth. A camp was set up while the guardsmen climbed to the top, where they performed rituals of worship to the peaks and witnessed what all interpreted as a favorable portent: seven out of a herd of wild deer leaping on the mountain peaks lost their footing and fell off the mountain, to land next to the camp, thus providing food for the hungry soldiers. The expedition started back on July 17 and finally arrived in the capital on September 17. After receiving their report, the emperor sent an edict to the Board of Rites and the Grand Secretariat: "Changbaishan is the important place where the ancestors originated. There are many marvelous traces there; the mountain spirit should receive investiture and permanent sacrifice, to reflect the intentionality of the gods in the prosperity of the state."[92]

Guardsmen reconnoitered in the northeast during the Sino-Russian conflicts over the northern borders and also helped gather data for the compilation of the Kangxi atlas. They adjudicated bureaucratic disputes, such as the Yellow River conservation project debates of 1688, and investigated corruption, as in the management of the official granaries at Tongzhou (1820). In 1753 the Qianlong emperor had an adjutant general check rumors that Manchu bannermen were illicitly moving into the Outer City. When Nayancheng was sent as a special commissioner to investigate the situation in Xinjiang after an uprising (1826), the emperor sent a Qianqing gate guardsmen with him to act as the "emperor's eyes and ears." Guardsmen were assigned to a wide variety of tasks, in a manner that is reminiscent of the Kangxi emperor's use of his bondservants, with the exception that guardsmen were also skilled soldiers.

Many individuals began their long careers by serving in the imperial guards. The non-Han presidents of the Six Boards, the head of the Lifanyuan, and the senior non-Han president of the Censorate appointed in 1669 had all begun in the imperial guards. Many members of the famous Tong descent group entered official careers through guards service. The Fuca provide perhaps the most illustrious example of a descent group winning imperial favor through guards service. The first Fuca to do so, Hašitun (d. 1663), was a member of the vanguard under Nurgaci who then joined Hongtaiji's imperial guards and was promoted to *nei dachen* in 1644. He survived the purge that followed Dorgon's death and served Fulin, winning a baronetcy from the emperor. Hašitun's eldest son, Mishan, served in the Kangxi reign as a minister of the Imperial Household Department, held the presidency of the Board of Revenue, and sat on the Deliberative Council of Princes and High Officials. By the time of his death in 1674, he had become one of the emperor's most trusted high officials.[93]

Three of Mishan's four sons began their careers with service in the imperial guards. His eldest son, Maska, was appointed to the Deliberative Council after meritorious action in the Galdan campaign. Mawu, the third son, served in the imperial guards, accompanied the emperor on the Galdan campaign, but was disgraced thereafter (1709) for conspiring with other inner-court officials in the Yinsi faction during the emperor's near-fatal illness. He later served in inner-court and banner posts and was made a chamberlain of the Imperial Guard in 1721. The fourth son, Lirongbao, inherited Mishan's baronetcy and served in a variety of guard posts, eventually winning promotion to colonel of the Vanguard Division (*qianfeng canling*) and colonel of the Guard Division (*hujun canling*). Disgraced in 1709 because of Mawu, he died in 1710 but was posthumously made a first-class duke when his daughter became empress (1736).[94]

The fourth generation of Fuca serving in inner-court and banner posts included Fuliang, Baoju, and Fuqing, who began as a guardsman, served in a succession of banner posts, including four years as a deputy lieutenant general (*fudutong*) in Tibet (1744–48). Fuqing was appointed *amban* to Tibet in 1749, during a period of crisis in its internal affairs. Fuqing and his colleague Labdon's decision to murder the ruler, 'Gyur med rnam rgyal, led to the gathering of a frenzied mob that stormed the Qing officials' residence. Fuqing tried to defend himself, then committed suicide. The eventual consequence of the death of the two *amban* was the strengthening of the Qing military presence in Lhasa.[95]

Fuheng, Fuqing's famous brother, entered the guards under favorable terms, as a brother of the empress. He achieved rapid promotion in inner-court offices, and by 1748, he was already president of the Board of Revenue and an associate grand secretary. His greatest achievements took place during the Jinquan campaign (1748), for which he was made a first-class duke and awarded a double-eyed peacock feather. He was one of the advisers who argued in favor of the pacification of the Zunghars, which incorporated Ili and Chinese Turkestan into the empire. Although his last campaign in Burma was unsuccessful, he was posthumously awarded a second-degree princedom after his death in 1770.[96]

The Qianlong reign saw a fifth generation of Fuca achieve high office through service in the guards. These Fuca—Mingren, Mingrui, Mingliang, Fuling'an, Fulong'an, Fukang'an, and Fuchang'an—marked the high point in the family's fortunes. Fukang'an and Fuchang'an, sons of Fuheng, held both inner-court and central government posts. Fukang'an attracted favorable notice through his military actions in the second Jinquan campaign (1773–76), then served in the 1780s and early 1790s in a number of provinces as governor-general. His reputation as a civil administrator was not good but he was recognized as "one of the most capable commanders of the imperial troops" and helped quell uprisings in Gansu (1784), Taiwan (1787), and the southwest (1795–96). Fukang'an led the Qing forces in their successful repulse of the Gurkha invasion of Tibet (1792). He was the only Manchu who was not an Aisin Gioro to receive a princely title.[97]

Because guardsmen, particularly those in inner-court posts, came under the emperor's personal scrutiny, service could bring swift appointment and rich rewards. From the emperor's point of view, the guards constituted an alternative tool of the imperial will to the civil service bureaucracy and thus enhanced the ruler's flexibility. From the perspective of the banner elite, employment in the imperial guards offered the prospect of upward mobility.

THE AISIN GIORO IN DECLINE

During the late eighteenth and nineteenth centuries, the rising fiscal burden of supporting a growing number of imperial kinsmen drove rulers to limit both the size and number of princely stipends. A new regulation, introduced in 1848, cut off the holders of the lowest princely title after three transmissions for *enfeng* titles and five transmissions for *gongfeng* titles.[98] The Qing also successively discounted princely stipends, paying only 50 to 60 percent of the stipulated sum. Stipends for unranked Aisin Gioro fell below—in 1740 only 81 percent—the amount promised. From 1762 to 1853, the subsidies for wedding and funerary expenses were "temporarily halted." The actual payments of subsidies granted in 1671 to unranked *zongshi* males (36 taels of silver a year) were much lower. In 1740 they were on average less than six taels apiece; in that same year, 78 percent of the silver and 70.4 percent of the rice payments went to the ranked nobles who constituted a tiny percentage of the imperial lineage.[99]

By the end of the dynasty, even the most privileged princes of the first and second rank were receiving only 50 percent of their nominal silver stipends and approximately 70 percent of the grain allotment. A few favored princes did continue to receive imperial bounty, in the practice called *jiaxian* or *shangxian*, whereby the court added honorific titles on top of the heritable rank. In the Kangxi and Yongzheng reigns, *jiaxian* was largely granted posthumously, to provide honor by raising the level of the funerary rituals. During the Tongzhi and Guangxu reigns, however, these awards—which amounted to raising stipends—were granted to several imperial princes.[100]

Economic discrimination may be the reason why *juelo* descendants had fewer concubines and increased at a slower rate (an average of 1.1 percent as opposed to 1.5 percent a year) than did their *zongshi* kinsmen. By the late nineteenth century, the average Aisin Gioro (including both *zongshi* and *juelo*) had only one wife, in sharp contrast to the late seventeenth century, when he might have had more than five.[101] A recent demographic study argues that female infanticide was practiced by the lower imperial nobility in the *zongshi*, estimating that perhaps 10 percent of all daughters born to the Aisin Gioro from 1700–1840 were "victims of infanticide" and that female infanticide increased in the late eighteenth century.[102]

Poverty emerged as a problem among the unranked *zongshi* in the eighteenth century. Father Parennin, writing in 1724, observed:

> It is good to caution you concerning the notions that you have formed about the princes of the blood in China: You will deceive yourself if you

compare them to those of Europe. . . . The princes of the blood of whom I speak are quite close to their origins; there are only five generations; their numbers nevertheless have so multiplied in such a short time that they are estimated today to be over 2,000; this multitude . . . above all those . . . who find themselves deprived of titles and employment, cannot be represented in a manner appropriate to their birth; it is this which makes a great contrast between princes of the same blood.[103]

Archival reports from the Imperial Clan Court include many petitions like the one in 1811 from Yongze, an unranked *zongshi*. The sole support of his widowed mother, he reported that he could not wait until the end of the year for his stipend and grain allotment. The court was embarrassed by many drunken and quarrelsome kinsmen: in one case, a man, repeatedly turned in by his widowed mother who could not control him when he was in his cups, was finally sentenced to permanent confinement for the remainder of his mother's life (he was the only son). The emperor himself demanded an investigation in another instance, when a *zongshi* used abusive language toward a matron in the Han Chinese quarter of the capital.[104] The *zongshi* even produced a gang leader.

Hunhun (*hun'er* in Peking dialect) were "knights errant," toughs of bannermen origins who operated within the Inner City. Anecdotes about them and their physical exploits cover the entire span of the dynasty. An example of this type was Alima, whose many illegal activities finally brought him to the Shunzhi emperor's attention. The emperor ordered that he be executed. Alima reluctantly agreed to submit to the imperial judgment but he refused to be killed outside the Xuanwu gate, where Han Chinese could view the proceedings. So he was executed in the Inner City.

The *zongshi* gang leader was Xiaochong, who led a large gang from the 1860s until his death in the middle of the Guangxu reign. His downfall came when a rival gang, led by Deng Jiawuhu ("Fifth-Tiger" Deng) invaded Xiaochong's territory. "Fifth Tiger" was himself registered in an Imperial Household Department banner. He was one of five equally ferocious brothers, known as "Big Tiger," "Second Tiger," and so on. By the late nineteenth century, the earlier method of settling gang disputes by one-on-one combat between the two gang leaders had been supplanted by gang fights outside the Di'an gate, where the gangs would assemble at two winehouses, armed with cudgels. Each side would send several men to engage the other gang in verbal insults and the confrontation would escalate into a brawl. Xiaochong challenged Deng Jiawuhu to such a confrontation and was killed in the fray. Deng Jiawuhu was arrested and executed shortly afterward for having beaten a commoner to death.[105]

Such incidents spurred the court to expel its black sheep from the capital. Attempts made during the Yongzheng and Qianlong reigns were half-hearted; it was the Jiaqing emperor who ultimately acted decisively. Although Yongyan had rejected a memorial in 1808 proposing that unranked *zongshi* be moved to Mukden, the continuing economic and social deterioration among these families prompted him to change his mind. In August 1812 the emperor ordered the military governor of Mukden, Hening, to begin planning the housing and family subsidies that would go to the *zongshi* households. Even at this date, *zongshi* were assigned houses within an enclosed area, with guards checking entry and exit just as in Peking. The dimensions of the houses that would be given to the *zongshi* are also extremely instructive: in contrast with the mansions of the princes, these were modest dwellings with a three-*jian* front room, side room of four *jian*, and a courtyard.[106]

The court wished to move kinsmen who were propertyless, kinsmen who were vagrants, and those who had committed crimes. They tried to entice volunteers to move away by offering additions to the normal stipend (two taels per year for *zongshi* over 15 *sui* of age; three taels for those aged 20 *sui* and older), and they promised that each household leaving Peking would receive the rent from 360 *mu* of land, which amounted to 21 taels a year. Not surprisingly, many *zongshi* preferred the pleasures of the capital: one such well-to-do individual, Guomin, committed suicide when the Imperial Clan Court tried to force him to move.[107] After a year of effort, officials of the Imperial Clan Court picked 70 households and sent them with a military escort to Mukden. Each household received a travel allowance and a flat sum of 15 taels, and carts for their belongings. The third batch, to be moved in 1815, included *zongshi* who had been arrested: in their case, the clan court officials argued that only half the travel allowance and nothing else should be bestowed.[108]

Aisin Gioro who committed crimes short of treason had their sentences lightened. Banishment to Sinkiang was changed to a pardon for Zhengfang, a beggar chief whose mother was an Aisin Gioro, because the emperor was impressed by her age and propriety.[109] There were Aisin Gioro con men like *zongshi* Dekjitai, who had been sent to imprisonment in Jilin for a fraud committed in 1823. When he was released in 1831, Dekjitai was permitted to reside in Mukden, but in 1852 he slipped out of the city. Although efforts to arrest him at first failed, he was eventually nabbed in Peking.

Imperial nobles were among the many who pushed opium sales in China to record levels during the nineteenth century. The court tried to strictly punish opium addicts. Imperial kinsmen had their sentences reduced from death for opium addiction to banishment to the Jilin garrison, where the criminal would be imprisoned for a two-year term and receive a beating of thirty strokes.[110] Information on punishments meted out to both *zongshi* and *juelo* kinsmen in 1907–9 show the full range of criminal activity, from manslaughter and assault to fraud and theft.[111]

The continuing economic degradation of most Aisin Gioro can be seen in information concerning their occupations and incomes at the close of the dynasty. A survey conducted in 1959 of Peking's Manchu population included three *juelo* descendants. One household subsisted on the annual stipend received during the last year of the dynasty, a total of 10 taels of silver. In the most prosperous case, the household had lived on the official salary of the grandfather before 1911. After the revolution, this family sold its estate and lived on the proceeds while the other two households became peddlers, laborers, and artisans. The stipend rolls of the Plain Red Manchu Banner stationed in Peking show 664 *juelo* drawing 1.4 taels a month, thirteen *zongshi* descendants with the same stipend, and 53 more favored *zongshi* drawing 2.1 taels a month.[112]

A LEAN ARISTOCRACY

The princes of the blood were a very tiny minority of the descendants of Nurgaci and his brothers, who constituted the *zongshi*. The 177 *zongshi* holding princely titles toward the end of the dynasty represented approximately 1 percent of the number of male *zongshi* alive at that time, and about 0.6 percent of the total number of Aisin Gioro males (including the *juelo*; table 1).[113] The princes occupying the upper six ranks, who enjoyed "the eight privileges," constituted less than 25 percent of the imperial nobility. The upper and lower nobility differed significantly in their characteristics. None of the *bafen* princes, as compared with 27 percent of the lower ranks, had obtained his title through examination. Of the *bafen* princes, 41 percent (as opposed to only 4 percent of the lower ranks) held their titles in perpetuity. The core of the high nobility in 1907 was thus a permanent hereditary elite, whereas many of the other princes were on the ladder of downward mobility.

There was significant variation in the ability of emperor's sons to found long-lived princely descent lines (table 2). The higher percentages enjoyed by princes of the first two generations is a result of the Qianlong emperor's award of the privilege of perpetual inheritance to conquest heroes, a privi-

Table 1. Sources of Princely Titles Held in 1907

Princely Rank[a]	By Exam	From Father	Perpetual Grant	Other	Total
1	0	1	9	0	10
2	0	0	2	0	2
3	0	5	0	0	5
4	0	3	0	0	3
5	0	10	1	0	11
6	0	5	5	0	10
7	0	4	0	0	4
8	3	2	1	1	7
9	0	1	1	2	4
10	8	1	0	1	10
11	1	2	1	0	4
12	4	1	1	0	6
13	1	3	0	0	4
14	3	2	0	0	5
15	0	3	1	0	4
16	0	6	0	0	6
17	10	5	0	0	15
18	7	49	1	0	57

[a]The eighteen ranks of princes of the blood draw on the list in H. S. Brunnert and V. V. Hagelstrom, *Present-Day Political Organization of China,* trans. A. Beltchenko and E. E. Moran (Foochow, 1911), nos. 10–27. Data on 1907 holders of princely titles come from Yang Xuechen and Zhou Yuanlian, *Qingdai baqi wang gong guizu xing shuai shi* (Shenyang, 1986), tables 5–8 on 472–85.

lege that was not given to Fulin's brothers. The princes in Yinzhen's generation suffered permanently from an unusually bitter succession struggle (see chapter 3): their representation in the nobility would be still lower had the Qianlong emperor not appointed a brother and two of his sons as heirs to vacant princedoms.[114]

The princes were thus disproportionately the heirs to the warrior heroes of the first three conquest generations: they occupied eight of the first-degree princedoms and all the other lower-ranking titles given in perpetuity. Even at the end of the dynasty (table 3), about 38 percent of all princely titles were held by descendants of the first two generations—a remarkable figure considering the operation of the reduction of noble rank with each

Table 2. The Continuity of Noble Rank among the *Zongshi*

Generation Of	Number of Nobles[a]	Percentage with Titled Descendants
Nurgaci	4	50
Hongtaiji	15	53
Fulin	7	28
Xuanye	3	67
Yinzhen	18	78
Hongli	1	100
Yongyan	7	86
Minning	3	100
Yizhu	5	100

SOURCE: *Zongshi wang gong shizhi zhangjing juezhi xici quanbiao* (1906), 1.24–39: the figures represent the population as of the end of 1906. The total number of ennobled imperial agnates in the *zongshi* recorded in this source is 177, a figure that varies slightly from the total (168) recorded in *Aixin juelo zongpu* (Fengtian, 1937–38); the former seems to include individuals resident in Mukden.

[a] Totals exclude the ruler, sons who did not survive to adulthood, and sons who were assigned as heirs to other descent lines, where they are counted.

hereditary transmission, which would have caused the greatest downward mobility in the descendants of these early ancestors.

This was a tiny imperial nobility. By ruthlessly reducing the number of princedoms that were inheritable, the Qing succeeded in reducing its fiscal burden. In many dynasties, imperial relatives who live on imperial subsidies become a significant drain on state finances. As already noted, the Qing rulers sharply differentiated between support of *zongshi* and *juelo* descendants. Only the first group was eligible for the princely ranks that conveyed special privileges, high stipends, and access to power; not every son of an emperor was given a princely rank.

From a small group of only 419 males registered in 1660, the *zongshi* grew to total 16,454 males in 1915, three years after the 1911 Revolution had ended the whole system of subsidies. We can compare the 10 Qing princes of the first rank with the 30 first-rank princes at the end of the Ming dynasty (out of 50 first-rank princedoms created) or, most strikingly, the 2 Qing second-rank princes with the 220 Ming holders of this title (out of 472) who remained in 1644. The holders of each of the lower noble ranks

Table 3. Distribution of Noble Rank among Descendants of
Imperial Sons, 1906

	Ranks		
	---	---	---
Generation Of	High (1–6)	Middle (7–11)	Low (12–18)
Nurgaci	3	2	11
Hongtaiji	8	5	38
Fulin	2	10	11
Xuanye	1	1	2
Yinzhen	9	4	30
Hongli	1	0	5
Yongyan	7	3	11
Minning	5	2	0
Yizhu	5	1	0
Total	41	28	108

SOURCE: *Zongshi wang gong shizhi zhangjing juezhi xici quanbiao*
(1906), 1.24–39.

in the Ming eight-rank system totaled "several tens of thousands."[115] At
the bottom of the hierarchy, the hordes of unranked Aisin Gioro contrast
with the Ming, when "every male descendant of every Ming emperor . . .
theoretically received some title of royalty and a corresponding emolument
from state funds."[116]

By 1915 the Aisin Gioro were estimated to number 73,418 persons. Estimates of the size of the Ming imperial clan around 1644 range from over
80,000, only slightly larger than the size of the Qing imperial clan, to over
200,000. Figures for 1740 and 1742 indicate that the total expended on the
stipends represented less than 1 percent of the silver in the Board of Revenue treasury. This total may have risen to 1.25 percent of tax revenues in
the mid-nineteenth century, but the contrast with the Ming—which by
1615 was paying its kinsmen stipends that were 143 percent of the annual
land tax revenues—is striking.[117]

To the layperson, aristocracies represent the triumph of birth over merit.
Comparison of the Manchu imperial princes with their Ming counterparts
underlines the degree to which Qing rulers introduced merit as a criterion

for the perpetuation of economic and status privilege among kinsmen. By ensuring that princely and noble titles would be limited to a few individuals, the throne produced a lean aristocracy that it could control. It employed imperial kinsmen and banner nobles in strategic posts to further imperial interests. As the core of the conquest elite, the aristocrats were a primary element in an intricate system of checks and balances that pervaded Qing administration.

Chapter 3   Sibling Politics

Imperial policies dealing with agnatic relatives were profoundly political in their inspiration and directly related to the competition for power, as Jennifer Holmgren demonstrates. Most Han Chinese rulers regarded their brothers and sons as the most serious threat to the throne and tailored their policies to discourage challengers. The Ming dealt with this problem by selecting the eldest son of the empress as heir apparent when he was very young. All other sons were banned from political participation and sent to reside for life on estates in the provinces.

The Qing strategy was very different. As the Toba Wei (ca. 400 – 500 A.D.), the Khitan Liao (970 – 1055), and the Mongol Yuan (ca. 1240 – 1300) rulers did, the Qing employed imperial kinsmen in governance. But they did not enfeoff sons and give them territories to hold, as the Mongols did. Nor did they follow the Khitan policy of bypassing closely related kinsmen to give substantive appointments to more distant agnates. Instead, the Qing rulers emphasized competence in making appointments, as the Toba Wei did, and insisted that "power and authority allocated to individual members of the ruling clan derive only from office-holding, and that in turn derives from service and loyalty as perceived by the emperor."[1]

The Toba Wei political organization focused on "protection of the privileged place of the emperor's paternal relatives in government, maintenance of non-Han supremacy in general, and employment of men who identify strongly with the centre of power."[2] The Qing pursued identical goals, but their historical circumstances dictated somewhat different strategies. In the late sixteenth and early seventeenth centuries, Nurgaci's brothers, sons, and nephews had been a major factor in his military success. Within the confines of Nurgaci's kin group, rewards of military command went strictly by performance. No one, not even the ruler's sons, could become a banner lord without successful generalship. As a result, *beile* enjoyed nearly absolute power over their own banners during the first half of the seventeenth century.

Hongtaiji and his successors confronted the problem of tempering the power of the banner lords while continuing to depend on their military leadership. Struggles over succession (see below) highlighted the banner lords' challenge to any system of centralized rule. The completion of the conquest in 1683 altered the political situation in several important ways. The emperors continued to whittle away at the autonomy enjoyed by the *beile*. The need for and the means to reward military heroes declined, even though conflicts on Qing borders continued for another seventy years. The criteria for princely status shifted to emphasize loyalty, bureaucratic efficiency, and, increasingly, adherence to normative standards of Manchu behavior.

The taming of imperial princedoms also proceeded from economic motives. The great princely estates created on the spoils of war (see below) were a thing of the past, and emperors now drew on their own estates in order to establish their sons in independent households. The new princely houses were poorer, and the hereditary transmission of princely ranks was curtailed. Even as emperors used new investitures to dilute the solidarity (and political orientations) of the lower five banner companies, they made sure that these princelings would be subordinated to the throne.

The triumph of the throne over the *beile*, achieved in the Yongzheng reign, ushered in another policy shift. Rulers selectively commemorated the conquest heroes of the Aisin Gioro as exemplars of Manchu martial traditions but required that heirs prove themselves worthy of these titles. Having eliminated their political power, emperors permitted the descendants of the "iron-capped princes" to bask in glory and enjoy the enormous estates acquired by their forefathers. Although all imperial kinsmen could also enter office by passing special examinations, imperial appointments favored closely related kin.

All imperial princes were required to reside in Peking. Beginning in the last years of the Shunzhi reign, they could absent themselves from the capital only with the emperor's consent. And the emperor controlled virtually every aspect of their lives. With few exceptions, princes' stipends and estates depended on imperial favor. Their estates were managed by stewards responsible to the throne. Their mansions could be confiscated or reallocated at imperial whim. They were forbidden to have close friendships with

Han Chinese officials. They could not marry, or give their daughters in marriage, without the emperor's approval. When they died, the emperor had the power to confirm the heirs to their hereditary titles.[3]

PRINCELY POLITICS IN THE EARLY QING
The Triumph of Father-Son Succession

In Jurchen society, family and tribal headship were determined primarily on the basis of merit. The Jurchen Jin and the Mongol Yuan dynasty alike had permitted brothers as well as sons to inherit the khanate.[4] Competition over the succession was a dominant aspect of Aisin Gioro interaction in the seventeenth century.

According to historical sources, the succession issue was first raised in 1622 when Nurgaci's sons asked their father whom he had chosen to succeed him as khan. Nurgaci replied that naming a successor would give that person added power, which he might abuse. Instead he suggested that the eight *beile* should select from amongst their group the one with the most talent and the greatest ability to lead and make him khan. Some historians ascribe Nurgaci's reluctance to his experience with his eldest son, Cuyeng (see below).[5]

When Nurgaci died, his authority was shared by the four senior *beile*, his sons Daišan, Manggultai, and Hongtaiji, and his nephew Amin, Šurgaci's second son. It was the eldest and most powerful of Nurgaci's sons, Daišan, who led the *beile* in electing Hongtaiji khan. The rituals that were performed on this occasion, however, suggest that the election did not give Hongtaiji the undisputed leadership position. Daišan and the other two senior *beile* led the assembled kinsmen in swearing an oath of submission, and Hongtaiji in turn performed the ritual obeisances symbolic of subordination to his two older brothers and cousin.[6]

Hongtaiji gradually reduced the power of the other "four great *beile*." Amin was disgraced and imprisoned in 1630 by a council of his peers, and his headship of the Bordered Blue Banner was given to his younger brother Jirgalang. Nurgaci's fifth son, Manggultai, was posthumously denounced for treason in 1635, his sister, brother, and son were executed, and his descendants removed from the imperial lineage. Yoto, Daišan's eldest son, was demoted in rank for his complicity in the plot.[7] Only Daišan survived Hongtaiji's reign.

Hongtaiji's death in 1643 sparked another succession crisis. An assembly of banner nobles and officials met in front of Hongtaiji's coffin to elect his successor. Dorgon, his brother Dodo, Daišan, and Hooge were nominated. Hooge was supported by the yellow banner officials, Dorgon by the white banners. The assembly compromised by selecting Hongtaiji's infant ninth son, Fulin, and appointing Jirgalang and Dorgon as regents. When Adali conspired against the collegial decision, he was executed.[8]

As regent, Dorgon consolidated his personal power. He removed his co-regent Jirgalang in 1647, on charges of usurping imperial prerogatives. Hooge died in prison in 1648. Dorgon's allies in the imperial lineage, Bolo, Nikan, and Mandahai, were promoted in princely rank. Dorgon became the sole regent, but after his death in 1650 he and his brother Dodo were posthumously condemned. Dorgon's adopted heir was returned to his natal family; Dodo's princedom was reduced in rank, and Ajige, their full brother, was stripped of his titles, imprisoned, and forced to commit suicide. The line of Bayara, Nurgaci's younger brother and a Dorgon ally, was cut off when Bayara's son Bayintu was imprisoned (1652) and expelled from the imperial lineage. In 1659 Mandahai, Bolo, and Nikan were all posthumously accused of appropriating Dorgon's property for personal use. Mandahai's and Bolo's descendants were deprived of all ranks; because Nikan had died in battle, his rank was permitted to continue.[9]

Fraternal succession was not an option when Fulin, the Shunzhi emperor, died of smallpox in 1661. The Shunzhi emperor's designation of an heir had broken with tradition. Since Fulin's successor was not yet seven years old, a regency was inevitable. Fulin's selection of four regents, none of whom were imperial agnates, also set a precedent.[10] Two (Ebilun and Oboi) belonged to the Bordered Yellow Banner, one (Suksaha) to the Plain White Banner, and the senior regent, Soni, to the Plain Yellow Banner.

The political struggle among the imperial princes continued in the first years of the Kangxi reign. Soni was too old to exert leadership. With Ebilun's support, Oboi became the dominant figure. After Soni's death in 1667, Oboi brought the third regent, Suksaha, to trial and had him and his family executed. In 1669, with the help of Soni's son Songgotu, the young Kangxi emperor succeeded in arresting Oboi for insolence.[11] Oboi's allies were purged. The line of Tabai, Nurgaci's sixth son, was cut off when Bambursan and Ekcin, Tabai's sons, were denounced and executed in 1669; Nikan's son Lambu was reduced to a prince of the fifth degree "for concealing the misdemeanors of his wife's grandfather Oboi."[12]

Princes and the Banners

The elimination of fraternal succession paralleled the throne's subjugation of banner lords. Before 1644, the banners were directly controlled by the banner *beile*, whose autonomous powers over the Manchu, Mongol, and Han Chinese units under their commands extended far beyond the battle-field. Banner companies were the *beile's* personal property, to be passed on to his sons without reference to the khan. The banner *beile* were co-sharers with the khan in the division of booty; they were empowered to engage in trade; they deliberated with the khan on all state matters.

Despite his exhortations for fraternal rule, Nurgaci himself had set the precedent for the struggle between the khan and the banner princes that followed his death. Political purges removed many individuals. When Šurgaci disputed his elder brother's right to primacy, Nurgaci had him executed (1611). Cuyeng, Nurgaci's eldest son, died in prison for his "treasonous plans." Of Nurgaci's four brothers, all active in the conquest, two were no longer represented among the princely houses, and few of Šurgaci's descendants became prominent. Nurgaci had sixteen sons who survived to adulthood. Half of them were either executed, forced to commit suicide, or posthumously disgraced; over another quarter (five out of sixteen) were either cut off for subsequent political crimes or occupied only peripheral posts.[13] Hongtaiji had eleven sons; eight either left no descendants or founded lines that never distinguished themselves.[14]

The imperial campaign to whittle away the autonomy of the banner princes proceeded along several paths. In the Shunzhi reign, the emperor's control of three banners—the Bordered Yellow, Plain Yellow, and Plain White—was confirmed. These became the "upper three banners" (*shangsan qi*). Within the lower five banners, companies were passed from father to son along with the princely titles, and the princes retained their traditional powers over their companies.[15] The loyalty of bannermen to their original banner lord was diluted through the expansion of the banners in the seventeenth and eighteenth centuries. One major vehicle for the creation of new companies was the practice of shifting emperor's sons into the lower five banners when they set up their own households. Reduction in rank with each generational transmission meant that eventually these companies would be returned to the emperor's upper three banners, but that process took several generations.

The throne's repudiation of the banner lord's right to command his own troops in battle was achieved after dismal performances by the princes appointed as commanders in chief of the banner forces during the rebellion of the Three Feudatories (1673–81): five princes lost their rank and another was fined the equivalent of a year's stipend.[16] In later campaigns the Kangxi emperor had the authority to appoint commanders. Xuanye's elder brother, Prince Yu, his younger brother Prince Gong, and his son Yinti were among the princes leading banner troops against the Mongol leader Galdan. During the second expedition (1693), the emperor had five of his sons leading different banner troops, while he himself commanded the main force. After the crushing defeat of Galdan under his personal leadership, he assigned his son Yinti (1718) to lead the army against Tsereng Araptan, Galdan's erstwhile ally.[17]

The bureaucratization of banner administration also helped the throne to triumph over the banner lords. The process had begun when Hongtaiji gave new powers to banner officials and encouraged the growth of a banner bureaucracy. Banner administration was taken away from the banner *beile* and put in the hands of a lieutenant general and deputy lieutenant general who were appointed by the emperor. The first appointments were made extemporaneously. In 1718 the Kangxi emperor ordered his seventh son, Yinyou, to manage the affairs of the three Plain Blue Banners while its lieutenant general was on campaign; for the same reason he appointed Yin'e, his tenth son, to manage the affairs of the three Plain Yellow Banners and put Yintao, his twelfth son, in charge of Manchu, Mongol, and Han Plain White Banner affairs. Yintao later (1722) became lieutenant general of the Manchu Bordered Yellow Banner. Yinli, Xuanye's seventeenth son, served successively as lieutenant general of the Manchu Bordered Red Banner, Han Bordered Blue Banner, and Mongol Bordered Blue Banner from 1724 to 1733.[18] While all these sons held princely titles, they were not the hereditary masters of the banners that they managed. Instead, they were now administrators, acting on behalf of the emperor.

The subjugation of the banner princes was completed by the Yongzheng emperor, who limited the number of bannermen controlled by a banner prince, bureaucratized recruitment of company captains, standardized the operations of the banners, and expanded the imperial surveillance system. The power to adjudicate disputes and punish bannermen, formerly enjoyed by banner princes, was transferred to the central government organs. The emperor also decentralized authority over the Manchu, Mongol, and Han banners. Cutting off the succession of Yolo, Prince An, he gave Yolo's banner companies to his own brother, Yinxiang, and warned the banner princes that "the state (*guojia*) has only one master."[19] After his reign "the ruler was able to make his word final in banner and state affairs."[20]

Secret Succession

The system of secret succession began in the Kangxi reign. Xuanye came to regret his decision to make the eldest son of his empress heir apparent, and in 1712 he removed Yinreng from the heirship. Factions formed around several sons eager to succeed him, and eventually eight more of Xuanye's twenty sons suffered punishment for their actions. Yinshi, the eldest, had been arrested in 1708 for attempting to use sorcery against Yinreng and stripped of his princedom; he died in confinement as did his brother Yinzhi. Yinsi and Yintang also died in prison, stripped of rank and expelled from the imperial lineage. Yin'e, Yintao, Yinti, and Yinqi all suffered demotions under Yinzhen's hand but were lucky enough to be rehabilitated during the Qianlong reign.[21]

The Kangxi emperor's bad experience with his heir apparent was a textbook illustration of the perils of combining the Han Chinese system of succession—naming the heir at an early age—and the non-Han conquest tradition of employing imperial kinsmen in governance. Since all of Xuanye's sons resided in Peking, they were avid observers of the ambivalent relationship between Yinreng and his father and were quick to seize on Yinreng's fall from grace to advance themselves or a brother in their father's favor. Princes became deeply engaged in court politics. After 1712 Xuanye refused to publicly name an heir, with the result that his deathbed designation of Yinzhen was clouded by rumors of fraud.[22]

To prevent similar succession crises in the future, Yinzhen introduced a system of "secret succession." He wrote the name of his heir and sealed the edict in a casket that he placed in the rafters behind a placard hanging in the Qianqing palace, to be opened only after his death. After his sons by the empress died in infancy, Hongli also refused to announce his successor's name. As far as we can tell, he did not decide on Yongyan, his fifteenth son, until 1773, when he secretly placed one copy of the edict designating his choice in the traditional spot while retaining one copy in a small box on his person.[23] Apparently the Grand Council was informed of his action, but there was no public acknowledgment of this act. Thereafter, according to the emperor's own recollections, he kept a close eye on Yongyan and on several occasions prayed to Heaven and the ancestors to confirm the wisdom of his choice. Hongli was the only Qing emperor to abdicate the throne. In 1796 Yongyan was installed as the Jiaqing emperor.

Several times in his reign, the Qianlong emperor reaffirmed the notion that merit and not birth order should be the primary criterion for the succession. Against officials who argued that public identification of the heir would stabilize court politics, Hongli cited the stability of his own succession. In rejecting pleas that he abide by the eldest son principle, he pointed to Yao, who selected not his own son but the most virtuous, Shun, to succeed him. Officials who petitioned the emperor on this issue aroused his anger. In 1778 he responded to a memorial on these lines by writing, "Whenever I receive petitions on the appointment of an heir, I observe that the majority wish profit for themselves; if they are old, then for their sons or grandsons. Outwardly they grasp precedent and claim to be instructing, but inwardly they are privately plotting self-gain."[24]

Secret succession prevailed for the rest of the dynasty. When Yongyan was on his deathbed in 1820, he summoned high officials and princes to have the casket containing his will opened before them. Inside was a document dated at the conclusion of the hundred-day mourning period for Hongli in 1799, designating his son Minning as his heir. Minning himself designated an heir only in 1846, again in secret. The public reading of his will took place as he lay dying at Yuanmingyuan. Yizhu died in 1861 at Chengde, where he had fled after the Allied Expeditionary forces entered Peking. According to the historical records, Yizhu was too weak to write the edict naming his heir, which was composed by Sushun and seven other ministers. In any case there was no choice, since the emperor had only one son.[25]

With Yizhu, imperial demography entered a new infertile phase. Yizhu was thirty years old when he died. Despite his eighteen consorts, he left only two children. His successor, Zaichun, had no children when he died of smallpox, a few months before his nineteenth birthday. The council hurriedly summoned by the two regents, Empresses Dowager Ci'an and Cixi, confronted a situation with no dynastic precedents. It seems to have been Cixi's decision to ignore generational rules in selecting the eldest son of Yihuan, Prince Chun (Yizhu's brother) as the next emperor. It was she who also selected the successor in 1908 when Zaitian, the Guangxu emperor, died childless.[26]

Princely Estates

The banner princes of the conquest generation acquired huge estates. In 1644 abandoned lands around Peking and lands belonging to members of the Ming imperial lineage, Ming nobles, and eunuchs were distributed to the Qing princes, meritorious officials, and bannermen. Three of these distributions in the Shunzhi reign affected the ownership of 160,000 *qing* of land in ten counties and departments in present-day Hebei province.[27]

Princely estates were also located around Ningguta, Jilin city, and other garrisons established in the northeast with the labor of banished criminals. Even at the end of the dynasty, when many princely estates had been dis-

sipated, there were over one hundred princely estates in the northeast totaling 2.7 million *mu*, over twice the size of the imperial estates around
Shengjing. The princely estates were spread over twenty-one different
counties and departments.[28]

Large pasturelands inside and outside the Great Wall were given to
princes so that they could maintain herds of horses for military use. Each
prince might own from several hundred up to a thousand horses and be
asked to provide three hundred or four hundred mounts for a particular
campaign. This tradition persisted into the 1730s, when a memorial from
Prince Ping complained that he had already sent five hundred horses to the
front lines; surely other *zongshi* princes could also contribute their share
of horses to the campaign.[29]

Prince Zhuang's estate totaled 78,000 *mu* scattered over twenty-five
counties in Zhili, 4,000 *mu* in Zhangjiakou and Chengde, 71,000 *mu* in Liaoning, and pasturelands totaling 324,000 *mu* in Shanxi. As Yang Xuechen
and Zhou Yuanlian point out, Prince Zhuang's properties constituted approximately 5.5 percent of the total taxable arable land for the empire in
1887. In 1723 when Yinzhen designated his brother Yinlu (1695–1767)
heir to Boggodo, Prince Zhuang, the prestige and wealth of this first-degree
princedom, which was founded on the battle merit of Šose, Hongtaiji's fifth
son, made others regard this act as an "extraordinary favor" and Yinzhen's
payoff to a loyal brother.[30]

The estate of Daišan, Prince Li, originally spread over eight counties in
Liaoning and totaled 98,682 *mu*. Since many of his sons won titles and
were awarded estates on their own merit, his descendants were exception-
ally well-off. Hooge, Prince Su, held princely estates totaling 80,053 *mu* of
land in nine counties of Fengtian prefecture, but this was only a portion of
his total holdings. A Japanese report of 1915 records that Prince Su's holdings included 32,070 *mu* of fields in Zhili and Fengtian, 1,700,000 *mu* in
Rehe, 1,260,000 *mu* of pastureland in Chahar, and some orchards, mountain areas, a forest, and a gold mine.[31] The estates of Jirgalang (Prince
Zheng) and Dorgon, Prince Rui, were also extremely large.

In most cases, moreover, the estates of the princes who had won their
titles through merit were not confiscated when an individual was disgraced
or demoted. For example Xingni, a great-grandson of Daišan, endured
several political vicissitudes, being stripped of his fourth-degree princedom for the second and final time in 1725. Throughout his career, however,
Xingni enjoyed the revenues of estates in Fengtian totaling almost 10,000
mu. The confiscation of Dorgon's estate after his death was an exception.
Dorgon owned between 1,000,000 and 2,000,000 *mu* of land, with a large

number of agricultural serfs; his heirs received 300,000 *mu* of land in the northeast and Hebei when Dorgon was politically rehabilitated in 1778.[32]

It was not confiscation but the erosion of an estate by inheritance that worked most strongly against the perpetuation of the great princely houses. Some princely houses expanded their holdings, but the majority divided their estates among a larger and larger number of descendants. Even though the title was passed on to one heir, he was responsible for ensuring that his brothers would have some economic security, and lands were parceled out in each generation. By 1911, the estate of Prince Zhuang had been divided eight times and held by thirty-four persons. The last prince Zhuang still owned 550,000 *mu* of land.[33]

Fenfu

Most imperial princes held their titles by imperial favor (*enfeng*) and they received much smaller estates from the emperor. *Fenfu* refers to the transfers of men, land, and goods that took place when an emperor decided to separate a son or brother from the palace family by providing him with a separate establishment. The granting of imperial properties in *fenfu* embraced the emperor's grandsons and even great-grandsons. Other imperial kinsmen were expected to receive a portion of their father's estate.

The Qing practice of *fenfu* was unique. Qing rulers transformed the granting of titles from an automatic right into a prize for meritorious conduct. The Kangxi, Yongzheng, and Qianlong emperors tended to be more generous toward their brothers. Although Xuanye made his brothers first-degree princes when they became fourteen, his sons were in their late teens and twenties before he awarded them first-, second-, and third-degree princedoms. Yinzhen invested two sons when they reached their early twenties and disinherited his third son, who "led a wanton life."[34] Hongli awarded princely titles to his sons when they were in their twenties and thirties.[35] Nor were the sons who eventually ascended the throne favored. The future emperor Yinzhen was twenty before he was made a *beile*. Hongli was twenty, Yongyan twenty-nine, and Minning thirty-one when they were first given titles. Yizhu became emperor at nineteen but was never a prince.[36]

Regulations, revised periodically during the dynasty, listed the items in a *fenfu*.[37] The archives of the Imperial Household Department and the Imperial Clan Court hold many memorials on the subject. Because the Qianlong emperor asked several times for information on precedents, we have fifteen complete lists of these bestowals, beginning with the 1667 *fenfu* of

Fuquan, Prince Yu, and continuing through the eighteenth century. These lists enable us to trace the major changes in the shape and size of a princely estate during the early Qing.[38]

Twenty-six imperial sons were invested as first-rank and fourteen sons as second-rank princes during the Qing dynasty. Yang Xuechen and Zhou Yuanlian use records housed in the First Historical Archives to reconstitute the land holdings of eight first-rank princes.[39] These princes include Fuquan, the second son of the Shunzhi emperor, given his title in 1667, and continue chronologically up to Prince Chun, father of the Guangxu emperor.

Fuquan, Prince Yu, received what became a standard assortment of grain estates, vegetable orchards, and fruit orchards. His holdings totaled approximately 70,000 *mu*. Yinshi, the Kangxi emperor's eldest son, received over 50,000 *mu* when he was granted a second-rank princedom in 1698. Both princes received larger estates than those given to Yinli, Prince Guo (1725); Hongzhou, Prince He (1733); and Yongxing, Prince Cheng (1789).[40] Only the grants to Mianxin, Prince Rui (subsequently Duan), the fourth son of the Jiaqing emperor, whose land holdings exceeded 50,000 *mu*, and Yihuan, Prince Chun, promoted to the first rank in 1872 with holdings totaling over 68,000 *mu*, seem to have matched the seventeenth-century estates. That these princes received lands at all was an exception to the rules made in the late Qianlong period whereby grants of income-yielding pawnshops replaced the grants of land.[41] By 1850 the ministers of the Neiwufu, or Imperial Household Department, were reporting that they could no longer provide lands for new princes without an infusion from the Board of Revenue.[42]

The Manchus had initially defined power as control over men. Grants of bannermen, serf-tenants, and servants were a constant but declining part of a prince's estate. Fuquan received ten Manchu, six Mongol, four Hanjun, and one bondservant company located outside the Great Wall in 1667. When Changying and Longxi were invested as first-degree princes in 1675, they received only six Manchu, three Mongol, three Hanjun, and one bondservant company. After 1779 these grants were further reduced to one Manchu, two Mongol, one Hanjun, and one bondservant company.

The number of stewards on grain estates was also gradually decreased, from twenty-six to eleven, with similar reductions in the grants of fruit and melon orchards. Initially princes received hundreds of serf-tenants who had "voluntarily" (*touchong*) entered this status; their numbers quickly dwindled. Fuquan received fifty households from the upper three banners stationed in Mukden; later princes got thirty. Fuquan was not allocated hunters (stationed in the northeast) who would send him game, but this feature became a regular part of subsequent bestowals. Princes were also assigned men who would send firewood, coal, and other supplies to their mansions in the capital. By the Qianlong reign, bestowals also included eunuchs who had served the princes within the palace.

The total grant of a *fenfu* can be seen in the provisions made by the Imperial Household Department in 1781 for a fourth-degree prince, the emperor's grandson Mianyi. In addition to the banner companies (three Manchu, one Mongol, and one Han), Mianyi received 400 bondservants, 8 stewards, 90 households attached to various parcels of land, and 159 items including 200 ounces of gold, 50,000 ounces of silver, silver dishes, court robes, jewels, and hats, as well as saddles, spears, bows, and arrows. Munificent as it was, this bestowal was significantly smaller than those of earlier times. Fuquan, for example, received 300 ounces of gold and 100,000 taels of silver in his 1667 *fenfu*. Originally the grants also included camels, horses, oxen, and sheep, but these had been commuted to silver payments. Still, Mianyi received as much silver as Yixin, who was invested as Prince Gong (a first-rank title) and given a separate establishment in 1852.[43]

The prince also received a mansion. Residences granted to princes were imperial property and reverted to imperial control if its occupant were stripped of his rank (see chapter 1). Their size and spatial arrangements were governed by sumptuary laws. Residences of first- and second-degree princes were called *wang fu*, were roofed with green tiles, and had a main reception hall with a throne and screen. Lesser princes resided in *fu*, which could not be roofed with green tiles and had no throne room. The number of rooms, paintings, and objects were all graded according to princely rank.[44]

Fenfu did not herald princely independence but rather the continuation, under somewhat constrained fiscal conditions, of palace life. The throne controlled the princely establishments through stewards appointed to manage the prince's affairs.[45] These stewards were responsible to the throne for the behavior of their masters; a prince's misdemeanor usually brought punishment for the servant as well (see chapter 5).

Imperial surveillance of the networking activities of princes was perfected in the early eighteenth century. Yinzhen had in 1724 lectured the assembled *zongshi* on the evils of factionalism:

> Over the years I have observed that the atmosphere of the *zongshi* is not good. Kinsmen frequently behave as though they were enemies. . . . How did they come to slander and fight, causing flesh and bone to be separated? . . . You *zongshi* regard your flesh and blood as enemies, having secret dealings with mother's faction (*dang*), wife's relations, and

with sons-in-law and others who should not meddle. . . . When I was
a prince, I was never overly intimate with Nian [Gengyao], Maternal
Uncle [Longkodo], with the family of the empress, and with the households of my in-laws. . . . Moreover I never tried to form close secret ties
with Manchu or Chinese high officials and persons responsible for inner-
court affairs and imperial guards.[46]

During the late Kangxi reign, even favored officials like Songgotu were arrested and imprisoned for taking part in factional politics at court.[47] The
fallout from the succession struggle continued in the Yongzheng reign. In
1724 Sunu, a fourth-generation descendant through Nurgaci's eldest son,
Cuyeng, was accused of creating dissension among Xuanye's sons in order
to avenge his ancestor. Sunu and his descendants were expelled from the
Aisin Gioro lineage. He, his family, and eight of his sons were banished,
while five other sons were placed in confinement. Even though the Jesuits
believed that Sunu's crime had been conversion to Christianity, the major
cause of his troubles was his advocacy of Yinsi.[48] Friendship with Yinsi,
whose name was changed by imperial order to Acina, a Manchu word
meaning "cur," also resulted in the expulsion of Yinzhen's eldest surviving
son, Hongshi, from the imperial lineage in 1726.[49]

Miande (1747–86) and his half brother Mian'en (1747–1822) were
raised in the palace when their father, Hongli's eldest son, died while still
in his early twenties. Miande was one of Hongli's favorite grandsons, but
the emperor did not hesitate to discipline him when he broke the prohibition against cultivating Han Chinese officials. In 1776 Miande was stripped
of his inherited second-degree princedom because he became friends with
a former department director in the Board of Rites named Qin Xiongbao.
The emperor ordered a secret investigation, which revealed that gifts had
been exchanged between the two men. Hongli noted that "this matter is
very consequential. Miande is studying in the inner court. He should be
careful of his conduct. He ought not to cultivate social relations with outsiders (*wairen*). . . . Happily this was quickly discovered. That it was not a
matter of long standing is the prince's good fortune. If we don't make an example [of him], the other imperial sons and grandsons will fear nothing
and gradually abandon our dynastic family laws."[50] When Miande's son,
Yichun, the emperor's first great-grandson, was born (1784), Miande was
partially forgiven and awarded a fourth-degree princedom. That the emperor exacted this kind of punishment on a favorite underlines the seriousness with which he, like other Qing rulers, viewed the formation of social networks linking Han Chinese officials and Aisin Gioro princes.

Princes were required to maintain a specified level of conspicuous consumption. Much of their estate was in illiquid form, and it is likely that many princes were financially hard-pressed. This was certainly true for Yongrong, the emperor's sixth son, who was adopted out as his uncle's heir in 1760. In 1763 deficits in his annual budget caused the emperor to order an accounting, which revealed that Prince Zhi's annual outlays, totaling over 15,500 taels, outran his income of over 12,860 taels. After itemizing all the prince's expenses (for rituals, food, fuel, etc.), the ministers of the Imperial Household Department concluded: "each year there is a deficit of 2,600 or 2,700 taels. . . . We stress that these are all expenditures of a routine nature and are definitely not extravagances. Moreover, even though he has been granted a separate household, the prince still attends the palace school and gets free meals and horses, and so forth, as do all the princes inside the palace. When he stops getting this support and everything has to be supplied by his own establishment, the deficit will grow." [51]

Fenfu was a form of premortem inheritance, but the property transferred was not all permanently bestowed. Since banner companies could be owned only by princes in the first six ranks, and most inherited titles were reduced with each generation, this part of a prince's estate eventually disappeared. [52] The rank and number of the guards and officials to which a prince was entitled also declined with rank. Personnel who became superfluous when a son inherited had to return to their original banner companies, although in one case Neiwufu officials suggested that an old guard be allowed to continue serving the family despite his inappropriately high rank. [53] Although residences were the princes' private property (as long as their inhabitants remained in good standing), sumptuary regulations and the diminution of titles through inheritance resulted in the eventual return of these mansions to the emperor.

Examples from the nineteenth century demonstrate that the emperor always held the right of eminent domain. When Prince Chun was forced to move from his first residence after his son became emperor, the court presented him with the mansion an imperial kinsman had inherited from Yongxing, Prince Cheng, and gave the kinsman another house. Prince Chun's first mansion had previously been the residence of Yoto's third son, then inhabited by Hongli's fifth son, Yongqi, and taken back when the third-generation descendant was stripped of his title. Similarly, the ministers of the Imperial Household Department scrambled to find appropriate substitute housing for other imperial agnates whose residences were handed over in 1861 to the British and French for use as embassies. [54]

SEGMENTATION WITHIN THE MAIN LINE

The growth of the Aisin Gioro forced emperors to search for ways to redefine the groups entitled to special favor. Emperors sought to "differentiate between the near and far" and favored closely related kinsmen. Segmentation, the creation of descent groups organized around individual rulers, was pursued by every ruler. The imperial discourse on personal names, discussed below, was at the core of imperial efforts to limit the innermost circle of kinsmen entitled to special favor. The Kangxi emperor began by hiving off "close branches" (*jinzhi*) from the rest of the main descent group, the *zongshi*. The Qianlong emperor identified a smaller group of "immediate kinsmen" (*jinpai zongzhi*) within the close branches. Only in the late nineteenth century, when the Xianfeng emperor died leaving just one son, was there a reverse movement to expand the size of this innermost group by extending the privilege of the common *pianpang* from two to four generations for the descendants of the Jiaqing emperor. Many of these immediate kinsmen performed valuable services for the dynasty during its last decades.

To set his name apart from his brothers', the Yongzheng emperor adopted the Chinese regulation prohibiting others from using the characters in his personal name. Of Yinzhen's brothers, only his favorite, Yinxiang, was posthumously exempted from the rule.[55] Alternatively the character in the emperor's name could be altered. When Yongyan was proclaimed the Qianlong emperor's heir apparent in 1795, a rare character pronounced "Yong" was substituted for the commonly used homophone in his name. The Daoguang emperor changed the first character of his name from *mian* to *min* for the same reason.

Removal of a common generational character undermined the ideal of fraternal solidarity. Hongli, the Qianlong emperor, protested in the following terms:[56]

> My brothers share the first character of their name with me. Now there have been requests to change their names. In my opinion, my and my brothers' names were all presented to us by the Kangxi emperor and entered into the imperial genealogy. If, just for my sake, the others all had to change their names, I would not feel at ease. . . . What I desire is that my brothers will all mend their virtue and exert themselves for the nation to supplement my deficiencies. This, not the trivialities of ritual, is the true principle of respecting the lord. This matter of changing names need not be carried out.

Hongli decreed that one stroke be omitted in the writing of his personal name to distinguish it from the names of his brothers. His grandson, the Daoguang emperor, relinquished even this distinction in 1826, when he ordered that the principle of omitting one stroke be applied to the generational character shared by his sons and future descendants, so that subjects who would not otherwise be able to use these characters would not be inconvenienced. Thereafter the characters in the personal names of emperors were not altered when they ascended the throne.

The imperial genealogy shows no pattern in the Manchu personal names of the first and second generation, nor in the apparently Chinese personal names awarded to the Shunzhi emperor's sons, although Nurgaci and his brothers shared some syllables of their personal names.[57] It was the Kangxi emperor who first adopted the Han Chinese practice known as *paiming*, by which the first character of each son's two-character name would be identical and the second character would share the same radical component. This practice, begun in 1672, was not uniformly observed until 1677.[58]

Generational characters and character elements (known as *pianpang*) marked the names in successive generations of close branches of the *zongshi* (table 4). Four rulers—Xuanye, Hongli, Minning (in 1826), and Yizhu (in 1857)—actually had the privilege of selecting these characters. According to the dynastic regulations, the Kangxi emperor "selected the 'day' character element and the 'jade' character element and had them entered into the red book [the record of Aisin Gioro births]."[59] His grandsons all shared the first character *hong* and the "day" element in the second character of their personal names. The next generation were named with the first character *yong* and a second character featuring the jade radical. The Qianlong emperor narrowed the circle of those who could receive *pianpang* to his own descendants.[60] A list of appropriate names from which the emperor could make his choice was apparently stored in the files of the Jingshifang, the subagency under the Neiwufu that was responsible for supervision of the daily lives of the emperor, his consorts, and his children.[61]

During the eighteenth century the *zongshi* were divided into lineage segments through the use of generational names (chart 1). The Kangxi emperor's descendants, who all shared a common generational name, were thus separated from the descendants of earlier Manchu rulers. Xuanye's descendants constituted the close branches of the *zongshi*. Within the close branches, the descendants of the Qianlong emperor were separated from the others by the use of a common radical (*pianpang*) in the second character

Table 4. Generational Elements in Personal Names of Imperial Descendants

Generation Of	Common First Character	Common Radical in Second Character
Taksi's sons	——	——
Nurgaci's sons	——	——
Abahai's sons	——	——
Fulin's sons	——	——
Xuanye's sons	*yin*	"to manifest" (113)
Yinzhen's sons	*hong*	"day" (72)
Hongli's sons	*yong*	"jade" (96)
Yongyan's sons	*mian*	"heart" (61)
Minning's sons	*yi*	"word" (149)
Yizhu's sons	*zai*	"water" (85)
Zaichun's sons	*pu*	"man" (9)

SOURCES: *Aixin juelo zongpu* (Fengtian, 1937–38); *Da Qing yudie.*
NOTE: Even though Zaichun, the Tongzhi emperor, was childless, the generational rules applied to the names of his uncle's grandsons.

of their personal names: they constituted the immediate kinsmen. This privilege was later extended from two to four generations for the descendants of the Jiaqing emperor.

The immediate kinsmen were not free to name their sons. In 1801 the Jiaqing emperor announced that he would personally name all the sons and grandsons of his brothers, those who shared the *pianpang* of his own descendants (see chart 1). Individuals outside this group—for example, the great-grandsons of his brothers—were to be named by the senior male of their branch.[62]

The Jiaqing emperor paid attention to infringements of the naming regulations. In 1808 he noted that a *zongshi* descendant named Mianhu had incorrectly used the "jade" radical (in the character *hu*), which was reserved for the personal names of the previous *yong* generation. Mianhu's name contravened the naming rules in two ways: first, he appropriated names reserved for close descendants, and second, he confused the generational name. The emperor ordered that the second character in Mianhu's name be altered.[63]

The seriousness with which Yongyan guarded his prerogative was clearly revealed in 1806, when he issued an edict dealing with the failure of

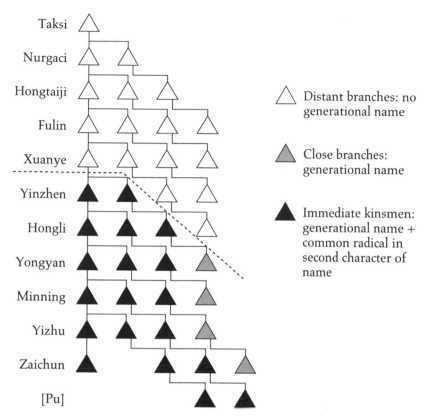

Taksi

Nurgaci

Hongtaiji

Fulin

Xuanye

Yinzhen

Hongli

Yongyan

Minning

Yizhu

Zaichun

[Pu]

△ Distant branches: no generational name

▲ Close branches: generational name

▲ Immediate kinsmen: generational name + common radical in second character of name

CHART 1. Significant segments within the main line of the Aisin Gioro. Sources: *Da Qing yudie* (Beijing, 1986); *Aixin juelo zongpu* (Mukden, 1937). Note: This chart portrays the emperors as forming a single descent line marked by naming rules; it ignores their birth order and represents all other sons of an emperor by a single symbol; thus, for example, the triangle next to Nurgaci represents his four brothers. The descent lines from distant branches are artificially truncated; in reality, they extend into thirteen or fourteen generations from Taksi. Note the absence of a triangle next to Zaichun since he was an only son. Zaichun's successor was his uncle Yihuan's son. It omits the last two emperors of the dynasty since their inclusion would not alter the pattern.

his nephew Mianyi to submit his two sons for imperial naming. Since the elder, Yimin, was born before 1801, Mianyi's omission in this instance was blameless (although the emperor criticized him for using the wrong *pianpang* in the second character of the boy's name). The birth of the second son, Yirong, in 1802, clearly should have been reported to the emperor. The emperor blamed the Imperial Clan Court for failing to inform all princes concerning the new regulations and ordered those responsible punished. But this was not the end of the matter. The emperor mused:

> Since [Mianyi] never received notification of the edict [of 1801], his fault can be excused. But he failed to use the "silk" radical in the character of his sons' names, as ordered by Father. Mianyi should be faithful to the principle, yet he illegally uses the "gold" radical in the names for his two sons. Thus he does not adhere to the rule for the close branches but behaves like the distant branches. What is in his heart? If he wishes to conduct himself like a distant relation, I will not regard him and treat him as a close nephew. When appointments to jobs are given to close relations, I will not have him serve.[64]

Genealogical records show that all but the last of Yinzhen's grandsons, born in 1745, shared the name attributes of immediate kinsmen (see chart 1) but that this privilege was not extended to Yinzhen's great-grandsons, who lapsed into the category of close branches, sharing a common generational name but not the *pianpang*. The same generational rules seem to have applied to Hongli's descendants. They were permitted to follow the naming practices of immediate kinsmen for two generations but then lapsed into the more distant category of close branches. In the early nineteenth century, when the Daoguang emperor ordered that the "word" radical be used as a *pianpang* for immediate kinsmen in his sons' generation to distinguish them from the lines of close branches, which continued to use the silk radical, he was again attempting to limit the size of this inner group.[65] The extension of the naming privileges for immediate kinsmen to include the Jiaqing and Daoguang emperors' great-great-grandsons (see chart 1) was the final modification to the naming policies that affected imperial agnates.

The groups formed by imperial decisions on the names of descendants did not conform to any of the kinship groups familiar to Han Chinese. Immediate kinsmen were not identical with the Han Chinese mourning circle (*wufu*), which was also based on degree of relationship (chart 2). The *wufu* system draws the major line between individuals within four generations (ascending and descending) as well as their descendants, and all other kinsmen. An individual is obliged to observe some degree of mourning for those in the first group, and not for others more distantly related. The group defined as immediate kinsmen by naming rules was much smaller than the boundaries of mourning kinsmen established in the *wufu* system.

Nor did the immediate kinsmen identified through naming practices coincide with the group defined by the emperor's prerogatives concerning the selection of a marriage partner. All *zongshi* descendants initially required the emperor's approval to marry, but in 1801 the Jiaqing emperor decreed

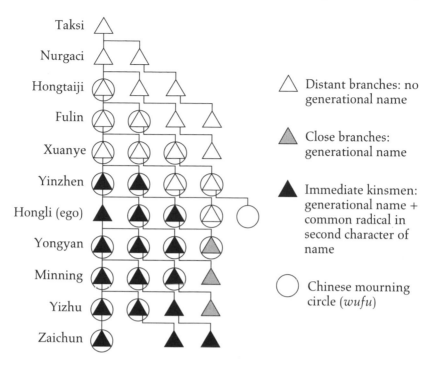

Taksi

Nurgaci

Hongtaiji

Fulin

Xuanye

Yinzhen

Hongli (ego)

Yongyan

Minning

Yizhu

Zaichun

△ Distant branches: no generational name

▲ Close branches: generational name

▲ Immediate kinsmen: generational name + common radical in second character of name

◯ Chinese mourning circle (*wufu*)

CHART 2.   Immediate kinsmen of the Aisin Gioro lineage and the Chinese mourning group. The relations within the mourning circle are diagrammed for Hongli, the Qianlong emperor. Source: The mourning circle information comes from Han-yi Feng, *The Chinese Kinship System* (Cambridge, 1967), diagram 4 on 42.

that he would follow the precedent of his father in only selecting brides for the descendants of the Yongzheng emperor, that is, for the descendants of his father's half brothers. Later he decided to limit this privilege to descendants in his sons' generation; only the descendants of the Qianlong emperor himself would continue to petition the emperor for wives into the third generation.[66] The circle of kinsmen for whom the emperor personally selected a bride was at that point still larger than the group identified as immediate kinsmen (chart 3).

The patterns in charts 1 through 3 further underline the non-Han nature of Qing imperial kinship. In the Ming dynasty, the line connecting one emperor to the next would have approximated the *zong* or eldest-son descent line. The Qing line of emperors not only moved significantly away from that pattern but also deviated from the Han Chinese generational sequence in the selection of Zaitian as emperor (see above). Neither of the

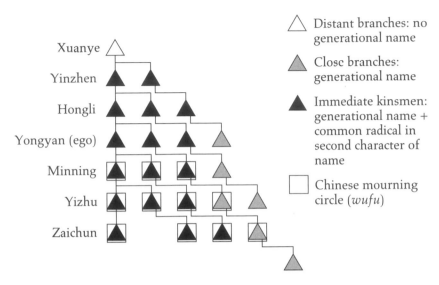

CHART 3. Immediate kinsmen of the Aisin Gioro lineage and the inner marriage circle for Yongyan. Source: *(Qinding) Da Qing huidian shilu* (Guangshu ed., 1976), j. 1.

lineage segments identified as the close branches or the immediate kinsmen corresponded to patterns of segmentation found in Han Chinese lineages. And they were completely different from the group for whom the Jiaqing emperor chose brides.

The historical shift from close branches to immediate kinsmen during the eighteenth and early nineteenth centuries, like the attempts to reduce the size of princely stipends (see chapter 2), was driven by the need to reduce the cost of supporting the Aisin Gioro. Many jobs were created for the *zongshi*. They could be appointed to the clansmen's corps of the imperial guards; they became clerks in the Imperial Clan Court. There were posts for them in the Six Boards and the Lifanyuan (court of colonial affairs). Hongli added new posts in the Censorate that were reserved for *zongshi*; Yongyan established a special examination for *zongshi* interpreters.[67] But there were limits to what could be done. As the Jiaqing emperor noted in 1813: "Shizu [the Shunzhi emperor] entered the passes to quell disorder and to settle the capital. The princes, dukes, and *zongshi* followed to assist government in Peking. Over 170 years have since passed. The eight banners grow more and more profuse, clustering around the capital district; the price of goods and land rises, this is a natural phenomenon. . . . How can we annually raise stipends? Nor can we employ the *zongshi* entirely, we must appoint Manchu, Mongol, and Han officials."[68]

There were simply too many kinsmen at court, and their numbers had to be reduced. This conclusion was very clearly expressed in an edict issued in 1802:

> Recently there are too many persons proffering their congratulations. We have to set some limits. From this year's imperial birthday and next year's New Year celebrations, *qinwang, junwang,* and *beile* [princes of ranks one through three] will be permitted to come forward to extend their greetings regardless of whether or not they are inner- or outer-court persons. But only inner-court *beizi* [princes of the fourth rank] and *gong* [dukes] will be allowed to come forward.[69]

The primary motivation behind these actions was to cut down the size of the kinship group whom the ruler would cultivate while heightening the attentions this group received. During the Kangxi reign, the major banquet hosted by the emperor on New Year's Day feted the banner nobility, Mongol princes, foreign ambassadors, and high officials; there was no separate banquet for the emperor's close kinsmen. The custom of hosting a separate banquet for his direct descendants and the first-rank princes began with the Qianlong emperor. Hongli also determined that the sacrifices in the Temple of the Ancestors should be made only by descendants belonging to this group. The Jiaqing and Daoguang emperors invited the imperial sons and close relatives (*qinfan*) to the banquet; these descendants became the "close branches and relatives" (*jinzhi qinfan*) from the Xianfeng reign onward.[70]

EMPERORS' SONS

We can examine what it meant to be a prince during the Qing dynasty by following the life course of an *age* or emperor's son. Even though a prince usually lived with his birth mother until the age of six *sui*, he acquired his own personal servants at birth.[71] The young prince had at least one wet nurse (*momo* in Manchu) and additional nurses (*mamari* in Manchu), responsible for his care.[72] As with commoners, however, his social existence began with the completion of the first month of life, when the "full month" (*manyue*) rituals were celebrated, and the princeling was put on the rolls of the Department of the Privy Purse (*guangchusi*). The Imperial Household Department would provide each prince with a daily ration of meat, vegetables, and grains; coal for heating and cooking; and candles. Each month he would receive ten taels of silver, an allocation of tea, and an annual allowance of gold, silver, textiles, and furs.[73]

Many Manchus and Mongols had no immunity to smallpox and realized that living in a Chinese city increased the likelihood that they would contract this dreaded disease. Smallpox was a major killer of infants. This fear was ameliorated after the Kangxi emperor, whose father died of smallpox, adopted the Chinese medical practice of variolation for his children and grandchildren in 1681. Variolation seems to have become standard practice in the palace, and a smallpox specialist was appointed to the Imperial Medical Department (*taiyiyuan*) in 1747. We know that the successful physician was rewarded with money, red satin, and a set of gold flowers (the Chinese term for variolation means "planting flowers").[74]

The first big change in a prince's life came when he entered school. The Manchus were slow to adopt the Han Chinese custom that sons should be formally schooled from the age of six. The Kangxi emperor did not begin formal lessons with Confucian lecturers until 1670, when he was already sixteen, but he was schooled from a much earlier age. His first Manchu-language lessons, for example, were from Sumalagu, a female servant of his grandmother, Empress Dowager Xiaozhuang (see chapter 5). Xuanye's crown prince began to read and write under his father's tutelage and did not study with official tutors until he was twelve.[75] The creation of a school where the emperor's sons, grandsons, and nephews might study together was only accomplished in the Yongzheng reign.[76]

Classes were held in the Shangshufang for princes (palace school; see map 3), which occupied the eastern wing of the Qianqing palace, where the emperor conducted the daily affairs of state. There were classrooms as well at the Xiyuan and Yuanmingyuan, so that instruction would not be interrupted when the emperor and his family moved to their villas. The princes were taught by Hanlin scholars from 5 A.M. to 4 P.M. throughout the year; the curriculum included lessons in Manchu, Mongolian, and Chinese as well as riding, archery, and other military subjects.[77]

Within the Palace School, the emperor's sons mingled with their paternal cousins and with selected sons of high banner officials (in Manchu, *haha juse*). With the emperor's permission, sons of princes who had already moved out of the Forbidden City could attend classes.[78] Court etiquette was relaxed within the classroom but dress and attendance were strictly regulated. There was no fixed term, and many princes seem to have been compelled to continue their studies into adulthood. The Jiaqing emperor reminisced about the "over twenty years" that he and his brother Yonglin studied together in the Palace School; the Daoguang emperor wrote about the "over thirty years" he spent in its classrooms. Yizhu, the

Xianfeng emperor, studied until he ascended the throne. His brother Yi-zong had been adopted out as heir to Miankai, Prince Dun, but still attended the palace school.[79]

Princes who were assigned ritual duties were expected to come to school after finishing their task; unexcused absences or early departures were to be reported to the emperor. The school could be used as a form of punishment: in 1855, after burying his mother, Yixin, Prince Gong, was ordered to give up all his posts and return to the Palace School to study.[80] Small wonder that there were delinquents: in 1770 the Qianlong emperor sent to the Palace School for his fourth son (Yongcheng) and was informed that he was absent because he was performing a sacrifice. But, the emperor observed, the sacrifice was scheduled for dawn and Yongcheng should have come to school instead of using his ritual duty as a pretext for absenting himself.[81] Yongcheng was thirty-one at the time.

When they entered school, the emperor's sons and grandsons left the female quarters and moved into "boys' houses." Sometimes they roomed together, at other times they were separately housed with their personal staff. A number of different compounds within the inner court served as residences for these young princelings during the early Qing (see chapter 1). Those that were first used, the Qiandongwusuo and the Qianxiwusuo, had the advantage (from the paternal perspective) of affording excellent control over the boys' movements, since these residences were located with their backs to the northern boundary of the wall that surrounded the entire palace and could be entered only through the east and west gates at the end of a long alleyway.[82]

The next phase of life for the emperor's sons or grandsons began when they were fourteen or fifteen, when the emperor was requested to select their brides from the draft of eligible maidens (see chapter 4).[83] Marriage signaled an increase in the allowances that princes received. Their monthly allowances, raised from 10 to 50 taels when they entered school, were raised again; their wives were given maidservants, daily food rations, and separate allowances as well. In 1826, the regulations stipulated that the emperor's sons would receive 500 taels of silver a month after their marriage; grandsons would receive 200, and great-grandsons 100 taels a month. The archival records, however, suggest that only a fraction of the stipulated allowance was actually paid by the early nineteenth century: married sons seem to have received only 100 taels a month in the 1850s and 1860s. Minning reminisced, "When I lived in the princes' hall [Agesuo], the stipend was very strained. Every evening we could only buy five griddle cakes (*shaobing*). The empress and I would each eat two, the last we would give to our eldest son; our servings of rice were only three bowls; how can this be called 'full'!"[84]

Princes continued to live in the Forbidden City or in the imperial villas until the emperor bestowed mansions on them. A separate establishment was a very expensive proposition and frequently delayed. Especially during the eighteenth century, married sons with titles still lived for years with their wives and children in the palace. Four emperors, Hongli, Yongyan, Minning, and Yizhu, never moved out of the palace before ascending the throne. Yongxuan was married for eighteen years and Yonglin for fourteen before they moved into their own private residences. Hongli's eleventh son, Yongxing, was forty-three before he received his own house.[85] Still others, like Yonghuang and Yongzhang, married but died before *fenfu*. Yonghuang's sons Miande and Mian'en were thus raised inside the palace. Miande married in 1765 but lived in the palace until 1779. Even after he received a mansion, Miande's son Yichun continued to live in the Shoukang palace. Mian'en also lived in the palace until 1779.[86]

There could be only one head of the imperial family residing within the Forbidden City, and that was the emperor. The emperor was the sole male of his generation who lived there. When a new emperor ascended the throne, his married brothers moved out (unmarried brothers were not regarded as adults). We have such an example in a memorial addressed to the new Daoguang emperor in 1821. In this document, the ministers of the Neiwufu proposed that Minning's brothers Miankai (Prince Dun, 1795–1839) and Mianxin (Prince Rui, 1805–28) be given princely mansions and moved out of the Agesuo, where they were residing with their families. According to the ministers, "to have two princes living for so long in close proximity to the imperial residence is not compatible with the state system (*guojia tizhi*)."[87]

Qing emperors also provided housing for their sons in Rehe and in the imperial villas northwest of Peking. The Kangxi emperor and his successors granted married sons parcels within the Changchunyuan, Yuanmingyuan, and Bishu shanzhuang so that they could move with him. Archival and historical records reveal that grandsons with their wives, adopted-in daughters of particularly favored brothers, and a number of more distantly related cousins lived in the palace.[88] Princes were therefore in close touch with one another and with their father. Co-residence fostered familial sentiments but also allowed the emperor to keep track of his sons' activities and to evaluate their personalities, talent, and moral development.

Ritual Attendants

Imperial princes were appointed for palace duty and assigned to one of six shifts, just like high officials. They attended the emperor on a daily basis while he was in residence and accompanied him when he traveled or when he sacrificed at the state altars. These assignments were taken seriously and exemptions were unusual: one such exemption in September 9, 1801, excused the emperor's brothers Yongxuan and Yongxing and his nephew Mian'en from the rota to perform the monthly sacrifice at the ancestral hall within the palace (Fengxiandian) because they were "too busy"—with the purge of Heshen.[89]

Princes were appointed as inspectors of state altars. An imperial prince supervised each of the two imperial cemeteries, living at the site during his three-year tour of duty; six princes were assigned to reside in Shengjing and sacrifice at the three ancestral tombs located there.[90] On imperial deathdays and at four other points during the year, the emperor would send other princes to sacrifice at the tombs; princes were also assigned to sacrifice at the Temple of the Ancestors on the first and fifteenth of each lunar month.[91] In fact, princes were assigned to perform a great variety of ritual duties. They coordinated the wedding arrangements for an emperor, planned imperial funerals, and escorted coffins to the imperial mausolea. They took part in shamanic rituals in the *tangzi* along with the shamans. They substituted for the emperor at all levels of state sacrifices, up to and including the most important sacrifice to Heaven (see chapter 6).[92]

Guardians of the Throne

Emperor's sons and other imperial princes were active in military affairs throughout the dynasty. One example is Xibao, the eighth prince Shuncheng, who led the Qing armies against the Eleuths (1731) and "distinguished himself" in these campaigns. He also served as lieutenant general of the Bordered Blue Manchu Banner and held posts in the Imperial Clan Court. Another *zongshi*, Fupeng, Prince Ping, was also for a time (1733) commander in chief of the Qing forces against the Eleuths. He too held a variety of posts in the Imperial Clan Court, banners, and sat on the Grand Council for a time.[93]

By the eighteenth century, the careers of the imperial clansmen were regularized. As young men, princes served in the clansmen's corps of the Imperial Guard (see chapter 2): ninety descendants of the main line were customarily appointed to this body.[94] During the nineteenth century several imperial clansmen, among them Lukang, Qiying, Yijing, and Zaiquan, the fifth prince Ding, held the strategic post of captain general of the Peking gendarmerie, the police forces of the capital.[95]

Aisin Gioro frequently filled the top banner posts of lieutenant general and deputy lieutenant general. Yinxi (1711–1758) and Yinbi (1716–1773), Kangxi's twenty-first and twenty-fourth sons, held various banner posts in the Yongzheng and Qianlong reigns. Yinxi was successively lieutenant general of the Manchu Bordered Red Banner (1733), Han Plain Yellow Banner (1735), and Manchu Plain White Banner (1740); Yinbi served as lieutenant general of the Mongol Bordered White Banner (1740) and of the Manchu Plain White Banner (1752). This tradition, recorded in the two editions of the *Baqi tongzhi* (General history of the eight banners), appears to have been continued in the 1860s and early 1870s, when Shiduo, Prince Li, served in a succession of banner posts. Princes Rui and Shuncheng as well as other imperial kinsmen occupied the lieutenant generalships of many different banners during the last fifty years of the dynasty.[96]

Princes appeared in leadership roles at times of military crises. The future Daoguang emperor, Minning, his brother, uncles, and cousins spontaneously defended the Forbidden City against attack by millenarian rebels in 1813. Imperial kinsmen were also prominent in the mid-nineteenth-century campaigns against the British, American, and other European powers. Yijing was the ill-fated choice to head the Manchu counteroffensive against the British invasion of the lower Yangzi delta in 1842; he had entered the bureaucracy through examination (see below) and held a variety of posts within the Imperial Household Department before being appointed to the military governorship of Mukden (1835) and the presidency of the Board of Personnel (1836). Yijing's disastrous Zhejiang campaign resulted in his imprisonment in the Imperial Clan Court (1842). Pardoned in 1843, he served on the empire's Inner Asian frontiers. Discharged as commandant of forces at Ili (1846) and exiled to Heilongjiang, he was recalled to service in 1852 and died in Xuzhou, where he was sent to defend the city against the Taiping rebels.[97] And in 1853 the fifth son of the Jiaqing emperor, Prince Hui, was commander in chief of the forces defending Tientsin and Peking from the Taiping rebels.[98]

High Officials

Throughout the dynasty, princes also participated in the highest councils of state. They sat on the Deliberative Council of princes and high officials

(*Yizheng wang dachen huiyi*), which functioned as the major decision-making body in the Manchu state from 1615 until at least 1673.[99] Although it was subsequently overtaken by the Grand Council (*junjichu*), so that it had only a nominal presence at the end of the eighteenth century, the process of consultation with princes continued. During the first three years of his reign the Yongzheng emperor had four "imperial assistants plenipotentiary" (*zongli shiwu wang dachen*), two of whom were his brothers Yinsi and Yinxiang. Appointed to oversee the Board of Revenue, Yinxiang discovered that nearly three million silver taels were missing from the treasury. Yinxiang also helped to map out the campaign against the Eleuths (1726) and was almost continually consulted on important government matters until his death in 1730.[100]

Yinxiang's prominent official career was directly linked to his close and cordial relations with Yinzhen. Yintao, who had been appointed to banner offices, also held numerous civilian posts during his long life. He served at various times in the administration of the Imperial Household, Imperial Clan Court, Board of Rites, and Board of Public Works. This kind of fraternal support had particular significance during political crises. When the Jiaqing emperor purged Heshen, he did so with the help of two brothers: Yongxuan, Prince Yi (1746–1832), supervised the Board of Personnel while Yongxing, Prince Cheng (1752–1823), supervised the Board of Revenue and served for a short time on the Grand Council. Replacing Heshen in these central posts, the two princes were charged with reorganizing the administration to obliterate Heshen's faction. At one point Yongxuan also concurrently held the posts of presiding controller of the Imperial Clan Court, chamberlain of the Imperial Guard, and lieutenant general of the Manchu Plain Red Banner.[101]

These two brothers set illustrious precedents for the career of Yixin, Prince Gong (1833–98), during the second half of the nineteenth century. Prince Gong, who "provided the channel through which the ideas of Restoration statesmen could be sanctioned and implemented" during the Tongzhi reign (1862–74), actually began to serve on the Grand Council, the major decision-making body, from 1853, when his brother, the Xianfeng emperor, was on the throne.[102]

Emperors' sons did not monopolize bureaucratic careers. In 1724 special schools were opened for imperial clansmen, and from 1744–52 imperial clansmen were permitted to sit for the metropolitan examination without qualifying in the lower exams. After 1799 imperial clansmen could compete at favorable quotas for the *juren* degree; those who succeeded then sat for the metropolitan or *jinshi* degree. In addition to this "orthodox" route to office, a certain number of secretarial posts in the Six Boards were earmarked for Aisin Gioro.[103]

An "unorthodox" route seems to have been the way in which *zongshi* Qiying began his long career in office. A member of the Plain Blue Banner, Qiying belonged to a distant branch of the imperial main line. Serving in a succession of secretarial posts in the Lifanyuan as well as the Six Boards, with many concurrent posts in the Peking gendarmerie and the Neiwufu, Qiying became military governor of Mukden before being appointed imperial commissioner to negotiate treaties with the British, and later with the Americans, French, Swedes, and Norwegians to conclude the Opium War. A favorite of the Daoguang emperor, he fell from power under Yizhu and was eventually ordered to commit suicide in 1858.[104]

Many Aisin Gioro qualified for official careers by passing special examinations (*kaofeng*; see chapter 2). Not all princes who placed in this examination were ambitious: Yongzhong (1735–93), a great-grandson of the Kangxi emperor, passed the examination in 1756, was awarded a tenth-rank noble title, and lived a leisured (and cultured) life with only nominal duties.[105] *Zongshi* Yilibu, a member of the Yellow Bordered Manchu Banner, won a *jinshi* degree in 1801 and served in a number of provincial posts before being appointed governor-general of Liangjiang (1840). Yilibu was appointed to negotiate with the British, who had occupied Dinghai. He was then ordered to attack the British position and stripped of his rank for failing to do so; his fortunes fluctuated as the court used him as a scapegoat for its anger over British recalcitrance. It was Yilibu's fate to sign the Treaty of Nanking (1842) and be posthumously condemned as a traitor.[106]

Sushun (1815–61), a descendant of Jirgalang, Prince Zheng, also had a very remarkable official career. He passed the examination in 1836 and was invested with a tenth-rank noble title: his bureaucratic career included service in banner posts, the Imperial Household Department, Censorate, Board of Works, Board of Rites, and Board of Revenue, in several of which he achieved the highest rank, while serving concurrently in the Grand Secretariat (1860–61). An active official who participated in treaty negotiations with the Russians (1859–60), Sushun was with the Xianfeng emperor when he died in Chengde and formed part of the regency that was overthrown by Empress Dowager Cixi and Prince Gong. He was arrested and executed by the victors.[107]

The nineteenth century in particular found many imperial kinsmen serving in a variety of offices. Aisin Gioro were occasionally appointed to posts in the provincial administration. Depei, a descendant of Jirgalang's younger brother, served in both central and provincial government posts under the Yongzheng and Qianlong emperors, achieving the governor-generalship of Huguang, Minzhe, and Liangjiang during his long career.[108] Sung Fu, another imperial clansman, served as governor-general of Huguang (1826–30). Aisin Gioro more commonly occupied central government offices. They were among the non-Han grand secretaries serving in the seventeenth and nineteenth centuries, a group that included *juelo* Baoxing, governor-general of Sichuan; *zongshi* Jingzheng, president of the Board of Revenue (1842–45); Xi'en, a *zongshi* who was president of the Board of Revenue (1852) and sent on a variety of investigatory missions by the Daoguang emperor; Zailing, a *zongshi* who served concurrently as a grand secretary while heading the Board of Personnel (1877–78); Linggui, who served in various posts within the Grand Secretariat during 1880–85; Fukun, president of the Board of Revenue and concurrently grand secretary (1885–92); and Linshu, president of the Board of Personnel and concurrently grand secretary (1892–95).[109]

Princes appointed to the Grand Council included Yinlu and Yinli (1735–36), Yaerheshan (1754–56), Yongxing (1799), and Guifang (1813–14). During the late nineteenth century at least one and on occasion several princes sat on the Grand Council at one time: Prince Gong served 1853–55, 1861–84, 1894–98; Shiduo, Prince Li, 1884–1901; Yikuang, Prince Qing, from 1903 until the 1911 Revolution.[110]

Princes also filled many of the non-Han presidencies of the Six Boards, the presidency of the Lifanyuan (which was reserved for a Manchu or Mongol), and the non-Han presidency of the Censorate. Year after year imperial clansmen occupied anywhere from one to five of the top eight posts for which they were eligible in the period before 1669 and after 1800. Imperial clansmen were not appointed to these posts (with rare exceptions) after 1669 when the Kangxi emperor took personal control of the government; with the exception of the first years of his reign (1722–25), the Yongzheng emperor also adopted the same policy and so too did the Qianlong emperor.[111]

Imperial princes also played significant roles in foreign affairs, particularly with the non-Han regions. Seven of the 120 persons who served as *amban* or imperial envoys in Lhasa from 1727 to 1910 were Aisin Gioro. An imperial prince, Šose, escorted the Dalai lama to Peking in 1653 and along part of his journey home, while another prince, Jirgalang, met and entertained the prelate at Qinghe.[112] The tenth son of the Kangxi emperor, Yin'e, was assigned to take the remains of the Jebtsundamba khutukhtu back to Tibet after he died in Peking in 1723. When the Panchen lama journeyed to Rehe in 1780, he was also met and escorted by an imperial prince.[113]

We began this chapter by contrasting the Han Chinese dynasties, which prevented imperial kinsmen from participating in government, with the conquest regimes, which followed a diametrically opposed strategy. Many Chinese historians argue that the cost of employing imperial princes in office was political instability, and fraternal competition was certainly a major element in court politics during the seventeenth century. At the same time, the Qing never experienced a usurpation of the throne or princes' revolts, as did the Ming.[114] More than any preceding dynasty, the Qing successfully synthesized Han Chinese bureaucratic techniques and non-Han fraternal alliances to resolve the perennial challenges of imperial kinsmen to the authority of the ruler, diminishing their autonomy while eliciting their military, political, and ritual support. Qing princes were transformed into pillars of the imperium, not its inevitable rivals.

Chapter 4   Imperial Women

Empress Dowager Cixi (1835–1908) is unquestionably the best known of the two dozen women who attained this preeminent rank at the Qing court. Thanks to the photographs and the many historical records that survived, we know a great deal about her. While her life was hardly typical, her career epitomizes what a daughter of the conquest elite could strive for.[1] Born in 1835 into the Yehe clan, she entered the palace on June 26, 1852, as a lowly consort of the sixth rank. Two years later she was promoted to the fifth rank; the following year, on April 27, 1856, she gave birth to the future Tongzhi emperor. The presentation of an anxiously desired son won her promotion to the fourth rank. Yet when the Xianfeng emperor died in 1861, she was only a third-rank consort.[2]

It was motherhood, and the alliance with Empress Ci'an and the deceased emperor's brother Yixin, Prince Gong, that first brought Cixi into a regency and subsequently enabled her to become dominant at court. As the birth mother of Zaichun, the child who succeeded to the throne, she was made empress dowager. Junior to Ci'an, she dominated the senior empress dowager by virtue of her personality. After serving an apprenticeship in affairs of state under Prince Gong, she publicly checked his authority in 1865 and showed that he served at her pleasure. By all accounts, her decision in 1875 to abrogate the customary rules of succession by selecting someone in her son's own generation to succeed him was uncontested by Yixin and the others present at the council of state. Luke Kwong's study of the Guangxu reforms portrays her as an intimidating personality who frightened the young Guangxu emperor. She had a part in the most significant decisions at court from the 1860s until her death in 1908.[3]

Cixi is the most famous but not the only Qing imperial matriarch who wielded power extending beyond domestic affairs. Although many historians view her as an exemplar of the "Wu Zitian" or usurping empress tradition, she fits more naturally into the context of non-Han rulership. According to Jennifer Holmgren's comparison, Han Chinese emperors banned imperial agnates from participation in government, turning instead to the male relatives of the empress for support against the bureaucratic elite. But, since maternal affines could threaten the throne's autonomy during regencies, the consort families had to be held in check. Power at the Han Chinese court "oscillated between . . . the emperor, the senior widow, and members of the bureaucracy."[4] Many Han rulers also tried to use their brothers-in-law to counter the power of maternal affines. Unlike any brother, a sister could not occupy the throne, so she was not a potential rival. Her husband and his kinsmen could serve as important allies for the ruler.

The non-Han state's court politics was very different. Because steppe states required adult rulers, regencies were uncommon, and marriage was no longer a key to control during regencies. Instead, non-Han rulers tended to use marriage as a device to cement alliances within their own conquest circle or with foreign rulers. Marriage with the conquered Chinese population was usually discouraged if not prohibited. The khan's wives became permanent members of the ruling house, along with his sisters and brothers. When there were regencies, "the empress in the Mongol-Yuan dynasty was seen as an individual to be entrusted with power and authority in the same manner as an imperial sister or brother."[5]

The Qing power structure resembled but did not mirror the structures of previous conquest regimes. As they did, Qing marriage policies prohibited intermarriage with the conquered Ming population (see below) and encouraged marriage with elites residing in the Inner Asian peripheries. Even though the Qing dynasty was not, strictly speaking, polygynous (the imperial consorts occupied distinctly unequal status, and there was only one empress at a time), its insistence that all sons were eligible to become emperor had the same effect as polygyny in deemphasizing the family of the empress. With the adoption of the father-son succession rule after 1643, the Qing had infants ascend the throne under regencies, as native Chinese regimes had. Regencies existed in the 1640s, the 1660s, the 1860s, from 1875 to 1889, and again from 1908 to 1912. Senior widows took political roles in each of these regencies, but, rather than rely on their own kinsmen as the native Chinese regimes did, the dowager empresses allied with their husbands' brothers. And as the Yuan did, the Qing broke the political threat posed by matrilateral kinsmen, but it accomplished this through a somewhat different series of marriage policies.[6]

Like the Chinese, Manchu society was patrilineal (descent groups were organized in terms of the male line), patrilocal (married couples resided with the groom's parents), and patriarchal (the senior male was head of household). Yet Manchu traditions gave women significantly greater freedom and authority. Manchu women were forbidden to bind their feet, so they were not crippled. Instead of being confined to the inner quarters, women walked in public places, rode horses, practiced archery, and participated in hunts. According to one pre-1644 source, "Women hold the reins, spur on horses, and are no different from men . . . if there is leisure, the wives and concubines are led into the hunt."[7] Women were occasionally active on the battlefield: a few even attained the title of banner lieutenant during the conquest. Women also held key roles in shamanic performances at court: like Korean women, they thus wielded "positive powers" in the ritual sphere. The shamans performing rituals in the Kunning palace (see chapter 7) were women.[8]

The example of Princess Hexiao is a case in point. She was the youngest (some sources say favorite) daughter of the Qianlong emperor. The princess dressed in man's clothing, practiced archery, and accompanied her father on the hunt, killing a deer on at least one occasion. One (perhaps apocryphal) account reports the proud emperor saying, "If you had been a boy, I would definitely have made you Heir."[9]

Manchu women initially had personal names. History records the names of Nurgaci's first and second wives, and at least one of his daughters. The Shunzhi emperor's sisters were named Yatu (1629–78) and Atu (1632–1700); one of his half sisters was Maketa (1625–63).[10] After the court moved to Peking, women's personal names disappear from the genealogical and archival records. Consorts were known by the title and rank they received. Consorts of high rank or those who became mothers received posthumous death names; lower-ranking childless consorts sometimes disappeared from the record books (see below). Daughters, even those who died in infancy, appeared in the Aisin Gioro genealogy (but not in Chinese genealogies). Daughters were called first princess, second princess, and so on, by their birth order. After their betrothal they were invested with the formal titles and rank by which they became known.

Manchu and Mongol nobles of both sexes had the right to divorce. Widows often married their husband's younger brother. The Jurchen practiced this form of marriage, the levirate, in order to keep the property a woman brought into the descent group from dispersal in the widow's remarriage.[11] Legally prohibited from at least Tang times, the levirate was regarded as a hallmark of barbarity by Chinese. The Ming dynasty founder had this to say about it:[12]

> the . . . *Ti* [that is, Mongols] entered China . . . and both within and without the Four Seas there was none who did not submit to them. Could this have been achieved by human power [alone]? Indeed when Heaven transferred [its mandate] to them, the rulers were intelligent and the subjects were sincere . . . . But . . . the rulers of the Yuan no longer observed the instructions of their ancestors . . . . Things went so far that a younger brother [could] marry . . . his [deceased] elder brother's wife, and a son [could] have relations with his [deceased] father's concubine. Those above became familiar with those below . . . . The result was that the rules of conduct between ruler and subject, husband and wife, elder and younger brothers broke down completely.

The levirate was forbidden in 1631 and 1636 by Hongtaiji. Although the ban was ignored in the marriages of Hongtaiji's half sister Mukushi to Eidu and then to his son, Turgei, and the sequential marriages of Hongtaiji's daughter Maketa to two sons of Ligdan Khan (1636, 1648), it held for the rest of the dynasty. The Manchus tolerated cross-generational marriages, which Chinese avoided, and like the Mongols they favored matrilateral cross-cousin marriages (marrying mother's brother's daughter), and the sororate (marriage to sisters). The result was a very dense kinship network within the women's chambers in the palace. Isaac Headland, describing the court of Empress Dowager Cixi, notes that among her ladies in waiting were an adopted daughter, born to her brother-in-law Yixin (Prince Gong); a niece; and another niece by marriage. The density of these interlocking relationships would not have been untoward two centuries earlier, in the Shunzhi reign, when Fulin's first empress was the niece and his second empress the grandniece of one of his father's empresses.[13]

MARRIAGE POLICY

After permitting intermarriage between bannermen and Han Chinese for more than a decade after their conquest, the Manchu rulers reversed themselves. In 1655 the Shunzhi emperor responded indignantly to a memorial from a Han Chinese official, who accused the emperor's servants of arousing anti-Manchu sentiments by purchasing girls in Yangzhou for the imperial harem. In his response, the emperor stated that "there have never been Han females in the palace under the house rules of Nurgaci and Hongtaiji."[14] As Ding Yizhuang notes, no one has yet discovered the actual regulation prohibiting intermarriage among the official records, although an edict issued toward the end of the dynasty in the Guangxu reign cites this dynastic rule. That such a rule did exist is confirmed by imperial edicts from the Kangxi reign onward, which reiterate the prohibition or permit exceptions. Ding's search of the archives has uncovered fifty-seven cases, running throughout the dynasty, of marriages between bannermen and commoners (i.e., Han Chinese). Most (forty-five of fifty-seven) involved bannermen marrying Han Chinese women. Of these, 74 percent were registered in the Imperial Household Department's bondservant companies. Twelve involved Hanjun banner daughters marrying Han Chinese. In one of these cases, the Qianlong emperor observed that the practice of Hanjun marrying commoners was of such long standing that it should be tolerated. He added, however, that the other banner groups must adhere to the Manchu regulations.[15] Manchu banner daughters were not given in marriage to Han Chinese husbands. Ding concludes that the Qing prohibition on intermarriage focused on wives: she argues that Manchu bannermen could buy Han Chinese concubines.

Like many other non-Han dynasties the Manchus practiced a form of political endogamy. Noting the oft-repeated claim that the Qianlong emperor married his favorite daughter to the head of the Confucius family, Du Jiaji uses Kong archival materials to prove that the real wife was the daughter of Grand Secretary Yu Minzhong.[16] The wives of emperors and princes came predominantly from a relatively small number of families belonging to the Mongol nobility and distinguished banner families. After 1653 brides for the Aisin Gioro were selected from banner officials' daughters aged thirteen to fourteen *sui,* who were required to present themselves at the palace in Peking before they could be betrothed to others. In this triennial draft of *xiunü* (beautiful women) some girls were immediately chosen to be wives or consorts for the princes or for the emperor himself. Others were appointed as ladies-in-waiting, serving for a five-year term: those who caught the emperor's eye during their service might be promoted into the harem. In contrast to the high social status of the *xiunü,* women selected through a separate annual draft for palace maids (*gongnü*) were daughters of bondservant officials in the upper three banners who served in the Neiwufu. They too might be promoted into the harem. Sixteen percent of the imperial consorts were originally palace maids.[17]

IMPERIAL CONSORTS

The highly stratified imperial harem seems to have been a Han Chinese structure that Manchu rulers adopted in the course of the seventeenth century. Preconquest marriages among the elite may have approximated a truly polgynous system. Before 1636 all of Hongtaiji's consorts were called *fujin*, the Manchu designation for the wife of a prince (*beile*).[18] Although Hongtaiji "rewrote" the historical record by posthumously promoting his birth mother to "empress" (*huanghou*), most of the women in his own as well as his father's harem were not retroactively fitted into the seven-rank system. Hahanajacing, who bore Nurgaci's first son, Cuyeng, was simply "first consort" (*yuanfei*); another, the mother of Manggultai and Degelei, was "successor consort" (*jifei*). Of Nurgaci's sixteen consorts, four were "side-chamber consorts" (*zefei*) and six, "ordinary consorts" (*shufei*).[19]

The same simple hierarchy continued in Hongtaiji's time. The majority (ten of fifteen) of his consorts were identified by the older terms of his father's generation. Over half of the consorts buried in the Shunzhi emperor's consort tomb were identified simply as *gege*, a Manchu term meaning "lady" that was later specific to princesses. Even in the late seventeenth century there were ordinary consorts among the consorts of the Kangxi emperor.[20]

After 1636 the emperor's consorts (throughout this chapter the term refers to the empress or to concubines) became differentiated into eight ranks, headed by the empress. As the emperor's wife, she occupied a position above the other seven status groups, the highest being *huangguifei*, then in descending order *guifei, fei, pin, guiren, changzai,* and *daying*. Food, clothing, jewelry, stipends, and maids were allocated to the consorts by rank, with minute gradations exemplifying a ranked hierarchy.[21]

Although the post-1636 consort ranks resemble the Ming system, the way in which the Qing system worked was very different and much more fluid. Unlike the Ming, which adhered to what might be called serial monogamy, the Qing did not limit the succession to sons of the empress.[22] Adding to the open-ended succession were practices that blurred the social distinctions among consorts. Imperial consorts of the first four ranks recruited through the *xiunü* draft came from the same social strata as empresses. Like empresses, they were invested with titles and performed domestic rituals signifying their incorporation into the harem. Consorts in ranks five through seven received no patents; they were frequently recruited through the maidservant (*gongnü*) rather than the *xiunü* draft and thus entered the palace without prior sacrifice at the ancestral altars. Even low-ranking consorts could be promoted to empress. Once promoted, these women received the same privileges accorded to those who had been invested with the title at marriage. Cixi offers an outstanding example of what was possible.[23]

The Qing strategy of integrating brides into the imperial descent group "involved denying, or at least underplaying, a consort's ability to claim rank and status in her own right . . . . The power of Ch'ing consorts and their families was greatly decreased by treating the emperors' sexual partners primarily as women and only secondarily as members of classes, ranked hierarchies, and families."[24] The process began with elimination of the dowry (the imperial household itself supplied the dowry), thus erasing any possibility that the emperor's in-laws could affect what happened to their daughter once she entered the inner court.

New consorts' identities were "written over," often many times, in the course of their lives in the palace. The father's clan and personal name and his official title were often omitted for low-ranking consorts. Bondservants' daughters who entered the harem with the fifth, sixth, or seventh rank were often referred to by only their clan name and rank. Higher-ranking consorts were given names, but these were not always unique: a 1734 list of palace inhabitants, for example, lists two consorts with the name Xiu, one holding the fifth and the other the seventh rank.[25] Furthermore, these names sometimes changed. One study of ten lower-ranking consorts of the Daoguang emperor shows that half had their names altered during their time at court.[26]

The example of Empress Dowager Cixi illustrates this point. When she entered the palace in 1853, she was called Lan (orchid), a name she shared with a consort of the Kangxi emperor and a consort of the Qianlong emperor.[27] Only after her promotion to *pin* in 1854 was Cixi's name changed to Yi (virtuous). After the birth of her son (1856), she was again promoted and became first Yi *fei*, then Yi *guifei*. Cixi, the name by which she is known, was the title conferred on her when she finally became empress dowager.[28]

Palace regulations made it virtually impossible for a consort to remain close to her natal kin. Visits home were rare and hedged with protocol, which demanded that a consort's parents and grandparents prostrate themselves before her instead of the reverse. Parental meetings, which were permitted when a consort was pregnant or when her parents were elderly, required imperial permission.[29] Court regulations aimed at limiting affinal interference in palace affairs prohibited casual social contacts between the inner quarters and the world outside. Consorts could not send servants to their family homes without special permission (see chapter 5) and were forbidden to give or receive anything from family members. The regulations were made clear in an edict issued in 1742 by the Qianlong emperor:

> With respect to the *taifei* [senior widowed *fei*], what they possess was all bestowed on them by the Kangxi emperor. All that the *fei* of Mother's

generation possess was bestowed on them by Father; similarly I have bestowed all that the empress possesses. Everyone should use these things frugally. It is not permitted to take objects owned in the palace to bestow on one's family. It is also not permitted to bring objects possessed by one's family inside the palace.[30]

Nor could the natal families of consorts try to curry favor by presenting gifts to other palace women. In 1856, when the "full month" of his first son was celebrated, the Xianfeng emperor angrily ordered that presents sent by Shou *guiren*'s mother be returned, noting, "The families of palace ladies are not permitted to have social dealings with the palace."[31]

Motherhood

The palace career of consorts depended on whether they could produce children. In the final analysis, it was motherhood that brought consorts honor and, in some cases, political power. The ultimate prize in the "motherhood stakes" for consorts was bearing a son who became emperor. The inclusion of consorts from the whole spectrum of banner society helped Qing rulers neutralize the political power of matrilateral kinsmen. The actual record of succession demonstrates that heirs were selected without regard to the rank or family background of their mothers. Of the eleven emperors who ruled from 1644 to 1911, only one (the Daoguang emperor) was actually the son of an empress. The birth mothers of the Yongzheng, Qianlong, and Jiaqing emperors came from lowly bondservant backgrounds and must have entered the palace through the "back door," that is, through the draft for maids.[32]

As soon as a consort became pregnant, special precautions were taken to ensure the health of the future child and its mother. The expectant mother received extra food rations; imperial physicians and midwives visited her at least once a month during the course of the pregnancy and more frequently in its final phases; baby clothes were prepared, and wet nurses and staff for the newborn child were hired. Archival reports on the 1821 pregnancy of Quan *guifei*, who gave birth to the future Xianfeng emperor, suggest that the bulk of the medical attention was focused on the last five weeks, when a physician and midwife were in constant attendance to await the onset of labor. By far the most-studied pregnancy was that of the future empress dowager Cixi. According to the archival materials, when Yi *pin* (Cixi's title in 1856) became pregnant, an edict was issued authorizing her mother to reside with her in the Chuxiu palace until the birth. After the New Year, the Imperial Household Department began to recruit additional staff for

Cixi's establishment: two nurses (see chapter 5), and four additional staff for domestic chores were added on the third day of the second month. As Cixi's pregnancy entered the ninth month, two midwives were assigned to watch over her, with two imperial physicians on call. Later four other physicians were assigned and put on rotas to provide around-the-clock staffing.[33]

Motherhood usually brought promotion, though rarely to the preeminent rank of empress. That was more generally conferred on his birth mother by a new emperor. If his mother predeceased him, a new ruler might honor his foster mother in this way. Fewer than half (eleven) of the twenty-four empresses during the Qing dynasty entered the palace with that rank. Virtually all the others were mothers or foster mothers of emperors.[34]

Widowhood and Regency

Women played significant political roles during the conquest period, when the rulers did not name their successors. In the struggle for primacy after Nurgaci's death (see chapter 3), the senior *beile* may have forced Nurgaci's senior widow Abahai, née Ula Nara, to "accompany the lord into death" (*xun*) because they feared the influence she might have exerted in favor of her sons, Dorgon and Dodo, who were also candidates for the khanate.[35] The *xun* custom was abolished during the Shunzhi reign.

Hongtaiji's mother was dead by the time he became the leader of the Manchus, and there was no strong maternal influence during his rule. Information concerning the "advice" he received from his consorts is likely to have been retroactively inserted into the historical record. After Hongtaiji died (1643), the mother of the infant who was enthroned as the Shunzhi emperor became an influential figure. Bumbutai was the daughter of a Khorchin Mongol prince named Jaisang, who claimed descent from Chinggis Khan. She was presented to Hongtaiji in 1625, when she was about twelve years old.[36] Bumbutai gave Hongtaiji three daughters and his ninth son. She was never made empress by Hongtaiji: in 1636, when he created new titles, Bumbutai was made a consort (*fei*) while Jere, her aunt, became empress. Only after the succession struggle between Hooge and Dorgon (see chapter 3) had resulted in the selection of a compromise candidate, Bumbutai's son Fulin, was she made Empress Dowager Xiaozhuang. After Jere died (1649), Bumbutai became the central female in the palace. Her political role during Fulin's infancy and the regency of his successor bears comparison with that of Empress Dowager Cixi, who dominated the last fifty years of the dynasty.[37]

During the Shunzhi regency, which lasted until Dorgon's death (1651), Empress Dowager Xiaozhuang worked closely with the regent, who was her brother-in-law: whether or not she actually married him (which would have meant reviving the prohibited levirate) is not possible to determine on the basis of the current evidence.[38] Bumbutai's influence on her son after 1651 is problematic. Scholars cite Fulin's divorce of his first and estrangement from his second empress, both of whom were Khorchin Mongol relations of Bumbutai, as evidence of strained relations between mother and son. Matters took a turn for the worse when the emperor became infatuated with a consort from the Donggo clan, and the circumstances of the consort's death in 1660 continues to evoke scholarly speculation. The emperor's own death the following year brought Bumbutai back into prominence in another regency, this time for her grandson Xuanye. The regency of Dorgon, who had been one of the candidates for the rulership in 1643, underlined the dangers of permitting an imperial prince to become regent. In 1661 Bumbutai allied herself with prominent Manchu nobles, all of whom had been active in the conquest, and none of whom were imperial kinsmen. She took charge of Xuanye's upbringing after his mother died in 1663. Unlike the four regents, who were deposed in 1669, Bumbutai continued to influence the Kangxi emperor until her death in 1688.

By 1861, when the death of the Xianfeng emperor brought another infant to the throne, the political situation at court had changed. The triumph of the throne over banner lords in the early eighteenth century ushered in a new cooperative phase in the ruler's relations with his kinsmen (see chapter 3). The empresses dowager Ci'an and Cixi worked closely with their spouse's half brothers, Princes Gong and Chun, during the Tongzhi and Guangxu regencies. In 1908, when another infant, Puyi, was put on the throne, his father, the second Prince Chun, served as regent, sharing power with the senior widow, who became Empress Dowager Longyu after Cixi's death. Longyu forced Prince Chun to retire after the onset of the 1911 Revolution; it was she who authorized the imperial decree announcing the abdication of the last emperor of the dynasty.[39]

The senior widows and the birth mother of the infant emperor played a prominent role in each of the regencies during the Qing dynasty. Even when imperial agnates were specifically rejected as regents during the infancy of the Kangxi emperor, the power of the throne was exercised by banner officials and not the kinsmen of the empress. Cixi's case is again instructive. Cixi was born into the Manchu Bordered Blue Banner. Her ancestors held middle-level banner and governmental posts for at least several generations before her birth. The highest office that her father,

Huizheng, achieved was that of circuit intendant (*daoyuan*). He was cashiered in 1853 for leaving his post during a Taiping advance and seems to have died not too long thereafter. Thanks to Cixi's success in winning favor with the Xianfeng emperor, the family was given a house inside the Xizhi gate (1856–57) and their registration was transferred into the more prestigious Manchu Bordered Yellow Banner.[40] None of her natal kinsmen won elevation to high office even after she became empress dowager.

This is not to say that Qing emperors did not employ matrilateral and affinal kinsmen in important posts. Tong Guogang, the Kangxi emperor's mother's brother, was one of the officials who negotiated the Treaty of Nerchinsk (1689) with the Russians. He and his younger brother Guowei participated in the highest councils of state. The Kangxi emperor himself took two of Guowei's daughters into his harem; one was promoted to empress shortly before she died. Throughout their long careers, however, there is no evidence that the Tong brothers were not simply loyal imperial servants.[41]

Tong Guowei's third son, Longkodo, may have come closest to intruding on the imperial prerogative. With an aunt and two sisters having entered the imperial harem during the Shunzhi and Kangxi reigns, Longkodo was linked to the Kangxi emperor through multiple ties of marriage. He began his career in the imperial guards and served for many years as the commandant of the Peking gendarmerie (see chapter 2). Apparently Longkodo participated in the factional rivalry over the succession issue in the last years of the Kangxi reign. His control over the Peking garrison was critical when the Kangxi emperor died (1722). Scholars suspect that Longkodo engineered Yinzhen's accession. Whatever the truth of these accusations, Longkodo did not long survive into the Yongzheng reign. He was purged in 1725, stripped of his honors and titles, and died in 1728 while under house arrest.[42] The lesson to be learned from Longkodo's disgrace was clear: the emperor had no intention of sharing power.

In the palace as in commoner society, women reached the pinnacle of status only after their sons had become adults. The senior woman in the palace, who was responsible for supervising the administration of the women's quarters, was normally a widow of the previous ruler, who held the title empress dowager. An emperor's death signaled a change of residence for his surviving consorts. Traditionally the empress dowager moved into one of a number of palaces, along with the other widowed consorts. The Kangxi emperor's grandmother, Empress Dowager Xiaozhuang, lived initially in the Cining palace but moved into the Ningshou palace after its completion in 1689.[43] Later, in the nineteenth century, the Jiaqing emperor's widows moved to the Shoukang palace, which was renovated for this purpose.[44] The palace also housed the widows of princes who had died before they moved out of the Forbidden City. A 1774–75 palace account notes that the wife and consort of the emperor's eldest son, Yonghuang (d. 1750), and the wives of his third son, Yongzhang (d. 1760), and his fifth son, Yongqi (d. 1766), were continuing to receive monthly silver allowances from the palace coffers.[45]

Filiality

"We rule the empire with filial piety."[46] The Kangxi emperor's pronouncement stimulated what Harold Kahn calls "veritable orgies of filial solicitude" on the part of Qing emperors.[47] It was not only the grand southern tours and the birthday banquets that revealed Qing emperors as filial sons: presenting himself at his mother's chambers every morning to inquire about her well-being (*qing'an*), an emperor expressed filiality on a routine daily level.

Emperors honored not only their own birth mothers but also kind senior consorts who had befriended them in childhood. When Hongli left his father's house to move into the Kangxi emperor's palace, he was only ten and a half. In later life, he bestowed various expressions of his affection and gratitude on the two consorts who took care of him.[48] Empress Xiaoquan died when her son Yizhu was less than nine years old. He was handed over to Jing *guifei*. This woman, née Borjigit, the daughter of Hualangga, a Mongol bannerman whose highest post was that of a second-class secretary in the Board of Punishments, entered the palace as a fourth-rank consort (*guiren*). She was promoted after giving birth to a son (1826) and was eventually the mother of three sons and a daughter.

Yizhu amply repaid his foster mother after he ascended the throne as the Xianfeng emperor. He paid his respects to her every day, as he would have to his real mother. He visited her during her last illness and promoted her to the rank of empress dowager in August 1855, shortly before she died. After she died, Yizhu appointed two princes, one of them being her own son Yixin (Prince Gong), to manage the funeral arrangements and announced his intention to spend the mourning period living at the Yangxindian. His devotion to her memory extended beyond death; she received domestic ancestral rites within the palace for the rest of the century (see chapter 8).[49]

Even though only one consort in each generation had the good fortune to be the mother of the next emperor, there were usually several who were lucky enough to have sons who became imperial princes. A widowed consort could not easily leave the palace to reside with her son. Ding *fei*, the mother of Xuanye's twelfth son, was given permission to do so by the Yongzheng emperor, but she had to return every New Year's to the palace to pay her respects. On her ninetieth birthday, the Qianlong emperor went to her son's mansion to congratulate her; she lived to the age of 97 *sui*.[50] Hongli himself was reluctant to make this a precedent. In 1736 he responded to the requests of his uncles Yinlu, Prince Zhuang, and Yinli, Prince Guo, that their mothers be allowed to leave the Ningshou palace to move into their sons' mansions. The emperor commented:

> Having heard their requests, I felt very uneasy. So I consulted the empress dowager and she feels even more strongly that this cannot be permitted. I have been mulling over this matter . . . . If we turn down their requests, we don't allow the two princes to demonstrate their filiality. If we agree to their request to shelter the senior widowed consorts in their mansions, then I will be deficient in receiving their nurturance. I am truly dissatisfied. Henceforth during the summer and winter festivals and at birthdays the two princes and other princes may each welcome widowed consorts into their mansions. They can reside there for a total of several months a year; the rest of the time they will live in the palace.[51]

Filiality was also the reason cited for promoting all of a late emperor's consorts. This practice seems to have begun with the Kangxi emperor, who promoted five of his father's widows. At the onset of his reign, Yinzhen promoted twelve of the Kangxi emperor's consorts, all but two of whom had produced sons. Six of these same women received further promotions when Hongli ascended the throne thirteen years later. In addition, Hongli announced that, in obedience to his mother's wishes, he would promote Yu *fei* who "served the late emperor for many years and produced the fifth son, who has already been invested as a first-rank prince by imperial grace." Both Yu *fei* and Qian *pin*, mother of the sixth son, were promoted one rank.[52] The promotion of widowed consorts became a custom with no relation to motherhood. The onset of the Xianfeng, Tongzhi, and Guangxu reigns saw large-scale promotions of many infertile consorts, including those in the lowest ranks.[53]

The promotion of widowed consorts of the ruler's father and, on occasion, grandfather satisfied the claims of generational seniority and expressed the ruler's filiality—toward his father. It did not, however, mean that all consorts were commemorated. The archival and other evidence suggests rather the opposite: in the court, as in commoner society, low-ranking childless consorts tended to fade into social anonymity.

Infertility and Oblivion

Despite its high quality, the Qing imperial genealogy, the *Da Qing yudie*, suffers from the same defect as the genealogies of Chinese commoners: it underreports consorts who did not bear children.[54] Evidence for this conclusion comes from a comparison of the *Da Qing yudie* with the last published imperial genealogy, the *Aixin juelo zongpu*, and the reconstitution of the imperial descent group by Tang Bangzhi.[55] Archival records offer further evidence, especially the annual lists for distribution of imperial gifts (*gong fen*), which list each palace resident and his or her servants, and the recorded burials of consorts in each imperial grave.

Comparison of the number of imperial consorts of each ruler recorded in the imperial genealogy with data on the women buried in the consort tombs that were built next to the imperial tumulus (see chapter 8) shows that in many cases the actual number of consorts found in graves significantly exceeds the number recorded in the imperial genealogy (table 5). All the higher-ranking consorts buried in the tombs were also recorded in the genealogy, whether or not they produced children for the lineage. The women in the graves who are missing from the genealogy occupied the fifth, sixth, and seventh ranks. Since the imperial genealogies recorded children who died on the day of birth, and the name of each child's mother, the women missing from the record are most likely to have been infertile.[56]

To make matters more complex, not all imperial consorts listed in the genealogy can be found in the list of women buried in the consort tombs. For example, among the consorts of the Kangxi emperor the genealogy lists two consorts of the fourth rank, six of the fifth rank, and four of lower rank who are missing from the burial lists, so the actual number of Xuanye's consorts probably exceeded the fifty-four in table 5.[57] There are similar discrepancies in the consort lists of the Jiaqing and Daoguang emperors.[58]

Still other kinds of records suggest that not all consorts received imperial burials. Many names of fifth-, sixth-, and seventh-ranking consorts found in the annual palace distribution (*gong fen*) lists prepared each winter in the twelfth lunar month cannot be matched with either the burial lists or the lists in the imperial genealogy. One example out of many is a consort identified in these palace distribution lists as Guo *guiren*. Guo *guiren* first appears on the palace distribution of 1734; she reappears in the lists for 1751, 1756, and 1767. A memorial concerning her death on September 24, 1761, is also preserved in the archives. Whose consort was she? She does not appear in the lists of women in the harems of the Kangxi and Yongzheng emperors, yet she could not have had this title in 1734 had she

Table 5. Imperial Consorts Recorded in the Genealogy and
Women Buried in Consort Tombs

Emperor (reign name)	Total in Genealogy	Total Burials	Omissions (percentage)
Shunzhi	19	32	41
Kangxi	39	54	28
Yongzheng	8	24	67
Qianlong	27	41	34
Jiaqing	14	14	0
Daoguang	8	20	60
Xianfeng	5	18	72
Tongzhi	5	5	0
Guangxu	3	3	0

SOURCES: *Da Qing yudie;* Chen Baorong, *Qing Xiling zong heng* (Shijiazhuang, 1987); Yu Shanpu, *Qing Dongling daguan* (Shijiazhuang, 1985).

not been a consort of the one or the other. At least twenty-three other women appear in the archival records as consorts but cannot be matched with the women whose names appear in the genealogy or the burial records.

If imperial consorts are underreported in the genealogies, the fertility of Qing consorts, since it is based on the incomplete figures, must be overstated. When the missing women are added to the list of consorts (table 6), the comparison of those consorts with the women who became mothers underscores one reality of palace life. Many consorts and, in most reigns the majority of consorts, bore the social stigma of infertility. Infertility spanned all consort ranks, from the empress on down, and no doubt its effects (including a woman's place in court society) were keenly felt. High-ranking consorts, however, did not vanish into social oblivion; in death as in life, they remained "on the record." Low-ranking consorts were not commemorated after death; their graves might be unmarked, and their names may never have been written into the genealogies.

The anonymity that absorbed the low-ranking consorts who were not fortunate enough to produce children or act as foster mothers extended into the symbolic life after death. As Fonssagrives shows in a study of the Qing western tombs, only empresses and consorts of the first three ranks were entitled to have a spirit tablet in the sacrificial hall in the Mudongling attached to the Daoguang emperor's tomb. In the Changfeiling attached to the Jiaqing emperor's mausoleum, only the spirit tablets of consorts of the

Table 6. Fertility of Qing Empresses and Consorts in the Historical Record

| Emperor | Number of Women[a] | Fertile Women | | Number of Children |
		Number	Percentage	
Shunzhi	32	11	34	14
Kangxi	54	30	55	55
Yongzheng	24	7	29	14
Qianlong	41	9	22	27
Jiaqing	15	7	47	14
Daoguang	21	7	33	19
Xianfeng	18	3[b]	17	3
Tongzhi	5	0	0	0
Guangxu	3	0	0	0

SOURCES: *Da Qing yudie; Aixin juelo zongpu* (Fengtian, 1937–38). The consort burials are taken from table 5.

[a] Totals include empresses and consorts.

[b] The emperor's second son, born in 1858, died on the same day.

first two ranks sit on thrones while those of lesser rank are arrayed on tables, and at the Taifeiling, attached to the Yongzheng emperor's mausoleum, only one first-ranked consort has this honor.[59]

Death and Property Rights

The emperor's right to dispose of the possessions of his consorts was both clear and complete. Empresses and imperial consorts' dowries were prepared by the Neiwufu and did not come from their natal families. Imperial consorts did not have private funds (*sifangqian*) at their disposal, as did commoner brides.[60] Their property rights were thus weaker than those of their subjects, as exemplified in the disposition of their possessions after death. It was customary to provide a deceased person with his or her favorite objects, clothing, and items of daily use to take into the otherworld. Imperial personages got imperial sendoffs. When Empress Dowager Cixi died in 1908, the value of the jewels and other costly items placed in her coffin, according to one estimate, totaled five million taels of silver.[61] Further possessions were burned as part of the extended funerary rites (see chapter 8). The articles that accompanied the empress into death symbolically paralleled the dowry (*zhuanglian*) with which a bride was endowed when she entered the household. Empress Dowager Xiaosheng was the great-granddaughter of an illustrious Manchu hero of the conquest, Eidu, and had entered Yinzhen's household while he was a prince, with a dowry supplied by her father.[62] In keeping with the sumptuary laws, the size of her dowry would be significantly smaller than the dowry supplied by the Imperial Household Department for an empress in a *dahun* or marriage of a reigning emperor. A detailed account of the dowry provided to Empress Xiaoding in the *dahun* of February 15, 1889, began with three gold *ruyi* (Chinese scepters) and went on through various items of clothing, furniture, dishes, utensils, bedding, and so forth. The trousseau took two hundred men to deliver. The Neiwufu also furnished the apartments of the emperor's consorts with additional gold and silver utensils and implements.[63]

The possessions of deceased persons that were buried with them and destroyed during their funeral rites were treated as their personal property, but it was the emperor who determined precisely what these articles would be. There is no archival evidence that private bequests were customary. That even low-ranking consorts had a considerable number of possessions is clear from the evidence of death inventories, dating from 1788 to 1874, held in the First Historical Archives.[64] The 1788 inventory is a typical example.

On May 25, 1788, Grand Secretary Heshen transmitted the imperial edict: the clothing, jewelry, and other possessions left by Rong *fei*, Hongli's Muslim consort who had died the previous day, should all be bestowed on inner-court personages, the senior princess, palace personnel, eunuchs, and maidservants. The possessions were arranged for imperial inspection on the twenty-sixth. Certain items were returned to the storehouse for future use; a scepter, earrings, court hat, robes, silver pots, basins, mirror, combs, and cloth were bestowed on the emperor's tenth daughter, who was engaged to Heshen's son. Hongli's third daughter, Princess Hejing, received a somewhat smaller number of court accessories, robes, and other clothing. A set of bedding, clothing, hair ornaments, and other items was placed on the corpse and in her coffin. A silver pot, basin, spoon, set of ivory chopsticks and a tray were arranged on the altar in front of the coffin for the hundred days of full mourning. Some of Rong *fei*'s possessions were distributed to ten consorts; still others were given to her own sisters. Silver was distributed to the members of her household staff. In addition the men servants received cloth and the women servants got items of clothing that she had owned.[65]

The death inventories all follow the same format. The number of articles in the death inventories ranged from a high of 1,014 items (in the inventory of a second-ranking consort) to a low of 106, held by a childless fourth-rank consort of the Jiaqing emperor.[66] All but one of the fourteen lists record the emperor's decision on what should be done with each item. In some of the lists, these decisions are written on thin yellow slips, pasted at the top. In others, the decisions are written in the margin above the item.

Analysis of the death inventories suggests that no imperial consorts had property that was theirs alone. It is true that the inventories all seem to focus on the possessions of childless consorts, so that we cannot be certain whether consorts who bore children would be allowed to deed some of their things to their descendants. At the same time, the emperor, not the consort, determined what should be given to Rong *fei*'s sisters as well as to her servants.

The death inventories also suggest that court accessories and court dress were not personal possessions but part of the collective property of the imperial household. As such, they were returned to the storehouses, to be recycled as needed. The lists all include many court accessories (scepters, robes, utensils, chests, etc.), which were returned to the Yangxindian storehouse. Even a "firepot" (*huoguo*) in the possession of one of Hongli's widowed consorts, Fang *taifei*, was returned to the kitchen of the emperor's residence, the Yangxindian.[67] The Yangxindian was where the palace workshops were located; archival documents show a wide variety of goods, from court hat finials, robes, face cloths, and bedding to chopsticks and combs being taken from the storehouse to become part of the dowry of princesses, underlining the likelihood that these objects were recycled.[68]

Aside from items among a consort's possessions that were sent into the storehouse for future use, items would be recycled among other palace women. The clothing of an elderly widowed consort might be given to other elderly consorts, the clothing of a younger junior consort to other junior palace ladies. But the court hierarchy did not preclude presenting the empress with something from a low-ranking consort's estate: for example, the empress, a second-rank consort, two princes' wives, and two of the emperor's daughters were among the recipients of hair ornaments from the childless Zhuang *fei*'s possessions after her death in 1811.[69] Underwear, socks, and shoes tended to be given to servants. The petty cash in the consort's estate would be divided among her servants.

IMPERIAL DAUGHTERS

In both Han Chinese and conquest dynasties, the politics of rulership influenced the status of princesses in clear and consistent ways. Imperial daughters, unlike virtually all others, retained membership in their natal families throughout their lives. Unlike other wives, they were economically, ritually, and socially superior to their husbands and their in-laws. As a consequence, "the sororal bond was transformed into an arm of the ruling line, reaching out into the wider community and establishing pockets of loyalty within other, potentially dangerous, lineages without the threat of domination or usurpation."[70] Although Qing princesses never shared regencies (as occurred in the Yuan dynasty), their marriages reinforced and reaffirmed Qing bonds with particular noble houses in the banner elite (see chapter 2). And their husbands became members of the imperial family.

Titles

The rank hierarchy for imperial daughters and sisters also evolved over the first half of the seventeenth century. Nurgaci's daughters were called *gege*, the Manchu term for "young lady." In 1636, Hongtaiji pronounced that the daughters of the empress would bear the title *gurun gungju* (state princess) with a rank that was equal to that of a first-degree prince. The daughters of consorts would become *hošoi gungju*, with a rank equivalent to that of a second-degree prince. These rules prevailed (with some notable exceptions) for most of the dynasty.[71] The title of princess, graded into seven ranks, was bestowed on daughters of the emperor and of princes in the first six ranks; another title (*zongnü*) was conferred on the daughters of lower-ranking princes. Titles were normally presented only at marriage.[72]

The granting of *gungju* titles to daughters of princes was gradually narrowed during the eighteenth century. By the early nineteenth century only daughters of the wives of first- and second-rank princes and one daughter of the wife of lower-ranking princes were granted a title and stipend. In 1864, the privilege was further limited to include only the daughters of high-ranking princes descended from the Qianlong emperor. Although one study of imperial houses lists one hundred Qing princesses, only sixty-two of them lived to marry. Of these, thirty or almost half married before the formal inauguration of the dynasty. Nine of these first- and second-rank princesses were daughters of imperial brothers.[73]

Princesses were not immune to gender discrimination. The general social valuation of boys above girls seems to have prevailed within the palace as well. The survival chances were markedly lower for girls than for boys (table 7). While the finding that almost a third of the emperor's daughters died in the first two years of life (table 8) is congruent with the high infant mortality patterns typical of many premodern societies, death from infectious disease probably did not discriminate by gender. There is absolutely no evidence that the cause of the differential mortality was female infan-

Table 7. Survival Rates of Qing Emperors' Sons versus Daughters

Emperor	Number of Sons	Survivors[a] (percentage)	Number of Daughters	Survivors[a] (percentage)
Shunzhi	7	42.8	6	16.7
Kangxi	34	55.9	20	40.0
Yongzheng	9	33.3	4	25.0
Qianlong	16	56.3	10	50.0
Jiaqing	4	75.0	9	22.2
Daoguang	8	75.0	10	50.0
Xianfeng	1	100.0	1	100.0

SOURCES: Da Qing yudie; Aixin juelo zongpu (Fengtian, 1937–38).
[a] "Survivors" are those who lived to marry.

Table 8. Age at Death of Emperors' Daughters, 1651–1900

Born In	Daughters (total)	Age at Death (in years)					
		0–2	3–5	6–15	16–25	26–30	30+
1651–1700	25	7	4	4	5	0	5
1701–50	9	7	0	0	0	0	2
1751–1800	13	3	3	2	2	2	1
1801–50	12	3	2	2	1	2	2
1851–1900	1	0	0	0	1	0	0

SOURCES: Da Qing yudie; Aixin juelo zongpu (Fengtian, 1937–38).

ticide. Without further information, the most reasonable assumption is that the heightened mortality of daughters in the palace was caused by the operation of an East Asian bias against girls, which produced "benign neglect."

Marriage

In contrast to Han Chinese ruling houses, non-Han rulers used marriage exchange as a normal part of foreign relations.[74] Qing princesses tended to marry in their mid-teens (table 9). The emperor selected their grooms. Although many of the great Manchu aristocratic houses—the Donggo, the

Table 9. Age at Marriage of Qing Princesses

Period	Number of Cases	Median Age
1601–50	19	11
1651–1700	13	15–16
1701–50	10	16–17
1751–1800	4	14
1801–50	5	15
1851–1900	4	19.5

SOURCE: *Da Qing yudie.*
NOTE: only emperors' daughters and princesses of the first two ranks are included in this table.

Suwan Gūwalgiya, the Niohuru, to name a few—married princesses (see chapter 2), the rulers favored Mongol grooms (table 10). The Qianlong emperor declared that this preference should be maintained, although he also permitted princesses to marry into distinguished banner families. His successor agreed. In 1817, reacting against the marriages of two Aisin Gioro princesses to bannermen, the Jiaqing emperor extended the ages of eligible Mongols from 18 *sui* to from 13 to 23 *sui*.[75] He ordered the Lifanyuan to circulate a notice among the thirteen banners in southeastern Inner Mongolia asking them to report the names of sons of *jasagh* or ruling nobles of a banner, together with their birth dates, their mothers' status, and biographical data for three generations of male forebears. All this information was passed to the Imperial Clan Court, which ranked the candidates and presented a list to the throne for the final decision.[76]

The stated preferences of the Qing emperors were realized in the actual matches, presented in table 10. The largest number of marriages, over 58 percent, were with Mongols; other scholars show that lower-ranking Aisin Gioro also married Mongol nobles in large numbers. The marriages also reveal that certain princely lines were especially favored.[77]

As the imperial lineage grew in size, the responsibility for wedding expenditures was increasingly divided between the Imperial Household Department and the princely households. From 1775, the marriages of princesses to court officials were arranged by the Neiwufu in conjunction with the Board of Rites. Marriages of princesses to Outer Mongols (*waifan*) were the primary responsibility of the Lifanyuan.[78] The Imperial House-

Table 10. Ethnicity of Qing Grooms of Princesses

Period	Marriages (number)	Manchu Grooms	Mongol Grooms	Hanjun Grooms
1601–50	24	7	17	0
1651–1700	13	3	6	4
1701–50	10	1	8	1
1751–1800	4	3	1	0
1801–50	5	2	3	0
1851–1900	4	4	0	0

SOURCES: Da Qing yudie; Tang Bangzhi, Qing huangshi sipu (Taipei, 1967).
NOTE: in the period 1601–50, some princesses married more than once, so the number of matches exceeds the number of princesses recorded in previous tables.

hold Department was also in charge of planning the betrothal and wedding banquets and preparing the dowry.[79]

The dowry for a princess had to match her preeminent status. Its size was codified in 1745 when the Qianlong emperor's third daughter was married. In general, princesses who married Outer Mongols got larger dowries than princesses who married banner nobles.[80] The size of the dowry or zhuanglian ranged from a total of 126 items, valued at over 12,000 taels, for a princess of the first rank down to 64 for a zongnü, the daughter of a an imperial prince of the sixth rank or below.[81] In addition to court robes and other clothing, jewelry, and accessories, the dowry included household linens, furniture, dishes, utensils, chests, and carpets, female attendants, maids, and dependent households. A princess who married a Mongol and moved to the steppe, was provided with camels, camel halters, horses, saddles, round-topped felt tents, covered passenger carts, and the other paraphernalia required for a pastoral existence. The groom and his parents received court dress, weapons, and saddled horses. Tents, saddled horses, and outfits were also given to the servants who accompanied the princess.[82]

A marriage settlement included much more than the items in the dowry. When the Shunzhi emperor's second daughter married in 1667, she was granted 8 imperial estates (zhuang) and 2 imperial orchards (yuan), each with a steward, totaling over 975 qing of land. In addition Princess Gongyi received houses in the capital, occupying a total area of 776 jian; 25 horses, 59 head of cattle, and 975 dependents.[83] By the late eighteenth century, pawnshops and other revenue-bearing assets had replaced grants of livestock, estates, and dependent households (see chapter 3 for parallel trend in princes' stipends).

The conjugal pair received a noble title. The groom's title was determined by his wife's, not the other way round (as was customary). The husband of a first-degree princess would be invested as a *gurun efu* (husband of *gurun gungju*) with a status equivalent to that of a fourth-degree prince. The husband of a second-degree princess enjoyed a status equal to that of a fifth-degree prince. That meant that his wife outranked him after 1786, when the household of a princess was given status parity with the household of a prince of the same rank.

Rites of Respect

Whereas marriage rituals for commoners emphasized the social superiority of the groom's family, the status of a princess turned normal superior: inferior relationships upside down. The bride's family decided on the match and initiated the rituals. When the groom was summoned to the palace to receive the imperial edict announcing the engagement, he performed the "three prostrations and nine knockings" (*sangui jiukou*) signifying his assent to the imperial order. These obeisances to the bride's parents were repeated by the groom, his agnates, and his female relatives at the palace during the banquets marking the betrothal and wedding. For her part, the princess omitted the customary rites of respect before her parents-in-law—indeed, they were expected to greet her on their knees.[84] When the couple visited the palace on the ninth day after the wedding, the groom had to perform his salutations outside the palace gates, while his wife entered the inner quarters to see the emperor, empress, and (if she was a consort's child) her mother.

Marital Protocol

Marriage to a princess was an "unsought honor" (see above). As an Aisin Gioro, the princess always outranked her husband. A Mongol noble family whose son married a Manchu princess acquired a bride "who became part daughter-in-law and part overlord to them."[85] The rules governing the behavior of princesses reflected the throne's assessment of the function of the marriage exchange.

Since a major motivation for marriage was to cement or reaffirm bonds between the imperial line and its noble allies, most princesses married to Outer Mongols were sent to reside with their husbands in Mongolia. Their inclination to return to the luxury of Peking was curbed. Princesses with aged parents could visit once every five years, other princesses usually made home visits once a decade. Their stay in Peking was limited to six months, although extensions could be obtained on grounds of ill health. Exceptions to these rules required imperial approval. In return, the court sent them gifts of fruits, rice, and foodstuffs during the years when they did not come to the capital.[86]

Relations with the Outer Mongols were important for the peace of the realm, and the Qing rules reflected the political situation. Some princesses and their husbands were allowed to reside in Peking, in a mansion bestowed on them by the emperor. The property would be drawn from the Imperial Household Department's sizable holdings of real estate in Peking (see chapter 1). When Princess Zhuangjing (*tob ginggun hošoi gungju*), the Jiaqing emperor's third daughter, became engaged to the Khorchin noble Sobnamdobjai in 1798, a 405-*jian* residence was renovated for the princess, at a cost to the Privy Purse of 18,000 taels of silver.[87] This second-rank princess received a substantially larger residence than the 320-*jian* mansion bestowed on her younger half sister (a first-rank princess). There seems to have been an inflation in these bestowals during the Jiaqing reign: Hongli's ninth daughter, a second-ranking princess, had received a house with only 199 *jian* of space when she married in 1772.[88] The mansions assigned to Shouxi *hošoi gungju* and Rong'an *gurun gungju*, who married in 1863 and 1873, were 377 and 300 *jian* respectively.[89]

A eunuch appointed by the Neiwufu supervised the establishment for the princess and her husband; the commandant (*zhangshi*) or steward in charge of the household of a first- or second-degree princess or prince was an official in the Imperial Household Department holding the eighth rank. Officers from the imperial guard commanded the guardsmen and Imperial Household personnel (eunuchs, maidservants, nurses) who served the princess during her lifetime.[90] Ten guard-households, nineteen eunuchs, and five nurses accompanied Zhuangjing *hošoi gungju* into her marriage; her younger half sister, Zhuangjing *gurun gungju*, who married a year later (1802), was assigned twelve guard-households, fifteen eunuchs, six nurses, and four maids.[91] These numbers shrank in the second half of the nineteenth century.[92]

Princesses and their husbands received stipends, calculated in rice, that were fixed according to rank. First-degree princesses residing in the capital received 400 taels, their husbands 300 taels, and a rice allowance of 200 *shi*. First-degree princesses who married Outer Mongols and resided in Mongolia received 1,000 taels of silver and 30 rolls of satin; their husbands received 300 taels and 10 rolls, but the difference may well have been offset by the fact that princesses remaining in the capital received a mansion and daily food rations as well. In 1841, the stipend was raised to 1,200 taels a year, obtained through rental properties and the interest income from a pawnshop.[93]

Whatever the regulations stipulated—stipends, goods, interest income or rental income from land and houses—in fact an emperor's daughters received much more, no doubt because they were part of court circles, receiving special presents on their birthdays and taking part in the grand celebrations marking the birthdays of the emperor, empress dowager, and empress.[94] In 1801 the Jiaqing emperor's third daughter, Princess Zhuang-jing, received a pawnshop, capitalized at 113,000 strings of cash, a 405-*jian* furnished mansion, the rental income from imperial estates (administered by local stewards [one and a half *zhuangtou*]) amounting to over 300 taels a year, and a lump sum of 10,000 taels of silver.[95] The emperor's fourth daughter, Zhuangjing *gurun gungju*, was married in 1802 to Manibadara, a Tümed prince. The pawnshop conferred on her was capitalized at 104,000 strings of cash; she had the rental income from land (two and a half *zhuangtou*) amounting to about 500 taels a year, other rental income of 132 taels a month, and a lump sum of 12,000 taels.

When an emperor's daughter could not live within her means, she appealed to the Privy Purse. Princess Shouxi, the eighth daughter of the Daoguang emperor, married in December 1863 and was awarded the right to an income of 2,180 taels. In less than a year, her unpaid debts caused the Neiwufu to petition and obtain an additional 800 taels on her behalf.[96]

Information dating from 1860 indicates that emperors substantially raised the marriage settlements of princesses in the mid-nineteenth century (table 11). Shou'an, a first-rank princess, was the fourth daughter of the Daoguang emperor, married in 1841 to a Mongol prince. At her death in 1860, she was receiving over 9,400 taels a year, over two and a half times the amount given to first-rank princesses in the first part of the nineteenth century. The Xianfeng emperor's daughter, first-rank princess Rong'an, received an identical marriage settlement when she married in 1873.[97]

Although the court had ruled that, once married, a princess must share punishments meted out to her groom, emperors found it difficult to treat their sisters so summarily.[98] Princess Hexiao, daughter of the Qianlong emperor, was married in 1790 to Fengshenyinde, the son of her father's crony Heshen. When Heshen was purged after the Qianlong emperor's death in 1799, Hexiao's financial situation was cushioned by the solicitude of her half brother, the Jiaqing emperor: archival records indicate that half

Table 11. Sources of Princess Shou'an's Income, 1860

	Amount (silver taels)	*Percentage of Income*
Pawnshop income	2,957.8	31.4
Land rents	1,200.0	12.7
House rents	1,560.0	16.6
Interest, cash dowry	1,200.0	12.7
Imperial subsidies	2,500.0	26.5
Total	9,417.8	100.0[a]

SOURCE: First Historical Archives, Beijing (557-5-66-4/3114).
[a] Total may not add up to 100.0 because of rounding error.

of Heshen's town and Jehol properties were given to the princess, who also received special grants in 1814, 1821, and 1822 to supplement her income.[99]

Imperial Inheritance

The emperor presented gifts when a princess gave birth to a daughter or a son, while a prince received these gifts only on the birth of a son.[100] Each imperial son, daughter, grandson, and granddaughter also received gifts from the throne. The sons of Qing princesses married to Mongol nobles inherited titles according to their mother's rank, along lines similar to the inheritance system among imperial princes. The principle of reducing rank with each transmission, found among the Aisin Gioro, also applied to Mongol noble titles. The rank of *efu* (imperial son-in-law) was inheritable in perpetuity by one son after his father died or at eighteen *sui;* other sons of his were invested as *taiji,* a Mongol noble title. The titles of the latter were transmissible only with imperial approval. After 1775 sons born to princesses of the two highest ranks living in the capital were invested with their father's titles when they reached thirteen *sui.*[101]

Efu participated in the elaborate social networks set up by the dynasty to integrate Mongolia into the empire (see chapter 2). They were expected to present themselves in Peking for imperial audience on a rotating basis that has been likened to the Japanese *sankin-kotai* system in its political effects. Sons born of these unions were also organized into rotas and expected to appear in Peking on regular occasions. After 1659, sons of princesses could be reared in Peking at court and sometimes attended the Palace School.[102]

Imperial Property

The distinctive status of a princess is reflected finally in the rituals accompanying her death. Unlike all other married women, even in death she was imperial and the disposal of her remains became the responsibility not of her husband but of her natal family. The bereaved widower was required to notify the emperor immediately when his wife died. The emperor could grant permission for the princess to be buried with her husband; for example, the Kangxi emperor's second daughter, who married a noble of the Balin banner, was buried in Inner Mongolia.[103] But permission of this kind was not always granted. When Princess Shou'an died in 1860, her husband, a Naiman noble named Demchugjab, wanted to bury his wife in his own home territory. The matter was handed over to the Lifanyuan for deliberation but it refused to issue a decision. The Neiwufu then took over the case and announced that "there is no precedent of this sort in our records." Archival files on the Kangxi and Yongzheng reigns were not in sufficiently good condition to be consulted; the Qianlong files were not complete. The department could cite one case of a second-rank princess buried in Mongolia, but "in the Jiaqing and Daoguang reigns, the princesses' tombs were all close to the capital and none was outside the passes." The department recommended that the Lifanyuan circulate a notice to the heads of the Mongol leagues asking them to report the particulars of any such tombs in their territories. Demchugjab's request was eventually turned down and Princess Shou'an was buried at imperial expense outside Peking.[104]

The funeral and interment expenses were paid by the emperor. Officials of the Imperial Household Department choreographed the funeral rites for the princess, directed the construction of her tomb, and disposed of her estate. Sometimes the tomb construction would be paid for out of the income that had been assigned to the princess; at other times, it would be paid directly by the Imperial Household Department.[105] After the hundred days' mourning period had passed, the maidservants and eunuchs attached to her household would return to the Neiwufu registers, with the exception of those assigned to guard her tomb. That the princess was considered "family"—a part of the imperial lineage—was also clear from the inclusion of closely related princesses in special grave rituals performed during the late nineteenth century.[106] From birth to death, the princess remained a member of her natal lineage.

The archival materials also show that on occasion, ritual incorporation of *efu* extended to the management of their death rituals. This was the case for Sebtenbaljur, who married the Qianlong emperor's third daughter. His father, Bandi, was a first-degree prince in the Khorchin Left Flank Center Banner. Sebtenbaljur himself was one of the Mongols selected for rearing in the palace; he entered the Palace School at the age of nine *sui*. Invested as a first-degree *efu* when he married Princess Hejing in 1745, he lived in Peking. He died in 1775, leaving his wife, a son, and several daughters, yet the funeral was arranged by officials from the Neiwufu who reported directly to the emperor. The emperor contributed 3,000 taels of silver toward funeral expenses.[107]

Did the objects bestowed on a princess constitute a true dowry, which is defined as a permanent transfer of property from the bride's family to the bride or to the new conjugal fund? Unlike imperial consorts (see above), princesses did have real dowries. Detailed accounts of the disposition of their estates through most of the nineteenth century show that jewelry, clothing, utensils, and other dowry goods of princesses were permanently transferred and inherited by their children. Other items were bestowed on princesses as lifetime grants, to be returned to the imperial household on their death. These included the grants of income from imperial estates, official pawnshops, and the personnel assigned to serve all the establishments. As with the *enfeng* princes (see chapter 3), the net effect of these policies was to prevent the new descent groups created by the unions from building autonomous bases of wealth and hence potential power. Each generation would remain dependent on the ruler for benefits.

The archival documents indicate that imperial policies with respect to the disposition of the properties settled on princesses became stricter as the demands on the imperial purse increased. When Princess Gongyi, a princess of the second rank, died in 1685, her estate was not returned to the throne. Not until 1733 was an inventory taken of the estate, and the eventual settlement was not reached until 1735, fifty years after her death. During that interval, the estate and its income were available to her husband and son: that she had at least one son is indicated by the report in 1736 that a widowed daughter-in-law of the princess lived in one of her houses. When the bulk of the land, housing, and dependents granted more than a half-century earlier was taken back into the Imperial Household Department, this daughter-in-law was "temporarily" allocated a house, twenty *qing* of income-yielding land, and forty-one dependents. The clear implication of the memorial is that on her death these too would revert to the Neiwufu.[108]

Did grooms retain a share of the property of their wives? As mentioned earlier, the stipend provided an *efu* was continued as long as he did not take a second wife. That his income was considered when his wife's estate was inventoried is suggested by a report of Princess Hejing's estate after her death on February 9, 1775. The cash on hand, 5,000 taels of silver, was to be used to help defray the funeral expenses. The capital and interest in the pawnshop that had been allocated to the princess totaled 30,000 taels; two years' interest from this pawnshop would be dedicated for the construction of the tomb. Since the widower would have an income equivalent to that of a marquis, he would not need to continue to receive the pawnshop income.[109]

When Princess Zhuangjing, the Jiaqing emperor's third daughter, died in 1811, the emperor decided to allow his son-in-law Sobnamdobjai to retain the services of three of the nineteen eunuchs who had been assigned to their establishment. Four of the ten guard-households assigned to her were reassigned to guard his daughter's tomb, but the other servants all returned to their original banners. The remainder of the cash dowry, 5,000 taels, and rental income from the imperial estates also reverted to the Imperial Household Department. The death settlement a few months later of the Jiaqing emperor's fourth daughter differed only in its details. Here too the emperor took back the income from the imperial estates and other rental properties. The six nurses, four maids, and six of his daughter's twelve guard-households were returned to their original banners; her husband, Manibadara, retained the fifteen eunuchs and the remaining six guard-households were assigned to her tomb.[110]

In 1811 the pawnshops that were part of the marriage settlement were given to the surviving husbands of the two princesses. Sobnamdobjai, the husband of Princess Zhuangjing, was also given her mansion. When he decided it was too big, the emperor gave him 3,000 taels so that he could purchase a house for himself. Apparently Sobnamdobjai chose another mansion, comprising 184 *jian*, owned by the imperial household. In 1820, he petitioned to return this house.[111] Why he did this is not known, although the case of Manibadara may provide one explanation. Manibadara had continued to reside in the mansion assigned to his wife after her death in 1811. In 1820, he petitioned requesting permission to return the large (316-*jian*) house because he could not maintain this residence while making payments on another house, purchased from the Neiwufu by his father.[112] *Efu* widowed in the late nineteenth century were not treated so well: the Xianfeng emperor took back the mansions and properties of three of the Daoguang emperor's daughters after their deaths in 1856, 1859, and 1860.[113]

Whatever widowers received, however, was "by imperial grace," and not an automatic property right. Grants of houses, land, domestic staff, and even grave-guardian households were the emperor's to give and to take away. The temporary nature of these grants is clear in a 1733 petition in the archives from the widow of a bannerman who had been assigned to maintain the grave of Princess Gongyi (the second daughter of the Shunzhi emperor, discussed above). Her husband, Suhe, had died ten years earlier; she had continued to sweep the grave and carry out sacrifices but was now unable to manage because of illness. Eventually most personnel assigned to the households of princesses were returned to their original banner registers.[114]

CONCLUSIONS

Qing succession policies resulted in a structural negation of the social status acquired by women at birth and ordinarily brought with them into marriage. Membership in the imperial lineage was the dominant factor in the status of imperial women. Women who married into the imperial family were socially and ritually severed from their natal families. Their imperial status overrode their roles as daughters and inverted the rituals respecting age and generation that were normal in commoner society. The Manchu success in separating imperial wives and consorts from their natal kin may help explain why, throughout the dynasty, imperial widows allied with their husband's brothers during the political crises produced by a minor ascending to the throne. Regencies featuring cooperation between empress dowagers and imperial princes were a recurring element in Qing rule, one that should be distinguished from the examples of usurping empresses found in Han Chinese dynasties.

The Qing incorporated the husbands of their daughters and sisters into the imperial lineage. These women retained their imperial identity in life and after death. Their husbands entered the functional equivalent (in Han Chinese society) of uxorilocal marriage: their status was fixed by their wife's rank, and they lived in houses provided by their father-in-law, on incomes that he provided. Throughout the rest of their lives they would be identified in official documents (and by the emperor) as *efu*. The term overrode the specific relationship between the reigning emperor and the individual. The Khalkha noble Tsereng (see chapter 2), for example, was a son-in-law of the Kangxi emperor, but he continued to be called *efu* by the Yongzheng and Qianlong emperors whom he loyally served. *Efu* were family as far as the Qing rulers were concerned. They received special treatment and were one of the groups of imperial relatives who were regularly feted during the New Year and in Chengde.

The Qing strategies of incorporation succeeded brilliantly in Tsereng's case. Although his marriage with a Qing princess lasted only four years before her untimely death, Tsereng went on to make major contributions to the Qing cause in campaigns against the Zunghars. Tsereng was unusual because he rose far above the rank he had received as an *efu*. Indeed, Tsereng reversed the normal expectation in winning posthumous promotion for his wife through his military victories. That she was important to him is suggested in his request, many decades after her death, that he be buried next to her in the suburbs of Peking, rather than in Tamir, the pasturelands in the Mongolian steppe that were his home.[115] At least partly in commemoration of Tsereng's deeds, his descendants were twice selected to marry princesses.

Looking at women's claims to imperial property gives us a valuable opportunity to consider the whole issue of the rights of imperial family members to the imperial estate. The sons and daughters of an emperor both held claims on the imperial resources. *Enfeng* princes received estates, princesses dowries. Both represented a temporary transfer of goods from the imperial house to a new conjugal unit. The imperial children were granted lifetime use of houses, servants, and stipends but these could and often were eventually taken back into the imperial estate. The descendants were thus never given an economic basis for independence from the throne. They had to renew their bonds with the court in each generation if they were to flourish.

Not even the emperor himself had permanent property rights. The Qing distinguished the emperor's property from the property of the state. The first was managed by the Department of the Privy Purse (see chapter 5), the latter by the Board of Revenue. A Qing emperor could of course bestow honors, office, and other public goods on whomever he pleased, but grants to kinsmen and many gift exchanges were financed from his own resources. The emperor was in some important respects the custodian and not the owner of the imperial resources. Many of his material goods were "inalienable possessions" of the Qing state. "Inalienable possessions," or state treasures, are objects that are "imbued with the intrinsic and ineffable identities of their owners" and confer power and legitimacy.[116] Such objects belong not to one individual, but to the ruling house. Like the crown jewels of England, they cannot (or should not) be given away.

The Qing regarded several types of objects as inalienable possessions of the imperial house. First was the pre-1644 state seal, the only one that Hongli did not have recarved. Then there were the objects linked to the imperial ancestral cult (see chapters 6 and 8). The jade tablets and seals of deceased emperors and empresses were preserved in the Temple of the Ancestors and the sacrificial halls of the imperial mausolea. Ancestral portraits and tablets were stored within the Shouhuangdian and installed in the altars erected in private palace residences. Imperial artifacts from earlier dynasties included approximately 152 portraits of Song, Yuan, and Ming emperors and empresses as well as Ming patents of investiture and seals. These had been discovered in 1644 by Qing troops and were stored in the Nanxundian, a hall within the inner court in the southwestern corner of the Forbidden City.[117]

More broadly, everything that had belonged to the emperor took on part of his charisma. And the imperial bestowal of court robes on Tibetan Buddhist prelates, Mongol nobles, and favorites should be understood as "the means by which authoritative relations were established."[118] By thus transferring part of his authority, embodied in the court robes, the emperor incorporated the recipients into a relationship of subordination. On another level, as Angela Zito argues, the ritualized "sharing" of imperial meals with palace ladies and officials performed the same symbolic function as did the distribution of death mementos (*yinian*) of a deceased ruler.[119]

Because imperial possessions were not ordinary goods, their owner, the emperor, could not always freely dispose of them. Imperial clothing, porcelain, furs, weapons, and objets d'art were stored within the palace in the Six Vaults, which were periodically weeded out. In 1736 Hongli ordered the Department of the Privy Purse to inventory the Six Vaults and to distribute old and worn-out items among banner officials, imperial guardsmen, and palace staff.[120] In 1800, when imperial finances were straitened by the White Lotus rebellion, the Imperial Household Department ministers proposed that "worn-out" and "spoiled" goods from the Six Vaults be sold. The Jiaqing emperor responded indignantly:

> The ministers of the Neiwufu have sent up lists of jade treasures, pearls, and porcelains that have been stored since the beginning of the dynasty and repeatedly request that merchants be invited to buy them. All are things it is forbidden to sell. With the exception of myself, the princes, and high ministers, who would dare to use these jades and treasures? All of these things have been stored as heirlooms for eternity. If we display them in the marketplace and sell them, regardless of the price, the effect on the court system (*chaoting tizhi*) . . . would be too shameful.[121]

In a similar sense imperial women were also "inalienable possessions" of the imperial house. Whereas marriage normally established a reciprocal social relationship between wife-givers and wife-takers, the Qing rulers from the Qianlong ruler onward did their best to ignore or reduce this particular social bond. Consorts were stripped of their prior identities. They entered the palace as brides with goods conferred on them by the emperor. Everything they owned came from the emperor. They were "reinvented" as imperial consorts. Their social relations with their natal families and even their children were controlled by the throne. The Qianlong emperor's reluctance to "honor filiality" by permitting senior widowed consorts to live with their sons outside the palace underlines the degree to which they were regarded as imperial property.

The same principles were applied to daughters. The emperor did not "give away" his daughters; he used them to obtain sons-in-law. The retention of daughters and the incorporation of consorts not only served a symbolic purpose of projecting the throne's absolute preeminence to the world outside the court but also advanced the political goals of the Qing rulers. The Qing succeeded in neutralizing the potential dangers from matrilateral kinsmen and in introducing important members of the conquest elite into the emperor's extended family. Shrewd marriage and inheritance policies enabled Qing rulers to avoid the political chasms that confronted their predecessors.

Chapter 5   Palace Servants

A study of servants provides rich insights into discourses of power. The emperor needed servants for both practical and symbolic reasons. They performed menial tasks and kept the large and complex imperial household smoothly functioning. They were also agents of the imperial will whom the emperor used to check elite political constituencies. But the number and nature of the palace staff were not primarily dictated by the burden of domestic or even political chores. As in other "forms of domination based on a premise or claim to inherent superiority by ruling elites," Qing ruler-ship required that the emperor maintain a lavish lifestyle.[1] His staff must be bigger and grander and more complex than anything lesser mortals might devise.

The palace staff came from widely varying backgrounds and social status. Many servants were bondservants or bannermen and could not be employed by commoners. Eunuchs were another group whose employment was governed by sumptuary laws. There were also Tibetans, Uighurs, and European Jesuits in imperial service. Although Jesuits may have conceived of their palace work as one form of missionizing, emperors used them as material testimony to the cosmopolitan nature of their rule. The diversity and size of the palace staff thus vividly reinforced the Qing claim to be world monarchs.

The projection of an imperial image was continually under challenge by palace servants, who shared many of the characteristics of the subordinate groups in James Scott's classic analysis of domination and resistance. Bond-servants and eunuchs occupied low-ranking status that could not be easily changed. In a hierarchy of master-servant relations that ran throughout society (see chapter 1), the power the emperor exercised over servants was unbounded. He could act in arbitrary and capricious ways, without challenge. The omnipresent implied threat of his unlimited power over servants gave them little recourse to anything other than veiled patterns of resistance.

Scott's description of the circumstances that cause subordinates and masters to wage a "silent struggle" will be familiar to students of the Qing court. Scott's analysis suggests strategies by which the court's depiction of itself and of its servants can lead us to a better understanding of the structure of Qing legitimation. The Imperial Household Department's rich documentation on palace servants provides ample evidence of the "private transcripts," the sentiments and actions that contrast sharply to the "public transcript" of masterful rulers and deferential servants that the throne projected.[2] The "off-stage" discourse of the dominant group and their subordinates—which fills the documents of the Neiwufu and the Imperial Clan Court—shows behavior that contradicts the image of a united first family exemplifying the highly touted virtues of filiality and fraternal affection. As long as the dominant group successfully projects the appearance of overwhelming coercive force, implicit rejections of the public discourse tend to remain underground. In the imperial discourse, eunuchs and bondservants should be hardworking and efficient, utterly loyal and devoted to the emperor. Yet the criminal cases display lazy, thieving, gossiping betrayers of the imperial trust, whose existence contradicts the central tenet of the Qing social order, namely that the emperor's persona commands complete obedience.

The tension between master and servant was built into the structure of palace administration and into its internal system of checks and balances. Since servants ran errands, delivered and received messages within the inner court, and controlled access to the individuals they served, they could manipulate the system for their own profit. Emperors worried about controlling palace servants. They feared lest eunuchs and others use their positions for private gain or transfer their primary loyalty from the ruler to their master or mistress. Eunuchs should be, first and foremost, agents of the imperial will. Obedience to a consort or prince should be subordinated to this prior loyalty. An attempt by prince or consort to break the law was reported to the throne. And any failure to enforce palace regulations on palace residents was rigorously prosecuted.

The emperor's desire to control the behavior of his family through rules enforced by palace servants introduced a dissonance between the nominal and actual hierarchy of power relations. Eunuchs in fact became extensions of the persons they served. Not only did eunuchs recreate amongst themselves the social hierarchy of their masters and mistresses, they embodied its gradations of rank and power as they carried out their duties within the palace. The emperor's eunuch was powerful within court circles, not only among his eunuch peers but also among the imperial consorts and other palace residents—supervising or "controlling" the imperial princes, princesses, and consorts on his master's behalf. The lack of symmetry between a eunuch's low status and actual delegated authority was a constant source of tension in the social relations between and among palace residents. Because it was willed by the emperor, nothing could be done by the courtiers to remedy the situation. When eunuchs showed any sign of disrespect toward their social superiors, they were decisively slapped down. Such behavior was extremely threatening to the emperor and the dynasty, because it challenged the hegemonic order. The imperial vision of a stratified social order assumed that this order was realized in real life: behavior that transgressed the social boundaries was intolerable because it suggested that this vision was a fiction.[3] "Holding the line" on status distinctions between master and servant was crucial. If princes did not receive the respect due their status, the emperor would not long survive. As the cases below show, emperors acted decisively to put down the social pretensions of eunuchs and bondservants.

Incidents sparked by insubordination, theft, and intrigue challenged the ruler's control of his court. The Qing emperors were keenly aware that the information they obtained through bureaucratic channels in the outer court frequently concealed the real facts; many studies show their efforts to pursue and uncover the "truth."[4] Episodes in the palace were especially upsetting when they revealed that rules were being ignored or broken without the emperor's knowledge, within the walls of his residence. As the examples show, the imperial response often blended frustration, aggravated suspicion, and a determination to get to the bottom of an affair.

PALACE PERSONNEL

Eunuchs

Throughout Chinese history, to act as agents of the imperial prerogative in the perennial competition for political dominance between the throne and the civil service bureaucracy, Han Chinese dynasties typically relied on eunuchs—castrated males, who were pariahs because they could not fulfill a Confucian society's most fundamental individual responsibility: they could not perpetuate the descent line. The same factor that made them pariahs made them valuable to rulers. As Torbert notes, "The eunuchs . . . willingly carried out even the most despicable or sacrilegious commands, yet they did not constitute a threat to the ruler." They were "the ideal servants" throughout Chinese history for emperors struggling to offset the political influence of maternal affines or of civil servants.[5] At the same time, infamous examples of eunuchs' abuse of power during the Tang and especially the late Ming dynasty sounded a cautionary note for the Manchus.

The Manchus continued to employ Ming palace eunuchs after they entered Peking. Under Dorgon's regency, eunuchs were barred from handling the revenues of the imperial estates and from participating in court audiences, but in 1653 Fulin, the Shunzhi emperor, created the Thirteen Eunuch Bureaus to supplant the Neiwufu as the unit of palace administration. Fulin probably hoped to use eunuchs to offset the independent power of the banner lords; he modified the Ming system, instituted joint management of palace affairs by bondservants and eunuchs, and appointed Manchus to the Thirteen Bureaus to check on eunuch officials. After his death, the Thirteen Bureaus were abolished, but eunuchs continued to be employed in the palace.[6]

Although the Yongzheng emperor is said to have ruled that bannermen should not be permitted to become eunuchs, the archival evidence shows that this prohibition was never completely honored.[7] A listing of the eunuchs enrolled in the Court Theatrical Bureau from 1740 to 1911 shows many came from banner registers. In 1811 the Jiaqing emperor complained that although the number of eunuchs in the palace had declined, more came from the banners. He attempted to recruit more eunuchs from the Han commoner population by offering them higher rates of compensation.[8]

The number of commoners who became eunuch-actors increased beginning in the 1820s. Of 441 eunuchs serving in the Court Theatrical Bureau, over 30 percent came from three counties in and around Peking. The metropolitan area of Wanping produced the single highest number of eunuchs; in the Daoguang and Tongzhi reigns, it was the native place for 41 and 50.9 percent, respectively, of the eunuchs joining the Court Theatrical Bureau. The locality with the second highest showing was Daxing county, in the eastern suburbs of the capital. Ranking a distant third was Qing county in southern Zhili.[9]

Life histories collected in post-1949 China give several explanations of why individuals became eunuchs. Li Lianying, the favorite of Empress Dowager Cixi, was born in a village in southern Zhili, in 1848, the second of eight children. Although his family claimed officials among their ancestors, Lianying's grandfather was a merchant and his father a leather worker. In 1854, the six-year-old Lianying fell into a hole and sprained his left knee. The injury caused him to limp; local doctors could not cure him. His father took the boy to Peking, where the family had a leather shop, the Yongdetang. The doctor he consulted foretold that Lianying was "out of the ordinary"; the boy should either enter Buddhist orders or become a eunuch. The parents vowed that if he were cured, they would follow the doctor's suggestions.[10]

Li Lianying's story echoes others explaining why sons were given to monasteries. Sickly boy children might be promised to the gods as a thank-offering for a cure: the notion seems to be that it was their "fate" to turn away from the normal life cycle. The case of You Chunhe, born in a village in eastern Hebei belonging to Prince Zhuang, follows another pattern. You's family had for generations been assigned to watch over the prince's ancestral graves. Driven out of the village by massive floods, You wandered into Peking in 1898 to look for work and was tricked into becoming a eunuch. Naïveté may have been the short-run reason why You fell into this trap—according to his account, he did not understand what he was assenting to when asked if he were willing to undergo castration—but the fundamental reason was poverty and the absence of any viable alternative.

Most people could accept "fate" and poverty as reasons for becoming a eunuch. But some individuals voluntarily chose to become eunuchs, presumably for the chance to acquire wealth and power. This motive seems to have drawn Zhang Xiangzhai, who entered the palace in 1891 and served two empresses dowager over twenty-two years. Zhang was born in a village in southern Hebei in 1876. During a severe drought in 1888, he and his brother sought refuge at a house whose master turned out to be a eunuch at court. When Zhang discovered the source of the household's comforts, he declared that he wished to castrate himself. Apparently his decision caused quite a stir, because although the district produced eunuchs, there had never previously been a case of a boy's voluntarily seeking this fate.[11]

Not everyone managed to enter the palace immediately. When Zhang Lande found that he could not enter the palace after castrating himself, he worked for a bannerman family, doing odd jobs for two ounces of broken silver a month until, after three years, a vacancy opened in the palace. Even though sumptuary laws forbade commoners to employ eunuchs, no one seems to have prosecuted the family.[12]

A 1751 edict fixed the number of eunuchs in palace service at 3,300. In actuality, the number of eunuchs on call was contingent on the number of imperial children at court and the number of imperial consorts. Each consort, son, or daughter was assigned a certain number of eunuchs, in keeping with the rank and age of the individual.[13] Princes and princesses were allowed to keep eunuchs after they married. The number of eunuchs em-

Table 12. Number of Eunuchs in Palace Service

Year	Number of Eunuchs	Source
1750	3,107	Archives 446-5-55/80
1774	2,864	Archives 446-5-55/219
1797	2,524	Archives 446-5-55/328
1799	2,802	Archives 446-5-55/336
1800	2,740	Archives 446-5-55/340
1842	2,216	Wang Shuqing
1874	1,596	Wang Shuqing
1887	1,693	Wang Shuqing
1922	1,137	Aisin Gioro Puyi

SOURCES: First Historical Archives, Beijing; Wang Shuqing, "Qing-chao taijian zhidu," *Gugong bowuyuan yuankan* 2 (1984): 8; Aisin-Gioro Pu Yi, *From Emperor to Citizen: The Autobiography of Aisin Gioro Pu Yi*, trans. W. J. F. Jenner (1964; reprint, New York, 1987), 62.

ployed in the palace reached its peak in the Qianlong reign (table 12). The most precipitous declines came in the second half of the nineteenth century, when the size of the imperial harem decreased under a series of infant rulers.

Eunuchs' society was sharply stratified. At the peak of the hierarchy were the eunuch-officials who were granted bureaucratic rank in 1722. After 1742, no eunuch could be promoted above the fourth rank, to "prevent them from meddling in court politics." [14] Of the roughly 3,000 eunuchs in palace service in the eighteenth century, only 10 percent, about 300, belonged to the eunuch elite, who held supervisory titles. [15]

As the head of the Jingshifang (office of eunuch affairs), the chief eunuch (*jingshifang zongguan taijian*) was at the top of the eunuch order. This office handled imperial edicts on all palace affairs. In addition to managing eunuchs, it was charged with carrying out rites and circulating documents among the subagencies of the Imperial Household Department. The chief eunuch was usually a veteran of thirty or more years' service in the palace and had often served the emperor when he was a prince. Even though he was under the jurisdiction of the ministers of the Neiwufu, and its accounting office controlled financial administration, the chief eunuch enjoyed a great deal of independent authority. [16] He supervised a staff of forty-four eunuchs, including eunuchs literate in Manchu and Chinese who staffed the Manchu and Chinese writing offices. Chief eunuchs often enjoyed extraordinary imperial favor in the form of gifts and private residences outside the palace.

Supervisory eunuchs (*shouling*) of lower rank (ranks seven and eight)—a total of 124—were assigned to the different gates within the Forbidden City and to imperial gardens, villas, major altars and temples, imperial mausolea, palace halls, and storehouses that constituted the palace domain. *Shouling* were also appointed to the imperial pharmacy, tea bureau, and the buttery. Different *shouling* managed the tea, medicine, and food services for the empress dowager; the affairs of each widowed consort of the major ranks; and the personal staffs of the emperor's children. There were even *shouling* in charge of the dog kennels and aviary. These supervisory eunuchs were responsible to the chief eunuch, who answered for their conduct to the Neiwufu ministers and the emperor.[17]

Alongside the official ranking system stood another status hierarchy, based on proximity to the emperor. The senior eunuchs in charge of the emperor's private residence, the Yangxindian, and the Ruyi gate enjoyed considerable authority, often rivaling that of the chief eunuch, because of their constant attendance on the ruler. Eunuchs in charge of other halls that the emperor frequented comprised an elite, standing above eunuchs in personal service to the empress, consorts, and imperial offspring. Although eunuchs in attendance on a princeling had a relatively humble status in the palace hierarchy, they could rise to the top if their charge became emperor.

Eunuchs assigned to a palace resident all ranked above eunuchs performing specialized services. Ordinary eunuchs were graded into three ranks with graduated stipends in rice and silver. Some eunuchs were employed as barbers, others as masseurs; still others were trained in medicine and treated members of the court. Other eunuchs were taught to recite Tibetan Buddhist sutras or to become Daoist monks. Eunuchs waited on the emperor in shifts; when the emperor retired, a "sitting watch" was kept by the night shift so that someone was always within call to carry messages or fetch objects and persons. Eunuchs were essential because the physician on duty was the only male who was permitted to remain within the inner court at night.

Bondservants

The Qing devised an ingenious new solution to the problem of insubordinate eunuchs. They used another low-status group, the bondservants, to control and supervise eunuchs. By introducing a new element, the bondservant, into the palace administration, Qing rulers expanded the system of checks and balances within the palace. Bondservants were part of the conquest group and as such were clearly separated from the subjugated Han Chinese population. Because they occupied the lower rungs of the banner population, they were not (at least in law) allowed to intermarry with other banner groups. They were thus multiply marginal to Qing society. Qing emperors found bondservants useful precisely because this marginality made them completely dependent on the throne for their status.

Bondservants, *booi* (belonging to the household) in Manchu, were a hereditarily servile people registered in the banners.[18] The status of *booi* was not very different from that of slaves, who were called *aha* in Manchu or *booi aha*. Both *aha* and *booi* were legally defined servile groups in the Qing. Most were descended from Chinese and other northeastern residents who had been taken captive during the conquest period and divided among the banner nobles, like other booty.[19] Whereas *aha* worked in fields, *booi* were in domestic service. Some bore arms and fought in battle during the conquest period alongside their masters. By 1636 they were enrolled in the developing banners as separate units.[20]

After the upper three banners—the Bordered Yellow, Plain Yellow, and Plain White—were taken over by the emperor, *booi* in these banners became the emperor's household servants. With the Manchu conquest their activities were "elevated from a family level to a state level of operations."[21] Bondservants were enrolled in special bondservant companies, headed by *guanling* (in Manchu, *booi da*) and *zuoling*. In its mature form, a bondservant banner was made up of twenty-nine (later thirty) companies.[22] Bondservant *guanling* (with their underlings) were assigned to manage the affairs of the emperor's consorts and grown sons. The empress dowager and empress were each assigned thirty *guanling*, who rotated in the post; the affairs of an emperor's son and his wife were handled by one *guanling*. Extra *guanling* would handle matters when the emperor and court moved to Chengde, traveled to the ancestral tombs, or resided in the imperial villas.[23] Especially in the early Qing, the Household Division staffed by bondservants was used to guard different parts of the Forbidden City.[24]

Booi in Palace Posts   The term *baitangga* apparently first meant "applicable, useful" but later came to denote an "errand boy, handyman, underling." According to Ye Zhiru, it was a catch-all term for unranked clerks in government offices, artisans, and doctors. Many *baitangga* were bondservants.[25] Archival documents show that *baitangga* were assigned to various kinds of duties.

By far the most numerous group of workers in the palace were the casual laborers, the *sula*. A Manchu term, *sula* can mean "idle, unemployed" and refers to bannermen without an official post. From the late seventeenth century, *sula* also referred to posts attached to the bondservant companies and carrying a small stipend. In 1708 150 *sula* posts were created under each *guanling*; this number was halved in 1735. Despite the low pay, *sula* posts were sought after.[26] *Sula* were hired on a short-term basis, apparently by the day, to perform varied tasks. After 1757 the Neiwufu ministers reported each month on how many *sula* had been hired. In July 1779, for example, *sula* carried trays of cakes and other offerings to the Buddhist altars; transported sacrificial vessels, musical instruments, and furniture from one place to another; swept the palace halls; and changed the water in the emperor's goldfish pond. The total number of *sula* hired that month was unusually high; 794 more laborers had been used than in June, because of the work involved in helping set up princely establishments for the emperor's eighth son, Yongxuan, Prince Yi, and his grandson Miande, Prince Ding. To move the hardwood furniture and other objects bestowed by the emperor on Yongxuan had required 246 *sula*, and another 30 to transport the ritual vessels for his *shentang* (shamanic altar).[27] To move the ritual and household goods of Miande had taken 284 *sula*, and an additional 64 *sula* to carry the fruit and cake trays commemorating his new household.

The demand for casual labor also varied by season. The first lunar month, which featured the annual gathering of officials at court, banquets for Mongol nobles, and New Year festivities, traditionally demanded large numbers of staff. So did the elaborate celebrations of the birthdays of the emperor, empress, and the empress dowager. Extra laborers were hired to pull up the grass and weeds in the "dog days" of summer. The size of the palace staff swelled during the winter solstice when the penultimate state sacrifice to Heaven took place, and in the last month of the year, when the court held numerous rites. When there were marriages of imperial grandsons managed by the Neiwufu, extra men had to be hired: such at least was the explanation in 1779 for the 1,167 extras hired during December. Extra heavy snowfalls might also require extra laborers: this was one of the factors leading to the 3,471 extra men hired in December 1781.[28]

Casual labor was one item that the Qianlong emperor kept his eye on: in 1774, for example, he ordered the agencies of the imperial household to review their need for casual laborers. The ministers suggested eight areas in which their numbers could be reduced, while defending other areas where the numbers were "barely sufficient; cannot be cut."[29] On April 5, 1778, the emperor ordered that the total number of *sula* employed in a given year should not exceed 50,000, and that the annual total should be

Table 13. Number of *Sula* in Palace Employment

Year[a]	Number of Sula	Number of Days in Reign Year[a]	Sula Employed (daily average)
1760–61	36,495	374	97.6
1800–1801	27,542	374	73.6
1820–21	32,429	354	91.6
1848–49	17,799	353	50.4

SOURCES: Reports from the ministers of the Imperial Household Department, found in Archives 446-5-55, nos. 323, 341, 429–33, and 531–34.

[a] Calculated from the lunar calendar used by the dynasty, which recorded events in terms of the reign year: 1760–61 and 1800–1801 were thirteen-month years, adjusting the lunar calendar to the solar cycle.

reported at the end of every year.[30] The 1778 edict continued to be implemented into the late nineteenth century. And the palace actually never used its full quota, which came to 133 to 141 laborers a day (table 13). By 1848 the number of *sula* being employed had been significantly reduced from the levels of earlier reigns.

Maidservants assigned to the palace residents were usually short-term inhabitants of the Forbidden City. Their status rested on the status of their master or mistress. Each member of the imperial family was assigned maids. The highest ranking female in the court was the emperor's nominal mother, the empress dowager. She had twelve "palace maids" (*gongnü*); empresses received ten maids, and so on down to the lowest ranking consort, a *daying*, who might have only one. Palace records show that despite exceptions—for example, Empress Dowager Cixi had twenty maids—the regulations were implemented most of the time.[31] The personal staffs of other imperial widows were often smaller than their allotment. For example, a 1751–52 list of the residents and staff in the Shoukang palace shows that Empress Dowager Cixuan (the Qianlong emperor's mother) had her full complement of maids, the third-ranking consort Yu had only six instead of eight maids, and several consorts of the seventh rank had only one instead of the nominal three.[32]

The number of maids in palace service depended on the size of the imperial household. During periods when there were many consorts and children, as in the Kangxi reign, there were also more maids. The archival documents show that the over 500 maids serving in the palace in 1734 represented a historical peak. During the Qianlong reign, the size of the household shrank as the emperor grew older. By the 1790s, only slightly more than 100 maids served in the palace. The number of maids increased from the Jiaqing reign onward. During the second half of the nineteenth century, between 150 and 200 maids were generally in palace service under Empress Dowager Cixi.

Maids were selected through an annual draft of the daughters of men in the upper three bondservant banners conducted by the Imperial Household Department. Each year, daughters who had reached the age of twelve *sui* were reported by the company captains for the draft and brought to the palace for inspection. After 1735, families residing far away from the capital and, after 1801, daughters of imperial wet nurses were exempted from the draft.[33] Parents became more and more reluctant to give their daughters to palace service. According to one source,

> When our daughters are taken into the palace . . . they are dead to us until they are twenty-five, when they are allowed to return home. If they are incompetent or dull they are often severely punished. They may contract diseases and die, and their death is not even announced to us; while if they prove themselves efficient and win the approval of the authorities they are retained in the palace and we may never see them or hear from them again.[34]

Nonetheless, the number of girls who were summoned was still very large. 2,092 banner daughters appeared for inspection in the 1736 draft; the number in the 1742 draft was 1,165 and hovered between 650 to 850 in the 1770s through 1831, falling below 500 thereafter.[35]

As could be anticipated, by far the largest group—in one draft, 82.3 percent—of girls brought up for the *gongnü* draft were daughters of *sula*. Another sizable group had fathers who "wore armor" (*pijia*) referring to foot soldiers in the banner forces; less than 5 percent belonged to other status.[36] A list of 110 maidservants in palace employment in September 1885 shows only a slightly different picture, with 33 percent from *sula*, 35 percent from foot soldiers, and 17 percent from Guards Division families.[37]

Banner girls selected as maids served a set term, during which they would receive a stipend and food allowances. Maids were generally young, frequently thirteen to fifteen years of age. Except for the very few who, despite prohibitions (see chapter 4) entered the emperor's harem, maids left at the end of five (later ten) years of service. The Kangxi emperor ordered that all maids thirty *sui* and over should be released to their parents to be married; the age limit was lowered to twenty-five by his son. On discharge at the end of their service they were rewarded with a lump sum of twenty taels of silver and released to their families to be given in marriage. And on occasion the emperors themselves arranged betrothals of bannermen to maids.[38]

Bondservant society was also complex and hierarchical. Bondservants in the upper three banners could serve in the Guards Division (*hujun*) and the Vanguard Division (*qianjun*). They could become banner officers, take the examinations and enter the bureaucracy, or fill important positions within the Neiwufu. Since the textile factories in Suzhou and Hangzhou were under this department, bondservants did not all work in Peking. Some bondservants held powerful supervisory posts, were wealthy, and owned slaves; a fictional depiction of the lifestyle of this bondservant elite can be found in the Qing novel *Honglou meng* (Story of the stone). Other bondservants occupied menial positions. And at the bottom of the Neiwufu bondservant banner population, below it, were the state slaves, or *sinjeku*.

State Slaves

The Manchu term *sinjeku* first appears in a 1622 order that the Han Chinese soldiers captured at Fushun should be enrolled in special *sinjeku* companies. After 1644 the *sinjeku* status became a punishment imposed on persons found guilty of major economic and political crimes. Enslavement was one of the most extreme forms of punishment in the Qing criminal code. Unlike *booi*, who could be manumitted by their masters, *sinjeku* were public property, and the masters to whom they were assigned were not permitted to sell them or grant them freedom.[39] Although the *sinjeku* were granted the same status under criminal law as the *booi* in 1738, they continued to rank below the bondservants.[40] By the Kangxi to Qianlong reigns, *sinjeku* were enrolled in all eight banners, but only those registered in the upper three banners were eligible for palace service.

Sinjeku came from diverse backgrounds. Many were unemployed bannermen or foot soldiers who were enslaved for bad debts, others were bannermen who failed to rectify deficits in government accounts while in office. One document presenting cases dating from 1661 to 1735 lists 170 individuals, whose wives, sons, sons' wives, and other family members—a total of 762 dependents—were converted into *sinjeku*.[41] With two exceptions all were bannermen. Seventy percent of those punished for bureaucratic crimes were Chinese bannermen (Hanjun), perhaps because they were favored for local administrative posts: 64 percent of these bannermen served in local or provincial posts, as compared to 16 percent of the Manchus. By contrast Manchus dominated the category of political crimes: 64 percent of this group belonged to Manchu banners, and only 14 percent were Chinese bannermen.[42] Some of the most illustrious conquest noble families had descendants who were so disgraced. Among those convicted of failing to compensate the government for deficits in official accounts were two descendants of Shang Kexi, Prince Pingnan, of conquest fame, and a descendant of the great Eidu, companion of Nurgaci.[43]

Of the Chinese bannermen enslaved for bureaucratic crimes, only 8 percent were assigned to the Imperial Household Department registers, as compared to 100 percent of the Manchu slaves. The same practice of sending Chinese bannermen to estates and the Manchus and Mongols to the capital companies under the imperial household prevailed for those guilty of political crimes. That Manchus and Mongols were favored over their Chinese banner counterparts—palace service meant easier living conditions and opportunities for winning redemption through imperial favor— is highlighted by the rare exceptions to this practice. The fall in 1718 of Zhutianbao, who had pleaded with the aged Kangxi emperor for the reinstatement of Yinreng as heir apparent, also brought down two Manchus in the Plain Red Banner. Zhutianbao's father and Changlai were permanently put in a cangue—a heavy wooden board placed around the neck, a sort of portable pillory; their twenty-four dependents were made *sinjeku*, barred from serving in the Forbidden City, and sent instead to the frontier to undertake hard duty.[44]

During the Yongzheng reign, Hanjun *sinjeku* were assigned to banner units on the imperial estates, where they tilled the vegetable and melon gardens; they performed "the most menial physical tasks" and occupied the lowest social status in the bondservant banners. The movement of state slaves into the Neiwufu's banner units also provided labor for imperial establishments.[45] Whereas most Chinese bannermen who became state slaves were placed on the imperial estates, virtually all Manchu and Mongol *sinjeku* were registered under the *guanling* of the Neiwufu, where they formed a labor pool for palace service. Women of *sinjeku* status were also assigned to the palace ladies and imperial children to light the lamps, fetch the "washing the face water," do needlework, and prepare noodles or cakes or offerings for the altars. In 1723 and 1736, a total of 5,193 *sinjeku* women were employed on such tasks in the Forbidden City; in 1750, the number had risen slightly, to include 5,440 persons. These figures did not include the *sinjeku* women performing similar chores at the imperial mausolea and palaces in Mukden, a total of 4,232 in 1681.[46]

Banner Servants

Wet nurses and nurses occupied the most prestigious status in the female side of the servant quarters. Each of the emperor's sons and daughters had at least two and sometimes three wet nurses.[47] An intimate relationship often developed between master and servant, giving occupants of these posts opportunities for upward mobility. Wet nurses—the Manchu term was *meme eniye,* abbreviated by imperial fiat in 1736 to *memeniye*—were selected from among the wives of bannermen (including bondservants). According to regulations, names of nursing mothers would be submitted by the banner captains and overseers. When a woman was chosen, her own child would be fed by another wet nurse specially selected for that purpose. Wet nurses tended to be fairly young—in one list of seventy-two candidates, the average age was slightly over thirty-one *sui*—and the status of their husbands seems to have represented the whole range of banner ranks, from the unemployed on up.[48]

Wet nurses were well treated. In 1651 the Shunzhi emperor conferred the honorary sixth rank of nobility on the husbands of his three wet nurses, along with the privilege of transmitting the title for three generations. The Kangxi emperor also bestowed a title on his father's wet nurse and ordered that she be buried with the honors due a duke's wife. Wet nurses received cemetery plots near the imperial mausolea, commemorative steles, cemetery guards, and fields whose rental income would be used for mortuary rites. The Qianlong emperor gave his wet nurses a modest residence and 1,000 taels of silver.[49]

Wet nurses' husbands tended to receive purely honorary posts, with some notable exceptions. Although Manduri, a bondservant in the Bordered Yellow Banner, won his freedom through battle valor, he probably owed his honorary title and post in the Imperial Household Department to his wife, who was the Shunzhi emperor's wet nurse. The ancestor of the author of *Honglou meng,* Cao Xueqin, was Cao Xi. Cao Xi received promotion and founded the Cao family fortune because his wife, née Sun, was the Kangxi emperor's wet nurse. A granddaughter of theirs eventually married a Manchu prince.[50]

The son of a wet nurse of the Yongzheng emperor, Haiboo, rose to become a minister of the Imperial Household Department and superintendent of the Suzhou Imperial Textile Factory. Caught embezzling 220,000 taels of silver in 1740 while serving in the latter office, Haiboo would by rights have been severely punished. Bannermen guilty of much lesser crimes had been executed or imprisoned, and their dependents enslaved. But, the emperor mused, "I think of the merit of his mother, who was my father's wet nurse ... if I completely confiscated Haiboo's estate, what would his wife and children live on? They would have nothing with which to carry on the rites for his mother." Eventually, almost two years later, the emperor concluded Haiboo's case: "He ought to be heavily punished, but I can't bear to do it. He is pardoned."[51]

Nurses (*mamari* in Manchu; *baomu* in Chinese) played a more supervisory role. All the palace dependents, the empress dowager included, had nurses assigned to their staffs. According to regulations, *mamari* were recruited from childless wives of men in the Neiwufu's bondservant divisions; in reality, some nurses had children. The post tended to be assigned to older women, who continued their duties for unspecified periods of time. As with wet nurses, we know most about *mamari* from the lucky individuals serving future emperors, who received a residence, silver, grave land, ritual lands, and grave guards from their grateful charges.[52]

Nurses could also enjoy close relationships with their charges. One example is Sumalagu, a Manchu woman who taught the future Kangxi emperor his first Manchu letters and later served his son Yintao. A serving woman on the staff of Xuanye's grandmother Empress Dowager Xiaozhuang, Sumalagu was sent to oversee the young child's well-being when he was being reared outside the palace. Manchu-language documents indicate that the empress dowager called Sumalagu *gege*, a polite term that was also applied to the princesses. The Kangxi emperor called her "mother" (*eniye*); his children referred to her as "mama," a term of respect for a woman in one's grandmother's generation. When Sumalagu died in 1705, Yintao insisted on performing many funerary rituals for her in person, saying, "She raised me since I was little, and I have not been able to repay her."[53]

Companions

When imperial sons and grandsons entered the Palace School, they were assigned "boy companions" (*haha juse*) and *anda* (both are Manchu terms). The boy companions seem in fact to have been older—over age seventeen and thus adults in the Qing world—and were not companions so much as personal servants who accompanied the young princes to their classes. Selected from the banners, the *haha juse* rotated in their duties, which continued even after their masters married and set up separate households. A memorial dated March 30, 1821, shows the emperor permitting Siyanggi, a boy companion to his fourth son, Mianxin, to be released from Mianxin's service in order to take up a position in the Board of Personnel. At the time of this memorial, Mianxin was approximately sixteen years old and was already married.[54]

The Manchu term *anda* originally meant "a sworn brother, bosom friend, friend from childhood." In the Qing it designated bannermen assigned to the Palace School who taught Manchu, Mongolian, and mounted archery to the imperial sons. By the early nineteenth century, *anda* with martial skills tended to come from the northeast: "although their archery and horse riding are pure and skilled, as persons they are rustic and people look down on them."[55] Language teachers, "known as *nei anda* . . . were normally selected from among those translators in the banners who had achieved *jinshi* ranking."[56]

Anda were also banner officers whom the emperor personally selected.[57] These *anda* functioned much as tutors did among the British aristocracy and were responsible for supervising the behavior of the princes. There seem to have been both "inner" (*dorgi*) and "outer" (*tulergi*) *anda*. Since outside *anda* accompanied the imperial sons when they traveled to the ancestral tombs to perform sacrifices, they may have performed a more ceremonial function. One memorial of 1774 shows that although the thirty-five-year-old fourth prince as well as his twenty-two-year-old and fourteen-year-old brothers were accompanied by outside *anda*, the two younger princes had their inner *anda* with them, suggesting a more supervisory or tutorial role for the inner *anda*. *Anda* were set apart from the other servants of the imperial family by their relatively high status. Examples of officers appointed to this post in the middle of the eighteenth century included second-class guardsmen in the Imperial Guard and colonels and lieutenant colonels in the Guards Division.[58]

Artists and Artisans

The imperial factories (*zhizaoju*) were founded in 1661 to manufacture clothing, objets d'art, and religious objects for court use and the gift exchanges that were an integral part of the system of rulership espoused by the Manchus (see chapter 8). In 1693 the workshops (*zaobanchu*) supervised by the Imperial Household Department were expanded into fourteen units, each specializing in the production of textiles, metal, glass, enamels, leather, icons, paintings, or printed books. At their peak in the Qianlong reign, there were thirty-eight workshops, located not only in the Forbidden City but also within the imperial villas. The imperial silk factories in Suzhou, Hangzhou, and Jiangning were also part of the same administrative system.[59]

Although civilians could be hired on a temporary basis, most artisans were probably recruited from the upper three bondservant banners.[60] Many were *sinjeku*. New artisans underwent a training period of three years; those with special talent would be recognized and rewarded.[61] In 1671 the quota was set at 450 artisans and 284 short-term laborers, but with peace and prosperity the actual numbers exceeded these ceilings. The Imperial Weaving and Dyeing Office itself employed over 800 persons by the early 1730s; there were 176 silversmiths, 105 coppersmiths, 170 leather workers, and over 300 tailors in the palace workshops. The number of artisans thus employed by the palace has been estimated at 10,000 persons, with 7,000 employed in the Hangzhou, Suzhou, and Jiangning workshops alone, and additional short-term and long-term temporary workers.[62]

In addition to recruiting artisans from servile statuses, the palace workshops employed skilled craftsmen from the Han Chinese commoner population. Furniture produced for the palace included "ornate, pseudo-rococo designs" reminiscent of the "Canton style" in furniture. Skilled glassblowers from Boshan, Shandong, introduced a new technique to make enameled glassware and painted enamels. Cantonese who had learned European glassmaking techniques were brought in to create the snuff bottles, ornaments, and objets d'art that the emperor bestowed on imperial relatives, high officials, and embassies from tributary states. The palace artisans produced enameled porcelains with European motifs, copied presumably from originals presented to the court. A notion of the volume of items produced is provided by a 1755 order for 500 snuff bottles and 3,000 other items to be used as gifts during the emperor's sojourn in Rehe.[63]

Chinese glass-making technology was apparently sufficiently advanced to make the production of enameled glassware a relatively simple matter. That was not the case with painted enamelware. The technique of painted enamelware, developed in mid-fifteenth century Flanders, was introduced into China through European presentations that caught the Kangxi emperor's eye. When the emperor sought skilled workers who could reproduce this technique, he had the governor of Guangdong province himself search for skilled artisans and inquired amongst the Jesuits. Father Ripa and Giuseppe Castiglione, whom the emperor ordered into the palace workshop, failed the test (perhaps deliberately); not until 1719, when a French enamel master, Jean Baptiste Gavereau, arrived, was "acceptable" enameled metal ware produced in the palace. Required for imperial use on all tours of the provinces, painted enamelware was used at funerals, births, weddings, at the first-rank sacrifices, and as gifts to worthy officials.[64]

Because of its long and intimate links with Han Chinese literati culture, painting at court was a form of patronage with which emperors wooed literati to the support of the new dynasty. Chinese artists were invited to the court from the Shunzhi reign; some were appointed to high office in the Kangxi reign. The over two hundred painters working in the palace from the late seventeenth through the eighteenth century included, especially before 1736, Hanlin academicians and degree-holders, as well as famous artists like Gao Shiqi (1645–1704), whose residence in the Nanshufang (southern study) lent luster to the court.[65] Among those hired specifically as court artists were the Jesuits. One of the most famous was Castiglione, who worked at the Qing court from his arrival on November 22, 1715, to his death on June 10, 1766. Castiglione developed a synthesis of Western and Chinese style (called *xianfa* in Chinese) and taught it to his students in the court painting academy. Castiglione painted imperial portraits, worked in enamel, jade, and lacquer, and provided Europeanized designs for the Qianlong emperor's villa, Yuanmingyuan. He rose to become chief painter at court and an official of the Neiwufu.[66]

Many other Europeans served at the Qing court from the late seventeenth to the late eighteenth centuries. The Jesuits sent priests who were skilled in various genres of painting. Father Benoit, writing in 1773, described the Yuanmingyuan, where "at the entrance to the gardens is located the Ruyi guan, which is the place where the Chinese and European painters, European watchmakers who create automations or other machines, gemstone workers and ivory makers work."[67] While the Jesuits undertook these labors as a means to the hoped-for Christian conversion of the ruler and thence of the whole population, the Qing emperors viewed their European staff as a palpable manifestation of their status as the rulers of a multiethnic empire, collecting tribute from all corners of the globe. From their point of view, the employment of Europeans in the palace workshops was proof of the correctness of their claims to be *khaghans*—the khans of khans—and not just emperors on the Chinese model. That these Europeans were at the beck and call of the emperor is very clear from another account of how Frère Attiret was suddenly called to Rehe in 1754 to paint the Zunghar chieftains who had come over to the Qing side.[68]

The artists, artisans, and other skilled persons working for the Imperial Household Department were truly international in their composition. About two hundred Tibetans, captured during the Jinquan campaigns, were brought to Peking during the Qianlong reign. Although most were stone masons who built a Tibetan-style watchtower in the Western Hills where the Qing troops could be drilled over terrain resembling the battleground in Sichuan, Tibetan craftsmen specializing in the production of silver, wooden, and painted religious art as well as Tibetan translators, dancers, and singers were also installed in workshops within the Forbidden City and enrolled in a Imperial Household Department banner company.[69]

There were also Uighurs working for the court. After 1759 Uighur craftsmen who were skilled in creating jade and gold objects, dancers, and singers were brought to Peking and were also enrolled in a banner company under the Neiwufu. During the Qianlong reign, over three hundred Uighurs worked for the court and resided in a "Uighur camp" inside the Tartar city.[70]

The actors employed by the palace fell under the jurisdiction of the Nanfu (court theatrical bureau), which was created about 1740. After 1751, when the emperor decided to recruit actors from Suzhou and Yangzhou, a Jingshan office was established for drama. During the 1820s the Nanfu and Jingshan were merged into the Shengpingshu, which trained eunuchs for theatricals and provided court entertainment. In its heyday during the Qianlong reign, there were "well over 1,000 actors providing entertainment for the imperial family."[71] The court's drama troupes trained and rehearsed within the Forbidden City, the imperial villas in the Western Hills outside the capital, and in the emperor's summer retreat at Rehe. Opera performances were not only a reflection of the ruler's personal taste but essential for the celebration of festive occasions such as imperial birthdays, weddings, banquets for the Mongol princes, and the annual observances at New Year's, the Lantern Festival, Dragon Boat Festival, Mid-Autumn Festival, and Guandi's feast day. Although noted opera companies and actors were invited to perform within the palace during the periods 1751–1827, 1850–61, and 1884–1911, eunuchs were the mainstay of the court's drama troupes. Eunuchs aged twelve or thirteen would be recruited for these companies and trained in the schools run by the palace staff. If they were successful, they might eventually be promoted to administrative and teaching posts within the Theatrical Bureau. Skill in acting was thus one route of upward mobility for the eunuch actors, as seen in the biography of Li Luxi, who was a longtime head of the Nanfu and its successor, the Shengpingshu, during the first half of the nineteenth century.[72]

THE PALACE BUREAUCRACY

Early Qing emperors often used the Imperial Household Department, or Neiwufu, to perform diplomatic and fiscal tasks that exceeded their primary responsibility of managing the emperor's household affairs. Staffed by banner personnel, this agency represented another check on the civil service officials in the outer court. The employment of bannermen also enabled Qing rulers to avoid the eunuchs' domination of palace administration. More than any previous dynasty, the Qing succeeded in controlling their palace servants and in mobilizing the Neiwufu to serve the throne.

The Neiwufu developed during the early seventeenth century from what seems to have been the personal household administration of Nurgaci. Some scholars believe it was created during the 1620s. By 1638 it was sufficiently institutionalized to merit a office building of its own in Mukden.[73] Temporarily supplanted by the Thirteen Eunuch Bureaus from 1653 to 1661, the Neiwufu was revived in the Kangxi reign and underwent extensive organizational expansion in 1667. The number of its officials, which stood at over 402 in 1662, had increased to 939 by 1722 and to 1,623 by 1796. Eventually, in the late nineteenth century, the department overlooked the operations of over 56 subagencies. From the middle of the seventeenth century through the rest of the dynasty, the Neiwufu also maintained offices in Mukden.[74]

The Neiwufu attained its "final, definitive form" in the Qianlong reign. Its mission as enunciated by the Yongzheng emperor was enshrined in a plaque over the entrance to its office: "Government and imperial household working in unison" (*Gongfu yiti*).[75] Under this rubric, it carried out a bewildering variety of activities. It was first and foremost the administrative unit in charge of palace affairs. It was in charge of the wardrobes, food, residences, and daily activities of the emperor and his family. It exercised jurisdiction over palace construction, security, rituals, and palace staff. But its activities extended far beyond the walls of the Forbidden City and the imperial villas. The Neiwufu was a major publisher, producing outstanding examples of printed works by imperial commission. It held monopoly rights over the profitable jade and ginseng trades. It ran textile factories in Hangzhou, Suzhou, and Jiangning that produced textiles for the court. Using the taxing powers of the state, it gathered precious objects such as sables, ermine, mink, and fox from parts of Mongolia and the northeast through the annual tribute system, reserving a portion for imperial use and disposing of the residue through the customhouses. The Imperial Household Department issued permits for the salt trade, the jade trade from Central Asia, and licensed "state merchants" to import copper for coinage during the early Qing. It issued loans at interest, acquired pawnshops, and derived revenues from its many rentals in the imperial city.[76]

Although the emperor's private funds, managed by the Guangchusi (department of the privy purse), were separated from the taxes collected by the Board of Revenue, its outer-court equivalent, these distinctions were not always honored. From the early eighteenth century, the Privy Purse received "surplus quotas" (*yingyu*) at the customhouses that taxed trade in the capital, Kalgan, Jiujiang, Hangzhou, Hushu (near Suzhou), and Canton. By the early nineteenth century, officials fearful of imperial wrath hastened to deliver approximately two million taels of silver in surplus quota each year, while the regular quota (*zheng'e*) paid into the Board of Revenue lay in arrears.[77] When officials' estates were confiscated, they frequently ended up in the hands of the Neiwufu. During the Qianlong reign, a Secret Accounts bureau in the Neiwufu collected large "fines" that officials imposed on themselves in recognition of their failure to live up to the requirements of their posts.[78] The tribute presented by emissaries from foreign countries and minority peoples within the empire became the private property of the emperor, just as the gifts he bestowed on the gift bearers were produced by the palace workshops. Finally, important elements of Qing relations with Tibet and Mongolia were handled by agencies such as the Sutra Recitation Office, lodged within the palace, rather than the Board of Rites. In all these ways, the Qing blurred the boundary between the emperor's personal affairs and the affairs of state.

The Neiwufu had its own bureaucratic regulations, which were compiled and revised at intervals throughout the dynasty.[79] Its highest officials, the ministers of the Imperial Household Department (*zongguan Neiwufu dachen*), eventually held the third rank in the eighteen-rank hierarchy of the civil service, but these officials were not Han Chinese degree-holders. The ministerial posts—there was no limit on the number of persons who could hold this title at any one time—were instead filled by Manchu princes with prior experience in the Imperial Guard (*shiwei*), especially in the position of chamberlain of the Imperial Guard (*lingshiwei nei dachen*), and by bondservants who had climbed up through service in the Neiwufu itself. The ministers thus came from quite different social status and backgrounds: some belonged to the Aisin Gioro lineage, others were of servile status. Mingling these individuals in the supervisory role served to ensure that no one group dominated the palace service.

Ministers had the overall responsibility for the functioning of the Imperial Household Department. Individual ministers were appointed on a rotating basis for one-year terms to supervise subsidiary units that were deemed to be especially sensitive, such as the Department of the Privy Purse, which was in charge of imperial revenues and expenditures as well

as the Six Vaults; the Department of Works (*yingzaosi*), the palace counterpart of the Board of Works and in charge of palace maintenance and repair;
and the Jingshifang, the unit that was in charge of the recruitment, appointment, and punishment of eunuchs. Ministers were appointed to manage the imperial villas and assigned to ritually important sites such as the
imperial cemeteries. Special supervisory officials (*guanli dachen*) were also
appointed to agencies such as the Imperial Buttery (*yuchashanfang*),
which prepared the food for the palace, the Imperial Dispensary (*yuyao-
fang*), and the Nanfu (after 1820, the Shengpingshu). They could be appointed to oversee the proper conduct of princely establishments.[80]

CONSPICUOUS CONSUMPTION

Qing rulers used bannermen, bondservants, state slaves, and eunuchs to
perform domestic tasks in the imperial household and to penetrate into
strategic areas in the Qing administration.[81] Their success in expanding
the imperial prerogative is undeniable, and important. The massiveness of
the palace establishment, however, was primarily dictated by a larger political agenda, familiar to students of kingship, the need to awe and impress
subjects.

The Qing Imperial Household Department employed more people and
engaged in many more activities than its counterparts in Europe. Its multitude of servants was not the only facet designed to awe foreigners and
Chinese alike: the type of servants it employed, notably the eunuchs, was
distinctive. The employment of eunuchs was strictly governed by sumptuary laws enacted from 1701 on. Only officials of the first two ranks and
nobles were permitted to have eunuchs. From the eighteenth century,
princely households were required to report the eunuchs in their employ
even though, after 1746, eunuchs who had been assigned to princes establishing separate households were no longer being directly paid by the Imperial Household Department.[82] To ensure that outside employers were not
harboring eunuch fugitives from palace service, nobles hiring a eunuch had
to first send the applicant's name, age, household registration, and personal
description to the two agencies in the Imperial Household Department that
were in charge of eunuchs' personnel files. Anyone who employed a eunuch who had absconded from the palace was himself investigated. Even
eunuchs who had obtained legitimate discharges were liable to punishment
and return to imperial jurisdiction.[83]

Pressure on curbing the number of eunuchs employed outside the palace seems to have increased from the Jiaqing reign. On May 15, 1799, and February 6, 1804, for example, the emperor reminded the princes that they should not exceed the quotas on the numbers of eunuchs in their households: any surplus eunuchs should be sent to the palace to be assigned to duties. In January 1819, complaining that the eunuchs appearing for palace service were too old ("twenty to thirty *sui* or older"), the emperor ordered an exchange: older eunuchs and those from areas outside Zhili should be sent to the princes' households, while the princes should each send the younger eunuchs ("under twenty *sui*") on their staffs to the palace, the number to be fixed by the prince's rank.[84] The drafting of eunuchs from princely households continued through the first part of the nineteenth century.[85]

The emperor's concern was heightened by what seems to have been a marked preference among eunuchs for the softer life of princely service. There were many cases of eunuchs fleeing palace service. Instead of asking for permission, some went home because of a sick parent; some overstayed their leave; but in their confessions the primary motive for absconding was fear of punishment after making a mistake while on duty. Despite the increasingly severe punishments, the casebooks show some eunuchs who had run away from their duties not just once or twice, but up to nine times.[86]

DOMINATION AND SUBVERSION: ARCHIVAL TRANSCRIPTS

We can discern the special concerns and anxieties of the rulers in the imperial injunctions written down in the palace regulations.[87] What emerges from their edicts is an overriding obsession with control and palace security. The lesson that Hongli, the Qianlong emperor, took from the eunuchs' excesses of the late Ming was that eunuchs' abuses emerged only when rulers failed to exert themselves in vigilance. He ordered that a history of the Qing palace regulations be compiled in order to ensure that his descendants would be familiar with the ancestral regulations that strictly controlled all eunuchs' activity. This project was begun in 1742, revised in 1759, and finally completed in 1769 as the *Guochao gong shi* (History of the Qing palace). Three copies of the work were made for deposit in the Qianqing palace, the Palace School, and the Southern Study. Later the work was copied into the *Siku quanshu*.[88]

The palace claimed jurisdiction over the servants who were employed (and paid) by princes and princesses living in their own establishments. Palace officials kept close tabs on the performance and behavior of those bondservants and eunuchs sent to manage the household affairs of the emperor's offspring, intervening to replace or punish those deemed unsatisfactory.[89] Servants who stole, assaulted one another, or fled from princely employers were eventually sent to the Judicial Department (*shenxingsi*) of the Imperial Household Department for judgment.[90]

The system of collective responsibility that applied to the civilian population also extended to palace officials. Eunuch supervisors, bondservant officials, even princes were held ultimately responsible for all matters (and personnel) under their jurisdiction, regardless of whether they had been directly involved. An example concerns the fourth daughter of the Jiaqing emperor, Princess Zhuangjing, who was married in 1802 to a Tümet Mongol prince, Manibadara. When the head of her guards was discovered accepting bribes, punishment was meted out not only to the principals but to her household steward, a minister, and a department director of the Imperial Household Department, who had been assigned to supervise her affairs.[91]

Palace security was a paramount concern. Entry and exit into the Forbidden City were subject to detailed regulation (see chapter 1). The first problem was to control the guards, who were supposed to keep all unauthorized persons from entering the grounds of the palace or the imperial villas. During the Yongzheng reign, an order prohibiting "grain shops" from selling liquor to soldiers on duty at the Donghua and Xihua gates into the Forbidden City was justified on grounds of palace security.[92] In 1766 the Qianlong emperor indignantly observed that when he went to visit the sickbed of his fifth son, he discovered the boy had received a fresh haircut from a barber who had a shop outside the Fuyuan gate. Noting that "the princes' hair should be cut by a eunuch-masseur," the emperor ordered the chief eunuch to investigate whether his other sons were also infringing the rules. "The Fuyuan gate is an area of the court, it is forbidden for outsiders to go in and out of it. If we permit the commoner barber to come to the prince's residence, the others can also summon people."[93] The chief eunuch and the *anda* of the fifth son were punished.

Strictures on persons entering the inner court applied to former palace servants. Maids were barred from revisiting the inner court after they left palace service. Servants taking sick leave were not permitted to return after they recovered. Male relatives of imperial consorts were required to ask formal permission to visit. By the Xianfeng reign, families of consorts were not allowed to "come in and out" of the palace, nor were they to send presents to their grandchildren (by the emperor).[94]

The court especially disliked the disruption and noise of large groups of outsiders entering for the annual imperial presentation of venison to the princes and high officials. As Yang Xishou reported in his 1755 memorial:

> The Forbidden City is an important place. It ought to be kept tranquil (*suqing*). Recently there have been quite a few underlings going in and out. On an occasion such as the time last year on the twenty-eighth day of the twelfth month, after Your Majesty bestowed mutton and deer meat on the princes and high officials, their servants who had been sent to take receipt of these gifts were crowded into the left side of the Wu-yingdian and suddenly pressed forward. Many of them dropped their parcels onto the ground . . . . Each year at year's end, [the emperor] gives the princes and high officials deer meat and other things . . . . The number of year-end presentations totals over three hundred. Those who come to bear the gifts away are not less than over a thousand. They jostle and drop things, which are stolen . . . . Henceforth, at the year-end distribution of deer meat, during the two days when it is distributed, all recipients should send their servants to come get it. It is not permitted to hire [outside] persons, which brings confusion. Have the captain general of the Guards Division of the banners assign a person to supervise the presentation of items that are in the Imperial Household Department storerooms. Escort the persons receiving the presents out of the gate. Thus those taking the gifts will not crowd around and we can avoid loss of the imperial gifts.[95]

There were several reasons why a scene such as the one described above would disturb the court. Large crowds provided an opportunity for thieves and others to mix in and pursue illegal activities. Worst of all, however, the confusion and jostling marred the tranquil atmosphere of the palace and symbolically polluted this sacred space, while the dropping of the imperial gifts was an act of lèse majesté. If imperial presentations were not conducted in awesome dignity, the whole point of the presentation was lost.

Security was always a difficult task, given the hundreds of persons who came into the Forbidden City every day. We have already described the system of belt tallies designed to check on workers. But how could one guard against theft on the job? Even if the item taken was trivial, such as the foodstuffs sent to Yongxuan's wife by her mother's family, the Neiwufu ministers reasoned, "if it had been other things that had been illegally consumed, how could it be tolerated?"[96] And there were certainly more serious incidents, some of which looked like insiders' fraud. On June 28, 1741, an official in charge of the silk vault inquired of the Neiwufu office about a document, issued the previous winter for 150 bolts of colored silk, which had never been returned to his office. It turned out that no such requisition had been sent by the ministers, whose forged signatures were eventually discovered on the form. Someone had managed to get away with a considerable amount of valuable material, and the ministers ordered an investigation and arrest of the persons responsible.[97]

In 1800 a young bannerman named Sandaizi was caught stealing a piece of jade. An employee of the Department of the Privy Purse's bullion vault, Sandaizi was helping to carry out objects from the storehouse for an imperial inspection when he hid a piece of jade in his clothing. After an audit disclosed that one piece of jade was missing, he tried to flee and was nabbed by the guards at the gate. It turned out that the stolen jade was of low quality, being assigned to the fourth grade (earlier the officials had recommended that all but first-grade jades in the storehouse should be sold), and Sandaizi received a correspondingly modified sentence of ninety strokes, exile for two and one-half years, and removal from the banner rolls.[98]

The system of mutual responsibility was at least partially successful in discouraging collusion. An 1832 memorial reported on a eunuch, Wang Deshun, who stole bolts of silk gauze from his post in the Anlanyuan because he wanted to send money to his family to help pay for his nephew's wedding expenses. When Wang was caught, he was confronted by his immediate superior, *fushouling* Zhang Jingui, who was his relative (*qinshu*). The two men were alone; Zhang let Wang go.[99]

One night in 1775 a thief was arrested inside the gate of the Ningshou palace. The emperor was horrified: "The palace is an important place. That thieves should dare to enter it and steal is a very evil matter." He ordered a detailed interrogation of the culprit: how had the man dared to enter the palace to steal? Did he have accomplices on the inside, and was he also responsible for the previous losses of silver from the vaults? Eventually not only the unsuccessful thief, but the chief eunuch as well as his underlings were punished; the three eunuchs who caught the thief were rewarded.[100]

That outsiders could independently penetrate the innermost recesses of the Forbidden City was alarming. Still worse was the discovery in 1851 of eunuchs smuggling in unauthorized persons. Bai Sanxi, who wanted to go home, smuggled out a belt tally from the Southern Study (his duty assignment) and gave it to Bai Da, who used it to enter the Forbidden City. Belt tallies and vouchers were the palace's attempt to curb pilferage, and the flouting of the system was always alarming.[101] The damage done in this case was minor, and all participants were punished; but reports of other incursions revealed the chilling prospect of an autonomous free-flowing society of service personnel that existed despite the best imperial precautions and most detailed rules.

Consider the brouhaha that ensued on the night of July 22, 1801, when a fire broke out at approximately 9 P.M. in a dormitory (in Manchu, *tadan*) outside the Baotai gate in the northeastern quadrant of the Forbidden City. The minister of the Imperial Household Department on duty, receiving a report from the night duty clerk, hastened to the palace, but the Shenwu gate was closed and he could not enter. The captain general of the Guards Division on duty, Danbadorji, had soldiers snuff out the fire, but a small house was destroyed. Since fires were greatly feared, a detailed investigation was ordered. The inhabitants of the dormitory were Wang Xi, a eunuch assigned to the Ningshou palace, Zhang Lao, a cook for the dormitory, and a *sula*, Si'er. The testimony of the cook proved to be the key to the case. Zhang Lao, a man of 58 *sui*, had been cooking at this dormitory for over twenty years. He said,

> On the southern side of the kitchen in the sleeping quarters are put miscellaneous equipment such as broken steamers and lamps, there are also leftover kaoliang stalks and rice husks to feed the pigs. No one lives there. In the courtyard are five pigs raised by eunuch Wang Xi, I feed them every day. On the eleventh of this month, at dusk, when I went to close the pigpen I saw that the pigs had gone into the sleeping quarters. When I went in to chase them out, I did not realize that the embers from the tobacco that I was smoking had fallen there. At the changing of the watch I heard someone outside shouting that there was a fire. We all went with the official and soldiers to stamp it out. I've thought about it and no one else entered, so it must have been my tobacco fire that lit the stalks.

The ministers decided that both Zhang Lao and Wang Xi were guilty— the first for starting the fire, and the second for infringing the prohibition on raising livestock inside the Forbidden City! The pigs were sold and the proceeds put into the government coffers. Moreover, the eunuch supervisors and chief eunuch were also punished; only Si'er escaped without punishment.[102]

Another glimpse of the normally subterranean servant world was obtained on June 15, 1760, when the body of an unknown person was discovered in the moat by the Jinshui bridge. Investigation revealed that the drowned man was a commoner, Li San. What was a commoner doing within the Imperial City? Testimony from the guards and the *sula* who were also assigned to prepare tea showed not only that he was well known, but that he was one of four commoners who, contrary to regulations, earned a living preparing tea for the guards at the nearby Taihe gate. Li San's father had "served seventy years at the gate," so the custom was one of long standing. Not only was he working in forbidden territory, he was sleeping in the dormitory used by the guards' servants. When the interrogators asked, "You are commoners, how dare you take up duties in the palace! Someone must have hired you to illegally substitute [for a bannerman]," they learned that the practice dated "from the Kangxi reign, we don't know what year. No one hired us, it's simply that our service to the guards is careful, cheaper, and more responsive than that of the officials." The benefits of palace employment were also spelled out: "Each day the guards give us their leftover food; at each festival they bestow presents, so we rely on this for a living, we didn't hire on to substitute." For the ministers who summarized the case, the fact that commoners who ought not to be working inside the palace were coming in and out without the least fear or constraint was "terrible." The discovery of these long-term illegal arrangements prompted the emperor to order each agency of the Imperial Household Department to check its employment lists to ensure against similar infringements. Commoners must be fired and replaced by *sula;* the dormitories must be checked to ensure that unauthorized persons were kept out.[103] This category included eunuchs' "sons."[104]

The illegal arrangements uncovered by the drowning of Li San were alarming because they raised questions concerning the extent to which the imperial will was defied or ignored. Other discoveries were more directly linked to theft of state property. On the night of July 25, 1820, an officer of the court coming on night duty saw a flock of sheep loose in an area of the palace where the animals should not have been wandering. His report sparked an investigation, that sought to discover whether government meat was being illegally siphoned off by the eunuchs of the Imperial Buttery, or whether the eunuchs were simply guilty of carelessness in carrying out their duties.[105] The suspicion of the first possibility, reinforced by previous incidents, was of course what always drove the emperor to demand more and more detail on these seemingly innocuous episodes.

Tracking the imperial concern for palace security has led us into the realm of what James Scott terms "hidden transcripts."[106] The imperial edicts concerning palace regulations and the criminal case reports in the archives provide direct insights into the emperor's response to the subversion of the normative order. In striking—the rulers would have said, dismaying—contrast to the official ideal, servants were not grateful recipients of their masters' instructions and orders but unruly, self-absorbed creatures who actively created a society of their own that the rulers only occasionally glimpsed. The dignity and tranquillity of the inner court, and hence of the master's peace, were upset when servants quarreled and loudly cursed each other. For obvious reasons, there were laws against servants pulling out weapons in quarrels with other palace personnel. A minor altercation about his duty assignment caused Liu Tianguang, a secretary in the Imperial Medical Department (*taiyiyuan*) to lose his temper and threaten to commit suicide. Unfortunately for Liu, a guard injured himself in grabbing the knife that Liu flourished, and Liu was punished for "conducting quarrels within the court."[107]

Less obviously, the law punished self-inflicted injury resulting from quarrels. Suicides were very closely investigated, lest there be a cover-up of fraud, theft, or murder.[108] When an angry servant killed another servant, not only the perpetrator but his nominal superiors were punished. In a case in 1798 a young eunuch was killed by his fellow worker. The murderer was immediately executed by strangulation; his supervisors were beaten; the chief of the Office of Eunuch Affairs and an assistant chief were stripped of their posts and beaten; and the chief eunuch was fined.[109]

Violence instigated by servants was not tolerated; neither was extortion. Eunuchs were not permitted to leave their employer's house without permission, precisely in order to deny them opportunities to move freely in commoner society seeking advantage. The difference between their nominally low social status and the social reality was clear in these cases and derived from the fact that, as servants who carried out the emperor's will, eunuchs had the authority to override the demands of any palace resident who tried to break palace rules. In 1778 Chief Eunuch Wang Chengxiang reported to the emperor that consort Ming *guiren* had asked Wang to send a eunuch to the residence of her elder brother. Wang had rejected her request, and the emperor supported his decision.[110]

Eunuchs were to ensure that their charges obeyed the regulations for the Qing imperial family and stayed out of trouble. Even the emperor's mother was supposed to ask for her son's consent before taking any action outside the Forbidden City. In 1736, shortly after he ascended the throne, Hongli scolded his mother's two senior eunuchs for failing to report her plans to repair the Shuntian prefectural Dongyue temple. He noted:

> All palace matters must have my approval. How can temple renovations be regarded as part of filiality? If the outside world learns that the empress dowager is repairing temples, monks will use their status as a pretext to make untimely demands for aid. We cannot let this become a custom. If in future there is an infant ruler who is ignorant of the rule concerning outside affairs, this may also cause harm to the state . . . .
> If there is a recurrence of this kind, where the senior eunuchs do not memorialize the throne before taking action, I will not treat it lightly.[111]

Hongli's desire to control all decisions on major projects is most instructive. Here is an emperor renowned for his filiality (see chapter 4) and famous for renovating temples (see chapter 1). The issue was not patronage of popular religion: as chapters 6, 7, and 8 point out, Qing emperors supported a wide variety of religions. Hongli was merely setting the tone for his reign. "All palace matters must have my approval" meant precisely that. No one, not even his beloved mother, was exempt.

Eunuchs were thus bound to serve their charges but also told to overrule them by invoking the imperial authority. Imperial authority gave them power outside the palace, and some tried to take advantage. Liu Fu was a eunuch in the employ of an imperial agnate without noble title. He visited the prefect in his home locality riding in a sedan chair, with a retinue. Liu stated that he was appearing on behalf of his deceased nephew, who had been beaten to death by a local scholar, and was asking the prefect to "speedily conclude the case." The prefect interpreted this request as an attempt to extort funds from the defendant in the murder case and arrested Liu. Even though Liu protested his innocence ("I sought some money to buy a coffin to bury the corpse"), his deposition showed that he had taken care to state his connection with the imperial family through his employer when introducing himself to the official, and he admitted that the reason for which he had requested leave—to visit his ancestral graves—was a pretext. The officials decided that Liu Fu should pay the penalty for extortion. They also ordered that his master be punished for failing to control his eunuch.[112]

The descriptions of eunuchs brought to trial for extortion reveal that it was not just their attempt to use their connections at court for personal profit that was objectionable. Equally repugnant to the masters, whose perspective dominates the documents, was the overstepping of social boundaries involved in taking on the appurtenances of their masters' rank. Liu Fu's entourage and his sedan chair aped the customary norm for officials and nobles. In perhaps the most famous extortion case of all, involving Chief Eunuch An Dehai, it was not just a symbolic but a real breaking down of boundaries that precipitated his arrest and execution.

An Dehai (1844–69) rose to become a favorite of Empress Dowager Cixi in the 1860s. In 1869 she sent him to supervise the Imperial Textile Factory at Nanking, a post heretofore reserved for bondservants. An Dehai went to his new assignment via the Grand Canal, on a boat flying the imperial insignia. "So encouraged was he by the respect which the over-awed officials of Zhili had shown him that he engaged women to play music on the boats and demanded services and bribes from local magistrates."[113] His activities in Shandong were reported to Peking by the governor, Ding Baochen, who arrested him for fraudulently claiming he was on an imperial mission. He and six other eunuchs in his party were speedily executed; the others were enslaved and banished to Heilongjiang. Historians interpret his demise as part of the inner court's political struggle between Cixi and Prince Gong; what is also clear is the degree to which the appointment of a eunuch to a post outside the palace heightened the tension resulting from the contradiction between his despised status and his real power.[114]

Some Chinese scholars note that the Qing dynasty did not experience usurpation of power by eunuchs until the second half of the nineteenth century, when a series of infant rulers ensured that real power lay in the hands of women. Although Empress Dowager Cixi's role in Qing rule is susceptible to several interpretations (see chapter 4), the gender constraints in Chinese society suggest that eunuchs were probably better able to monopolize access to the ruler under the Empress Dowager Cixi than they could under emperors.[115]

Departing from the traditional view of eunuchs as greedy unscrupulous parasites, scholars in the People's Republic of China portray them as a miserable, isolated pariah class, cut off from the mainstream, whose old age was likely to be economically precarious and lonely.[116] Of course, some eunuchs supervised other palace servants, attained high posts, and got rich. When one eunuch, Liang Jiugong, was implicated in a crime in 1712, his slaves and servants successfully concealed some of Liang's estate for several decades by registering Liang's farms and houses under the servants' names. Zhang Xiangzhai, another eunuch, was a well-to-do owner of a number of silk stores in Peking and Tientsin after he left the palace in 1913; he also served as a bank manager in his second career.[117]

The majority of eunuchs, however, never attained supervisory ranks or won favor with a powerful palace resident. They were always vulnerable to arbitrary punishments ranging from money fines, calculated in terms of a eunuch's monthly stipend, all the way up to execution. Beatings were very common, as were sentences to cut grass (zhacao), sometimes for life. Eunuchs were occasionally put in confinement. More frequently, they were banished to Heilongjiang.[118] The most frequent prosecution was for runaway eunuchs, who would be confined to the palace area and assigned to cut grass for a year. A second attempt to flee was always treated with greater severity: in 1779 the ministers noted that whereas the punishment for first-time escapees was to cut grass for one year, then transfer to a unit outside the palace, the punishment for the second try should be three years of grass cutting, then assignment outside the palace. The more normal sentence, found in another two-time loser's case of 1796, seems to have been two years, and banishment to Ili as a slave, for a third failed attempt. These kinds of sentences could be combined with beatings and periods in the cangue.[119]

The emperor could and did confer honors, estates, and privileges on "meritorious" servants.[120] At certain times he could and did pardon criminals (including servants). He could and sometimes did chastise servants for trivial offenses: unseemly behavior in the emperor's presence during the sacrificial ritual, or while his procession was passing by.[121] Virtually anything that caught the emperor's attention was dangerous. The question, "What were the reasons for today's sacrificial meat being raw and tough?" brought punishment not only for the eunuchs who were in charge of the preparations and their supervisors, but recommendations extending punishment to officials of the Imperial Buttery, their supervisors, and the ministers of the Imperial Household Department. That may have been because of an earlier incident in 1731, when eunuchs had in fact sold the meat provided for imperial sacrifices to get money.[122]

The right to punish was an imperial monopoly. The emperor would not tolerate attempts by others to take the prerogative on themselves. Earlier we noted that eunuchs assigned to supervise the household staffs of princesses were reported (and punished) for excessive use of force on underlings. The injunctions also applied to the emperor's relatives and consorts. In a notorious case in 1778, the Qianlong emperor summoned his grand councillors and the princes to the western hall of the Yangxin palace to pronounce on the punishment of one of his concubines, Dun *fei*. Dun *fei*, née Wanggiya, was the daughter of a banner lieutenant general. Entering the harem when she was seventeen, this consort was successively promoted in 1768, 1771, and 1774 before giving birth to the emperor's tenth daughter (1775). Her beating of a maidservant to death was "a rare occurrence," indeed the first case of its kind, and hence important for setting an example for others.

The emperor noted, "I have the authority of life and death in the empire, but I have never beat a servant to death in a rage . . . previously when the eunuchs Hu Shicai and Ruyi angered me, I punished them lightly with twenty to forty strokes." "Matters concerning people's lives are not to be lightly handled"; both "human sentiment and the law" must be satisfied. The ruler must not show favoritism in such a case: "even though Dun *fei* received my favor, now she has committed an offense . . . no special exceptions will be made." Dun *fei* was reduced one rank; the eunuchs who were in supervisory posts were also punished, and the consort was ordered to pay half of their fines as well as a compensatory sum of 100 taels to the parents of the deceased maid.[123]

The Manchu rulers were also very sensitive to abrogations of the status hierarchy. Eunuchs were of low status; the Kangxi emperor once stated, "eunuchs are only good for performing menial tasks within the palace and nothing else." In 1769 the Qianlong emperor, infuriated at what he considered to be the overeducation of eunuchs in the Eunuch School, said that "literacy only makes it easier for eunuchs . . . to satisfy their own greed and ambitions . . . . All they need to be able to do is to recognize a few characters and that's all."[124] Eunuchs should not be permitted to use their positions to inflict punishments on those who were their social superiors. When Prince Lü died in 1763, his title was given to Yongcheng, the fourth son of the Qianlong emperor. Yongcheng, in deference to the wishes of his new foster mother, retained Zong Fuqing in charge of household affairs. But the eunuch "suddenly put himself forward without restraint, recklessly took on an air of self-consequence, and behaved with unrestrained indulgence." He ordered third- and fourth-rank Imperial Household Department officials to kneel before him, scolded them, "and treated them as though they were nothing." He even had banner corporals beaten: as the Neiwufu minister Yinglian pointed out, "Although the corporals (*lingcui*) are of low rank, they are still bannermen," and "a eunuch is not the person who ought to beat them." If unchecked, such behavior would cause other eunuchs in the household to "also become more reckless in their behavior"; Zong must be punished as a warning to others.[125]

The normative order was upset not only when social inferiors took it on themselves to punish their nominal superiors, but when servants became too friendly with each other. Consider the Xianfeng emperor's comments in 1855 when he punished low-ranking consort (*changzai*) Bin. Not only did she cruelly mistreat a maid, she was guilty of "chatting and joking" with a eunuch. Consort Bin was stripped of her rank and demoted to maidservant status. In his edict the emperor warned palace residents (eunuchs as well as palace women) against fraternization.[126]

Palace women (including consorts and maids) were prohibited from setting up fictive kin relations with eunuchs. Any palace woman who called a palace eunuch by terms like "uncle" or "brother" would be severely punished, and her relatives as well. The Qing rulers also repeatedly ordered that eunuchs should not be permitted to collect for idle gossip. Eunuchs should not mingle freely with the transport workers employed on the emperor's visits to Chengde or elsewhere, lest they transmit gossip about the inner court to outsiders. The rulers sought to control information concerning the inner court by ordering that eunuchs from the palace not be allowed to mingle with those employed in princely households. Even the eunuch supervisors were ordered not to enter their masters' rooms when they had no business, to stand around, or to chat.[127]

Worst of all were the instances when eunuchs or servants forgot themselves so far as to impinge on the imperial dignity. Such an instance occurred during a congratulatory rite within the inner court in 1801 when Chief Eunuch Zhang Jinxi not only failed to instruct the eunuch supervisors on their proper place but dared to stand along with the imperial sons at the head of the steps. As the memorialist requesting punishment put it, "This amounts to disorder (*luan*) and is not just a case of error."[128]

The concept of order, used frequently in Confucian discourse on the civilizing mission of rulership, is pregnant with meaning concerning the ideal society, in which individuals realize and live up to the normative content of their social roles. The reverse, chaos or disorder, results when individuals overstep the boundaries of their place in society. Observing the concept, eunuchs' behavior toward officials and commoners should be as proper as toward the princes and the emperor. As the Kangxi emperor wrote, "Eunuchs are the lowest status, persons like ants: how dare they not stand up when they see an official or guard? To bow slightly while squatting is extremely ill-behaved. Henceforth let them stand up respectfully." Another time some eunuchs sat down at a banquet while the assembled princes and high officials were still standing. This too was a breach of the rules that was punished.[129]

The "overstepping of bounds" by eunuchs was clearly manifested when they donned unauthorized clothing. As noted in chapter 1, the sumptuary dress code that governed officials, princes, and palace inhabitants was jealously preserved by the rulers, who monopolized the right to make exceptions. The Kangxi emperor had strenuously objected when he saw young eunuchs wearing the red hats reserved for their masters. In the same vein, chief eunuchs and others might wear leopard skin hats but not leopard skin jackets. Remarking that "ceremonial clothes are graded to distinguish superior from inferior," the Xianfeng emperor prohibited eunuchs from wearing robes embroidered with the "rivers and mountains" motif unless they were imperial gifts.[130]

The imperial response to (admittedly rare) instances of social inversion can be seen in the young Qianlong emperor's edict, shortly after his father's death in 1735, punishing his father's chief eunuch. The edict begins:

> There is . . . an unchanging etiquette for superiors and inferiors that should be respectfully implemented . . . . How can one override this? Eunuchs are rustic ignorant people of very low status who, upon entering the palace, receive ranks not because of their merit but as an act of imperial grace . . . . You [eunuchs] should think about your place and be respectful, you should pay attention and constantly be in fear and trembling, so as to forever receive the imperial grace and escape punishment . . . now, because the princes are still young, you behave negligently. For example, Su Peisheng is an ignorant fellow. He obtained Father's favor and was made a chief eunuch of the fourth rank, not through his own merit. Yet he did not have the proper gratitude, and he dared to behave recklessly. Sometimes he does only a half-kneel in front of my brothers when he "pays respects," or he joins his hands; he even sits down and converses with Prince Zhuang, he is without any propriety! [131]

What angered the emperor was the unwonted familiarity between "the Kangxi emperor's son, my brother," and a mere eunuch. It reminded him of other abuses that he himself had witnessed: an imperial agnate who called a eunuch "uncle"; a banquet at which the hapless Su Peisheng sat down to eat with his masters. According to the emperor this behavior was "sedition"; to those who would claim that he was focusing on trivia he warned, "small sparks can set a prairie afire, drops of water if they are not blocked can become a river in the end." Eunuchs must behave respectfully toward princes, officials, palace ladies, and the wives of the princes. The chief eunuch must display the deference to superiors that, clearly, the Yongzheng emperor's favor had led Su Peisheng to forget.

Hongtaiji's antler chair. Naitō Torajirō took this photograph in the former Qing capital of Mukden (Shengjing) before World War II. His photograph shows that the chair had a finial, which is missing from what is probably the same chair in the collection of the Shenyang Provincial Museum today. The poem inscribed on the chair back was apparently the work of the Qianlong emperor. This chair may be the first of a number of such pieces commissioned by Qing emperors (see chapter 1). Naitō Torajirō, *Naitō Kōnan zenshū*, vol. 6 (Tokyo: Chikuma shobō, 1972), 6:593.

Giuseppe Castiglione, "Ayusi Assailing the Rebels with a Lance." Handscroll, 1755. National Palace Museum, Taipei. Ayusi, a Zunghar, won the emperor's commendation for his exploits in a surprise night attack by Qing forces on the Zunghar camp at Gädän-Ola in 1755. Here, in one of several paintings of Ayusi ordered by the emperor, he wears a half-length coat of mail, leather protective plates over his thighs, and a winter court hat with a one-eyed peacock feather. For more on these and similar portraits of Qing military heroes, see Ka Bo Tsang, "Portraits of Meritorious Officials: Eight Examples from the First Set Commissioned by the Qianlong Emperor," *Arts asiatique* 47 (1992): 69–88 (see chapter 1 for a discussion of the larger project of which they were a part).

Portrait of Yinli, Prince Guo (1697–1738). Hanging scroll. Ink and color on silk. 158.8 × 88.9 cm. One of the Yongzheng emperor's favorite brothers is painted in an informal pose; the inscription is dated to the first month of summer 1731. A bilingual seal, superimposed on the inscription, gives the prince's title in Manchu: "hošoi genggiyen cinwang" (see chapter 3 for a description of this prince's political career). S 1991.95. Courtesy of the Arthur M. Sackler Gallery, Smithsonian Institution, Washington, D.C.

Photograph of Empress Dowager Cixi, on her way to a morning audience. The empress dowager is surrounded by ladies-in-waiting. The two eunuchs leading the procession are Cui Yugui (*left*) and Li Lianying (*right*). For background information on these photographs, see Lily Kecskes, "Photographs of Tz'u-hsi in the Freer Gallery Archives," *CEAL Bulletin* 101 (1993): 87–91 (see chapter 4 for a discussion of Cixi's political career). Negative no. SC-GR 275. Courtesy of the Arthur M. Sackler Gallery, Smithsonian Institution, Washington, D.C.

Opposite: Princess Shou'en, 1831–59. Hanging scroll. Ink and colors on silk. 188.6 × 102.1 cm, 314.7 × 142.5 cm overall. The portrait is said to depict the fifth daughter of the Daoguang emperor, Princess Shouzang (1829–56); the Sackler Gallery identifies it as the sixth daughter, Princess Shou'en. There is no inscription, so a definitive identification of the woman in formal court robes cannot be made. Note the three earrings in each ear, characteristic of bannerwomen's dress; the rich fur-edged vest, worn over a dragon robe, is itself covered at the throat by a

(*continued*)   fur-edged capelet. The court necklace is supplemented by two other necklaces, draped across each shoulder and crossing at center front and back. The fur hat, worn over a headband decorated with pearls, is ornamented with three gold phoenixes and an elaborate finial. The omission of hands and feet is very typical in female ancestor portraits (see chapter 8 for a discussion of the use of these portraits in rituals). S 1991.122. Courtesy of the Arthur M. Sackler Gallery, Smithsonian Institution, Washington, D.C.

Photograph of the interior of the Temple of the Ancestors (Taimiao) in Peking, taken by Hedda Morrison. A rare glimpse of the interior of the Qing Temple of the Ancestors (see chapters 1 and 6 for discussions of its ritual importance). The arrangement of the altars was replicated in other formal settings, for example in the sacrificial halls at the tombs. The spirit tablet would be placed on throne chairs set behind the altar tables when actual sacrifices were offered. Hedda Morrison Collection. Harvard-Yenching Library, Harvard University, Cambridge, Massachusetts.

Spirit pole, photographed in the former Qing capital of Shengjing by Naitō Torajirō. According to Naitō (673), the pole stood in the residence area of the Qingning palace; the men standing next to it are members of the palace staff. The Qing
emperor and imperial kinsmen performed rituals at spirit poles (see the description in chapter 7). Naitō Torajirō, *Naitō Kōnan zenshū*, vol. 6 (Tokyo: Chikuma
shobō, 1972), 6:586.

Tangka with Qianlong as Mañjuśrī, the bodhisattva of compassion and wisdom. This is one of several known *tangkas* featuring the Qianlong emperor at the center, symbolizing his claim to be a manifestation of Mañjuśrī, a major deity in Tibetan Buddhism (see chapter 7 for a discussion of the significance of these *tangkas*). The Palace Museum, Beijing, People's Republic of China.

Amitāyus, dated 1770. Qing dynasty, Qianlong period. Bronze. One of the hundreds of Amitāyus produced as birthday presents for the Qianlong emperor's mother on her eightieth birthday, this piece is discussed by Terese Tse Bartholomew, "Sino-Tibetan Art of the Qianlong Period from the Asian Art Museum of San Francisco," *Orientations* 22, no. 6 (1991): 41. B60 B140. The Avery Brundage Collection. Asian Art Museum of San Francisco.

Funerary cover. China, eighteenth or nineteenth century. Gold-colored satin-weave silk with gold metallic thread. Called *tuolo jingbei* (dharani coverlets), these cloths were wrapped around the bodies of deceased emperors, empresses, and higher-ranking consorts before encoffinment (see chapter 8). 85.12.0661. The Jacques Marchais Museum of Tibetan Art.

Part 3

QING COURT RITUALS

Chapter 6   Rulership and Ritual Action in the Chinese Realm

In recent years, a growing body of secondary literature has analyzed the complex ways in which rituals interact with politics in historical contexts across the globe. Rituals, defined by one scholar as "symbolic behavior that is socially standardized and repetitive," structure our sense of reality and our perception of the world.[1] Ever-changing, rituals mask their construction in patterns of continuity. Rituals are the major device by which rulers and ritual specialists attempt to legitimate political systems by fusing potent cultural symbols into a sequence of gesture, music, and voiced utterances that stirs our emotions.

Cultural symbols make up the language of ritual, which is powerful precisely because it is ambiguous and multivalent. The same ritual can say different things to different people. Because "the hallmark of power is the construction of reality," rituals are important in the creation of a hegemonic order, that is, a widely accepted system of beliefs concerning the origins of power and the ethical correctness of the social order.[2] Rulers of politically stable societies rely not merely on coercion but on ideological systems that present the existing political structure as "authoritative and God-given."[3] Some rituals, especially those involving audiences (see below) are "public transcripts," performances of deference, that not only project the self-image of the dominant elite but also seek to convince the subordinate groups of the crushing weight of authority embedded in the ideology behind the rite. As displays of domination, they affirm and thus help maintain the hierarchical order and the status quo.[4]

Of course, no individuals ever existed in complete alienation from the times and the society in which they were born. Rulers were no exception. Although they were entirely capable of manipulating rituals for specific political ends, they were simultaneously captives of their own culture. The two stances are not necessarily incompatible. It is impossible to know whether an emperor "believed" in a religion or a political ideology. The historian's task is instead to describe actions, statements, and their consequences.

The actions and statements of the Qing rulers certainly advanced their political goals. The chapters that follow examine three major ritual arenas in which Qing rulers participated. Chapter 6 focuses on what many historians call the Confucian ritual arena (and which some of them take to be the entirety of Qing ritual). When the Manchus entered the Ming territories, they skillfully drew on Confucian rituals to help win over former Ming officials and the populace. Confucian scholars viewed rituals as an essential and perhaps the primary task of the late imperial Chinese state, a major "means of both legitimizing political power and exerting administrative control."[5] One historian argues that "Anyone who works extensively with Ming documents . . . cannot avoid the conclusion that proper government in the Ming view was largely a matter of performing proper rituals."[6] The Qing were quick to demonstrate that they were prepared to carry on the Ming state rituals. One of the first actions they took on entering Peking was to order former Ming officials to prepare and perform the funerary rites for the last Ming emperor.

But Confucian rituals could never exert a monopoly on the rituals of a conquest state. There was first of all the rulers' determination to maintain a separate cultural identity: distinct rituals were essential, to match that identity. State rituals evolved to meet the shifting demands of empire and drew on different symbolic systems to address different subject peoples. Qing policies and practices associated with shamanism and Tibetan Buddhism will be treated in chapter 7.

Nurgaci had appealed to shamanic deities in his early campaigns and created state rites for a Manchu "heaven" that paralleled but was not identical to the Han Chinese *tian*. This should not be surprising: concepts of heaven as a deity existed from early times among the Turks and Mongols as well as Northeast Asian peoples.[7] The first major title claimed by Nurgaci, in 1616, was the Mongol *khan* (in Manchu, *han*). The Manchu-language text describing this event states that "the assembled princes and high officials raised Taizu [(Nurgaci's temple name) as] 'Enlightened' (*kundulen*) *han*."[8] Hongtaiji cultivated high Tibetan Buddhist prelates even as he explicitly drew on Chinese canons such as the *Liji* (Record of rites) and declared himself emperor, *huangdi*.[9] Hongtaiji's acquisition of the "seal transmitting the state" (*chuan'guoxi*) after defeating the Chahar leader Ligdan Khan was hailed as concrete proof that he had received the Mandate of Heaven. The "jade seal" or *qas boo*, as it was called in Mongolian, was believed to have been the state seal since Han times. Lost during the Jurchen conquest of Kaifeng, the seal was rediscovered in 1294 and was given to Temür's mother. The last emperor of Yuan took it with him when he fled China.[10]

After 1644, Qing rulers blended religious elements into images of rulership aimed at the different subject peoples living along their Inner Asian frontier. Manchus were urged to retain their traditional shamanic rituals and beliefs, despite the real changes made in both by the eighteenth-century codification of shamanism. The emperor presented himself to Han Chinese as the heir to the Chinese dynastic tradition, a Confucian monarch. Tibetan Buddhism provided a different vocabulary of legitimation for the Mongols and Tibetans who were brought under the Qing umbrella. The only subjects who were immune to such appeals by virtue of their religion were the Muslims. Fletcher notes that the Islamic worldview "challenged the very cornerstone of imperial order: the emperor's ultimate authority." Because Islam did not allow unbelievers to act as patrons of the faith, "the rule of the unbeliever could be accepted only as a temporary thing."[11] The emperor preached religious tolerance for the Uighur and other Muslim elements in the empire. The Qianlong emperor, for example, provided funds for the construction of the mosque dedicated to Amîn Khoja in Turfan, one of Xinjiang's most famous mosques. Qing patronage and protection of Islam in the eighteenth century gave way under fiscal pressures in the nineteenth century to a policy that was much less favorable toward Muslims. Han migration was encouraged after 1864 and exacerbated relations between Muslim and non-Muslim in the locality. The late eighteenth-century sectarian feuds among Muslims, which the emperor tried to arbitrate, gave way a century later to Han versus Muslim fighting in Yunnan, Gansu, and Shaanxi. In Xinjiang the weakened Qing authority was challenged by an invasion from Kokand, led by a descendant of the pre-Qing rulers of Altishahr (the northern half of Xinjiang).[12]

The artful manipulation and synthesis of Han and non-Han models of rulership was not new with the Qing. Early Manchu rulers studied the examples of the Jin and the Yuan dynasties. Although Khubilai, the first Mongol to become emperor of China, was elected *khaghan* (khan of khans) at a traditional Mongol assembly (*khuriltai*) in 1260, he shortly thereafter issued a Chinese-language edict announcing his new Chinese-style reign name. In 1272 he took on a dynastic name (Yuan) and renamed his capital city to accord with Chinese norms. At the same time, Khubilai drew on the Buddhist model of kingship, which he proclaimed in the language of the Tibetans, Uighurs, and other central Asians. Langlois concludes that "these two systems of legitimacy coexisted, giving the regime in China a split or double image."[13]

The Qing ruler was concurrently Chinese emperor, khan of khans, and Buddhist reincarnate. These titles were neither identical in meaning nor subsumed under the title of emperor, at least in its traditional sense before 1644.[14] In the Qing as in the Yuan case, different languages communicated distinct messages. The rituals stemming from the Chinese model of rulership take up most of the standard Chinese-language compendium of the dynasty's collected regulations, *Da Qing huidian*. Compartmentalization of communications toward the Manchus, Mongols, Tibetans, Uighurs, and Han Chinese went hand in hand with cultural policies that promoted the distinctiveness of each. As such, the Qianlong vision of a multicultural empire was fundamentally at odds with a Confucian emphasis on acculturation.

The themes of chapters 6 and 7 come together in chapter 8, which analyzes the private or "domestic" rituals of the Qing court, in which imperial women as well as princes and emperors participated.[15] State rituals were only one part of the complete ritual calendar, which also included rites commemorating imperial birthdays, deathdays, and the ordinary festival days that marked each season of the year for commoners. The rituals performed by Confucian, popular religious, Chinese Buddhist, Tibetan Buddhist, shamanic, and Daoist religious specialists for the imperial court were an eclectic blend of the various belief systems patronized by Qing rulers. The domestic rituals of the court thus perfectly reflected the cosmopolitan and diverse mixture of peoples and cultures that comprised the empire. Here in the imperial precincts, and perhaps only here, they all found a home. These private rites speak eloquently to the multicultural nature of the Qing imperial enterprise.

STATE RITUALS

Confucian state rituals were presented in the *Da Qing huidian*. These rituals were under the jurisdiction of the Board of Rites and were organized into five groups. The first, "auspicious rites" (*jili*), totaled 129 ceremonies, including the sacrifices to Heaven, Earth, and lesser deities at the suburban altars, the sacrifices to imperial ancestors and to the rulers of previous dynasties, rituals performed at the imperial tombs, and the imperial tour of inspection, *feng* and *shan* sacrifices at Taishan and Songshan, rituals at the *mingtang* (hall of light), and promulgation of the calendar.[16] The 74 "joyous rites" (*jiali*) included the accession ceremony, the imperial audience, reception of embassies, and the congratulatory rituals acknowledging the status of the empress dowager, empress, and other court personages. Among the 18 "military rites" (*junli*) were military review of the troops, rites performed when troops were led on campaign by the emperor, and those attending a victory. The 20 "guest rites" (*binli*) included not only the submission of tribute by vassal states but the rituals to be performed at court by Outer Mongol nobles and nobles in the imperial lineage. The 15 "rites of misfortune" (*xiongli*) were funeral rituals for individuals of different status.

The ceremonies under the Board of Rites might also be classified in terms of their function. One whole group of ceremonies marked "sacrifices" (*siji*) to deities and the imperial ancestors. Another group observed political rituals such as the accession ceremony, audiences, reception of envoys, and review of troops. Yet a third set of rituals covered stages in the life cycle, in particular marriage and death.[17] In the first group, the emperor communicated with the deities as a supplicant on behalf of the people. In the second, he received the recognition due the Son of Heaven. In the third, he acted as an individual who was also the head of his own household and lineage.

All these ceremonies paid special attention to the fixing of hierarchies of status. Sacrifices were grouped into three classes, and ranked within each class, affirming a hierarchy of status within the supernatural as in the secular world, in which inferiors acknowledged their submission to superiors. Even the act of sacrifice itself can be interpreted as a sign of submission by the emperor to the deity.[18] The audience rituals symbolized not only the acquiescence of subordinated groups to the emperor, but the status differentials among subordinated subgroups of family members, nobles, officials, ambassadors, and others. Ritual prescriptions for marriage and death stipulated the ceremonies proper for each major social status in Qing society. What were the messages that these rituals sought to convey?

PRINCIPLES OF RULE

Ritual action within the Chinese political tradition reflected two primary and to some extent conflicting strands: "rule by virtue" and "rule by heredity." The rituals of the Chinese state were artfully crafted to seem ageless and eternal but in reality had evolved with the development of a centralized bureaucratic state. In the Shang and Zhou periods, state rites were based on the notion of the ruler as the exemplar of virtue. This ideal was personified by the mythical ruler Yao, who selected not his son but the most worthy man, Shun, to succeed him. Shun, however, passed the throne to his own son. The principle of rule by heredity contested the principle of rule by virtue, and the Shang rulers tried to reconcile the two by claiming special access through the royal ancestors to the world of the deities. The Zhou, who conquered the Shang territory, introduced a new emphasis on the Mandate of Heaven, which could be taken away from a ruling house if the king failed in virtue.[19]

"Rule by virtue" was presented in the ancient canonical tradition as a genuinely transformative form of kingship, whereby the ruler's example inspired emulation by his subjects and thus laid the basis for a virtuous society. Adherence within China to a tradition of succession by descent created a conflict between the ideal and reality. With the introduction during the Later Han dynasty of the cyclical theory of history, each state was conceived as having a finite life and thus being only one of a succession of states to rule China.[20] Although the institutionalized custom of having a new dynasty write the history of its predecessor testifies to the incorporation of the cyclical theory in political thought, state rituals tended not to dwell on its implications for the ruling house but instead stressed the more optimistic notion of the Mandate of Heaven. As the recipient of the Mandate of Heaven, the emperor had the primary responsibility to sacrifice on behalf of the people in order to ensure that Heaven favored the empire with the conditions required for good harvests and peace.

The Mandate of Heaven was always to some extent at odds with the religious expression of rule by heredity, the worship of imperial ancestors. Rulers of China mostly accepted the principle of succession within a descent group. The imperial ancestral temple, called *zongmiao* or Taimiao, was equal to the highest state altars in Han times, and the power to worship the spirits of past rulers was a jealously guarded prerogative.

Worship of imperial ancestors did not cease with the seventh-century placement of the sacrifice to Heaven as the most important state ritual. The Ming and Qing both designated the Taimiao as a first-rank altar (see map 2 for the location of the Temple of the Ancestors and other main altars). During the Qing dynasty, "reporting rituals" (*gaoji*) were performed at the Taimiao before all major political events and after all the family changes: births, marriages, and deaths, of the emperor's family. There was also a long tradition of presenting sacrifices to the rulers of past dynasties both at their tombs and before their tablets. The Qing sacrifices at the Temple to Rulers of Successive Dynasties (*lidai di wang miao*) fell into the second rank of state sacrifices.[21]

In 1644 Manchu forces entered Peking, after they were invited into China proper by the Ming general Wu Sangui. Wu, who had been summoned to defend the capital from the rebel Li Zicheng, was too late; by the time the Manchu banners rode into Peking, the last emperor of the Ming was dead. The Qing were thus spared the crime of regicide.[22] While proclaiming their intention to aid the Ming, they methodically hunted down and exterminated all the claimants to the Ming throne.[23] The day after their entry into the city, the young Shunzhi emperor, who had inherited the throne from his father a year earlier, took part in an enlarged accession ritual to mark the occasion. The primary event was a sacrifice to Heaven at the altar to Heaven erected by the Ming. After the sacrifice was performed, the emperor was seated on a throne in an enclosure to the east of the altar. The imperial seal was placed in front of him on a table; the assembled officials performed the full obeisance of "three kneelings and nine kowtows." The enthronement and obeisances were repeated within the Forbidden City of the Ming rulers, where a throne was erected at what later became the Taihe gate: here the congratulatory memorial (*hebiao*) was read before the emperor ascended the throne.[24]

The principle of rule by heredity became part of the accession rites after 1644. Even though Heaven retained its preeminence, Qing accession rituals gradually placed more and more emphasis on filiality. The system of secret succession that the Manchus eventually adopted only intensified the need to display filiality, both during and after the lifetime of the father. Elsewhere, I analyze these ritual changes, which began with the accession ritual of 1735.[25] The symbolism of the 1735 accession ritual redefined "rule by virtue" to infuse the emperor's designated heir with imperial qualifications. Because the emperor was free to choose his successor among all his sons, he could arguably select the ablest. In the language of the accession rite, "merit" was equated with virtue and its most conspicuous quality was filial piety. In contrast to the rituals of earlier dynasties, which gave prominence to the direct transmission by locating the primary accession ritual at the coffin of the previous ruler, the later Qing ritual emphasized the enthronement ceremony.

Sitting on the Throne

The symbolic significance in the Chinese ritual vocabulary of "facing south" harks back to classical precedent. According to the *Analects*, the mythical emperor Shun, who "ruled by inactivity," performed only one action: he faced south.[26] By the late imperial period, the throne in the Taihedian was integrated into a complex cosmology. The term for the palace, Zijincheng, linked it to the *ziwei*, the cluster of stars surrounding the center of Heaven, the pole star. When the emperor, the "pole star" of the earthly realm, faced south (as does the star) and assumed the ruling position in the secular counterpart to the center of Heaven, he thus drew on the symbolic capital of the Chinese cosmological system to reinforce his legitimacy.[27]

Initially the term "to go to the imperial position" probably had a more general meaning, which incorporated the action of sitting on a throne to receive obeisances. The political symbolism of this act was widely understood not only in Chinese society but in the steppe world. John of Plano Carpini, a Franciscan sent by Pope Innocent IV to the emperor of the Tartars, arrived at Karakorum in 1245 A.D. in time to witness the traditional Mongol assembly that elected Güyüg, a grandson of Chinggis, *khaghan*. He tells us that a central feature of the ceremony that followed the election was the seating of Güyüg on a throne to receive the submission of tribal chieftains.[28] The ancient history of this custom suggests that even though the bilingual Veritable Records of Nurgaci were extensively revised in the eighteenth century, its illustrations of a seated Nurgaci receiving the submission of former foes may be historically accurate.[29] There were thus historical precedents in both the steppe and the Han Chinese world for selecting this ritual to signify political submission.

Written accounts of the 1626 accession rite emphasize the obeisances of the princes and ministers, who thus signified their consent to his election. Records of the 1643 accession portray a young heir who was unsure of whether he should reciprocate when his uncles knelt before him in homage.

> When Shizu [the Shunzhi emperor] mounted the throne he was only seven *sui* . . . the assembled princes, *beile*, civil and military officials all knelt to welcome him. The emperor entered the hall. He said to the officials, "You uncles and elder brothers have come to bow in congratulations. Should I respond likewise? Or should I sit and receive the obeisances?" The officials answered, "You should not respond likewise." Thereupon Jirgalang, Prince Zheng, and Dorgon, Prince Rui, led the assembled inner and outer princes, *beile, beise* (fourth-rank princes), dukes, and civil and military officials in the three kneelings and nine kowtows rite.[30]

In 1661 another child, Xuanye, "ascended the precious throne" (*sheng baozuo*); the same phrase was used in 1722. Not until 1735 was the heir described as "going to the imperial position" and "mounting the throne" (*ji huangwei; sheng zuo*). The two phrases were repeated in the accession rites of the Daoguang, Xianfeng, and Tongzhi emperors.

The Collected Regulations of the Qing adopted the Ming term for the rite of accession, *dengji*, which literally means "to mount the ultimate." In reality, as a perusal of the Veritable Records shows, the more common phrase, used before 1722 and frequently thereafter, was one that meant "to go to the imperial position" (*ji huangdi wei*). In the Veritable Records the term "to go to the imperial position" first appears to describe Hongtaiji's actions in October 8, 1626, when he formally succeeded to the rulership after Nurgaci's death. This term is repeated in the context of every subsequent accession before 1908, as opposed to the less frequently used *dengji*.[31]

The act of mounting the throne in the Taihedian became the act that completed the accession ritual. Meyer argues that the fact that Empress Dowager Cixi never dared sit on this throne "makes clear what the ritual signifies. It makes a claim to total authority. Performing the rituals is what legitimates the assumption of power"—and we might add, underlines the uniqueness of the emperorship.[32]

The culmination of the accession ritual combines two actions of great symbolic value in Chinese society: the act of facing south, described above, and of sitting on the throne to receive the obeisances of the princes and officials. This second action—sitting to receive obeisances—was the focal point of ceremonies within the palace that served to publicly reinforce the relative status of family members. At the New Year and on other occasions, an emperor prostrated himself before his mother, who was seated on a throne; the empress prostrated herself before her mother-in-law and husband; the consort prostrated herself before the empress.

Christian Jochim argues that ritualized obeisances are "acts both of humility and privilege."[33] By kneeling and kowtowing before Heaven and his imperial ancestors, the emperor partakes of their numinous power; by kneeling and kowtowing before the emperor, ministers, princes, and others participating in an audience ritual partake of the powers flowing through the emperor. The emperor's obeisance to his mother carries a somewhat different symbolic message, one that reifies the hierarchical relationships within families that lie at the core of the Confucian order.

The symbolic significance of sitting to receive ritual homage was broadly understood in Chinese society. The same action confirms the submissiveness of the young bride to her new parents-in-law, the subordination of a concubine to her husband's wife, of a maidservant to her mistress. By extension we find in Chinese society the symbolic vesting of authority in both a specific chair and in the pose itself. By at least Song times some of the legitimacy conferred by this symbolically charged act had been transferred to the chair itself. Chan Buddhist monasteries during the funeral of an abbot placed the deceased man's portrait in the "dharma seat"—the seat occupied by the abbot—until a new successor was installed, thus drawing on the same symbolic vocabulary found in discussions of the throne in the Taihedian.[34]

The argument that Chinese ritual culture gave primacy to performance of the act rather than to a specific throne or chair can be supported by popular religion, where deities in Chinese temples are portrayed in a seated position, to receive the worship of the people. The tablets denoting Heaven and the imperial ancestors in the Temple of the Ancestors were also "seated" on thrones during rituals.[35] Deities in the popular religion are depicted in this seated pose to the present day. The popular woodblock prints known as *zhima*, which continue to be produced in the People's Republic of China, show the deity in a seated frontal pose, "like a statue in a Chinese temple": "This effect is no accident, since prints of this type (some authors have called this an 'iconic' print) were the focus of domestic religious ceremonials and received offerings, such as incense, from family members."[36] As with deities, so with the emperor—or perhaps the statement should be reversed. When the new emperor sat on the throne and received the obeisances of the nobles and officials, he was performing a ritual action that not only echoed those of ordinary persons in the society but also replicated that of the gods in Chinese popular religion.

The accession ritual is the first of the "joyous rites," all of which followed the same patterned sequence of ritual actions and carried them into the realm of the annual ritual calendar. The ceremonial audience (*dachao*), which was held at the "three great festivals" of the year—New Year's, the emperor's birthday, and the winter solstice—was an occasion at which the body politic recreated the cosmic order. Within the courtyard of the Taihedian, as elsewhere in the empire, imperial nobles, civil and military officials, and tributary emissaries garbed in court robes faced in the direction of the capital and performed obeisances. This ritual creation of "a symbolic universe" was "a microcosmic representation of the social-political cosmic order" and reaffirmed the Confucian world order. Other analyses of the audiences given to tributary states support Jochim's interpretation.[37]

Significantly, the act that made an heir the emperor—seating himself on the throne and receiving the acclamation of the nobles and officials—is static. As we noted, the authority derived from this action was strengthened by explicit parallels between the secular and the cosmic order. The image conveyed through this culminating act is one in which a seated ruler receives the symbolic submission of his "subjects," represented not by the people but by the conquest elite and the civil service bureaucracy. What has happened to the Confucian model of the transformative nature of virtuous rule? The implication is that the ruler should "rule by inaction." The symbolic structure of the rite expresses the Confucian preoccupation with the fixing (some would say freezing) of the Chinese sociopolitical order. Since Chinese history is full of power struggles between the ruler and the bureaucracy, we may speculate as to whether the emphasis placed on this aspect of emperorship itself implied the bureaucracy's unspoken desire: that an emperor reign but not rule.

By Ming times Chinese political culture had developed a distinctive emphasis on the primacy of bureaucratic governance. Ray Huang's powerful indictment of late Ming rule shows an emperor whose attempts to rule were ably deflected by his highest officials. Their ideal model was a noninterventionist ruler. Since the creative possibilities of imperial leadership were more than offset by the dangers of arbitrary and whimsical edicts, it was far better to follow precedent and give bureaucrats the leading role in policy making. Bitter disputes over ritual issues in the sixteenth century exemplify the dominance of Confucian ritual specialists and the weakness of the throne on issues of ritual.[38]

Whereas the late Ming emperors were quite ineffectual, the early Qing rulers were not. From 1661 to at least 1800, a succession of decisive emperors significantly increased the powers of the throne over the bureaucrats. An analysis of how they succeeded in breaking through the bureaucratic constraints that frustrated the late Ming emperors is beyond the scope of this chapter. Some factors include the separation of a conquest elite from the civil service and the employment of conquest nobles in an inner court. In the ritual realm (see below and chapters 7 and 8), Qing rulers moved outside Confucian frameworks to tap other symbolic systems. They confined Confucian ritual specialists to the altars that had been customarily worshiped by the Ming. Even though these altars could and were reproduced in the new outposts of empire, the emperors also sanctioned the reverse: Tibetan Buddhist temples and shamanic altars were erected in Peking and in the major administrative centers dotting the periphery. The imperial patronage of multiple religious traditions gave Qing rulers a freedom denied emperors in the Chinese ritual tradition.

Filiality and State Sacrifice

Of the two ideological bases for imperial rule, rule by virtue was by far more difficult for rulers to substantiate. Each dynasty claimed rule by virtue was the reason for its founding, but what of subsequent accessions? The Qing rulers tried to conflate rule by virtue and rule by birth by defining virtue in terms of filiality. Filiality was explicitly identified by the Kangxi emperor as one of the key traits that a ruler must possess. He stated, "We rule the empire with filial piety. That is why I want to exemplify this principle for my ministers and my people—and for my own descendants."[39] The emperor himself prominently displayed his filial sentiments during the illness and death of his grandmother in 1687. Some historians suggest that Xuanye's repudiation of Yinreng, his heir apparent, stemmed from Yinreng's marked lack of filial feeling during Xuanye's illness in 1690. Yinzhen's filial piety and Yinzhi's conspicuous lack of this quality are also said to have weighed in the eventual selection of Yinzhen as the heir. Similarly, Hongli, angered at what he considered to be insufficient mourning on the part of his eldest and third sons upon the death of his empress in 1748, later explicitly barred them from the succession.[40] From his pronouncements, we know that Hongli drew on the Kangxi precedents in his own lavish display of filiality toward his mother.[41]

Qing rulers adopted Han Chinese traditions of ancestor worship, then modified them. In 1636, when Hongtaiji took on the Chinese title of emperor and the dynastic name of Qing, he awarded his principal ancestors the title of king (*wang*). After 1644, these titles were upgraded to emperor. A Chinese-style ancestral temple was constructed by Hongtaiji in Mukden, the capital from 1625 to 1644; after 1644, the Qing erected their ancestral tablets in the former Ming Taimiao in Peking.

Qing ancestral worship was largely a continuation of Ming practice. Like the Ming, the Qing distinguished between the Taimiao, which was a first-rank altar of the state, and the private or familial Fengxiandian (hall of the ancestors), which was located in the inner court of the Forbidden City. In the Taimiao, located outside the Wu gate, the focal ancestor was Taizu (Nurgaci) and his empress; the tablets for earlier ancestors were housed in a separate back hall.[42] The Fengxiandian housed only the tablets of the emperors and empresses beginning with Taizu.[43] Both of these ancestral halls differed from those of commoners in not housing the tablets of collateral descendants.

Rituals performed at the Taimiao included the *meng* rites in the first, fourth, seventh, and tenth lunar months, and the *xia* sacrifice at the end of the year. During these rituals, the ancestral tablets normally housed in niches in the back hall were placed on the altar in the south-facing main hall. The same kinds of musical instruments, dancers, choir and offerings stipulated for the other first-rank altars were provided for these rites. These calendrical rituals were supplemented by offerings made on the first and fifteenth of each lunar month before the separate shrines in which the spirit tablets of each emperor and his empresses were installed.

In an earlier article, I describe the construction of the mausolea that housed the remains of an emperor and his empresses.[44] Each tomb was constructed with its own sacrificial hall for the spirit tablets of those buried within. Like the deities of the popular religion who were entered into the official register of altars, imperial ancestors received additions to their death names that were inscribed on the tablets, most frequently when a new emperor ascended the throne. These tablets received offerings on the first and fifteenth of each month; in addition, officials were sent on individual death-days and at Qingming, Zhongyuan (the fifteenth day of the seventh month), the winter solstice, and the end of the year to perform sacrifices at the mausolea. Additional rituals would be performed on an ad hoc basis, so that a total of as many as thirty rites might be carried out at a tomb in one year.[45]

The Qing expanded the sphere of ancestor worship by increasing the numbers of past emperors who participated in the first-rank sacrifice to Heaven. Earlier dynasties erected only the spirit tablet of the dynastic founder as an ancillary object of worship (*pei*) in this ritual. When the Shunzhi emperor performed the sacrifice in 1644, the Altar to Heaven did not include any of his ancestors' tablets. The tablet of Nurgaci was added in 1648, and in 1657, the emperor issued an edict justifying the addition of Hongtaiji's tablet. Noting that "in filiality, nothing is more important than revering one's parent," Fulin praised his father's achievements and ordered that the tablet receive ancillary sacrifice at the sacrifices to Heaven, Earth, and the prayer for grain.[46]

Once the addition of ancestors as objects of ancillary worship was construed as an expression of filiality, each new ruler had to add his father's tablet to the state altars. Shunzhi's was added in 1666, Kangxi's in 1723, and so on until 1850. Because the Daoguang emperor's will explicitly forbade further additions, no doubt because at that point the *pei* tablets exactly matched the tablets installed in the rear hall of the Taimiao, the Daoguang tablet was the last to be included in the grand sacrifices.

Imperial ancestors also provided dynastic legitimation within the notion of *zhengtong*. The concept developed out of the Han synthesis of Confucianism with *yinyang* and five-elements theory. In Han times, *zhengtong* referred to the line of orthodox or legitimate succession within a royal house or family. During the Tang and Song, the term came to be applied to tracing a legitimate line of rulership from antiquity to the present. Although not all dynastic founders accepted the notion—Khubilai is said to have rejected it in favor of the model of universal rulership posited by Chinggis Khan—many who wished to establish a new Chinese ruling house tried to manipulate the system to their advantage by adopting dynastic names and symbols that fit into the *zhengtong* framework. Hok-lam Chan argues, for example, that this was the reason why the twelfth-century Jurchen adopted "Great Golden" (*da Jin*) for their state name.[47]

Zhengtong substituted "political descent" for descent by blood. It asserted that legitimacy crossed over descent lines and could be transmitted from one ruling house to another. What Wechsler calls a shift from worship of "lineal ancestors" to "political ancestors" took place and was reflected in ritual. The court undertook to support (and control) ancestral rituals for the rulers of preceding dynasties. It also expanded the foundations of imperial legitimacy by reasserting "the hallowed notion that the empire was not the perpetual monopoly of one house only."[48]

When Qing troops entered Peking in 1644, they designated a descendant of the Ming imperial house to act as the prime officiant of rituals at the Ming tombs. The justification for a new ruling house to honor its predecessors' ancestors could be found in the Book of Rites. From the Zhou dynasty, each new ruling house selected descendants of two previous dynasties (*er wang hou*) who would be honored with noble titles and given ritual functions in the new state. The *er wang hou* policy was supplemented by direct sacrifices to the spirits of former rulers. In later dynasties the number of former rulers who were so honored varied greatly. The Zhou rulers placed two of the Shang royal ancestors in the Zhou pantheon, perhaps because of the matrilateral relationship the Zhou founder enjoyed with the Shang royal family. In 657, the Tang began to sacrifice on a regular basis to the spirits of the mythical emperors Yao, Shun, Yu and Tang, as well as to the Zhou rulers Wenwang and Wuwang and the founder of the Han dynasty, Gaozu. The Qing dynasty added rulers from the two Jin dynasties, northern and southern dynasties, and the five dynasties. Initially the sacrifice was to be performed once every three years at the tomb or a location associated with the ruler, but eventually the sacrifices were performed in a temple dedicated to the emperors and kings of previous dynasties (*Lidai diwang miao*).[49]

RITUAL AND IMPERIAL PREROGATIVE

In the last months of his reign, Hongli had included ritual performance among the activities to be assigned to his son after abdication. Because of his old age, "he was no longer up to the strenuous 'ascendings and descendings, obeisances and bowings requisite for the expected reverence' at the grand sacrifices."[50] And Hongli was true to his word: the ritual calendar confirms that after his abdication in 1795, he never again personally presided at the grand sacrifices.[51]

Hongli's decision to delegate the sacrifices at the most important altars of the state religion raises an important issue for historians, who argue that the sacrifice to Heaven was one of the pillars of the Confucian ideology that supported the Qing state. The political significance of sacrificing to Heaven was well known. By the Tang dynasty a new emperor, "to express fully the legitimate nature of his power," had to personally perform the sacrifices to Heaven and Earth at the suburban altars shortly after his accession. The pivotal position of the emperor in harmonizing human society with the cosmos hinged on his ritual performance at the state altars: "it was upon his performance that the interconnection of the cosmos depended. While these rituals constituted the cosmic cycle, they also became proof of the emperor's fitness to rule as the man who could . . . show the unity of Heaven and Earth."[52]

This direct link with Heaven, enjoyed by no one else, enhanced the emperor's authority, as did the seventh-century decision to worship only one rather than several Heavens. Anyone other than the emperor who performed this ritual committed "high treason" and signaled his "intention to usurp the prerogative and to seize the throne of the sovereign."[53] That was certainly the motivation behind the sacrifice to Heaven performed by Fulin in 1644 after the banner troops had captured Peking.

All state rites were under the emperor's direct control. The nature of imperial participation varied with the status of the ritual act. Imperial supervision over worship at the altars of deities of the second and third ranks in the state religious hierarchy rarely went beyond approval of the dates of worship. In the second rank were sacrifices presented at eleven other altars; the third and lowest rank of state sacrifices were those at a further twenty-nine temples and other religious sites. Since some altars required more than one annual sacrifice, the state ritual calendar included well over fifty ritual performances a year.[54]

By the end of the Kangxi reign (1722) the first-rank sacrifices included the sacrifice to Heaven during the winter solstice, the sacrifice to Earth during the summer solstice, prayers for a good harvest at the Qiniandian in the Altar to Heaven complex, performed during the first month; sacrifices at the Altar of Land and Grain in the first ten days of the second and eighth months; and sacrifices at the Temple of the Ancestors at the beginning of each quarter and at the end of the year. In 1742, prayers for rain, performed in the fourth month at the Altar to Heaven, were added to the first-rank rituals. Each grand sacrifice was preceded by three days' abstinence and, at least in theory, was to be performed by the emperor himself as well as his officials.[55] Although the grand sacrifices included sacrifices performed at the ancestral tombs at several points during the year, those were normally performed by a high-ranking imperial kinsman, and not by the emperor.[56]

Whereas earlier rulers tended to be lackadaisical about performing sacrifices, Qing rulers took the statement by Confucius seriously: "If I am not present at the sacrifice, it is as though there were no sacrifice."[57] The passage from the *Analects* encapsulated the Kangxi emperor's attitude toward ritual performance. In 1711, having recovered from a slight indisposition, he reversed a previous edict delegating the sacrifice to Heaven: "Only by personally conducting the rite may I display sincerity of intent (*chengxin*)." On his deathbed in 1722, he reiterated much the same sentiment in his instructions to his son Yinzhen, whom he appointed to perform the grand sacrifice: "I cannot personally attend the suburban sacrifice to Heaven. I order you to reverently perform in my stead. You must be sincere, reverent, and strict in observing the rules of abstinence; only thus will you be able to display my sincerity in sacrificing."[58] In the words of his grandson Hongli, "The ruler is the Son of Heaven, he should make reverence for Heaven and concern for the people his first task. Only thus will he obtain Heaven's favor."[59] The Jiaqing emperor expressed his reverence by attempting to personally sacrifice at altars of not only the first but also the second rank. In 1802 he ordered that palace memorials from the Board of Rites and Court of Sacrificial Worship that concerned the grand sacrifices to Heaven, Earth, or the ancestors be put at the head of their group for imperial perusal. Further, eunuchs were to provide a basin so that the emperor could wash his hands before reading ritual memorials.[60]

Monopolization of the ritual did not mean that the emperor was personally required to perform the ritual. From the Han to the Tang dynasty, when the ruler's monopoly of the imperial ancestors was the more important symbol of imperial power, a new ruler was required to personally worship at the ancestral temple at least once, but most of the time the sacrifices were performed by others. The same custom seems to have been followed after the seventh century, when the sacrifices to Heaven and Earth were raised in importance.[61] Although the Qing rulers were by comparison extremely diligent in discharging their ritual duties, they also regarded delegation of the sacrifice as in no way an infringement of the imperial prerogative.

Even with the best of intentions, it was virtually impossible for an emperor to carry out all the prescribed rituals. After the seventeenth century an infant emperor could not personally perform the sacrifices at first-rank altars before he personally took charge of the government after "coming of age." Although the young Kangxi emperor performed some (but not all) of the grand sacrifices before his marriage in October 1665 and assumption of personal rule in August 1667, the later infant emperors did not. Neither the Tongzhi nor the Guangxu emperors of the late nineteenth century were allowed to preside at grand sacrifices until after they married and assumed personal rule.[62]

Other imperial activities interfered with the ritual schedule. The Kangxi emperor was touring Jiangnan on the first of his six southern tours during the winter solstice of 1684; in 1695 and 1696 he was leading troops against the Zunghar leader Galdan. The death of his first empress (June 6, 1674) interrupted his ritual activities (state rituals could not be performed by persons in mourning) for several months; when his second empress died (March 18, 1678) there was a similar if shorter hiatus. When his beloved grandmother died on January 27, 1688, the emperor again devoted himself to mourning observances. He did not personally perform any of the first-rank rituals until the sacrifice to Earth during the summer solstice.[63] From the late 1680s there were also annual migrations north of the Great Wall to Chengde: in 1714, for example, the emperor left Peking on June 2 and did not return until November 6.[64]

And finally, old age and illness struck even the most robust men. The Kangxi emperor, about to sacrifice to Heaven in 1786, noted, "This year I am already sixty. If when I conduct the rite, those on both sides help a little, that's all right."[65] The Qianlong emperor wrote apologetically about his limited ritual activities:

> In Qianlong 45 [1780] I attained my seventieth year; fearing lest in the grand sacrifices there would be error in the ritual, I had my sons go separately before the tablets to pour libations and make offerings of silk . . . the Altars to Heaven and to Earth are both grand sacrifices. And the sacrifice to Heaven in the southern suburbs is especially important. . . . It is not that I am remiss in this matter; it is essential in matters linked with the grand sacrifices to exercise care and sincerity. There must be no error in the rite. . . . Consider that I have already passed through eighty-four springs and autumns, and am fourteen years past [1780]. Although I desire to invite the kindness of broad Heaven, and to exert myself as of old, my risings and bowings unavoidably fall rather behind yesteryear's.[66]

The Veritable Records indicate that delegation of sacrifices at even the first-rank altars was common. In 1684 and 1694, for example, Xuanye presided at only four of the ten grand sacrifices; in 1704 he sacrificed only three times and in 1714, only twice.[67] In short, the emperor exercised his prerogative only about one-third of the time.

Despite the growth of imperial rhetoric concerning the close identification of the sacrifices at the first-rank altars of Heaven and earth with the emperorship, Chinese historical tradition and the actions of Qing rulers indicate that it was not, in fact, essential for the emperor in person to carry out the ritual each time. The act of sacrificing to Heaven was apparently not coterminous with emperorship. Heaven, it seemed, would accept sacrifices performed by substitutes. An emperor should at a minimum perform the sacrifice to Heaven once. Most Qing emperors actually tried to discharge their ritual obligations on a regular basis whatever the Confucian ritual framework allowed, rather than delegate them to others. What they jealousy guarded was the imperial prerogative to fix the ritual calendar itself. More broadly, the emperor's sacral power was defined less by his sacrificial actions than by his power to fix space and time.

The first and most important exercise of imperial prerogative lay in the fixing of the ritual calendar. The close links of this act with rulership have been noted by Jacques Gernet: "Chinese emperors held total power over the organisation of society and the universe, and space and time. . . . The emperor imposed order on the world through inauguration ceremonies, the diffusion of the calendar, the bestowal of titles and names, the classification of the various cults and deities, the diplomas he granted them. . . . The Chinese emperors combined, in their persons, functions and aspects in which the profane and the sacred were indistinguishable."[68] From the state's perspective, this, and not the popular "almanac," was the first calendar of the dynasty. Prepared by the Board of Rites, the ritual calendar listed the major state and domestic sacrifices for the year ahead.[69] Once approved by the emperor, this calendar was disseminated to all the government offices in the empire. The emperor's centrality to this ritual calendar was signified in his ultimate power to determine, from the alternative dates presented by the Board of Astronomy, the specific times of ritual performance. Thus the emperor set the appropriate conjunctions between the people and the deities.[70]

The ritual calendar grew over the course of the dynasty. The calendar for the fifty-first year of the Qianlong reign (1786) lists sixty-two different sacrifices, as compared with eighty-three sacrifices for the thirty-first year of the Guangxu reign (1905).[71] Of the thirty-eight altars listed in the 1905 ritual calendar 55 percent were devoted to popular deities such as Guandi, dragon gods, and river gods. And 28 percent were temples honoring meritorious generals and officials, including heroes of the conquest period such as Eidu and Tong Tulai. One of these new temples, the Zhaozhongci (temple to glorify loyalty), was erected in 1724 inside the Chongwen gate at the wall dividing the imperial from the southern city. Here the tablets of princes, high officials, soldiers, and others who helped the dynasty were presented with sacrifices in the second month of the spring and autumn. Six years later another temple, the Xianliangci (temple to meritorious and virtuous officials) was established outside the Di'an gate in the northeast of the imperial city, to honor "those Manchu and Chinese high officials who have striven mightily on our behalf but have not yet received sacrifices."[72]

IMPERIAL DELEGATION OF SACRIFICES

The emperor named persons to perform the first-rank sacrifices in his stead, but these sacrifices, in particular the sacrifice to Heaven, remained closely tied to the emperorship. If an individual was qualified by birth and virtue (the implication of allowing him to perform a ritual acceptable to Heaven), what was to prevent him from usurping the throne?

The historical shifts in the ritual assignments given to the emperor's closest kinsmen mirrored the evolving relations between the throne and the princes. The Kangxi emperor consistently bypassed his sons to appoint others to perform the grand sacrifices (table 14). The heir apparent, Yinreng, was the sole exception. Xuanye instead delegated the grand sacrifices to Manchus occupying either the top posts in the central government bureaucracy or nobles whose full title, chamberlain of the Imperial Guard and inner-court high minister (lingshiwei nei dachen), reflected their importance in the emperor's extrabureaucratic councils.

The prominence of this inner-court group is even more striking in the list of persons appointed to perform the grand sacrifice to Heaven (table 15). With the exception of Bahundai, all the others held the title of chamberlain of the Imperial Guard and inner-court high minister. Fushan served in this post, normally given to six or more persons at any one time, from 1680 to 1708; Tong Guowei from 1682–98; Poerpen from 1684–1711; Alingga, from 1701–16; Marsai, from 1714–31; Efei from 1702–9, Urjan served briefly in 1719, and Bahundai himself served in this post from 1701–23.[73]

All these men were descended from famous heroes of the conquest period. The only imperial kinsman, Efei, was a great-grandson of Amin, one of the "four great beile" of the 1620s. Bahundai was the grandson of Irde, who had been made a first-rank marquis. Fushan, who inherited the

Table 14. Performers of Grand Sacrifices during the Kangxi Reign

Date[a]	Ritual Performer	Source
1684–85	Duke Tong Guowei, Chamberlain	*DQSL* 5:174
	Yizang'a, Board President	*DQSL* 5:204
	Samha, Board President	*DQSL* 5:208
	Hangai, Board President (twice)	*DQSL* 5:219
	Bahundai, Lieutenant General	*DQSL* 5:231
1694–95	Duke Tong Guowei, Chamberlain (four times)	*DQSL* 5:769, 789, 800, 803
	Duke Fushan, Chamberlain	*DQSL* 5:774
	Kulena, Board President	*DQSL* 5:792
1704–5	Efei (agnate), Chamberlain (twice)	*DQSL* 6:177, 207
	Heir Apparent Yinreng (twice)	*DQSL* 6:177, 188
	Wenda, Censorate President	*DQSL* 6:180
	Duke Poerpen, Chamberlain	*DQSL* 6:215
	Shulu, Censorate President	*DQSL* 6:193
1714–15	Funing'an, Board President	*DQSL* 6:546
	Yintebu, Board President	*DQSL* 6:548
	Duke Alingga, Chamberlain	*DQSL* 6:552
	Duke Furdan, Chamberlain (five times)	*DQSL* 6:555, 558, 563, 565, 577

SOURCE: *Da Qing shilu* (Beijing, 1986).

[a] Calculated from the lunar calendar used by the dynasty, which recorded events in terms of the reign year: 1760–61 and 1800–1801 were thirteen-month years, adjusting the lunar calendar to the solar cycle.

dukedom in 1664, was a great-grandson of the famous Yangguri. Duke Tong Guowei, the emperor's maternal uncle, was a general whose family had played prominent roles in the conquest. Poerpen, who inherited his first-class dukedom in 1652, was a son of Tulai and a grandson of Fiongdon, the founder of the Suwan Güwalgiya lineage. Alingga, who received his dukedom in 1786, was the fifth son of Ebilun and a descendant of the famous Eidu, founder of the Niohuru fortunes. Marsai inherited the dukedom of his grandfather, Tuhai, a general under the young Kangxi emperor. Urjan, also an imperial agnate, was descended from Yolo, one of Nurgaci's grandsons.[74]

Even though the Kangxi emperor preferred to depute the most solemn sacrifice in the state calendar to nobles with no claim on the throne, he was not averse to assigning other ritual duties—sacrifices to Earth, the ances-

Table 15. Men Appointed to Sacrifice to Heaven during the Kangxi Reign

Year[a]	Appointee	Source
1684	Bahundai, Lieutenant General	DQSL 5:231
1691	Fushan, Chamberlain, Imperial Guard	DQSL 5:692
1694	Tong Guowei, Chamberlain, Imperial Guard	DQSL 5:800
1695	Fushan, Chamberlain, Imperial Guard	DQSL 5:831
1696	Heir Apparent Yinreng	DQSL 5:913
1701	Heir Apparent Yinreng	DQSL 6:98
1702	Poerpen, Chamberlain, Imperial Guard	DQSL 6:132
1703	Efei, Chamberlain, Imperial Guard	DQSL 6:170
1705	Heir Apparent Yinreng	DQSL 6:241
1706	Heir Apparent Yinreng	DQSL 6:276
1708	Alingga, Chamberlain, Imperial Guard	DQSL 6:350
1709	Alingga, Chamberlain, Imperial Guard	DQSL 6:392
1717	Marsai, Chamberlain, Imperial Guard	DQSL 6:694
1718	Marsai, Chamberlain, Imperial Guard	DQSL 6:753
1720	Marsai, Chamberlain, Imperial Guard	DQSL 6:821
1721	Yinzhen, Prince Yong	DQSL 6:854
1722	Duke Urjan	DQSL 6:901

SOURCE: *Da Qing shilu* (Beijing, 1986).

tors, and to Confucius—to his offspring. All but the youngest sons performed state rituals at their father's behest. One scholar notes that Yinzhen, the future Yongzheng emperor, sacrificed on twenty-two, his elder brother Yinzhi on twenty occasions.[75]

Changes in imperial preference occurred during the Yongzheng reign (table 16). In place of the Manchu banner nobles favored by his father, Yinzhen appointed only Aisin Gioro princes of the first and second rank, including more distantly related kinsmen. Some, like Guanglu, Chong'an, and Fupeng, were distant collateral cousins. Guanglu was a great-grandson of the Shunzhi emperor, Chong'an a fourth-generation descendant of the great Daišan, and Fupeng a fifth-generation descendant of Yoto. Yinzhen also appointed close kinsmen for important ritual tasks. Of the two brothers whom he appointed to perform the grand sacrifice, Yinlu supported his succession and Yinbi, born in 1716, was a mere child when the Kangxi emperor died. Hongzhi, Prince Heng, was the heir of another brother (Yinqi), whom the emperor "tolerated."[76] The most surprising appointment was that of Hongchun, Prince Tai, son of Yinzhen's full brother Yinti, who had

Table 16. Performers of Grand Sacrifices during the
Yongzheng Reign

Date[a]	Ritual Performer	Source
1727–28	Chong'an, Prince Kang	*DQSL* 7:866
	Yinlu, Prince Zhuang	*DQSL* 7:896
1729–30	Guanglu, Prince Yu	*DQSL* 8:78
	Prince Ping, Fupeng	*DQSL* 8:97
1731–32	Yinbi (brother)	*DQSL* 8:385
	Yanhuang, Prince Xian	*DQSL* 8:404
	Guanglu, Prince Yu	*DQSL* 8:424
	Hongzhou (son)	*DQSL* 8:446
	Yinlu, Prince Zhuang	*DQSL* 8:471
1733–34	Hongchun, Prince Tai	*DQSL* 8:700
	Hongzi, Prince Heng	*DQSL* 8:714
	Yinbi, Prince Cheng	*DQSL* 8:727

SOURCE: *Da Qing shilu* (Beijing, 1986).

[a] Calculated from the lunar calendar used by the dynasty, which recorded events in terms of the reign year.

been his major rival for the throne. In 1733, when Hongchun performed the sacrifice to Earth on behalf of the emperor, his father lay in prison, stripped of his titles and freedom since 1726.[77] Finally, Yinzhen appointed one son, Hongzhou, to perform a first-rank sacrifice.

Hongli continued his father's practice and delegated sacrifices at first-rank altars to Aisin Gioro (table 17). Hongli appointed an uncle (Yinbi, Prince Cheng) and two brothers (Hongyan, Prince Guo, and Hongzhou, Prince He) to stand in for him at the sacrifices, as well as more distantly related agnates such as Prince Su, a fourth-generation descendant of Hongtaiji, and Prince Yu, a fourth-generation descendant of Dodo. In 1769, for example, the Qianlong emperor personally sacrificed to Earth during the summer solstice and to Heaven during the winter solstice; he sacrificed to the Altars of Land and the Harvest in the second month and performed two of the five first-rank sacrifices at the Temple of the Ancestors. The rest of the over sixty ritual performances scheduled during the year were delegated to his sons and imperial kinsmen.[78]

By the early nineteenth century, the choice of ritual performers was narrowed further to members of close branches, those descended from Hongli (see chapter 2). This was the gist of an 1808 edict ordering the grand

Table 17. Performers of Grand Sacrifices during the
Qianlong Reign

Date[a]	Ritual Performer	Source
1759–60	Yinbi, Prince Cheng	DQSL 16:372
	Hongyan, Prince Guo	DQSL 16:468
	Hongzhou, Prince He	DQSL 16:580
	Guanglu, Prince Yu	DQSL 16:612
1769–70	Guanglu, Prince Yu (twice)	DQSL 19:8, 189
	Yinbi, Prince Cheng (twice)	DQSL 19:89, 223
1779–80	Jihena, Prince Cheng	DQSL 22:418
	Hongwei, Prince Li	DQSL 22:507
	Hongchang, Prince Cheng	DQSL 22:587
	Xiuling, Prince Yu	DQSL 22:617
1786–87	Yongxi, Prince Su	DQSL 24:747
	Yonggao, Prince Heng	DQSL 24:823
	Yonglang, Prince Yi	DQSL 24:903

SOURCE: *Da Qing shilu* (Beijing, 1986).

[a]Calculated from the lunar calendar used by the dynasty, which recorded events in terms of the reign year.

secretaries to call on three of Yongyan's brothers (Princes Yi, Cheng, and
Qing), or his nephew Prince Ding when someone was required to sacrifice
at the first- and second-rank state altars. A more distant agnate, Prince Su,
was added in 1816 when Prince Yi and Prince Cheng were excused on account of their age (they were in their seventies). The shrinking pool of el
igible first- and second-degree princes forced the Daoguang emperor to order that a third-ranking prince could be appointed to sacrifice if needed.[79]
The Jiaqing emperor's injunction to limit this privilege to close branches
continued to be honored into the 1870s (table 18).[80]

Minning and his successors were forced by the increasing paucity of imperial siblings (Yizhu was the last ruler with brothers) to name first- and
second-degree princes from more distantly related collateral branches of
the imperial lineage. Moreover, a succession of infant rulers in the late
nineteenth century meant that all the eleven sacrifices at first-rank altars
had to be performed by princely appointees. Three successive generations
inheriting Dorgon's title, Prince Rui, were appointed to perform grand sacrifices during the Daoguang (1821–50), Tongzhi (1861–75), and Guangxu
reigns (1876–1908); descendants of Hooge, Prince Su, Daišan, Prince Li,

Table 18. Performers of Grand Sacrifices in Selected Years, 1825–1908

Year	Appointee	Source
1825	Miankai, Prince Dun	DQSL 34:257
	Yiwei, emperor's son	DQSL 34:302
1830	Mianyu, Prince Hui	DQSL 35:541
	Yiwei, emperor's son	DQSL 35:583
1835	Mianyu, Prince Hui	DQSL 37:6
	Yishao, Prince Ding	DQSL 37:24
1840	Mianyu, Prince Hui (twice)	DQSL 38:4, 5
	Zairui, Prince Cheng	DQSL 38:18
	Renshou, Prince Rui	DQSL 38:100
1845	Miange, Prince Zhuang	DQSL 39:184
	Renshou, Prince Rui	DQSL 39:194
	Mianyu, Prince Hui	DQSL 39:252
1854	Yixin, Prince Gong (twice)	DQSL 42:14, 382
1858	Yixin, Prince Gong (six times)	DQSL 43:765, 768, 867, 1039, 1172, 1227
	Yizong, Prince Dun (three times)	DQSL 44:778, 859, 999
	Huafeng, Prince Su	DQSL 43:932
1860	Yizong, Prince Dun (three times)	DQSL 44:466, 677, 797
	Yixin, Prince Gong (three times)	DQSL 44:628, 874, 1048
	Shido, Prince Li	DQSL 44:946
	Qinghui, Prince Keqin	DQSL 44:993

Dodo, Prince Yu, and Jirgalang, Prince Zheng, were included among the ritual performers (see table 18).

The Sacrifice for Rain

The sacrifice for rain personifies the problems created for rulers by adherence to a doctrine of rule by virtue. Most of the sacrifices at first-rank altars aimed at the maintenance of cosmic harmony; no specific object was sought from the deities and indeed, as the Kangxi emperor complained, the prayers tended to fit a stereotypic mold, dictated by precedent.[81] Imperial charisma—or the lack of it—was not clearly tested. The exception to this generalization was the prayer for rain.

The link between Chinese rulers and prayers for rain reached back to ancient times. During the third century B.C. to the first century A.D., sto-

Table 18—*Continued*

Year	Appointee	Source
1867	Yizong, Prince Dun	*DQSL* 49:474
	Zaidun, Prince Yi	*DQSL* 49:476
	Puxu, Prince Ding (twice)	*DQSL* 59:510, 625
	Puzhuang, *beile*	*DQSL* 49:572
	Dezhang, Prince Rui (twice)	*DQSL* 49:580, 767
	Shido, Prince Li (twice)	*DQSL* 49:673, 847
	Yixin, Prince Gong (twice)	*DQSL* 49:710, 898
1870	Te-chang, Prince Rui (twice)	*DQSL* 50:801, 912
	Yixin, Prince Gong (twice)	*DQSL* 50:809, 1166
	Yizong, Prince Dun	*DQSL* 50:824
	Chengzhi, Prince Zheng	*DQSL* 50:876
	Zaidun, Prince Yi	*DQSL* 50:883
	Yihui, Prince Fu	*DQSL* 50:944
	Benge, Prince Yu (three times)	*DQSL* 50:981, 1034, 1099
1884	Longqin, Prince Su (twice)	*DQSL* 54:466, 641
	Benge, Prince Yu	*DQSL* 54:468
	Zaidun, Prince Yi (twice)	*DQSL* 54:477, 574
	Zaiyun, Prince Zhuang	*DQSL* 54:519
	Kuibin, Prince Rui (three times)	*DQSL* 54:532, 769, 798
	Yizong, Prince Dun	*DQSL* 54:696
	Yikuang, Prince Qing	*DQSL* 54:853

SOURCE: *Da Qing shilu* (Beijing, 1986).

ries circulated about a seven-year drought that began after Tang, the founder of the Shang dynasty, killed the last ruler of the preceding Xia dynasty. When the gods of the mountains and rivers demanded a human sacrifice, Tang prayed to the deity that controlled rain, Shangdi, announcing his willingness to take the burden of wrongdoing on his own person, and to become the sacrifice. Heaven responded with a great rain.[82]

The North China plain on which the capital, Peking, is located experiences periodic droughts that cause severe famine, such as the ones reported in the late nineteenth and early twentieth centuries.[83] Emperors kept an eye on the rainfall and received reports even when they were absent from the capital. As Pierre-Etienne Will notes, a drought was a "progressive calamity" for which preventative measures in the form of famine relief could be and were implemented, at least during the heyday of Qing rule.[84]

While they took practical measures to alleviate food shortages and dampen soaring grain prices, emperors felt obliged to simultaneously pursue rituals that would bring rain. That they did so is not surprising when we consider the cosmological claims on which emperorship rested. The failure of prayers to elicit rain detracted from an emperor's charisma, his "kingly virtue" (*de*). Unlike other state rites, this one prayer demanded an immediate and physically apparent cosmological response.

The prayer for rain was not initially a regular state ritual of the first rank, or, from the historical perspective, a Confucian ritual. The story about Tang and his sacrifice to Shangdi dates only from the Early Han. During the preceding Warring States period, shamanic rituals for rain seem to have featured the Yellow Emperor and a mythical figure, Chi You. After the Han, Daoist masters were frequently featured as successful rainmakers, and this tradition persisted into late imperial times.[85]

The Qing emperors conducted prayers for rain within the precincts of the Altar to Heaven. The Shunzhi emperor first personally conducted these rites in 1657 and 1660 during periods of drought in North China. According to the Collected Regulations, prayers were also performed by the Kangxi emperor in 1671, 1678, 1679, 1680, 1687, 1689, and 1717. In 1742 the prayer for rain became an annual first-rank ritual, to be performed in the fourth lunar month, the "first month of spring" (*mengchun*).[86] This fourth-month ritual was called the "regular" prayer for rain (*changyu*), to distinguish it from special prayers (*dayu*), to be conducted in times of crisis.[87]

The prayer for rain was initially called the *yusi* (sacrifice for rain). It was penitential in nature and thus eschewed the normal practices linked with rituals performed at the Altar to Heaven. It was preceded by the observance of three days of abstinence by the emperor, princes, and accompanying officials. During this period it was forbidden to slaughter livestock. On the day of the prayer, the emperor wore "plain clothes" (*sufu*), the same kind of clothing worn during mourning. He showed humility by walking instead of riding in a sedan chair. The imperial regalia were not displayed; music was not played; and there were no ancillary objects of worship (*pei*).[88]

The replacement of the *yusi* by the *changyu* ritual in 1742 symbolically amounted to routinizing the rite and demoting it in the ritual hierarchy. The major object of worship was still Heaven (*huang tian shangdi*), at the Altar to Heaven, but now the spirits of the imperial ancestors were added as ancillary objects of sacrifice. In this and other respects, the routinization of the prayer for rain did away with the penitential nature of the *yusi.* Like the other first-rank rites, all of which were classified as "auspicious" (*ji*) in nature, the *changyu* was performed wearing *lifu*, court dress for ritual occasions. Music was played; the regalia were displayed. In the prayer and the sacrificial songs accompanying the rite, the emperor reported his deep concern about the difficulties of ordinary people in sowing and reaping. He prayed that Heaven would recognize his sincerity and reward the people with rain and sunshine in the proper measure. If rain did not fall after this ritual, sacrifices were to be made three times to the altars of Tianshen (heaven deity), Diqi (earth deity), the hall dedicated to Taisui (planet Jupiter), and the Altar of Land and Grain.

The altars to Tianshen, Diqi, and Taisui were all classified in the middle rank of state sacrifices. They were located within the enclosure of the Altar to Agriculture (*xian nong tan*) in the Outer City. The subsidiary tablets in the altar to Tianshen were dedicated to the deities of the clouds, rain, wind, and thunder; those in the altar to Diqi were dedicated to mountains and rivers of the area around the capital. Taisui was "an important and powerful spirit governing the passage of time," which each year moved through one of the twelve constellations of the astrological zodiac, completing a circuit once every twelve years. The Ming was the first dynasty to establish an altar and to offer regular worship to the spirit; the Qing continued the practice. The eastern and western wings of the Taisuidian were dedicated to the "moon generals" (*yuejiang*) of the four seasons.[89] From the Shunzhi reign, officials were sent during floods or droughts to pray at these altars for succor, and sacrifices at these altars occurred in conjunction with prayers for rain from 1657 onward.

Prayers for rain were also conducted at other temples around Peking, and the accretion of these altars illustrates how popular cults entered the state sacrificial register. The Black Dragon Pool Temple (*heilongtansi*) was erected in 1681 at a site on Gold Mountain (Jinshan) over 30 *li* to the northwest of the capital city, because the dragon god there was said to be efficacious. Kangxi's calligraphy was engraved on stone and awarded to the temple. After prayers here brought good rain for the capital in 1724, the Yongzheng emperor presented his calligraphy and awarded the temple the privilege of using yellow tiles (the imperial color) on its roof. According to an edict issued by Hongli in 1738, "The dragon god of the Heilong pool favors the people . . . whenever the capital district needs rain, prayers here are answered. The ordinary people believe in the merit of this enlightened deity in moistening the fields and permitting the crops to ripen."[90] The Qianlong emperor proposed to show reverence by adding more characters to the deity's name. A 1740 memorial from Yinlu, Prince Zhuang, noted, "In the past, whenever there has been anxiety about drought, praying several times for rain at the Black Dragon Pool has always brought a response. Now the capital district lacks rain; we request that nine Daoist priests respectfully pray for rain at the Black Dragon Pool." [91]

The deity of the White Dragon Pool (Bailongtan) was given a title, "Gloriously Numinous and Broadly Beneficent Dragon God" (*zhaoling guangji longshen*), in 1781. Its sacrifices were performed by local officials selected by the governor general of Zhili. We are not told what meritorious action earned the additional characters "universally benefiting" (*puze*) added in 1817. [92] A more important rain god seems to have been the dragon god of the Jade Spring Mountain (Yuquanshan). A temple to this deity had been built within the Jingmingyuan. In 1744 the god received the title "Merciful and Protecting Dragon God" (*huiji ciyou longshen*). In 1751 the emperor recognized the importance of the water flowing from the spring for the capital and ordered that its altar be entered in the sacrificial register on a par with the altar to the deity of the Black Dragon Pool. He delegated the Neiwufu minister in charge of the Yuanmingyuan to perform the sacrifices. The addition of the characters "numinous protector" (*linghu*) in 1801 came with the following comment:

> The dragon god temple at Yuquanshan has repeatedly responded to prayers for rain and has been enrolled on the list of state altars for a long time. Recently, because the rain was relatively light after the summer solstice, I personally went to pray for rain on the seventeenth of this month. That day there was a light rain. The next day there was ample rainfall. This continued for a day, then cleared, thus further verifying the deity's efficaciousness. [93]

Yet another temple was enrolled in 1812. According to the edict,

> Kunming Lake's dragon god in the Broadly Moistening Efficacious Rain Temple (*guangrun lingyu ci*) has an efficacy that is well known. On the twenty-ninth day of the third month [May 9], because the farmers are yearning for rain, I went there to offer incense. When I returned to the villa, the rains came and continued for ten days . . . at the time of the last drought I again went to light incense and pray. Immediately clouds gathered, and in the afternoon there was rain. The fields were soaked. Today we have again obtained rain. The god favors us and responds to prayers. [94]

Temples to various deities were erected in the imperial villas. Worried lest the gods of rivers (*shui fu*) be angered at their exclusion, the Jiaqing emperor ordered in 1812 that the tablets of Tianhou, the empress of Heaven, and gods of rivers be placed in a new temple. This was a formal act of imperial recognition, like the 1786 order to send officials to make sacrifices to the river and wind gods for sufficient water to enable the grain tribute boats to make a speedy passage northward to the capital.[95] The duty to perform the regular sacrifices in the spring and autumn for all these temples was transferred in 1770 from the Board of Rites to the Neiwufu.

Drought spurred the emperor to order rituals in many different religious traditions. Daoist rites were performed in the Dagaodian (hall of high heaven), a Ming structure that was renovated during the Yongzheng and Qianlong reigns. The supreme deity in this hall was the Jade Emperor, who was worshiped as a nature god who could send or withhold rain.[96] Buddhist rites were performed at an altar outside the Jueshengsi, or the Dazhongsi, which seems to have been the site of a popular cult to the dragon king. A memorial from 1783 that orders nine monks to chant the "Great cloud requesting rain sutra" for seven continuous days at this altar sends imperial princes at the same time to pray for rain at a Daoist altar erected at the Zhanlisuo.[97] Even Muslim rituals seem to have been performed for rain; one document from 1796 orders that rewards be distributed in thanks for rain to the Buddhist, Daoist, and Muslim clerics whose prayers had been answered.[98]

According to the Collected Rituals, Heaven frequently responded promptly when the emperor prayed. In 1657 we are told that the emperor had not even returned to his palace from the Altar to Heaven after performing the rite when a "great rain" began. In 1660 clouds gathered even as the emperor prayed, and rain fell for three days. There was a similarly favorable and immediate response to the emperor's prayers in 1671, 1678, 1686, and 1735.[99] But prayers at altars of the popular dragon god cults also produced "immediate" results. We have already noted the additions of several of these altars to the Qing official register, usually because of their efficacy. In 1801 the Jiaqing emperor noted that after he went to light incense at the altar, "immediately that day there was a slight rainfall, and the next day, a large downpour that continued for several days before clearing. This further proof of efficacy (*ling*) prompts me to reverently add characters to the name of the Jade Spring dragon god."[100]

Since they were a Confucian portent of bad government, droughts also required emperors to respond in a Confucian manner by seeking correction from officials. The Kangxi emperor noted in 1711:

> Since the spring, despite ample rainfall there has been no wind . . . . now the weather is very dry. Clouds arise but they disperse. From ancient times when there is error in human affairs the harmony of Heaven is affected. Perhaps there has been error in governance; I may have been found wanting in my personnel appointments. Among the officials

factions may have formed. Perhaps the unworthy occupy official posts
. . . you Grand Secretaries should consult with the ministers and memo-
rialize in detail.[101]

In view of our knowledge concerning the factions surrounding imperial
sons at that time, we can well understand the ministers' response: "Having
respectfully read Your Majesty's edict," they wrote, "we could not avoid
trembling."[102] Despite their protestations of innocence, the drought continued. On June 20 the emperor ordered three days of prayer beginning
June 21: during this period, when there would be no hunting in Chengde,
capital officials should pray earnestly and temples should chant sutras. The
emperor criticized the Manchu president of the Board of Rites for laziness
and negligence and ordered that the president of the Board of Revenue,
Muhelun, pray in Beiheno's place (June 22). Two days later, the emperor
offered to return to Peking but was saved from doing so by the onset of
rains, on June 26.[103]

In 1711 the Kangxi emperor did not perform the prayer for rain, but his
exchanges with the high ministers underlined the degree to which it was
assumed that the efficacy of the prayers rested on the emperor's charisma:
in Chinese, his "kingly virtue" (*de*). Hongli used this precise term in the
bad famine year of 1744 when the government faced a second year of a
drought that had begun in the summer of 1743. Through 1743 and the
early months of 1744, the emperor discussed with his officials how to re-
lieve the food shortages. Their efforts produced a substantial relief program
that significantly eased the food scarcities in Zhili province. But the practical implementation of famine relief did not preclude parallel efforts to obtain rain through prayer. That year, the emperor announced, he would personally carry out the *changyu* rite. He also directed that prayers be offered
at the Guandi temple, City God temple, Black Dragon Pool Temple, and
several others.[104] Because of the drought crisis, this prayer could not be
considered routine; the emperor would adopt the hallmarks of full peni-
tence (no music, no imperial regalia, no carriage, no *lifu*).

When weeks passed after the *changyu* rite without rain, the emperor's
anguish increased. On June 12, when he went to pay his respects to the empress dowager at the Changchunyuan, she walked from her quarters to the
Dragon God temple in the villa grounds to add her prayers for rain. The
emperor reported: "Today the Empress Dowager walked from her palace to
the Dragon God temple in the villa grounds to devoutly pray. As I listened
reverently I was alarmed and awestruck (*huang kong, zhan piao*). This is
all [due to] my being unvirtuous (*bu de*). Being unable to summon Heaven's

harmony, I have dragged Mother to exertion. Having arrived at this extremity, as a son, I have no way in which I can pardon myself."[105] And still there was no rain. On June 16 the emperor personally composed a sacrificial prayer and sent a prince to pray at the temple to the wind god (*feng shen miao*). The emperor's exertions were finally brought to a happy conclusion with the onset of a heavy rainfall in the evening of June 26, 1744: it soaked the ground and permitted late grain and bean crops to be sown.[106]

Nature was even more cruel to Hongli in the drought year of 1759, when he again personally performed the *changyu* rite as a full penitential ritual. Again, there was no rain after the rite was performed on May 3. By May 7 the emperor was ordering the Board of Punishments to check the criminal dockets to ensure that there was no miscarriage of justice. On June 6 the emperor went to the Black Dragon Pool Temple to pray for rain; he ordered that sutras be chanted in temples in and near Peking while officials prepared to implement famine relief. On June 16 he personally sacrificed at the Altars of Land and the Harvest, wearing a rain hat and plain clothes (*sufu*) to show his contrition. That same day he issued an edict suggesting that the persistent drought might be caused by misgovernment, indicating his willingness to leave no stone unturned in his efforts to restore cosmic harmony.

The drought persisted. As the emperor prepared for the grand sacrifice at the Altar to Earth at the summer solstice, he modified the normal ritual procedures to reflect the crisis. No carriage would be used; the imperial regalia would not be erected. Despite these measures, the sacrifice to Earth on June 22 brought no rain. The emperor again issued orders that punishments in criminal cases be lightened. And still there was no rain. Finally, on June 30, the emperor announced that since all the normal measures had failed, he would observe strict abstinence and carry out a *dayu* ritual, on July 5. Much to everyone's relief, rain began to fall that evening and into the next day, ending the drought crisis.[107]

The prayer for rain, or *dayu*, was performed as a last-ditch ritual response to a prolonged drought. In theory it was scheduled only after three prayers for rain at the altars cited above had not brought relief. In reality, as we have seen, it tended to take place after appeals to various local dragon gods had been ineffectual. The ritual was performed only twice during the dynasty, first in 1759, then in 1832, when repeated prayers at other altars, including the Altar to Earth, had not brought sufficient rain.[108] The blame for drought lay squarely on the shoulders of the ruler: as the Daoguang emperor said, "I tremble as I consider the causes of the drought: the fault must be mine."[109] The *dayu* climaxed a series of governmental and ritual actions by the emperor that attempted to reform government and persuade Heaven to yield. Each time there were political ramifications. In 1800, for example, it won a pardon for the scholar-official Hong Liangji (1746–1809). Hong had been exiled to Ili for his political opinions, but the prolonged drought necessitated "the ritual granting of amnesties to propitiate Heaven." When a pardon was granted to Hong, rain fell that afternoon; the emperor blamed himself for having punished a remonstrating official.[110]

All the pre-1742 prayers for rain at the Altar to Heaven, and the *dayu* rites thereafter, were personally conducted by the emperor and shared the same structure. Unlike the *changyu* ritual, these were penitential rituals. The ancestral tablets were omitted; the emperor and participants wore plain clothes. Rain tassels were attached to the caps.[111] Slaughter of livestock was forbidden; the emperor and his court observed three days of abstinence. During the rite itself, the imperial regalia were not erected; no music was played. The emperor eschewed the use of his carriage to walk from the Hall of Abstinence to the Altar to Heaven.

As we have observed, the rituals for rain in the Peking district went far beyond the framework of the state altars, to encompass all the major religious traditions of the empire and move altars from the popular religion into the state sacrificial registers. The search for efficacy tended to encourage a multiplication of ritual performances and ritual sites, as we can see when we examine the ritual actions taken to get more rain during 1807.[112] The winter of 1806–7 saw sparse snowfall, and scanty spring rains. Altars set up during late March and April brought some rain but not nearly enough. The emperor decided to carry out the *changyu* ritual personally; he followed this with further prayers at various local altars. From March 22 to June 19 of that year, the Jiaqing emperor had prayers for rain performed on four occasions at the altars to Tianshen, Diqi, and Taisui, on ten different occasions at the Black Dragon Pool altar, and twice at the Jueshengsi. He sent an official to pray at the White Dragon Pool altar in Miyun county, and had an altar erected at the Shangaoshuizhang within the Yuanmingyuan and either he or his sons went to pray there eight times, both to ask and give thanks for rain.

But there could also be too much of a good thing. In 1801, as we have noted above, the emperor's prayers for rain were answered. By late July the emperor was in a quandary: there was too much rain. As the emperor explained in an edict, a new ritual solution was required:

> From the first *xun* of the sixth month, the capital district has had steady rain. It has rained continuously for two *xun* and still it has not cleared.

The Yongding River has overflowed and caused damage, and the waters do not recede. I am beset with anxiety and my fear mounts. I have consulted the *huidian* but it only has the ritual praying for rain in the Altar of Land and Grain. There is no prayer for clearing, but floods and droughts are both disasters, and ought to be treated in the same way . . . on the twenty-sixth day of this month [August 5] I will go to the Altar of Land and Grain to pray for clearing. Earlier on the twenty-second I will enter the Palace of Abstinence. I will observe the three days of abstinence from the twenty-third . . . the twenty-seventh, twenty-eighth, and twenty-ninth are days of abstinence for the autumn sacrifice. On the first [August 9], after the ritual is completed, if the skies have cleared and the mud has dried I will return to reside in the Yuanmingyuan. If at that time there is still no clearing, I must remain inside the Palace of Abstinence for several days until the weather clears.[113]

The accretion of imperial prayers for rain to dragon gods and other deities raises interesting questions concerning evolving notions of Qing rulership. We began by noting that the Qing perpetuated an uneasy balance between the potentially contradictory principles of rule by virtue and rule by heredity. The prayer to Heaven at the Altar to Heaven was based on the assumption that rain or drought was Heaven's response to virtuous rule. Emperors made the direct linkage between their own virtue (*de*) and the response of Heaven. When Hongli put the prayer for rain on the annual ritual calendar in 1742, he enlisted the imperial ancestors in soliciting the favors of Heaven for their descendant. The *changyu* ritual like the other first-rank rites thus represented an attempt to amalgamate rule by virtue and rule by heredity.

The political challenge to imperial legitimacy posed by drought dissuaded emperors from relying solely on Confucian rituals. Emperors presented offerings to popular dragon gods and summoned Buddhist, Daoist, and even Muslim clerics to invoke rain through prayers and rites. Such actions were part of a long history of state-society interaction, whereby the state systematically incorporated popular local cults into the state religion and attempted to harness their magical efficacy into the service of the regime. *Ling,* the term which has been translated as "efficacy" in this chapter, refers to the magical powers of deities, which exists irrespective of the *de* of rulers. As Kenneth Pomeranz notes, state incorporation resulted in "normalization," that is, in reducing the *ling* of a cult or shrine. In structural terms, *ling* became weaker as it moved up the spatial hierarchy. The state was thus engaged in a Sisyphean task: it tried to take over the *ling* of popular cults, but the takeover weakened the very efficacy it sought, so new cults and shrines had to be continually added.[114]

De, "kingly virtue," is, in Confucian terms, as magically powerful as *ling* in constructing an ideal society. *De* inspires subjects to fulfill their proper social roles: "if the prince is a genuine man of virtue, then all officials, fathers, and husbands will perforce follow his example." In ancient Confucian thought *de* is in itself sufficient to produce the correct social order. Incorporation of popular deities into the state religion should not be needed. That it occurred was an implicit recognition of the chimerical nature of rule by virtue alone—and a reflection of the realpolitik dictating imperial action.

Qing rulers did not like to openly discuss the gap between Confucian rites and rituals required to keep the state in good order. Kenneth Pomeranz's study of the Handan Rain Shrine focuses on a prolonged drought in 1867, which drove the Tongzhi emperor to send the president of the Board of Rites to perform sacrifices at this ancient shrine. Despite borrowing a rain-producing tablet to take to the capital, the state "overtly denied that anything other than the virtue of the person praying could move the gods."[115] Faced with a concrete test of their rulership, emperors were happy to govern with the help of *ling*, but they did not want to talk about it.

Chapter 7 Shamanism and Tibetan Buddhism at Court

Shamanism and Tibetan Buddhism were major elements in Qing policies that incorporated the peoples of Northeast and Inner Asia into the empire. The emperors identified shamanism with Manchu tradition and used shamanism in the creation of Manchu identity. Patronage of Lamaist Buddhism enabled the rulers to promote a model of kingship with deep resonance in Inner Asia. Both found a place in the life of the court.

SHAMANISM

Contemporary analyses of shamanism or what Jane Atkinson calls "shamanship" have moved a significant distance away from the assumptions and interpretations found in Mircea Eliade's classic 1951 work.[1] Discarding Eliade's assumption of a unitary model, which he called "classic" shamanism, and its corollary, that shamanism was a cultural product of prestate societies, frees specialists to consider the great diversity of shamanic practices that are found in an equally bewildering range of political systems, from nonurban groups living a pastoral existence to colonized subjects to, for example, Koreans and Taiwanese in contemporary times.

Shamanism persists in twentieth-century North Asia.[2] The term *šaman* (*saman* in Manchu) is found in every Tunguso-Manchurian and also in some Mongol and Turkic languages.[3] Shamanship operates in a world dominated by nature deities, some of whom are ancestral spirits. The world in which humans live is the middle realm; above in the sky is another world of the deities, while below the earth lies the kingdom of the dead. A river or a "world-tree" is the path between upper and lower worlds. With the aid of bird, animal, and ancestral spirits, shamans summon deities to come down the world-tree into their presence.[4] And the tree links the middle realm to the upper world. When people pray to the gods, they go to a sacred tree in the forest or use a specially prepared pole (in Manchu, *somo* or *siltan moo*) for the ritual.

The Jurchen ancestors of the Manchus practiced shamanism by the eleventh century A.D.[5] Like other Tungus people, they probably worshiped many deities in the natural world as well as part-human, part-animal ancestral deities. Recent studies of Manchu folklore recited by storytellers and old shamans in Northeast China reveal the names and characteristics of many of these spirits.[6] The creation story features a "heaven mother," Abka *hehe*, who symbolizes the good in the world. Stories of her battle with evil in the person of the deity Yeluli were recited in many parts of the northeast. One legend tells of a goddess named Uludun *mama*, alternatively known as Aoyazun, who gave birth to all living things and created heaven, earth, mountains, and streams ("Uludun" means "light of the sun"). Another divides the responsibility of creation: Heaven mother created things; the fire god created light and warmth; and the willow gave birth to humankind.[7]

Manchu legends say that originally heaven had no form. Its earliest embodiment was as a pregnant woman shaped like a willow. Manchus revere the willow, which represents fecundity; they say that humans emerged out of the willow, which grows without exhaustion. When Abka *hehe* fought with Yeluli, many benevolent deities died. As Abka *hehe* tried to flee, Yeluli caught her by her battle skirt, which was made of willow leaves. Some of these leaves broke off and fell to earth, where they gave rise to living creatures. A Fuca shamanic prayer describes how a great flood destroyed all living beings except for one human, who survived by holding on to a willow branch. Fodo *mama*, or Folifodo *mama* (Willow mother) is worshiped by many Manchu clans.[8]

Veneration of crows and magpies was also deeply embedded in Jurchen culture. Several Jurchen clans identify the crow as their ancestor, and crows were one of the sacred birds on whom a shaman could call for help. In the Manchu epic about the great shaman Wubuxiben *mama*, the crow was a companion of Heaven. It died after eating a black herb, was transformed into a black horse, and became a messenger bringing warnings and bad news. The huge flocks of crows in the park in Peking surrounding the Temple of the Ancestors were probably descended from the crows attracted to the palace by the food offerings in the compound of the Kunning palace (see below).[9]

The magpie (*saksaha*) is also a sacred bird, sometimes identified as the maidservant of Heaven mother. The magpie plays a key role in Manchu legends of their origin and of Nurgaci's rise to power. It was a magpie who dropped the red fruit that caused the heavenly maiden Fekulen to conceive and give birth to Bukuri Yongson, the founding ancestor. A magpie allowed Bukuri Yongson's descendant to escape from his pursuers by landing on his head, causing them to think the figure they saw in the distance was a dead tree: "thus, future generations all love the magpie and are forbidden to harm it."[10] The pole or sacred tree pierces heaven or connects it to the earth. In some versions, nine branches must be left on the spirit pole, because there are nine heavens. The magpie—some would say, the crow—is the primary deity receiving offerings in these sacrifices, even though the ritual is identified as a sacrifice to heaven.[11]

The Jurchen had two kinds of shamans. One type included individuals "selected" by a deity; they underwent a "shamanic illness" until they agreed to the god's demands. Such "transformational" shamans could treat persons of any clan, unlike the hereditary shamans who specialized in performing rites for their own clan.[12] In Jilin, Qiqihaer, and Dairen, hereditary shamans were called *sama*; in some cases they were regarded as outcasts, and all of them were male. These "patriarchal" shamans performed rituals to the ancestors of the kinship groups. Another type of shaman were those who had been "called," the *daxian*: this group included both men and women. The *daxian* set up altars in their own houses and were consulted as healers. Both types received training.[13]

Records of the pre-1644 period indicate that the Jurchen-Manchus called upon shamans to heal sickness. When *beile* Dodo became ill, he summoned the shaman Jingguda to his house, but Jingguda's efforts at a cure failed and Dodo died. Apparently Hongtaiji did not believe in the shaman's ability to heal and forbade shamans to practice their arts. Company captains could be punished for failing to enforce the ban.[14] Still, shamanic rites continued to be performed in attempts to cure illness: one archival record notes that June 10, 1685, was an auspicious day for the "seeking good fortune" rite on behalf of the emperor's sixth son, Yinzuo, who nonetheless died five days later. Archival records also show that sacrifices were offered on behalf of an emperor's sons after their recovery from smallpox variolation.[15]

The shaman was a healer of the sick, and someone who could bring the dead back to life. Many Tungus peoples believed that humans have several (often three) souls. When one of these souls is missing, either because it is lost or because some evil spirit has taken it away, the person becomes ill and may die. The shaman can force spirits who stole a sick person's soul to give it back and may journey to the underworld trying to redeem the spirit of the dead and bring them back to life. For Eliade, this trance-journey was the quintessential core of shamanism.[16]

The Manchu understanding of the trance-journey is revealed in a Manchu-language transcription of an oral story called "The Tale of the Nišan Shamaness."[17] In this folk epic an official whose only son, Sergudai, has died while hunting, is advised to consult a shaman to bring the boy back to life. He enlists the services of a shaman called Teteke, who asks some village (male) shamans to help her in the ritual. Teteke requires bells, a rooster, a dog, bean paste, and paper. The bean paste and paper are used to pay off or bribe various individuals in the underworld. The rooster and dog are payment for extension of Sergudai's life. The epic describes Teteke's journey to the land of the dead, where she bargains for the life of the boy with a relative of the Lord of the Underworld. Teteke's spiritual helper in this dangerous journey is Omosi *mama*, the willow goddess, whose full name is Folifodo omosi *mama*. When the shaman is awakened from her trance, Sergudai also regains consciousness.

The dress worn by Manchu shamans was very characteristic.[18] The professional shaman wore an apron; a cap, made of feathers symbolizing the ability of the shaman to fly to the world of the deities; a belt, on which bells dangled; and a knife, to which metal links were attached at the hilt and along one edge. He or she also held two long wooden sticks, with metal bells attached at their tips. Perhaps the most important part of a shaman's equipment was the drum.

Jurchen offered the spirits grain, beans, millet cakes, home-brewed wine, fish, and meat. In the early days wild game was offered as a sacrifice but after 1644 the court substituted seasonal presentations of live fish and fowl for the larger game. The primary animal sacrifice was the pig.

Imperial Rites

Nurgaci and his successors created shamanic state rituals. By the seventeenth century, the Jurchen belief in multiple heavens was supplanted by one Heaven (Abka *ama*, Abka *han*), now a male supreme deity: whether this new concept of Heaven was the direct result of Chinese influence is impossible to determine, but the conceptual change also mirrored the process of political centralization within the Jurchen polity. As the ruler gave noble titles and bureaucratized his rule, Heaven's name also changed. By 1660 prayers were addressed to "the highest Heaven-khan," *dergi abkai han*.[19] The court performed shamanic rituals that paralleled but did not intersect with the Han Chinese state rituals to Heaven. According to the eighteenth-century compendium on Manchu shamanism,

> The Manchus from ancient times have revered Heaven . . . thus when we established a base in Shengjing, we respectfully built the *tangzi* (shamanic shrine) in order to sacrifice to Heaven. . . . Although we subsequently erected the altar [to Heaven] and temples where we separately sacrificed to Heaven, the Buddha, and gods, we dared not alter the old customary ceremonies of sacrifice. When our ancestors settled the [North China] plain and moved the capital, they still respected the sacrificial customs of the past.[20]

In contrast to the Chinese custom, the worship of Heaven was performed by ordinary Manchus and imperial officials alike.[21]

In worshiping Heaven, the Manchus followed the Jin and Mongol precedents. Jin rulers worshiped Heaven in shamanic rituals and, like the Mongols, made military decisions based on shamanic divination.[22] There was thus already a form of state shamanism during the twelfth century under the Jurchen Jin state and in the thirteenth century under Chinggis Khan. Chinggis Khan had always worshiped Mönke Tenggeri, the "supreme god of early Mongolian shamanism," and ascribed his success in battle to Heaven's favor.[23]

Nurgaci's appeals to Heaven paralleled those of Chinggis. He cited Heaven as the arbiter of right and wrong. Heaven would give the victory in battle to the cause that was just. The Manchu records show that Nurgaci worshiped Heaven and the flags in 1593 before his campaign against the Yehe. In 1616 he reported the "seven grievances" (justifying his attack on the Ming) to Heaven. Later, Nurgaci cited his victories as proof that Heaven had chosen him to become ruler.[24] Later rulers continued this tradition. In 1644 the regent, Dorgon, led the *beile* to worship Heaven before leading the Manchu banners into China. The rites, which consisted of the three kneelings and nine kowtows to Heaven and, separately, before the flags (presumably to a god of war), were performed at a temple (*tangzi;* in Manchu, *tangse*) which was erected in the capital. Similar rituals were performed by the Kangxi emperor before departing the capital on the campaign against Galdan.[25]

Traditionally the worship of Heaven took place in spring and summer. The addition of a New Year rite may have stemmed from a desire to emulate the Han Chinese practices of the Ming court. In place of the Chinese sacrifice to Heaven during the winter solstice, Manchu rulers worshiped Heaven at the *tangzi* on New Year's day. According to the Manchu-language records, the precedent was set by Nurgaci in 1624. With Hong-taiji, these rites became a regular part of the shamanic ritual calendar and took place before a spirit pole erected in the courtyard of the *tangzi*. Monthly rituals were also added in the 1640s.[26] During Hongtaiji's reign, major events in the kingdom were also reported to Heaven.[27]

Tangzi *Rituals*

The *tangzi* was the site for state shamanic rituals during the Qing dynasty. The term may have originated in the portable "god boxes" (*tangse*) in which the figures of the deities were placed during an earlier era, when the Jurchen were mobile hunters. After the ancestors of Nurgaci settled in a palisaded village, their deity altar (*tangse*) faced southeast and was constructed in an octagonal shape because the shamans taught that all the spirits of nature came from an eight-sided, nine-layered heaven. According to one scholar, when Nurgaci defeated rival Jurchen tribes, he had his troops destroy their *tangse*. Eventually Nurgaci's *tangse*, with his clan's protective deities, supplanted all the others, although tribes who had voluntarily joined Nurgaci's cause were allowed to worship their own gods.[28]

Under Hongtaiji, commoners and officials were forbidden to erect *tangse* for ritual purposes: the *tangse* became the monopoly of the ruler. There was a *tangzi* in Hetu Ala, and another in the eastern capital, before the capital was moved to Mukden. In Mukden, the *tangzi* was located to the east of the palace. In Peking, work on building a *tangzi* inside the Inner City to the southeast of the palace began almost immediately after the Manchu troops occupied the capital. Because this temple was damaged during the Boxer rebellion and its neighborhood became the site of the foreign diplomatic legations, a new *tangzi* was established in the southeastern corner of the imperial city in December 1901.[29]

The *tangzi* in Mukden and Peking included four sites for ritual performance. At the northernmost edge of the walled compound in Peking (the place of honor) stood a rectangular sacrificial hall (*shendian, xiangdian*), in which Sakyamuni Buddha (Fucihi), Guanyin (Fusa), and Guandi (Guwan i beise) received sacrifice at the New Year, on the eighth day of the fourth month, when they were washed in the ceremony of "bathing the Buddha" (*xifo*), and in the spring and autumn. The introduction of these deities may well have predated Nurgaci, since Buddhism was known to the Jurchen since at least the Jin dynasty. These "guest deities" were not traditionally worshiped by ordinary Manchus.[30]

South of the sacrificial hall stood the "round hall" (*yuandian*), whose octagonal structure marked it as a lineal descendant of the earlier *tangse*. The two deities worshiped in this pavilion bore noble titles such as *taiji* and *beise*. In contrast with Sakyamuni, Guanyin, and Guandi, who were *enduri*, these deities were called *weceku*. According to Charles de Harlez, *enduri* were "les esprits de premier ordre," with power to manipulate the forces of nature. *Weceku* were "les génies domestiques, protecteurs du foyer et de la famille, mais surtout les âmes des ancêtres auxquels ce dernier rôle est spécialement attribué."[31] *Weceku* were thus ancestral deities. Niohon *taiji*, also called Niohon Abka (green heaven), and Uduben *beise* (first ancestor) were the objects of the New Year sacrifices; the sacrifices preceding military campaigns; monthly sacrifices; and an annual sacrifice to the horse deity.[32]

Directly south of the round hall stood the stone plinth that held the emperor's spirit pole during the spring and autumn rites. It stood in the center and slightly to the north of twelve rows of plinths for the spirit poles erected by the princes. Another octagonal structure, located in its own enclosure in the southeastern corner, was dedicated to Šangsi *enduri*, an agricultural deity, who received sacrifices on the first day of each month.[33]

The sacrifice of animals to Heaven, called *metembi* in Manchu, was distinguished from other sacrifices called *wecembi*. The *metembi* ritual did not include the *tiaoshen* or shamanic dance (see below). Performed on the day after the monthly rites and the grand sacrifice at spring and autumn, the sacrifice to Heaven began with preliminary offerings of incense, water, and cakes to the morning and evening deities, who were placed on the west and north *kang* (heated raised platforms along the walls of the room). The spirit pole in the south courtyard was lowered and cleaned. The shaman presented a sacrificial pig and washed grain, along with appropriate prayers to Heaven, while the emperor knelt facing the spirit pole. After the pig was slaughtered, its blood, viscera, and flesh were presented as offerings to Heaven. A third presentation of grain and pork occurred after the pork was cooked. This presentation of cooked rather than raw flesh was a distinctive Manchu custom, which differed from the custom at the state altars.[34] At the conclusion of the ritual, the pig's neck bone was attached to the top of the spirit pole while the viscera, flesh, and grain were piled into the offering plate at the top of the pole for crows and magpies to consume. The pole was then raised. The remaining pork was consumed by the emperor and other participants.[35]

The *tangzi* rituals were state rituals for the conquest elite. The participants were Manchu nobles, banner officials, and Manchu civil and military officials of high rank.³⁶ As noted above, the objects of worship in the *tangzi* were carefully separated. Buddhist and Chinese deities enjoyed the highest rank but did not feature in the central rituals, which were directed to Heaven and to the protective deities of the Jurchen housed in the *yuandian.* The peripheral status of the agricultural deity, Šangsi *enduri,* was also reflected in its location and ritual calendar. The most important shamanic rite, the *wecembi* (*beideng ji*), was never performed there. The worship of Heaven itself culminated in actions borrowed from the Confucian state rites, the three kneelings and nine prostrations.

The worship of Heaven at the *tangzi* can also be interpreted as a clan ritual for the Aisin Gioro. This aspect of the ceremony was embodied in the spirit poles for the emperor, his sons, and the imperial princes. After the emperor performed the sacrifice during the great spring and autumn rites, the princes would set up their spirit poles and offer their sacrifice. This practice contrasted with the practice of other Manchu descent groups, whose spirit pole was monopolized by the main house.³⁷

Palace Rites

The *tangzi* rites overlapped with those performed within the women's quarters in the Qingning palace in Mukden and after 1644 in the Kunning palace in Peking. Palace rites were the responsibility of the Office of Shamanism (Shen fang), an agency under the Imperial Household Department that employed 183 shamans (all of them women) and eunuchs to assist them.³⁸ Before the 1660s the palace rituals were performed for the Aisin Gioro by their wives and by the ruler's consorts.³⁹ Later, shamans were selected from the wives of high officials belonging to Gioro households of the upper three banners.

With the exception of offerings to the horse god, who was worshiped in a separate temple erected in the northwestern corner of the Forbidden City, shamanic rituals were carried out in the Kunning palace. Images of Sakyamuni, Guanyin, and Guandi were placed on the western *kang* to receive daily offerings of incense, water, and cakes at dawn. Because Chinese Buddhism prohibited animal sacrifice, the images of Buddha and Guanyin were removed from the *kang* before the shamans sacrificed two pigs before Guandi.⁴⁰

Scholars have long puzzled over the origins and meanings of the three *weceku* who received offerings on the north *kang* during the daily evening services. Recent fieldwork among northeastern shamans helps us better understand Monggo, Murigan, and Nirugan *weceku.* According to these studies, Monggo was originally a protective deity, Katun *noyan*, worshiped by the Jurchen who lived along the Sungari and Mudan river systems. Murigan seems to have been a mountain god worshiped by Jurchen living north of the Amur River, while Nirugan were ancestral paintings.[41] The *weceku* received daily pig sacrifices, supplemented once a quarter by the presentation of live wildfowl or fish. Once a quarter both the morning and evening deities also received additional offerings of oxen, horses, gold, silver, and silk and cotton cloth.[42]

Only the *weceku* received the *wecembi* rite. After the pork was offered to gods and ancestors during the evening rites, the shaman would dance and sing the sacred songs and prayers in a darkened closed room. She would call the gods by name to come down and accept the sacrifices that had been prepared for them: "What we call is the god, those who wait are the children. The sacrifices are ready and the persons respectfully pray and express thanks."[43]

The daily sacrifices in the Kunning palace and the calendrical rituals performed in its courtyard were the imperial correlate of the household rites performed by ordinary bannermen. The altars were located in the residence of the empress and underlined the primacy of the wife in the rituals. Additionally, the rituals marked the boundaries for the emperor's conjugal family unit as defined by Manchu laws of inheritance. Emperor's sons who were minors had black pigs sacrificed on their behalf in the Kunning palace. When they married, however, they had to perform their own sacrifices in their conjugal residences, even though they resided within the Forbidden City. New domestic altars for the *weceku* were installed in their mansions when they moved out of the palace.[44]

Other palace rituals replicated commoners' rites. The "seeking good fortune" (*qiufu*) ritual, performed when a prince married and at the end of every year, was, along with the raising of the spirit pole to worship Heaven, part of the annual sacrifice to ancestors performed by bannermen (see below).[45]

Shamanic rituals at court were also modified to accommodate the requirements of state ritual. The slaughter of black pigs, an integral part of the *wecembi* rites, occasionally conflicted with the prohibition on killing during the three days of abstinence observed before sacrifice at the first-rank altars of the state. According to a 1742 memorial drawn up by the ministers of the Neiwufu, "formerly [shamanic] sacrifices could not be conducted in the palace on the days when the regulations forbid the killing of living creatures . . . in the Kangxi reign it was determined that if the day when the pole was raised at the *tangzi* and grand sacrifice conducted for the ancestors [coincided] with a day when living creatures should not be killed in order to obtain rain, the latter rule should not apply. In Yongzheng 11 [1733] an edict was issued that reversed this decision."[46] The same memorial disclosed that the Kangxi emperor had personally raised the pole and conducted the grand sacrifice only once, in 1670, and that the Yongzheng emperor had performed the rite once, in the autumn of 1723. Were their successors more diligent? The regulations of the Board of Rites issued a century later cite imperial decisions concerning shamanic sacrifice during days of abstinence that indicate that the Qianlong and Jiaqing emperors did personally participate in the *tangzi* rituals.[47]

The Shamanic Code

The Qianlong emperor's avowed concern for the perpetuation of a separate Manchu identity naturally embraced the Manchu traditional religion, which he feared was disappearing. The Manchu prayers were sometimes no longer comprehensible; the emperor inspected and corrected the texts of family prayers submitted by the princes.[48] The *hesei toktobuha manju we-cere metere kooli bithe* was compiled in Manchu in 1747 by an imperial commission chaired by an Aisin Gioro prince. In 1777 the emperor ordered it translated into Chinese for incorporation into the Four Treasuries (*Siku quanshu*). A committee headed by Agui and Yu Minzhong produced the Chinese-language edition, the *Qinding Manzhou jishen jitian dianli*, in 1780. Later commercial editions of this code were produced and apparently circulated among ordinary citizens. One of these, an 1828 edition entitled *Manzhou tiaoshen huanyuan dianli*, compiled by Punian, is still extant. A comparison of the Manchu and Chinese texts shows that the Manchu-language edition included more detailed illustrations with explanations, reflecting the court's hope that it would be used as a guide to praxis.[49]

The rituals described in the shamanic code combined shamanic elements with Buddhist and popular religious practices. Court shamanism strongly emphasized ancestor worship. By bureaucratizing the recruitment of women as shamans and by replacing trance with the lighting of incense, presentation of offerings, obeisances, and kowtows, the court removed the ecstatic element from all the rituals except the palace evening services. The dilution of shamanic elements is evident in Xiaoshi's description of *tiao-shen*, which cited the chanting of Tibetan sutras before Tibetan Buddhist statues within the Forbidden City.[50]

The Qianlong emperor's goal, the preservation of Manchu shamanic rituals, was not fully realized. Even the Mukden specialists had to be taught the Manchu shamanic prayers for the grand sacrifice scheduled during the Jiaqing emperor's visit in 1818. Nonetheless, the compilation and dissemination of the work had a significant impact on the shamanic rituals practiced by the banner population; many households accepted it as a standard of Manchu culture. One study recently discovered that even Hanjun families performed the prescribed shamanic rituals.[51] Many Manchu shamans interviewed in the early twentieth century were able to reproduce only the Chinese transliteration of the original Manchu prayers, and shamanism seems to have become largely a thing of the past for banner families residing in Peking. A 1981 survey of six *mukûn* (clans) living in the northeast showed, however, that some clan shamans were still performing shamanic rites according to the prescriptions in the *Qinding Manzhou jishen jitian dianli.*[52]

The dissemination of the shamanic code promoted the Aisin Gioro family rites among ordinary Manchus, even though older traditions lingered among shamans living on the northern border with Russia and in isolated localities along the Ussuri and Sungari rivers. The court used the banner organization to implement compliance with the shamanic code. It forced other surname groups to remove their own clan ancestors from the altars and was probably responsible for increasing worship directed to Heaven.[53] The degree to which court-prescribed shamanism influenced the shamanic practice of bannermen can be measured by the revival, during the Opium War era, of ecstatic shamanism. According to the "god books" (*shenben*) kept by many banner lineages, the clan gods returned after a long absence to "seize" the shamans, who performed shamanic rituals discouraged by the Qing court. Some god books describe deceased shamans returning on the backs of tigers; others the return of gods in dreams. Similarly, the end of the dynasty in 1911 permitted clans living in the more remote parts of the northeast to openly practice shamanic rituals that had been repressed by the court.[54]

The influence of the Qing shamanic code can still be discerned in the shamanic rituals performed by kinship groups in Northeast China. Echoing fieldwork observations from the early twentieth century, these descriptions of the annual sacrifices performed by members of the *mukûn* to household gods and ancestors include many of the rituals recorded in the code, such as the raising of the spirit pole and the "seeking good fortune" rite.[55]

The Qing emphasis on clan rituals meant that the hereditary clan shaman was favored over the "called" or professional shaman. And the prestige of both types of shaman declined, since the head of a household or his wife could perform regular sacrifices to the ancestors (although some households still called on professional shamans for healing and communication with the world of the dead).[56] Women performed the domestic shamanic rituals, just as they do in contemporary Korean households.[57]

Shamanism and State Building

Shamanism was one of a set of cultural policies that changed the societies of people living on the Siberian frontier. The Manchu rulers directed intensive efforts to control the hunting and fishing groups living on the lower reaches of the Amur after the Treaty of Nerchinsk. In the seventeenth century Daur, Oroqen, Evenk, and other peoples were enrolled into the banners as "new Manchus" (*ice manju*). *Ice manju* were sent to Ningguta for training, then assigned to new garrisons built along the Qing-Russian frontier. A decision in 1692 to move the Xibo, who had been subordinates of the Khorchin Mongols, from the Mongol to the Manchu banners, had far-reaching consequences for the Xibo, who were sent to garrisons in Shengjing, Peking, and Xinjiang in the eighteenth century. The Xibo were eventually dispersed all over the northeast, Peking, Dezhou (Shandong), and Xinjiang, and Manchu supplanted their own spoken language, Mongolian, as the first or native speech. The Xibo community in Xinjiang became one of the few that still retained fluency in Manchu in the early twentieth century.[58]

The Xibo experience can be generalized for the northeast. Banner schools were established that taught Manchu to Tungus and Altaic-speaking peoples. The result was a "Manchuization" of the northeastern population. Manchu provided the vehicle through which these peoples heard Chinese literary works read aloud in villages; Manchu funerary and marriage customs influenced their practices. When Shirokogoroff visited this region in 1915–17, he found strong traces of Manchu influence. During the Qing, he notes, "The Manchu language became indispensable to the northern Tungus. . . . Manchu books, Manchu fashions, and Manchu ideas became the standards for the northern Tungus."[59] Other contemporary surveys of northern Tungusic peoples such as the Negidal, Nanay (Nanai), Ul'chi, Udegey, and Orochi living on the Amur River cite the Manchu influence in shamanic rituals as well as in clothing styles, the structure of the winter dwelling, furnishings, decorative motifs, and hairstyles, including the Manchu queue for men and the Manchu hairdo for women.[60]

Promotion of shamanism reinforced Qing legitimacy among the northeastern tribes. Just as the Mongols deified Chinggis Khan, so too did Manchus circulate legends about Nurgaci.[61] In existence since the seventeenth century, these legends were probably revised and elaborated during the dynasty. One collection of these stories, *Nan bei han wang zhuan,* was a banned book in the Qianlong reign; the other, *Ruzhen pu ping,* was a late Qing collection of stories from Heilongjiang, written down by a *xiucai* (first degree-holder).[62] A team of scholars collected over one hundred versions of these Nurgaci stories in counties in Heilongjiang, Jilin, and Liaoning in 1984. The legends relate how Fodo *mama* sent her sacred dog to guide Nurgaci to a cave, where she revealed herself to him and instructed him on how to organize the eight banners. Another story tells how a deity taught the Jurchen how to plant buckwheat during a food crisis in the Later Jin state. Others describe the birds and tigers coming to protect Nurgaci when he was born; in one story, a mother eagle uses her wings to sweep the ground of snow and warms him with her feathers. Nurgaci's battle exploits, disseminated through such oral legends, were also enshrined in shamanic rituals at the Kunning palace. Shamanic prayers cited Ugunai, the grandfather of the Jin dynasty founder, and linked the Aisin Gioro to the Jin ruling house. The "Mihu mahu" dance that is performed on imperial birthdays, for example, featured the successful combat between Nurgaci and his foes, represented as masked performers dressed in bearskins and sheepskins. The presence of similarly garbed dancers performing in front of the Taihedian during an imperial wedding suggests the wider presence of these motifs in other court rituals.[63]

The Manchu imprint on the cultures of Northeast Asian peoples remains evident today, long after the end of the Qing dynasty. The Manchu general Sabsu lives in a Daur folktale about a cannon that would fire only upon the Russians and not upon the Manchu forces. Other folktales explain the creation of Qiqihar and talk about how a Daur general helped the Daur avoid payment of freshwater pearls as tribute to the Qing court. An oral story about "Ny Dan the Manchu Shamaness," written down in 1985, reveals the Daur perspective on their encounter with the Qing. In this story, Ny Dan is summoned to the Qing imperial palace after two "lama priests" have failed to bring the crown prince back to life. Although these priests try to prevent her meeting with the emperor, she evades them by flying into the palace on her hand drum. Ny Dan travels to the lower world, finds the crown prince's soul, and brings it back to the human world. The Tibetan Buddhist priests then get the emperor to ask her to retrieve the soul of his younger sister. Ny Dan replies that she cannot do this because the sister has been dead for too long and her flesh is decomposed. In a fury, the emperor has Ny Dan killed by throwing her into a well. The sky darkens after Ny Dan's death and there is no light until the emperor conducts propitiary rituals. Thereafter, Manchus must make offerings to the Eagle Deity who was Ny Dan's spirit helper. And Ny Dan can still be heard drumming and dancing at the bottom of the well.[64]

"Ny Dan the Manchu Shamaness" touches on several issues in the cultural exchange between the Daur and the Qing court. The emperor needs the shamanic assistance that Ny Dan can provide. She has tremendous powers, she flies into the palace, she successfully retrieves the crown prince's soul, and her unjust death causes darkness to fall on earth. The Tibetan Buddhist priests at court who plot against Ny Dan and eventually cause her death represent the forces of Tibetan Buddhism that flourished under Qing patronage (the Daur resisted conversion and remained faithful to shamanism). The emperor in this story is neither omniscient nor wise. He is irritated because Ny Dan doesn't obey palace rules concerning entry into the Forbidden City. He asks Ny Dan for unreasonable things, such as the retrieval of his long-dead sister. He can be gulled by the "lama priests." And he has arbitrary secular power. Despite her shamanic prowess, Ny Dan is put to death by his orders.[65]

TIBETAN BUDDHISM

In the seventeenth century the reconversion of Mongols to Tibetan Buddhism profoundly altered both Mongol and Tibetan political affairs. Mongol chieftains vied with one another to patronize the religion and thereby enhance their own legitimacy, while the dGe lugs pa order established a theocracy in Tibet with Mongol military assistance. The Manchu rulers had to compete with Mongol khans for regional hegemony and they too turned to Tibetan Buddhism for legitimacy. The history of Tibetan Buddhist patronage by the Qing court is thus closely intertwined with the successful Manchu campaign to extend their control over the Mongols, who constituted their greatest potential threat.

Buddhism and the Mongols

Buddhism was of course known to the steppe nomads from very early periods. Non-Han rulers adopted Buddhism as "a counter-philosophy against the state Confucianism of the Chinese ruling class" or, as the founder of the Khitan empire declared, because "Buddhism is not a Chinese religion." [66] Even before the establishment of the Yuan dynasty in 1260, there was a Tibetan state preceptor (*guoshi*) at the court of Möngke Khan in Karakorum, and the Bureau of Buddhist and Tibetan Affairs (*xuanzhengyuan*) supervised 360 Buddhist monasteries. The appointment of hPags pa as state preceptor in 1260 gave the Tibetan Sa skya pa order the dominant position at Khubilai's court as well as overall religious authority over the Yuan empire.[67] Tibetan motifs influenced Chinese Buddhist painting, sculpture, and ceramics not only in North China but in the southern Song capital of Hangzhou.

The Ming dynasty renewed relations with Tibet in the 1390s. Shortly after he took the throne, the Yongle emperor invited the head of the Karma pa order to visit Nanjing and conferred the title of state preceptor on the prelate in 1406. This and subsequent exchanges with Tibetan prelates enabled the Ming emperor to enlist the cooperation of Tibetan regional powers in protecting the trade routes that supplied the Ming armies with Inner Asian horses.[68] The early Ming government sponsored twelve temples and incorporated Tibetan Buddhist offices into the local administration of Xining. Active cultivation of relations with Tibetan prelates ended with the Jiajing reign (1522–66), when Mongols supplanted the Ming as the dominant power in the Amdo region and under Altan Khan began to harass the Chinese frontier.[69]

Yuan interactions with Tibet rested on the "lama-patron" model of the ideal relationship of sacred and secular rule. The khan acknowledged the superior spiritual leadership of the religious leader, who in turn acknowledged Khubilai as protector of the faith. The religious leader was a spiritual father to the secular ruler, an "object of worship" as well as "an object of patronage." The emperor's role was to protect, with military force if necessary, the Lamaist church, and to promote the propagation of the faith through various means, including publication and study of the Buddhist canon. Benefits would accrue to the country as a whole, since the Buddhist deities would in their turn preserve the state against natural disasters, foreign invasions, and domestic unrest.[70]

Under the Yuan, Tibet had been indirectly ruled by Sa skya pa prelates. For the first time "the principle of a lama as head of state had been established in Tibetan political theory, and an important new cultural pattern was set into movement."[71] Reliance on external patronage was a political strategy pursued by the Tibetan orders, who would enlist their patron's military forces to enhance their own authority within a weak and decentralized Tibetan polity. Tibet's forbidding terrain and isolation tended to insulate the religious orders from the full consequences of their alliances with outside rulers. Until the seventeenth century, these powers were generally unwilling or unable to incorporate Tibet into their own empires.

In the late sixteenth century, Mongol leaders searching for a means of expanding their political authority turned to Tibetan Buddhism and revived the lama-patron relationship. In 1578 Altan Khan, the eastern Mongol ruler, met with bSod nams rgya mtsho (1543–88), head of the dGe lugs pa, an order formed during the fourteenth century. Traditional shamanism had been revived among the Mongol tribes; Altan Khan's conversion to the dGe lugs pa can be interpreted as an attempt to expand his authority in his conflict with his nominal superior, Tümen Khan. Altan Khan accepted bSod nams rgya mtsho as his "spiritual guide and refuge" and conferred the title "Dalai lama" on him. In exchange the lama recognized the khan as "Protector of the Faith."[72]

Thereafter virtually every ambitious Mongol leader tried to bolster his political authority with recognition from high Tibetan clerics. Before bSod nams rgya mtsho died in 1588, he predicted that he would be reincarnated in Mongolia. His successor, the fourth Dalai lama, Yon tan rgya mtsho (1588–1617), was a fourth-generation descendant of Altan Khan. Appreciation of the political potential of "living Buddhas" (in Mongolian, *khubilgan*) brought a succession of other Mongol infants identified as rebirths, reincarnations of lamas sent to Mongolia in the late sixteenth century by bSod nams rgya mtsho.[73]

Following the 1585 conversion of Abdaï Khan, the Tüshiyetü khanate, one of three khanates ruling the Khalkha tribes of Mongolia, first patronized monks of the Sa skya pa. Zanabazar (1635–1723), the first Jebtsundamba (in Tibetan, rJe btsun dam pa, meaning "precious saint") was born to the wife of the Tüshiyetü khan. Special signs attending his birth permitted monks to identify the infant as the incarnation of Tāranātha, a monk belonging to a dissident branch of the Sa skya pa sect who had missionized in Mongolia and founded a monastery there. Although the young prince received the title "He Who Brandishes the Banner of Sa skya" in 1639, he studied at the dGe lugs pa monastery of Kumbum (sKu 'bum in Tibetan, Ta'ersi in Chinese) in Amdo and received consecrations from the Panchen *erdeni* (literally, precious Panchen) at Tashilhunpo (rKra shis lhun po) and the Dalai lama in Lhasa. It was the fifth Dalai lama, Ngag dbang bLo bzang rgya mtsho (1617–82), who gave the young monk the title rJe btsun dam pa khutukhtu. Returning home in 1651, this "living Buddha" became the major religious figure for the Khalkha, who called him "great enlightened one" (Bogdo or Ondör Gegen). He ensured the triumph of the dGe lugs pa in northern Mongolia and was the "source and inspiration for a renaissance of Buddhist art and culture."[74] The Jebtsundamba residence in Urga (the modern Ulan Bator), became the most important religious center in northern Mongolia, a major printing center for religious books. More important, from the Qing point of view, was the prelate's enormous prestige, which permitted him to take an active role in Khalkha negotiations with the Russians as well as the Qing, and his hagiography credits him with the Khalkha decision to submit to the Qing court.[75]

Oirat and Khosot Mongol nobles in Amdo and Khams had embraced Buddhism during the Yuan dynasty. Since the Yuan had favored the Sa skya pa, that was the sect that dominated the monasteries and temples erected in that period. During the seventeenth century the Khosot ruler Guši Khan became an adherent of the dGe lugs pa and promoted the expansion of the faith among ordinary people who had followed shamanism. As dGe lugs pa monks penetrated the region, many formerly Sa skya pa monasteries shifted their allegiance to the dGe lugs pa, although Sa skya pa and Kagyü pa monasteries survived in Amdo until the 1950s.[76]

The Khosot and Zunghar nobles had competed with one another to build dGe lugs pa monasteries, endowing them with pasture lands and *shabinar* or households of herdsmen. Kumbum, the monastery erected at the birthplace of the dGe lugs pa founder, Tsong kha pa (1357–1419), was constructed by the Zunghar Batur Khongtaiji. The Torgut khan, whose territory overlapped with that of the Khosot, cooperated with the Khosot to build a powerful monastic establishment around the adopted son of the Khosot ruler Baibagas. This son, Ziyabandi, returned in 1639 from study in Tibet to become a major religious leader among the western Mongols. Ziyabandi's monasteries and *shabinar* were destroyed by the Zunghar leader Galdan, but Galdan and his successors, each in their turn, continued to build new monasteries and to endow them with pastures and *shabinar*.[77]

Reincarnate Lineages

What attracted Mongol and Manchu rulers to Buddhism? To answer this question, we must survey the evolution of the concept of the Buddhist king. Buddhism provided two role models for secular rulers. One was the *dharmarājā*, the king who upholds the Buddhist law within his state. This concept continued to be part of the church-state discourse during the seventeenth and eighteenth centuries and was adopted by the Qianlong emperor himself. The other was the concept of the *cakravartin*. This model, found throughout the Buddhist world, emerged in China after the fall of the Han dynasty (202 A.D.). The *cakravartin* is a world conqueror, a universal ruler.[78] Beginning with Emperor Wu of the Liang dynasty (502–57 A.D.), who took Buddhist vows and patterned himself on the *cakravartin* ideal, Chinese rulers enhanced their legitimacy with recourse to Buddhist devotions.

Cakravartin kingship was modified by the introduction into Tibetan Buddhism of the notion of reincarnated lines of spiritual descent. According to Turrell Wylie, "*Reincarnation* . . . is uniquely Tibetan in conceptualization" and should be distinguished from the concept of incarnation (in Tibetan *sprul sku*), which existed from the early days of Mahāyāna Buddhism.[79] Reincarnation, "to exist again" (in Tibetan *yang-srid*), enlarges on the concept of incarnation by positing that each hierarch will be reborn in the person of his successor and has the power to select (and foretell) the circumstances of his rebirth. A reincarnate hierarch is thus simultaneously a manifestation of a deity and the embodiment of all his previous lives.[80]

Although there is some debate concerning the exact dating of the first reincarnate lama in what came to be called the "rosary of bodies," Wylie and others cite the Karma pa lineage and the critical role played by its third hierarch, Rang byung rdo rje (1284–1338). The first occurrence can thus be dated to the late thirteenth or early fourteenth century. Wylie observes that the innovation was motivated by the internal politics of Tibet, in which monastic succession was frequently within a given family. Acceptance of the notion of reincarnate lineages amounted to institutionalization of charisma and facilitated the transition from "charisma of person" to "charisma of office" within Tibetan monastic orders.[81]

The concept of a reincarnate lineage of hierarchs was subsequently adopted by the other major religious orders in Tibet. It was frequently combined with the earlier notion that some individuals, especially high-ranked lamas, were "emanations" or incarnations of bodhisattvas or Buddhas. The head of the dGe lugs pa order, for example, is believed to be simultaneously the "emanation" of the bodhisattva Avalokiteśvara and the rebirth of his predecessors all the way back to the fourteenth-century founder, Tsong kha pa.[82]

The notion of reincarnate lineages was adopted by secular rulers. The Yuan inserted the lineage of Chinggis into a Buddhist framework, claiming that Khorichar-Mergen, Chinggis's ancestor, was the reincarnation of the Indian Padmasambhava, who is credited with bringing Buddhism to Tibet. Seventeenth-century Mongol chronicles later claimed that one of Chinggis's distant ancestors had moved from Tibet into Mongolia. The genealogy of Mongol rulers was thus grafted on to the Tibetan Buddhist notion that one could be simultaneously an "emanation" of a bodhisattva or Buddha. Chinggis became a protective deity of Tibetan Buddhism, a "bodhisattva lord" (*dafu dagui pusa shengzhu*). Some also identified Chinggis as the son of Indra, the king of the gods, or of Vajrapani, with whom Indra was equated.[83]

The notion of a reincarnate lineage was transferred to the secular realm in yet another way, by conflation with the Chinese *zhengtong* (see chapter 6). Altan Khan identified himself as a reincarnation of Khubilai; others laid claim to the charisma of Chinese emperors like Tang Taizong. Thus Ligdan Khan, the last Chahar ruler and a Tibetan Buddhist patron, styled himself (in Mongolian) "the Saintly, Ingenious Chinggis, Dayiming, the Wise, the One Who Completely Vanquishes Directions, the Powerful Cakravartin, Great Tayisung, the God of Gods, Indra of the Universe, the Dharma King Who Turns a Golden Wheel."[84]

Ligdan Khan's self-identification invoked the name of Chinggis Khan. During the Yuan dynasty, Chinggis was the first of the "four great emperors" (Chinggis, Ögödei, Güyüg, Möngke) who were worshiped in shamanic rituals in the imperial ancestral temple. After the fall of the dynasty, the Chinggis cult was centered on rituals performed at Ejen khoroo, the *naiman chaghan ger* (tents of worship) located on the south bank of the Yellow River in the Ordos. Since all but the Zunghar aspirants to the title of *khaghan* claimed descent from Chinggis, it is not surprising that his relics, housed in Ejen khoroo, were seized by Ligdan Khan when he declared himself "khan of khans."[85]

The expanded concept of reincarnate lineages stimulated Inner Asian rulers to attempt to combine religious and secular authority in a new concept of the foundations of rulership. The possibilities of this new model were appreciated by the Manchus and incorporated into their state-building efforts. Lord Macartney, visiting the Qing court in 1793, recorded in his diary that a "Tartar" (i.e., Manchu) visitor told him "that the present Emperor is descended from . . . Kublai Khan. . . . The Mongols who then fled into the country of the Manchu, intermarried and mixed with them, and from one of these alliances sprung the Bogdoi Khans, who invaded China in 1640, and have reigned over it ever since."[86] Another diary entry notes that according to Qing courtiers, "the emperor was descended from Kublai Khan and believed that the soul of Fo-hi [Buddha] had 'transmigrated into his imperial body.'"[87]

Tibet

During the early seventeenth century, as Nurgaci and Hongtaiji unified the northeast, a similar unification occurred further west under the leadership of Guši Khan. Succeeding to the headship of the Khosot and the title "Oirat Khan" in the 1620s, Guši Khan led an Oirat army to take over Amdo and Khams. Proclaimed the Dharmarājā or "king of Tibet," Guši Khan made the fifth Dalai lama the secular as well as religious ruler of Tibet (1642). Mongol patronage enabled the dGe lugs pa sect to win out over its internal rivals, other great monastic orders such as the rNying ma pa and the Sa skya pa. Although he initially shared power with the regent and Gusi Khan, the fifth Dalai lama expanded his own authority by presenting himself as Avalokitesvara through the performance of rituals, the erection of the Potala and other structures on religiously significant sites, and the writing of biographies of his predecessors that stressed the reincarnate lineage.[88] The huge palace-temple in Lhasa known as the Potala was named after the divine palace, residence of the "Lord of the World," Lokesvara, in his Buddhist manifestation as Avalokitesvara. The significance of the fifth Dalai lama's achievement has been explained by two scholars:

> The Dalai lamas now came to be consciously identified as manifestations of this most popular of Tibetan Buddhist divinities. A similar idea of divine kingship, but in an entirely non-Buddhist context, had been attributed to the early kings of Tibet . . . although they have since become mingled, the two ideas, that of a lama conceived of as a reincarnation of his predecessor, and that of a lama or a ruler conceived of as a manifestation of a popular divinity, are really quite distinct.[89]

The unification of religious and secular rule in the person of the Dalai lama was thus a political innovation that began with the fifth Dalai. The success of dGe lugs pa missionizing in Amdo, Khams, and Mongolia laid the basis for the great influence wielded by the Dalai lama in seventeenth-century Inner Asia. The Dalai lama issued titles and seals that formalized the accession of Mongolian khans. He could and sometimes did order Mongol troop movements outside Tibet; he could also make peace between warring Mongol tribes, and his influence over the Mongols surpassed the influence of the Qing court.[90]

The assumption of a protectorate over Tibet was a by-product of Qing efforts to curb the Zunghars. The Qing allied themselves with the Khosot. When in the 1690s the Kangxi emperor moved troops into the far west to counter the Zunghar leader Galdan, he seized the opportunity to strengthen Manchu control over his Khosot allies. Adopting the policy of "divide and rule," the Qing appointed rivals to military posts under the supervision of the commander of the Green Standard troops.[91]

Controversy over the authenticity of the sixth Dalai lama, Tshang dbyangs rgya mtsho (1683–1706), sparked a Khosot Mongol takeover of Tibet (1703).[92] The Khosot Mongol leader, Lajang Khan, deposed the sixth Dalai lama and put his own candidate in this position in 1707. The Kangxi emperor eventually supported Lajang's choice (1710) but Mongol chieftains in Kokonor instead supported another youth, who had been authenticated as the genuine rebirth by the state oracle of Tibet. The controversy provided the pretext for the Zunghar invasion of Lhasa. Lajang died before Qing troops could respond to his appeal for aid, and this first expedition ended in defeat for the Qing. A second force, however, reached Lhasa in 1720 and expelled the Zunghars. The Qing took advantage of this opportunity to further their own interests. Even though they were quick to proclaim the seating of the candidate supported by the Kokonor Mongols as (seventh) Dalai lama, actual power was handed over to a council of ministers. Khams and Amdo, in southeastern Tibet, were detached and put under the control of the governor of Sichuan. The rebellion of Lobsang Danjin, the Khosot Mongol chieftain (1723), was stimulated by Lobsang's perception that the Qing had reneged on a promise to return control over Tibet to the Khosot. After Lobsang was defeated, the Qing gave his territory to his rival and asserted suzerainty over Kokonor, which they renamed Qinghai. In 1725 the emperor split Khams into two units, leaving the western half under the control of central Tibet but administering the eastern half through local tribal leaders.[93]

The Qing control over Tibetan affairs was initially extremely indirect. Enmity among the Tibetan nobles nominated to a governing council by the Qing court brought civil war (1727–28); the victor of the war ruled with Qing support until his death in 1747. In 1750, when his successor was killed by the two Qing representatives of the emperor in Tibet, and the *amban* were themselves attacked and killed by a Tibetan mob, the Qing intervened again, and increased the power of the imperial envoys. A small Chinese garrison, first established in 1721 but withdrawn from 1723–28 and 1748–50, was restored with 1,500 bannermen and soldiers from the Green Standard armies stationed in the west.[94]

Qing Patronage

Manchu patronage of Tibetan Buddhism began before 1621, when Nurgaci appointed a lama as the state preceptor of the Manchu *gurun*, establishing a precedent for his successors. The rulers maintained relations with several rival Tibetan Buddhist orders until the Qianlong reign. Hongtaiji invited the Dalai lama to come to Mukden and lavishly entertained his emissaries in 1642–43, but his most memorable action, the adoption of the Mahākāla cult, favored the rival Sa skya pa order. The Shunzhi emperor received the Dalai lama in Peking in 1653, but as Xiangyun Wang has noted, Yinli, Prince Guo's 1732 invitation to two prelates of the rival Karma pa order to come to Peking for a theological debate indicates that the dGe lugs pa had not yet won a monopoly position at the Qing court.[95]

Hongtaiji followed precedents established by Khubilai and Ligdan Khan when he embraced the Mahākāla cult. The *yi-dam* ritual transferred to Hongtaiji the powers of Mahākāla, a seven-armed warlike deity known as a Protector of the (Buddhist) Law. Grupper notes the political significance of his initiation: "through Tantric consecration . . . Abahai successfully bypassed genealogical restrictions and rose to the most exalted political status of Inner Asia: Emperor of the Mongols."[96] Qing acceptance of a notion of sovereignty that had been created by Mongols "significantly eased" Mongol submission to the Manchus.

Hongtaiji's Mahākāla temple, the Shishengsi, was completed in 1638. Four branch temples, set at the compass points, were built in 1643–45 to house four other deities. The temple complex was extended in an "architectonic representation of the Buddhist cosmological order," and the entire realm was put under the protection of the deity.[97] In 1694 the Mahākāla image was moved from Mukden to Peking, where it was installed in the former residence of Dorgon. Repaired in 1776, the Pudusi was staffed by Mongol lamas. In late Qing times it was the only Tibetan Buddhist temple in the capital where the services were conducted in Mongolian.[98]

The Kangxi, Yongzheng, and Qianlong emperors renovated or built a total of thirty-two Tibetan Buddhist temples within Peking and erected multilingual inscriptions recording the history (some going back to the Liao dynasty) of each site. The first temple was the Huangsi, built to accommodate the fifth Dalai lama and his entourage during his visit to the capital in 1653.[99] The most famous was the Yonghegong, which was located in the northeastern quadrant of the Inner City (see map 2). This princely residence of the Yongzheng emperor was converted into a Lamaist temple in 1744 by his son. Normally closed to the public, its operations were the responsibility of the Lifanyuan (court of colonial affairs). The Yonghegong became a teaching center and academy for the Yellow Sect. During the eighteenth to the mid-nineteenth centuries, it housed five hundred to six hundred Mongol, Manchu, and Tibetan monks, as well as palace eunuchs who were occupied in sutra recitation and ritual performance. The monks also accompanied the troops on campaign. In the eyes of ordinary Peking residents in the twentieth century, the Yonghegong monks were noted for the masked dance-ritual (*tiaobuzha*) performed for three days at the end of the year. This rite was observed by Manchu princes, Mongols, and banner-men during the Qing.[100]

Qing emperors built eleven Lamaist temples in Chengde. The Putuo-zongcheng was a temple modeled on the Potala, the residence of the Dalai lama in Lhasa. The Xumifushou temple was built to house the sixth Pan-chen lama, bLo bzang dpal ldan ye shes (1738–80), during his visit in 1780. Based on the Panchen *erdeni*'s home monastery of Tashilhunpo, it became a center for the chanting of sutras and dharanis by Tashilhunpo lamas.[101]

The third major Lamaist center in China proper that was built up with imperial donations was Wutaishan. Wutaishan became a religious center for the tribes of Inner Mongolia, and the court sponsored the publication of Mongolian language guidebooks to the pilgrimage site. During the Kangxi reign ten Chinese Buddhist monasteries here were converted into monasteries for Tibetan Buddhism. The number of Tibetan Buddhist mon-asteries increased to twenty-six during the Yongzheng reign, and six more were added by the Qianlong emperor.[102]

The Qianlong emperor worried about the religious condition of the Manchus. At least six temples, located in the capital, in Chengde, and at the imperial villas and cemeteries, were specifically erected during the Qian-long reign to house Manchu monks, recruited from the banner registers.[103] Imperial subsidies were also bestowed to build monasteries in the periph-eral regions that were added to the Qing empire. Sometimes these monas-teries were erected as the residence of a reincarnate lineage. Others served as Buddhist centers for a region. The great monastery at Dolonor, north of Peking, was erected during the Kangxi reign and became designated as the center of Buddhism for southern Mongolia.[104] The court funded monas-teries in Guihua (the Mongol Köke Khoto), in the territory of the Tümet Mongols; it built or renovated monasteries in Amdo. The monastic estab-lishment in Amdo was extremely large. During the Qing, its most promi-nent monasteries, which each housed over 1,000 monks, were as large as the largest dGe lugs pa monasteries in central and western Tibet. One scholar estimates that in 1958 Qinghai, which encompasses most of Amdo, had 869 Tibetan Buddhist monasteries with approximately 60,000 monks.[105]

The Qing emperors sponsored massive compilation and translation projects, which made Peking a major center of Tibetan Buddhism. In the course of the dynasty, more than 230 Tibetan Buddhist works were trans-lated into Mongolian under Manchu and Mongol princely sponsorship. Under the Kangxi emperor, the Mongolian Kangyur produced under Lig-dan Khan was revised and edited in 1717–20 by a commission of scholars recruited from all the banners. Calligraphers "who command the Mongol script well" were called to Dolonor in the summer of 1718, and the imperial red edition was printed in 108 volumes in 1720. The Tibetan Tripitaka was translated into Mongolian and Manchu during the Qianlong reign; many of these writings, printed in Peking in the neighborhood behind the Songzhusi temple, were widely distributed among the Mongol tribes.[106] There were even translations from the Chinese to Tibetan: one example is the (apocryphal) Sūraṅgama sutra (in Chinese, *Lengyan jing*), which the Qianlong emperor ordered translated by Rol pa'i rdo rje. Perhaps because the results "delighted Qianlong," the emperor ordered that one hundred copies each of the Tibetan and Mongolian versions be distributed to temples and monasteries in the capital, Chengde, Shengjing, and the Mongolian banners.[107]

Qing Administration of Tibetan Buddhism

Qing policies facilitated the penetration of Buddhism among the Mongols. Eventually perhaps 30 to 60 percent of men in Inner Mongolia and more than 30 percent of all Mongol males in Outer Mongolia were lamas living in monasteries.[108] By the early part of the Qianlong reign, there were nearly 2,000 monasteries and temples in Mongolia, with 800 monasteries in southern Mongolia, 136 monasteries in the Khalkha lands, and a further 500–600 in Amdo, Gansu, Sichuan, Xinjiang, and Shanxi.[109] The monasteries were established on sites revered in Mongol shamanism, coopting the traditional spirits into the new religion. Tibetan Buddhist monasteries became "the *de facto* centralized state institution" of a decentralized nomadic society.

The Qing court limited the size of the priesthood by setting quotas on the issuance of ordination certificates. Lamaist affairs were supervised by a subagency of the Lifanyuan. They created an administrative hierarchy of clerical ranks, which coexisted alongside a similar hierarchy of "Tibeto-Mongol" origin.[110] A Tibetan title, such as *khanpo*, which initially designated the administrator of a monastic school, was transplanted to the monasteries of Inner and Outer Mongolia; new titles, such as *jasagh da lama* (grand prince of the church) and *jasagh lama* (prince of the church) were introduced by the Qing. Unlike the *khanpo*, the *jasagh da lama* and *jasagh lama* combined secular with religious authority. Seven of the most powerful monasteries were designated as banner units, separate from the secular banners, with the head of the monastery, the *jasagh da lama*, wielding judicial and administrative power. In cases where a "living Buddha" controlled a population of more than 800 persons, a banner (*jasagh*) lama under him would exercise these secular functions. This merger of spiritual and secular rule had ample antecedents. Both the Yuan and Ming dynasties, for example, had appointed Buddhist monks to administer the Xining region.[111]

Qing rulers began in the late seventeenth century to assert their right to confer recognition on the reincarnate hierarchs (*khubilgan* in Mongolian). In the new religious hierarchy created after 1691, each title had to be personally bestowed by the emperor. Eventually there were 14 *khubilgan* in Peking, 19 in northern Mongolia, 157 in Inner Mongolia, and 35 in the Kokonor region, for a total of 243. The Qing tried to avoid recognizing reincarnations from powerful Mongol descent groups (for example, the court did not permit a Mongol Jebtsundamba after the second incarnation), but sons of Mongol nobles were firmly entrenched in the upper echelons of the priesthood.[112] Attempts to bureaucratize the process by which rebirths were identified culminated in 1792, when the Qianlong emperor ordered that the dGe lugs pa hierarchs should henceforth be selected by drawing names out of a golden vase. Two vases were made: one was sent to Lhasa, and the other retained in the Yonghegong in Peking.[113]

The relationship of prominent Tibetan prelates to the Qing ruler was couched in the language of tribute. They, too, fell under the system of *chaogong* administered by the Lifanyuan.[114] For his part, the Qianlong emperor attempted to communicate with these prelates (as with his other non-Han subjects) in their own language. He once wrote:

> In 1743 . . . I began to practice Mongolian. In 1760 . . . I pacified the Uighurs and acquainted myself with Uighur. In 1776, after the two pacifications of the Jinquan [rebels] I became roughly conversant in Tibetan. In 1780, because the Panchen lama was coming to visit, I also studied Tangut. Thus, every year when the rota of Mongols, Uighurs and Tibetans came to the capital for audience, I used their own language and did not rely on an interpreter . . . to express the idea of conquering by kindness.[115]

We have already described how the Manchus presented the fifth Dalai lama with the documents and seal recognizing his title. They also wooed the "second supreme dignitary" of the dGe lugs pa order, the Panchen rinpoche.[116] The first Panchen lama, bLo bzang chos kyi rgyal mtshan (1569–1662), was recognized as an incarnation of Amitābha by the fifth Dalai lama, who thereby raised the prestige of the dGe lugs pa. His title, Panchen *bogdo* (great scholar) was given to him earlier (1645) by Guši Khan, and his home monastery was Tashilhunpo. In 1703 the Kangxi emperor conferred on him the title Panchen *erdeni*. According to some scholars, the Yongzheng emperor attempted to make a "donation" of gTsang, the region dominated by Tashilhunpo, and of western Tibet to the Panchen, in a ploy designed to divide the authority of the Dalai lama, but the Panchen "prudently accepted only a part of the donation."[117]

Although the two dGe lugs pa reincarnate lineages each dominated a region of Tibet and competed to some degree for influence within the Tibetan monastic world, they also strongly supported each other and thus strengthened the authority of the dGe lugs pa order. The head of each lineage provided legitimacy by recognizing the rebirths of the other lineage, acting as the tutor and initiator into the esoteric rituals for the young *yang srid*. Thus, for example, bLo bzang served as the fifth Dalai lama's tutor and presided over his ordination ritual. His rebirth, born in 1663, was formally recognized four years later by the fifth Dalai, who also administered (1670) the Shamo initiation. The same pattern was followed for his successors: each received (at least in theory) recognition and ordination from the Dalai. In turn, from the time of the sixth Dalai lama, who received the Shamo initiation from the fifth Panchen, new rebirths of the Dalai lama would receive recognition and ordination from the Panchen lamas. When the Khosot leader Lobzang Khan deposed the sixth Dalai lama in 1707, it was thus natural that he would call upon the fifth Panchen lama to confer the Shamo initiation upon his candidate.[118]

Although the Qing maintained close relations with the Dalai lama, Panchen *erdeni*, and Jebtsundamba (invested in 1693 as a *da lama*), these three prelates enjoyed an independent authority that posed an obstacle to Qing control of Tibetan and Mongol affairs.[119] The Qing court attempted to diffuse clerical authority by expanding the number of reincarnate lines, especially lines born in the former Tibetan kingdom of Amdo (Kokonor in Mongolian), the native place of the first and second lCang skya khutukhtu who played important roles at the Qing court during the eighteenth century. Xiangyun Wang observes that many of the prelates whom the lCang skya introduced to the court, reincarnate lamas like the dG'aldan Siregetü khutukhtu, Ra kho khutukhtu, A skya khutukhtu, sTong 'khor, and the 'Jam dbyangs bzhad pa, were natives of this buffer zone between Mongolia and central Tibet. These hierarchs were tied to Kumbum and Labrang, the two major monastic centers of Amdo, and through teacher-student relations to the major dGe lugs pa schools in central Tibet.[120]

The Qing emperors raised the rank of the lCang skya reincarnate hierarchs and placed them just below the Dalai lama, Panchen lama, and Jebtsundamba khutukhtu. The first lCang skya khutukhtu, Ngag dbang bLo bzang chos ldan (1642–1715), met the Kangxi emperor during the attempts (1687) by Xuanye and the Dalai lama to arbitrate the dispute between two Khalkha khans. In 1693 the emperor summoned the lCang skya to Peking and invested him as a *da lama,* with authority over the Khalkha Lamaist church. He aided the Kangxi emperor in diplomatically pacifying the Oirat chieftains after Galdan's defeat. Promotions in rank followed, until he was invested with the title lCang skya khutukhtu (1705) and made a state preceptor in 1706. To increase his influence in Inner Mongolia, the Yongzheng emperor built a summer residence for the lCang skya in Dolonor. This was the Huizongsi monastery, built with funds from the imperial treasury, which served as a center for lamas from each Inner and Outer Mongol banner. During the winter the lCang skya khutukhtu lived in Peking, in the Songzhusi, a temple built for him by Kangxi.[121]

The life of the second lCang skya, Rol pa'i rdo rje (1717–86), exemplifies the Qing Mongol and Tibetan policy. In a sense, the Yongzheng and Qianlong emperors created the second lCang skya khutukhtu: the first removed the young boy from his home monastery in Amdo and brought him to Peking, to be educated in the palace school alongside the imperial princes; and the second accepted Rol pa'i rdo rje as his spiritual teacher. Rol pa'i rdo rje became the most favored Tibetan prelate in Peking. Hongli assigned him to ensure a smooth succession after the death of the seventh Dalai lama bsKal bzang rgya mtsho in 1757; he served as interpreter for the Panchen lama during the latter's visit to Chengde (1780). Rol pa'i rdo rje is credited with persuading the Jebtsundamba to remain neutral in the 1756 Chingunjav revolt, and his magical rituals were credited with Qing victory in the second Jinquan campaign (1771–76), which enabled the dGe lugs pa to wipe out the rival Bon sect in this locality. Rol pa'i rdo rje was also a distinguished scholar who headed the translation of the Tanjur (bsTan 'gyur) into Mongolian and the Buddhist canon into Manchu.[122]

Manchu patronage of lamaism made "political good sense," but there is also evidence that some emperors were believers. According to one scholar, Xuanye, raised by a Khorchin Mongol grandmother, the empress dowager Xiaozhuang, "was the first of the Manchu emperors to display a personal religious interest in Lamaism."[123] The Yongzheng emperor had an image of himself depicted as a lama installed in the Songzhusi.[124] Although Yinzhen was said to be "but slightly interested" in Tibetan Buddhism, Wang notes that he was "the best among all emperors of China" in his understanding of Buddhist theology, and known among Mongols and Tibetans for his reconstruction of Tibetan Buddhist monasteries in Amdo. His brother Yinli, Prince Guo, was a Tibetan Buddhist scholar and patron.[125]

Despite disclaimers protesting that his patronage was merely a matter of state policy, conversations recorded by Rol pa'i rdo rje's biographers and the emperor's own actions suggest that Hongli was a genuine student of Tibetan Buddhism. He learned Sanskrit and Tibetan from Rol pa'i rdo rje, who bestowed the Samvara initiation on him in 1745. In 1780, when the Panchen lama granted the emperor the Mahākāla and Cakrasamvara initiations, the latter ritual climaxed Hongli's birthday celebrations and signified that he "had entered the Buddhist realm."[126]

The Qianlong emperor was said to practice Buddhist meditations daily. The Zhongzhengdian, a hall in the northwestern corner of the Forbidden City, had in 1690 been dedicated to sutra recitation as well as the production of religious paintings and images. The Sutra Recitation Office in this hall, which was under the Neiwufu, became the emperor's primary office for dealing with Tibetan Buddhist matters. In addition, Hongli erected a private chapel, the Yuhuage, to the south of the Zhongzhengdian. The Yuhuage was patterned after the Buddha hall of the famous mTho gling temple in Tibet, said to have been erected in the tenth century. Besides being furnished with Tibetan Buddhist iconography, the chapel featured a shrine to the Kangxi emperor, enclosing his spirit tablet.[127] Hongli's mausoleum was built during his lifetime under his supervision, and the walls of the underground hall leading to the coffin chamber were ornamented with Buddhist deities and texts in Sanskrit. Tibetan-language sutras and Sanskrit dharani were incised into the east and west walls of the underground sarcophagal chamber (digong), and the walls were ornamented with bas-reliefs of bodhisattvas and guardian deities.[128] In this most private place the Qianlong emperor, who is widely regarded as culturally Chinese, asserted his commitment to Tibetan Buddhism.

Art historians note the hundreds of Buddhist objects lavished by Hongli upon his mother on her birthdays. She was a pious devotee who embroidered a hanging of the Green Tara, made up of over seven thousand pieces of satin, which is still preserved in the Yongyou hall of the Yonghegong.[129] The Qing court exercised a major influence on the Tibetan Buddhist religious objects produced during the eighteenth and nineteenth centuries. One scholar argues on the basis of stylistic and technical evidence that a significant proportion of the Tibetan metal ritual objects from this period were Sino-Mongolian in origin and cites nineteenth-century accounts of Chinese workshops in the major monastic centers of Dolonor, Ganden, Wutaishan, and Chengde, as well as along the borders of eastern and northeastern Tibet.[130]

Archival records in Peking contain annual inventories of the hundreds of ritual objects that were produced in the palace workshops and received as gifts from important lamas, Mongol nobles, and imperial relatives. These records, which extend from 1747 into the late nineteenth century, reveal an extensive system of gift exchange in which the Qing emperors participated as donors and recipients. Although the details of this system are beyond the scope of the present study, its general significance lies in highlighting the extent to which Tibetan Buddhism provided the commodities as well as a vehicle for the court's incorporation of the Mongols and Tibetans into the empire.[131]

Under imperial sponsorship, elements of Mongol and Chinese popular religion were added to Tibetan Buddhism. One example is the insertion of the folk deity Guandi into Tibetan Buddhist altars as "sacred emperor Guan" during the Jiaqing and Daoguang reigns. In Guandi temples erected in the northern border provinces and Manchuria, trilingual inscriptions identified the Chinese deity as the Tibetan Vaisravana, the guardian king of the north, who was also equated with Gesar Khan, protector of warriors and herds. Gesar, who was identified from the fourteenth and fifteenth century with the royal family of gLing, a small kingdom in northeastern Tibet, was celebrated in epics among Mongols and Tibetans as a conqueror of demons. After the late sixteenth century, Gesar's image crept into the Buddha halls in Mongolia, where ordinary people frequently confused him with Guandi. A prayer declaring that Guandi was the great protective deity of the empire was composed by the lCang skya khutukhtu, printed in Tibetan, Manchu and Mongolian, and widely distributed.[132]

Qing involvement in Tibetan Buddhism also led to the continued evolution of the relationship between the sacred and secular realms encapsulated in the lama-patron model. This relationship is represented in some *tangkas* produced during the Qianlong reign. Two recent illustrated catalogs of objects in the Palace Museum, Beijing, join an earlier catalog presenting pieces in the collection of the National Palace Museum, Taipei. Together with a catalog illustrating objects in the Yonghegong, Beijing, and another presenting the collection of the State Museum of Ethnology in Munich, they enable us to evaluate the significance of the Qing-Tibetan Buddhist relationship through an examination of its material artifacts.[133]

Modifications in the Lama-Patron Relationship

Many *tangkas,* or Buddhist religious paintings, produced during Hongli's reign depict the Qianlong emperor as the bodhisattva Mañjuśrī.[134] Although we do not have a definitive account of the total number of these *tangkas,* we have at latest count at least six and perhaps seven such *tangkas,* held by museums in Sweden, Beijing, Shenyang, and in the Potala.[135]

The iconography of the *tangkas* and the symbolic significance of what is represented in them has been analyzed by David Farquhar:

> we see Ch'ien-lung . . . in the raiment of a hieromonk-reincarnation with the characteristic cap and monastic robes; his left hand holds the Wheel of the Law . . . and his right hand is in the gesture of argument . . . ; he is surrounded by many Buddhist saints, gods, and goddesses. . . . An inscription in Tibetan under the central figure makes it clear that we are viewing not simply a portrait, but the representation of a deity, "The sagacious Mañjuśrī, the guardian of men, great and sublime being, King of the Law, Thunderbolt . . . having a good destiny, and satisfying all desires." [136]

Although Farquhar reproduces only one *tangka* in his article, the six *tangkas* that are now known to exist all share the critical iconographic features that he identified. Each shows the emperor as the central figure in a religious setting. In each painting he sits on a lotus pedestal, wearing the robes of a lama. Several of the *tangkas* depict him in the identical pose described by Farquhar, while others show him holding a round gold object studded with jewels in his left. Some of the *tangkas* show the flaming sword on a lotus flower and the sutra, symbols associated with Mañjuśrī, to the left and right of his throne. Many include an offering table in front of the throne, with an inscription. All the *tangkas* depict the spiritual lineage of Rol pa'i rdo rje, the emperor's religious teacher, who is depicted directly above the emperor. The rest of the *tangka* is filled with other Buddhist deities, including the protective deities who are painted at the bottom of the *tangka.*

The Qianlong *tangkas*—thus far no counterparts for other Qing emperors have been found—deserve to be studied on their own merits as historical artifacts. We must confine ourselves here to a preliminary discussion of their political significance. Farquhar's study argues that these *tangkas* were part of a court-sponsored image-making directed to the Mongol followers of Tibetan Buddhism and centered on the Wutaishan pilgrimage. He notes that the Kangxi emperor made this pilgrimage five times, the Qianlong emperor six times, and the Jiaqing emperor once. That the effort predated

Qianlong is clear from the first Mongol-language guidebook to Wutaishan, published in 1667, which referred to the Qing ruler as "reincarnation of Mañjuśrī, sublime lord, who makes the world prosper."[137] The success of this propaganda effort can be measured by the common use in Tibetan chronicles of "Mañjuśrī" when referring to the Qing emperor.[138]

The Qianlong reign marks the culmination of earlier trends that attempted to combine religious and secular authority in one person. In this respect, both the Qing emperor and the Dalai lama had moved out of the former confines of the "lama-patron" relationship that constituted the classic model of "dual rule" animating relations between Tibetan orders and secular rulers. Whereas the "dual rule" model posited a dyarchy, the new model transcended the former distinctions between the religious and lay worlds, and that was as true of the Dalai's position as of the emperor's. Ruegg notes that "the *bla ma* as Ruler-Bodhisattva . . . may in fact combine both functions. Moreover, the *rgyal po* as Dharma-King (*chos kyi rgyal po*) could on his side be conceived of as the manifestation of a Bodhisattva."[139]

Ruegg's analysis underlines the inherent ambiguity that characterized the relationship of the Qing emperor to the Dalai lama, Panchen lama, and other reincarnate lamas of Tibetan Buddhism. All occupied statuses whose symbolic content had been transformed, creating confusion in the traditional lama-patron relationship. It is no wonder then that Tibetan-language accounts of the Qing-Tibetan relationship vary widely from Han Chinese accounts. The wide variation in "readings" of the same event can be seen most dramatically in accounts of the 1780 visit of the Panchen lama to Chengde and Peking.

In 1780 the Qianlong emperor was celebrating his birthday in his summer capital, Chengde. The Panchen lama journeyed to Chengde, where he met with the emperor. During his five weeks in Chengde, he consecrated palaces and temples; he preached to the monks and court; he initiated the emperor and others into esoteric tantras. As Angela Zito shows us,[140] the Tibetan- and Chinese-language sources each present a carefully structured account of the entire episode, beginning with the "invitation," and concluding with a detailed description of the visit itself. The different accounts reflect the different audiences for these records. The Tibetan records cast the meeting in terms of the lama-patron model, emphasize the veneration (rightfully) accorded to the Panchen lama by the emperor, and underline the superior position of the teacher. Chinese accounts, by contrast, stress the rituals of subordination performed by the Panchen as part of the ceremonial etiquette of imperial audience. Since the meeting combined the emperor's religious concerns with (from his perspective) a reification of his status as universal monarch, it is virtually impossible and inappropriate to interpret the event in strictly hierachical terms. The meaning to be derived from it depended on one's cultural perspective. When Tibetan monks referred to the Qing emperor as "Mañjuśrī," the context in which they used that appellation included the constellation of Buddhas and bodhisattvas as organized in the tantric teachings, in which there was the possibility of simultaneous myriads of manifestations of each spiritual being. For the Tibetan Buddhists the Qing emperor's recognition of the Dalai lama as "Avalokiteśvara" symbolized the emperor's acceptance of their religious framework, just as acceptance of the Panchen lama as "teacher" was implied in the services that he performed for the emperor and his court.

Four murals painted on the walls of the Potala depict this relationship. The first shows the meeting of the Yongle emperor with the fifth Karma pa hierarch. The hierarch, on his *dharma* seat, is lecturing to the monks; next to him sits the emperor. Another mural depicts the meeting of the fifth Dalai lama with the Shunzhi emperor. The author notes that the emperor, dressed in court robes, is solidly ensconced in the center and superior position, with the Dalai lama on his right; but the mural pictures the emperor as half the size of the Dalai. A third mural shows the meeting of the thirteenth Dalai lama, Thub bstan rgya mtsho (1876–1933), with the Empress Dowager Cixi. Here the Dalai kneels before the empress and offers her an Amitāyus. A final mural shows Cixi seated in the central position and the Dalai (and emperor) at her right side, thus (from the Chinese point of view) firmly establishing the hierarchy of superior-inferior relationships for all to see.[141]

Another product of this complex relationship exists in the Sasum Namgyal (chapel of the victory over the three worlds), which was formerly used by the seventh Dalai lama. In this room hangs a *tangka* of the Qianlong emperor as Mañjuśrī, which is said to have been presented on the occasion of the coronation of the eighth Dalai lama in 1762. Beneath this *tangka* sits a quadrilingual plaque, inscribed in Tibetan, Chinese, Manchu, and Mongolian, proclaiming, "May Emperor Kangxi live for thousands and thousands of years." This plaque was apparently presented to the seventh Dalai lama to commemorate the sixty-first anniversary of Kangxi's ascent of the throne. The plaque is surrounded by statues of prominent lamas, including the seventh Dalai lama, the fourth and sixth Panchen lamas, and other Tibetan lamas. On the wall to the left are cases holding the Manchu edition of the Kangyur.[142] The artifacts in this room summarize the early Qing-Tibetan relationship but in precisely what way? On the one hand, the Kangxi plaque symbolizes a major appeal of Tibetan Buddhism for Qing rulers, the hope that prayers would be efficacious in promoting long life. The Kangyur reminds the Dalai lama of the signal services performed by Qing emperors as propagators of the faith. On the other hand, the *tangka* itself is the most significant object in the room. It embodies the transition that had taken place in the image of rulership under the Qianlong emperor, who represented himself as an incarnate ruler, Mañjuśrī, Chinggis, and Tang Taizong in one. That this incarnate ruler confronted a mirror image in the Dalai lama points to the ways in which the Qing-Tibetan relationship enriched Qing resources in creating legitimacy.

Chapter 8   Private Rituals

If sacrifices at the state altars were about rulership, and Qing religious patronage was about politics, the private rituals were about the court as a household, a family writ large. An eclectic mixture of shamanic, Daoist, Chinese Buddhist, Tibetan Buddhist, and popular religious traditions, the palace's rituals took place within the space of the inner court. They marked important stages in the lives of Qing emperors and their families, commemorated their ancestors, and symbolically linked them to their subjects. These ritual events, the subject of this chapter, not only reveal a normally hidden dimension of court life, they also illustrate the way in which rituals created a solidary community that cut across other social boundaries.

PRIVATE VERSUS PUBLIC RITUAL

Most of the public rites performed by the emperor took place at the state altars in the suburbs of Peking, outside the walls of the Forbidden City, or within the three state halls in the outer court of the Forbidden City (see chapter 1 and map 3). Although the emperor and other members of his family also worshiped at altars within the inner court, most of these acts were not cited in the public record. The accounts from several different sources for the emperor's activities punctuating the last and first days of the Chinese year point up this omission.

According to the Veritable Records, on the thirtieth day of the twelfth lunar month in the tenth year of his reign (February 14, 1885) the Guangxu emperor "went to the Baohedian and feted the Mongol princes, sons-in-law, civil and military officials, the Korean ambassador and deputy ambassador . . . at 5 p.m. he went before Empress Dowager Cixi and performed the rites." Comparing this account with the more than twenty ritual actions that an archival ritual document lists for the emperor on the same day, we can begin to measure the difference between the court's domestic or private ritual activities and those of a more public nature.[1]

According to archival documents, on the last day of the year, February 14, 1885, the emperor first worshiped at the altar to "Heaven and Earth"—not the suburban state altars, but the altar located in the Yangxindian. This altar was also featured in the imperial wedding of a reigning emperor. On the day after his new empress entered the palace, the couple prostrated themselves before this altar.[2] The emperor also lit incense before deities in the Buddha halls (*Fotang*) scattered throughout the palaces; he worshiped Daoist deities at shrines in the imperial garden and the Qin'andian; he sacrificed to "Almighty Heaven" (in Manchu *dergi abkai han*, in Chinese *hao tian shangdi*) in the Tianqiongbaodian. In the Kunning palace, the emperor lit incense at the shamanic altars and before a shrine dedicated to Zaojun, the kitchen god.

The kitchen god's altar stood in a corner above the stoves. In popular religion the kitchen god was the lowest-level official in the supernatural bureaucracy, installed in the kitchen to both protect and observe the individuals in the family: this location was especially appropriate because among ordinary Chinese, the family or *jia* is defined as those who share a stove. On the twenty-third day of the twelfth month, it was customary for Chinese households to send off the kitchen god with sweets to ensure that he would report favorably to the Jade Emperor on the household's activities during the year. The Qing court followed this custom, presenting special offerings of a fat sheep, fruit, vegetables, cakes, soups, tea, and sugar before the altar on that day. The good-natured flavor of these ceremonies in the court is reflected in a report of the Qianlong emperor, who "used to sacrifice to the Kitchen God in person, beating a drum and singing a popular song called 'The emperor in search of honest officials,' with the Court drawn up in two rows, and ending with a discharge of crackers to speed the god on his way."[3] On New Year's eve and New Year's day, small and large firecrackers were set off at various inner-court gates and sites to punctuate the sendoff of the kitchen god and the first rites of the year.[4]

New Year's day entailed another long list of ritual activities for the emperor. In addition to revisiting many of the altars visited on the previous day, the emperor also went to the Qianqing palace's eastern wing to kowtow before a portrait of Confucius. He kowtowed in the Imperial Pharmacy before the medicine god. After breakfast, he went outside the Shenwu gate to light incense at the Daoist altars of the Dagaodian. On New Year's eve and New Year's day, the portraits of deceased emperors were unrolled and hung in the Shouhuangdian, rebuilt in 1749–50 on the model of the Tai-miao (temple of the ancestors) in the northeastern corner of Jingshan. Here the emperor presented special offerings.[5]

Again, we can compare this long list—twenty-two activities before breakfast—with the version offered in the Veritable Records:

> The emperor went to the Fengxiandian [hall of the ancestors] to perform rites. He sent an official to perform the rites in the back hall of the Tai-miao. He led the princes, civil and military officials to the gate of the Cining palace to present congratulations to the empress dowager. Then he went to the Taihedian and received congratulations. He proceeded to the Dagaodian and the Shouhuangdian to perform rites. He went to the Zhuxiu palace to pay his respects to the empress dowager. He went to the Qianqing palace and feted the close branches.[6]

The emperor's complete schedule of activities on New Year's day shows that the public rites did not necessarily take precedence over private ceremonies. On this day, the emperor arose shortly after midnight. Between 1:30 and 2 A.M. he performed private rituals; at 2 A.M. he sacrificed to the ancestors in the Fengxiandian. The public ritual over, he performed private rites in the Yangxindian, Kunning palace, and Qianqing palace before emerging at 4 A.M. to perform the public rites at the *tangzi*. The weaving of public and private rites continued through his busy morning: visits to Buddhist altars in the inner court preceded his public presentation of congratulations in front of the empress dowager's residence; the emperor's reception of congratulations from princes and ministers was followed by private rituals at the Dagaodian and visits to various Buddhist temples.[7]

The participation of the women of the imperial family is yet another way in which the private rituals of the court differed from the public rites. State rituals, with the single exception of the sacrifice to the silkworm deity, which the empress led, were the prerogative of men. The private rites, by contrast, involved the women as well as the men of the imperial household; the senior woman, generally an empress dowager, led them. The altars visited were all within the inner court. Most of them were also on the emperor's list. But the ritual schedule of the empress dowager was much shorter than the emperor's.

Domestic worship featured much more prominently in the rituals performed by the palace women than in the rituals performed by the emperor. The separate rituals performed by the women of the court for the last and first days of the year in 1885 and 1886 present a point of comparison. On the last day of the year in 1885, Empress Dowager Cixi led the consorts in the senior generation first to the Tianqiongbaodian to worship "almighty Heaven," then to the Qin'an hall to light incense to Xuantian shangdi. She then went to light incense in front of the portraits of her mother-in-law, her husband's foster mother; her husband, the Xianfeng emperor (temple name, Wenzong); and her son, the Tongzhi emperor (Muzong). She lit incense at shrines in the flower garden; the consorts (without Cixi) concluded the rituals by lighting incense before the spirit tablets of Tongzhi's empress and Ci'an.[8] On New Year's day, the first action of the empress dowager was a visit to the Shouhuangdian, where she lit incense; the rest of the ritual schedule repeated the previous day's actions.

The palace ladies, led by the empress dowager, lit the incense and performed the obeisances to send off the smallpox goddess after a successful variolation; they also performed domestic ancestral rites. Just as the emperor commemorated his father's birthday and deathday with ritual, so did the deceased emperor's surviving consorts. On Wenzong's birthday, the empresses dowager led several of these widows in lighting incense before his portrait in the Dongnuange. On Wenzong's deathday, the empresses dowager lit incense in the Shouhuangdian and the Dongnuange; after these rites, they went to the Zhuxiu palace and lit incense before the memento shrine (*yinian kan*) standing there. Similar commemorative rituals were carried out by his widows for the Tongzhi emperor on his deathday.[9]

A comparison of the ritual schedules of 1854 with those of 1885 show that while each emperor worshiped at the major altars in the Yangxindian, Kunning palace, and Qianqing palace, he also included altars of lesser importance that he had selected.[10] On New Year's day, imperial princes and palace officials were sent to light incense at altars in six other palace sites.[11] For the rest of the year the lighting of incense at the inner-court altars was a regular part of the private ritual activities of the court.

The Qing rulers and their ladies donated money and offerings to monasteries and temples of every description in Peking and its suburbs for services commemorating imperial birthdays and deathdays (see below); they sponsored prayers to bring rain (see chapter 6) and the blessings of longevity. Virtually every palace residence and certainly every imperial villa had its own Buddhist altars, and sometimes its own temples. The Enyousi, located just outside the northwestern corner of the Changchunyuan, was a Buddhist temple erected by Yinzhen in honor of his father; next to it was the Enmusi, which Hongli erected in 1777 in honor of his mother. To supplement the Tibetan Buddhist chapels within the Forbidden City and the Yonghegong, which functioned in part as a shrine to the Yongzheng emperor (see below), the Yanshousi and the Zhengjuesi were erected within the imperial villas in the northwestern suburbs. The Yongzheng emperor and his successors erected Daoist altars to the Dipper (*doutan*) and dragon-god temples to rain deities, as well as temples dedicated to Guandi and to Niangniang, a female North China goddess. Shrines to the earth god, which existed in the palace, were also part of the religious landscape.[12]

These religious activities entailed the expenditure of enormous quantities of labor and other resources. An account book of 1796 records a total of twenty-six incense burners at altars within the Forbidden City alone, and their numbers probably increased in the nineteenth century. By the end of the dynasty, the court was observing forty-eight birthday and death anniversaries, each requiring monks and offerings. Not surprisingly, emperors began to cut back on ritual expenditures. In 1753 Hongli ordered that the number of Daoist priests serving in the Yuanmingyuan be cut in half; these priests had been recruited during the Yongzheng reign from the bannermen who served as *sula* (see chapter 5). In 1839 the Daoists and eunuch-monks who had been caring for the Yuanmingyuan altars were all released from their duties.[13]

THE RITUAL CALENDAR

Surviving archival records show that many of the popular religious practices found in the late nineteenth-century court were already present in the Shunzhi reign. A bilingual prayer to the kitchen god dated May 21, 1659, is one of the earliest preserved in the archives. Its text reads: "First day of the fourth month, sixteenth year of the Shunzhi reign: words of sacrifice to the god of the stove, commissioned by the emperor. 'Let daily drink and food be supplied to the stove god. Let it be done in the place where the fire is set. Present sacrifices of silk, livestock, and wine in the first month of summer. May the god look in the mirror and accept [the offerings].'"[14]

The sacrifice to the kitchen god was part of a calendrical ritual cycle that was observed by commoners. Other prayers from the Shunzhi reign show sacrifices in the first month of spring to the door god, enjoining him to carefully supervise the comings and goings of persons and ensure that the doors were opened at daylight and closed at dusk, and in the first month of winter to the god of the well, praying that he will "make the water from the spring clear and clean."[15]

The reference to "looking in the mirror" recurs in many of these early prayers, not just to household deities in the popular religion, but also in addresses to the ancestors of the imperial lineage. "Looking in the mirror"—in Manchu, *bulekušembi*—seems to be related to the shaman's use of mirrors in communicating with the deities. Mirrors appear on the shaman's costume among Tungus peoples: the early twentieth-century Russian scholar S. M. Shirokogoroff noted that "When there is no costume, the shaman can perform with the mirror alone, while when there is no mirror or its substitute, no performance is possible." [16] The mirror helps to "place" the spirit that is being summoned and thus enables the shaman to receive the deity's communications. A 1670 prayer to the ancestors at the Fengxiandian ends with the words "May the deities of the Fengxiandian look in the mirror" (in Manchu, "feng siyan diyan enduringge se bulekušereo"). The phrase recurs in a 1688 prayer to the ancestors that reports the addition of honorifics to the posthumous name of Hongtaiji's second empress, and its Chinese-language counterpart is still found in prayers of the early eighteenth century. [17]

The shamanic influence on court rites was not surprising, given the Manchu religious tradition. Although shamanic rites were performed at court throughout the dynasty, their primacy was gradually eroded. Worship at the *tangzi*, the first New Year activity for emperors from the Shunzhi period, was dropped from first to second place by the Qianlong emperor. [18] As the shamanic rites faded from the court, sacrifice to the ancestors took their place. It was the Qianlong emperor who added worship at the Fengxiandian as the first imperial action of the New Year schedule. He was the first to sacrifice before the imperial portraits in the Shouhuangdian and in the back hall of the Temple of the Ancestors. None of these events was featured during the Kangxi or Yongzheng reigns.

It was also the Qianlong emperor who first worshiped at the Daoist altars in the Dagaodian on New Year's day. The Dagaodian, located in the southwestern corner of Jingshan, directly north of the Forbidden City, was initially called the Dagaoxuandian (hall of high heaven). It was built during the Ming and repaired in 1730 and 1746. Here the supreme Daoist deity, the Jade Emperor, was worshiped as a god who could send or withhold rain and snow. A stop at the Dagaodian became an enduring feature of the emperor's New Year schedule. [19]

By the late nineteenth century, many Peking customs marking the passing of the old year and the coming of the new were followed at court. The imperial family pasted "good fortune" (*fu*) characters to different palaces and garden structures; erected door gods to defend against heterodox influences; offered congee to the Buddhas on the eighth day of the twelfth month; and sent off the kitchen god on the twenty-third. Firecrackers were set off during the last day and first day of the year to ritually purify the inner court. Like ordinary residents of Peking, the emperor ate *jiaozi* dumplings on New Year's day and offered *yuanxiao* (round dumplings symbolizing good fortune) on altars to mark the end of the New Year festivities on the fifteenth day of the first month.

The household rituals at New Year's were part of a year-long schedule, sanctioned by custom, that was designed to protect and obtain future good fortune for the inhabitants of the inner quarters behind the Qianqing gate. At Qingming special offerings were placed on the domestic ancestral altars. The spring and autumnal equinoxes were marked by private rituals and special offerings. The Ullambara or "Hungry Ghosts" festival on the fifteenth day of the seventh month was marked by the lighting of incense at the domestic ancestral altars and the release of specially made lanterns on the waters at the Changchunyuan and Yuanmingyuan.[20] Just as changes in the status or identity of the head of household affect the religious activities of commoners, so too with the emperor. When an imperial wedding—the marriage of a reigning emperor—took place, the household god was renewed, to symbolize the advent of his adulthood. When the emperor died, the private rituals of the New Year were suspended; the kitchen god could not return until after the first hundred days of mourning had passed.[21]

In addition to the popular calendrical rituals, the court maintained regular offerings at various altars. A ritual schedule for the Guangxu reign lists six altars, with the eastern and western Buddha halls of the Yangxindian receiving the greatest attention. Incense was lit on these altars seven times during the twelfth month, six times during the first month, and from four to five times a month the rest of the year. The other sites, where incense was lit four or five times during the twelfth month and at least twice a month the rest of the year, were the back hall of the Temple of the Ancestors, the Dongnuange and Xinuange of the Qianqing palace, and the Fanzonglou, a Tibetan Buddhist chapel in the northwestern part of the Forbidden City dedicated to the worship of Mañjuśrī. Altars to Taisui and Heaven and Earth received attention only in the twelfth month and at the New Year.[22]

The court ordered the chanting of sutras at many of these sites. During the twelfth month, Tibetan dignitaries and monks chanted sutras for four days in the Baohuadian, a hall in the northwestern compound dedicated to Buddhist images. In the Nanyuan, the large hunting park south of Peking, stood the Yongmusi, where a high lama and forty priests chanted sutras for twenty-one days during the last month of the year.[23] As we shall see below, sutra recitations were also ordered to commemorate the birthdays and deathdays of emperors and empresses.

COURT PATRONAGE

Whereas the court followed popular customs in its observance of the annual round of festivals, it was unique in the scale of its religious patronage of shamanic, Daoist, Chinese Buddhist, and Tibetan Buddhist clergy. As we noted earlier, worship at the Daoist altar within the palace in the Tianqiongbaodian was a standard feature of the New Year's rituals. The Daoist scriptures for the other altars in the Qin'an palace and the Dagaodian were stored in this hall. At the Yuanmingyuan, the Yongzheng emperor installed forty-four Daoist priests and a head Daoist, Lou Jindan, in the Daguangmingdian after its repair in 1733, conferring on Lou the third official rank and stipends with which to perform on the emperor's birthday and at eleven other points in the year. The court also patronized the Guangmingdian, located in the western part of the imperial city. Under the Ming, this temple was called the Wanshougong; the Qianlong emperor renovated it and changed its name. Daoist rites were performed here and at the Dongyuemiao in the eastern suburbs.[24]

The imperial family presented offerings at many Buddhist temples in the Peking area and in Chengde. On New Year's day, imperial princes and officials were sent to light incense on the emperor's behalf at over a dozen nearby temples.[25] Sutra recitations were one way to acquire merit in Buddhism. During the late seventeenth and early eighteenth centuries, a sutra recitation office was created and housed in the Zhongzhengdian, a hall located in the northwestern corner of the palace. Eventually this office, the first in the court to deal solely with Tibetan Buddhist affairs, was supervised by imperial princes and was part of the Neiwufu's Zhangyisi (department of ceremonial). The Zhongzhengdian became the nucleus of the Tibetan Buddhist activities at court, not only conducting sutra recitations under high lamas, but also casting Buddha images and other religious paraphernalia.[26]

A large number of temples received regular subsidies from the palace. One document from 1854 shows that the court spent 126.7 taels of silver supporting the religious activities of 1,516 Tibetan Buddhist monks for one month. Within the inner court, lamas—some of them eunuchs trained for this purpose—chanted sutras in the Zhongzhengdian and the neighboring Yuhuage, a Tibetan Buddhist chapel erected by the Qianlong emperor. Together, the two chapels employed 1,106 lamas in these rites and had the lion's share of these funds. Other recitations took place in the Yong'ansi, located in Beihai, Tangshan, lying north of the capital, the Zhaomiao, a temple in the Western Hills erected by the Qianlong emperor, the Yan-shousi, and the Sumeru land.[27]

Some of the events sponsored by the court were also seasonal in nature. Each year, on the sixth day of the first month, at the Hongrensi, a temple located on the western shore of Beihai, Tibetan lamas put on ritual dress and danced before a Mongol audience in praise of "Sor Baling"; another performance at this temple on the eighth, dedicated to Maitreya Buddha, also seems to have been directed at Mongols. Monks at the Hongrensi also recited sutras from the fourth to the eighth day of the first month, as did four hundred lamas in the Enmusi; the ranking lama at this temple also recited sutras on the twenty-first, as did monks at the Ciyousi.[28] On the eighth day of the fourth month, celebrated as Buddha's birthday, offerings were presented at the Yongningsi, located in the Changchunyuan, and the palace theatrical troupe performed. Sutra recitations for the Qianlong emperor's birthday in 1798 were carried out at the Wanshousi, a Ming temple in the northern suburbs of Peking; at the Fayuansi, a temple in the imperial city, built by the Kangxi emperor; the Guangjisi, a temple in the northwestern part of the Tartar city that had been renovated by the Kangxi emperor; and the Huguosi (protect the nation temple), which was situated in the same district.[29]

LIFE CYCLE RITUALS

Birthdays

The normal religious routines were magnified during the celebration of the birthday of the empress dowager or the emperor. The *wanshou qingdian*, or full-scale imperial birthday celebration, was held only seven times during the course of the dynasty: on the Kangxi emperor's sixtieth birthday (1713), the Qianlong emperor's eightieth birthday (1790), his mother's sixtieth and eightieth birthdays (1751, 1771), the Jiaqing emperor's sixtieth birthday (1819), and Empress Dowager Cixi's fiftieth and sixtieth birthdays (1884, 1894). These were extraordinary public events and, in the case of Xuanye and Hongli, marked the achievements of their long reigns. Special as well as ordinary imperial birthdays were occasions for public and private rituals such as sutra recitations, opera performances, banquets, and the presentation of extravagant gifts.

Although mourning obligations dominated court rituals for three years after the death of an emperor (discussed below), the accession of a new emperor was marked by the addition of special religious rites on his birthday.

In 1736, while the court canceled the New Year festivities because it was still in mourning for the Yongzheng emperor, Yinlu and other ministers of the Neiwufu suggested that twenty-four Daoist priests and a Daoist official perform rites in the Dagaodian for a period of thirty-six days around the new emperor's birthday. These Daoist rites, which continued through the Qianlong reign, were supplemented by Tibetan Buddhist and Chinese Buddhist rituals. Records from 1796, after the Qianlong emperor had abdicated in favor of his son, show that two thousand Tibetan lamas were employed in chanting the "Long life sutra" (*Wanshoujing*) at the Hongrensi for the four days leading up to (and including) his birthday. The sutra recitation, which was repeated annually through the year after his death, cost over 1,758 taels of silver each year.[30] That this became customary practice for every new emperor is suggested by the staging in 1799 and 1820 of the same recitation at the Hongrensi for the Jiaqing and Daoguang emperors on their birthdays.[31]

Birthday celebrations tended to become more elaborate over time. The Qianlong emperor's birthday in 1798 was also commemorated at six other Buddhist temples where 218 monks chanted for nine days. The Daoguang emperor's birthday had not only the monks of the Hongrensi, but other high-ranked Tibetan monks entering the palace to chant the Amitāyus sutra in the Yangxindian and the Zhongzhengdian.[32]

Sutra recitation was also a feature of birthday celebrations for empresses dowager. At the Yanshousi (extend long life temple), which he had erected for his mother's sixtieth birthday, the Qianlong emperor assembled priests to chant sutras "for the eminent, prolonged, and extensive happiness of my mother and for her long life without measure." On his mother's seventieth and eightieth birthday, the Qianlong emperor had the highest Tibetan dignitary in Peking, the lCang skya khutukhtu, lead a thousand lamas from various temples in chanting the Sukhāvatīvyūha or Amitāyus sutra, designed to ensure rebirth in the Pure Land. He bestowed a set of nine Buddhas and a complete set of Amitāyus figures on his mother for her sixtieth birthday; for her seventieth birthday, she received over nine thousand statues of Buddhas, bodhisattvas, Amitāyus, tara, and lohans, in multiples of nine (nine being a homophone for eternity, i.e., long life). Ten thousand Amitāyus statues, signifying wishes for long life and rebirth in the Western Paradise, were made for Hongli's own sixtieth birthday. Funds for these "birthday presents" were contributed by the court: on the emperor's seventieth birthday, the princes and officials clubbed together to present a total of 2,233 Amida Buddhas costing over 321,000 taels of silver.[33]

Marriage

Marriage, like death, is by definition a public event, which involves not just the bride and groom but the social recognition of their union by their community. Elsewhere, I describe the public rituals marking the marriage of a reigning emperor, called *dahun*.[34] Those rites were outlined in the regulations of the dynasty, the *Da Qing huidian* and the *Da Qing tongli*, compiled during the Qianlong reign. Here I turn to the private rituals, performed within the confines of the inner court, that accompanied the public marriage ceremonies.

The private rituals seem to conform closely to the popular customs attending marriage among commoners in North China.[35] The Imperial Household Department searched among the wives of its officials to select women who had "complete families" (living husbands, sons) and whose horoscopes matched those of the bride to form the entourage that went to the bride's house to bring her to the palace on her wedding day. The "phoenix carriage" that transported the bride to her new home was purified with Tibetan incense. The bedchamber for the new couple was decorated in red, the felicitous color used for weddings. Grain (symbolizing fertility) was deposited there in a vessel called a "precious vase" (*baoping*, a pun on "precious harmony"). A *ruyi* (a Chinese scepter; its name is a pun on "fulfillment of wishes") was placed on each of the bed's four corners. The bride's wedding outfit, which was brought to her from the palace, consisted of a "dragon and phoenix in harmony robe," a "double happiness" headdress, hairpins ornamented with *ruyi* and with the characters for "double happiness."

Other popular customs appeared in the imperial marriage (*dahun*) of 1872. The bride stepped into the sedan chair carrying an apple whose name was a homonym for peace (*pingguo*). She stepped over a saddle (a pun on *an*, "peace") when she descended from the sedan chair and entered the courtyard of the Qianqing palace. In the bridal chamber the bride's hair was combed into the style suited to a matron; additional hairpins with the characters for "good fortune" (*fu*) and "honor" (*gui*) were inserted into her hair. At this point, the bride donned the court necklace, thus completing her transformation into an empress. The couple were made to eat "many sons and grandsons" cakes, served on a round (for harmony) platter; on the wedding night, they were served "long-life" noodles.

The rituals that were perhaps unique to the court were those performed before the shamanic altar in the Kunning palace. In the case of the Tongzhi emperor's *dahun*, the Imperial Household Department ministers decided that the deities should be moved out of the Kunning palace over a month before the nuptials to permit renovation of the altar. The wedding took place on October 16, 1872; the gods were reinstalled in the palace on October 25 and the emperor and empress performed the "seeking good fortune" rite (*qiufu*; see chapter 7) on the following day.[36]

Commoner brides and bridegrooms worshiped tablets representing Heaven and Earth and bowed before the ancestral tablets. The imperial newlyweds lit incense and performed the "three kneelings and nine prostrations" before a "heaven and earth" offering table and an "auspicious gods" offering table set up in a hall of the Kunning palace. They kowtowed before the shamanic altars, then offered incense and kowtowed to the kitchen god. The couple visited the Shouhuangdian, where they lit incense and prostrated themselves before portraits of past emperors and empresses.

Commoners normally had the bride bow before her new parents-in-law. In the case of the *dahun* the father-in-law was deceased. Both the Tongzhi emperor and his bride performed the three kneelings and nine prostrations before the senior empress dowager Ci'an and the mother empress dowager Cixi, in the central halls of their separate palace residences. The empress led the other consorts in performing the same ritual before her husband in his residence, the Yangxindian. Finally, in her own palace, the Chuxiugong, the empress herself sat on a throne while the princesses, consorts, and court ladies acknowledged her new status by performing the same rituals of submission before her.

Nor was that the full extent of the marriage rituals. Before receiving the symbolic submission of the consorts and princesses, the new empress went to light incense and worship at the Buddhist altar, the memento shrine, and the gods installed in her new residence. She thus performed rituals before the multiple deities, originating in several different religious traditions, that ruled over the Qing inner court. In comparison, the imperial consorts performed a simplified set of rituals when they entered the palace. They visited not the Shouhuangdian but the various palaces of the inner court to worship before the portraits of the Xianfeng emperor's mother, his foster mother, the portrait of the Xianfeng emperor, and the spirit tablet of his first empress. This was their "worship of the ancestors," and the primary feature of their ritual introduction to the inner court.

Marriage supplanted the classical capping ceremony as the ritual that transformed a boy into an adult. For the Kangxi, Tongzhi, and Guangxu emperors, the *dahun* also signified the end of regencies and the assumption of personal rule. The "new beginning" was symbolized in the renewal of the gods, a tradition that was normally performed at the New Year. During the twelfth month of every year, the deities installed in the shamanic altars of the Kunning palace were moved to the *tangzi*. When they returned after the New Year to the palace, there were rites "opening" the new gods and praying for good fortune in the coming year. In 1872, however, the rituals first removing and then reinstalling the gods were performed to highlight the wedding of the Tongzhi emperor.[37]

Establishing a Separate Household

In contrast to the birthday celebratory rites, which focused on Buddhist and Daoist services, the maturation and coming of age of young princes were tied to shamanic rituals. Archival records show that when a prince established a separate household, household deities were installed in his new residence, and the prince was expected to perform the monthly sacrifice to gods and Heaven there. Interestingly, a Buddhist ritual with the same intent of "asking the god to enter the house" was performed when a princess married and was awarded a mansion in the capital to reside in.[38] When the prince married, the "seeking good fortune" rite to the deity of fortune and fertility, Folifodo omosi *mama enduri*, was performed. Unlike ordinary bannermen, who could not continue the Jurchen tradition, the imperial lineage permitted sons to establish separate households after marriage, at a time determined by the emperor (see chapter 3). Princes who had already established a separate household were generally expected to separately perform the monthly sacrifices at the Kunning palace. In the *tangzi*, the princes of the blood erected their own spirit poles and sacrificed to Heaven after the emperor.[39]

Illness

By the mid-eighteenth century, Tibetan Buddhist rituals may have supplanted shamanic efforts to cure illness. When the emperor's third son, Yongzhang, lay ill in September 1760, his great-uncle, Prince Zhuang, reported in his capacity as a minister of the Neiwufu that the lCang skya khutukhtu had been consulted concerning the sutras to be read on his behalf. The khutukhtu, selecting one that would be beneficial for the lung disease that Yongzhang had contracted, moved to a house close to the prince's mansion. He and ten lamas recited the sutras for two days in an effort to improve Yongzhang's health. Unfortunately, the patient died two days later.[40]

Funerals

The biggest change in Manchu funerary customs, which does not appear in the Qing official record, was the abandonment of cremation during the late seventeenth century. Nurgaci, Hongtaiji, and Fulin were all cremated, as were their consorts who died before 1661. Thereafter rulers and most of their consorts were buried. There were exceptions: one of Hongtaiji's consorts was cremated after her death in 1674; recent excavations of a Qing princess who died in Mongolia in 1678 show that she was cremated; and two of Yongzheng's sons who died in childhood, the second in 1728, were cremated and their ashes put into jars that were buried with no tumulus.[41]

The new precedents that prevailed for the rest of the dynasty were set in 1688 during the mortuary rites for the emperor's beloved grandmother, empress dowager Xiaozhuang. The emperor cut off his queue, an action previously performed only upon the death of the ruler. He abandoned plain silk and insisted on cotton mourning clothes. Refusing to move the coffin out of the palace for the New Year festivities, Xuanye instead canceled the festivities. Despite the rigors of the Peking winter, he lived in a tent to "watch by the coffin" throughout the mourning period. By eventually installing his grandmother's spirit tablet in the Taimiao, he broke the Ming regulation allowing only one empress to be admitted into the ancestral hall.[42]

The public and private distinction between rituals performed by the court is also present in the funerals of emperors and empresses. In a previous study, I traced the sequence of events constituting the public funerary rites presented in the *Da Qing huidian* and *Da Qing tongli*.[43] Although the private rituals performed during the funeral of an emperor or empress replicated many customs linked with Peking, it also introduced distinctive new elements, which in at least one instance won acceptance among ordinary households.

Most of the private rituals performed during an imperial funeral were non-Confucian practices that were observed by ordinary Peking families. The body of the deceased was washed and clothed in court dress (*chaofu*), the most formal official attire. Clothing found in the grave of Empress Dowager Cixi suggests that these garments might be embroidered with auspicious characters for "long life," "good fortune," and with Buddhist symbols. The body was then wrapped in five layers of *tuolo jingbei* (dharani coverlet), silk shrouds into which were woven "secret" dharani (religious incantations believed to have magical powers) in Sanskrit and Tibetan. These dharani included formulaic passages that were familiar to Chinese as well as Tibetan Buddhists.[44] The dharani coverlet of an emperor or empress was made of gold silk damask embroidered with five shades of gold; that for other ranks may have been gold on a white background. There were also dharani coverlets that had gold characters on a red background: perhaps these were intended for consorts of the fifth rank and below, whose coffins were lacquered red. Imbued with an efficacy derived from having had scriptures and dharani chanted over them by an incarnate Buddha, these shrouds were believed to have the power to absolve the deceased from the misdeeds of life and enable the spirit to go to the Western Paradise. Eight additional layers of silk satin embroidered with dragons were wrapped over the five layers of dharani coverlet, making a total of thirteen layers of silk cloth.[45]

After the relatives of the deceased changed into mourning garb, they went to notify the gods. In commoner society, this was accomplished by reporting to the local earth deity, who was a member of the supernatural bureaucracy. When an emperor died, the ritual of notification was performed before the ancestors at the Fengxiandian, but also at sixty sites throughout the empire to gods of the popular religion and to emperors of earlier dynasties. We have a list of these sites from the funeral of the Qianlong emperor in 1799: they included the god at Changbaishan (the Manchu ancestral home), the god of the Sungari river; the gods of Xiyu and Huashan in Shaanxi and Sichuan; the gods of Taishan, Kuaiji shan, and Hengshan; the gods of the Northern Ocean (Beihai), Eastern Ocean (Donghai), and Southern Ocean (Nanhai); and the mausolea of the Han, Tang, Song, Yuan, and Ming emperors.[46]

The coffin of a deceased emperor or empress was made of *nanmu*, a Chinese hardwood. After lying in state for two weeks, the coffin was usually moved into temporary storage to permit workmen to cover the coffin with forty-nine coats of lacquer, and a final coat of gold lacquer. The coffin itself seems to have had Tibetan and Sanskrit dharani written over its surface.[47] Because the lacquering could not take place when the temperatures were too cold, the coffin frequently remained above ground for many months, and sometimes for years. As long as the coffin remained uninterred, the deceased was in a liminal state and needed spiritual protection. When the Yongzheng emperor died, his coffin was moved after nineteen days to his former residence, the Yonghegong (see map 2), and remained there until interment in March 1737. This mansion, Yinzhen's residence from 1694–1722, was refurbished. While the coffin rested in Yinzhen's former bedchamber, the Yongyoudian, sutra recitations were conducted in the main and back halls by six Chinese Buddhist monks and eight Daoist monks. A portrait of Yinzhen was hung in the Yongyoudian, and sacrifices were conducted before it.[48]

The burning of paper money, furniture, servants, houses, and other items is a persistent element in Chinese funerals, and the Qing emperors followed the same practices. A tremendous quantity of paper ingots, paper money, and paper clothing was burned. The paper goods themselves were a major expenditure: the total cost of this item alone for the first year of Cixi's funerary rites is estimated to have been 1.2 million taels of silver. But in imperial funerals, actual clothing and furniture was burned in awesome quantities. Amiot's description of the funeral procession in 1777 of the Qianlong emperor's mother, Empress Dowager Xiaosheng, describes the scene:

> camels and horses, two by two, loaded with provisions as if for a long trip: beds, utensils, provisions, etc. After them came the carts, the rolling chairs, the sedan chairs, armchairs, chairs, stools, cushions, trunks, basins, and all the articles of the toilette. All this marches in file for twenty-eight rows. Articles of use, jewels, all that the princess used while she lived, like mirrors, fans, etc . . . were carried separately by the servants, forming several ranks, after which was carried, with much respect, the little stick which she used during her old age.[49]

Sacrificial offerings marked each of the rituals performed while the coffin lay in state, was moved to temporary storage, and finally interred, three years after her death. In addition to animal sacrifices, wine, and paper money, the deceased person's clothing, furniture, utensils—in theory, everything used by the person, with the exception of articles that were given as mementos to relatives and high officials—were burned as offerings to the deceased, who would thus have the use of these items in the next life. One scholar has calculated that over 770 items of clothing were burned during nineteen separate rites performed up to the first anniversary of the Qianlong emperor's death. A total of 734 items of this kind were burned during the funeral of the Guangxu emperor.[50]

Sutras and dharanis were a central element in the funeral services that Daoist, Chan, and Lamaist Buddhist monks performed simultaneously at different altars within the villas and palaces of the inner court. While the Yongzheng emperor's coffin lay in state at the Qianqing palace, 108 lamas chanted. On the first anniversary of his death, 108 lamas were assigned to chant sutras for twenty-one days at the Yuanmingyuan. The funeral services were led by the highest religious dignitaries. The lCang skya khutukhtu, Rol pa'i rdo rje, personally performed the funeral rites for seven days when the Qianlong emperor's mother died in 1777.[51]

The number and frequency of the sutra recitations performed during the funeral of an emperor seem to have increased in the eighteenth and nineteenth centuries. During the funeral of the Xianfeng emperor (1861) Daoist services were scheduled for three days in the Qianqing palace, as well as twenty-one days of sutra recitations by 108 Tibetan Buddhist monks. And 108 Tibetan Buddhist monks officiated at the rites preceding the transfer of the coffin to the Guandedian; the day after this move, a new round of sutra recitations began, employing 80 lamas.[52] During the Tongzhi emperor's funeral in 1875, the move of the coffin from the Qianqing palace to temporary storage in the Guandedian signaled the beginning of a cycle of recitations. First were the religious services performed by the coffin. For twenty-one days 80 Tibetan Buddhist monks recited sutras; then for seven days 48 Chan Buddhist monks recited sutras; the Tibetan Buddhist and Chan Buddhist monks rotated every seven days in their recitations for a period of over ten weeks. The penultimate recitation was performed by 108 Tibetan and 25 Chan Buddhist monks. The recitation schedule was repeated in 1908 for the funeral of Empress Dowager Cixi; for the funeral of the Guangxu emperor in the same year, there were 108 Tibetan Buddhist and 108 Chan Buddhist monks reciting in nine-day segments while forty-nine coats of lacquer were applied to the coffin. In addition, monks performed rituals for the feeding of hungry ghosts; they accompanied the coffin when it was sent to the tombs, and each night, after the evening libations were poured, they chanted mantras while circumambulating the coffin.[53]

Meanwhile, Chinese Buddhist, Tibetan Buddhist, and Daoist services on behalf of the deceased emperor were also being performed in temples and Daoist altars. For the Tongzhi emperor's funeral, two hundred Tibetan Buddhist monks chanted for seven days in three temples in the Songzhusi, Fayuansi, and Zhizhusi. The last two temples, located in the imperial city near Jingshan, were erected by the Kangxi emperor and housed Mongol monks who translated and printed "liturgical books" in Tibetan and Mongolian. These sutra recitations were also performed for the Guangxu emperor and Empress Dowager Cixi.[54]

The funerals of emperors and empresses were important political and ritual events, and much of the funerary service for these personages remained in the public realm. The reverse is true of the funerary rituals for other imperial family members. In general, the lower the rank, the more private the rites that were performed. Archival records permit us to examine these rites in some detail, in order to assess both the immutable and the variable elements in private commemoration.

Whether the death of an imperial consort was a public or private affair depended ultimately on the decision of the ruler. Although the emperor tended to follow the generational rules customary in Chinese society, participating in the funerary rituals of the consorts in his mother's and grandmother's generation, this was by no means always the case. The young Qianlong emperor, for example, ignored the deaths of some of his father's and grandfather's consorts, while honoring others by pouring libations before their coffins. Some consorts who had borne a son were so honored, and their deaths listed in the Veritable Records, while the funerals of others enjoying equal rank were omitted.[55]

In commoner society, and generally within the imperial harem, mothers were honored above infertile wives (see chapter 4). Bearing the emperor's children, however, did not guarantee that the mother would enter the Veritable Records after death. In accordance with custom, the emperor did not participate publicly in the funerals of his own consorts, but a very broad range of options allowed him to choose which deaths he would honor. In some cases, his decisions were based on personal feelings. In others, he honored a consort because of his affection for her children. Yu *guifei*, who bore the Qianlong emperor a son, received no mention when she died at the age of 79 *sui*; by contrast, the death of the childless Yu *fei* in 1774 brought a suspension of court business for three days.[56] When Xin *fei* died in 1764, the emperor ordered that she be given the funeral of a second- rather than third-ranking consort, and he appointed three sons and a grandson to be the principal mourners—this despite the fact that she had borne him only two daughters. For Fulehun *huangguifei*, the mother of the future Jiaqing emperor and five other children, the funerary rites when she died in 1775 involved the shaving of heads, doffing of cap ornaments and jewelry, and donning of mourning dress among her children and their spouses.[57] Shu *fei*, mother of a son who did not survive to adulthood, nonetheless had two imperial sons, two grandsons, and two sons-in-law appointed to mourn for her when she died in 1777. The Veritable Records, which provide the details, show that at least part of the funerals of these imperial consorts occurred in the public arena.[58]

The encoffinment, presentation of funerary offerings, the eventual movement of the coffin out of the residence, and the interment of the coffin were parts of the funerary rites that would normally be performed in public (and entered in the Veritable Records) for emperors or empresses. Although the size and scale of these rites varied, certain persistent elements characterized the funerals of men and women in the imperial family. The body of a deceased consort would have a pearl put into its mouth, the Manchu set of three earrings attached to each ear, and would be clothed in dragon robes and a phoenix headdress. The body would be wrapped in layers of colored silk embroidered with dharani, and further outer layers of silk. Into the coffin, which for high ranking consorts could be made of *nanmu*, was placed other clothing, underclothes, jewelry, and perhaps a *ruyi*. The coffin would then be moved to the *ji'an suo* (place of auspicious rest), where it would lie in state and receive daily offerings. During the late Qing era the *ji'an suo* was located outside the Forbidden City, northeast of the walled enclosure that was Jingshan.

Each princely mansion, like the palace and imperial villas, had a place where the coffins and mortuary paraphernalia were stored, which was euphemistically called the "place of good fortune" (*jixiang suo*). Ordinary Manchus called the board on which a dead person was placed the "board of good fortune" (*jixiang ban*); similarly the "place of good fortune" became the *ji'an suo*, and the conveyance in which the coffin was moved the "sedan chair of good fortune" (*jixiang jiao*).[59] After a period of lying in state, the coffin would sometimes be interred, but might also be temporarily stored. During the Kangxi reign, coffins were frequently stored in Gonghua, which lay north of Peking on the banks of the Sha River. This was where the coffins of Xuanye's first and second empresses were stored until work on Jingling, the tomb, was completed. During the Qianlong reign, coffins were sometimes stored in the Guandedian, which stood on Jingshan. When the Yongzheng emperor decided to build his tomb in an area to the southwest of the capital, coffins were stored at Zaobali, a new temporary storage place that was closer to the site of the western tombs. During the Daoguang reign, Jing'anzhuang, which was located about 100 *li* away from the capital, became a favored coffin depository for his consorts. Later, in the Guangxu reign, imperial coffins were deposited in Tiancun, a village on the western outskirts of Peking.[60]

Regardless of whether or not their deaths were inscribed in the Veritable Records, all consorts received funeral rituals that are described in archival records. Extensive archival records describe the last illness and death in December 1740 of Cheng *fei*, a consort of the Kangxi emperor who had given him a son; but the Veritable Records have no mention of any of these events.[61] They also omit any mention of Iletu *fei* (Xuan *fei*), who died on September 12, 1736.

Iletu *fei* was a consort of the Kangxi emperor, a Khorchin Mongol "mother's brother's daughter"—she was the daughter of the brother of one of the Shunzhi emperor's consorts. Being childless, she had no descendants, and the emperor appointed his twenty-third son, Yinqi (1714–85), Prince Cheng, to perform the role of chief mourner. Many of the observances performed in the public arena for an emperor or empress were performed for the consort: the prince and his wife put on mourning clothes, as did the maids, eunuchs, and nurses in Iletu *fei*'s residence. Although the prince did not cut his queue, the staff adopted this customary sign of mourning. The consort's Khorchin kinsmen also donned mourning garb. The princes, princesses, and palace staff were assembled in mourning dress for libations and offerings for three days, after which, at a time selected by the Board of Astronomy, the coffin was moved into temporary storage, then buried. The seven-day intervals after death that were normally marked by rituals were compressed so that the culminating "grand sacrifice" (*da ji*) was performed a month after Iletu *fei* died, but the customary hundred-day period marking the period of most intense mourning was observed with daily offerings of a table of fruit and one of cakes. The customary rituals marking the first anniversary of death were also performed.[62]

Iletu *fei*'s funeral is not mentioned in the Veritable Record. Nor of course do we read about the Daoist and Buddhist rites that were performed. After the coffin was closed, lamas circumambulated the coffin, chanting dharani. Daoist rites were performed at an altar within the inner court. Tibetan Buddhist monks chanted sutras for the soul of the deceased at rites marking the first month, hundred days, and full year after death. These seem to be the essential points for sutra recitation in the funerary sequence.

The rank of the consort and whether or not she had borne children, determined the number of monks, and the number of days of recitation. A childless fourth-rank consort (*guiren*) of the Yongzheng emperor, dying in 1760, had 20 monks circumambulating the coffin, 40 Tibetan Buddhist monks, 24 Chan Buddhist monks, and 24 Daoist priests chanting masses for seven days; another fourth-rank consort had 48 Tibetan Buddhist monks and a head monk chanting for three days after her death in 1761. A first-rank consort, dying in 1860, received thirty-five days of sutra recitation by 108 Tibetan Buddhist and 48 Chan Buddhist monks, whereas a fourth-rank consort dying the following year had only fourteen days of recitations by 40 Tibetan Buddhist and 24 Chan Buddhist monks. But funerary rites for all ranks tended to become more elaborate over the course of the dynasty. The 1885 funeral of Yu *fei*, a childless consort of the Xianfeng emperor, included seventy days of sutra recitations and a performance of the service for hungry ghosts and sutra recitations on two successive days after the encoffinment.[63]

As head of his household and the imperial lineage, the emperor also concerned himself with the deaths of his sons, daughters, brothers, kinsmen, and their dependents. The emperor could choose to take public notice of these deaths. When his younger brother Longxi died in 1679, the Kangxi emperor led the high officials in pouring libations and wailing before the coffin. Although he did not personally attend the interment (because "it would not be convenient for the widow"), he visited the coffin before it was buried and performed rites at the grave afterwards.[64]

When his younger brother Hongyan became seriously ill in 1765, the Qianlong emperor promoted him to the second princely rank, hoping that Hongyan's pleasure would bring about a speedy recovery. After he died, Hongli ordered that he be buried with the rites of a first-rank prince and designated one of his own sons to don mourning garb, but he did not personally attend the rites. This symbolic gesture, however, Hongli extended to his favorite brother, Hongzhou. The emperor had visited him during his illness, sending a court physician to tend the patient; when, against hope, his brother died, the emperor poured libations before the coffin, designated two of his own sons to don mourning, appropriated 10,000 taels for the funeral expenses, and appointed Prince Cheng to head a committee to manage the funeral.[65]

Seniority of generation was a major element shaping the funerary rituals, but here too imperial sentiment significantly modified the actual proceedings. Fathers were not supposed to participate in the funerals of their sons; after all, dying before one's parent could be construed as an extremely unfilial act. When his eldest son, Yonghuang, died at the age of 22 *sui* in 1750, the Qianlong emperor issued a statement of his grief that appears in the Veritable Records (see chapter 3). He posthumously bestowed a first-rank princedom on Yonghuang and ordered that he be buried with the rites appropriate to his new rank. Because he "could not bear" that the body be buried after the customary three days' interval, the emperor ordered that the coffin be retained for five days and suspended court business for that time. He went every day before the coffin to pour libations and saw the coffin finally depart the palace for temporary storage. The day after it was moved, he went to the hall in Jing'anzhuang where it had been deposited and poured libations there.[66]

Deaths of infants, of lower-ranking consorts, and of princes' dependents tended to be omitted from the Veritable Record but they nonetheless commanded the attention of the emperor through the actions of the Imperial Household Department and the Imperial Clan Court. The death of a prince's wife would produce a grant of silver for funerary expenses; the death of a consort or child would elicit the designation of principal mourners from the imperial family as well as the performance of funeral rites that included sutra recitations, services for the hungry ghosts, and the other private Daoist, Tibetan Buddhist, and Chinese Buddhist rites described above. As noted above, the emperor could and often did order the Imperial Household Department to manage the funeral proceedings; he also kept an eye on the private affairs of his descendants even after they had married and established separate households. When the mother of one of his grandsons died, the emperor, worried that Mianhui and his wife were too young to manage their own affairs (Mianhui was thirty at the time), appointed a steward from the Neiwufu.[67]

Descriptions of funerary customs in Peking in the 1920s and 1930s show that some court practices crept into the usages of ordinary residents in the capital. The dharani coverlets were presented to high officials and by the late Qing seem to have become a Peking funerary custom. Takeda Masao, reporting on Manchu and Han customs in the 1930s, wrote that dharani coverlets were used by "everybody" "regardless of their status."[68] Those who could afford it hired Tibetan Buddhist priests to chant sutras for the deceased or alternatively included lamas, Daoist priests, and Buddhist monks in the funeral service. According to one writer, sutra recitation was reckoned in terms of a cycle of three days, called "matshed sutras" (*pengjing*). Ordinary households might pay for only one cycle, while wealthy households hosted up to nine *pengjing* for their dead.[69]

DOMESTIC ANCESTRAL WORSHIP

The emperor also carried out a form of domestic ancestral worship. The Guangxu emperor, for example, lit incense before (in this order) portraits of the Xianfeng emperor's mother (Xiaoquan Cheng *huanghou*) and foster mother (Xiaojing Cheng *huanghou*); the Xianfeng emperor (Wenzong) and the Tongzhi emperor (Muzong). Finally, he lit incense in front of spirit tablets for the Xianfeng emperor's first and second empresses.

Several aspects of the private ancestral rituals are noteworthy. The first is that the rituals did not take place at the Taimiao, the first-rank ancestral altar in the state religion, nor at the Fengxiandian, which was the more informal "family" ancestral hall, which held tablets for these individuals. Rites performed in the Taimiao and the Fengxiandian on New Year's day belonged to the public rather than the private realm and were recorded in the Veritable Records. These imperial ancestral temples installed the spirit tablets of deceased emperors and empresses as part of the funerary rites.

And the formal ancestral sacrifices of the imperial family did not exclude the recent dead, as those of commoners did.[70]

Unlike the Taimiao and Fengxiandian, which were centers of collective worship, the altars for domestic ancestral rites were in private residences. During the reigns of the Yongzheng, Qianlong, Jiaqing, and Daoguang emperors, a private altar stood in the eastern Buddha hall (*dongfotang*) in the imperial villa, the Yuanmingyuan. Within the Forbidden City, the primary private altar was the eastern Buddha hall of the Yangxindian. When the Jiaqing emperor died, tablets for him and his empress were placed not only in the eastern Buddha hall of the Yangxindian but also in the eastern Buddha hall of the Fengsanwusi, his residence within the Yuanmingyuan. Later there was a proliferation of sites. The portrait of the Xianfeng emperor's mother, Empress Xiaoquan, seems to have hung originally in the Zhongcui palace: her son came here on New Year's day 1854 to light incense. By the Guangxu reign, however, the portrait hung in the Chengqian palace, alongside an image of the Buddha and a shrine holding her spirit tablet; the portrait of Empress Xiaojing, who acted as a foster mother to the Xianfeng emperor, hung in the Yuqing palace. Both of these palaces were located in the block east of the Qianqing palace, whereas the spirit tablets of the Xianfeng emperor's first and second empresses were installed in the Jianfu palace, in the western block.

The practice of commemorating particularly loved ancestors within the palace residences of the inner court probably originated in the early Qing. We know that the Yongzheng emperor installed the spirit tablets of his father and his natural mother in the eastern Buddha hall of his private residence, the Yangxindian. Yinzhen also seems to have installed a spirit tablet for his father in Xuanye's former princely residence, which he transformed into a Buddhist temple, the Fuyousi.[71] The records indicate that the Xianfeng emperor performed rites before the portrait of his grandfather, Renzong, in the Dongnuange of the Qianqing palace.[72] By the Guangxu reign, this pavilion had portraits of the Xianfeng and Tongzhi emperors, before whom rituals were performed.

Both spirit tablets and portraits, sometimes both, were the objects of private worship in the inner court. The portrait, called a *shengrong* or *yurong* (literally, the "sacred" or "imperial" countenance), seems to have been hung and rituals performed before it while the coffin awaited burial. The portrait of the Yongzheng emperor was hung and worshiped in his former bedchamber in the Yonghegong before his interment. The Xianfeng emperor's portrait was hung in the Dongnuange of the Qianqing palace and the Shouhuangdian in the last days of the year, several years before the interment. Similarly, worship before the portrait of the Tongzhi emperor, hung in the last days of the lunar year of his death, preceded his burial by over four years.[73]

In the Taimiao and Fengxiandian, the ancestral hierarchy was fixed and organized around the founder of the dynasty, Nurgaci. By contrast, the private rites focused on those ancestors who were closest in ascending generations to the living emperor. The number of generations of ancestors worshiped depended on the individual ruler. Although the Yongzheng emperor seems to have worshiped before the tablets of only his parents, the Qianlong emperor retained his grandparents' tablets while adding those of his parents to the private altars. By the time the Jiaqing emperor died in 1820, the eastern Buddha hall at the Yangxindian held the tablets of the Kangxi, Yongzheng, and subsequent emperors and their empresses; the tablets of Kangxi, Yongzheng, and their wives were transferred to the Shouhuangdian by the Daoguang emperor.[74] What would have remained were the tablets of the Qianlong emperor and his successor. Thus the Daoguang emperor's domestic worship was limited to his father and grandfather. The ritual schedules for the Tongzhi and Guangxu emperors do not mention rites before portraits of ancestors beyond the third ascendant generation.

As part of the funerary ritual, the ancestral tablet of a deceased emperor and his spouse, the natural mother of the successor, would be created by the palace workshops and installed in shrines in these halls; the spirit tablets of the new emperor's grandfather and grandmother would be moved and ritually installed before the imperial portrait in the Shouhuangdian or, for those in Yuanmingyuan, before the imperial portrait in the Anyou palace within the grounds of the villa. Portraits along with jade seals and tablets (*yuce, yubao*) inscribed with the posthumous name seem to have also been installed in Mukden, along with the Veritable Records of the deceased ruler's reign; in the case of the Xianfeng emperor his portrait was eventually moved from the Qianqing palace to the Bishu shanzhuang in Chengde, where the emperor had died.[75]

Resembling the domestic ancestral cult of commoners in its focus on the more recent dead, this private worship also differed from popular practice in deliberately selecting some favored ancestors while omitting others. For example, the Yongzheng emperor put the spirit tablet of his mother on his private altar while ignoring the Kangxi emperor's first three empresses. Similarly, when his son placed the spirit tablets of his father and natural mother in the eastern Buddha hall after he ascended the throne, he omitted that of his father's first empress. Neither the Daoguang emperor nor his first two empresses were commemorated in the private rites performed by the Guangxu emperor, which included Daoguang's third empress and one of his consorts.[76]

The deathdays of emperors and empresses were also commemorated by both public and private rites, performed by the emperor and senior women. The private rites began even before the formal interment of the imperial coffin: for example, the Tongzhi emperor ended rituals marking his father's third death anniversary by lighting incense before Wenzong's portrait, even though Wenzong was not interred until the following year. Within the palace, incense would be lit before the portrait, spirit tablet, or other symbolic object.[77]

Ancestors' deathdays were acknowledged in both public and private ritual; the commemoration of birthdays seems to have been a matter of personal choice and evolving tradition. We know something about the evolution of these birthday rituals because of the young Qianlong emperor's request in 1736 for a review of the precedents. Apparently this practice originated in 1723 with the Yongzheng emperor, who commanded that incense be lit in the back hall of the Fengxiandian on the birthdays of his father and natural mother, Empress Xiaogong. The Qianlong emperor ordered that henceforth this should be done for all the rulers from Nurgaci down to his father: he also abolished the ritual observance for Empress Xiaogong.[78]

What began as a private ritual—the Yongzheng emperor was "breaking the rules" by favoring his natural mother over the senior empresses—became by the end of the dynasty a public, standardized rite for close male ancestors. The Veritable Records for 1871 record that the reigning Tongzhi emperor "went to the Fengxiandian and the Shouhuangdian and performed rites" on the birthdays of his father and grandfather, but not for more distant ancestors.[79] What the Veritable Records do not mention are the other rituals performed in the inner court on that day. After the public rites, the emperor proceeded to the Dongnuange of the Qianqing palace, where he lit incense before Wenzong's portrait, where a special offering of twenty items had been placed. These birthday observances could be made not only before portraits and spirit tablets, but also before a stupa or reliquary: for example, the Guangxu emperor commemorated the birthday of Empress Dowager Xiaosheng by lighting incense before her "hair stupa" (*fata*). This hair stupa (now part of the Palace Museum collection) was made of gold in the shape of Mount Sumeru, the sacred Buddhist mountain, and incised with auspicious symbols and words. An Amitāyus of gold was put inside it, alongside a gold casket containing Hongli's mother's hair. Created shortly after the empress dowager's death in 1777 out of her gold patent and seal, the completed stupa was installed in the Buddha hall of the Shoukang palace.[80]

Yinian, or "mementos," consisted of the clothing and other personal effects of a deceased person. Although some of these objects were burned during the funeral, it was customary to distribute some *yinian* to relatives, close friends, and servants. A portion may also have been stored in the palace. The archaeological evidence shows that *yinian* were deposited in the grave of Nurgaci's great-great-grandfather (the focal ancestor of the Aisin Gioro) when his remains were reinterred in a new tumulus in 1658, so the custom of saving *yinian* may have existed among the Jurchen ancestors of the Manchus. The *yinian* of Nurgaci and Hongtaiji were certainly preserved above ground, in temples in Shengjing, and are still extant.[81]

The list for the distribution of the Guangxu emperor's effects in 1909 survives and enables us to see who received the emperor's *yinian.* By 1909, the list of persons receiving mementos had expanded beyond imperial relatives and servants, to include major Han Chinese officials. Fifty-six men and three women received *yinian;* the female recipients were the empress dowager, Longyu; Jin *guifei,* a widow of the Tongzhi emperor; and Princess Rongshou, Prince Gong's eldest daughter, who had been taken into the inner court by Cixi. The list of male recipients was headed by the new emperor, who received a hat, robe, and jacket. The majority of the men, who included prominent officials such as Yuan Shikai and Xu Shichang, received a hat, a dragon robe, and a dragon surcoat. There was a special hall in each princely mansion called the *yinian dian,* in which these imperial mementos were preserved.[82]

Not all of an emperor's personal effects were burned or given away. What was left over was retained at the palace. A 1756 inventory of the *yinian* of the Kangxi and Yongzheng emperors lists court hats, hat finials, court robes (*chaopao*), dragon robes (*longpao*), court surcoats (*gua*), court belts and accessories, court necklaces, rosaries (*nianzhu*), socks, and shoes. Presumably these were what remained after sets of mementos had been distributed. It appears that some of the personal effects of an emperor could be worshiped. An edict dated July 25, 1867 (Tongzhi 6/6/24) orders that objects belonging to the Daoguang emperor: his white jade belt buckle, forming the characters for "good fortune" and "longevity" (*fu shou*), and his cap finial of gold inlaid with pearls be put in a red sandalwood casket, along with a gold Buddha inlaid with pearls, and objects belonging to the Xianfeng emperor: two plaits of his hair; a gold dragon inlaid with pearl; a painting by Ding [Guan]peng, the court painter; and a vermilion brush. The casket containing these mementos of the two emperors was moved into a niche in the eastern Buddha hall of the Yangxindian, where it became the focus of worship. This was probably the *yinian kan* (memento shrine) Empress Dowager Cixi worshiped on her husband's deathday.[83]

Birthdays and deathdays brought sutra recitations before the private ancestral altar. In addition to the sutra recitations accompanying the funerary rituals, changes were made in the commemoration of the now deceased emperor's birthday. After the death of the Xianfeng emperor, the three days of sutra chanting in the Zhongzhengdian and Hongrensi, performed during his life, became a monthly service conducted by seven lamas, performed in the Cining palace. In the period before the interment, sutra recitations were also performed for seven days on the deathday. On the deathday of the Jiaqing emperor's first empress, eunuch lamas chanted sutras in the Yuqing palace. While Empress Xiaoquan's portrait hung in the Zhongcui palace during her son's reign, eunuch lamas came to this place to chant sutras each year on her birth- and deathdays. Before 1845, these palace recitations apparently extended beyond the circle of recently deceased ancestors. In that year, sutra recitations on birthdays and deathdays were reduced, probably as a cost-cutting measure. By the late nineteenth century, however, even the sutra recitations for Empress Xiaozhuang, the Kangxi emperor's beloved grandmother, were gone from the private ritual schedule of the court.[84]

GRAVE RITUALS

Qing emperors and empresses were interred in elaborate underground tombs, which were part of a mausoleum complex featuring a "spirit road," stele pavilion, and sacrificial halls modeled on the Taihedian, the main audience hall in the Forbidden City. The tombs of the imperial ancestors before the Shunzhi emperor were located in the homeland; subsequent rulers were buried in the eastern and western cemeteries found northeast and southwest of Peking.[85] Ritual observances at these mausolea and the tombs of the Ming emperors were important parts of state rites, as extensive studies by J. J. de Groot and others demonstrate.[86] In this section, we focus instead on the grave rituals of lesser members of the imperial family.

The mausolea of the imperial family were constructed according to a highly detailed set of sumptuary regulations that fixed the size of the tomb, sacrificial hall, the memorial stele, and all the other features that constituted the Chinese imperial tomb tradition. Tombs for personages of different rank had different names. Only an emperor or empress could be interred in a *ling* (imperial tomb); other lower-ranking consorts were buried in a *yuanqin*, or, in Manchu a *fei yamun* (*fei* refers to consorts). The mausolea were given euphemistic names while their future tenant was still alive: an emperor's tomb was a "ten-thousand year auspicious site" (*wannian jidi*) and a tomb for prince or princess was a "site of good fortune" (*fudi*).[87] The mausolea of princes and princesses, whose tombs were usually not under the supervision of the Imperial Household Department were also called *yuanqin*, although the colloquial name for them was *fen*.[88]

If the main design of an imperial tomb was to emphasize the unique status of its occupant, the clustering of brothers' tombs around their perimeters expressed the fraternal sentiments that were also typical of Manchu imperial culture. In the 1650s, the throne permitted imperial aunts, uncles, and meritorious high ministers to be buried on the outskirts of the Yongling, Fuling, and Zhaoling. When the eastern cemetery (*dongling*) was first opened during the late seventeenth century, the Kangxi emperor allowed the tomb of his brother Longxi (d. 1679) to be erected outside its walls. Eventually the graves of six sons of the Shunzhi and Kangxi emperors were clustered together in this spot which was called the "princes' cemetery" (*wangyeling*).[89] Yinzhen gave his brother Yinyu a burial plot of one hundred *mu* south of the western cemetery (*xiling*); four other brothers, including his favorite, Yinxiang, also lie there outside the cemetery walls.[90]

Princes were normally expected to manage their own funerary rituals. An emperor, however, could always make exceptions. In 1794, Hongli received a report on the funerary arrangements for the wife of a favorite grandson, Mianyi. He assigned a Neiwufu official, Yilingga, to help the prince's steward find a "cheap" grave site close to the tomb of Mianyi's adoptive father, and Grandpa may well have footed the bill. For the most part, however, princes' tombs were "spread all over the vast plains around the Metropolis."[91]

An emperor normally shared his tomb with his empresses, and occasionally some of his consorts. From the Kangxi reign onward, an emperor's resting place was not reopened after his burial. Empresses who died before their spouse would eventually lie in his *digong* or underground tomb but most empresses who survived their husbands were buried in a separate *ling* adjacent to the main mausoleum. The exception was the mother of Fulin, whose grandson, the Kangxi emperor, honored her wish to be buried close to her descendants rather than in Shengjing. An appendage of the Zhaoling, which is situated in Mukden, the Zhaoxiling is actually located just outside the eastern tombs, south of the Shunzhi emperor's tomb, the Xiaoling. Initially the site was designated as a "temporary" depository for the empress dowager's coffin; the mausoleum itself was not completed until 1724.[92]

The mother of the Qianlong emperor, who was promoted to the rank of empress dowager by her son, died in 1777, long after her husband; her coffin lies in a separate tomb, the Tai dong (east) ling, constructed by her son. Similar separate *ling* house the remains of the Jiaqing emperor's second empress, who outlived her husband by thirty years, and Ci'an and Cixi, the widows of the Xianfeng emperor. Two empresses were denied burial next to their spouses: the Qianlong emperor signified his displeasure with his second empress by ordering that she be accorded the burial of a first-rank consort. Although the Xianfeng emperor had shown his affection and gratitude by raising his foster mother, Daoguang's widow, to the rank of empress dowager, he felt impelled to "obey" his father's hierarchical arrangements rather than his own when she died; she was not given a separate *ling* but buried in the consorts' tomb attached to the Muling.[93] Conversely, in the tombs of the Kangxi, Yongzheng, and Qianlong emperors lie the remains of several first-rank consorts, *huangguifei*, who had predeceased their spouses.[94]

During the Kangxi reign, interment of an empress' coffin was not delayed until the death of the emperor. Work on the Jingling, the mausoleum of the Kangxi emperor, began after the death of his first empress. Construction began in 1676 and was completed in 1681. By that time, Kangxi's second empress had also died, and the coffins of these two women, which had been stored at Gonghua, located to the north of the capital city, were buried. The tomb was reopened thereafter in 1689, 1700, and 1723 for the interment of the Kangxi emperor, his third and fourth empresses, and one of his first-rank consorts.[95] Construction of the Tailing, the Yongzheng emperor's mausoleum, began in 1730 and was not completed until 1737, two years after the emperor's death; the coffins of his first empress and a favorite first-rank consort, who had died in 1731 and 1725, were taken from temporary storage at temples and simultaneously interred with the emperor's in 1737.

What of the lower-ranking consorts? In chapter 4, we talked about women who acted as foster mothers for young princes and thereby gained promotion. The Qianlong emperor rewarded two of the Kangxi emperor's first-rank consorts (*huangguifei*), who had taken care of him when he entered the palace to live with his grandfather, by erecting a special tomb for them. Forty-eight other consorts were buried from 1681 onward in a mausoleum attached to the Jingling.[96] *Fei yuanqin* attached to the mausolea in the eastern and western imperial cemeteries followed the precedents set during the late seventeenth century in serving as the burial place for virtually all the imperial consorts who were not interred in the central tomb with the emperor.[97]

Perhaps the most neglected burials were those of children. Their fathers rarely built separate tombs for them. Some infants were buried next to their mothers: this was the case for the Kangxi emperor's eighteenth son, Yinjie, who died at the age of seven. Yinzhen's first son, who died in 1704, and his eighth son, who died in 1728, were first buried with no tomb. Only after their brother Hongli came to the throne did they receive first-rank burials.[98] Yonglian, Hongli's eldest son by his empress, merited a mausoleum of his own because he was posthumously proclaimed heir apparent. When her second son, Yongcong, died at the age of two, he was simply buried in his brother's tomb. Hongli's ninth, tenth, thirteenth, fourteenth, and sixteenth sons, all of whom died in infancy or childhood, were also buried in Yonglian's tomb, which now lies in ruins. Similarly, the graves of the Jiaqing emperor's daughters were clustered in the countryside near the western cemetery.[99]

The Daoguang emperor's first daughter, who died in 1819 before he ascended the throne, was initially buried together with his first wife (not her natural mother). In 1827 this daughter's coffin was moved and interred in a "princess's tomb" (*gongzhu yuanqin*) located outside the Dongling. The emperor's second daughter, second son, and third son, all of whom died in infancy, were also buried here, while his third daughter is buried near the western cemetery, where Daoguang's tomb lies.[100]

Since the Qing rulers practiced a system of deathbed succession, it is not surprising to find rearrangements of tombs as the rank of a prince changed, or a consort's rank was altered. When the Yongzheng emperor posthumously promoted Yinxiang's mother from the third to the first rank, her coffin was moved out of the *yuanqin* and installed in the burial chamber of the Jingling. Perhaps the most striking example of the movement of coffins accompanying promotion in rank concerns the Daoguang emperor's first wife. When she died in 1808, the Jiaqing emperor favored her (and thus his son) by ordering that a lavish tomb be built. Minning's ascent to the throne necessitated that the coffin of his wife, posthumously invested with the rank of empress, be moved into the mausoleum in which he would eventually lie. She was reinterred in the new mausoleum constructed in the eastern cemetery in 1827, then, after this tomb proved to be faulty (water seeped into the burial chamber), reburied in 1845 in the Muling, located in the western cemetery.[101]

When a tomb was designated as a *ling*, households were assigned to guard the grave and to maintain its various buildings and monuments. A *ling* was normally enclosed by a wall and closed to all except designated imperial officials and relatives. A descendant of the Ming imperial lineage was given a noble title and the responsibility of performing sacrifices at the Ming tombs, which were also under Qing protection. Descendants of the Aisin Gioro lineage were sent in rotation to "guard" the eastern and western cemeteries and the three mausolea in Manchuria where the Qing ancestors were buried.[102] Sacrifices at these graves were part of the state ritual, unlike the graves of princes and princesses that lie outside the walls of the imperial eastern and western cemeteries. Nonetheless, the emperor could assign banner households to guard the princely tombs and order annual grave rites. In addition, outlying graves could be incorporated into the rituals performed during the funeral of an emperor. When the coffin of the Daoguang emperor was taken to the western cemetery in 1852, imperial princes were sent to pour libations at the nearby graves of the Jiaqing emperor's third, fourth, fifth, and ninth daughters, the Daoguang emperor's third daughter, and several princes.[103] During the funerals of the Tongzhi and Guangxu emperors, the same rites were performed at the graves of daughters of Qianlong and Daoguang.[104]

RITUAL PARTICIPANTS

As we have seen above, the inner-court rituals encompassed not only the emperor, his consorts, and children, who inhabited the palaces within this part of the Forbidden City, but a much wider circle of kin, including affines, daughters, brothers, and more distantly related members of the imperial lineage. The marriages and funerals of Aisin Gioro were events in which the emperor played an important role as the supreme head of the lineage; as we have seen in other chapters, he selected brides for princes, received reports concerning births of kinsmen and thus exercised powers surpassing those held by the head of a commoner lineage. In return, the princes played important administrative roles in the inner court's rituals, some of which extended into areas of governance; the activities of the sutra recitation office in the Zhongzhengdian are a case in point. The rituals thus served a number of purposes, all at the same time: they enabled a ruler to exhibit personal sentiment, which was constrained by the regulations governing public ceremonial; they reinforced the larger kinship groups of agnates and affines who participated in court society; and beyond that, they allowed the emperor and his family to pursue private worship and underline commonalities linking them not only to Han Chinese society but also to the Manchu and Mongol elites who were their allies.

Conclusion

Several major factors shaped Manchu institutions and state rituals. The first was a strong and persistent impulse to create and retain a separate cultural identity. Citing the Jurchen Jin dynasty as a model of the dangers of assimilation, Nurgaci and his successors enacted cultural policies enshrining Manchu martial traditions, dress, and language. At the same time the Jurchen developed skills of a different sort to create stable alliances with neighboring Mongol tribes. The Mongol-Manchu alliance was vital to Manchu success through at least the middle of the eighteenth century and formed a conscious element in the culture of the Qing conquest elite. Finally, Jurchen leaders had to appeal explicitly to Han Chinese elites to rule the Ming territories.

The Jurchen who reinvented themselves as Manchus had to perpetuate a separate cultural identity, maintain effective multiethnic coalitions, and induce specific peoples to acquiesce in Manchu rule. The simultaneity of these political demands produced a kind of political schizophrenia in 1635 and 1636, when Hongtaiji proclaimed first a Manchu identity and then the establishment of a Chinese-style dynasty. Later, after 1644, attempts to realize all these potentially conflicting goals produced the spatial, functional, and linguistic compartmentalization described in chapters 1 and 2.

Manchu stood alongside Chinese as an official language of the dynasty. Although Peking, the former Ming capital, became the primary seat of Qing government, Hongtaiji's former capital, Mukden, and Rehe (Chengde), a former Jin capital, were given secondary capital status. Banner forces in Peking and in the other Ming cities were residentially and socially segregated from the conquered Ming Chinese population. A Ming-style civil service administered the Ming territories while bannermen under the Lifanyuan administered the Inner Asian peripheries. A system of checks and balances ensured that the Han Chinese degree-holders, who represented the majority of officials, would be offset by bannermen occupying the post of governor-general (with jurisdiction over provincial governors) and half the presidencies of the central government ministries. The influence of the civil service itself was checked by creating an inner court, dominated by imperial relatives and bannermen, whom the emperor could look to for counsel.

Whether learned indirectly, through Jin and Yuan precedents, or through direct contacts with the Ming administration, bureaucratic principles were the single most important aspect of the Chinese political culture that the Manchus adopted. Bureaucratization as a process, represented in the replacement of hereditary leaders by appointed officials, took place systematically across a wide range of social institutions and became a hallmark of Qing administration. Chapter 2 described the growth of a banner administration that assumed many of the prerogatives of the banner lords and supervised the banner nobility. Incorporated into the banners and exposed to bureaucratic administration, Mongol leaders were transformed from short-term, ad hoc allies into permanent subjects. Differences between the Qing treatment of the *waifan* Mongols and the Inner Mongols, who were fully incorporated into the banners, were ones of degree rather than of kind.

Bureaucratization was also the primary tool for resolving the issues of dynastic politics, treated in chapters 2 and 3. The Qing could employ kinsmen in governance precisely because the throne had eliminated their autonomy. All Aisin Gioro were subject to imperial surveillance and evaluation by the Imperial Clan Court, which controlled membership in the imperial lineage and meted out rewards and punishments. The throne ranked merit above birth order in selecting heirs to noble titles. Most titles were reduced in rank with each generational transfer, so that the vast majority of bannermen and imperial kinsmen were unranked and received only minimal stipends from the state. The throne further divided imperial princes by heaping glory on the descendants of conquest heroes while reserving official appointments for more closely related descendants or for those who passed the examinations.

Qing rulers also sought to control imperial consorts and mothers, discussed in chapter 4. By eschewing the Han Chinese succession principle, recruiting imperial consorts from a wide social spectrum of banner families, and permitting sons of lower-ranking consorts to become emperor, the Manchus reduced the possibility of powerful maternal lineages that could dominate the throne. Rulers selected their successors on the basis of merit and delayed naming an heir until their deathbeds. Like other non-Han dynasties, the Qing used marriage exchanges as a key element in creating and reaffirming alliances with Mongol nobles. Sisters and daughters retained their membership in the imperial family. The privilege accorded princesses inverted the normal gender relationship in Chinese society and was a striking example of imperial preeminence.

Manchu rulers also bureaucratized the palace administration, surveyed in chapter 5. A highly diversified staff that included European artists, Muslim doctors, and Mongol musicians reflected, rulers thought, the cosmopolitan nature of the Qing empire. Having identified eunuchs' dominance at court as the cause of the Ming decline, the Qing created an intricate system of checks and balances in the palace service. Low-status eunuchs supervised low-status maidservants and other eunuchs but were themselves under the scrutiny of bondservant officials and imperial princes who held the highest positions in the Neiwufu. The success of the Qing scheme did not, however, remove concerns about "the servant problem," and emperors recognized the tremendous capacity for subversion inherent in even the most docile domestics.

The chapters in part 3 highlighted certain problems raised by rituals of rulership. Chapter 6 analyzed the symbolic language of state rituals in terms of the Confucian discourse on sources of legitimation. The Qing tried to resolve the tension between "rule by virtue" and "rule by descent" by combining the two. The state was the family writ large, and the ruler was the exemplar of family values. Filiality became a major component of the virtue required for rulership: the key moment in the accession rite, the act of enthronement, replicated family rituals. The kowtows performed before the ruler by his officials echoed the ritual kowtows of children in front of their parents.

Another issue concerned legitimation and ritual performance. More than earlier rulers, Qing emperors emphasized their personal participation in the grand sacrifices, yet even they frequently delegated this task to others. According to Confucian ideology, the cardinal act of rulership was not the actual sacrifice, but the determination of when the sacrifice would take place. The ritual heart of rulership lay in the power to set the ritual calendar and therefore, symbolically, cosmic time. Not that this concept was without some ambiguity: we could not otherwise explain the Kangxi emperor's careful avoidance of his agnates when delegating grand sacrifices, or the policy reversal by his son and grandson. Moreover, ritual performance did not simply exist in the symbolic realm but was tied to concrete secular phenomena such as the weather. Confucian ideology, which blamed drought on a ruler's lack of virtue, forced Qing rulers—who had to confront the periodic droughts of North China—to resort to what Kenneth

Pomeranz describes as "magic," that is, prayers to dragon gods who could bring rain.[1] When the performance of penitential rituals failed to bring rain, rulers could not afford the luxury of ideological consistency. Nor, given their multicultural stance, should the issue of consistency even arise.

Chapter 7 explored some ways in which Manchu rulers used rituals to create images of rulership for the different subject peoples of their empire. The court identified shamanism as the traditional religion of its ancestors and sponsored shamanic state and family rituals at court throughout its dynastic life. Shamanism became a source of legends legitimating the Manchus and the Aisin Gioro lineage. Even as it subsidized and tried to perpetuate shamanic rituals, the court's patronage altered traditional shamanic practices: after the late eighteenth century, a shamanic code commissioned by the Qianlong emperor was disseminated to bannermen as a guide to practice. The code, based on court rituals, helped systematize and reshape what had been a very fluid and diverse belief system. The totemic deities of other clans were replaced by the Aisin Gioro deities; the "ecstatic" shaman was displaced by the hereditary clan shaman. That the shamanic code did not completely unify and standardize shamanic practices does not negate its historical importance.

Qing patronage of Tibetan Buddhism, also treated in chapter 7, helped incorporate Mongolia into the empire. Nurgaci and Hongtaiji's courtship of high prelates coincided with the efforts of other Inner Asian leaders to seek legitimacy through their patronage of the religion. The lama-patron relationship was transformed when Qing troops invaded Lhasa in 1720 and became the dominant military power in the region. Even as Tibetan Buddhism penetrated Mongol society and transformed it, the appearance of reincarnate lineages and subsequently of a theocracy in Tibet stimulated the Qianlong emperor to recast his image in the Tibetan Buddhist world. Representations of the emperor as Mañjuśrī vied with representations of the Dalai lama as Avalokiteśvara; secular and spiritual validations were merged in an Inner Asian vocabulary of rulership.

The private rituals of the imperial family, described in chapter 8, were typical of the compartmentalization of imperial institutions. They were an eclectic blend of the many cultural traditions that the emperors had promoted among their subjects. Household rituals common to Han Chinese families took place within the palace, alongside shamanic and Tibetan Buddhist rites. Grave worship tried to reconcile fraternal sentiment with the ritual separation demanded of the ruler. Barred from the Taimiao or the Fengxiandian, palace women could commemorate loved ones at Chinese Buddhist altars in the inner court. Similarly, rulers could express their private sentiments and ignore the strict ritual rankings of the public altars in the privacy of their residences.

This study of the imperial lineage and imperial household also speaks to larger generalizations concerning the nature of the Qing period. The archival documents show that Qing emperors were perennially conscious of their own cultural identity, which was separate from the identity of Han Chinese subjects. The several varieties of ethnocentric and culturalist discourse that preceded modern Chinese nationalism circulated amongst these subjects, and not amongst the conquest elite.[2]

In the same vein, generalizations that identify the Qing as a phase in China's progress toward nationhood are nationalist in inspiration and ahistorical. James Millward demonstrates that interpretations of figures like Xiang *fei*, the eighteenth-century Muslim consort of the Qianlong emperor, are barometers of evolving Chinese national identity but have little to do with historical reality.[3] Similarly, proof that the Qianlong emperor did not marry one of his daughters to a descendant of Confucius does not refute but rather confirms the Manchus' self-projection as monarchs on the Chinese model.[4]

The explicit theme to be found in many recent scholarly articles and books is that the Qing advanced China's accommodation of many divergent peoples and cultures into what has now become a multiethnic nation state. This assertion may well be true, yet it is an unanticipated consequence of Qing policies and actions, which focused on quite a different set of goals. The archival documents of the palace administration show that Qing emperors pursued policies aimed at expanding their personal authority and power. To resolve the problem of holding together a multiethnic empire, the ideology of rulership developed during the early reigns followed paths trod by earlier non-Han dynasties. The Qing success may well have created the territorial precedents for a modern nation-state encompassing China and Inner Asia, but such a political concept was never the Qing rulers' goal.

This study proposes an alternative interpretation of the historic significance of this dynasty. It agrees with earlier scholars who identify the Qing as the greatest dynasty in Chinese history. The Qing found solutions to many perennial issues in court politics plaguing earlier dynasties. Tracing the evolution of the imperial lineage and the social dynamics within the imperial household supports the argument that the Qing triumphed precisely because they were not a Han dynasty. Qing strategies were in many respects exactly the opposite of those found in a Chinese ruling house. The rulers separated the conquerors from the conquered and relied on a system that used various groups to check one another. Even as they favored close relatives over nonkin, emperors found ways to ensure that these kinsmen did not challenge the throne's authority. Imperial sisters and daughters retained their membership in the imperial family; palace consorts sided with the imperial line, and not with their natal families. Historical judgments vilifying Cixi as a usurping empress in the Han Chinese mode should be reexamined. Cixi can instead be compared to the strong empress dowagers of the early Qing, and her joint rule with Princes Gong and Chun may be seen as a historical repetition of the Manchu tradition of cooperation between imperial widows and their brothers-in-law.

Equally distinctive was the Qing contribution in creating a long-lasting union of the Inner Asian peripheries with China. As Thomas Barfield reminds us, this was an achievement denied to earlier steppe and Chinese regimes.[5] He would argue that its origins in the northeast produced this dynasty's sensitivity to regional cultures, its flexibility in administrative arrangements, and its ability to synthesize bureaucratic principles with non-Han traditions. These were the factors that enabled the Qing rulers to consolidate political authority in a wide variety of circumstances and to achieve a long-lasting political merger of Inner Asia and East Asia.

Qing rulers from the eighteenth century onward may have tried to preserve the distinctive cultural traditions of major subject peoples, but their policies had unanticipated consequences that are directly relevant for the twentieth-century nation-state. The Qing restructured the social hierarchies of Tibetan, Uighur, Mongol, and northeastern society by eliminating opponents and rewarding allies, removing autonomous sources of power and prestige for local elites, and forcing them into relationships of dependence. The dGe lugs pa sect of Tibetan Buddhism was triumphant over its rival monastic orders within Tibet and among Mongols, but it had to give up autonomy over rebirths, whose selections now required confirmation from Peking. The local notables of the Tarim basin, the *begs*, were confirmed in their leadership roles, but their hereditary right to office and their authority were eroded. The demarcation of territories for each tribe imposed curbs on the free movement of Mongol pastoralists; new social identities were created by the banner organization. Northeastern tribes were Manchuized, incorporated into the banners, and moved around the empire.[6]

Levels of literacy among peripheral populations rose as a direct consequence of Qing policies. Banner schools educated the sons of the local elites in several languages. While imperially commissioned multilingual dictionaries in Manchu, Mongolian, Tibetan, Uighur, and Chinese were as much the products of imperial self-glorification as practical aids to learning, these efforts were symptomatic of the many grammars and other language texts that were written during the Qing era. The impact of the educational drive was profound for Mongolian and Manchu, which had primarily been spoken rather than written languages. Writing down and identifying a "standard" vocabulary narrowed the diversity of spoken variants; increasing literacy stimulated production of a written literature. The *pax Mandjurica* saw an efflorescence of Mongol literature and cross-fertilization of peripheral cultures: important commentaries on Tibetan Buddhist texts by the Mongol Rol pa'i rdo rje is an example. And the center of this cultural boom was Peking, which became an important center of Tibetan Buddhist printing during the Qing.[7]

The Qing impact on the cultures of the peripheries had an economic dimension as well. The establishment of one empire created conditions conducive to trade. Russian and Chinese trade flowed into the northeast, where iron implements and guns were traded for furs and other valuable local products. The court's tributary system itself encouraged commoditization of ginseng, marten skins, and the freshwater pearls of the region, just as the creation of large garrisons to defend the region led ultimately to expansion of agriculture. Similarly, the need to provision garrisons in Xinjiang increased Han Chinese migration into the region. Han Chinese merchants penetrated into Mongolia as well; by the end of the Qing dynasty, the pressure of Han Chinese migration and economic competition had raised tensions between Mongols and the Han Chinese.[8]

Qing policies stimulated social, cultural, and economic changes in the peripheries that encouraged the growth of ethnic identities among the Mongols, Uighurs, and Tibetans. Under Qing rule, the focus of primary identities had begun to shift from tribal units to larger social groups. Literacy created a body of writings that these people could now tap for the creation of a self-conscious *ethnos*. Resentment against Han Chinese traders and settlers ensured that northeastern peoples, Mongols, and Uighurs would not readily subscribe to a definition of nation that put the Han at its center. The breakaway movements of the post-1911 period are testimony to the fact that we cannot simply equate the Qing empire with a nation-state called China.

The history of Chinese nationalism and the internal struggle between a multiethnic constitutional definition of the state and Han nationalism are subjects that go far beyond the scope of this book, which supplies a historical perspective on the Qing contribution to these modern phenomena. The emergent nationalism of the late nineteenth and early twentieth centuries should not prevent us from recognizing the particular genius of the Qing. The last emperors of China were true innovators. Their rule represents a creative adaptation to problems of rulership that was not simply a repetition of the dynastic cycle. A more detailed analysis of their policies and the historical consequences is required before we can fully appreciate the value of the Qing contribution.

Appendix 1
Names of Qing Emperors and the Imperial Ancestors

Personal Name	Reign Names[a]	Temple Name	Posthumous Names[a]	Life Dates
Taksi	—	Xiezu	Xuan, Iletulehe	—
Nurgaci	Tianming, Abkai Fulingga[b]	Taizu	Gao, Dergi[c]	1559–1626
[Hongtaiji][d]	Tianzong, Abkai Sure[b] Chongde, Wesihun Erdemungge[e]	Taizong	Wen, Genggiyen Su	1592–1643
Fulin	Shunzhi, Ijishūn Dasan	Shizu	Zhang, Eldembure	1638–61
Xuanye	Kangxi, Elhe Taifin	Shengzu	Ren, Gosin	1654–1722
Yinzhen	Yongzheng, Hūwaliyasun Tob	Shizong	Xian, Temgetulehe	1678–1735
Hongli	Qianlong, Abkai Wehiyehe	Gaozong	Chun, Yongkiyangga	1711–95
Yongyan	Jiaqing, Saicungga Fengšen	Renzong	Rui, Sunggiyen	1760 1820
Minning	Daoguang, Doro Eldengge	Xuanzong	Cheng, Šanggan	1782–1850
Yizhu	Xianfeng, Gubci Elgiyengge	Wenzong	Xian, Iletu	1831–61
Zaichun	Tongzhi, Yooningga Dasan	Muzong	Yi, Filingga	1856–75
Zaitian	Guangxu, Badarangga Doro	Dezong	Jing, Ambalinggū	1871–1908
Puyi	Xuanzong, Gehungge Yoso	—	—	1906–1911

SOURCES: Bo Yang, *Zhongguo di wang huanghou qinwang gongzhu shixi lu* (Beijing, 1986), 1:246–48; Chieh-hsien Chen, "A Study of the Manchu Posthumous Titles of the Ch'ing Emperors," *Central Asiatic Journal* 26, nos. 3–4 (1982): 187–92; Jerry Norman, *A Concise Manchu-English Lexicon* (Seattle, 1978), 319.

[a] The first name is Chinese, the second Manchu.

[b] To call this a "reign name" is anachronistic.

[c] Nurgaci's Manchu posthumous name was originally "horonggo" (see Chieh-hsien Chen, "Manchu Posthumous Titles," 188–89).

[d] "Hongtaiji" was probably a title and not a personal name (see Pamela K. Crossley, *The Manchus* [Oxford, 1997], 208).

[e] Reign name during 1636–43.

Appendix 2
Imperial Princely Ranks

The English-language translations of the titles below are taken from H. S. Brunnert and V. V. Hagelstrom, *Present-Day Political Organization of China*, trans. A. Beltchenko and E. E. Moran (Foochow, 1911), hereafter BH.

1. *Heshe qinwang* M. *hošoi cin wang.*[a]   Prince of the Blood of the first degree (BH 16)
2. *Dolo junwang,* M. *doroi junwang.*[b]   Prince of the Blood of the second degree (BH 17)
3. *Dolo beile,* M. *doroi beile.*   Prince of the Blood of the third degree (BH 18)
4. *Gushan beizi,* M. *gūsai beise.*[c]   Prince of the Blood of the fourth degree (BH 19)
5. *Feng'en zhenguo gong,* M. *kesi be tuwakiyara gurun be dalire gung.* Prince of the Blood of the fifth degree (BH 20)
6. *Feng'en fuguo gong,* M. *kesi be tuwakiyara gurun be aisilara gung.* Prince of the Blood of the sixth degree (BH 21)
7. *Burubafen zhenguo gong.*   Prince of the Blood of the seventh degree (BH 22)
8. *Burubafen fuguo gong.*   Prince of the Blood of the eighth degree (BH 23)
9, 10, 11. *Zhenguo jiangjun.*   Noble of the imperial lineage of the ninth rank, grades one through three (BH 24)
12, 13, 14. *Fuguo jiangjun.*   Noble of the imperial lineage of the tenth rank, grades one through three (BH 25)
15, 16, 17. *Fengguo jiangjun.*   Noble of the imperial lineage of the eleventh rank, grades one through three (BH 26)
18. *Feng'en jiangjun.*   Noble of the imperial lineage of the twelfth rank (BH 27)

NOTES

[a]In Manchu *hošoi* means "region, area"; *cin wang* is a transliteration of the Chinese title, used in the Ming dynasty.
[b]In Manchu *doroi* means "gift."
[c]In Manchu *gūsai beise* means "prince of the banner," *gūsa* being the Manchu word for banner.

Notes

ABBREVIATIONS

Archival and Published Sources

Archives *First Historical Archives, Beijing*

AJZP	*Aixin juelo zongpu*
BMST	*Baqi Manzhou shizu tongpu*
BQTZ	*(Qinding) Baqi tongzhi*
BQTZXB	*(Qinding) Baqi tongzhi xubian*
DQHD	*(Qinding) Da Qing huidian*
DQHDSL	*(Qinding) Da Qing huidian shili*
DQHDT	*(Qinding) Da Qing huidian tu*
DQSL	*Da Qing shilu*
DQTL	*(Yuzhi) Da Qing tongli*
DQYD	*Da Qing yudie*
ECCP	Arthur W. Hummel, *Eminent Chinese of the Ch'ing Period (1644–1912)*
QGXZ	*Qinding gongzhong xianxing zeli*
ZNXZ	*Qinding zongguan Neiwufu xianxing zeli*

Reign Titles and Personal Names of the Qing Emperors

Abbreviation	*Reign Name*	*Personal Name*	*Reign Dates*
SZ	Shunzhi	Fulin	1644–61
KX	Kangxi	Xuanye	1662–1722
YZ	Yongzheng	Yinzhen	1723–35
QL	Qianlong	Hongli	1736–95
JQ	Jiaqing	Yongyan	1796–1820

Reign Titles and Personal Names of the Qing Emperors (*continued*)

Abbreviation	Reign Name	Personal Name	Reign Dates
DG	Daoguang	Minning	1821–50
XF	Xianfeng	Yizhu	1851–61
TZ	Tongzhi	Zaichun	1862–74
GX	Guangxu	Zaitian	1875–1908
XT	Xuantong	Puyi	1909–12

INTRODUCTION

1. On Nurgaci, see Yan Chongnian, *Nuerhachi zhuan* (Beijing, 1983) and *Tianming han* (Changchun, 1993); Teng Shaozhen, *Nuerhachi pingzhuan* (Shenyang, 1985). On Hongtaiji, see Sun Wenliang and Li Zhiting, *Qing Taizong quan zhuan* (Changchun, 1983), reissued under the title *Tianzong han: Chongde di* (Changchun, 1993). Also Pamela K. Crossley, *The Manchus* (Oxford, 1997), chs. 3, 4; also her *A Translucent Mirror: History and Identity in the Transformation of Qing Imperial Ideology* (Berkeley, forthcoming).

2. Ping-ti Ho, "The Significance of the Ch'ing Period in Chinese History," *Journal of Asian Studies* 26, no. 2 (1967): 191.

3. Kai-wing Chow, "Narrating Race, Nation, and Culture: Imagining the Hanzu Identity in Modern China," presented at the conference, "Narratives, Art, and Ritual: Imagining and Constructing Nationhood in Modern East Asia," University of Illinois, Champaign-Urbana, November 15–17, 1996; Benedict Anderson, *Imagined Communities: Reflections on the Origin and Spread of Nationalism* (London, 1991). Also Brackette F. Williams, "A CLASS ACT: Anthropology and the Race to Nation Across Ethnic Terrain," *Annual Review of Anthropology* 18 (1989): 401–44.

4. For Chinese writings on race, and the concept of the yellow race, see Frank Dikötter, *The Discourse of Race in Modern China* (Stanford, 1992), 55–57.

5. Both quotes are from Dikötter, *The Discourse of Race*, 124.

6. Prasenjit Duara, *Rescuing History from the Nation: Questioning Narratives of Modern China* (Chicago, 1995), 3.

7. See the shrewd observations by Pamela K. Crossley, "Thinking About Ethnicity in Early Modern China," *Late Imperial China* 1 (1990): 4–5 on the persistence of this model among Western scholars. The retroactive drawing of the modern boundaries of the nation-state backward into historical time, which is also evident in Chinese-language historical analysis, is a typical component of modern historical writing: see Partha Chatterjee, *The Nation and Its Fragments: Colonial and Post-Colonial Histories* (Princeton, 1993), ch. 5. For a detailed analysis of different historical works in the nationalist mode, see Duara, *Rescuing the Nation*, ch. 1.

8. Mary C. Wright, *The Last Stand of Chinese Conservatism: The T'ung-chih Restoration, 1862–1874* (Stanford, 1957); see critique in Pamela K. Crossley, *Orphan Warriors: Three Manchu Generations and the End of the Qing World* (Princeton, 1990), 224–25.

9. Crossley, *Orphan Warriors*, 225.

10. Pamela K. Crossley and Evelyn S. Rawski, "A Profile of the Manchu Language in Ch'ing History," *Harvard Journal of Asiatic Studies* 53, no. 1 (1993): 63–102.

11. Alexandra Pozzi, "A Journey to the Original Places of Manchu People (1982)," *ZentralAsiatische Studien* 20 (1987): 208.

12. See Anderson, *Imagined Communities*, ch. 5; Einar Haugen, "Dialect, Language, Nation," *American Anthropologist* 68 (1966): 922–35; Crossley, "Thinking About Ethnicity," 22–23.

13. Ernest Gellner, *Nations and Nationalism* (Ithaca, 1983); Anderson, *Imagined Communities*.

14. The recent Chinese-language literature on this subject is surveyed in Evelyn S. Rawski, "Re-envisioning the Qing: The Significance of the Qing Period in Chinese History," *Journal of Asian Studies* 55, no. 4 (1996): 834–35. See David Farquhar, "The Origins of the Manchus' Mongolian Policy," in *The Chinese World Order: Traditional China's Foreign Relations*, ed. John K. Fairbank (Cambridge, Mass., 1968), and his "Mongolian vs. Chinese Elements in the Early Manchu State," *Ch'ing-shih wen-t'i* 1, no. 6 (1971): 11–23.

15. Crossley, *The Manchus*, 9–10.

16. Crossley, "Thinking About Ethnicity"; Tsung-i Dow, "The Confucian Concept of a Nation and Its Historical Practice," *Asian Profile* 10, no. 4 (1982): 347–61.

17. Quoted in Yuan Hongqi, "Qianlong shiqi de gongting jieqing huodong," *Gugong bowuyuan yuankan* 3 (1991): 85.

18. See Kai-wing Chow, *The Rise of Confucian Ritualism in Late Imperial China: Ethics, Classics, and Lineage Discourse* (Stanford, 1994), 224–25; Lynn Struve, ed. and trans., *Voices from the Ming-Qing Cataclysm* (New Haven, 1993), 1–5.

19. Crossley, *The Manchus*, 22–23.

20. The secondary literature is summarized in Rawski, "Re-envisioning the Qing," 836–38.

21. For a brief survey of some of this primary source material, see Rawski, "Re-envisioning the Qing."

22. Feng Erkang, *Qingshi shiliao xue chugao* (Tianjin, 1986), 31–39.

23. Stevan Harrell, Susan Naquin, and Deyuan Ju, "Lineage Genealogy: The Genealogical Records of the Qing Imperial Lineage," *Late Imperial China* 6, no. 2 (1985): 37–47.

24. Beatrice S. Bartlett, *Monarchs and Ministers: The Grand Council in Mid-Qing China, 1723–1820* (Berkeley, 1991); Susan Naquin, *Shantung Rebellion: The Wang Lun Uprising of 1774* (New Haven, 1981) are two examples of archive-based research.

25. These articles are cited in Crossley and Rawski, "Profile of the Manchu Language."

CHAPTER 1: THE COURT SOCIETY

1. Herbert Franke, "The Jin dynasty," in *Alien Regimes and Border States, 907–1368,* ed. Herbert Franke and Denis Twitchett (Cambridge, 1994), 270. The non-Han multiple capitals system left its mark on the Chinese political order: see Nancy Shatzman Steinhardt, *Chinese Imperial City Planning* (Honolulu, 1990), 166–67, on how the founder of the Ming dynasty (1368–1644) was influenced by the Yuan precedent of multiple capitals to attempt to set up a three-capital system.

2. Denis Twitchett and Klaus-Peter Tietze, "The Liao," and table 5, "Capital Cities," in *Alien Regimes and Border States, 907–1368,* ed. Herbert Franke and Denis Twitchett (Cambridge, 1994), 43–153, xxix; Steinhardt, *Imperial City Planning,* 123–28.

3. For a concise description and contemporary photographs of Nurgaci's capitals, see Giovanni Stary, Nicola Di Cosmo, Tatiana A. Pang, and Alessandra Pozzi, eds., *On The Tracks of Manchu Culture, 1644–1994: 350 Years After The Conquest of Peking* (Wiesbaden, 1995), 1–17, map on 26; and Li Fengmin and Lu Haiying, "Qingchao kaiguo de yi ducheng—Hetu ala," *Zijincheng* 81 (1994): 10–12. Also Yan Chongnian, "Qingchu sijing yu ducheng sanqian," in his *Yanbuji* (Beijing, 1989), 365–93. For a description of Fe Ala, which was Nurgaci's first headquarters, see Yan Chongnian, "Hou Jin ducheng Fei ala boyi," *Qingshi yanjiu tongxun* 1 (1988): 30–33; Tong Yonggong and Guan Jialu, "Qianlong chao Shengjing zongguan neiwufu de sheli," *Gugong bowuyuan yuankan* 2 (1994): 19–23.

4. Philippe Forêt, "Making an Imperial Landscape in Chengde, Jehol: The Manchu Landscape Enterprise" (Ph.D. diss., University of Chicago, 1992), 10 and ch. 7. See also Yan Chongnian, "Kangxi huangdi yu Mulan weichang," *Gugong bowuyuan yuankan* 2 (1994): 9.

5. Yuan Shenbo, "Qingdai kouwai xinggong de youlai yu Chengde Bishu shanzhuang de fazhan guocheng," *Qingshi luncong* 2 (1980): 287–88.

6. Zhang Zhiqiang, "Jilin zhi Shengjing yizhan shulüe," *Lishi dang'an* 4 (1993): 87–89; Wan Sizhi, "Cong Bishu shanzhuang shuo 'Kang Qian shengshi'—jian lun Buerni zhi fan yu shanzhuang de xingjian," *Qingshi yanjiu* 2 (1993): 1–9; Wang Shuyun, *Qingdai beixun yudao he saiwai xinggong* (Beijing, 1989), 4.

7. Hu Rubo, "Mulan weichang yu weichang diming," *Diming zhishi* 4 (1991): 32–33; Yan Chongnian, "Kangxi huangdi yu Mulan weichang."

8. Yuan Shenbo, "Qingdai kouwai xinggong," 288–89. Chengdeshi wenwuju and Renmindaxue, Qingshi yanjiusuo, *Chengde Bishu shanzhuang* (Beijing, 1980), 40–49; Wang Zhonghan, "'Guoyu qishe' yu Manzu de fazhan," in *Manzu shi yanjiu ji,* ed. Wang Zhonghan (Beijing, 1988), 198.

9. Yuan Shenbo, "Qingdai kouwai de xinggong," 290–93.

10. Yan Chongnian, "Kangxi huangdi yu Mulan weichang," 10, 25.

11. *Chengde Bishu shanzhuang*, 47. Wang Caiyin, "Kangxi, Qianlong huangdi xiai weilie yu xiaolu huodong," in his *Gugong jiu wen yi hua* (Tianjin, 1986), 64–68.

12. Wang Shuyun, *Qingdai beixun yudao he saiwai xinggong* (Beijing, 1989), 27–28. Tibetan tribute was also dealt with at Chengde: see memorial of the Xianfeng reign (hereafter XF) 11/3/28 (May 7, 1861) [First Historical Archives, Beijing (hereafter, Archives) 446-5-55/568] as an example.

13. *Chengde Bishu shanzhuang*, 43; *Memoirs of Father Ripa during Thirteen Years' Residence at the Court of Peking in the Service of the Emperor of China*, trans. Fortunato Prandi (London, 1846), 66, 70, 72, 74–79. Father Ripa states (66) that the emperor took thirty thousand men with him to Chengde. For a synopsis on the Kangxi emperor's thoughts on hunting, see Jonathan Spence, *Emperor of China: Self-Portrait of K'ang-hsi* (New York, 1974), 7–23; Meng Zhaozhen, *Bishu shanzhuang yuanlin yishu* (Beijing, 1985), 5. Forêt, "Making an Imperial Landscape," chs. 5, 7.

14. Anne Chayet, *Les Temples de Jehol et leurs modèles tibétains* (Paris, 1985), 28–33, fig. 5; on bSam-yas, see David L. Snellgrove and Hugh Richardson, *A Cultural History of Tibet* (New York, 1968), 78–79; Yuan Shenbo, "Qingdai kouwai de xinggong," 314.

15. Forêt, "Making an Imperial Landscape"; Ning Chia, "The Lifanyuan and the Inner Asian Rituals in the Early Qing (1644–1795)," *Late Imperial China* 14, no. 1 (1993): 60–92.

16. See map 1. In 1820, Chengde was thus part of Zhili, despite its location.

17. Wan Yi, "Qianlong shiqi de yuanyou," *Gugong bowuyuan yuankan* 2 (1984): 19. This visit of the Panchen lama is described in *The Visit of the Teshoo Lama to Peking: Ch'ien Lung's Inscription*, trans. Ernest Ludwig (Peking, 1904). See also Chayet, *Temples de Jehol*, 25–52; Yuan Shenbo, "Qingdai kouwai de xinggong," 315–18.

18. Wan Yi, "Qianlong shiqi de yuanyou"; Silas H. L. Wu, *Passage to Power: K'ang-hsi and His Heir Apparent, 1661–1722* (Cambridge, Mass., 1979), 51, 154, 179; Osvald Sirén, *Gardens of China* (New York, 1949), 117; Yan Chongnian, "Kangxi jiao zi," in *Qing gong yishi*, ed. Zheng Yimei et al. (Beijing, 1985), 10–13.

19. Juliet Bredon, *Peking* (Shanghai, 1922), 256; Cécile and Michel Beurdeley, *Giuseppe Castiglione: A Jesuit Painter at the Court of the Chinese Emperors*, trans. Michael Bullock (Rutland, 1971), 65. Shu Mu, Shen Wei, and He Naixian, eds., *Yuanmingyuan ziliao ji* (Beijing, 1984), 361–62; Zhao Shu, "Yuanmingyuan baqi yingfang shulüe," *Manzu yanjiu* 4 (1994): 32–35.

20. Sirén, *Gardens of China*, ch. 9; Dai Yi, "Qianlongdi he Beijing de chengshi jianshe," in *Qingshi yanjiu ji*, Zhongguo renmin daxue Qingshi yanjiu suo (Beijing, 1988), 6:1–37. Also Wan Yi, "Qianlong shiqi de yuanyou"; Huang Ximing, "Zijincheng gongting Yuanlin te jianzhu tesi,"*Gugong bowuyuan yuankan* 4 (1990): 38–46.

21. Meng Zhaozhen, *Bishu shanzhuang yuanlin yishu* (Beijing, 1985), 4;

Dai Yi, "Qianlongdi he Beijing," 12–16; Beurdeley and Beurdeley, *Giuseppe Castiglione*, 65–75. On the impact in Europe, see Maggie Keswick, *The Chinese Garden* (New York, 1980), 9; *Lettres édifiantes et curieuses concernant l'Asie, l'Afrique et l'Amérique, avec quelques relations nouvelles des missions et des notes géographiques et historiques*, ed. M. L. Aimé-Martin (Paris, 1843), 4:121.

22. Osvald Sirén, *The Imperial Palaces of Peking* (1926; reprint, New York, 1976), 1–4. For Peking's earlier history, see Steinhardt, *Imperial City Planning*, 4–19, 154–59.

23. Dai Yi, "Qianlongdi he Beijing." Hou Renzhi and Jin Tao, *Beijing shihua* (Shanghai, 1980), ch. 7. On water control over the Yongding River during the Kangxi reign, see Ding Jingjun, "Kangxi yu Yongdinghe," *Shixue yuekan* 6 (1987): 33–36.

24. Howard J. Wechsler, *Offerings of Jade and Silk: Ritual and Symbol in the Legitimation of the T'ang Dynasty* (New Haven, 1985), 109–17; Jeffrey F. Meyer, *The Dragons of Tiananmen: Beijing as a Sacred City* (Columbia, S.C., 1991), ch. 1. The Altar to Heaven was where combined rites to Heaven and Earth were performed from 1377 to 1530 during the Ming dynasty. On this and other historical shifts, see Nancy Shatzman Steinhardt, "Altar to Heaven Complex," in *Chinese Traditional Architecture*, ed. Nancy Shatzman Steinhardt et al. (New York, 1984), 139–49.

25. Steinhardt, *Imperial City Planning*, 124, 170–71. On the plans of earlier Manchu capitals, see Hosoya Yoshio, ed., *Chūgoku tōhokubu ni okeru Shinchō no shiseki* (Tokyo, 1991), 57, 63, 105, 123, 127, 131, 138, 140, 168, which has sketches of the spatial layouts of many seventeenth-century tribal centers in the northeast, including Fe Ala and Hetu Ala; Shenyang gugong bowuyuan, *Shengjing huang gong* (Beijing, 1987), 17–23. The authors argue that a distinctive Jurchen building style can be seen evolving in the early seventeenth-century capitals of Nurgaci.

26. *Da Qing shilu* (Beijing, 1986 [hereafter *DQSL*]), 40.9ab, 40.11a, 40.14ab; Frederic Wakeman, Jr., *The Great Enterprise: The Manchu Reconstruction of Imperial Order in Seventeenth-Century China* (Berkeley, 1975), 1:480; Lawrence D. Kessler, *K'ang-hsi and the Consolidation of Ch'ing Rule, 1661–1684* (Chicago, 1976), 15–16. On the cultural differences between the Inner and Outer Cities, see Li Chiao, "Qingdai Beijing neiwai cheng shehui shenghuo xisu zhi yi," *Ming Qing shi yuekan* 12 (1987): 33–35.

27. Hou Renzhi and Jin Tao, *Beijing shihua*, 174–75.

28. Hou Renzhi and Jin Tao, *Beijing shihua*, 176–80; Jin Qizong, "Jing qi de Manzu," *Manzu yanjiu* 3 (1988): 63–66; Li Chiao, "Qingdai Beijing neiwai cheng," 35.

29. Du Jiaji, "Qingdai baqi lingshu wenti kaocha," *Minzu yanjiu* 5 (1987): 83; on the locations of these banner offices, see Wu Changyuan, *Chen Yuan shilüe* (1788; reprint, Beijing, 1981), 94, 124, 128, 130; Alison Jean Dray-Novey, "Policing Imperial Peking: The Qing Gendarmerie 1650–1850" (Ph.D. diss., Harvard University, 1981), 62–63.

30. *Xiaoting xulu* (1909; reprint, Beijing, 1980), 384; Yang Naiji, "Qianlong Jingcheng quantu," *Gugong bowuyuan yuankan* 3 (1984): 21. The Russian banner company is studied by Wu Yang, "Qingdai 'Eluosi zuoling' kaolüe," *Lishi yanjiu* 5 (1985): 83–84; see also Mark Mancall, *Russia and China: Their Diplomatic Relations to 1728* (Cambridge, Mass., 1971), 205–6. On the Uighur camp, see Zhang Yuxin, "Qingdai Beijing de Weiwuerzu," *Xinjiang shehui kexue* 4 (1984): 92–97. On the Tibetan community, which still lives in the northwestern suburbs, see Chen Qingying, "Guan yu Beijing Xiangshan Zangzuren de zhuanwenji shiji jizai," *Zhongguo Zangxue* 4 (1990): 104–15.

31. Archives 557-5-66-5/4119 has contracts of the Guanfangzuku from the Yongzheng to Qianlong reigns. These are large woodblock printed forms in both Manchu and Chinese. Archives 5557-5-66-5/4126 are account books dating from 1794 to 1848. The accounts itemize the lots owned by the emperor, by district, and name the tenants and rents. Archives 557-5-66-5/4120 includes twenty-seven contracts of the Jiaqing reign, some of bannermen giving up rentals, others recording the sale of a house from one bannerman to another. Archives 557-5-66-5/4121 includes fifty-seven contracts of the Daoguang period. Archives 557-5-66-5/4122 include twenty-six sales contracts and one mortgage. The above are merely a sample of the archival holdings concerning this office.

32. Liu Xiaomeng, "Cong fan qiwenshu kan Qingdai Beijing chengzhong de qimin jiaochan," *Lishi dang'an* 3 (1996): 83–90; Zhang Deze, *Qingdai guojiu jiguan kaolüe* (Beijing, 1984), 183; Li Pengnian et al., *Qingdai zhongyang guojia jiguan gaishu* (Harbin, 1983), 118; Preston M. Torbert, *The Ch'ing Imperial Household Department: A Study of Its Organization and Principal Functions, 1662–1796* (Cambridge, Mass., 1977), 114.

33. Du Jiaji, "Yongzhengdi jiwei qian de fengqi ji xiangguan wenti kaozhe," *Zhongguoshi yanjiu* 4 (1990): 84–89. Information on the 1750 and 1909–11 maps is in Hou Renzhi, ed., *Beijing lishi diluji* (Beijing, 1985), 41–42, 47–48; the 1846 information comes from a map, 920.21.48, held by the Far Eastern Department, Royal Ontario Museum, Toronto, Canada. I am indebted to James Hsu of the Far Eastern Department, who kindly gave me a draft of his manuscript, "Shijiu shiji Beijing neicheng jiedaotu," which compares the 1846 map with the Hou Renzhi maps. On the 1750 map, see Yang Naiji, "'Qianlong jingcheng quantu' kaolüe," *Gugong bowuyuan yuankan* 3 (1984): 8–24.

34. Archives 446-5-55/350, memorial dated Jiaqing reign (hereafter JQ) 8/1/23 (February 14, 1803).

35. Zhongguo diyi lishi dang'anguan, "Xianfeng nianjian bufen wang gong fudi," *Lishi dang'an* 3 (1994): 26–31. See also Archives 446-5-55/354, memorial dated JQ 9/3/21 (April 30, 1804), presenting estimates of the renovation costs in providing housing for *zongshi* and *juelo*.

36. Isaac Taylor Headland, *Court Life in China: The Capital, Its Officials, and People* (New York, 1909), 330; Sirén, *The Imperial Palaces of Peking*, 25–42. See the map of the imperial city ca. 1750 in Hou Renzhi, *Beijing lishi ditu ji*, 43–44, and the magnificent photographs of the palaces taken during the

Boxer expedition by K. Ogawa and published under the title *Photographs of Palace Buildings of Peking* by the Imperial Museum of Tokyo (Tokyo, 1906).

37. Tong Yue, "Qing Shengjing Taimiao kaoshu," *Gugong bowuyuan yuankan* 3 (1987): 24–25. Steinhardt, *Imperial City Planning*, 177–78, 14, fig. 2 on 3; Meyer, *Dragons of Tiananmen*, 68–73, 62–68.

38. Wang Daocheng, "Beihai yu Qianlong," *Qingshi yanjiu* 2 (1992): 75–77; L. C. Arlington and William Lewisohn, *In Search of Old Peking* (1935; reprint, New York, 1967), 81–82, 127, 123, 204; J. J. Heeren, "Father Bouvet's Picture of Emperor K'ang Hsi (With Appendices)," *Asia Major*, 1st s., 7 (1932): 558.

39. Florence Ayscough, "Notes on the Symbolism of the Purple Forbidden City," *Journal, North China Branch of the Royal Asiatic Society*, n.s., 52 (1921): 64; Yu Zhuoyun, ed., *Palaces of the Forbidden City*, trans. Ng Mausang et al. (New York, 1984); Stephen Markbreiter, "The Imperial Palace of Peking," *Arts of Asia* 8, no. 6 (1978): 66–77. The Yang line of palace architects was descended from a native of Jiangxi who was called to Nanking during the Hongwu reign to help in palace construction. This family maintained its hereditary specialization for five hundred years. See Zhu Qiqian, "Yang Shilei shijia kao," in *Yuanmingyuan ziliao ji*, 102–4.

40. On these and other matters, see Zheng Lianzhang, *Zijincheng cheng chi* (Beijing, 1986).

41. Markbreiter, "Imperial Palace of Peking"; Steinhardt, *Imperial City Planning*, 172–74.

42. John E. Wills, Jr., "Museums and Sites in North China," in *Ming and Qing Historical Studies in the People's Republic of China*, ed. Frederic Wakeman, Jr. (Berkeley, 1980), 13–14.

43. Zhou Suqin, "Qingdai Shunzhi, Kangxi liangdi zuichu de qingong," *Gugong bowuyuan yuankan* 3 (1995): 45–49.

44. Beatrice S. Bartlett, *Monarchs and Ministers: The Grand Council in Mid-Qing China, 1723–1820* (Berkeley, 1991), 25–26, 30, 46, 65, 178. For an analysis of earlier struggles between an inner and outer court, see Andrew Eisenberg, "Retired Emperorship in Medieval China: the Northern Wei," *T'oung Pao* 77, nos. 1–3 (1991): 51.

45. Shan Shiyuan, "Qing Gong Zhoushichu zhizhang ji qi dang'an neirong," *Gugong bowuyuan yuankan* 1 (1986): 7–12. The development of palace memorials and the transmission procedure is described in Silas H. L. Wu, *Communication and Imperial Control in China: Evolution of the Palace Memorial System, 1693–1735* (Cambridge, Mass., 1970), ch. 5.

46. Stephen Markbreiter, "The Imperial Palace of Peking: The Inner Court," *Arts of Asia* 9, no. 1 (1979): 103–15. Zhang Naiwei, *Qing gong shuwen* (1937; reprint, Beijing, 1988), 340 ff. Unless otherwise specified, all references are to this edition. The Yangxindian was also the last Qing emperor's residence: see Aisin-Gioro Pu Yi, *From Emperor to Citizen*, trans. W. J. F. Jenner (1964; reprint, New York, 1987), 64.

47. Liu Lu, "Kunning gong wei Qingdi dongfang yuanyin lun," *Gugong*

bowuyuan yuankan 3 (1996): 72–77; Qi Feng, "Jiaotaidian," *Zijincheng* 6 (1981): 6–8; Xu Qiqian, "Qingdai baoxi luetan," *Gugong bowuyuan yuankan* 3 (1995): 62–66; Ayscough, "Notes on the Symbolism"; Zhang Naiwei, *Qing gong shuwen*, 283–93; see H. S. Brunnert and V. V. Hagelstrom, *Present-Day Political Organization of China*, trans. A. Beltchenko and E. E. Moran (Foochow, 1911), no. 79a.

48. Puren, "Wan Qing huangzi shenghuo yu dushu xiwu," *Zijincheng* 2 (1989): 26; Zhang Naiwei, *Qing gong shuwen*, rev. ed. (Beijing, 1990), 720–22. See Archives 446-5-55/130, memorial of Qianlong reign (hereafter QL) 26/5/25 (June 27, 1761) on the conversions of other palace buildings into princes' residences.

49. There seems to have been quite a squeeze at court during the QL reign. See Archives 446-5-55/124, memorial dated QL 25/4/18 (June 1, 1760), fixing a date for the fourth and fifth sons, Yongcheng and Yongqi, to move from their quarters in the Yuanmingyuan into new quarters in the palace. Similarly, in 446-5-55/430, memorial dated JQ 25/7/26 (September 3, 1820), some of the new Daoguang emperor's brothers were moved out of the Xiefangdian (see text below) into quarters in the Jingren palace and inside the Qianqing gate, so princes actually lived in a wide array of the palaces within the Forbidden City.

50. See Zhang Naiwei, *Qing gong shuwen*, 315–17; quote on 206; Tong Yue and Lü Jihong, *Qing gong huangzi* (Shenyang, 1993), 43.

51. See Zhang Naiwei, *Qing gong shuwen*, 142–44 for a history of the Xiefangdian; Archives 446-5-55/245 records the 1779 move of the emperor's son Yonglin and his grandson Mianyi into the Sansuo after their marriages. Tong and Lü, *Qing gong huangzi*, 41–43.

52. Xu Kun, "Qing chu huangshi yu douzhen fangzhi," *Gugong bowuyuan yuankan* 3 (1994): 91–96, 90. Xu notes that many of Fulin's children and his kinsmen died of smallpox (as the Shunzhi emperor himself did), and that Hongtaiji had begun the practice of having "smallpox avoidance places." Zhang Jinfan and Guo Chengkang, *Qing ruguan qian*, 423 report on Hongtaiji's flight from smallpox in 1632. Variolation did not always "take"; Bai Xinliang, "Qianlong jiating mian mianguan," 3–4, reports on the death of Hongli's seventh son from smallpox; the Tongzhi emperor too died of smallpox even though he had received variolation when a child.

53. Data for calculating the emperor's schedule come from Zhongguo diyi lishi dang'anguan, *Kangxi qijuzhu* (Beijing, 1984), vols. 1, 3. In 1714 (which had 355 days) the emperor spent 5 percent of his time in the Forbidden City, 36.9 percent in the Changchunyuan, 39.2 percent in Chengde, and 18.9 percent on the road.

54. *Lettres édifiantes*, 4:221. I have taken the liberty of changing Benoit's spelling of Chinese place-names to the pinyin rendering used in this book.

55. Wan Yi, "Qianlong shiqi de yuanyou," 17–18.

56. Evelyn S. Rawski, "Re-envisioning the Qing: The Significance of the Qing Period in Chinese History," *Journal of Asian Studies* 55, no. 4 (1996): 829–50 discusses the work by Farquhar and others. See also Liu Xiaomeng,

"Manzu qixing shiqi suo shou Menggu wenhua de yingxiang," *Shehui kexue zhanxian* 6 (1994): 169–75.

57. *Taizong shilu, juan* ([hereafter j.]) 25, dated Tianzong 9/10/13 (November 22, 1635); on the meaning of *gurun* in the early seventeenth century, see Pamela K. Crossley, *A Translucent Mirror: History and Identity in the Transformations of Qing Imperial Ideology* (Berkeley, forthcoming); Wang Zhonghan, "Guanyu Manzu xingcheng zhong de jige wenti," in his *Manzushi yanjiu ji* (Taiyuan, 1988), 6–8. On the unresolved debates concerning the meaning of "Manju," see Giovanni Stary, "The Meaning of the Word 'Manchu': A New Solution to an Old Problem," *Central Asiatic Journal* 34, nos. 1–2 (1990): 109–19.

58. Jin Taofang, "Cong Nuzhenyu dao Manzhouyu," *Manyu yanjiu* 1 (1990): 46–52, 36; S. Robert Ramsay, *The Languages of China* (Princeton, 1987), 227–29. Hanson Chase, "The Status of the Manchu Language in the Early Ch'ing" (Ph.D. diss., University of Washington, Seattle, 1979).

59. Pamela K. Crossley and Evelyn S. Rawski, "A Profile of the Manchu Language in Ch'ing History," *Harvard Journal of Asiatic Studies* 53, no. 1 (1993): 70–75; Qiao Zhizhong, "Hou Jin Manwen dangce de chansheng ji qi shixue yiyi," *Shehui kexue zhanxian* 3 (1994): 155–60; Liu Ziyang and Zhang Li, "'Manwen laodang 'Taizong chao' zongxi," *Manyu yanjiu* 2 (1992): 66–73, 1 (1993): 65–77; Guan Xiaolian, "Qing Kangxi chao Manwen zhupi zouzhe chuyi," *Lishi dang'an* 1 (1994): 84–90. On the language capabilities of early Qing officials, see Chase, "The Status of the Manchu Language," ch. 1. Tong Wanlun is conducting a painstaking line-by-line comparison of the Manchu and Chinese-language versions of the veritable records for Nurgaci's reign; see his "'Manzhou shilu' (Manwen) de mimi (1)," *Manyu yanjiu* 1 (1993): 78–86. For a survey of recent scholarship, see Guan Jialu and Tong Yonggong, "Zhongguo Manwen ji qi wenxian zhengli yanjiu," *Qingshi yanjiu* 4 (1991): 29–36.

60. Aixinjuelo Yingsheng, "Tantan Manyu de jingyu," *Manyu yanjiu* 1 (1987): 2–15, 73; 2 (1990): 22–36, 2(1991): 3–15, 2 (1992): 1–17, 2 (1993): 25–34, 24; 1 (1994): 15–23,36; 1 (1995): 13–20; Zhang Hong, "Qianlong chao 'Qinding Xin Qingyu,'" trans. Cheng Dakun, *Manyu yanjiu* 2 (1993): 79–84, 55; 2 (1994): 68–77, 50; 2 (1995): 51–58. Also Chase, "The Status of the Manchu Language," ch. 2; Wu Xuejuan, "Tan Qingdai Manwen dang'an zhong de gongwen taoyu," *Manyu yanjiu* 1 (1992): 119–24, 89.

61. Ji Yonghai, "'Da Qing quanshu' yanjiu," *Manyu yanjiu* 2 (1990): 42–50; Crossley and Rawski, "Profile of the Manchu Language," 83–87; Aixinjuelo Yingsheng, "Tantan Manyu de jingyu," *Manyu yanjiu* 2 (1992): 1–17. On the five-language dictionary, *han-i araha sunja hacin-i hergen kamciha manju gisun-i buleku bithe*, see Imanishi Shunju, "Gotai Shinbunkan kaidai," in *Gotai Shinbunkan yakkai*, ed. Tamura Jitsuzō et al. (Kyoto, 1966), 17–29. Qing emperors were bilingual and trilingual through at least the first half of the dynasty. The Qianlong emperor tried to learn each of the five languages of

his major subject peoples: see Jin Baosen, "Qiantan Qianlong dui fazhan Manwen de gongxian," *Qingshi yanjiu* 1 (1992): 78–80.

62. Zhang Hong's study, "Qianlong chao 'Qinding Xin Qingyu,'" is based on the Manchu-language materials in the "Heitudang" in Liaoning. See also Liao Ning and Tong Yonggong, "Qianlong huangdi yu Manyu diming," *Diming congkan* 6 (1987): 33–34; Tong Yonggong and Guan Jialu, "Qianlong chao 'Qinding xin Qingyu' tanxi," *Manzu yanjiu* 2 (1995): 66–70.

63. See the detailed discussion of "capital speech" vs. other spoken dialects by Aixinjuelo Yingsheng, "Tantan Manyu de jingyu." For a discussion of the impact of Manchu on the Chinese spoken in Peking, see Stephen Wadley, "Altaic Influence on Beijing Dialect: The Manchu Case," *Journal of the American Oriental Society* 116, no. 1 (1996): 99–104.

64. Xu Shuming, "Qing qianqi Heilongjiang diqu de sanzuo xincheng—Aigun, Moergen he Qiqihaer," *Qingshi yanjiu tongxun* 3 (1988): 17–18; Zhang Jie, "Qingchu zhaofu xin Manzhou shulue," *Qingshi yanjiu* 1 (1994): 23–30.

65. Badarongga, "Manzhouyu yu Dawoeryu de guanxi," *Manyu yanjiu* 2 (1993): 35–38; Ding Shiqing, "Lun Dawoeryu zhong de Manyu jieci," *Manyu yanjiu* 1 (1990): 53–60. Sergei M. Shirokogoroff, *Social Organization of the Northern Tungus* (Shanghai, 1929), 73–85; Zhang Jie, "Qingdai Manzu yuyan wenzi zai dongbei de xingfei yu yingxiang," *Beifang wenwu* 1 (1995): 63–68. On the movement of *ice manju* into Shengjing, see Jiang Xiangshun, "Shenyang Manzu de bianqian," *Dongbei difang shi yanjiu* 1 (1990): 59. On the "Manchuization" of Hanjun, see Teng Shaozhen, *Qingdai baqi zidi* (Beijing, 1989), ch. 2.

66. "Heilongjiang jiji zhengli yanjiu Manyu," *Dalu xinwen*, December 31, 1993, A11. The village, Sanjia zicun, Fuyu county, was identified by a team sent by the Heilongjiang Manchu Language Research Institute in cooperation with the Central Minorities Institute, Beijing.

67. Pamela K. Crossley, "Manchu Education," in *Education and Society in Late Imperial China, 1600–1900,* ed. Benjamin A. Elman and Alexander Woodside (Berkeley, 1994), 353–55.

68. *(Qinding) Da Qing huidian shili* (Guangxu ed., 1976 [hereafter DQHDSL]), j. 1, edict of QL 32.

69. Edicts dated 1767, 1806, and 1823 touch on this subject in *DQHDSL,* j. 1. The names of the descendants of all Aisin Gioro are included in the Imperial Genealogy and the *Aixin juelo zongpu* (hereafter *AJZP*), printed in Fengtian in 1937–38. For a discussion of Manchu naming practices, see Chieh-hsien Chen, *Manchu Archival Materials* (Taipei, 1988), 182–85.

70. John Vollmer, *In the Presence of the Dragon Throne: Ch'ing Dynasty Costume (1644–1911) in the Royal Ontario Museum* (Toronto, 1977), 9. See 16–28, from which the following discussion is drawn.

71. On the significance of the stirrup, see Charles P. Chevenix-Trench, *A History of Horsemanship* (New York, 1970), 64–66.

72. *Taizong Wen huangdi shilu,* 32.8–9b; 34.26b–27; Zhang Jinfan and Guo Chengkang, *Qing ruguan qian guojia falü zhidu shi* (Shenyang, 1988), 458–61; Schuyler V. R. Cammann, *China's Dragon Robes* (New York, 1952), 51.

73. Wakeman, *Great Enterprise,* 2:976–77. *Gaozong Chun huangdi shilu,* 919.11–13b. Also Cammann, *China's Dragon Robes,* 50, quotes from the emperor's preface in the *Huangchao liqi tushi,* completed in 1759. See Zhang and Guo, *Qing ruguan qian guojia falü,* 458–61 on the dress code before 1644.

74. Zhang Jinfan and Guo Chengkang, *Qing ruguan qian,* 459; Wakeman, *Great Enterprise,* 1:646–50.

75. Bao Chunli, "Cong tifa zhidu kan Qingchao de minzu zhengce," *Nei Menggu minzu shiyuan xuebao (zhexue, shehuixue)* 3 (1991): 66–70, 87.

76. *DQHDSL,* j. 1114, edict dated 1759.

77. *DQHDSL,* j. 1114.

78. *Shizu Zhang huangdi shilu,* 54.18b; cited in Wakeman, *Great Enterprise,* 2:75.

79. Vollmer, *In the Presence of the Dragon Throne,* 31ff, 69–75. Cammann, *China's Dragon Robes;* for an appraisal of Cammann's work, see John R. Finlay, "Chinese Embroidered Mandarin Squares from the Schuyler V. R. Cammann Collection," *Orientations* 25, no. 4 (1994): 57–63.

80. Cammann, *China's Dragon Robes,* 4–9; Ka Bo Tsang, "The Dragon in Chinese Art," *Arts of Asia* 18, no. 1 (1988): 60–67.

81. Similar hierarchical rankings were spelled out in the dress code for consorts and wives of officials: see Cammann, *China's Dragon Robes,* chs. 7, 12. See Archives 446-5-55/434, memorial of Daoguang reign (hereafter DG) 1/6*(July 1821) reviewing dress codes for imperial progeny.

82. Cammann, *China's Dragon Robes,* 170–75; Henny Harald Hansen, *Mongol Costumes* (London, 1993).

83. Stefan Sokol, "The Asian Reverse Bow: Reflex and Retroflex Systems," *Arts of Asia* 24, no. 5 (1994): 146–49.

84. Wakeman, *Great Enterprise,* 1:46, 236; Ning Changying, "Lun Manzu de sheliu xisu," *Manzu wenhua* 16 (1992): 66–68.

85. Wang Zilin, "Qingdai gong ya," *Gugong bowuyuan yuankan* 1 (1994): 86–96. As Sokol, "Asian Reverse Bow," notes, a bow's "pull" is the degree of force required to extend the bow a certain distance.

86. Cited in Wang Zhonghan, "Guoyu qishe," 200.

87. Wang Zhonghan, "Guoyu qishe," 197.

88. Reported in Zuo Buqing, "Manzhou guizu de shangwu jingshen ji qi minmie," *Gugong bowuyuan yuankan* 3 (1989): 32–37.

89. Wan Yi et al., eds., *Qingdai gongting shenghuo* (Hong Kong, 1985), no. 170 on121. Wang Zilin, "Qingdai gong ya," 87; Ruo Jing, "Qianlong di chiyu huangzi xianxi qishe," in *Qing gong yishi,* ed. Zheng Yimei et al. (Beijing, 1985), 57–59. On antler horn chairs, see Hu Desheng, "Qianlong lujiaoqi," *Wenwu* 7 (1986): 84–85. My thanks to Jan Stuart, who gave me this reference. Hu states that a Kangxi antler chair was kept at the Bishu

shanzhuang, and that three such chairs were made during the Qianlong reign. According to Li Fengmin and Lu Haiying, eds., *Gugong zaqu* (Shenyang, 1996), 125–27, Hongtaiji also had three antler chairs, made from his own kills; one still survives in the Shenyang Palace Museum and its photograph appears on 14 in Shenyang gugong bowuyuan, *Shenyang gugong bowuyuan wenwu jingpin huicui* (Shenyang, 1991). See Xu Ke, *Qing bai leichao* (1917; reprint, Taipei, 1966), 2:20 on the initiation of examinations in archery for *zongshi* by the Qianlong emperor.

90. Reported in Zhang Naiwei, *Qing gong shuwen*, 385. Yihuan was born in 1840; eighth brother, Prince Zhong, in 1844, and ninth brother, Prince Fu, in 1845. Fourth sister, Shou'an *gurun gungju*, was born in 1826, married in 1841, and died in 1860 at thirty-three years of age.

91. Wang Zhonghan, "Guoyu qishe," 198. Since a Chinese child is one *sui* at birth, the emperor would have been younger than age twelve by Western reckoning. There is a painting by Giuseppe Castiglione of the Kangxi emperor aiming his bow at a deer, in the Musée Guimet, and a painting of the Qianlong emperor aiming an arrow at a bear, in Wan Yi, *Qingdai gongting shenghuo*, pl. 168 on 119.

92. Zhaolian, *Xiaoting zalu* (Beijing, 1980), 13–14; Xu Ke, *Qing bai leichao*, 56; Wu, *Passage to Power*, 37.

93. Kaye Soon Im, "The Rise and Decline of the Eight Banner Garrisons in the Ch'ing Period (1644–1911): A Study of the Kuang-chou, Hang-chou, and Ching-chou Garrisons" (Ph.D. diss., University of Illinois, 1981), 15; Spence, *Ts'ao Yin and the K'ang-hsi Emperor*, 130–31, 148. On Xuanye's ambidexterity, see Heeren, "Father Bouvet's Picture," 560; the description of the emperor's strength with the bow comes from Spence, *Emperor of China*, 147–48. Xuanye's archery skills are clearly superior, since the strongest bow had a pull of eighteen. According to Chieh-hsien Ch'en, "Introduction to the Manchu Text Version of the Ch'ing Emperors' Ch'i-chü-chu (Notes on the Emperors' Daily Activities)," *Central Asiatic Journal* 17, nos. 2–4 (1973): 127, the Manchu-language diaries provide information on archery contests that is omitted from the Chinese-language version.

94. *Ts'ao Yin and the K'ang-hsi Emperor*, 130–31.

95. *DQSL*, j. 192, Kangxi reign (hereafter KX) 38/3/27; *DQSL*, j. 117, KX 23/11/3; *DQSL*, j. 41, KX 12/1/20. Also reported in Kessler, *K'ang-hsi and the Consolidation*, 107.

96. Zhaolian, *Xiaoting zalu*, 432, 515; Wang Zhonghan, "Guoyu qishe," 199.

97. From an imperial poem, cited by Wang Zhonghan, "Guoyu qishe," 199.

98. Wang Shuqing, "Qingdai gongzhong shanshi," *Gugong bowuyuan yuankan* 3 (1983): 57–64. Each occupant of the palace had a food ration. Efforts to cut down on costs can be seen in a memorial dated QL 59/11/2 (November 24, 1794), Archives 446-5-55/317.

99. Wu, *Manzu shisu*, 430–32; Yuan Hongqi, "Qing Qianlong di de changshou yu shanshi," *Lishi dang'an* 4 (1993): 135; Spence, "Ch'ing," in *Food*

in Chinese Culture: Anthropological and Historical Perspectives, ed. K. C. Chang (New Haven, 1977), 281.

100. Wu Zhengge, *Man Han quanxi* (Tianjin, 1986), 3–6.

101. Wu Zhengge, *Manzu shisu yu Qing gong yushan* (Shenyang, 1988), 244–46.

102. Wu Zhengge, *Manzu shisu*, 147–48 has a long list of specific foods sent to the court before 1861; 249–56 looks at the *xiaocai* archive of 1774–78. *Xiaocai* (small dishes) refers to what the Qianlong emperor ate on a daily basis, apart from banquets. See also a Manchu-language memorial of QL 1/10/6 (November 8, 1736) [Archives 446-5-55/7] on the Hami melons presented by Uighur Prince Amin. For the taboo on dog meat, see Li Yanping, "Manzu yinshi wenhua," *Manyu yanjiu* 2 (1994): 82. Li explains that the taboo may derive from the hunting culture traditions of the ancestors of the Manchus: the reason Manchus gave for this prohibition was because Nurgaci had been aided at critical points in his early career by a dog.

103. *Memoirs of Father Ripa*, 49–50. On the elaborate system of tribute, see Dong Jianzhong, "Qing Qianlong chao wang gong dachen guan yuan jingong wenti chutan," *Qingshi yanjiu* 1 (1996): 40–66.

104. On lichee, see Archives 467-4-85/1869, a *shangtan* (bestowal list) dated QL 62/intercalary 6/18 (!) (August 10, 1797).

105. Spence, "Ch'ing," 282–84, describes the official regulations for banquets and notes that more research is needed on the Manchu banquets. This research has been supplied by Wu Zhengge, *Manzu shisu*, 230–31. Wu's thesis, that the rulers preserved Manchu cuisine and served it at banquets, goes against the assertion of some scholars, who say that the banquets were "completely Chinese": see, for example, Ju Deyuan, "Qing gong dayan liyi he shantan," *Zijincheng* 5 (1981): 34–36.

106. The largest banquets recorded were those held in 1713 at the Changchunyuan to celebrate the emperor's sixtieth birthday; the 1718 banquet celebrating his sixty-fifth birthday, held at the Qianqing palace; the 1785 banquet to fete the elders held at the Qianqing palace, and the 1795 banquet when five thousand elders were guests. See Wang Shuqing, "Qingdai gongzhong shanshi," 63; Liu Guilin, "Qian sou yan," *Gugong bowuyuan yuankan* 2 (1981): 49–55.

107. *Lettres édifiantes*, 4:224–25.

108. Xu Qixian, "Qingdai huangdi de yongshan," *Zijincheng* 4 (1980): 10; Wang Shuqing, "Qingdai gongzhong shanshi," 60. These daily menus are found in Archives 467-4-85/2220, *shantan* (menus) of the Qianlong reign. Manchu pastries are still made and sold in Peking: Li Ke, "Jingwei xidian: Huicuiyuan," *Renmin ribao*, October 11, 1991; Yuan Hongqi, "Qing Qianlong di de changshou yu shanshi"; Li Guoliang, "Bishu shanzhuang yushan zatan," *Gugong bowuyuan yuankan* 1 (1988): 83–85.

109. On the provisioning in Peking, see *Qinding zongguan neiwufu xianxing zeli* (Peking, 1937 [hereafter ZNXZ]). A Manchu-language memorial (Archives 446-5-55/7), dated QL 1/9/12 (October 16, 1736), notes that al-

though twenty-four milk cows have been assigned to the empress dowager, the twenty-four catties of milk they produced each day had to suffice to provide cream, sour milk, and milk curd for the young imperial daughters as well. Shortfalls were supplemented from the herd of one hundred cows assigned to the emperor. The ministers requested that the size of the herds be increased, but they were turned down. A 1741 memorial discussing the provisioning of milk to the imperial entourage indicates that the system of supplying seventy-five milk cows and rotating them to ensure a continuous abundant supply of milk for the Tea Bureau was devised during the early eighteenth century by the Kangxi emperor: see 446-5-55/33, dated QL 6/5/17 (June 29, 1741). The herds also had to be deployed during southern tours: see 446-5-55/2, memorial dated QL 48/11/24 (December 17, 1783) making arrangements for sheep and cows to be deployed along the route of the 1784 southern tour (ZNXZ). For changes in regulations from 1707 to 1761 concerning the number of milk cows allocated to imperial sons and grandsons after marriage, see 446-5-55/128, memorial dated QL 26/2/7 (March 13, 1761).

110. Xu Qixian, "Qingdai huangdi de yongshan"; Wang Shuqing, "Qingdai gongzhong shanshi," 60.

111. Evelyn S. Rawski, "The Imperial Way of Death: Ming and Ch'ing Emperors and Death Ritual," in *Death Ritual in Late Imperial and Modern China*, ed. James L. Watson and Evelyn S. Rawski (Berkeley, 1988), 228–53; Chieh-hsien Ch'en, "A Study of the Manchu Posthumous Titles of the Ch'ing Emperors," *Central Asiatic Journal* 26, nos. 3–4 (1982): 187–92.

112. Liu Xiaomeng, "Manzu qixing shiqi," 172–73; Ji Yonghai, "Qingdai cehao kaoshi," *Manyu yanjiu* 2 (1993): 69–78.

113. Owen Lattimore, *The Mongols of Manchuria: Their Tribal Divisions, Geographical Distribution, Historical Relations with Manchus and Chinese, and Present Political Problems* (New York, 1934), 29, argues that the eastern Mongols felt that they were co-equals with the Manchus as founders of the Qing empire. "Bogdo" was conferred by the Mongol princes on Hongtaiji in 1636; see Chen Xiaoqiang, "Cong Menggu lama Neiqiaotuoyin yishi de huodong kan Manzhou Qing zhengfu quan dui Zang zhuan Fojiao de fuzhi he xianzhi," *Qinghai minzu xueyuan xuebao (shehui kexue ban)* 4 (1991): 40. Charles R. Bawden, *The Jebtsundamba Khutukhtus of Urga: Text, Translation and Notes* (Wiesbaden, 1961), 45–46. On the historical use of the term Khaghan (*qaghan*) in Turkic history, see Michael R. Drompp, "Supernumerary Sovereigns: Superfluity and Mutability in the Elite Power Structure of the Early Türks (Tu-jue)," in *Rulers from the Steppe: State Formation on the Eurasian Periphery*, ed. Gary Seaman and Daniel Marks (Los Angeles, 1991), 2:92–115. On the Russian term, see Mancall, *Russia and China*, 45.

114. Chieh-hsien Ch'en, "Introduction to the Manchu Text Version of the Ch'ing Emperors' Ch'i-chü-chu (Notes on the Emperor's Daily Activities)," *Central Asiatic Journal* 17, nos. 2–4 (1973): 126; Xiaoshi, *Yongxian lu* (Beijing, 1959), 137; Takao Ishibashi, "The Formation of the Power of Early Ch'ing Emperors," *Memoirs of the Research Department of the Tōyō Bunkom* 48 (1990):

1–15. See also Xu Ke, *Qing bai leichao*, "Chengwei," IV, 5. Memorials dated JQ 4/3/18 (April 22, 1799) [Archives 446-5-55/332] and JQ 4/10/22 (November 19, 1799) [446-5-55/335].

115. The Manchu-language palace memorials of the Kangxi reign, published in Taipei, include many memorials using these terms: see Guoli Gugong bowuyuan, *Gongzhong dang Kangxi chao zouzhe* (Shilin, 1977), vols. 8, 9. The prayer cited above is taken from the Manchu text on a *yuce* dated April 22, 1661, in the Wason Collection at Cornell University.

116. Mu Sou, "Manzu qing'an li," *Zijincheng* 38 (1987): 31–32.

117. Wen C. Fong, "Imperial Patronage of the Arts," in *Possessing the Past: Treasures from the National Palace Museum*, ed. Wen C. Fong and James C. Y. Watt (New York, 1996), 555.

118. Fong, "Imperial Patronage," 560; Hironobu Kohara, "The Qianlong Emperor's Skill in the Connoisseurship of Chinese Painting," in *The Elegant Brush: Chinese Painting Under the Qianlong Emperor 1735–1795*, ed. Ju-hsi Chou and Claudia Brown (Phoenix, 1985), 56–73. On the size of the emperor's collection and on his brushes, ink, etc., see James C. Y. Watt, "The Antique-Elegant," in *Possessing the Past*, 537–43, 549.

119. Examples are found in Watt, "The Antique-Elegant," pls. 302, 305–6, 308–11; also 509, 513, 515–16, 518–19.

120. National Palace Museum, *Catalogue of a Special Exhibition of Hindustan Jade in the National Palace Museum* (Taipei, 1983), 83–93.

121. Beurdeley and Beurdeley, *Giuseppe Castiglione*, 79–88; Nie Chongzheng, "Tan Qingdai 'Ziguangge gongchenxiang,'" *Wenwu* 1 (1990): 65–69; Ka Bo Tsang, "Portraits of Meritorious Officials: Eight Examples from the First Set Commissioned by the Qianlong Emperor," *Arts asiatique* 47 (1992): 69–88; Zeng Jiabao, "Ji fenggong, shu weiji: Qing Gaozong shiquan wugong de tuxiang jilu—gongchenxiang yu zhantu," *Gugong wenwu yuekan* 93 (1990): 38–65.

122. Wei Tong, "'Huang Qing zhigongtu' chuangzhi shimo," *Zijincheng* 72 (1992): 8–12.

123. Zhongguo diyi lishi dang'anguan, *Yuanmingyuan: Qingdai dang'an shiliao* (Shanghai, 1991), 2:1530.

124. Beurdeley and Beurdeley, *Giuseppe Castiglione*, 119–23; Chuang Chi-fa, "The Emperor's New Pets: Naming Castiglione's 'Ten Champion Dogs,'" trans. Mark Elliott, *National Palace Museum Bulletin* 23, no. 1 (1988): 1–13.

125. Wu Hung, "Emperor's Masquerade—'Costume Portraits' of Yongzheng and Qianlong," *Orientations* 26, no. 7 (1995): 25–41. Another portrait of Yinzhen in a European wig also exists and appears as fig. 8 in Wu's article.

126. Wu Hung, "Emperor's Masquerade," 30.

127. Wu Hung, *The Double Screen: Medium and Representation in Chinese Painting* (Chicago, 1996).

128. Wu Hung, "Beyond Stereotypes: The Twelve Beauties in Qing Court

Art and the 'Dream of the Red Chamber,'" in *Writing Women in Late Imperial China*, ed. Ellen Widmer and Kang-i Sun Chang (Stanford, 1997), 330.

129. Wu Hung, *Double Screen*, 209–10.

130. Wu Hung, *Double Screen*, 229.

CHAPTER 2: THE CONQUEST ELITE
AND THE IMPERIAL LINEAGE

1. Pamela K. Crossley, "*Manzhou yuanliu kao* and the Formalization of the Manchu Heritage," *Journal of Asian Studies* 46, no. 4 (1987): 779.

2. Crossley, "*Manzhou* and the Formalization." For a recent attempt to trace changes in Jurchen/Manchu kinship organization, see Gao Bingzhong, "Dongbei zhutun Manzu de xueyuan zuzhi—cong shizu dao jiazu zai dao jiahu de yanbian," *Manzu yanjiu* 1 (1996): 16–24.

3. Pamela K. Crossley, "The Qianlong Retrospect on the Chinese-Martial (hanjun) Banners," *Late Imperial China* 10, no. 1 (1989): 63–107.

4. A detailed analysis of the creation and evolution of the banner system during its first decades is provided by Zhang Jinfan and Guo Chengkang, *Qing ruguan qian guojia falü* (Shenyang, 1988).

5. Fang Chao-ying, "A Technique for Estimating the Numerical Strength of the Early Manchu Military Forces," *Harvard Journal of Asiatic Studies* 13, no. 1 (1950): 192–214. Meng Lin, "'Manwen laodang' yu Menggushi yanjiu," *Nei Menggu shehui kexue* 4 (1987): 85–86.

6. Zhao Kai, "Qingdai qigu zuoling kaobian—jianlun youguan Qingdai baoyi de rogan wenti," *Gugong bowuyuan yuankan* 1 (1988): 3–11, 20; Wu Yang, "Qingdai 'Elusi zuoling' kaolue," *Lishi yanjiu* 5 (1985): 83–84; Wang Huo, "Qingdai baqi zhong Gaoliren mingzi de yuyan he minsu tezheng," *Manzu yanjiu* 2 (1995): 43–49.

7. Wang Zhonghan, "Qingdai baqi zhong de Man Han minzu chengfen wenti," *Minzu yanjiu* 3 (1990): 36–46; 4 (1990): 57–66.

8. See Pamela K. Crossley, *Orphan Warriors: Three Manchu Generations and the End of the Qing World* (Princeton, 1990).

9. Zhou Yuanlian, "Guan yu shiliu shiji sishi—bashi niandai chu Jianzhou Nüzhen he zaoqi Manzu shehui xingzhi wenti," *Qingshi luncong* 1 (1979): 161–71.

10. Yang Xuechen and Zhou Yuanlian, *Qingdai baqi wang gong guizu xing shuai shi* (Shenyang, 1986), 47.

11. Yang Xuechen and Zhou Yuanlian, *Qingdai baqi*.

12. This point is made by Wang Zhonghan, "Guan yu Manzu xingcheng zhong de jige wenti," in his *Manzu shi yanjiuji* (Taiyuan, 1988), 6, and Zhang Jinfan and Guo Chengkang, *Qing ruguan qian*, 187.

13. Zhang Jinfan and Guo Chengkang, *Qing ruguan qian*, 211–15; Du Jiaji, "Qingdai zongshi fenfengzhi shulun," *Shehui kexue jikan* 4 (1991): 94.

14. Zhao Zhiqiang, "Yongzheng chao Junji dachen kaobu," *Lishi dang'an* 3 (1991): 93–104. Joint rule differs from "dyarchy" (see John K. Fairbank, *Trade*

and Diplomacy on the China Coast: The Opening of the Treaty Ports, 1842–1854 [Cambridge, Mass., 1953], 40–41). Dyarchy posits shared rule between two groups but the Qing system of shared rule included representation from the Mongols, Tibetans, and Turkic-speaking Muslims as well as the Han Chinese.

15. Zhang Jinfan and Guo Chengkang, *Qing ruguan qian;* Mark C. Elliott, "Resident Aliens: The Manchu Experience in China, 1644–1760" (Ph.D. diss., University of California, Berkeley, 1993); and Kaye Soon Im, "The Rise and Decline of the Eight Banner Garrisons in the Ch'ing Period (1644–1911): A Study of the Kuang-chou, Hang-chou, and Ching-chou Garrisons" (Ph.D. diss., University of Illinois, 1981).

16. Arthur W. Hummel, *Eminent Chinese of the Ch'ing Period (1944–1912)* (Washington, D.C., 1943 [hereafter *ECCP*]), 247. See his biography in *Baqi Manzhou shizu tongpu* (Fengtian, 1937–38; hereafter *BMST*), 1.1b–2b.

17. For Eidu, see *ECCP,* 221–22; *(Qinding) Baqi tongzhi* (1944; reprint, Shenyang, 1989 [hereafter *BQTZ*]), 6:3706–7; *BMST,* 5.1b–2b; for Fiongdon, see *ECCP,* 247; *BQTZ,* 3:1544, 6:3693–95; *BMST,* 1.1b–2b; Crossley, *Orphan Warriors,* 42–44; for Hohori, see *ECCP,* 291, *BQTZ,* 3:1589, 6:3953–54; *BMST,* 8.1a–2b; for Hurhan, see *ECCP,* 275; *BQTZ,* 6:2857–59; *BMST,* 19.8a–9b; for Anfiyanggu, see *ECCP,* 13; *BQTZ,* 6:4118–20.

18. Yang Xuechen and Zhou Yuanlian, *Qingdai baqi,* 45; *(Qinding) Da Qing huidian* (1899; reprint, Taipei, 1976 [hereafter *DQHD*]) j. 12; Wolfgang Franke, "Patents for Hereditary Ranks and Honorary Titles during the Ch'ing Dynasty," *Monumenta Serica* 7 (1942): 38–67. The English translations of the Ming military terms are taken from Charles O. Hucker, *A Dictionary of Official Titles in Imperial China* (Stanford, 1985); on the Qing Manchu titles, see Elliott, "Resident Aliens."

19. The ranks are listed in H. S. Brunnert and V. V. Hagelstrom, *Present-Day Political Organization of China,* trans. A. Beltchenko and E. E. Moran (Foochow, 1911), no. 944. Yang Xuechen and Zhou Yuanlian, *Qingdai baqi,* 45–46 for evolution of system.

20. See Lawrence D. Kessler, *K'ang-hsi and the Consolidation of Ch'ing Rule, 1661–1684* (Chicago, 1976), 71–73 for Xuanye's purge of the Oboi regents. Kessler erroneously awards Ebilun the ducal title; see *BQTZ,* 3:1549 and *(Qinding)Baqi tongzhi xubian* (1799; reprint, Taipei, 1968 [hereafter *BQTZXB*]), 47:19289–90 for the hereditary succession of Eidu's title.

21. Huang Pei, "Qingchu de Manzhou guizu (1583–1795)—Niohulu zu," in *Lao Zhenyi xiansheng bazhi rong Qing lunwen ji* (Taipei, 1986), 629–64.

22. *BQTZXB,* 7:19275–76.

23. *BQTZ,* 6:3953–54, *BQTZXB,* 47:1901–2.

24. *BQTZ,* 6:4118–20.

25. *BQTZ,* 6:3857–59; *BMST,* 19.8a–9b.

26. *BQTZ,* 1:29–31, 1:25–27, 1:77, 1:171. Hohori's line seems to have held only one hereditary captaincy in the first division of the Manchu Plain Red Banner: see *BQTZ,* 1:92.

27. See Yang Xuechen and Zhou Yuanlian, *Qingdai baqi*, table on 61–63.

28. On marriage, see Evelyn S. Rawski, "Qing Imperial Marriage and Problems of Rulership," in *Marriage and Inequality in Chinese Society*, ed. Rubie S. Watson and Patricia B. Ebrey (Berkeley, 1991), 170–203.

29. Yang Xuechen and Zhou Yuanlian, *Qingdai baqi*, 63–75, table on 75–76.

30. Owen Lattimore, *The Mongols of Manchuria: Their Tribal Divisions, Geographical Distribution, Historical Relations with Manchus and Chinese and Present Political Problems* (New York, 1934), ch. 7; Henry Serruys, "The Čahar Population During the Ch'ing," *Journal of Asian History* 12 (1978): 58–79; Hidehiro Okada, "Origin of the Čahar Mongols," *Mongolian Studies* 14 (1991): 155–79.

31. Tong Guijiang, "Qingdai Menggu guizu juezhi suoyi," *Minzu yanjiu* 1 (1987): 63–70.

32. Charles R. Bawden, *The Modern History of Mongolia* (New York, 1968), ch. 2; Junko Miyawaki, "The Qalqa Mongols and the Oyirad in the Seventeenth Century," *Journal of Asian History* 18 (1984): 136–73.

33. Yuan Shenbo, "Kaerke Menggu jasake de shezhi yu yanbian," *Qingshi yanjiu tongxun* 2 (1988): 1–10.

34. Zahiruddin Ahmad, *Sino-Tibetan Relations in the Seventeenth Century* (Rome, 1970), chs. 8, 9; Thomas J. Barfield, *The Perilous Frontier: Nomadic Empires and China* (Oxford, 1989), 277–93.

35. Bawden, *Modern History of Mongolia*, 105–7; Zhao Yuntian, "Guan yu Qianlong chao neifu chaoben 'Lifanyuan zeli,'" *Xibei shidi* 2 (1988): 122–25.

36. Zhang Jinfan and Guo Chengkang, *Qingdai ruguan qian*, 273–75, 356–87; Guo Chengkang, "Qingchu Menggu baqi kaoshi," *Minzu yanjiu* 3 (1986): 51–58.

37. Aleksei M. Podzneyev, *Mongolia and the Mongols* (1892), trans. John Roger Shaw and Dale Plank (Bloomington, 1971), chs. 4, 6.

38. Bawden, *Modern History of Mongolia*, 56; Robert A. Rupen, "The City of Urga in the Manchu Period," *Studia Altaica: Festschrift für Nikolaus Poppe zum 60. Geburtstag am 8. August 1957* (Wiesbaden, 1957), 157–69; Podzneyev, *Mongolia and the Mongols*, 46; M. Sanjdorj, *Manchu Chinese Colonial Rule in Northern Mongolia*, trans. Urgunge Onon (New York, 1980), 110.

39. Kang Youming, "Man Meng guizu lianmeng yu Qing diguo," *Nankai xuebao* 2 (1986): 59–66.

40. Tong Guijiang, "Qingdai Menggu guizu," 67.

41. *DQHD*, j. 66; Chia Ning, "The Li-fan Yuan in the Early Ch'ing Dynasty" (Ph.D. diss., Johns Hopkins University, 1992), 110–13, 126–28; see her table on 130 for stipends of Mongol nobles.

42. Tong Guijiang, "Qingdai Menggu guizu," 65.

43. Bawden, *Modern History of Mongolia*, 103–5; *BQTZXB*, 7:19263–64, *ECCP*, 15–16; Nie Chongzheng, "Tan Qingdai 'Ziguangge gongchenxiang,'" *Wenwu* 1 (1990): 65.

44. Bawden, *Modern History of Mongolia*, 83; also his "The Mongol Rebellion of 1756–1757," *Journal of Asian History* 2, no. 1 (1968): 1–31.

45. *ECCP,* 755–57; Bao Guiqin, ed., *Qingdai Menggu guanshi zhuan* (Beijing, 1995), 711–14.

46. Meng Yunsheng, "Beijing de Menggu wangfu," *Manzu yanjiu* 3 (1989): 51–55. The author is a descendant of Tsereng and a grandson of Prince Nayentu. This article describes seven other Mongol princely houses that had residences in Peking and remained active until the end of the dynasty.

47. Crossley, "The Qianlong Retrospect"; Zhang Jinfan and Guo Chengkang, *Qingdai ruguan qian,* 302–11, 318–26; Xie Jingfang, "Baqi Hanjun de mingcheng ji hanyi yange kaoyi," *Beifang wenwu* 3 (1991): 84–88.

48. *BQTZ,* 3:1590; *BQTZXB,* 47:19403–4; *ECCP,* 499.

49. On the three generals, see Kessler, *K'ang-hsi and the Consolidation,* ch. 4. On the Tongs, see Pamela K. Crossley, "The Tong in Two Worlds: Cultural Identities in Liaodong and Nurgan during the 13th–17th Centuries," *Ch'ing-shih wen-t'i* 4, no. 9 (1983): 21–46. Sun Chengyun, the only other Hanjun groom, was a third-generation bannerman whose father, a general, had helped defeat the Eleuths in the famous battle of Jao Modo (1695): see *ECCP,* 2:682.

50. Hou Shouchang, "Kangxi muxi kao," *Lishi dang'an* 4(1982): 100–105.

51. *DQHD,* 12.1b.

52. Pamela K. Crossley, "An Introduction to the Qing Foundation Myth," *Late Imperial China* 6, no. 2 (1985): 21. According to Liu Housheng and Chen Siling, "'Qinding Manzhou jishen jitian dianli' pingzhe," *Qingshi yanjiu* 1 (1994): 68, the first time that "Aisin Gioro" appears is in documents dated 1612.

53. Tong Wanlun, "Lun Manzu sanxian nü shenhua de xingcheng yu jiazhi," *Minzu yanjiu* 3 (1992): 33. See Crossley, "*Manzhou* and the Formalization." The myth is reported by E. T. Williams, who observed that the trees in the compound housing the Taimiao were inhabited by a colony of magpies: see his "Worshipping Imperial Ancestors in Peking," *Journal, North China Branch of the Royal Asiatic Society* 70 (1939): 49.

54. See the biography of Sabsu in *ECCP,* 2:630; Chang Jiang and Li Li, *Qing gong shiwei* (Shenyang, 1993), 197–98; Liu Housheng, "Changbaishan yu Manzu de zuxian chongbai," *Qingshi yanjiu* 3 (1996): 93–96, notes that the last emperor, Puyi, also worshiped at the altar of this temple in 1934.

55. J. J. M. de Groot, *The Religious System of China* (Leiden, 1892–1910; reprint, Taipei, 1969), 3:1353–54.

56. The Temple of the Ancestors in Mukden was located in the southeastern corner of the walled city: see fig. 147 on 170–71 in Nancy Shatzman Steinhardt, *Chinese Imperial City Planning* (Honolulu, 1990).

57. On Yongling, see Li Fengmin, Lu Haiying, and Fu Bo, eds., *Xingjing Yongling* (Shenyang, 1996) and de Groot, *Religious System,* 3:1354–56. On Fuling, see Li Fengmin and Lu Haiying, eds., *Shenyang Fuling* (Shenyang, 1996); on Zhaoling, see Li Fengmin and Lu Haiying, eds., *Shengjing Zhaoling* (Shenyang, 1994).

58. The edict, cited by Zhang Jinfan and Guo Chengkang, *Qing ruguan*

qian, 446, is dated Tianzong 9/1/*dingxiu* (March 14, 1635): *Taizong Wen huangdi shilu,* 22.6ab.

59. Zhang Jinfan and Guo Chengkang, *Qing ruguan qian,* 446–47.

60. For information on the compilation, see Ju Deyuan, "Qingchao huangzu zongpu yu huangzu renkou chutan," in *Ming Qing dang'an yu lishi yanjiu: Zhongguo diyi lishi dang'anguan liushi zhounian lunwenji* (Beijing, 1988). On procedures for reporting births to princes and princesses living in the Forbidden City, see Archives 446-5-55/39, memorial from Neiwufu ministers dated QL 7/6/17 (July 18, 1742), which notes that they will submit a listing of all births to the Imperial Genealogy Bureau (Yudieguan) for the next edition of the imperial genealogy.

61. Zhang Jinfan and Guo Chengkang, *Qing ruguan qian,* 447–49.

62. Li Li, "Lun Qingchu yizhang zhi zhi de yanbian," *Liaoning daxue xuebao* 5 (1992): 42–46.

63. Ju Deyuan, "Qingchao huangzu zongpu," 433. According to Lai Huimin, "Qingdai huangzu de jingji shenghuo," Zhongyang yanjiuyuan *Jindaishi yanjiusuo jikan* 24 (1995): 485, only Aisin Gioro living in Peking and Shengjing received stipends.

64. Yan Ziyou, "Qingchao zongshi fengjue zhidu chutan," *Hebei xuekan* 5 (1991): 67–74; Du Jiaji, "Qingdai zongshi." On Manchu rank names see Ya Lu, "Tan Qingdai zongshi fengjue dengji," *Manyu yanjiu* 2 (1990): 112–13.

65. *BQTZ,* 2:976–79; presented in tabular form in Ju Deyuan, "Qingchao huangzu," table 6 on 428–29. A picul is a unit of volume, equivalent to 2.7 bushels. By the late Qing period, these stipends were being discounted and princes actually received only 50 to 60 percent of the stipulated sums.

66. *DQHD,* j. 1, notes that petitions to receive a posthumous name may be submitted on behalf of other princes and highest-ranking officials; on the general elite practice of conferring posthumous names, see de Groot, *Religious System,* 1:175.

67. Brunnert and Hagelstrom, *Political Organization,* nos. 17–27a.

68. Daišan's biography is found in *ECCP,* 214. See also *BQTZ,* 6:3536–39.

69. *BQTZ,* 3:1423–26; *AJZP.*

70. The regulations concerning the imperial nobility are printed in *DQHDSL,* j. 1; see also *BQTZ,* 3:1421. Yan Ziyou, "Qingchao zongshi," 69 makes generalizations about changes in 1653 which cannot be confirmed by the standard primary sources.

71. *AJZP.* This list of failed lines includes those of Hongtaiji's second, third, and eleventh sons, and of Shunzhi's seventh son. Examples include the sixteenth son of the Kangxi emperor, Yinlu, who became the heir to Boggodo, Prince Zhuang; the sixth son of the Yongzheng emperor, Hongyan, who became the heir to Prince Guo, his uncle; Hongli's fourth and sixth sons, and Yongyan's fifth son.

72. *DQHDSL,* j. 2.

73. *DQHDSL,* j. 2.

74. *DQHDSL*, j. 2, section on investiture by inheritance (*xifeng*).

75. *DQHDSL*, j. 2. For memorials concerning imperial scrutiny of the candidates for succession, see Archives 550-6-9-1/779, QL through Tongzhi (hereafter TZ) reigns. See 446-5-55/565, memorial of XF 10/1/6 (February 24, 1871) designating an heir for Prince Ruimin.

76. *DQHDSL*, j. 2, section on inherited titles.

77. Hongli's favor was indeed great. Hongli's sentimental attachments prompted exemption from reduction in rank for Mianlun, his brother's grandson, and Yichun, his first great-grandson. See *DQHDSL*, j. 2.

78. Edict of QL 41/10/4 (November 14, 1776) from *Gaozong Chun huangdi shilu*, 1018:657, cited by Wu Yuqing, *Qingchao bada qinwang* (Beijing, 1993), 3

79. *DQHDSL*, j. 2, edicts dated QL 32 and QL 39. The resulting compilation was the *Zongshi wang gong shizi zhangjing juezhi xici quanbiao*: see preface dated Guangxu reign (hereafter GX) 32/12/8 (January 21, 1907) in GX 33 (1907) edition, which states that the first compilation in the Qianlong reign was revised after 1781 but then untouched until 1898. Between 1898 and 1900, before the Boxer Uprising, the manuscript went through five drafts with checks on the then-complete archival records.

80. The names of the thirty-four *zongshi* ennobled before 1634 is found in Yang and Zhou, *Qingdai baqi*, 39–40; on the political fortunes of this group, see the biographies of these figures in *ECCP*.

81. *Gaozong Chun huangdi shilu*, QL 43/1/9 (February 5, 1778).

82. Ibid.

83. The only remaining title in the first two princely ranks was Prince Qing's. This title, descended from Hongli's seventeenth son, Yonglin (1766–1820), did not have the privilege of perpetual inheritance; it was Yikuang, the heir to the estate in 1830, who regained high princely rank through his activities as an official in the Zongli yamen: *ECCP*, 2:964–65.

84. *Gaozong Chun huangdi shilu*, QL 43/3/2 (March 29, 1778).

85. *DQHDSL*, j. 2, edict dated 1830.

86. Pamela K. Crossley, "Manchu Education," in *Education and Society in Late Imperial China, 1600–1900*, ed. Benjamin A. Elman and Alexander Woodside (Berkeley, 1994), 353–54.

87. *DQHDSL*, j. 2.

88. Here and elsewhere in this discussion I rely on Chang Jiang and Li Li, *Qing gong shiwei*.

89. See Zhaolian, *Xiaoting zalu* (Beijing, 1980), 93–94, 378–79.

90. See the imperial edicts and regulations on this subject in *Qinding gongzhong xianxing zeli* (1856 ms; reprint, Taipei, 1979 [hereafter *QGXZ*]), j. 1, 4, entitled "Gate prohibitions" (*Menjin*); further information can be found in *Qinding Liubu chufen zeli*, 31.1b–2b. See Alison Dray-Novey, "Policing Imperial Peking: The Ch'ing Gendarmerie, 1650–1850" (Ph.D. diss., Harvard University, 1981) for an analysis of the Peking gendarmerie, which shared the

security task; also Qin Guojing, "Qingdai gongting de jingwei zhidu," *Gugong bowuyuan yuankan* 4 (1990): 66–68.

91. Memorial dated QL 38/11/5 (December 18, 1773) [Archives 446-5-55/215]; memorials dated QL 41/12/27 (February 4, 1777) and JQ 24/2 (March 1819), printed as nos. 127 and 245 in Zhongguo diyi lishi dang'anguan, *Yuanmingyuan: Qingdai dang'an shiliao* (Shanghai, 1991), 1:191–201, 471. On security in the Yuanmingyuan, see memorial no. 74, dated QL 41/12/27 (June 28, 1756), published in *Yuanmingyuan*, 1:79–81; memorial dated XF 1/6/4 (July 2, 1851) [446-5-55/540].

92. Cited in Chang Jiang and Li Li, *Qing gong shiwei*, 197; on the whole expedition, see 193–98.

93. Chang Jiang and Li Li, *Qing gong shiwei*, 148–50; ECCP, 580–81.

94. ECCP, 568, 580–81; Chang Jiang and Li Li, *Qing gong shiwei*, 150–51.

95. ECCP, 249–51; L. Petech, *China and Tibet in the Early XVIIIth Century: History of the Establishment of Chinese Protectorate in Tibet* (Leiden, 1972), 213–18; Wu Fengpei and Zeng Guoqing, *Qingdai zhu Zang dachen zhuanlüe* (Xuchang, 1988), 18–24.

96. ECCP, 252–53; Chang Jiang and Li Li, *Qing gong shiwei*, 152–53.

97. ECCP, 253–55.

98. DQHDSL, j. 2.

99. Ju Deyuan, "Qingchao huangzu," table 8 on 1:432. In 1742, 81 percent of the silver and 70.8 percent of the rice payments went to princes of the blood. Archives 550-6-9-2/1579, dated 1838, includes many petitions by *zongshi* and *juelo* asking for grants to pay expenses of deaths and weddings.

100. Archives 550-6-9-1/265, report of the Imperial Clan Court in 1907; the grain allotment refers only to the sums received by first-rank princes. Yan Ziyou, "Qingchao zongshi fengjue," 71.

101. James Lee, Cameron Campbell, and Wang Feng, "The Last Emperors: An Introduction to the Demography of the Qing (1644–1911) Lineage," in *Old and New Methods in Historical Demography*, ed. David S. Rehen and Roger Schofield (Oxford, 1993), fig. 195 on 374. The actual difference in population growth, 1660–1915, is probably much greater: see Ju Deyuan, "Qingchao huangzu zongpu," for Ju's estimates of the actual population in 1915, table 5 on 427.

102. James Lee, Wang Feng, and Cameron Campbell, "Infant and Child Mortality among the Qing Nobility: Implications for Two Types of Positive Check," *Population Studies* 48 (1994): 400. This study used data from the *Da Qing yudie* (hereafter DQYD); "lower nobility" are defined as the *sipin zongshi*, see 404 n.30.

103. *Lettres édifiantes et curieuses concernant l'Asie, l'Afrique et l'Amérique, avec quelques relations nouvelles des missions et des notes géographiques et historiques*, ed. M. L. Aimé-Martin (Paris, 1843), 3:366–67.

104. Archives 550-6-9-1/899, DG 3/5/19, 550-6-9-1/898, JQ 23/11/28. In the latter case, the father of the culprit was punished because he had permitted

his sons to live outside the Tartar city. Archives 550-6-9-3/1839 has an 1839 petition from *zongshi* Heling of the Bordered Red Banner asking for help in collecting a bad debt. Archives 550-6-9-3/2937 contains Manchu-language recommendations for 1838 to fill vacancies.

105. Jin Qizong, "Jingqi de Manzu," *Manzu yanjiu* 4 (1988): 61–62.

106. Li Fengmin, "Jiaqing huangdi she zongshi ying," *Zijincheng* 4 (1988): 46, 37; Ju Deyuan, "Qingchao huangzu," 435. A *jian* is a traditional measure of rooms, defined as the space between pillars.

107. Li Fengmin, "Jiaqing huangdi," 46.

108. Li Fengmin, "Jiaqing huangdi," 46; Archives 550-6-9-1/135 item 3, 550-6-9-1/904, palace memorial dated JQ 20/1/28. The move revealed instances where families seem to have neglected to report all births: see 550-6-9-1/135, item 14, dated JQ 20/1, in which a widowed mother petitions that her infant son and she be permitted to move to Mukden along with her sole surviving adult son; item 15 in the same bundle concerns the addition of two of her grandchildren to the list of family members assigned to move.

109. Joanna Waley-Cohen, *Exile in Mid-Qing China: Banishment to Xinjiang, 1758–1820* (New Haven, 1991), 197. Criminals had their stipends halved: see Lai Huimin, "Qingdai huangzu," 485.

110. Archives 550-6-9-1/900, XF 2/2/6 (March 26, 1852); XF 7/2/7 (March 2, 1857); *ZNXZ*, 1884 ed., 4.1a–4b.

111. See appendix 4 in Yang Xuechen and Zhou Yuanlian, *Qingdai baqi*, 467–71.

112. Minzu wenti wu zhong congshu, Liaoning sheng bianji weiyuan hui, *Manzu shehui lishi diaocha* (Shenyang, 1985), 123–24, 124–29. The data on banner stipends are for 1918, when the bannermen were demobilized.

113. The total number of *zongshi* males is estimated at 16,454 and the total of *juelo* at 11,430 in 1915 by Ju Deyuan, "Qingchao huangzu," table 1 on 422 and table 2 on 423. The numeration of princes is taken from *Zongshi wang gong shi zhi zhang jing jüe zhi xi ci chuanbiao*, 1:24–39; if the slightly lower totals presented in appendix 5, Yang Xuechen and Zhou Yuanlian, *Qingdai baqi*, 472–85 are used, there would be 41 princes in the top six ranks and 127 in the lower twelve ranks.

114. Yinzhen's sixth son, Hongyan, was appointed to succeed his uncle Yinli, Hongli's son Yongcheng became Yintao's successor, and another son, Yongrong, succeeded to the princedom of Yinxi: DQYD, AJZP.

115. Estimates from Zhao Yi, "Mingdai zongshi renkou yu zonglu wenti," *Ming Qing shi yuekan* 11 (1986): 24; figures for the sixteenth century are provided by Zhang Dexin, "Mingdai zongshi renkou fenglu ji qi dui shehui jingji de yingxiang," *Ming Qing shi yuekan* 4 (1988): 25–30.

116. Hucker, *The Traditional Chinese State*, 9. Information on the generational continuity of the Ming princedoms is found in Bo Yang, *Zhongguo diwang huanghou qinwang gongzhu shixi lu* (Peking, 1986), 2:695–708.

117. Zhao Yi, "Mingdai zongshi renkou yu zonglu wenti," *Ming Qing shi yuekan* 11 (1986): 28–29, table 1 estimates that the Ming imperial lineage

numbered over 200,000 by late Wanli times, i.e., the early seventeenth century; Zhang Dexin, "Mingdai zongshi renkou fenglu ji qi dui shehui jingji de yingxiang," *Ming Qing shi yuekan* 4 (1988): 26 estimates that the lineage numbered 80,000 in 1604 and 221,667 in 1644. Ju Deyuan, "Qingchao huang-zu," 428–29, 435, table 8 on 432, 431; Zhang Dexin, "Mingdai zongshi renkou," table on 28.

CHAPTER 3: SIBLING POLITICS

1. Jennifer Holmgren, "Political Organization of Non-Han States in China: The Role of Imperial Princes in Wei, Liao, and Yuan," *Journal of Oriental Studies* 25, no. 1 (1987): 5.

2. Holmgren, "Political Organization," 4.

3. Archives 550-6-9-1/606 has two petitions. The petitioner in the first, dated August 1859, asks for a three-month leave in order to escort the coffin of his relative to Mukden for burial and guarantees that he will return directly after the interment. In the second petition, dated September 1861, Shengbao, a member of the guards, asks for a month's extension of leave to care for the stricken Prince Su. Both petitions confirm that these regulations continued to be observed during the late Qing.

4. On Mongol succession, see John D. Langlois, Jr., introduction to *China Under Mongol Rule*, ed. John D. Langlois, Jr. (Princeton, 1981), 8.

5. Sun Wenliang and Li Zhiting, *Qing Taizong quanzhuan* (Changchun, 1985), 141–42; Wang Sizhi, "Hongtaiji siwei yu chu da beile de maodun," *Lishi dang'an* 3 (1984): 79–84; Liu Shizhe, "Nuerhachi shiqi de zongshi fanzui de chufa," *Beifang wenwu* 1 (1992). 69–76. Although many studies use the Chinese transliteration of Nurgaci's eldest son's name, the Manchu-language documents show that it was "Cuyeng," not "Cuyen": see *uksun i wang gung sai gungge fassan be iletulere ulabun.*

6. Sun Wenliang and Li Zhiting, *Qing Taizong,* 147. Liu Ziyang and Zhang Li, "Manwen laodang 'Taizong chao' zongxi," *Manyu yanjiu* 2 (1995): 60 present Manchu-language material, edited out of the Veritable Records, that shows Hongtaiji behaving as an equal with the other senior *beile* on ritual occasions. Moreover, in 1632 he was still acknowledging the superior status of his elder brothers in family rituals. For a different interpretation from the one offered in the text, see Teng Shaozhen, *Nuerhachi pingzhuan* (Shenyang, 1985), 331–32.

7. On Šurgaci, see *ECCP,* 694; Matsumura Jun, "Syurugachi kō," in *Nairaku Ajia, Nishi Ajia no shakai to bunka,* ed. Mori Masao (Tokyo, 1983), 275–302; and Yan Chongnian, *Nuerhachi zhuan* (Beijing, 1983), 280–82. On Cuyeng see Yan Chongnian's work, 282–84; and *ECCP,* 212–13. On Amin, *ECCP,* 8–9; Wang Sizhi, "Hongtaiji siwei," 81–82. *ECCP,* 562–63; *ECCP,* 935; Wang Sizhi, "Hongtaiji siwei"; Liu Shizhe, "Qing Taizong shiqi."

8. Zhou Yuanlian and Zhao Shiyu, *Huangfu shezheng wang,* 122–32; Lawrence D. Kessler, *K'ang-hsi and the Consolidation of Ch'ing Rule, 1661–1684* (Chicago, 1976), 13; *ECCP,* 443.

9. On Hooge, see *ECCP,* 280–81. On Dorgon, see *ECCP,* 215–19; on Dodo, *ECCP,* 215; on Ajige, *ECCP,* 4–5. On Bayara, see *ECCP,* 598. Robert Oxnam, *Ruling from Horseback: Manchu Politics in the Oboi Regency* (Chicago, 1975), 45–47; *ECCP,* 16–17, 270–71, 590–91.

10. Yang Xuechen and Zhou Yuanlian, *Qingdai baqi wang gong guizu xingshuai shi* (Shenyang, 1986), 207.

11. Kessler, *K'ang-hsi and the Consolidation,* 64–73; *ECCP,* 599–600, 663–64.

12. Oxnam, *Ruling from Horseback,* 175–76, 179, 196; *ECCP,* 591.

13. Cuyeng was executed in 1615; Manggultai and Deggelei were posthumously condemned (1635); Babuhai was executed in 1643; Ajige was forced to commit suicide (1652); Dorgon and Dodo were posthumously disgraced (1651); and Fiyanggu was probably executed (1636). The hereditary transmission of Tangguldai's and Tabai's titles was cut off after the second generation; the descendants of Abai, Laimbu, and Babutai never rose above the lower ranks of the imperial nobility and were cut off from 1681 to 1735: see *uksun i wang gung sai gungge faššan be iletulere ulabun; BQTZ,* 2d ed., 273:19225–28, 19191–203, 19140–59, 19219–20, 19159–74.

14. According to the Qing imperial genealogy Loge, Gebohui, Bombogar, and an unnamed eighth son were childless; Yebushu, Gaose, Changshu, and Taose and their descendants never rose above the eighth rank. See *BQTZXB,* 273:19220–21, 19187–88, 19221–22, 19223–25.

15. Hosoya Yoshio, "Shinchō ni okeru hakki seido no sui-i," *Tōyō gakuhō* 51, no. 1 (1968): 1–43.

16. Yang Xuechen and Zhou Yuanlian, *Qingdai baqi,* 183–84. See also Kessler, *K'ang-hsi and the Consolidation,* 88–89, 103–4. On Yolo, see *ECCP,* 934–35; on Oja, *BQTZ,* 6:3623.

17. *DQYD; AJZP;* see Fuquan's biography in *ECCP,* 251–52. Yang Xuechen and Zhou Yuanlian, *Qingdai baqi,* 190–91. *DQYD; AJZP.*

18. *DQYD;* Guan Jialu and Tong Yonggong, "Cong 'Xiang hongqi dang' kan Yongzheng de zhengchi qiwu," in *Ming Qing dang'an yu lishi yanjiu: Zhongguo diyi lishi dang'anguan liushi zhounian lunwenji* (Beijing, 1988), 2:669–70.

19. Meng Sen, *Qingdai shi* (Taipei, 1962), 86; Feng Erkang, *Yongzheng quan* (Beijing, 1985), ch. 8; Li Xianqing and Zhang Shaoxiang, "Qing Shizong xiaoruo zhuwang qizhu shili de douzheng," in *K'ang Yong Qian sandi pingyi,* ed. Zuo Buqing (Beijing, 1986), 304–15.

20. Pei Huang, *Autocracy at Work: A Study of the Yongzheng Period, 1723–1735* (Bloomington, 1974), 164–84; quote on 184.

21. Silas H. L. Wu, *Passage to Power: K'ang-hsi and His Heir Apparent, 1661–1722* (Cambridge, Mass., 1979). See also Feng Erkang, "Kangxi chao de chuwei zhi zheng he Yinzhen de shengli," *Gugong bowuyuan yuankan* 3 (1981): 12–24; *DQYD; AJZP;* Yang Qijiao, "Kangxi yizhao yu Yongzheng cuanwei," *Qingshi luncong 1992* (Shenyang, 1993), 131–35; Yang Zhen, "Yinti chujun diwei wenti yanjiu," *Qingshi luncong 1992* (Shenyang, 1993), 107–22.

22. For an example of the scholarly speculation that continues to surround Xuanye's will, see Jiang Xiangshun, "Kangxi di wannian lichu zhi mi," *Manzu yanjiu* 1 (1995): 40–45.

23. Bai Xinliang, "Lun Qianlong mimi jianchu," *Gugong bowuyuan yuankan* 2 (1989): 5.

24. Cited in Bai Xinliang, "Lun Qianlong mimi jianchu," 9; also Zhang Yufen, "Qianlong jianchu shimo," *Liaoning shifan daxue xuebao (sheke ban)* 2 (1988): 77–82.

25. On Minning, see Bai Jie and Zhang Ping, "Jiaqing cusi yu Daoguang jiwei zhi zhenxiang," *Qingshi yanjiu* 3 (1994): 97–100; Zhang Yufen, "Daoguang jiwei, xuanchu ji," *Zijincheng* 2 (1994): 40–41. On Yizhu, see *ECCP*, 380; Wang Shuqing, "Qingdai de huangquan douzheng," *Gugong bowuyuan yuankan* 4 (1981): 65–73.

26. See biographies of Cixi, Zaichun, and Zaitian in *ECCP*, 297, 299–300, 730–33. An extended account of the 1875 council that was convened after Zaichun's death is provided in Zuo Shu'e, *Cixi taihou* (Changchun, 1993), 129–32.

27. Li Yanguang and Li Lin, "Qingdai de wangzhuang," *Manzu yanjiu* 1 (1988): 46–51. Chen Yufeng, "Dongbei huangzhuang shengchan guanxi de yanbian," *Shixue jikan* 2 (1988): 27–32. A *qing* of land is equivalent to over sixteen acres.

28. Guan Jialu and Tong Yonggong, "Cong 'Sanxing dang' kan Qingdai Jilin guanzhuang," *Lishi dang'an* 2 (1991): 80–86; Wang Gesheng, "Qingdai dongbei 'wangzhuang,'" *Manzu yanjiu* 1 (1989): 25–27.

29. Yang Xuechen and Zhou Yuanlian, *Qingdai baqi*, 222 citing a 1733 memorial by Fupeng, a fifth generation descendant of Yoto; see 217–21 for background on the distributions.

30. Yang Xuechen and Zhou Yuanlian, *Qingdai baqi*, 242–50; *ECCP*, 925.

31. Yang Xuechen and Zhou Yuanlian, *Qingdai baqi*, 257–59.

32. See Yang Xuechen and Zhou Yuanlian, *Qingdai baqi*, 267, on Xingni's estate. On Dorgon, see Yang Xuechen, "Qingdai de baqi wang gong guizu zhuangyuan," in *Manzushi yanjiu ji*, ed. Wang Zhonghan (Taiyuan, 1988), 146–49; Li Yanguang and Li Lin, "Qingdai de wangzhuang," *Manzu yanjiu* 1 (1988): 46–51; Wang Gesheng, "Qingdai dongbei 'wangzhuang.'"

33. Yang and Zhou, *Qingdai baqi wang gong*, 217–21, 242–50, 269.

34. Here and in the rest of this discussion, ages are calculated in the Western mode unless otherwise specified. Data taken from *DQYD, AJZP*, Tang Bangzhi, *Qing huangshi sipu*, j. 3; *ECCP*, 919.

35. But in 1759 Hongli's sixth son, Yongrong, at age fifteen was made the heir to Yinxi, Prince Zhenjing.

36. Liang Xizhe, *Yongzheng di* (Changchun, 1993), 293; Sun Wenliang, Zhang Jie, and Zheng Quanshui, *Qianlong di* (Changchun, 1993), 571; Guan Wenfa, *Jiaqing di* (Changchun, 1993), 579; Sun Wenfan, Feng Shixx, and Yu Boming, *Daoguang di* (Changchun, 1993), 470; Xu Liting, *Xianfeng, Tongzhi di* (Changchun, 1993), 417–18.

37. *DQHD*, j. 1; *DQHDSL*, 1198.9a–13b. Whereas the assignment of banner companies had occurred immediately upon investiture during the Shunzhi through the Yongzheng reigns (Hosoya Yoshio, "Shinchō ni okeru hakki seido no sui-i"), during the Qianlong reign the assignment seems to have occurred later, when a prince received a separate establishment.

38. Archives 446-5-55/3, memorials dated QL 1/2/16 (March 27, 1736) and QL 1/2/18 (March 29, 1736); 446-5-55/4, memorial dated QL 1/3/14 (April 24, 1736), and 446-5-55/5, memorials dated QL 1/4 and 1/4/16 (May 26, 1736) discuss the *fenfu* of Yinbi, Prince Cheng; Hongzhou, Prince He, and Yinreng's son Duke Hongwei. Archives 446-5-55/123 QL 25/1/25 (March 12, 1760), lists the *fenfeng* of Yongrong, Hongli's sixth son, who was adopted out as an heir to Xuanye's twenty-first son, Yinxi. It also includes information on the *fenfu* of *beile* Mianyi. Archives 446-5-55/242, memorials QL 44/3/24 (May 9, 1779) concern the *fenfu* of Yongxuan, Prince Yi, and Mian'en, Prince Ding. Archives 446-5-55/255, QL 46/10/26 (December 11, 1781), for the *fenfu* of Mianyi, Prince Rong, includes a full list of earlier *fenfu* in 1699 and 1731. Archives 446-5-55/321, QL 60/9/11 (October 23, 1795) gives full lists of *fenfu* for 1667, 1675, 1698, and 1760. Archives 446-5-55/321, QL 60/10/9 (November 19, 1795) presents the *fenfu* for Hongli's eleventh son, Yongxing. Archives 557-5-66-4/3114 has a full set of *fenfu* documents but they could not be GX 13/11/19 (January 2, 1888), which is the date on the accompanying memorial.

39. Yang Xuechen and Zhou Yuanlian, *Qingdai baqi*, 270–82. Li Yanguang and Li Lin, "Qingdai de wangzhuang," 50, also have some partial figures for princely estates in the northeast.

40. Yang Xuechen and Zhou Yuanlian, *Qingdai baqi*, 271. Archives 557-5-66-4/3114, memorial dated QL 60/9/11 (October 23, 1795) from Neiwufu ministers, seeking an imperial decision on what should be given to Yongxing. Archives 446-5-55/321, memorial dated QL 60/10/9 (November 11, 1795) lists all the items, including 200 taels of gold and 50,000 taels of silver, that would be awarded to this son. Archives 467-4-95/2378 lists the court jewels, robes, and other items given to Yongxing's son Mianzong when he married in 1789. Yongxing was at that time still living in the palace.

41. As a memorial of QL 1/4/25 (June 4, 1736) [Archives 446-5-55/5] indicates, the practice of investing funds and earmarking the interest for certain expenditures was used during the Yongzheng reign to provide wedding subsidies for bannermen. Beatrice Bartlett, *Monarchs and Ministers: The Grand Council in Mid-Ch'ing China, 1723–1820* (Berkeley, 1991), 83, notes that the Yongzheng emperor also gave Zhang Tingyu a pawnshop. Archives 446-5-55/436, memorial of DG 1/12/10 (January 2, 1822) reports six pawnshops with a total capital of 340,000 strings managed by the Neiwufu. Archives 557-5-66-4/3114 presents extremely detailed information on all the items provided by different Neiwufu agencies for the 1859 *fenfu* of Yihuan, Prince Chun. See 446-5-55/242, memorial dated QL 44/3/24 (May 9, 1779) on two pawnshops awarded to Yongxuan and one pawnshop awarded to Mian'en; 446-5-55/254 discusses the capitalization and interest income from pawnshops given to Yon-

grong, Prince Chih (1772), Yongxuan, Prince Yi (1779), and Mian'en, Prince Ding (1779); 446-5-55/574, memorials dated XF 11/12/18 (January 17, 1862) and TZ 1/12/4 (January 22, 1863) on current silver balances in accounts of Prince Zhong and Prince Fu. For more on imperial pawnshops, see Wei Qingyuan, *Ming Qing shi bianzhe* (Beijing, 1989), 70–257; Ye Zhiru, "Qianlongshi neifu diandangye gaishu," *Lishi dang'an* 2 (1985): 92–98.

42. Archives 446-5-55/539, memorial dated DG 30/12/29 (January 30, 1851), reports a severe depletion of imperial estates.

43. Archives 446-5-55/255, dated December 11, 1781; according to the memorial submitted by Neiwufu ministers, these presentations followed the precedent set in 1730 when *beile* Yinxi was given a separate establishment. On Prince Gong, see 446-5-55/542, memorial dated XF 2/4/19 (June 6, 1852). Prince Gong also received twelve milk cows as part of his princely estate.

44. Jin Jishui and Zhou Shachen, *Wang fu shenghuo shilu* (Beijing, 1988), 7–8.

45. Discussions of princely estates can be found in Archives 446-5-55/3, QL 1/2 (March 1736), Manchu-language memorial on selecting bondservants to manage the household affairs of two lower-ranking princes; 446-5-55/3114, undated memorial on the retention of the *haha juse* of Yongcheng, the former Prince Lü, to manage the household affairs of his successor; 446-5-55/257, memorial of QL 47/1/22 (March 5, 1782) on interviewing candidates for the manager of Mianyi's household.

46. *Shizong Xian huangdi shilu*, 1:369, Yongzheng reign (hereafter YZ) 2/8/22 (October 8, 1724).

47. The factional element in court politics runs through Wu, *Passage to Power*, also see Lin Qian, "Lun Kangxi shiqi de pengdang ji qi dui Qingchu zhengzhi de yingxiang," *Songliao xuekan* 1 (1984): 33–39. On Songgotu, see *ECCP*, 663–66.

48. Chen Yuan, "Yong, Qian jian feng Tianzhujiao zhi zongshi," *Furen xuezhi* 3, no. 2 (1931): 1–35; *ECCP*, 692–94. Sunu and his family are also described in the *Lettres édifiantes et curieuses concernant l'Asie, l'Afrique et l'Amérique, avec quelques relations nouvelles des missions et des notes géographiques et historiques*, ed. M. L. Aimé-Martin (Paris, 1843), 3:366, 468.

49. Yang Zhen, "Yongzheng shazi bianyi," *Qingshi yanjiu* 3 (1992): 41–46; Luo Lida, "Yongzheng chunian de huangzi jiaodu," *Qingshi yanjiu* 2 (1993): 93–94.

50. *Gaozong Chun huangdi shilu*, 21:376–77, QL 41/1/2 (February 20, 1776). On the favor shown to Yonghuang's descendants, see Guo Chengkang et al., *Qianlong huangdi quanzhuan* (Beijing, 1994), 690, 696. Miande and Mian'en received all the privileges of palace residents, including daily food allowances. Their wedding expenses were paid by the emperor: see memorials dated QL 26/2/7 (March 13, 1761) [Archives 446-5-55/128] planning their weddings.

51. Archives 446-5-55/155, QL 28/10/26 [November 30, 1763]. Yongrong's ritual expenses totaled over 4,000 taels, or over 26 percent of his annual in-

come. Yongrong's mansion was an extremely expensive drain on the imperial purse: see 446-5-55/125, memorial of QL 25/7 (August 1760) on renovations to Yongrong's mansion totaling over 36,000 taels; 446-5-55/259, memorial of QL 47/5/7 (June 17, 1782) on repairs to his front gate totaling over 15,000 taels; and 446-5-55/278, memorial of QL 50/5/17 (June 23, 1785) on repairs to Yongrong's study, totaling almost 500 taels.

52. See the examples provided, dated 1724, in Hosoya, "Shinchō ni okeru hakki seido no sui-i," 33.

53. Archives 557-5-66-4/3114, in the princely household of *beile* Mianhui, son of Yongcheng, Prince Lürui. Although the memorial is undated, it probably took place after Yongcheng's death in 1777 and before Mianhui's own death in 1801.

54. Puren, "Wan Qing fengwang," 41. Archives 446-5-55/567, memorials dated November 22 and December 7, 1860.

55. *ECCP*, 923; Xiaoshi, *Yongxian lu*, 58. Xiaoshi errs in his dating of the change of character on 8: the Kangxi emperor was still alive on KX 61/1/8 (Feb. 22, 1722). Subsequent records, including *Zongshi wang gong shizhi zhangjing juezhi xici quanbiao*, write the *yin* in Yinxiang's name using the non-imperial character.

56. *DQHDSL*, j. 1.

57. Common syllables in the names of Taksi's sons, some linguists argue, suggest Nurgaci instead of "Nurhaci": Taksi's other sons were Murgaci, Surgaci, Yargaci, and Bayara: *AJZP, DQYD*.

58. For detailed discussions of the imperial genealogy, the *Da Qing yudie*, see Ju Deyuan, "Qingchao huangzu." The Kangxi emperor's own sons did not all bear names with the common generational character and *pianpang: DQYD*.

59. *DQHDSL*, j. 1. Xu Ke, *Qing bai leichao* (1917; reprint, Taipei, 1966), 4:66.

60. *DQHD*, j. 1: "names of *zongshi* must avoid the emperor's name and those of his sons [in the radical element of the second character]." The only exceptions made to these rules were in the four instances when Yinzhen and Hongli appointed their brothers and sons to be "adopted" as heirs to great princedoms.

61. The Jingshifang was founded by the Kangxi emperor in 1677. Its other responsibilities included oversight of palace maintenance and security and supervision of eunuchs and maidservants. See Li Pengnian et al., *Qingdai zhongyang guojia jiguan gaishu* (Harbin, 1983), 124. *DQHDSL*, j. 1, records the Qianlong emperor as inquiring into the security of these name lists after finding another imperial agnate with the name he had bestowed on his seventh son.

62. See the discussion concerning the naming of his brother Yongxing, Prince Cheng's grandson Yishou's second son, in *DQHDSL*, j. 1.

63. *DQHDSL*, j. 1.

64. Edict in *DQHDSL*, j. 1. Note however, that the name given by the emperor to Yongrong's grandson (Yiqi) did not share the *pianpang* of "immediate kinsmen."

65. The ruling must have occurred after the birth of Minning's third son in 1829 and before the birth of his fourth son in 1831 because the *pianpang* of the first three sons uses the silk radical that is supplanted by the word radical in the names of subsequent sons born 1831 and after: *DQYD, AJZP.* As a consequence of this alteration in policy, the emperor decreed (1833) that the name of one nephew, a son of his younger brother Mianxin, be changed from Yiyue (with the silk radical) to Yizhi (with the word radical): *DQHDSL,* j. 1.

66. *DQHDSL,* j. 1.

67. Zhaolian, *Xiaoting zalu,* 206–7, 33; Xu Ke, *Qing bai leichao,* 3:88–89.

68. Quote from Veritable Records cited in Li Fengmin, "Jiaqing huangdi," 46.

69. *Renzong Rui huangdi shilu,* 5:840, dated JQ 25/1/2 (February 15, 1802). The rest of the edict stipulates which banner and civil officials may also enter the court on these occasions.

70. Xu Ke, *Qing bai leichao,* 1:46; *Gaozong Chun huangdi shilu,* 2:326–32 for 1739, 19:602–603 for 1795; *Renzong Rui huangdi shilu,* 2:433 for 1803; *Xuanzong Cheng huangdi shilu,* 2:1 for 1824; *Wenzong Xian huangdi shilu,* 2:1 for 1853; *Muzong Yi huangdi shilu,* 5:1 for 1866; *Dezong Jing huangdi shilu,* 2:574 for 1880.

71. The future Kangxi emperor was sent out of the palace for fear that he would contract smallpox: his former residence, made into a temple (the Fuyousi) by his successor, lies just outside the palace walls on the western side, north of the Xihua gate. See Zhang Qixiang, "Qianlong di," *Zijincheng* 9(1981): 22–24.

72. Regulations on selection of wet nurses is found in *DQHDSL,* j. 1218, and *ZNXZ,* Accounting (*kuaiji*) section, 3.46b–47a; recruitment will be discussed in chapter 5. See Tong Yue and Lü Jihong, *Qing gong huangzi* (Shenyang, 1993), 40–41; Xu Ke, *Qing bai leichao,* 1:1–2.

73. The archives include many records of the monthly allowances for the emperor's sons and daughters under the category "Age dengwei dibu."

74. See Liang Qizi, "Ming Qing youfang tianhua cuoshi zhi yanbian," in *Tao Xisheng xiansheng jiu zhi rongqing zhu shou lunwen ji Guoshi yilun* (Taipei, 1987), 239–53 for information on variolation and the Kangxi emperor's role in disseminating the practice; also Xu Kun, "Qingchu huangshi yu douzhen fangzhi," *Gugong bowuyuan yuankan* 3 (1994): 91–96, 90. Liu Yuduo, the man appointed as a smallpox specialist in 1747, was one of two outstanding Muslims who served in the Taiyiyuan: see Yang Daye, "Qing gong Huizu yuyi Zhao Shiying he Liu Yuduo," *Lishi dang'an* 4 (1995): 126. *ZNXZ,* Guangchusi, 4.88a, notes that the gold flowers were no longer given after 1730.

75. Kessler, *K'ang-hsi and the Consolidation,* 57; Wu, *Passage to Power,* 31–32, 36, 44; Yan Chongnian, "Kangxi jiao zi," in *Qing gong yishi,* ed. Zheng Yimei et al. (Beijing, 1985), 10–13, describes the crown prince's studies at the Wuyizhai, constructed on the grounds of the Changchun villa in the western suburbs.

76. Although the term *shangshufang* appears in 1693, when the emperor

appointed the Manchu Xuyuanmeng to it (Wu, *Passage to Power*, 70), the designation of the building described above was the act of the Yongzheng emperor so could not have predated 1723 (Harold L. Kahn, *Monarchy in the Emperor's Eyes: Image and Reality in the Ch'ien-lung Reign* [Cambridge, Mass., 1971], 118; Zhang Naiwei, *Qing gong shuwen* [1937; reprint, Beijing, 1988], 200).

77. For a description of the classroom routine in the early eighteenth century, see Kahn, *Monarchy*, 116–19, Zhang Naiwei, *Qing gong shuwen*, 200–201; Xu Ke, *Qing bai leichao*, 7:15–16. There is also a summary description of the school and its curriculum in Wang Caiyin, *Gugong jiuwen yihua* (Tianjin, 1986), 39–42.

78. Archives 446-5-55/430, memorial dated JQ 25/6/27 (August 5, 1820), transmitting an edict that Miandi, son of Yonglin, attend the Palace School and assigning a eunuch to serve him.

79. See these imperial commentaries on poems in Zhang Naiwei, *Qing gong shuwen*, 206. The Qianlong emperor's recollection of the twenty years that he and his brother Hongzhou spent studying together (Kahn, *Monarchy*, 101) also suggests that they attended the Palace School into their twenties. On Yizhu and Yizong, see Puren, "Wan Qing fengwang fenfu," *Zijincheng* 52 (1989): 40–41.

80. Dong Shouyi, *Gong qinwang Yixin dazhuan* (Shenyang, 1989), 511. Similar anecdotes appear in Tong Yue, *Qing gong huangzi*, 46–47.

81. Edict recorded in Zhang Naiwei, *Qing gong shuwen*, 205.

82. Zhang Naiwei, *Qing gong shuwen*, 330–31.

83. Although the regulations (*Qinding zongrenfu zeli*, 2.4ab, 2.5a) stipulate fifteen *sui*, the archival records show that some princes were fourteen when they married: examples include Qianlong's son Yonglin and his grandson Mianzong (Archives 446-5-55/245). Yixin, Prince Gong was 18 *sui* at his marriage: Dong Shouyi, *Gong qinwang*, 509. These weddings were planned by Neiwufu and paid for by the emperor. See 446-5-55/79, memorial dated QL 15/9/27 (Manchu-language memorial of same date, 446-5-55/80), on Yongzhang's wedding; 467-4-95/2378, documents dated QL 31 (1766) on Yongji's wedding; 446-5-55/245, Manchu-language memorial dated QL 44/11/18 (December 25, 1779) on Mianhui's wedding; 446-5-55/244, memorial of QL 44/7/10 (August 21, 1779) on Mianyi's wedding.

84. Quote from Zhang Naiwei, *Qing gong shuwen*, 144; regulations on princely stipends are recorded in *Zongguan neiwufu xianxing tiaoli Guangchusi* (Taipei, 1972), 4.98; ZNXZ, Guangchusi, 4.86b. Actual payments are found in monthly silver accounts in Archives 467-4-85/294 (XF 3), 467-4-85/303 (TZ 1). Puren, "Wan Qing fengwang," 4, also notes the significant reduction of princely incomes in the middle of the nineteenth century.

85. Archives 467-4-85/2103, dated 1795. Yixin, Prince Gong, and Yihuan, Prince Chun, both set up separate households when they were nineteen: Dong Shouyi, *Gong qinwang*, 510; Zhang Qixiang, "Qianlong di," *Zijincheng*, no. 9 (1981): 24. On the expense of repairing and renovating princely mansions, see 446-5-55/145, memorial of QL 28/12/26 (January 28, 1764), on repairs total-

ing almost 29,000 taels on Yongcheng's mansion, and 446-5-55/424, memorial of JQ 24/2/16 (March 11, 1819), on renovations to Mianxin's house totaling almost 1,000 taels.

86. *Gaozong Chun huangdi shilu*, 13:967, QL 15/3/15 (April 21, 1750) on Yonghuang's death. Archives 446-5-55/244, QL 44/8/23 (October 2, 1779) on Miande's *fenfu*; 446-5-55/243, QL 44/5/3 (June 16, 1779) and 446-5-55/244, QL 44/8/23 (October 2, 1779) on Mian'en's *fenfu*. Archives 446-5-55/254, QL 46/9/28 (November 13, 1781) has a memorial directing Yichun to move out of the Shoukang palace shortly before his wedding. Archives 446-5-55/123, QL 25/3/29 (May 14, 1760) has a memorial on Yongzhang's move out of the inner court into the Agesuo; this third son of Hongli died later that year.

87. Archives 446-5-55/433, DG 1/4/18 (May 18, 1821).

88. Archives 446-5-55/214, memorial dated QL 38/9/29 (November 13, 1773) lists three sons and a grandson, Miande, as denizens of the "inner court" and asks if court robes for the spring and summer rites should be made for these princes; the emperor ordered that they be made.

89. Archives 446-5-55/343; *Qinding wang gong chufen zeli*, 3.4b–5a stipulates that a fine of six-months' stipend will be meted out to princes who without excuse fail to appear at the Taimiao when they are assigned to accompany the emperor at a sacrifice. On the purge of the Heshen faction, see Li Shangying, "Jiaqing qinzheng," *Gugong bowuyuan yuankan* 2 (1992): 40–42. Delinquency in ritual duties was a problem of long standing: see 446-5-55/321, memorial dated QL 13/5/26 (June 1, 1748), ordering the Imperial Clan Court to make recommendations on how to deal with the princes who excused themselves from participation in the sacrifice during the summer solstice.

90. Assignment to guard the ancestral tombs could also be used as punishment: Yinti, the fourteenth son of the Kangxi emperor, was sent by his brother the emperor to guard Jingling in 1724. Yinti's biography is in *ECCP*, 930–31; *DQYD*.

91. These duties are spelled out in the *DQHD*, j. 1. On the Qing tomb administration, see J. J. M. de Groot, *The Religious System of China* (1892–1910; reprint, Taipei, 1969), 3:1339; and 549-4-93/465, 155-4-16-2/155.

92. Ritual assignments for the grand sacrifice, 1768–74 are listed in Archives 155-4-16-3/2949. Archives 446-5-55/219 has Manchu-language memorials from the Zhangyisi (Department of Ceremonial) dated QL 39/12/25, which list ritual assignments (January 26, 1775). See also 446-5-55/337, JQ 5/3/6 (March 30, 1800); 550-6-9-1/886, memorial of DG 13/8/6 (October 26, 1833) selecting a first-degree prince to escort Empress Xiaozhen's coffin to the tombs. Archives 550-6-9-1/886, memorial of DG 19/7/4 (August 12, 1839) selects princes to sacrifice at the Jingling on Empress Xiaoyi's deathday. Archives 550-6-9-1/886, memorial dated DG 23/10/24 (December 15, 1843) provides a replacement for a sick prince assigned to sacrifice at the tombs. Archives 446-5-55/613, memorial dated GX 1/9/24 (October 25, 1875) assigns princes to pour libations at certain tombs of princes and princess along the route of the funeral cortege of the Tongzhi emperor, to Dongling. The above are a sampling

of the issues treated in these memorials. Xu Ke, *Qing bai leichao*, 1:12 cites the Kangxi emperor's ordering his son to represent him in visiting the home of a deceased high minister to pour libations and wail.

93. Xibao's biography is in *ECCP*, 264–65; Yang Xuechen and Zhou Yuanlian, *Qingdai baqi*, 267–68.

94. H. S. Brunnert and V. V. Hagelstrom, *Present-Day Political Organization of China*, trans. A. Beltchenko and E. E. Moran (Foochow, 1911), no. 99.3; Jonathan Spence, *Ts'ao Yin and the Kangxi Emperor: Bondservant and Master* (New Haven, 1966), 49–50.

95. Alison Dray-Novey, "Policing Imperial Peking: The Qing Gendarmerie, 1650–1850" (Ph.D. diss., Harvard University, 1981), 51–56.

96. *BQTZ*, j. 107–8; *BQTZXB*, j. 322. Zhongguo diyi lishi dang'anguan, "Qingmo bufen baqi dutong lüli," *Lishi dang'an* 4 (1989): 36–45.

97. *ECCP*, 377–78; Qian Shipu, *Qingji zhongyao zhiguan*, 7, 8; on the Zhejiang campaign to retake Ningpo, see Frederic Wakeman, Jr., "The Canton Trade and the Opium War," in *Cambridge History of China: Late Ch'ing 1800–1911, Part 1*, ed. John K. Fairbank (Cambridge, 1978), 204–5.

98. Susan Naquin, *Millenarian Rebellion in China: The Eight Trigrams Uprising of 1813* (New Haven, 1976), 179–83. On Prince Hui, see *ECCP*, 968.

99. See Du Jiaji, "Dui Qingdai yizheng wang dachen huiyi de moxie kaocha," *Qingshi luncong* 7 (1986): 115–24.

100. *DQYD*; Silas H. L. Wu, *Communication and Imperial Control in China: Evolution of the Palace Memorial System, 1693–1735* (Cambridge, Mass., 1970), 69, 79, 80, 84–85. See the emperor's eulogy, 90.

101. *DQYD*; Tang Bangzhi, *Qing huangshi sipu* (Taipei, 1967), 158–59; *ECCP*, 962–63, 963–64.

102. Mary C. Wright, *The Last Stand of Chinese Conservatism: The T'ung-chih Restoration, 1862–1874* (Stanford, 1957), 50; Qian Shifu, *Qingji zhongyao zhiguan nianbiao* (Beijing, 1977), 44–51; Dong Shouyi, *Gong qinwang Yixin dazhuan* (Shenyang, 1989); Zhongguo diyi lishi dang'anguan, *Yuanmingyuan: Qingdai dang'an shiliao* (Shanghai, 1991), no. 428–430, 744–45, on Prince Gong's threatened disgrace, September 9–10, 1874.

103. Ping-ti Ho, *The Ladder of Success in Imperial China: Aspects of Social Mobility, 1368–1911* (New York, 1962), 22–24.

104. *ECCP*, 130–34; Qian Shipu, *Qingji zhongyao zhiguan*, 9–12.

105. *ECCP*, 962.

106. *ECCP*, 387–89.

107. *ECCP*, 666–69; Qian Shipu, *Qingji zhongyao zhiguan*, 17. On the examination, see *DQHD*, j. 1, under *kaofeng*.

108. Yang Xuechen and Zhou Yuanlian, *Qingdai baqi*, 260.

109. Information on the Grand Secretariat is obtained from Qian Shipu, *Qingji zhongyao zhiguan*, 7–11, 13, 25–36.

110. In addition Zaifeng, Prince Chun, and third-degree prince Youlang served short terms in the last few years of Qing rule. Qian Shifu, *Qingdai*

zhiguan nianbiao, 1:2–132 for grand secretaries, 1:135–156 for Grand Council members.

111. Qian Shifu, *Qingdai zhiguan nianbiao,* 1:158–332. The concentration of Aisin Gioro in the top posts increased after administrative reforms in 1901.

112. Wu Fengpei and Zeng Guoqing, eds., *Qingdai zhu Zang dachen zhuanlüe* (Lhasa, 1988); Zahiruddin Ahmad, *Sino-Tibetan Relations in the Seventeenth Century* (Rome, 1970), 172, 174, 181.

113. Xiaoshi, *Yongxian lu* (Beijing, 1959), YZ 1/2/8 (March 14, 1723); Zhao Yuntian, *Qingdai Menggu zheng jiao zhidu* (Beijing, 1989), 278–79; Wang Jiapeng, "Minzu tuanjie de lishi huajuan—liushi Banchan huaxiang," *Zijincheng* 2 (1990): 11–13.

114. Frederic Wakeman, Jr., *The Great Enterprise* (Berkeley, 1985), 1: 335–37.

CHAPTER 4: IMPERIAL WOMEN

1. A list of the biographical studies should include Sue Fawn Chung, "The Much Maligned Empress Dowager: A Revisionist Study of the Empress Dowager Tz'u-Hsi in the Period 1898 to 1900" (Ph.D. diss., University of California, Berkeley, 1975); Zuo Shu'e, *Cixi taihou* (Changchun, 1993); Yu Bingkun et al., *Xitaihou* (Beijing, 1985); Bao Chengguan, *Yixin Cixi zhengzheng ji* (Changchun, 1980).

2. Yu Bingkun, *Xitaihou,* 56–61; Zhang Shiyun, "Yipin yu ximi wen," *Lishi dang'an* 1 (1994): 131–32; *AJZP.*

3. See Yixin's biography, *ECCP,* 380–84; Luke Kwong, *A Mosaic of the Hundred Days: Personalities, Politics, and Ideas of 1898* (Cambridge, Mass., 1984).

4. Jennifer Holmgren, "Imperial Marriage in the Native Chinese and Non-Han State, Han to Ming," in *Marriage and Inequality in Chinese Society,* ed. Rubie S. Watson and Patricia B. Ebrey (Berkeley, 1991), 68. See also Jennifer Holmgren, "A Question of Strength: Military Capability and Princess-Bestowal in Imperial China's Foreign Relations (Han to Ch'ing)," *Monumenta Serica* 39 (1990–91): 31–85.

5. Holmgren, "Imperial Marriage," 86.

6. See Evelyn S. Rawski, "Qing Imperial Marriage and Problems of Rulership," in *Marriage and Inequality,* ed. Rubie S. Watson and Patricia B. Ebrey (Berkeley, 1991), 170–203, on how the Qing dealt with the potential problem of powerful maternal affines.

7. Wang Peihuan, *Qing gong hou fei* (Shenyang, 1993), 129, citing the *Jianzhou wenxian lu;* also see 130–33 on the hunt, 133–34 on ice-skating.

8. Kaye Soon Im, "The Rise and Decline of the Eight Banner Garrisons in the Qing Period (1644–1911): A Study of the Kuang-chou, Hang-chou, and Ching-chou Garrisons" (Ph.D. diss., University of Illinois, 1981); Zhang Wei, "Qingdai Manzu funü de shenghuo," *Zhongguo dianji yu wenhua* 3 (1994):

76. For examples of the political influence of Jurchen wives, see Wang Dong-fang, "Zaoqi Manzu funü zai jiating zhong de diwei," *Liaoning daxue xuebao* 5 (1994): 67; Laurel Kendall, *Shamans, Housewives, and Other Restless Spirits* (Honolulu, 1985).

9. Zhaolian, *Xiaoting xulu* (Beijing, 1980), 515. See also Wang Laiyin, "Hexiao gongju—Qianlong di de zhangshang mingzhu," in *Qing gong jie mi*, ed. Zheng Yimei et al. (Hong Kong, 1987), 112–15.

10. Histories of Chinggis and Khubilai Khan record the personal names of their wives: see Paul Ratchnevsky, *Genghis Khan: His Life and Legacy*, trans. Thomas Haining (Oxford, 1991), 31, 67; Morris Rossabi, *Khubilai Khan: His Life and Times* (Berkeley, 1988), 225–26. See *ECCP*, 598, 300, 302, 304.

11. For a description of twentieth-century Mongol practices, see Lawrence Krader, *Social Organization of the Mongol-Turkic Pastoral Nomads* (The Hague, 1963). Ratchnevsky, *Genghis Khan*, 125–26 discusses the influence of the mother on Mongol succession in the Chinggisid dynasty. On the Jin dynasty Jurchen, see Jing-shen Tao, *The Jurchen in Twelfth-Century China: A Study of Sinicization* (Seattle, 1976), 12–13; on pre-1644 Manchu laws, see Zhang Jinfan and Guo Chengkang, *Qing ruguan qian guojia falü zhidu shi* (Shenyang, 1988), 490–96.

12. Henry Serruys, "Remains of Mongol Customs in China during the Early Ming Period," *Monumenta Serica* 16(1957): 149–50.

13. Isaac Taylor Headland, *Court Life in China: The Capital, Its Officials, and People* (New York, 1909), 205; *AJZP*.

14. Rawski, "Qing Imperial Marriage," 181–82 incorrectly identifies the memorialist as Li rather than Ji Kaisheng. In the modern edition of the *DQSL* the passages are to be found in *Shizu Zhang huangdi shilu*, 3:725.

15. Ding Yizhuang, "Shilun Qingdai de Man Han tonghun," paper presented at the Association of Asian Studies Annual Meeting, Chicago, April 14, 1997. A ban on marriages between Mongol women and "inner-realm" persons (i.e., Han Chinese) is found in the *Menggu lüli*: see Zhao Yuntian, "'Menggu lüli' he 'Lifanyuan zeli,'" *Qingshi yanjiu* 3 (1995): 106.

16. Du Jiaji, "Qianlong zhi nü jia Kongfu ji xiangguan wenti zhi kaobian," *Lishi dang'an* 3 (1992): 98–101.

17. Rawski, "Qing Imperial Marriage," table 5.3 on 188.

18. Wang Shuqing, "Qingdai hou fei zhidu zhong de jige wenti," *Gugong bowuyuan yuankan* 1 (1980): 38; Jiang Xiangshun, "Qing Taizong de Chungde wu gong hou fei ji qita," *Gugong bowuyuan yuankan* 4 (1987): 67–71. According to Jiang, the five women selected for titles were all Mongols, part of the marriage exchanges that brought important allies into the Manchu camp.

19. The data cited throughout this discussion of titles come from the *DQYD* and *AJZP*.

20. *DQYD*; on the burials, see Yu Shanpu, *Qing Dongling da guan* (Shijiazhuang, 1985), 51. True polygyny was practiced by the Khitan rulers: see Jennifer Holmgren, "Marriage, Kinship, and Succession under the Ch'i-tan Rulers of the Liao Dynasty," *T'oung Pao* 72 (1986): 44–91.

21. The investiture of empresses and consorts is described by Wang Pei-huan, *Qing gong hou fei*, ch. 3; Rawski, "Qing Imperial Marriage," 191–93.

22. See Rawski, "Qing Imperial Marriage," 185–93. For Ming strategies for reducing the power of matrilateral kinsmen, see E. Soullière, "The Imperial Marriages of the Ming Dynasty," *Papers on Far Eastern History* 37 (1988): 1–30.

23. Rawski, "Qing Imperial Marriage"; Robbins Burling, *The Passage to Power: Studies in Political Succession* (New York, 1974), 112.

24. Rubie S. Watson, "Afterword: Marriage and Gender Inequality," in *Marriage and Inequality in Chinese Society*, ed. Rubie S. Watson and Patricia B. Ebrey (Berkeley, 1991), 349.

25. Archives 155-4-16-2/1599; these women were probably widows of the Kangxi emperor.

26. Yu Shanpu, "Daoguang hou fei yuannü duo," *Zijincheng* 1 (1994): 18–20. Yu bases his study on archival documents and has uncovered data absent from the genealogies.

27. A Lan *changzai* appears in the palace distribution list for 1734 (Archives 155-4-16-2/1599) among the names of the widows of the Kangxi emperor; in 1751 and 1756, a Lan *daying* appears on the list of consorts for the Qianlong emperor (467-4-85/1254, 1251) who seems to have been promoted to *guiren* (1767 list, 155-4-16-1/642). Yu Bingkun, "Cixi rugong shijian, shenfen he fenghao," in *Xitaihou*, by Yu Bingkun et al. (Beijing, 1985), 56–58.

28. Yu Bingkun, "Cixi rugong," 58; Wan Yi, "Cong Cixi shengzi kan Qing gong lou xi," in *Xitaihou*, 63.

29. Wang Guangyao, "Qingdai hou fei shengqin yu Qing gong kefang," *Zijincheng* 2 (1991): 14.

30. *Qinding gongzhong xianxing zeli chüan* 1, QL 6/12/7 [January 13, 1742].

31. Edict dated XF 6/4/23 (May 26, 1856) in *Qinding gongzhong xianxing zeli*, Guangxu ed., 1.111ab.

32. Table 5.1 on 172 in Rawski, "Qing Imperial Marriage"; the table errs in assigning C2 as the rank of Zaichun's mother; it should be C3. Also see 186–87.

33. Wang Peihuan, *Qing gong hou fei*, 140–43; Wan Yi, "Cong Cixi shengzi," 63–70.

34. See Rawski, "Qing Imperial Marriage," table 4.3 on 188.

35. Zhou Yuanlian and Zhao Shiyu, *Huangfu shezheng wang Doergun quanzhuan* (Changchun, 1986), 44–45.

36. Sechin Jagchid, "Mongolian-Manchu Intermarriage in the Ch'ing Period," *Zentralasiatische Studien* 19 (1986): 70; Dong Baocai and Zhang Xiaochang, "Boerjijite Xiaozhuang—Qing jiechu nü zhengchi jia," *Zhongyang minzu xueyuan xuebao* 3 (1989): 8–11; Li Hongbin, "Xiaozhuang Wen huanghou," in *Qingdai di wang hou fei zhuan*, Manxue yanjiu hui (Peking, 1989), 1:70–74; Shang Hongkui, "Qing 'Xiaozhuang Wen huanghou' xiaoji (Qingshi zhaji yize)," *Qingshi luncong* 2 (1980): 275–77.

37. The historical parallels extend to accusations that Xiaozhuang killed her

son's favorite concubine: see Zhang Xiaohu, "Dong'e fei siyin xintan," *Qingshi yanjiu tongxun* 3 (1990): 25–32.

38. For a review of the debate, see Zhou Yuanlian and Zhao Shiyu, *Huangfu shezheng wang,* 424–33. Other views are expressed by Li Hongbin, "Xiaozhuang Wen huanghou," 71–72, Liu Lu, "Lun Hou Jin yu Qingchu huangshi hunyin duixiang de yanbian," *Qingshi yanjiu* 3 (1992): 17–23, and the article by Dong Baocai and Zhang Xiaochang, "Boerjijite Xiaozhuang," 9.

39. Howard L. Boorman and Richard C. Howard, eds., *Biographical Dictionary of Republican China* (New York, 1970), 3:81–82.

40. Wang Daocheng, "Cixi de jiazu, jiating he rugong zhi chu de shenfen," *Qingshi yenjiuji* 3 (1984): 187–220.

41. On the Tong lineage, see chapter 2. Also *ECCP*, 794–96.

42. *ECCP*, 552–54; Hou Shouchang, "Kangxi muxi kao," *Lishi dang'an* 4 (1982): 100–105.

43. Archives 446-5-55/7, memorial dated QL 1/9/12 [October 16, 1736]. See Zhang Naiwei, *Qing gong shuwen,* 841–60, 895–922.

44. Archives 446-5-55/430, memorial dated JQ 25/8/6 [September 12, 1820]; see also Zhang Naiwei, *Qing gong shuwen,* 925–37.

45. Archives 155-4-16-4/4432, monthly accounts dated QL 39 to QL 40 (1774–75); 467-4-85/1254, which includes a list of residents of the Shoukang palace ca. 1751: among them were the widow of Yongzheng's third son Hongshi (d. 1735). Even granddaughters were brought to live in the Forbidden City: see a Manchu-language memorial of QL 47/2 (March 1782) [446-5-55/257] which has Hongli's ninth daughter's daughter moving in after her mother's death.

46. Silas H. L. Wu, *Passage to Power: K'ang-hsi and His Heir Apparent, 1661–1722* (Cambridge, Mass., 1979), 52.

47. Harold L. Kahn, *Monarchy in the Emperor's Eyes: Image and Reality in the Ch'ien-lung Reign* (Cambridge, Mass., 1971), 89; see also Evelyn S. Rawski, "The Creation of an Emperor in Eighteenth-Century China," in *Harmony and Counterpoint: Ritual Music in Chinese Context,* ed. Bell Yung, Evelyn S. Rawski, and Rubie S. Watson (Stanford, 1996), 157–61.

48. One of the concubines, Dunyi *huangguifei,* produced a daughter, but the child died within a month of her birth: *DQYD*. Hongli built a special tomb located alongside the Jingling for these two women: see Xu Guangyuan, "Jingling shuang fei yuanqin," *Zijincheng* 42 (1987): 37.

49. *Wenzong Xian huangdi shilu,* XF 5/7/1 (August 13, 1855), 42:896; j. 51 for 1852, j. 171 for August 1855; also Zhang Naiwei, *Qing gong shuwen,* 408.

50. Yu Shanpu, *Qing Dongling daguan,* 80.

51. Taken from the Veritable Records and cited in Zhang Naiwei, *Qing gong shuwen,* 853–54. Despite the filial rhetoric, these widows were left behind when the court fled during the Allied Expeditionary Force's occupation after the Boxer Uprising, 1900: E. T. Williams, "Worshipping Imperial Ancestors in Peking," *Journal, North China Branch of the Royal Asiatic Society* 70 (1939): 48.

52. See memorials dated QL 1/4/11 (May 21, 1736) [Archives 446-5-55/5].

53. *DQYD; AJZP.* The next-of-kin of the concubines were required to submit memorials to "give thanks for imperial grace" for the promotions: two Manchu-language examples, dated JQ 1/1/5 (February 13, 1796), can be found in Archives 446-5-55/323. One of them concerns the promotion of Yongyan's mother to the rank of empress.

54. Ts'ui-jung Liu, "The Demography of Two Chinese Clans in Hsiao-shan, Chekiang, 1650–1850," in *Family and Population in East Asian History,* ed. Susan B. Hanley and Arthur P. Wolf (Stanford, 1985), 16.

55. Tang Bangzhi, *Qing huangshi sipu.* See also the list compiled by Wang Peihuan, *Qing gong hou fei,* 330–53 of all imperial empresses and consorts: since Wang draws on archival materials elsewhere in his book it is puzzling that his list omits low-ranking consorts, especially those of the Qianlong (thirteen omissions), Daoguang (two omissions), and Xianfeng emperors (two omissions).

56. The information that is currently available to me does not permit complete matching of burial names with the names obtained from the *DQYD, AJZP,* and archival documents, for reasons that are outlined in the discussion that follows.

57. Chen Baorong, *Qing xiling congheng* (Shijiazhuang, 1987), 113; twenty-eight of the consorts in the consorts' tomb do not appear in the genealogy, while ten of the lower-ranking consorts listed in the genealogy do not appear in the burial lists. Even if we assume a perfect identity between these ten consorts and the burial lists, we would emerge with a total of fifty-eight and perhaps sixty consorts.

58. A fifteenth fifth-ranking consort of the Jiaqing emperor is listed in the published imperial genealogy; the archives list a sixth-ranking consort for the Daoguang emperor who is absent from the genealogies and the burial lists. A similar conclusion for the Qianlong emperor's consorts is drawn by Bai Xinliang, *Qianlong zhuan* (Shenyang, 1990), 490, where he states that Hongli had at least ten consorts before his accession, and could have had "no less" than 40 consorts.

59. E. Fonssagrives, *Si-ling: Etudes sur les tombeaux de l'ouest de la dynastie des Ts'ing* (Paris, 1907), 35–38, 56–71, 105–8.

60. See Rubie Watson, "Wives, Concubines, and Maids," 251 n.11, also Rubie Watson, "Afterword," 356–57.

61. Yu Shanpu, *Qing Dongling daguan* (Shijiazhuang, 1985), 167.

62. See edict dated DG 2/1/12 [February 3, 1822], *Qinding gongzhong xianxing zeli* 1.78b–79a: "Henceforth when emperor's sons and grandsons marry, the father of the bride when preparing the dowry should not be extravagant but frugal, in keeping with our old and simple Manchu customs. In future, present the list of dowry items for inspection. If there are luxurious or extravagant items which I find unacceptable, they will be returned and there will be punishments. Have this edict recorded by the ministers of the Imperial Household Department. Hand over this decree after the betrothal (*zhi hun*) to the bride's father to read and obey."

63. Li Pengnian, "Guangxu de dahun beiban haoyong gaishu," *Gugong bowuyuan yuan k'an* 2 (1983): 83–84. The archival materials concerning this wedding are described in Xin Hao, "Guangxu dahun dianli dang'an," *Lishi dang'an* 2 (1985): 132–33.

64. Archives 467-4-85/2104 and 2105.

65. Rong *fei*, who was childless, was the real person who was transformed into the mythic "Fragrant concubine" (Xiang *fei*), the Qianlong emperor's great love. For a close study of the evolution of this legend, see James A. Millward, "A Uyghur Muslim in Qianlong's Court: The Meanings of the Fragrant Concubine," *Journal of Asian Studies* 53, no. 2 (1994): 427–58.

66. This statement is based on a counting of the items in six of the fourteen death inventories found in Archives 467-4-85/2104 and 2105.

67. Fang *taifei* died JQ 6/8/30 [October 7, 1801]; her death inventory is in Archives 467-4-85/2104.

68. Dowry lists in Archives 467-4-85/2102 include the dowry for the 1770 marriage of the Qianlong emperor's seventh daughter, Princess Hejing, to Lhawangdorji, a Khalkha Mongol; the 1792 marriage of the emperor's granddaughter (by his sixth son) to an Outer Mongol prince; and the 1797 marriage of his granddaughter (by his eleventh son) to a Khorchin Mongol noble. Archives 467-4-85/1246 includes the dowry list of the 1786 marriage of another granddaughter (by his eleventh son) to Aokhan Mongol prince Dewedorji. Like the death inventories, most of the dowry lists have slips of paper indicating where each item in the dowry will be obtained, or naming the Neiwufu subagency responsible for obtaining the item.

69. Zhuang *fei*'s death inventory is in Archives 467-4-85/2104.

70. Holmgren, "Imperial Marriage," 67, on Chinese dynastic patterns.

71. The second rank was also bestowed on the daughter of Kong Youde, a Ming general who was rewarded for surrendering to the Qing in Liaoyang: see Liu Lu, "Qingchao Hanzu gongju—Kong Sizhen," in *Qing gong jie mi*, ed. Zheng Yimei et al. (Hong Kong, 1987), 109–11.

72. On the system of titles and ranks, see Zhang Jinfan and Guo Chengkang, *Qing ruguan qian*, 448–49; H. S. Brunnert and V. V. Hagelstrom, *Present-Day Political Organization of China*, trans. A. Beltchenko and E. E. Moran (Foochow, 1911), nos. 14, 35. On the exceptions to the general rules to the bestowal of first-rank titles, see Wang Shuqing, "Qingdai gongzhu," *Gugong bowuyuan yuankan* 3 (1982): 31–33; also Archives 467-4-85/2102, on the 1797 marriage of Prince Cheng's fifth daughter. Neiwufu officials managing the households of princes who neglected to obtain imperial permission before betrothing their daughters were punished: see memorial dated QL 50/2/5 (March 15, 1785) [446-5-55/279].

73. *DQHDSL*, j. 1; see the edicts of QL 46 (1881), JQ 12 (1807), and DG 11 (1831) in j. 2. The contrasting Sung policy is described in John W. Chaffee, "The Marriage of Sung Imperial Clanswomen," in *Marriage and Inequality*, ed. Rubie S. Watson and Patricia B. Ebrey (Berkeley, 1991), 133–69. Statistics

derived from listing of princesses in Bo Yang, *Zhongguo di wang huanghou qinwang gongju shixi lu* (Taipei, 1986), 2:827–37.

74. Holmgren, "A Question of Strength."

75. *Qinding zongrenfu zeli*, 2.7ab; Qianlong's 1751 edict, 2.6a. See also *Qinding Lifanbu zeli*, 25.10b.

76. The regulations are found in *Qinding zongrenfu zeli*, 2.1ab, *Qinding Lifanbu zeli*, 25.2a–3a. See Jagchid, "Mongolian-Manchu Intermarriage," 82.

77. Hua Li, "Qingdai de Man-Meng lianyin," *Minzu yanjiu*, no. 2 (1983): 52. A memorial dated QL 7/7/29 (August 29, 1742) [Archives 446-5-55/39] announces five betrothals, two of which are to sons of *efu*. The findings of table 8 contradict somewhat those of Jennifer Holmgren, who used information in the *Qingshi gao* to describe a waning of marriage exchanges between the emperor and the Mongols after 1683; see her "A Question of Strength," 70–71.

78. ZNXZ, 1937 ed., Zhangyisi, j. 4.48a–58b covers the marriages of princesses of lower rank. The archival documents are full of the details concerning these marriage rituals: Archives 446-5-55/39, memorial dated QL 7/7/29 (August 29, 1742), announces five betrothals and 467-4-85/2378, dated JQ 7/10/17 (November 12, 1802) on the wedding banquet for Princess Zhuangjing, to be hosted by the empress and held in the Chuxiu palace. Other arrangements for specific marriages are found in 467-4-85/2102 and 467-4-85/1246. Archives 557-5-66-4/3778 has a document dated QL 60/3/15 (May 3, 1795) reporting the arrangements for the marriage of Hongli's granddaughter (by his eleventh son). Archives 446-5-55/33, a memorial from Neiwufu ministers dated QL 6/6/8 (July 20, 1741) concerns the marriage of a granddaughter of the Kangxi emperor and shows how the court split the wedding costs with her father, Prince Dun.

79. See the Neiwufu lists in Archives 467-4-85/2102, dating from the eighteenth and early nineteenth centuries; a section entitled "Matters relating to the marriages of princesses," ZNXZ, 1937 ed., Zhangyisi, 3.40a–58b. Dowries are also discussed in some detail in Wan Yi, "Hexiao gongju de zhuanglian," in *Qing gong jie mi*, 119–24. Fathers of daughters holding the lowest ranks had to foot the bill for betrothal feasts and the wedding procession: see memorial dated QL 7/7/11 (August 11, 1742) [446-5-55/39] concerning the marriage of the daughter of a *zongshi* or unranked male descendant of the main line. In some cases, the prince would be asked to supply the maids and dependent households assigned to the princess: see memorials dated QL 7/11/9 (December 5, 1742) [446-5-55/41], QL 7/7/29 (August 29, 1742) [446-5-55/39].

80. See the regulations differentiating dowries and marriage rites of princesses marrying *waifan*, in ZNXZ, 1937 ed., Zhangyisi, 4.53b–58b. A summary of the precedents for grants to lower-rank princesses is provided in a memorial dated QL 40/12/6 (January 26, 1776) [Archives 446-5-55/224].

81. Wang Shuqing, "Qingdai gongzhu," 36. During the nineteenth century, the cost of the dowry was reduced by the use of less gold and silver or of silver rather than gold: see ZNXZ, 1937 ed., Zhangyisi, 3.47a.

82. Dowry lists for the nineteenth century include those for Princesses Shou'en (1844, Archives 557-5-66-4/3778), Shouzhuang (1863, 467-4-85/2380), and Rong'an (1873, 467-4-85/2380).

83. Archives 446-5-55/5, memorial dated QL 1/5/10 (June 18, 1736), reporting an inventory of that year. Although the livestock and dependents may have increased in the almost seventy years that had elapsed since the princess married, the estates were most likely precisely those granted to her in 1667.

84. These rules were relaxed in 1841; see *DQHDSL*, j. 325, which presents the precedents in the evolving regulations governing marriages of princesses; Jagchid, "Mongolian-Manchu Intermarriage," 84. Archival documents outlining the rites for the marriages of princesses Hejing, Shou'an, Shouxi, Shouzhuang, and lower-ranking princesses are found in Archives 467-4-85/2102. The 1863 marriage of Princess Shouxi is also covered in 467-4-85/2102 and 467-4-85/2380.

85. Jagchid, "Mongolian-Manchu Intermarriage," 84.

86. See regulations in *Qinding Lifanbu zeli*, 25.4b–6b; Archives 446-5-55/8, memorial dated QL 1/12/31 (since there was no thirty-first day, here translated as 1/12/30, i.e., January 30, 1737) concerns sending fruit to Khorchin princess Chunxi. The princess, daughter of the Kangxi emperor's younger brother Changying, married in 1690 and lived until 1741.

87. Memorials dated JQ 3/11/21 (December 27, 1798) [Archives 446-5-55/330]; JQ 16/3/13 (April 4, 1811) and JQ 16/4/27 (June 17, 1811) [446-5-55/390].

88. Memorials dated JQ 16/6/2 (July 21, 1811) [Archives 446-5-55/390] and QL 38/11/5 (December 18, 1773) [446-5-55/215]. The variability of these grants is apparent in other examples: see the memorial dated QL 46/5/10 (July 1, 1781) (446-5-55/253) discussing the purchase of a larger house by a Khalka Mongol groom, second-degree prince Yundundorji, who was about to marry a palace-reared *gege*. The prince was living in a ten-*jian* house that was clearly too small to serve as a residence for the couple. The Neiwufu recommended a ninety-*jian* house owned by the throne. Because of debts accumulated by the prince's father, the house was temporarily rented to the prince with the goal of eventual purchase on an installment plan deducting payments from his stipend.

89. Inventories of the estates, dated 1866 and 1875, in Archives 557-5-66-4/3114.

90. *ZNXZ*, 1937 ed., Zhangyisi, 3.46a–47a. See Brunnert and Hagelstrom, *Political Organization*, nos. 43, 45, 46; these are the same terms for persons appointed to princesses' establishments.

91. Memorials dated JQ 16/4/7 (May 28, 1811) [Archives 446-5-55/390], JQ 16/6/2 (July 21, 1811) [446-5-55/390].

92. See Archives 557-5-66-4/3114 for the inventories of the estates of Shouxi *hošoi gungju*, who married in 1863, and Rong'an *gurun gungju*, married in 1873.

93. Examples of stipends for Princesses Shouxi and Shouzhuang are to be

found in Archives 467-4-85/2102. Wang Shuqing, "Qingdai gongzhu," 36; Jagchid, "Mongolian-Manchu Intermarriage," 79–80.

94. Archives 467-4-85-1869, memorial dated JQ 13/2/12 (March 8, 1808) lists the presents for the third and fourth daughters of the Jiaqing emperor on their birthdays. Both had been married six to seven years earlier. Archives 467-4-85-1869, memorial dated GX 21/1/27 (February 21, 1895), lists presents for Princess Rongshou on her forty-first birthday. Archives 557-5-66-4/3114, includes Princess Rongshou's name in the list of imperial relatives who will appear at court to congratulate Empress Dowager Cixi on her birthday in 1901.

95. The imperial estates administered by Neiwufu are described in Preston Torbert, *The Ch'ing Imperial Household Department: A Study of Its Organization and Principal Functions, 1662–1796* (Cambridge, Mass., 1977), 84–89.

96. Archives 557-5-66-4/3114.

97. The income-yielding assets of Rong'an are detailed at her death in 1875: see Archives 557-5-66-4/3114.

98. Edict dated QL 22 (1757): "Henceforth when *efu* are stripped of their title for having committed an offense, the *gege* will also be stripped of her title." *DQHDSL*, j. 2.

99. Feng Zuozhe, "You guan Heshen jiazu yu huangshi lianyin de jige wenti," *Gugong bowuyuan yuankan*, no. 1 (1987): 11–15, 20; also his "Hexiao gongju yizhi dian di," in *Qing gong jie mi*, ed. Zheng Yimei et al. (Hong Kong, 1987), 116–18; Wang Laiyin, "Hexiao gongju—Qianlong di de zhangshang mingzhu," in *Qing gong jie mi*, 112–15. Archives 446-5-55/332, memorial dated JQ 4/4/27 (May 31, 1799) presents a Manchu-language "thanks for imperial grace" from *efu* Fengshengyinde in the palmy days before Heshen's purge.

100. *ZNXZ*, 1937 ed., Guangchusi, 4.87ab.

101. *Qinding Lifanbu zeli* 3.2b–4b. For correspondence of *efu* ranks to ranks of princes, see Wang Shuqing, "Qingdai gongzhu," 31–32; *DQHDSL*, j. 2.

102. Jagchid, "Mongolian-Manchu Intermarriage," 81; Zhao Yuntian, "Qingdai de 'bei zhi efu' zhidu," *Gugong bowuyuan yuankan*, no. 4 (1984): 33–34.

103. See Mo Zhuang, "Report from China: Pearl Robe Discovered in Tomb," *Oriental Art* 31, no. 4 (1985–86): 452–53. Princess Rongxian was buried in a double coffin; her husband was cremated.

104. Memorials dated TZ 1/3/2 (March 31, 1862) and TZ 1/3/27 (April 25, 1862) [Archives 446-5-55/571], TZ 1/5/3 (May 30, 1862) [446-5-55/572].

105. See the Manchu-language memorial dated QL 25/3 (April/May 1760) [Archives 446-5-55/125], which reviews the precedents on imperially managed funerals for princesses; 446-5-55/220, Manchu-language memorial dated QL 40/1/11 (February 10, 1775), reporting the thanks of widower Lhawangdorji at the imperial grace and describing funeral plans. Archives 446-5-55/565 includes memorials on the management of the death rituals for Shou'an *gurun gungju*, who died in 1865; memorials dated GX 1/1/19 (February 24, 1875) and GX 1/3/28 (May 3, 1875) [446-5-55/611] report on arrangements for the fu-

neral of Rong'an *gurun gungju*. An early example of the imperial construction of princesses' tombs is found in a memorial dated YZ 10/12/9 (January 24, 1733) reporting on construction of a tomb for Princess Chunyi, tenth daughter of the Kangxi emperor [446-5-55/2].

106. See memorial dated DG 30/8/27 (October 2, 1850) [Archives 446-5-55/537], in which the emperor was asked to decide whether libations should be poured at the tombs of imperial princes belonging to the close branches (see chapter 3) and high ministers, after the coffin of the Daoguang emperor was escorted to the western tombs. A list of sixteen tombs along the route was presented: to the four selected from this list, the emperor added the tombs of four of the Jiaqing emperor's daughters, and a daughter of the Daoguang emperor.

107. On Sebtenbaljur, see Hua Li, "Qingdai de Man Meng lianyin," 50. On the marriage, see memorial dated QL 26/7/12 (August 11, 1761) [Archives 446-5-55/132]; on Sebtenbaljur's funeral, see memorials dated QL 40/4/14 (May 13, 1775) [446-5-55/221] and QL 40/5/17 (June 14, 1775) [446-5-55/222].

108. Memorial dated QL 1/5/10 (June 18, 1736) [Archives 446-5-55/5].

109. Manchu-language memorial dated QL 40/1/11 (February 10, 1775) [Archives 446-5-55/220]. Hejing was a first-rank princess, the seventh daughter of the Qianlong emperor.

110. Archives 446-5-55/390, memorials dated JQ 16/5/7 (June 27, 1811); 446-5-55/391, memorial dated JQ 6/5/28 (July 18, 1811), JQ 16/6/2 (July 21, 1811); 557-5-66-4/3114 cites the settlement of Zhuangjing *gurun gungju*'s estate as a precedent for the settlement of Shou'en *gurun gungju*'s estate in 1859.

111. Archives 446-5-55/344, report on the pawnshops assigned to Zhuangjing *hošoi gungju* as a basis for recommendations on the death settlement; 446-5-55/390, edicts dated JQ 16/3/13 (April 4, 1811), JQ 16/4/7 (May 28, 1811), JQ 16/5/7 (June 27, 1811); 446-5-55/431, petition dated JQ 25 (1820); also 446-5-55/344. This was Zhuangjing *hošoi gungju*.

112. Petition of 1820 in Archives 446-5-55/431.

113. Archives 557-5-66-4/3114, which points out the precedents.

114. Archives 446-5-55/5, memorial dated QL 1/5/10 (June 18, 1736).

115. Bao Guiqin, ed. *Qingdai Menggu guanshi zhuan* (Beijing, 1995), 711–14. Tsereng's wife, a second-rank princess, died in 1710, forty years before Tsereng's own death. In 1733 she was posthumously promoted to the first rank by the Yongzheng emperor as a reward to Tsereng for his military victories against the Zunghars. When Tsereng died, the emperor granted 10,000 taels of silver to cover the funeral expenses, declared that he would personally pour funerary libations before Tsereng's coffin, and ordered that Tsereng be buried next to his wife with all the honors due a first-rank prince of the Aisin Gioro main line.

116. Annette B. Weiner, *Inalienable Possessions: The Paradox of Keeping-While-Giving* (Berkeley, 1992), 4.

117. See Xu Qiqian, "Qingdai baoxi luetan," *Gugong bowuyuan yuankan* 3 (1995): 63; Zhang Naiwei, *Qing gong shuwen*, 395–400 on the pre-Qing arti-

facts. Eventually the ancestral portraits of pre-Qing rulers were taken to Taiwan. See Li Lincan, "Gugong bowuyuan de tuxiang hua," *Gugong jikan* 5, no. 1 (1970): 51–61; and Jiang Fuzong, "Guoli gugong bowuyuan zang Qing Nanxundian tuxiang kao," *Gugong jikan* 8, no. 4 (1974): 1–16.

118. Bernard Cohn, "Cloth, Clothes, and Colonialism: India in the Nineteenth Century," in *Cloth and Human Experience*, ed. Annette B. Weiner and Jane Schneider (Washington, D.C., 1991), 310; see also 312–16.

119. Angela Zito, "The Imperial Birthday: Ritual Encounters Between the Panchen Lama and the Qianlong Emperor in 1780," presented at the "Conference on State and Ritual in East Asia," Paris, June 28—July 1, 1995, and organized by the European/North American Committee for Scholarly Cooperation in East Asian Studies.

120. Manchu-language memorial of QL 1/2 (March 1736) in Archives 446-5-55/3; bilingual memorial of QL 1/4/29 (June 8, 1736) in 446-5-55/5. A memorial of JQ 1/5/13 (June 17, 1796) [446-5-55/324] identifies five princes who were assigned to audit the Six Vaults.

121. Memorial of JQ 5/14/22 (June 14, 1800) for the edict (Archives 446-5-55/338); see also the initial proposal, memorial of JQ 5/4/26 (May 19, 1800) (446-5-55/337) and the follow-up memorial of JQ 5/9/14 (June 30, 1800) (446-5-55/339), in which the ministers cite a QL precedent for selling off low-quality jades from the Six Vaults.

CHAPTER 5: PALACE SERVANTS

1. James C. Scott, *Domination and the Arts of Resistance: Hidden Transcripts* (New Haven, 1990), 12.

2. Scott, *Domination and the Arts*, preface and ch. 1.

3. James C. Scott, *Weapons of the Weak: Everyday Forms of Peasant Resistance* (New Haven, 1985), ch. 8.

4. For an example, see the Kangxi emperor's conversations with officials in imperial audience presented in the appendix to Silas H. L. Wu, *Communication and Imperial Control in China: Evolution of the Palace Memorial System, 1693–1735* (Cambridge, Mass., 1970), 127–48.

5. Quotes from Preston M. Torbert, *The Ch'ing Imperial Household Department: A Study of Its Organization and Principal Functions, 1662–1796* (Cambridge, Mass., 1977), 1–2; see also 3–4, 9; and Lawrence D. Kessler, *K'ang-hsi and the Consolidation of Ch'ing Rule, 1661–1684* (Chicago, 1976), 4.

6. Torbert, *Imperial Household Department*, 22–25; Kessler, *K'ang-hsi and the Consolidation*, 26–27.

7. Many personnel records in Archives 467-4-85/1017, for example, list individual eunuchs with banner registrations; other archival records list eunuchs who were from commoner households—Han Chinese households outside the banner system.

8. Edict of JQ 16/2/19 (March 13, 1811) in *QGXZ*, 1.571–58b. Scrutiny of the personnel lists of the Court Theatrical Bureau and its precursors suggests

an additional complication, namely that eunuchs from Han Chinese civilian (*min*) household registers were being enrolled under the bondservant banners of the Neiwufu once they were employed in the bureau: see Wang Zhizhang, *Qing Shengpingshu zhilüe* (1937; reprint, Taipei, 1981), ch. 5. On the higher rates, see *QGXZ*, 1.68b–69a, regulations dated JQ 18/10/24 (November 16, 1813).

9. Data from Wang Zhizhang, *Qing Shengpingshu zhilüe*, ch. 5.

10. Cai Shiying, *Qing mo quanjian Li Lianying* (Hebei, 1986), ch. 1. According to Ye Zhiru, "Cong huangshi wangfu nüpu diwei kan Qingdai shehui de fuxiu luohou," *Gugong bowuyuan yuankan* 1 (1988): 22, before 1779, young boys were recruited from poor households and castrated inside the palace. After that date, the palace recruited castrated boys owned by princely households or recommended by officials for palace service. But the palace continued to have an official in charge of castration: see Dan Shi, *Yige Qing gong taijian de caoyu* (Beijing, 1989), 91.

11. Yang Zhengguang, *Zhongguo zuihou yige da taijian* (Beijing, 1990), 6. A similar motivation is reported for An Dehai, one of Empress Dowager Cixi's favorites in the 1860s: see Dong Shouyi, *Gong qinwang Yixin dazhuan* (Shenyang, 1989), 297.

12. Yang Zhengguang, *Zhongguo zuihou yige da taijian*, 18–21.

13. Archives 446-5-55/242, QL 44/3/24 (May 9, 1779), on the *fenfu* precedents of Yongxuan and his son Mian'en; 557-5-66-4/3114, QL 60/9/11 (October 23, 1795), on *fenfu* of the emperor's eleventh son, Yongxing, Prince Cheng.

14. Wang Shuqing, "Qingchao taijian zhidu," *Gugong bowuyuan yuankan* 3 (1984): 58. This injunction is clear in the regulations: see *QGXZ*, j. 4.

15. Luo Chongliang, "Cong dang'anguan cailiao kan Qianlong nianjian taijian de chutao," *Qingshi yanjiu tongxun* 4 (1986): 21. Luo is counting the number of eunuchs in *shouling taijian* and above. The exact number and distribution of these posts is found in Wang Shuqing, "Qingchao taijian zhidu," 4–7.

16. Tang Yinian, *Qing gong taijian* (Shenyang, 1993), 16–19; Torbert, *Imperial Household Department*, 42–43.

17. Wang Shuqing, "Qingchao taijian zhidu," 4–7 lists the assignments; see *QGXZ*, 1.100a, giving a 1839 list of the different temples to which eunuchs were assigned. See Torbert, *Imperial Household Department*, 39–51.

18. See Wei Qingyuan, Wu Qiyan, and Lu Su, *Qingdai nüpu zhidu* (Peking, 1982); Zuo Yunpeng, "Qingdai qixia nüpu de diwei ji qi bianhua," *Shanxi shi daxuebao* 1 (1980): 42–51.

19. On the ethnic backgrounds of *booi*, see Torbert, *Imperial Household Department*, 17. On voluntary enslavement and the sale of persons, see Wei Qingyuan et al., *Qingdai nüpu zhidu*, ch. 3.

20. Zuo Yunpeng, "Qingdai qixia nüpu," 46.

21. Kessler, *K'ang-hsi and the Consolidation*, 28.

22. Torbert, *Imperial Household Department*, 61; according to Fu Ketong, "Cong neizuoling he guanling tandao Qingdai xinzheku ren," *Qingshi*

tongxun 3 (1986): 9, there were a total of thirty *guanling* by the middle of the Kangxi reign.

23. The three lowest-ranking consorts, *guiren, changzai,* and *daying,* were not assigned *guanling;* see regulations in *ZNXZ,* 1841 ed., first *ce.*

24. See H. S. Brunnert and V. V. Hagelstrom, *Present-Day Political Organization of China,* trans. A. Beltchenko and E. E. Moran (Foochow, 1911), no. 97 on 104.

25. Jerry Norman, *A Concise Manchu-English Lexicon* (Seattle, 1978), 24; Ye Zhiru, "Conghuangshi wangfu," 22, 25.

26. On *sula,* see Norman, *Concise Manchu-English Lexicon;* Torbert, *Imperial Household Department,* 37; Ye Zhiru, "Cong huangshi wangfu," 25. A chronological review of the regulations is provided in *ZNXZ,* 1841 ed., first *ce.* For a description of efforts by the Qianlong emperor to relocate poor *sula* to vacant farmland in the northeast, see Diao Shuren, "Lüe lun Qianlong chao jingqi sula de yizhu," *Beifang wenwu* 2 (1994): 65–68.

27. Archives 446-5-55/244, memorial dated QL 44/7/20, covering the accounts for the sixth month, which in the Western calendar was July 13– August 11, 1779. In addition to princes Yi and Ding, an unnamed *zhenguogong* was also setting up his own establishment in the same month; he did not receive furniture and ritual vessels from the emperor but did receive fruit and cakes. Although Fu Kedong ("Cong neizuoling he guanling," 9) states that *sula* were manual laborers who were paid a tael of silver a month, the archival accounts all record use of *sula* by the occasion, suggesting hire by the day.

28. The monthly reports are found in Archives 446-5-55/246 for 1779/80 and 446-5-55/256 for 1871/82. On weeders, see memorial dated QL 5/16/5 (July 28, 1740) [446-5-55/29].

29. Archives 446-5-55/218, memorial from Neiwufu ministers dated QL 39/4/2 (May 11, 1774).

30. Archives 446-5-55/323, reports of 1796.

31. *QGXZ,* Guangxu edition, 3.1. On Cixi's staff, see Archives 467-4-85/1246, undated list.

32. Archives 467-4-85/1254, list of personnel at the Shoukang palace. The maids listed had entered palace service in the years 1733 to 1751, so we know that the list was made after September 27, 1751, and before 1760, when the emperor's fourth daughter was married.

33. See Shan Shiyuan, "Guanyu Qing gong de xiunü he gongnü," *Gugong bowuyuan yuankan* 2 (1960): 97–103. The regulations on the draft are found in *DQHDSL,* j. 1218 and *ZNXZ, kuaiji,* j. 4. For further exemptions, see the regulations cited in the previous footnote. Wet nurses' daughters were also exempted from the draft in an imperial decision of JQ 5/11/26 (January 10, 1801) [Archives 446-5-55/339].

34. Isaac Taylor Headland, *Court Life in China: The Capital, Its Officials, and People* (New York, 1909), 13. Headland identifies this quotation—of sentiments common to most parents who had to submit their daughters to the *gongnü* draft—as coming from Empress Dowager Cixi's parents, an extremely

unlikely source, since she was not from a bondservant family and entered the palace as a consort and not a maidservant.

35. Memorials for QL 1/11/22 (December 23, 1736) [Archives 446-5-55/7], QL 6/12/24 (January 30, 1642) [446-5-55/36], QL 7/4/6 (May 10, 1742) [446-5-55/37], QL 39/1/18 (February 18, 1774) [446-5-55/217], QL 40/12/23 (February 12, 1776) [446-5-55/224], QL 50/12/23 (January 22, 1786) [446-5-55/281], QL 60/12/25 (February 3, 1796) [446-5-55/322], JQ 8/12/26 (February 7, 1804) [446-5-55/353], DG 11/12/23 (January 25, 1832) [446-5-55/466], DG 25/12 (January, 1846) [446-5-55/523], GX 11/12 (January, 1886) [467-4-85/1017]. Sixteen sample name lists from which the selections were made are found in 467-4-85/1253.

36. The calculations cited were based on a listing of 113 girls for the *gongnü* draft, one of sixteen such lists found in Archives 467-4-85/1253; the categories *xiansan* and *sula* were merged, since they are equivalent: see Brunnert and Hagelstrom, *Political Organization*, no. 732a; Sun Wenliang et al., eds., *Manzu da cidian* (Shenyang, 1990), 343–44. On *pijia*, see Torbert, *Imperial Household Department*, 64.

37. Palace distribution list dated GX 11/8/16 (September 24, 1885) in Archives 467-4-85/1246.

38. See the memorials of 1734 in which Prince Zhuang reported on the betrothal of a maid to Police Lieutenant Jilantai of the Plain White Manchu Banner, and several other matches, in Guoli gugong bowuyuan, *Wenxian congbian* (1930; reprint, Taipei, 1964), 2:1038. My thanks to Susan Naquin for this reference. There is also an exceptional case of imperial recognition for long service: the Kangxi emperor ordered an old servant of Empress Dowager Xiaozhuang to be buried near the tomb of her mistress: see Yu Shanpu, *Qing Dongling daguan* (Shijiazhuang, 1985), 224.

39. See Joanna Waley-Cohen, *Exile in Mid-Qing China: Banishment to Xinjiang, 1758–1820* (New Haven, 1991), 39, 62, 166.

40. Torbert, *Imperial Household Department*, 65–66. For a general description of the development of this status, see Ye Zhiru, "Kang, Yong, Qian shiqi xinzheku ren de chengfen ji renshen guanxi," *Minzu yanjiu* 1 (1984): 34–46.

41. Archives 446-5-55/5: the cases are part of a review ordered by the new Qianlong emperor on December 10, 1735, as explained in a cover memorial dated July 2, 1736.

42. The same picture appears in a list of twenty-one cases dating from 1700 to 1831 (Archives 446-5-55/7): Hanjun dominated the list of those punished for defalcations, Manchus the list of those punished for crimes. Of the Hanjun who were made state slaves, 90 percent were placed on estates; all the Manchus and Mongols were enrolled in Neiwufu companies.

43. Shang Chongchu and Shang Chongnian both occupied posts as magistrates of departments before being punished for defalcations; Arbangga was punished for his father's bad debts. They are among the 109 cases found in Archives 446-5-55/5. On Shang Kexi and Eidu, see *ECCP,* 221–22, 635–36.

44. On the Zhutianbao case, see Silas H. L. Wu, *Passage to Power: Kangxi*

and His Heir Apparent, 1661–1722 (Cambridge, Mass., 1979), 158–61; see also *ECCP,* 925. The memorial presenting the dossiers of Zhuduna and Changlai (Archives 446-5-55/5) records that the enslaved dependents of both men were eventually awarded to Xuanye's grandsons Hongshu and Hongsheng.

45. Fu Kedong, "Cong neizuoling he guanling"; Torbert, *Imperial Household Department,* 61. On the Yongzheng policy, see Ye Zhiru, "Kang, Yong, Qian shi," 42–43; Waley-Cohen, *Exile in Mid-Qing China.*

46. Figure for 1736 from Archives 446-5-55/5, a memorial from Neiwufu ministers responding to the emperor's request that they deliberate on whether *sinjeku* wives from the upper three banners assigned to palace duties should receive imperial gifts; all the other figures, based on archival records, are quoted from Ye Zhiru, "Cong huangshi wangfu nüpu xiaren," 22.

47. Archives 155-4-16-1/636, list of palace allowances for JQ 7 (1802). The fourth daughter cited here was married in JQ 7/11/19 (December 13, 1802). The 1832 list as well as one for 1830 are found in 467-4-85/1246.

48. See Puyi's testimonial to his wet nurse in Aisin-Gioro Pu Yi, *From Emperor to Citizen,* trans. W. J. F. Jenner (1964; reprint, New York, 1987), 70–74; also Cao Chenqing, "Puyi rumu Wang Jiao shi," *Zijincheng* 48 (1988): 40; *DQHDSL,* 1218.11ab, *ZNXZ, kuaiji,* j. 4. The formal list of wives in the upper three Neiwufu banners cited is one of fourteen found in Archives 467-4-85/1254. The lists are not dated.

49. Two long memorials review the precedents on grants to wet nurses; see the memorial dated QL 1/7/19, in Archives 446-5-55/6, and the memorial dated JQ 25/20/29, in 446-5-55/431; Yu Shanpu, *Qing Dongling,* 223–24. Yang Naiji, "Qing di de naimu yu baomu," *Yendu* 6 (1987): 39–40; and Torbert, *Imperial Household Department,* 73, also cite relevant edicts from the Jiaqing and Daoguang emperors.

50. Torbert, *Imperial Household Department,* 72–73; Manduri's biography is in *BQTZ,* 6:3759; on the Cao family, see *ECCP,* 742.

51. *DQSL,* 120.41–42, QL 5/intercalary 6/14 (August 6, 1740) and 167.5a, QL 7/5/17 (June 19, 1742). Also Torbert, *Imperial Household Department,* 73.

52. Some empresses dowager did not in fact have four nurses (Hongli's mother ca. 1751–52 had three: Archives 467-4-85/1254), but other palace distribution lists from 1830 show four nurses: 467-4-85/1246. Archives 446-5-55/6 for QL 1/7/19, 446-5-55/451 for JQ 25/10/29, 446-5-55/570 for XF 11/10/15. The QL 1/7/19 memorial lists the descendants of the emperor's nurses, who were supposed to be childless. But see a memorial dated JQ 11/25/1 (446-5-55/432), which prosecutes the banner officials who falsely reported that a potential candidate for a nurse's post was childless when she really had two daughters: in this case, the regulations were upheld.

53. Reported by Yang Zhen, "Sumalagu yu Kangxi di," *Gugong bowuyuan yuankan* 1 (1995): 39.

54. Found in Archives 446-5-55/433; in the edict, the emperor orders that the replacement candidates be brought before him for an interview.

55. Zhaolian, *Xiaoting xulu,* 432.

56. Kahn, *Monarchy*, 119.

57. Memorial dated QL 40/11/29 (January 19, 1776) [Archives 446-5-55/223], on the subject of providing Mianyi, grandson of the Qianlong emperor, with *haha juse* and *anda* when he entered school. Norman, *Concise Manchu-English Lexicon*, 17; Shang Hongkui et al., eds., *Qingshi Manyu cidian* (Shanghai, 1990), 23; Du Jiaji, "Qingdai de huangzi jiaoyu," *Gugong bowuyuan yuankan* 2 (1990): 89. It may be significant that the memorials in which these posts are discussed are in Manchu. According to his memoirs, the last Qing emperor's *anda* was a chief eunuch: see Aisin-Gioro Pu Yi, *From Emperor to Citizen*, 64.

58. On their recruitment, see memorial dated QL 44/3/10 (April 25, 1779) [Archives 446-5-55/242], one dated QL 39/4/17 (May 26, 1774) [446-5-55/218], and an undated memorial concerning the selecting of companions for *beile* Zaizhi in 557-5-66-4/3114. On the *anda* accompanying princes traveling to the imperial tombs to perform sacrifices, see memorials dated QL 38/10/29 (December 12, 1773) [446-5-55/214], QL 39/2/13 (March 24, 1774), [446-5-55/217], and QL 40/2/19 (March 20, 1775) [446-5-55/220]. A Manchu-language memorial dated QL 58/10/4 (November 7, 1793) [446-5-55/313] discusses the appointment of an *anda* to accompany Yonglin, the emperor's seventeenth son, when he escorted the coffin of a second-rank consort to the tombs; Yonglin was twenty-seven at the time.

59. Ye Zhiru, "Cong huangshi wangfu nüpu xiaren," 21. On the location of the workshops under the *zaobanchu* see Liu Liang-yu, "Chinese Painted and Cloisonné Enamel: Introduction, The Imperial Workshops," trans. Mary Man-li Loh, *Arts of Asia* 8, no. 6 (1978): 83–85. Also Wu Zhaoqing, "Qing Neiwufu huojidang," *Wenwu* 3 (1991): 89–96, 55, which describes the archives of the palace workshops.

60. A memorial, dated YZ 6/2 (1728) [Archives 557-5-66-4/3118], approves a petition by the Department of the Privy Purse (*guangchusi*) to hire civilian artisans and stipulates seasonal wage rates for long-term workers. On the development of the workshops, see Liu Liang-yu, "Chinese Painted and Cloisonné Enamel."

61. The Yongzheng emperor, for example, awarded ten taels of silver to each artisan responsible for a specially fine piece of lacquerware: Zhu Jiajin, "Yongzheng Lacquerware," *Orientations* 19, no. 3 (1988): 28–39. Here the term *jiali* refers to bondservant bannermen who were trained at the palace workshops, as opposed to artisans hired from outside.

62. Ye Zhiru, "Cong huangshi wangfu nüpu xiaren," 21–22.

63. Tian Jiaqing, *Classic Chinese Furniture of the Qing Dynasty*, trans. Lark E. Mason, Jr. and Juliet Yung-yi Chou (Hong Kong, 1996), fig. 46 on 43; Yang Boda, "A Brief Account of Qing Dynasty Glass," in *The Robert H. Clague Collection, Chinese Glass of the Qing Dynasty, 1644–1911*, ed. Claudia Brown and Donald Rabiner (Phoenix, 1987), 71–86; for examples of enameled porcelain pieces with European motifs, see National Palace Museum, *Special Exhi-*

bition of Ch'ing Dynasty Enamelled Porcelains of the Imperial Ateliers (Taipei, 1992), pls. 73, 131, 135, 143, and 144, all made during the Qianlong reign.

64. Chang Lin-sheng, "Introduction to the Historical Development of Qing Dynasty Painted Enamelware," *National Palace Museum Bulletin* 25, nos. 4–5 (1990): 3–10; Chang Lin-sheng, "Qing Dynasty Imperial Enamelled Glassware," *Arts of Asia* 21, no. 3 (1991): 102; Liu Liang-yu, "Chinese Painted and Cloisonné Enamel."

65. Daphne Lange Rosensweig, "Painters at the Early Qing Court: The Socioeconomic Background," *Monumenta Serica* 31 (1974–75): 475–87; Howard Rogers, "Court Painting under the Qianlong Emperor," in *The Elegant Brush: Chinese Painting Under the Qianlong Emperor, 1735–1795*, ed. Ju-hsi Chou and Claudia Brown (Phoenix, 1985), 303–17; She Ch'eng, "The Painting Academy of the Qianlong Period: A Study in Relation to the Taipei National Palace Museum Collection," also in *The Elegant Brush*, 318–42.

66. Yang Boda, "Castiglione at the Qing Court—An Important Artistic Contribution," *Orientations* 19, no. 11 (1988): 44–51.

67. *Lettres édifiantes et curieuses concernant l'Asie, l'Afrique et l'Amérique, avec quelques relations nouvelles des missions et des notes géographiques et historiques,* ed. M. L. Aimé-Martin (Paris, 1843), 4:221. George Loehr, "European Artists at the Chinese Court," in *The Westward Influence of the Chinese Arts from the 14th to the 18th Century,* ed. William Watson (London, 1972), 33–42. On the location of the court painters during the Yongzheng and Qianlong reigns, see Yang Xin, "Court Painting in the Yongzheng and Qianlong Periods of the Qing Dynasty," in *The Elegant Brush: Chinese Painting Under the Qianlong Emperor, 1735–1795,* ed. Ju-hsi Chou and Claudia Brown (Phoenix, 1985), 343–57.

68. *Lettres édifiantes,* 4:44–45. Jesuits also introduced European cartography to the Qing court: for a discussion of their cartographic activities, see Cordell D. K. Yee, "Traditional Chinese Cartography and the Myth of Westernization," in *The History of Cartography,* vol. 2, book 2, ed. J. B. Harley and David Woodward (Chicago, 1994), 170–202. The significance of the title *khaghans* is discussed in chapter 1.

69. Chen Qingying, "Guan yu Beijing Xiangshan Zangzuren de quanwen ji shiji jizai," *Zhongguo Zangxue* 4 (1990): 104–15.

70. Zhang Yuxin, "Qingdai Beijing de Weiwuerzu," *Xinjiang shehui kexue* 4 (1984): 92–97.

71. Throughout this discussion, we rely on Colin Mackerras, *The Rise of the Peking Opera, 1770–1870: Social Aspects of the Theatre in Manchu China* (Oxford, 1972), quotes on 116–23, 154–57.

72. Mackerras, *The Rise of the Peking Opera,* 120–21; see also 155–56 on Li Luxi's successors.

73. Chang Te-ch'ang, "The Economic Role of the Imperial Household in the Ch'ing Dynasty," *Journal of Asian Studies* 31, no. 2 (1972): 245–46, citing a genealogy of a bondservant official. For other descriptions of the origins, see

Li Pengnian et al., *Qingdai zhongyang guojia jiguan gaishu* (Harbin, 1983), 100–101, and Zhang Deze, *Qingdai guojia jiguan kaolüe* (Beijing, 1984), 173–74. Torbert, *Imperial Household Department*.

74. Kessler, *K'ang-hsi and the Consolidation*, 28; Torbert, *Imperial Household Department*, 28–29. On the Shengjing or Mukden offices, see Zhang Deze, *Qingdai guojia jiguan kaolüe*, 192; Tong Yonggong and Guan Jialu, "Shengjing shang sanqi baoyi zuoling shulüe," *Lishi dang'an* 3 (1992): 93–97.

75. Chang Te-ch'ang, "Economic Role," 249, 250.

76. Torbert, *Imperial Household Department*, ch. 4.

77. Chang Te-ch'ang, "Economic Role," 257, tables 5, 6 on 258–59, 260–61.

78. Nancy Park, "Corruption and Its Recompense: Bribes, Bureaucracy, and the Law in Late Imperial China" (Ph.D. diss., Harvard University, 1993).

79. For a discussion of the different editions of the Neiwufu regulations, see the bibliographic entry under ZNXZ.

80. Details on the organization and staffing of the Neiwufu agencies is found in Zhang Deze, *Qingdai guojia jiguan kaolüe*, 172–97; Li Pengnian et al., *Qingdai zhongyang guojia*, 100–129. On appointing ministers to look after the affairs of princely establishments, see Archives 446-5-55/257, memorial dated QL 47/1/22 (March 5, 1782) concerning the *fenfu* of imperial grandson Mianyi. The emperor was worried lest the prince splurge all of his resources immediately after moving into his own mansion. The memorialist discusses the appointment of several experienced retainers to Mianyi's staff and notes that "Each princely household receives an edict assigning a Neiwufu *dachen* to overlook household matters."

81. Jonathan Spence, *Ts'ao Yin and the K'ang-hsi Emperor: Bondservant and Master* (New Haven, 1966); Ellen Soullière, "Reflections on Chinese Despotism and the Power of the Inner Court," *Asian Profile* 12, no. 2 (1984): 130–45.

82. See the Manchu-language memorial dated QL 28/12/17 (January 19, 1764) in Archives 446-5-55/145. In it Neiwufu ministers also argue that receiving the particulars on all eunuchs employed in princely households will enable the agency to change the quotas and reduce them if desired.

83. See the cases of eunuchs Sun Jinzhong and Fang Gui, dismissed from the palace for illness, who later tried to work for princes: QL 47/6/28 (August 6, 1782) in Archives 446-5-55/259. Even though Fang was guiltless, the ministers suggested that he should be sent for hard service at the outer garrisons. The regulations are reiterated in a memorial dated JQ 23/2/28 (April 4, 1818), in Archives 446-5-55/421. Absconding was one of the three most frequent crimes (the other two being acts of violence and theft) cited for punishment of eunuchs: see the cases listed in a memorial dated QL 6/10/23 (November 23, 1741) [446-5-55/35] and QL 28/12/17 (January 19, 1764) [446-5-55/145], describing punishments imposed from 1714 to 1764. See samples of these reports for JQ 25/6/24 (August 2, 1820) in 446-5-55/430 and XF 6/10 (December 1856) in 550-6-9-1/606.

84. Edicts of JQ 4/4/11 (May 15, 1799), reported in *QGXZ*, 1:77–78; JQ 23/12/24 (January 19, 1819) in Archives 446-5-55/423.

85. See memorials of JQ 25/11/5 (December 10, 1820), Archives 446-5-55/432, which drafted eunuchs from princely households for service in the Shoukang palace; DG 11/8/18 (September 23, 1831), 446-5-55/465, which proposed to make up shortages of eunuchs in the palace from the staffs of the princely households; DG 30/2/5 (March 18, 1850), to the same effect.

86. Absconding eunuchs are the topics of memorials dated QL 1/11/10 (December 11, 1736) [Archives 446-5-55/7], QL 44/8/9 (September 18, 1779) [446-5-55/244], JQ 1/7/7 (August 9, 1796) and JQ 1/7/22 (August 24, 1796) [446-5-55/324], JQ 9/1/17 (February 27, 1804) [446-5-55/354], JQ 18/10/26 (November 18, 1813) [557-5-66-1/407], JQ 25/5/17 (June 27, 1820) [557-5-66-1/407], DG 24/12/8 (January 15, 1845) [446-5-55/519].

87. In addition to the cases cited below from Neiwufu archives this section draws on the imperial edicts recorded in *QGXZ*, which exists in several editions, and those recorded in *Guochao gong shi*, ed. Ortai and Zhang Tingyu (1769; reprint, Beijing, 1987).

88. Zuo Buqing, "Kang Yong Qian shiqi gongwei jilüe—'Guochao gong shi,'" *Gugong bowuyuan yuankan* 4 (1984): 38–42.

89. In a Manchu-language memorial dated QL 47/5/6 (June 16, 1782) [Archives 446-5-55/259] Neiwufu obtained the emperor's permission to punish the head eunuch of Prince Yi's household for unjustified cruelty toward underlings. See the similar case against Zong Fuqing, in a memorial dated QL 28/12/6 (January 8, 1764) [446-5-55/145]. Of course, eunuchs caught stealing from the palace were also punished: a sample case of a eunuch caught stealing jade altar vessels from the Yonghegong is reported in JQ 5/5/11 (July 2, 1800) [446-5-55/338].

90. See, for example, the case of eunuch Wang Lun, who stole silver from his employer, Prince Yi, reported in a memorial dated QL 7/5/9 (June 11, 1742) [Archives 446-5-55/38], and eunuch Zhang Fu, punished when a fire began in the Buddha hall of (Prince) Yichun's mansion, in a memorial dated JQ 1/5/17 (June 21, 1796) [446-5-55/324]. See Torbert, *Imperial Household Department*, 45–47.

91. Memorial dated JQ 8/7/15 (August 31, 1803), in Archives 446-5-55/352; in a similar case, reported on JQ 8/5/8 (June 26, 1803) [446-5-55/351], another Neiwufu minister was punished for failing to inform the emperor of his sister's sale of a pearl bracelet.

92. Manchu-language memorial, dated YZ 11/12/24 (January 28, 1734) [Archives 446-5-55/2].

93. Edict of QL 31/2/5, presented in *QGXZ*, 1.53–54. A contemporary report of the persistent tradition can be found in *Renmin ribao*, Overseas edition, October 30, 1990, 8. Eunuchs who did not report unauthorized entries were also punished. See Archives 446-5-55/333, memorial dated JQ 4/5/6 (June 8, 1799). In the interrogation of Heshen's eunuch Heshitu, Heshitu admitted en-

tering the Ningshou palace. The eunuch in charge of the palace and other responsible eunuchs were all punished.

94. Edicts dated QL 6/12/7 (January 13, 1742), JQ 4/11/6 (December 2, 1799), JQ 13/15/7 (June 30, 1808), DG 12/8/3 (August 28, 1832), XF 6/4/23 (May 26, 1856), in the Xianfeng ed. of QGXZ, 1.11b–13b, 1.27b–28a, 1.40a–41a, 1.46ab, 1.96b–97b, 1.111ab.

95. Memorial from Yinlu, Prince Zhuang, dated QL 20/1/11 (February 21, 1755) [Archives 446-5-55/99].

96. QGXZ, j. 1, edict dated QL 26/7/1 (July 31, 1761).

97. Archives 446-5-55/33, memorial dated QL 6/5/19 (July 1, 1741).

98. Memorial dated JQ 5/5/4 (June 25, 1800) [Archives 446-5-55/338].

99. Memorial dated DG 12/5/23 (June 21, 1832), reprinted in Zhongguo diyi lishi dang'anguan, Yuanmingyuan: Qingdai dang'an shiliao (Shanghai, 1991), 1:511–13.

100. QL 40/8/23 (September 17, 1775) [Archives 446-5-55/223]. In a similar case in 1862, a thief was found on the roof of a palace building at dawn by Guards Colonel Fuquan: TZ 1/2/13 (March 13, 1862) [446-5-55/571].

101. XF 1/6/16 (July 14, 1851) [Archives 446-5-55/540]; see Torbert, Imperial Household Department, 45 on the smuggling out of state-owned silk that prompted the voucher system.

102. JQ 6/6/14 (July 24, 1801) [Archives 446-5-55/342].

103. QL 25/5/21 (July 3, 1760) [Archives 446-5-55/124].

104. Case dated JQ 5/5/21 (July 12, 1800) [Archives 446-5-55/338], fining eunuch Wang Wenzi, assigned to the Shoukang palace, who let his "son" Yongyu stay overnight in his dormitory.

105. JQ 25/6/23 (August 1, 1820), in Archives 446-5-55/430. The 1750 map of the imperial city shows a cattle paddock, a horse paddock, and several stables but no specific sheep pen.

106. Scott, Domination and the Arts of Resistance.

107. Memorial of QL 51/9/30 (November 20, 1786) [Archives 557-5-66-1/407]. Liu was ordered beaten and sent to bitter labor in Heilongjiang.

108. See memorials dated QL 1/6/17 (July 15, 1736) [Archives 446-5-55/6], QL 6/4/12 (May 26, 1741) [446-5-55/32], QL 7/4/12 (May 16, 1742) [446-5-55/38], and JQ 4/5/13 (June 15, 1799) [446-5-55/333].

109. Memorial dated JQ 3/6/3 (July 15, 1798) [Archives 446-5-55/330]. In another case in 1819, a maid who beat a younger maid to death was ordered beaten, then decapitated; her eunuch supervisor was dismissed. The sentence was considered to be relatively light because the court decided it was not premeditated: memorial dated JQ 24/2/8 (March 3, 1819) [446-5-55/424].

110. Tang Yinian, Qing gong taijian, 17–18.

111. Tang Yinian, Qing gong taijian, 27, citing Guochao gong shi.

112. Memorial dated QL 20/3/26 (May 5, 1755) in Archives 446-5-55/99. See also memorial dated QL 1/12/17 (January 17, 1737) [446-5-55/8] for another case of suspected extortion.

113. ECCP, 724.

114. See memorial dated TZ 8/8/11 (September 16, 1869) from Ding Baochen, in Archives 557-5-66-1/458; Xu Shiyan and Li Dongshan, *Da taijian An Dehai zhi si* (Jilin, 1986).

115. Yang Zhengguang, *Zhongguo zuihou yige da taijian*, 24; Tang Yinian, *Qing gong taijian*, 27, notes that even in Cixi's case, much of what has been said about the power of her chief eunuch, Li Lianying, is unsubstantiated. On the daily routines of the empress dowager, see the interviews with Geng Jinxi, a eunuch who served her in the Ningshou palace: "Taijian tan wanglu," *Zijincheng* 1–2 (1980): 42–44, 40–41.

116. See Ye Zhiru, "Cong huangshi wangfu nüpu," 22, Shi Kekuang, *Zhongguo huan guan mishi* (Beijing, 1988). On eunuch graveyards in Peking, see Lu Qi and Liu Jingyi, "Qingdai taijian Enjizhuang yingdi," *Gugong bowuyuan yuankan* 3 (1979): 51–58.

117. Memorial dated YZ 11/4/22 (June 4, 1733), in Archives 446-5-55/2; Yang Zhenguang, *Zhongguo zuihou yige da taijian*, 4.

118. See memorials in Archives 446-5-55/35, QL 6/10/23 (November 30, 1741), reporting on fourteen eunuchs serving out weeding sentences at Wengshan, also known as Jingshan; 446-5-55/145, QL 28/12/17 (January 19, 1764), reviewing the cases of eleven eunuchs sentenced to "eternally weed" at another locale; 446-5-55/463, DG 11/3/6 (April 17, 1831), listing eunuchs sent to Heilongjiang; 446-5-55/464, DG 11/7/5 (August 12, 1831), reporting on eunuchs who had been sent to Dasheng'ula to serve their terms; and 446-5-55/537, DG 30/8/29 (October 4, 1850), reviewing seventeen cases of eunuchs banished to Heilongjiang.

119. Memorials in Archives 446-5-55/7, QL 1/11/10 (December 11, 1736); 446-5-55/244, QL 44/8/9 (September 18, 1779); 446-5-55/324, JQ 1/7/7 (August 9, 1796), JQ 1/7/22 (August 24, 1796); 446-5-55/354, JQ 9/1/17 (February 27, 1804); 446-5-66-1/407, JQ 18/10/26 (November 18, 1813) in Manchu; 557-5-66-1/407, JQ 25/5/17 (June 27, 1820); 446-5-55/519, DG 24/12/8 (January 15, 1845).

120. These rewards were in addition to the institutionalized condolence money for servants; see, for example, Archives 155-14-16-4/4399, memorial dated QL 17/1/5 (February 19, 1752), on silver given to supervisory eunuchs to help their parents or siblings. In a memorial dated QL 1/2/11 (March 22, 1736) [446-5-55/3], 170 eunuchs are proposed for honors.

121. Memorial dated QL 1/3/12 (April 22, 1736) [Archives 446-5-55/4]; the regulation that was invoked in this case also stipulated punishments for "those who . . . when the emperor's carriage is entering or departing, recklessly shout and shove."

122. Memorial dated JQ 6/11/10 (December 15, 1801) in Archives 446-5-55/344; the 1731 incident is reported in Torbert, *Imperial Household Department*, 45.

123. QL 43/11/8 (December 26, 1778) in QGXZ, 57–63. The emperor ordered that his edict be disseminated to all palace inhabitants, and in addition recorded in the Palace School and the Jingshifang.

124. Torbert, *Imperial Household Department*, 48–50.

125. Memorial dated QL 28/12/6 (January 8, 1764) [Archives 446-5-55/145]; the emperor ordered Zong Fuqing beaten 100 strokes and sent to Heilongjiang. In addition, senior guards and bondservants in the household were punished for failing to report Zong's misdeeds. A similar case can be found in 446-5-55/259, QL 47/5/6 (June 16, 1782), sending the head eunuch of Prince Yi to Heilongjiang for repeatedly beating *sula* without justification.

126. Edict of XF 5/6/18 (July 31, 1855) in *QGXZ*, 1.109a–110a.

127. On the Kangxi precedents, see edict dated KX 16/8/1 (August 28, 1677), KX 40/3/7 (April 14, 1701), KX 44/2/3 (February 25, 1705), KX 54/2/27 (April 1, 1715) and KX 60/10/12 (November 30, 1721) in *Guochao gong shi*, 6, 11, 12, 15. The edict prohibiting eunuchs from the palace from mingling with those in princely households is dated JQ 18/10/11 (November 3, 1813) and is in *QGXZ*, 1.66a.

128. Memorial dated JQ 6/11/18 (December 23, 1801) [Archives 446-5-55/344].

129. Edicts dated KX 20/1/6 (February 23, 1681) and KX 21/7/8 (August 10, 1682), in *Guochao gong shi*, 7; also reported in Torbert, *Imperial Household Department*, 46.

130. Edict of KX 38/9/20 (November 11, 1699) in *Guochao gong shi*, 1.27b–28a; of XF 2/1/8 (February 27, 1852) in *QGXZ*, 1.108b.

131. Edict of YZ 13/10/11 (November 24, 1735) recorded in *QGXZ*, 15–25.

CHAPTER 6: RULERSHIP AND RITUAL ACTION
IN THE CHINESE REALM

1. David Kertzer, *Ritual, Politics, and Power* (New Haven, 1988), 9. See also Clifford Geertz, "Centers, Kings, and Charisma: Reflections on the Symbolics of Power," in *Rites of Power: Symbolism, Ritual, and Politics Since the Middle Ages*, ed. Sean Wilentz (Philadelphia, 1985), 13–38; David Cannadine and Simon Price, eds., *Rituals of Royalty: Power and Ceremony in Traditional Societies* (Cambridge, 1987).

2. Kertzer, *Ritual, Politics, and Power*, 5.

3. David Cannadine, introduction to *Rituals of Royalty*, 2.

4. James C. Scott, *Domination and the Arts of Resistance: Hidden Transcripts* (New Haven, 1990), chs. 2, 3.

5. Richard J. Smith, "Ritual in Qing Culture," in *Orthodoxy in Late Imperial China*, ed. Kwang-ching Liu (Berkeley, 1990), 282–90; quote on 288.

6. Charles Hucker, *The Traditional Chinese State in Ming Times (1368–1644)* (Tucson, 1961), 68.

7. Mori Masao, "Tōketsu ni okeru kunshu kan," in *Nairaku Ajia, Nishi Ajia no shakai to bunka*, ed. Mori Masao (Tokyo, 1983), 94–132; Herbert Franke, *From Tribal Chieftain to Universal Emperor and God: The Legitimation of the Yuan Dynasty* (Munich, 1978), 16–19.

8. Taken from the *manju i yargiyan kooli*, j. 4, in *Qing shilu* (reprint, Bei-

jing, 1986), 1:182, with a Manchu, Chinese, and Mongol text. The Chinese text reads differently: "Taizu established the calendar and took the imperial position."

9. The first Manchu translation of the *Liji* was ordered in 1653; see Hanson Chase, "The Status of the Manchu Language in the Early Qing" (Ph.D. diss., University of Washington, Seattle, 1979).

10. Sun Wenliang and Li Zhiting, *Qing Taizong quanzhuan* (Changchun, 1983), 261; Franke, *From Tribal Chieftain*, 42–46; Xu Yang, "Huangtaiji xide chuan'guoxi," *Manzu yanjiu* 3 (1994): 11–12. But note (chapter 1) that this seal's symbolic value was downplayed in later years; it does not appear as a prominent feature of the imperial seal collection.

11. Joseph Fletcher, "The heyday of the Ch'ing order in Mongolia, Sinkiang and Tibet," in *The Cambridge History of China: Late Ch'ing 1800–1911, Part 1*, ed. John K. Fairbank (Cambridge, 1978), 407. Pamela K. Crossley, "Review Article: The Rulerships of China," *American Historical Review* 97, no. 5 (1992): 1468–83. On a slightly different subject population, the so-called Sino-Muslims, see Jonathan N. Lipman, "Hyphenated Chinese: Sino-Muslim Identity in Modern China," in *Remapping China: Fissures in Historical Terrain*, ed. Gail Hershatter, Emily Honig, Jonathan N. Lipman, and Randall Stross (Stanford, 1996), 97–112.

12. On shifts in Qing policy toward Xinjiang Muslims, see James A. Millward, "Beyond the Pass: Commerce, Ethnicity, and the Qing Empire in Xinjiang, 1759–1864" (Ph.D. diss., Stanford University, 1993). On the Qianlong emperor's support of the building of the Amîn Khoja mosque, see Hu Ji et al., *Tulufan* (Shaanxi, 1987): my thanks to Jim Millward for this citation. On the late Qing Muslim uprisings, see Kwang-ching Liu, "The military challenge: the north-west and the coast," in *The Cambridge History of China: Late Ch'ing 1800–1911, Part 2*, ed. John K. Fairbank and Kwang-ching Liu (Cambridge, 1980), 211–43.

13. John D. Langlois, Jr., introduction to *China Under Mongol Rule*, ed. J. D. Langlois (Princeton, 1981), 3–7; quote on 7. On the use of the *khuriltai* by Chinggis, see Paul Ratchnevsky, *Genghis Khan: His Life and Legacy*, trans. Thomas Haining (Oxford, 1991), 108.

14. For a new understanding of the evolving conception of emperorship during the Qing dynasty, see Pamela K. Crossley, *A Translucent Mirror: History and Identity in the Transformations of Qing Imperial Ideology* (Berkeley, forthcoming). I explain the significance of the emperor's Buddhist identity in the next chapter.

15. The term "domestic" refers here to the rituals marking imperial birthdays and deathdays that dotted the ritual calendar; these will be discussed at length in chapter 8.

16. The *feng* and *shan* were sacrifices to Heaven and Earth, performed by the first emperor, Qinshihuang, at Taishan. See Susan Naquin and Chün-fang Yü, eds., introduction to *Pilgrims and Sacred Sites in China* (Berkeley, 1992), 13, 66.

17. Angela Zito, " Grand Sacrifice as Text/Performance: Writing and Ritual in Eighteenth-Century China" (Ph.D. diss., University of Chicago, 1989); James L. Hevia, "Emperors, Lamas, and Rituals: Political Implications in Qing Imperial Ceremonies," *Journal of the International Association of Buddhist Studies* 16, no. 2 (1993): 243–78; Evelyn S. Rawski, "The Imperial Way of Death," in *Death Ritual in Late Imperial and Modern China*, ed. James L. Watson and Evelyn S. Rawski (Berkeley, 1988), 228–53; Margareta T. J. Greissler, "The Last Dynastic Funeral: Ritual Sequence at the Demise of the Empress Dowager Cixi," *Oriens Extremus* 34, nos. 1–2 (1991): 7–35; Evelyn S. Rawski, "Qing Imperial Marriage and Problems of Rulership," in *Marriage and Inequality in Chinese Society*, ed. Rubie S. Watson and Patricia B. Ebrey (Berkeley, 1991), 170–203.

18. Howard J. Wechsler, *Offerings of Jade and Silk: Ritual and Symbol in the Legitimation of the Tang Dynasty* (New Haven, 1985), 121.

19. Wechsler, *Offerings of Jade and Silk*, ch. 1; Sarah Allen, "Drought, Human Sacrifice and the Mandate of Heaven in a Lost Text from the *Shang Shu*," *Bulletin, School of Oriental and African Studies, London University* 47 (1984): 523 39.

20. Hok-lam Chan, "'Ta Chin' (Great Golden): the origin and changing interpretations of the Jurchen State Name," *T'oung Pao* 77, nos. 4–5 (1991): 253–99.

21. *DQHDSL*, j. 423 on sacrifices at the Taimiao and j. 433 on those at the Lidai di wang miao.

22. See the analysis by Sarah Allen ("Drought, Human Sacrifice," 532) on the paradox that Heaven bestows the Mandate of Heaven on a virtuous ruler, yet that man, in order to found a new dynasty, commits regicide.

23. Frederic Wakeman, Jr., *The Great Enterprise* (Berkeley, 1985).

24. *Da Qing Shizu Zhang huangdi shilu*, 9.1a–5b, Shunzi reign (hereafter SZ) 1/10/1 (October 30, 1644).

25. Evelyn S. Rawski, "The Creation of an Emperor in Eighteenth-Century China," in *Harmony and Counterpoint: Ritual Music in Chinese Context*, ed. Bell Yung, Evelyn S. Rawski, and Rubie S. Watson (Stanford, 1996), 150–74.

26. Jeffrey F. Meyer, *The Dragons of Tiananmen: Beijing as a Sacred City* (Columbia, S.C., 1991), 40.

27. Ellen Uitzinger, "Emperorship in China," in *De Verboden Stad: Hofculture van de Chinese keizers (1644–1911)* (Rotterdam, 1990), 72.

28. In Christopher Dawson, *Mission to Asia* (Toronto, 1980), 63–64.

29. *Manzhou shilu*; on the rewriting of this record, see Liu Housheng, "Cong 'Jiu Manzhou dang' kan 'Manwen laodang' zhong de wei yu cuo," *Qingshi yanjiu* 4 (1991): 20–28. According to Changbaishanren, the thrones used before 1644 differed from those used during the dynasty. For a description of the evolution of thrones used by the Manchus, see his "Qingdai baozuo," in *Suoji qinggong*, ed. Wei Jiangong et al. (Beijing, 1990), 159–64.

30. Xu Ke, *Qing bai leichao* (1917; reprint, Taipei, 1966), 7–8.

31. The term "mounting the ultimate" (*dengji*) appears in the Veritable

Records to describe the accession rites of the Yongzheng emperor (*Shengzu Ren huangdi shilu*, j. 1, KX 61/11/19), the Tongzhi emperor (*Wenzong Xian huangdi shilu*, j. 6, XF 11/10/8), the Guangxu emperor (*Dezong Jing huangdi shilu*, j. 3, GX 1/1/20), and the Xuantong emperor (*Xuantong zhengji*, j. 2, GX 34/11/9). On the Ming rites, see *Da Ming huidian*, Board of Rites j. 3, 45.

32. Meyer, *Dragons of Tiananmen*, 54.

33. Christian Jochim, "The Imperial Audience Ceremonies of the Ch'ing Dynasty," *Society for the Study of Chinese Religions*, no. 7 (1979): 99.

34. T. Griffith Foulk and Robert H. Sharf, "On the Ritual Use of Ch'an Portraiture in Medieval China," *Cahiers d'Extrême-Asie* 7 (1993): 149–219.

35. See E. T. Williams, "The State Religion of China During the Manchu Dynasty," *Journal, North China Branch of the Royal Asiatic Society* 44 (1913): 33, and his article "Worshipping Imperial Ancestors in Peking," *Journal, North China Branch of the Royal Asiatic Society* 70 (1939): 50, 53. Illustrations of the thrones on which tablets were placed to receive sacrifice are found in Ishibashi Ushio, *Tentan* (Tokyo, 1958), 22, 23, 34, 35, 55; see also 297–98.

36. Song-nien Po and David Johnson, *Domesticated Deities and Auspicious Emblems* (Berkeley, 1992), 11.

37. Jochim, "Imperial Audience," 92; James Hevia, "Sovereignty and Subject: Constructing Relations of Power in Qing Imperial Ritual," in *Body, Subjectivity, and Power in China*, ed. Angela Zito and Tani Barlow (Chicago, 1994), 181–200.

38. Ray Huang, *1587: A Year of No Significance* (New Haven, 1981); Joseph S. C. Lam, "Ritual and Musical Politics in the Court of Ming Shizong," in *Harmony and Counterpoint: Ritual Music in Chinese Context*, ed. Bell Yung, Evelyn S. Rawski, and Rubie S. Watson (Stanford, 1996), 35–53.

39. Cited in Silas H. L. Wu, *Passage to Power: Kangxi and His Heir Apparent, 1661–1722* (Cambridge, Mass., 1979), 52.

40. Wu, *Passage to Power*, 4, 12, 51, 181–82; Yu Shanpu, *Qing dongling daguan* (Shijiazhuang, 1985), 57–58; Bai Xinliang, "Lun Qianlong mimi jianchu," *Gugong bowuyuan yuankan* 2(1989): 4.

41. Harold L. Kahn, *Monarchy in the Emperor's Eyes: Image and Reality in the Qianlong Reign* (Cambridge, Mass., 1971), 89–92; Harold L. Kahn, "The Politics of Filiality: Justification for Imperial Action in Eighteenth-Century China," *Journal of Asian Studies* 26, no. 2 (1967): 203.

42. See *(Qinding) Da Qing huidian tu* (reprinted with *DQHD*, 1976 [hereafter *DQHDT*]), j. 7; both this source and *DQHDSL*, j. 423, contradict the assertion by Williams, "Worshipping Imperial Ancestors," 54, that the focal ancestor for rituals in the main hall of the Taimiao was Shizu, the Shunzhi emperor. There was also a Taimiao in Mukden (Shengjing), which emperors visited during their eastern tours, but according to one scholar, the Mukden temple may not have had spirit tablets, nor were officials sent there to conduct the reporting rituals noted above: see Tong Yüe, "Qing Shengjing taimiao kaoshu," *Gugong bowuyuan yuankan* 3(1987): 27.

43. The charts for sacrifice in the *DQHDT*, j. 7 list tablets in the Fengxian-

dian; the statement in Rawski, "Imperial Way of Death," 233, implying the inclusion of tablets to the ancestors before Nurgaci is incorrect.

44. Rawski, "Imperial Way of Death," 234–38.

45. Zhongguo diyi dang'anguan, Qingdai di wang lingqin (Beijing, 1982), 2.

46. DQHDSL, j. 422; DQHDT, j. 1. Several late Qing descriptions of the altar note the inclusion of the imperial tablets: Henry Blodget, "The Worship of Heaven and Earth by the Emperor of China," Journal, American Oriental Society 20 (1899): 62; S. E. Meech, "The Imperial Worship at the Altar of Heaven," The Chinese Recorder 47, no. 2 (1916): 115; Williams, "State Religion of China," 29.

47. Hok-lam Chan, "'Ta Chin' (Great Golden): The Origin and Changing Interpretations of the Jurchen State Name," T'oung Pao 77, nos. 4–5 (1991): 253–99. On Qing additions to the Lidai diwang miao, see (Yuzhi) Da Qing tongli (hereafter DQTL), 1824 ed., 1.5b.

48. Wechsler, Offerings of Jade and Silk, 136.

49. DQTL, 1759 ed., 9.9b–10b lists 163 previous rulers who received sacrifice from the Qing.

50. Kahn, Monarchy, 230.

51. Gaozong Chun huangdi shilu, for 1796–99 period.

52. Wechsler, Offerings of Jade and Silk, 26, 108; quote from Angela Zito, "Re-Presenting Sacrifice: Cosmology and the Editing of Texts," Ch'ing-shih wen-t'i 5, no. 2 (1984): 52; also see her "Grand Sacrifice as Text/Performance."

53. Wechsler, Offerings of Jade and Silk, 108, 122; C. K. Yang, Religion in Chinese Society (Berkeley, 1961), 128.

54. For a listing of the state sacrifices and their ranking, see DQHDSL, j. 415.

55. The state rituals are authoritatively described in the DQHD and DQTL. They have been studied by many authors, including Williams, "State Religion of China."

56. Rawski, "Imperial Way of Death," 235.

57. Quoted in Wechsler, Offerings of Jade and Silk, 26.

58. Edict dated KX 50/11/10 (Shengzu Ren huangdi shilu, 248:15b); 1722 edict KX 61/11/9 (ibid., 300:3b–4a).

59. Dated QL 51/11/2 (Gaozong Chun huangdi shilu, 1268:2ab).

60. Taichangsi zeli, j. 1; Beatrice Bartlett, Monarchs and Ministers: The Grand Council in Mid-Ch'ing China, 1723–1820 (Berkeley, 1991), 253.

61. Wechsler, Offerings of Jade and Silk, 108–15, 123–35.

62. See, for example, the Veritable Records for 1664, when the emperor performed three of the nine great sacrifices: Shengzu Ren huangdi shilu, j. 11–13, 1664 can be compared with 1867 and 1870, before Zaichun assumed personal control, and 1873, after the end of the regency. In 1867 and 1870 the emperor performed none, and in 1873 he personally performed all the great sacrifices (Muzong Yi huangdi shilu, j. 194–220, 274–301, 348–62). For the Guangxu emperor, where the same contrast applies, see Dezong Jing huangdi shilu, j. 177–200 for 1884, and j. 569–85 for 1907.

63. The emperor's personal ritual performances (but not those he delegated to others) are recorded in *Kangxi qijuzhu:* see 1:145–87, 1:345–94, 2:1579–704, and 3:1705–822 for 1674–75, 1678–79, 1688–89, and 1689–90.

64. *Shengzu Jen huangdi shilu*, 258.15ab (KX 53/4/20), 260.7ab (KX 53/9/30).

65. Quote from edict dated KX 50/11/10, *Shengzu Jen huangdi shilu*, 258.15ab.

66. Edict dated QL 59/5/22, *Gaozong Chun huangdi shilu*, 1453.11a–15a.

67. *Shengzu Jen huangdi shilu*, j. 114–18 (KX 23); j. 162–65 (KX 33); j. 214–18 (KX 43); j. 258–61 (KX 53).

68. Jacques Gernet, *China and the Christian Impact*, trans. Janet Lloyd (Cambridge, 1985), 105.

69. The term "domestic" refers here to the rituals marking imperial birthdays and deathdays that dotted the ritual calendar; these will be discussed at length in chapter 8.

70. Williams, "State Religion of China," 14. On state calendars in general, see Richard J. Smith, "A Note on Qing Dynasty Calendars," *Late Imperial China* 9, no. 1 (1988): 123–45.

71. Both calendars are to be found in Archives 495-14-1/50 (Board of Rites).

72. Quote from the Qianlong emperor, in an edict dated QL 51/3/20 (*Gaozong Ch'un huangdi shilu*, 251.6b–7a), DQHDSL, j. 448, 449.

73. BQTZ, 5:2870–902; 2873–93; 2875–907; 2895–911;2909–27; 2896–3904; 2915; 2897–919.

74. For biographical information on Bahundai, see BQTZ, 3:1550–51 (the Chinese phonetic rendering of his name in this source uses a different third character from the one in the *DQSL*), Fushan, BQTZ, 3:1535–36 and on Yangguri, *ECCP*, 898–99; Tong Guowei, *ECCP*, 795–96; Poerpen (the characters used to render his name differ from those in the *DQSL*), BQTZ, 3:1536, and on his ancestors, *ECCP*, 247; Alingga, *ECCP*, 220; Marsai, *ECCP*, 265 and his ancestor, *ECCP*, 784; Efei, BQTZ, 3:1488; Urjan BQTZ, 3:1440 and his ancestor, *ECCP*, 934–35.

75. Feng Erkang, "Kangxi chao de chuwei zhih zheng he Yinzhen de shengli," *Gugong bowuyuan yuankan* 3 (1981): 19.

76. *ECCP*, 331.

77. On Yinti, see *ECCP*, 930–31.

78. The information here is drawn from two overlapping but not identical lists: Archives 155-4-16-3/2949, a "record of grand sacrifices" (*da ji dang*) covering QL 33/10 to QL 39/12, and the Veritable Records (*DQSL*, 32:11759–33:12153); the archival record includes events, such as birthdays of ancestors, and the names of persons appointed to perform lower-ranking sacrifices, omitted in the Veritable Records, while the Veritable Records includes some of the first-rank rites missing from the archival document.

79. *Taichangsi zeli*, j. 1.

80. A memorial dated GX 1/12/24 (Archives 446-5-55/614) seeking the

name of someone to perform the rites at the Shouhuangdian, stipulates, "the person must be a *beile* of the "close branches." The 1808 and 1816 edicts cited are found in *Taichangsi zeli*, Daoguang ed., j. 1, held by the National Central Library, Taipei.

81. The complaint was voiced in 1689 (KX 28) concerning the prayer to be burned during the prayer for a good harvest at the Qiniandian; see *DQHDSL*, j. 419.

82. Allen, "Drought, Human Sacrifice," 528. The link to sacrifices for rain does not contradict similar efforts made in other localities: see Kenneth Pomeranz, "Water to Iron, Widows to Warlords: The Handan Rain Shrine in Modern Chinese History," *Late Imperial China* 12, no. 1 (1991): 62–99. That similar efforts continue in contemporary China is clear from Kathryn Lowry, "Between Speech and Song: Singing Contests at Northwest Chinese Festivals," in *Contests*, ed. Andrew Duff-Cooper (Edinburgh, 1990), 6:61–79. Lowry studies singing contests during festivals to local gods and rain gods in Gansu, the People's Republic of China.

83. For their periodicity, see tables 1–2 on 41, 43 in Walter H. Mallory, *China: Land of Famine* (New York, 1926).

84. Memorials reporting rainfall for the Peking area are found for JQ 1/6/12 (July 16, 1796) Archives 446-5-55/324; JQ 6/2/21 (April 3, 1801), 446-5-55/341. Pierre-Etienne Will, *Bureaucracy and Famine in Eighteenth-Century China*, trans. Elborg Forster (Stanford, 1990).

85. Mark Lewis, *Sanctioned Violence in Early China* (Albany, 1990), 185–95; Judith M. Boltz, *A Survey of Taoist Literature: Tenth to Seventeenth Centuries* (Berkeley, 1987), 41, 66, 93–4, 96, 97, 150, citing Daoist adepts of the second to twelfth centuries A.D.

86. Here and throughout the discussion, *DQHDSL*, j. 420 (unnumbered pages); also see *DQTL*, 1759 ed., 1.43b–49b. 1824 ed., 1.47b–55a.

87. See *DQTL*, 1759 ed., j. 1 for a description of the *dayu* ritual.

88. *DQHDSL*, j. 420, describing the first *yusi*, performed in 1657.

89. Meyer, *Dragons of Tiananmen*, 106; also cited in L. C. Arlington and William Lewisohn, *In Search of Old Peking* (1935; reprint, New York, 1967), 116–17. See *DQHDSL*, j. 440, on middle-rank altars.

90. *DQHDSL*, 244.6a. The temple was classified in the third rank of state altars. On the linkage of dragons to weather and rain, see Zhao Qiguang, "Dragon: The Symbol of China," *Oriental Art*, n.s., 37, no. 2 (1991): 72–80.

91. Memorial dated QL 5/5/16 in Archives 446-5-55/28; *DQHDSL*, 444.6a–7a.

92. *DQHDSL*, 444.7a–8a.

93. *DQHDSL*, 444.8a–9b.

94. *DQHDSL*, 246.10ab.

95. *Gaozong Chun huangdi shilu*, 1247.18ab, QL 51/1/25 (February 23, 1786); also 1257.19b–21b, QL 51/6/25 (July 20, 1786). A similar story is presented in Zhaolian, *Xiaoting zalu* (1909 preface; reprint, Beijing, 1980), 1:

28, concerning the Jiaqing emperor and the building of an embankment in 1803–4.

96. Zhang Naiwei, *Qing gong shuwen* (Beijing, 1990), 961; Arlington and Lewisohn, *Old Peking*, 132; Williams, "State Religion of China," 38. See Boltz, *Survey of Taoist Literature*, 122, 140, 196 for outstanding Daoist rainmakers in earlier times.

97. Memorial dated QL 48/5/4 (June 3, 1783), in Archives 446-5-55/258; on the popular cult, see Li-ch'en Tun, *Annual Customs and Festivals in Peking*, trans. Derk Bodde, 2d ed. (Hong Kong, 1987), 12 n.1.

98. Memorial dated JQ 1/6/12 (July 16, 1796), Archives 446-5-55/324.

99. *DQHDSL*, j. 420; *Gaozong Chun huangdi shilu*, 584.10a–590.17b, covering the period QL 24/4/4 (April 30, 1659) to QL 24/6/13 (July 6, 1659); Xu Ke, *Qing bai leichao*, 1:20.

100. *DQHDSL*, 246.7a–10a.

101. *Shengzu Ren huangdi shilu*, 246.4a, KX 50/4/19 (June 4, 1711); Xu Ke, *Qing bai leichao*, 1:42–45, 7:25.

102. *Shengzu Ren huangdi shilu*, 246.4a, 5a (KX 50/4/19, 50/4/22).

103. *Shengzu Ren huangdi shilu*, 246.5b–9b (KX 50/5/5, 50/5/7, 50/5/9, 50/5/10, 50/5/11, 50/5/12, and 50/5/13).

104. *DQHDSL*, j. 420, dated QL 9.

105. *Gaozong Chun huangdi shilu*, 216.3ab (QL 9/5/2). The term *bu de* could also be translated as "uncharismatic."

106. *Gaozong Chun huangdi shilu*, 217.2ab (QL 9/5/17, reporting events of QL 9/5/16).

107. The 1759 travails are reported in *Gaozong Chun huangdi shilu*, 584.10a to 588.24a (QL 24/4/4 to QL 24/6/13). See Xu Ke, *Qing bai leichao*, 1:20 who cites the emperor's actions in 1759 as exemplary in "displaying sincerity toward Heaven" (*zhi cheng ge tian*).

108. *Xuanzong Cheng huangdi shilu*, 213.2b–215.5a, covering the period DG 12/6/2 (June 29, 1832) to DG 12/7/2 (July 28, 1832).

109. *Xuanzong Cheng huangdi shilu*, 213.8ab.

110. Benjamin Elman, *Classicism, Politics, and Kinship: The Ch'ang-chou School of New Text Confucianism in Late Imperial China* (Berkeley, 1990), 288–89; *ECCP*, 374.

111. In addition to the Veritable Records, see Xu Ke, *Qing bai leichao*, 1: 42–45.

112. For the narrative see *Renzong Rui huangdi shilu*, 174.36a (JQ 12/2/14, March 22, 1807) to 179.30a (JQ 12/5/14, June 19, 1807). Also cited in Xu Ke, *Qing bai leichao*, 7:25.

113. In a memorial dated JQ 6/6/19 (July 29, 1807) in Archives 557-5-66-4/3778.

114. Pomeranz, "Water to Iron," 63; P. Steven Sangren, *History and Magical Power in a Chinese Community* (Stanford, 1987), ch. 11.

115. Pomeranz, "Water to Iron," 63.

CHAPTER 7: SHAMANISM AND
TIBETAN BUDDHISM AT COURT

1. Jane M. Atkinson, *The Art and Politics of Wana Shamanship* (Berkeley, 1989), and her review article, "Shamanisms Today," *Annual Review of Anthropology* 21 (1992): 307–30; Mircea Eliade, *Shamanism: Archaic Techniques of Ecstacy*, trans. Willard R. Trask (Princeton, 1964); and Nicholas Thomas and Caroline Humphrey, eds., *Shamanism, History and the State* (Ann Arbor, 1994).

2. See Roberte N. Hamayon, "Shamanism in Siberia: From Partnership in Supernature to Counter-power in Society," in *Shamanism, History, and the State* (Ann Arbor, 1994), ed. Nicholas Thomas and Caroline Humphrey, 76–89. Hamayon divides Siberian shamanism into three categories derived from the ecology.

3. G. M. Vasilevič, "The Acquisition of Shamanistic Ability Among the Evenki (Tungus)," in *Popular Beliefs and Folklore Tradition in Siberia*, ed. V. Dioszegi (Bloomington, 1968), 341; on Turkic forms of shamanism, see V. Basilov, "Shamanism in Central Asia," in *The Realm of the Extra-Human: Agents and Audiences*, ed. Agehananda Bharati (The Hague, 1976), 149–57; N. A. Alekseev, "Shamanism among the Turkic Peoples of Siberia: Shamans and Their Religious Practices," in *Shamanism: Soviet Studies of Traditional Religion in Siberia and Central Asia*, ed. Marjorie M. Balzer (Armonk, N.Y., 1990), 49–109.

4. Tao Lifan, "Qingdai gongting de saman jisi," *Xibei minzu yanjiu* 1 (1992): 221–32; Sergei M. Shirokogoroff, "General Theory of Shamanism Among the Tungus," *Journal, North China Branch of the Royal Asiatic Society* 54 (1923): 246–49; Vasilevič, "Acquisition of Shamanistic Ability," 342–43.

5. Eliade, *Shamanism*, 497. Shamanism seems to have been the religion of the twelfth-century Jurchen: see Jing-shen Tao, *The Jurchen in Twelfth-Century China* (Seattle, 1976), 12–13.

6. Fu Yuguang, *Samanjiao yu shenhua* (Shenyang, 1990); Fu Yuguang and Meng Huiying, *Manzu samanjiao yanjiu*; Meng Huiying, *Manzu minjian wenhua lunji* (Shenyang, 1990); Fu Yingren, *Manzu shenhua gushi* (Harbin, 1985). Wang Honggang, "Manzu samanjiao de sanzhong xingtai ji qi yanbian," *Shehui kexue zhanxian* 1 (1988): 187–93.

7. Fu Yuguang, *Samanjiao yu shenhua*, 214: Uludun's story comes from a recitation by a *da saman*, Fu Qiye, in Sunwu county, Heilongjiang, 1936. Meng Huiying, *Manzu minjian wenhua lunji*, 238–40.

8. Fu Yuguang, *Samanjiao yu shenhua*, 76; Meng Huiying, *Manzu minjian wenhua lunji*, 208, 211; Fu Yuguang, "Samanjiao tian qiong guannian chu kao," *Heilongjiang minzu congkan* 3 (1987): 35–42; also "Qing gong tangzi jisi biankao," *Shehui kexue zhanxian* 4 (1988): 210.

9. L. C. Arlington and William Lewisohn, *In Search of Old Peking* (1935; reprint, New York, 1967), 69. According to Xu Ke, *Qing bai leichao* (1917;

reprint, Taipei, 1966), 11:97, there were many crows at the Taimiao, as there are in the Forbidden City today. Li Fengmin and Lu Haiying, eds., *Gugong zaqu* (Shenyang, 1996), 29–31, cite Jinliang, who found flocks of crows still thronging to the palace in Shenyang in 1928–31.

10. Taken from the *daicing gurun i fukjin doro neihe bodogon*, ch. 2.

11. Yan Chongnian, "Manzhou shen'gan sishen kaoyuan," *Lishi dang'an* 3 (1993): 81–85; Inoue Ichii, "Shinchō kyūtei samankyō," 80; Tao Lifan, "Qingdai gongting," 224; Luo Qi, "Manzu shenhua de minzu tedian," *Manzu yanjiu* 1 (1993): 76–85 notes that the magpie cult expanded after 1644. Fu Yuguang, *Samanjiao yu shenhua*, 54 differs from Yan Chongnian, stating that the sacrifice at the spirit pole is primarily directed to the sacred crow.

12. Wubing'an, "Saman shijie de 'zhenshen'—saman," *Manzu yanjiu* 1 (1989): 65–67; the term "transformational shamanism" comes from Caroline Humphrey, "Shamanic Practices and the State in Northern Asia: Views from the Center and Periphery," in *Shamanism, History, and the State*, ed. Nicholas Thomas and Caroline Humphrey (Ann Arbor, 1994), 198.

13. Akiba Takashi, "Sama no fusai to daisen no fujutsu—Manshū fuzokutō sa hōkoku," *Minzokugaku kenkyū* 1, no. 2 (1935): 237–57; Humphrey, "Shamanic Practices," 198.

14. Jiang Xiangshun, "Qing chu gongting de saman jisi," *Beifang wenwu* 2 (1988): 72; see Zhang Jinfan and Guo Chengkang, *Qing ruguan qian guojia falü zhidu shi* (Shenyang, 1988), 221 on punishment of company captain Bartai for this offense.

15. Archives 446-5-55/423 dated JQ 23/12/15 (January 10, 1819), presents memorials in the files from earlier reigns that are linked to the issue of shamanic rituals performed on behalf of or by the emperor's sons: memorial dated KX 24/5/9 (June 10, 1685). Archival documents on provisions for these sacrifices include memorials dated QL 25/3/1 (April 16, 1760), QL 25/3/21 (May 6, 1760), QL 25/3/29 (May 14, 1760) [446-5-55/123]; QL 44/4/28 (May 7, 1779) [446-5-55/244]; QL 60/11/18 (December 28, 1795) [446-5-55/322]; and the long summary of precedents in memorial dated JQ 23/12/15 (January 10, 1819) [446-5-55/423].

16. Mircea Eliade, *Shamanism: Archaic Techniques of Ecstasy*, trans. Willard R. Trask (Princeton, 1974), 4. More recent scholarship questions his emphasis on the celestial journey and notes the importance of the shaman's travels to both the lower as well as the upper world; see Atkinson, *Wana Shamanship*, ch. 10.

17. Margaret Nowak and Stephen Durrant, *The Tale of the Nišan Shamaness: A Manchu Folk Epic* (Seattle, 1977), 35. See Meng Huiying, *Manzu minjian wenhua lunji*, 141–83 for a study of folktales concerning Nišan saman circulating in the 1980s. Kevin Stuart, Li Xuewei, and Shelear, eds., *China's Dagur Minority: Society, Shamanism, and Folklore* (Philadelphia, 1994), 89–102, present a variant form of the epic, entitled "Nisang yadgan," which circulated among the Daur. In the 1980s a second epic was discovered: see Tatjana A. Pang and Giovanni Stary, "On the Discovery of a Manchu Epic," *Central Asi-*

atic Journal 38, no. 1 (1994): 58–70; Fu Yuguang, *Samanjiao yu shenhua*, 279–86.

18. Photographs of shamanic dress and instruments housed in the imperial palace (Qingninggong) in Mukden were published in Akamatsu Chijo and Akiba Takashi, *Manmō no minzoku to shūkyō* (Kyoto, 1941), 29–37 and Murata Jirō, "Shin-nei-kū no saiki (Shin kūshitsu syamanizumu sono san), *Manmō* 16, no. 3 (1935): 61–72; they are recognizably the same as the sketch of a Manchu shaman in Walther Heissig, *The Religions of Mongolia*, trans. Geoffrey Samuel (Berkeley, 1970), 18. Shamans pictured in performance in 1933–34 Manchuria also wore similar dress: see Akiba Takashi, "Sama no fusai to daisen no fujutsu"; Wang Honggang and Fu Yuguang, "Saman shen'gu tansuo," *Beifang wenwu* 1 (1992): 49; Eliade, *Shamanism*, ch. 5.

19. The 1660 prayer can be found in Archives 467-4-85/112 and is dated SZ 17/3/1 (April 10, 1660). On earlier beliefs about the heavens, see Fu Yuguang, "Samanjiao tian qiong guannian"; Meng Huiying, *Manzu minjian wenhua lunji*, 211–13. A multiplicity of heavens also characterized Mongol shamanic belief before the reign of Chinggis Khan: see Sechin Jagchid, "Chinggis Khan in Mongolian Folklore," in his *Essays in Mongolian Studies* (Provo, Utah, 1988), 300. Fu Yuguang, "Qing gong tangzi jisi biankao," 208; Wang Honggang, "Manzu samanjiao de sanzhong xingtai," 189, 192. The echoes of these earlier beliefs are reported by Eliade, *Shamanism*, 9, who notes that "Heaven" has seven or nine "sons" and "daughters" who are subordinate to him and who occupy lower heavens.

20. *Qinding Manzhou jishen jitian dianli*, 1.3ab. See Nicola di Cosmo, "Manchu Rites and Ceremonies at the Qing Court: A Study Based on the *Manjusai wecere metere kooli bithe, The Code of Sacrifices and Rituals of the Manchus*," in *State Ritual in China*, ed. Joseph McDermott (Cambridge, forthcoming). For an analysis of Nurgaci's use of the term "Heaven," see Gui Fu and He Shimin, "Nuerhachi de zongjiao zhengce yu qi baye," *Nei Menggu shida xuebao* (*zhexue shehui kexue ban*) 1 (1990): 84–89. According to Fu Yuguang, "Qing gong tangzi," 208, the rites to heaven predate shamanic ancestral rituals.

21. Inoue Ichii, "Shinchō kyūtei samankyō shiden ni tsuite," in *Haneda hakase shoju kinen Tōyōshi ronsō*, Haneda hakase shoju kinen kai (Kyoto, 1950), 91. According to Fu Yuguang, "Qing gong tangzi," 208, the oldest shamanic rites were not directed at the ancestors but at Heaven.

22. Fu Yuguang and Meng Huiying, *Manzu samanjiao yanjiu* (Beijing, 1991), 35–48.

23. Jagchid, "Chinggis Khan in Mongolian Folklore," 300; see Humphrey, "Shamanic Practices," 210–18 for an extensive analysis of the political role of shamanic prophecy in Mongol politics.

24. Ueno Saneyoshi, "Dōshi saishi kō," in *Shigaku kenkyū kinen ronsō*, Hiroshima bunrika daigaku, shigakka kyōshitsu (Hiroshima, 1950), 337–38; Murata Jirō, "Dōshi (Shin kūshitsu syamanizumu sono ichi)," *Manmō* 16, no. 1 (1935): 96–98; Ishibashi Ushio, *Peipin no samankyō ni tsuite* (Tokyo, 1934), 81–84. Gui Fu and He Shimin, "Nuerhachi de zongjiao."

25. Zhaolian, *Xiaoting zalu* (1909; reprint, Beijing, 1980), 232.

26. Murata Jirō, "Dōshi," 95–96, says that the New Year rites were discontinued for a period during the early Shunzhi reign; Inoue Ichii, "Shinchō kyūtei samankyō," 82–83.

27. Jiang Xiangshun, "Qing chu gongting," 73.

28. Jiang Xiangshun, "Qing gong samanjisi ji qi lishi yanbian," *Qingshi yanjiu* 1 (1994): 72. A variant explanation is offered by Bai Hongxi, "Qinggong tangzi ji tanji," *Manzu yanjiu* 3 (1995): 61–63.

29. Fu Yuguang and Meng Huiying, *Manzu samanjiao yanjiu*, 50–51. The authors point out that the particular shape of the *tangse* was specific to Nurgaci's clan; other clans used other shapes. Fu Yuguang, "Qing gong tangzi"; Jiang Xiangshun, "Qing gong samanjisi," 72; Murata Jirō, "Dōshi," 99–100; Inoue Ichii, "Shinchō kyūtei samankyō," 87.

30. Eliade, *Shamanism*, 496–500; on Buddhism in Jin times, see Herbert Franke, "The Forest Peoples of Manchuria: Kitans and Jurchens," in *The Cambridge History of Early Inner Asia*, ed. Denis Sinor (Cambridge, 1990), 419; Fu Yuguang, *Samanjiao yu shenhua*, 135. See Xiaoshi, *Yongxian lu*, 75 on the emperor's ritual performance at the *tangzi* during the New Year; his description omits the worship of heaven. On the Guandi cult in China, see Prasenjit Duara, "Superscribing Symbols: The Myth of Guandi, Chinese God of War," *Journal of Asian Studies* 47, no. 4 (1988): 778–95.

31. Charles de Harlez, "La Religion nationale des Tartares orientaux, Mandchous et Mongols, comparée è la religion des anciens Chinois," *Memoires couronnés et autres mémoires* 40 (1887): 13. But note that *enduri* included the Manchu deity Folifodo omosi *mama* and Heaven (Abka *enduri*).

32. On the meanings of these *weceku*, see Fu Yuguang, "Qing gong tangzi jisi," 208–9; Inoue, "Shinchō kyūtei samankyō," 84–85; Guo Shuyun, "Manzhou jishen jitian dianli lunzhe," *Shehui kexue jikan* 5 (1992): 81–82; Mitamura Taisuke, "Manshū syamanizumu no saishi to shukushi," in *Ishihama sensei koki kinen Tōyō gaku ronshū*, ed. Ishihama sensei koki kinen kai (Osaka, 1958), 544; Fu Yuguang, *Samanjiao yu shenhua*, 135–36. Although many of the scholars cited in this section describe the *tangzi* rituals, the clearest and most specific analysis of the separate altars within the compound is provided by Du Jiaji, "Cong Qingdai de gongzhong jisi he tangzi jisi kan samanjiao," *Manzu yanjiu* 1 (1990): 45–49.

33. Murata Jirō, "Dōshi," 102–6; Inoue Ichii, "Shinchō kyūtei samankyō," 60–63; Guo Shuyun, "Manzhou jishen jitian dianli," 82.

34. According to one story, the custom of presenting cooked flesh began only in the reign of Hongtaiji: see Murata Jirō, "Shin nei-kū no saiki," 69–70. The feeding of the birds at the top of the spirit pole goes back to the pre-1644 period: see Jiang Xiangshun, "Qing chu gongting," 75.

35. Ishibashi Ushio, *Peipin no samankyō*, 48–52.

36. *Libu zeli*, 112.3a notes that the emperor is accompanied at the New Year by imperial princes in the first six ranks, Manchu nobles, Manchu presidents of the Board of Rites and the Board of War, and banner lieutenant generals. The

emphasis here thus differs from that of Inoue Ichii, "Shinchō kyūtei saman-kyō," 89–90: he argues that as the *tangzi* became a national temple in the 1636–44 period, religious participation was confined to the imperial lineage.

37. Du Jiaji, "Cong Qingdai de gongzhong jisi," 47; *Libu zeli* 112.3a; *Qinding Manzhou jishen jitian dianli*, 1.4a–5a. Archives 446-5-55/423, dated JQ 23/12, collects nineteen Manchu-language memorials on the subject of shamanic sacrifice by emperor's sons dated from KX 17 (1678) on; see also 446-5-55/244, dated QL 44/4/28 (May 7, 1779) and 446-5-55/252, dated QL 46/4 (1781). Pamela K. Crossley, *Orphan Warriors: Three Manchu Generations and the End of the Qing World* (Princeton, 1990), 188 describes Gūwalgiya Jin-liang's view of the clan mansion in Peking: he "sought out Wenxiang's mansion in the northeast quarter . . . it was uninhabited. . . . Several intersections away, he found the mansion of the Suwan Gūwalgiya main lineage. . . . The spirit pole of the Suwan Gūwalgiya clan stood forlornly in the courtyard."

38. Du Jiaji, "Cong Qingdai de gongzhong jisi," 48; Juliet Bredon, *Peking: A Historical and Intimate Description of Its Chief Places of Interest* (Shanghai, 1922), 181–82.

39. Inoue Ichii, "Shinchō kyūtei samankyō," 75–77; Du Jiaji, "Cong Qing-dai de gongzhong jisi," 48. On the female shamans, see *Qinding Manzhou jishen jitian dianli*, 1.5b, which thus implicitly admits to the commonality of kinship between the Aisin Gioro and other Gioro descent groups. On the artificial creation of an imperial lineage, see Crossley, *Orphan Warriors*, 32–33. On consorts performing in shamanic rites, see Jiang Xiangshun, "Lun Qing gong saman," *Shenyang gugong bowuyuan yuankan* 1 (1995): 63.

40. Inoue Ichii, "Shinchō kyūtei samankyō," 81, 84–86, Inoue cites a taboo against sacrifices to the horse god in the front hall of the Kunning palace. Du Jiaji, "Cong Qingdai de gongzhong jisi," 49.

41. Guo Shuyun, "Manzhou jishen jitian dianli," 81–82; Fu Yuguang, *Samanjiao yu shenhua*, 135–36.

42. The sacrificial calendar of the Kunning palace with the number of pigs required for the third month of JQ 8 (1803) may be found in Archives 557-5-66-4/3778.

43. Jiang Xiangshun, "Qing chu gongting," 74. For descriptions of Manchu dances, and their componentsin shamanic rites, see Li De, "Manzu wudao tangai," *Manzu yanjiu* 1 (1995): 66-74. Giovanni Stary, " 'Praying in the Darkness': New Texts for a Little-Known Manchu Shamanic Rite," *Shaman* 1, no. 1 (1993): 15–30 translates shamanic prayers, collected in Jilin in 1981, that were uttered during this ritual. The phrase "praying in the darkness" (*tui-bumbi*) refers to the prayers uttered by the shaman.

44. *Qinding Manzhou jishen jitian dianli* 1.4a–5a; Archives 446-5-55/424, document dated JQ 24/2/16 (March 11, 1819). See the communication sent to the Zhangyisi on the number of "fine pigs" required for the Kunning sacrifices in 1803, 557-5-66-4/3778. On the *weceku* installed in princely mansions, see archival documents on provisions for these sacrifices, memorials dated QL 25/3/1 (April 16, 1760), QL 25/3/21 (May 6, 1760), QL 25/3/29 (May 14,

1760) [446-5-55/123]; QL 44/4/11 (May 26, 1779) and QL 44/4/28 (June 12, 1779) [446-5-55/243]; QL 44/4/28 (June 12, 1779) [446-5-55/244]; QL 60/11/18 (December 28, 1795) [446-5-55/322]; and the long summary of precedents in a memorial dated JQ 23/12/15 (January 10, 1819) [446-5-55/423]. Fu Kedong, "Baqi Manzhou de jishen lisu," *Manzu yanjiu* 3 (1989): 23–24.

45. Du Jiaji, "Cong Qingdai de gongzhong jisi," 46–47; also reported in Xiaoshi, *Yongxian lu* (1752; reprint, Beijing, 1959), 75–76; *Zongguan neiwufu xianxing tiaoli Guangchusi*, 2.49a.

46. Archives 446-5-55/37, Manchu-language memorial dated QL 7/3/7 (April 11, 1742).

47. *Libu zeli*, 1844 edition, 112.2a, 4a.

48. Crossley, *Orphan Warriors*, 28–29.

49. Murata Jirō, "Shin-nei-kū no saiki," 61; Liu Housheng and Chen Siling, "'Qinding Manzhou jishen jitian dianli' pingzhe," *Qingshi yanjiu* 1 (1994): 66–70.

50. Xiaoshi, *Yongxian lu*, 15–16. On the work itself, see Feng Ergang, *Qing shi shiliaoxue chugao* (Tianjin, 1986), 54. See also Xu Ke, *Qing bai leichao*, 26–28. On the evolution of Manchu clan groups from the Ming to the Qing, see Li Shutian and Yin Youshan, "Ula Manzu hala xintan," *Qingshi yanjiu* 3 (1992): 8–16, 23.

51. Document dated JQ 23/4/4 (May 8, 1818) in Archives 446-5-55/421; Jin Qizong, "Jing qi de Manzu," *Manzu yanjiu* 1 (1989): 58–63.

52. Cao Lijuan, "Hanjun baqi jisi gewu bianzhe," *Manzu yanjiu* 1 (1993): 86–90; Wang Honggang, "Manzu samanjiao de sanzhong xingtai," 191–92; Fu Yuguang, "Qing gong tangzi jisi," 210.

53. Fu Yuguang and Meng Huiying, *Manzu samanjiao yanjiu*, 58–59, cite oral legends about the arrest of shamans and the prohibition of clan deities during the Qing enforcement of their shamanic code.

54. Fu Yuguang and Meng Huiying, *Manzu samanjiao yanjiu*, 60–62; on 85–89 they describe "wild rites" of trance and possession.

55. Minzu wenti wuzhong congshu, Liaoning sheng bianji weiyuan hui, *Manzu shehui lishi diaocha* (Shenyang, 1985), 13; Fu Yuguang, *Samanjiao yu shenhua*, 113; Muercha and Zhan Kun, "Manzu de 'mama koudai' ji 'kaisuo' xisu de tantao," *Manzu yanjiu* 1 (1989): 77–79. Jin Baochen, "Samanjiao zhong de shengtiao chongbai," *Heilongjiang minzu congkan* 1 (1989): 57–59, studies the function of the rope in shamanic ritual and discusses its use in the shamanic sacrifices performed in the Kunning palace during the Qing dynasty, 58–59. On the early twentieth-century rites, see Akamatsu Chijo, "Manshū hatanin no ie-matsuri," *Minzokugaku kenkyū* 1, no. 2 (1935): 224–29 and Oyama Hikoichi, "Samankyō to Manshūzoku no kazoku seido," *Minzokugaku kenkyū* 7, no. 2 (1941): 174–75.

56. Wubing'an, "Saman shijie de 'zhenshen,'" 65.

57. Inoue Ichii, "Shinchō kyūtei samankyō shiden ni tsuite," in *Haneda hakase shoju kinen Tōyōshi ronsō*, ed. Haneda hakase shoju kinen kai (Kyoto, 1950), 76. Jiang Xiangshun, "Qing chu gongting," 73 calls the domestic rites

"kowtow" rites; Akamatsu Chijo, "Manshū hatanin no ie-matsuri." On Korean shamanism, see Laurel Kendall, *Shamans, Housewives, and Other Restless Spirits* (Honolulu, 1985).

58. Wu Yuanfeng and Zhao Zhiqiang, "Xibozu you Keerqin Mengguqi bianru Manzhou baqi shimo," *Minzu yanjiu* 5 (1984): 60–66.

59. Sergei M. Shirokogoroff, *Social Organization of the Northern Tungus* (Shanghai, 1929), 86. See also Zhang Jie, "Qingchu zhaofu xin Manzhou shulue," *Qingshi yanjiu* 1 (1994): 23–30, and his "Qingdai Manzu yuyan wenzi zai dongbei de xingfei yu yingxiang," *Beifang wenwu* 1 (1995): 63–68; Badarongga, "Manzhouyu yu Dawoeryu de guanxi," *Qingyu yanjiu* 2 (1993): 35–38. Badarongga is himself a Daur; he recounts reading the "Three Kingdoms" in Manchu as a child.

60. See the essays on these tribes in M. G. Levin and L. P. Potapov, eds., *The Peoples of Siberia*, trans. and ed. Stephen Dunn (Chicago, 1964), 685–761; the Russian original was published in 1956 by the Academy of Science, Moscow.

61. Elizabetta Chiodo, "The Book of the Offerings to the Holy Činggis Qagan: A Mongolian Ritual Text," *Zentralasiatische Studien* 22 (1989–91): 190–220. Chiodo transcribes a text found in 1958, which has been cited as evidence that a cult of Činggis existed in eastern Mongolia until the time of Ligdan Khan. See Almaz Khan, "Chinggis Khan: From Imperial Ancestor to Ethnic Hero," in *Cultural Encounters on China's Ethnic Frontiers*, ed. Stevan Harrell (Seattle, 1994), 248–77.

62. Meng Huiying, *Manzu minjian wenhua lunji*, 16–39.

63. Luo Qi, "Manzu shenhua," 80. The "Mi-hu ma-hu" is reported along with several other dances drawing on the exploits of Nurgaci in Arlington and Lewisohn, *Old Peking*, 48; on 119 they describe a ritual at the *tangzi* at year's end to commemorate the Aisin Gioro ancestor who was rescued by the magpie. On the dance performed during the wedding, see pl. 61 on 46–47 in Wan Yi et al., eds., *Qingdai gongting shenghuo* (Hong Kong, 1985).

64. "General Sabusu's Cannon," "The Wind Blows Bukui Away," and "The Pearls," in *China's Dagur Minority: Society, Shamanism, and Folklore* (Philadelphia, 1994), ed. Kevin Stuart, Li Xuewei, and Shelear, 122–23, 110–11, 128. Kun Shi, "Ny Dan the Manchu Shamaness," in *Religions of China in Practice*, ed. Donald S. Lopez, Jr. (Princeton, 1996), 226–28.

65. See Kun Shi, "Ny Dan the Manchu Shamaness," 225.

66. Larry W. Moses, *The Political Role of Mongol Buddhism* (Bloomington, 1977), 36; Karl Wittfogel and Feng Chia-sheng, cited in Anatoly M. Khazanov, "The Spread of World Religions in Medieval Nomadic Societies of the Eurasian Steppes," in *Nomadic Diplomacy, Destruction and Religion from the Pacific to the Adriatic*, ed. Michael Gervers and Wayne Schlepp (Toronto, 1994), 24.

67. Ts'un-yan Liu and Judith Berling, "The 'Three Teachings' in the Mongol-Yüan Period," in *Yüan Thought: Chinese Thought and Religion Under the Mongols*, ed. Hok-lam Chan and William Theodore de Bary (New York, 1982), 482–83; Yün-hua Jan, "Chinese Buddhism in Ta-tu: The New Situation and

New Problems," in *Yüan Thought*, 394, 398; Chün-fang Yü, "Chung-feng Ming-pen and Ch'an Buddhism in the Yüan," in *Yüan Thought*, 420.

68. Elliot Sperling, "Early Ming Policy Toward Tibet: An Examination of the Proposition that the Early Ming Emperors Adopted a 'Divide and Rule' Policy Toward Tibet" (Ph.D. diss., Indiana University, 1983). On the gifts produced in Peking and given to Tibetan prelates, see Heather Karmay, *Early Sino-Tibetan Art* (Warminster, England, 1975); Zhu Jiajin, "Gugong suo zang Ming Qing liangdai you guan Xizang de wenwu," *Wenwu* 7 (1959): 14–19; Xizang wenguan hui, wenwu pucha dui, "Dazhaosi zang Yongle nianjian wenwu," *Wenwu* 11 (1985): 66–71; one of the Yongle textile *tangkas* was sold in 1994 at Christie's and is described in Pratapaditya Pal, "An Early Ming Embroidered Masterpiece," *Christie's International Magazine* (May–June 1994): 62–63. Sheila C. Bills, "Bronze Sculptures of the Early Ming (1403–1450)," *Arts of Asia* 24, no. 5 (1994): 73–87, notes (73) that many outstanding bronze sculptures have imperial inscriptions of the Yongle and Xuande reigns. Similarly, J. Lowry, "Tibet, Nepal, or China? An Early Group of Dated Tangkas," *Oriental Art* 19, no. 3 (1973): 306–15 looks at four fifteenth-century *tangkas*, three of them with Chinese-language inscriptions and concludes (314) that various factors "weigh the probability slightly in favour of a Chinese provenance."

69. Zheng Weiguang, "Mingchao zhengfu zai Hehuang diqu de Zangzhuan Fojiao zhengce shulun," *Qinghai shehui kexue* 2 (1989): 93–96; Pu Wencheng, "Zangquan Fojiao chupai zai Qinghai de zaoqi quanban ji qi gaizong," *Xizang yanjiu* 2 (1990): 107–12, 125; T. Wylie, "Lama tribute in the Ming dynasty," in *Tibetan Studies in Honour of Hugh Richardson: Proceedings of the International Seminar on Tibetan Studies, Oxford, 1979*, ed. Michael Aris and Aung San Suu Kyi (Warminster, 1980), 335–40.

70. Zahiruddin Ahmad, *Sino-Tibetan Relations in the Seventeenth Century* (Rome, 1970), 96–98; Samuel Grupper, "Manchu Patronage and Tibetan Buddhism during the First Half of the Qing Dynasty: A Review Article," *Journal of the Tibet Society* 4 (1984): 49.

71. Geoffrey Samuel, *Civilized Shamans: Buddhism in Tibetan Societies* (Washington, D.C., 1993), 490. Moses, *Political Role of Mongol Buddhism*, chs. 1, 2. Giuseppe Tucci, *The Religions of Tibet*, trans. Geoffrey Samuel (Berkeley, 1980), 27, 40–41.

72. Moses, *Political Role of Mongol Buddhism*, 92–98; Tucci, *Religions of Tibet*, 41: because his two predecessors were retroactively also given this title, bSod nams rgya mtsho became known as the third Dalai lama. On the political ascendency of the dGe lugs pa within Tibet, see Ahmad, *Sino-Tibetan Relations*, ch. 3.

73. Cai Zhichun, "Menggu lama guizu xingcheng chutan," *Minzu yanjiu* 1 (1987): 52.

74. Patricia Berger, "'A Buddha from Former Times': Zanabazar and the Mongol Renaissance," *Orientations* 26, no. 6 (1995): 53; "After Xanadu," in *Mongolia: The Legacy of Chinggis Khan*, edited by Patricia Berger and Terese

Tse Bartholomew (San Francisco, 1995), 50–75. Zanabazar was the Mongol pronunciation of the reincarnate prelate's Sanskrit religious name, Jinanavajra. See also Zhang Xixin, *Qingdai si da huofo* (Beijing, 1989), 32–39; Junko Miyawaki, "The Qalqa Mongols and the Oyirad in the Seventeenth Century," 147–52; Gilles Béguin, "Mongolian Art Treasures from the 17th–19th Centuries," *Oriental Art* 39, no. 4 (1993–94): 14–21; Teresa Tse Bartholomew, "The Legacy of Chinggis Khan," *Orientations* 26, no. 6 (1995): 46–52; Robert A. Rupen, "The City of Urga in the Manchu Period," *Studia Altaica: Festschrift für Nikolaus Poppe zum 60. Geburtstag am 8. August 1957* (Wiesbaden, 1957), 157–69.

75. Charles R. Bawden, *The Modern History of Mongolia* (London, 1968), 69–77, provides the narrative of these activities. See Bawden's translation, *The Jebtsundamba Khutukhtus of Urga: Text, Translation and Notes* (Wiesbaden, 1961), 45–46.

76. Pu Wencheng, "Zangzhuan Fojiao," also his "Qinghai de Menggu zu siyuan," *Qinghai shehui kexue* 6 (1989): 102–9.

77. Chen Guoguang, "Xi Menggu fojiao jingji de xingrong," *Xinjiang shehui kexue* 4 (1987): 103–11.

78. Balkrishna G. Gokhale, "Early Buddhist Kingship," *Journal of Asian Studies* 26, no. 1 (1966): 15–22; S. J. Tambiah, *World Conqueror and World Renouncer: A Study of Buddhism and Polity in Thailand Against a Historical Background* (Cambridge, 1976), ch. 4; Arthur F. Wright, *Buddhism in Chinese History* (Stanford, 1959), 50–51.

79. Turrell Wylie, "Reincarnation: A Political Innovation in Tibetan Buddhism," *Proceedings of the Csoma de Körös Memorial Symposium Held at Mátrafüred, Hungary, 24–30 September 1976*, ed. Louis Ligeti (Budapest, 1978), 579.

80. Barbara N. Aziz, "Reincarnation Reconsidered—Or the Reincarnate Lama as Shaman," in *Spirit Possession in the Nepal Himalayas*, ed. John T. Hitchcock and Rex L. Jones (New Delhi, 1976), 347. Aziz differs from Wylie in using *sprul sku* as the equivalent of the reincarnate lama; see also Geoffrey Samuel, *Civilized Shamans: Buddhism in Tibetan Societies* (Washington, 1993), 493–95.

81. "Reincarnation," 580, 584, 586. See also Samuel, *Civilized Shamans*, 494.

82. Samuel, *Civilized Shamans*, 281–82; Almaz Khan, "Chinggis Khan: From Imperial Ancestor to Ethnic Hero," in *Cultural Encounters on China's Ethnic Frontiers*, ed. Stevan Harrell (Seattle, 1994), 253; Liang Bing, *Chengjisi han ling yu Erduosi* (Huhehaote, 1988). On Tsong kha pa, see David L. Snellgrove and Hugh Richardson, *A Cultural History of Tibet* (New York, 1968), 182–83.

83. Xing Li, "Lamajiao de Mengguhua," *Heilongjiang minzu congkan* 4 (1993): 93; Herbert Franke, *From Tribal Chieftain to Universal Emperor and God: The Legitimation of the Yuan Dynasty* (Munich, 1978), 64–65.

84. Heissig, *Religions of Mongolia*, 30–31; Hidehiro Okada, "Origin of the

Čaqar Mongols," *Mongolian Studies* 14 (1991): 167–68. A slightly different translation of Ligdan Khan's titles is provided by Bawden, *Modern History of Mongolia*, 34. The edition of the Mongolian Kanjur commissioned by Ligdan Khan in 1628–1629 is described by Lokesh Chandra, *Buddhist Iconography* (New Delhi, 1988),1:8. On Altan Khan as Khubilai, see Moses, *Political Role of Mongol Buddhism*, 96.

85. Khan, "Chinggis Khan: From Imperial Ancestor to Ethnic Hero," 252; Jagchid, "Chinggis Khan in Mongolian Folklore."

86. G. M. Macartney, *An Embassy to China: Being the journal kept by Lord Macartney during his embassy to the Emperor Ch'ien-lung, 1793–1794,* ed. J. L. Cranmer-Byng (London, 1962), 130.

87. James L. Hevia, *Cherishing Men from Afar: Qing Guest Ritual and the Macartney Embassy of 1793* (Durham, 1995), 108.

88. Yumiko Ishihama, "On the Dissemination of the Belief in the Dalai Lama as a Manifestation of the Bodhisattva Avalokitesvara," *Acta Asiatica* 64 (1993): 38–56. On the internal rivalries in Tibet, see Dan Martin, "Bonpo Canons and Jesuit Cannons: On Sectarian Factors Involved in the Ch'ien-lung Emperor's Second Goldstream Expedition of 1771–1776 Based Primarily on Some Tibetan Sources," *The Tibet Journal* 15, no. 2 (1990): 3–28.

89. Snellgrove and Richardson, *A Cultural History*, 200.

90. Michael Khordarkovsky, *Where Two Worlds Met: The Russian State and the Kalmyk Nomads, 1600–1771* (Ithaca, 1992), 15, 126, 152. Ahmad, *Sino-Tibetan Relations*, 101–152. Wuyunbilege, "Heshite han ting de jianli guocheng," *Nei Menggu shehui kexue* 4 (1988): 70–74.

91. Hanguanquejia, "Jian tan Qingchao qianqi Qinghai Menggu de tong-zhi," *Qinghai minzu xueyuan xuebao (shehui kexue ban)* 3 (1988): 33–36.

92. The role of the sGo mang school at 'Bras spungs (Drepung) in stirring up the Khosot over this issue has been analyzed by Ishihama Yumiko, "Jūhachi seiki shotō ni okeru Chibetto bukkyōkai no seijiteki tachiba ni tsuite," *Tōhō gakuhō* 88 (1989): 1–15.

93. Luciano Petech, *China and Tibet in the Early XVIIIth Century: History of the Establishment of Chinese Protectorate in Tibet* (Leiden, 1950), chs. 3–7; Katō Naoto, "Lobjang Danjin's Rebellion of 1723; with a Focus on the Eve of the Rebellion," *Acta Asiatica* 64 (1993): 57–80; Martin, "Bonpo Canons and Jesuit Cannons," 6.

94. Petech, *China and Tibet*. On the delicate tripartite relations among the Zunghars, the Dalai, and the Qing court in the 1730s, see Ma Lin, "Qianlong chunian Jungeer bu shouci ruZang aocha shimo," *Xizang yanjiu* 1 (1988): 62–69. The same author discusses the changing relationship between the Qing court and the Dalai lama in "Cong liyi zhi zheng kan zhu Zang dachen tong Dalai lama ji Xizang difang zhengfu shezheng de guanxi," *Qinghai shehui kexue* 6 (1980): 95–101.

95. The chronicle of Sino-Tibetan relations is presented in Ahmad, *Sino-Tibetan Relations*, 152–62. See Chen Xiaoqiang, "Cong Menggu lama Neiqiaotuoyin yishi de huodong kan Manzhou Qing zhengfu quan dui Zang

zhuang Fojiao de fuzhi he xianzhi," *Qinghai minzu xueyuan xuebao (shehui kexue ban)* 4 (1991): 39–44 on an earlier Mongol dGe lugs pa priest who visited Hongtaiji. Xiangyun Wang, "Tibetan Buddhism at the Court of Qing: The Life and Work of lCang-skya Rol-pa'i-rdo-rje (1717–1786)" (Ph.D. diss., Harvard University, 1995), 73–74.

96. Samuel Grupper, "The Manchu Imperial Cult of the Early Qing Dynasty: Texts and Studies on the Tantric Sanctuary of Mahākāla at Mukden" (Ph.D. diss., Indiana University, 1979), 146.

97. Samuel Grupper, "Manchu Patronage," 53. Zhao Zhiqiang, "Beita Falunsi yu Mengguzu, Manzu, Xibozu guanxi shulun," *Manzu yanjiu* 3 (1991): 79–86, describes the 1778 conversion of one of the six Tibetan Buddhist temples in Shengjing into a temple dedicated to Manchu-language sutra recitation.

98. Grupper, "The Manchu Imperial Cult," 165; Arlington and Lewisohn, *Old Peking*, 127–28; Juliet Bredon, *Peking: A Historical and Intimate Description of Its Chief Places of Interest* (Shanghai, 1922), 182–85; Wang Yao, "The Cult of Mahākāla and a Temple in Beijing," *Journal of Chinese Religions* 22 (1994): 117–26. According to Wang Yao, Dorgon built four additional temples to Mahākāla in the suburbs of Peking (122).

99. Zhang Xixin, *Qing zhengfu yu lamajiao* (Xuchang, 1988), 115; the author uses a list of Lamaist temples recorded in the Lifanyuan archives. Rainer von Franz, *Die unbearbeiteten Peking-Inschriften der Franke-Lauferschen Sammlung* (Wiesbaden, 1984), studies and translates the multilingual inscriptions at eleven of these temples. The archives include many memorials concerning expenditures to on temple repairs: one example is Archives 446-5-55/7, memorial dated QL 1/9/24 (October 29, 1736) on repairs to temples in the imperial villas. The 1653 visit of the Dalai lama is also described in *The Visit of the Teshoo Lama to Peking: Ch'ien Lung's Inscription*, trans. Ernest Ludwig (Peking, 1904), 2–3. See also Robert J. Miller, *Monasteries and Culture Change in Inner Mongolia* (Wiesbaden, 1959), 77–78.

100. Wei Kaizhao, *Yonghegong man lu* (Honan, 1985), chs. 1, 4, 5. For a close description of the iconography of the temple, see Ferdinand D. Lessing, *Yung-Ho-Kung: An Iconography of the Lamaist Cathedral in Peking* (1942; reprint, Taipei, 1993). Cheryl M. Boettcher, "In Search of Manchu Bibliography" (Master's thesis, University of Illinois, 1989), 53–54, notes that Walter Fuchs found some Tibetan Buddhist temples founded by Qing emperors still functioning in Jehol and Peking in the 1930s, with Manchu monks chanting sutras in the Manchu language.

101. Chengde shi wenwuju and Zhongguo renmin daxue, Qingshi yanjiu suo, *Chengde Bishu shanzhuang* (Beijing, 1980), 146–56; Wang Lu and Tian Fang, "Chengde wai ba miao yu Xizang de guanxi," *Zhongyang minzu xueyuan xuebao* 4 (1988): 35; Huang Chongwen, "Xumifushou zhih miao de jianli ji qi lishi yiyi," *Xizang yanjiu* 3 (1989): 80–83; Li Tongqing, "Cong Bishu-shanzhuang he waibamiao de jianzhu tesi kan Qing wangchao de minzu zhengce," *Zhongyang minzu xueyuan xuebao* 4 (1988): 37–39.

102. Zhang Xixin, *Qing zhengfu,* 116–17; Wang, "Tibetan Buddhism at the Court of Qing," 103–8; David M. Farquhar, "Emperor As Bodhisattva in the Governance of the Qing Empire," *Harvard Journal of Asiatic Studies* 38, no.1 (1978): 5–34.

103. Wang Jiapeng, "Qianlong yu Manzu lama siyuan," *Gugong bowuyuan yuankan* 1 (1995): 58–65, presents a list of these temples and the number of monks supported at each in a table on 62.

104. Miller, *Monasteries and Culture Change,* ch. 2; Zhang Xixin, *Qingdai sida huofo,* 44–45; Wang, "Tibetan Buddhism at the Court of Qing," ch. 4. On the Buddhist bronzes produced at Dolonor, see Teresa Tse Bartholomew, "The Legacy of Chinggis Khan," *Orientations* 26, no. 6 (1995): 48.

105. Pu Wencheng, "Qinghai de Mengguzu siyuan," *Qinghai shehui kexue* 6 (1989): 102–9. The comparison of Qinghai and Tibetan monastery size is made by Ishihama Yumiko, "Jūhachi seiki shotō ni okeru Chibetto bukkyōkai," 2; 1958 figures from Lamaozhaxi, "Qinghai lamajiao siyuan jingji de goucheng yinsu chutan," *Qinghai shehui kexue* 6 (1988): 98.

106. Lü Minghui, "Qingdai Beifang geminzu yu zhongyuan Hanzu de wenhua jiaoliu ji qi gongxian," *Qingshi yanjiu ji,* no. 6 (1988): 130–31; Heissig, *Religions of Mongolia,* 33; Walther Heissig, *Die Pekinger lamaistischen Blockdrucke in mongolischer Sprache; Materialen zur mongolischen Literaturgeschichte* (Wiesbaden, 1954); Boettcher, "In Search of Manchu Bibliography," 54; Lokesh Chandra, *Buddhist Iconography,* 1:8–9. Li Zhitan, "'Dazangjing' zang, Manwen ban xiancun gugong," *Wenxian* 4 (1991): 286–87 describes finding in 1950 the print blocks for the Manchu edition of the Buddhist canon.

107. Baron A. von Staël-Holstein, "The Emperor Ch'ienlung and the larger *Shūramgasūtra,*" *Harvard Journal of Asiatic Studies* 1, no. 1 (1936): 136–46; distribution of the copies is discussed in a memorial dated QL 36/5/1 (June 13, 1771) [Archives 446-5-55/333].

108. Miller, *Monasteries and Culture Change,* 27; Moses, *Political Role of Mongol Buddhism,* ch. 4, 8; Heissig, *Religions of Mongolia,* 29–31; Cai Zhichun, "Menggu lama guizu," 51.

109. Xu and Zhou, "Qingchao zhengfu," 59. Amdo was administratively placed under an *amban* stationed in Xining after the Qing invasion of Lhasa: see Geoffrey Samuel, *Civilized Shamans,* 89–91.

110. Xu Xiaoguang and Zhou Jian, "Qingchao zhengfu dui lamajiao li fa chutan" *Nei Menggu shehui kexue* 1 (1988): 55–59; Miller, *Monasteries and Culture Change,* 50–56.

111. Cai Zhichun, "Menggu lama guizu," 54; Zhang Weiguang, "Mingchao zhengfu zai Hehuang diqu de Zang zhuan Fojiao zhengce shulun," *Qinghai shehui kexue* 2 (1989): 93–96. On Qing policies see Chen Yuning and Tang Xiaofang, "Qingdai lamajiao zai Mengguzu diqu de tequan ji qi rongluo," *Qinghai shehui kexue* 5 (1988): 98–102.

112. Miller *Monasteries and Culture Change,* 63–67; Heissig, *Religions of Mongolia,* 34; Cai Zhichun, "Menggu lama guizu," 51.

113. A photograph of the Yonghegong vase is published in Du Jianye et al., eds., *Yonghegong: Palace of Harmony* (Hong Kong, n.d.), 37.

114. Li Fengzhen, "Qingdai Xizang lama chaogong gaishu—jian pingli chasun Xizang chaogong shi waijiao he maoyi guanxi de miulun," *Xizang Zangxue* 1 (1991): 70–81.

115. Cited in Yuan Hongqi, "Qianlong shiqi de gongting jieqing huodong," *Gugong bowuyuan yuankan* 3 (1991): 85.

116. Chen Qingying, "Si zhi jiushi Banchan dashi yi ji damen de lingta," *Qinghai shehui kexue* 3 (1989): 89–97; Tucci, *Religions of Tibet*, 42. The first Panchen is also often known as the fourth Panchen because his clerical predecessors were posthumously granted the title; the subsequent Panchen rebirths cited below can thus alternatively be referred to as the fifth, sixth, etc. Panchen lamas.

117. Quote from Snellgrove and Richardson, *A Cultural History*, 220. See also Zhang Xixin, *Qingdai si da huo fo*, 32; Tucci, *Religions of Tibet*, 42; Heissig, *Religions of Mongolia*, 29.

118. Chen Qingying, "Si zhi jiushi Panchen dashi"; Dou'gecairangzhaga, "Banchan shixi de chan sheng ji lishi banchan de zhuanshi guocheng (1)," *Xizang yanjiu* 1 (1991): 75–86.

119. Sechin Jagchid, "Mongolian Lamaist Quasi-Feudalism during the Period of Manchu Domination," *Mongolian Studies* 1 (1974): 35–37, 39–42.

120. Wang, "Tibetan Buddhism at the Court of Qing," ch. 6; Heissig, *Religions of Mongolia*, 34; Samuel, *Civilized Shamans*, 87–91; Zhazha, "Shishu Labulengsi yu Qingchao zhongyang zhengfu de guanxi," *Xizang yanjiu* 4 (1991): 123–28.

121. Heissig, *Religions of Mongolia*, 33; Miller, *Monasteries and Culture Change*, 81–82.

122. Wang, "Tibetan Buddhism at the Court of Qing," chs. 5, 7, 8; Zhang Xixin, *Qingdai si da huo fo*, 40–47; Grupper, "Manchu Patronage," 48; Martin, "Bonpo Canons and Jesuit Cannons." Rol pa'i rdo rje's Tibetan-language biography has been translated into Chinese: see Tuguan Luozang jieji nima, *Zhangjia guoshi Robiduoji zhuan*, trans. Chen Qingying and Ma Lienhua (Beijing, 1988).

123. Heissig, *Religions of Mongolia*, 33.

124. This is presumably a different painting from the album painting described by Wu Hung, "Emperor's Masquerade—'Costume Portraits' of Yongzheng and Qianlong," *Orientations* 26, no. 7 (1995): 30, pl. 6e on 31.

125. Wang, "Tibetan Buddhism at the Court of Qing," 316–17, 73–74.

126. The full text of the discourse "On lamaism" is presented in Lessing, *Yung-Ho-Kung*, 36–61. On the statue of Rol pa'i rdo rje ordered by the emperor, see Wang Jiapeng, "Zhangjia hutuketu xiang xiaokao—jian tan Qianlong huangdi yu Zhangjia guoshi de guanxi," *Gugong bowuyuan yuankan* 4 (1987): 88–93, 48. Also Wang Jiapeng, "Gugong yuhuage tang yuan," *Gugong bowuyuan yuankan* 1 (1990): 50–62; Grupper, "Manchu Patronage," 55;

Wang, "Tibetan Buddhism at the Court of Qing," 293–94. On the events of 1780, see Wang Lu and Tian Fang, "Chengde wai ba miao," 34–36; Huang Chongwen, "Xumifushou zhi miao de jianli," 80–83; *The Visit of the Teshoo Lama*. Daily recitations of the sutras in the Xumifushou seem to have continued after 1780: see memorial dated QL 46/2/19 (March 13, 1781) [Archives 446-5-55/251] reporting the cost of these recitations. On depictions of the Panchen, see Wang Jiapeng, "Minzu tuanjie de lishi huazhuan—liushi Panchen huaxiang," *Zijincheng* 2 (1990): 11–13.

127. Wang Jiapeng, "Zhongzheng dian yu Qing gong Zang zhuan fojiao" *Gugong bowuyuan yuankan* 3(1991): 58–71; Wang Jiapeng, "Gugong yuhuage"; the mTho gling is described in L. Austine Waddell, *Tibetan Buddhism* (New York, 1972), 283. Arlington and Lewisohn, *Old Peking*, 57.

128. For a description of the Yuling, Hongli's mausoleum, see Di yi lishi dang'an guan, *Qingdai di wang ling qin* (Beijing, 1982), 35–36; Yu Shanpu, *Qing dongling daguan* (Shijiazhuang, 1985), 94–100.

129. Du Jianye et al.,*Yonghegong*, 52.

130. John Clarke, "A Group of Sino-Mongolian Metalwork in the Tibetan Style," *Orientations* 23, no. 5 (1992): 65–75.

131. The documents can be found in Archives 467-4-85/311 on through /329, beginning QL 12 (1747) and extending into the Guangxu reign.

132. Heissig, *Religions of Mongolia*, 99–101; Xing Li, "Lamajiao de Mengguhua," *Heilongjiang minzu congkan* 4 (1993): 93–94; Snellgrove and Richardson, *A Cultural History*, 178. A *tangka* of "sacred emperor Guan" still hangs in one of the halls of the Yonghegong: see Du Jianye et al., *Yonghegong*, 118.

133. Palace Museum, *Cultural Relics of Tibetan Buddhism Collected in the Qing Palace* (Hong Kong, 1992); Nie Chongzheng et al., eds., *Qingdai gongting huihua* (Hong Kong, 1996); *Masterpieces of Chinese Tibetan Buddhist Altar Fittings in the National Palace Museum* (Taipei, 1971); Du Jianye et al., *Yonghegong*; Huang Xiuhui et al., *The Catalogue of Tibetan Artifacts Exhibition* (Taipei, 1994).

134. Harold L. Kahn, *Monarchy in the Emperor's Eyes: Image and Reality in the Ch'ien-lung Reign* (Cambridge, Mass., 1971), pl. 11 on 184; Farquhar, "Emperor as Bodhisattva," 7 uses the same illustration, which Kahn had obtained from Guoli Gugong bowuyuan, *Qingdai di hou xiang* (Peking, 1931). Most recently, a different *tangka*, held by the National Palace Museum, Beijing, was reproduced as fig. 19 on 41 in Wu Hung, "Emperor's Masquerade."

135. Reproductions of the six *tangkas*: (1) pl. 3, *ce* 3, in *Qingdai di hou xiang*, which was reproduced by both Kahn and Farquahar; (2) pl. 32 on 56 in *Cultural Relics of Tibetan Buddhism Collected in the Qing Palace;* (3) fig. 19 on 41 in Wu Hung, "Emperor's Masquerade"; (4) 223 in *Yonghegong;* (5) *tangka* hanging in the Sasum Nagyal chapel in the Potala, which is reproduced in *Zijincheng* 4 (1991): 26; (6) pl. 17 in Lessing, *Yung-Ho-Kung*, which notes that the *tangka* is part of the Hedin Expedition Collection in the State Ethnographic

Museum, Stockholm. Farquhar, 8 n.9 cites yet a seventh *tangka*, which was reproduced by Hemmi Baiei and Nakano Hanshirō, *Manmō no ramakyō bijutsu* (Tokyo, 1943), pl. II-16, which I have not yet seen.

136. Farquhar, "Emperor as Bodhisattva," 6.

137. Farquhar, "Emperor as Bodhisattva," 24, 30–31. Farquhar adds that the Chinese-language guides to Wutaishan omit these references to the emperor as Mañjuśrī.

138. Farquhar, "Emperor as Bodhisattva," 28–29 n.81; Wang, "Tibetan Buddhism at the Court of Qing," 316–17.

139. D. Seyfort Ruegg, "*Mchod yon, yon mchod* and *mchod gnas/yon gnas*: On the Historiography and Semantics of a Tibetan Religio-Social and Religio-Political Concept," in *Tibetan History and Language: Studies Dedicated to Uray Geza on His Seventieth Birthday*, ed. Ernst Steinkellner (Vienna, 1991), 450.

140. Angela Zito, "The Imperial Birthday: Ritual Encounters Between the Panchen Lama and the Qianlong Emperor in 1780," presented at the "Conference on State and Ritual in East Asia," organized by Committee for European/North American Scholarly Cooperation in East Asian Studies, Paris, June 28–July 1, 1995.

141. Liu Yi, "Cong lamajiao bihua kan Xizang yu Ming Qing zhongyang zhengfu de guanxi," *Lishi daguan yuan* 5 (1993): 8–11.

142. Lin Jing, "Lasa lansheng," *Zijincheng* 65 (1991): 26; Victor Chan, *Tibet Handbook: A Pilgrimage Guide* (Chico, 1994), 106–7.

CHAPTER 8: PRIVATE RITUALS

1. *Dezong Jing huangdi shilu*, 3:852–55; essentially the same account appears in Guoli gugong bowuyuan, *Qingdai qijuzhu: Guangxu chao* (Taipei, 1987), 23:012327–32. The archives holds a butterfly folded outline of the ritual sequence dated GX 10/12/30 (February 14, 1885) [Archives 467-4-85/2303] in a packet entitled "Ji zhu" (sacrificial prayers). See also Wan Yi, "Qingdai gongsu yu jingshi minsu," in *Zhongguo gudu yanjiu* (Hangzhou, 1986), 2:75–82; Fang Yujin, "Qing di zai zheng yue chuyi zhe yitian," *Zijincheng* 5(1981): 37.

2. Archives 467-4-85/2303 on rites performed on the last day of the year; the *du hun* wedding rites are outlined for the Tongzhi emperor's wedding in a bound book with yellow brocade covers, entitled "Dahun li dang, Tongzhi 11/9/15" (Ritual record of the da hun, October 16, 1872) in 467-4-85/2379. On the worship of Heaven and Earth in shamanism, see Sechin Jagchid, "Chinese Buddhism and Taoism during the Mongolian Rule of China," *Mongolian Studies* 6(1980): 61. Whereas the archival document for GX 11 and 12 states that the emperor lit incense at the "Heaven and Earth altar" (*tian di tan*), Fang Yujin states that the emperor burned a paper effigy of the "Heaven, Earth, three realms god" (*tian, di, sanjie shen*): see his "Qing di zai zheng yue."

3. L. C. Arlington and William Lewisohn, *In Search of Old Peking* (1935;

reprint, New York, 1967), 49; see account dated QL 26/12/22 (January 16, 1762) [Archives 467-4-85/2338]. On the food offered to the kitchen god see a memorial dated QL 12/23/60 (January 12, 1795) [467-4-85/2297], and a similar list for the Guangxu reign, in 467-4-85/2302; Feng Zuozhe, "Qing gong ji 'zao,'" *Zijincheng* 11 (1982): 28. On shamanic offerings, see Akamatsu Chijo, "Manshū hatanin no ie matsuri," *Minzokugaku kenkyū* 1, no. 2 (1935): 224.

4. Fang Yujin, "Qing di zai zheng yue," 37; Zhang Naiwei, *Qing gong shuwen*, rev. ed. (Beijing 1990), 659–65, 691. Records of where, when, and how many crackers should be set off are found in archival records for 1831–35 in Archives 155-4-16-2/1303.

5. Zhang Naiwei, *Qing gong shuwen*, 955–56; Arlington and Lewisohn, *Old Peking*, 126; offerings list in Archives 467-4-85/2338. Other materials for the Guangxu reign [467-4-85/2302] indicate that the ten altars in the hall also received daily offerings of brick tea.

6. *Dezong Jing huangdi shilu*, 3:856–69, GX 11/1/1 (February 15, 1885). See also *Qingdai qijuzhu: Guangxu chao*, 23:012333–012336.

7. Fang Yujin, "Qing di zai zheng yue." Although this short article has no bibliographic citations, it differs only in detail from the archival documents cited above.

8. Memorial dated GX 10/12/30 (February 14, 1885) [Archives 467-4-85/2303].

9. On the smallpox rite, see Wan Yi and Huang Haitao, *Qingdai gongting yinyue* (Hong Kong, 1985), 32. Memorials in Archives 467-4-85/2299 for Wenzong; in 467-4-85/1017 for Muzong.

10. Memorial dated XF 3/12/30 (January 28, 1854) [Archives 467-4-85/2298]; GX 10/12/30 (February 14, 1885) [Archives 467-4-85/2303].

11. Archives 467-4-85/2303.

12. Carroll Brown Malone, *History of the Peking Summer Palaces under the Ch'ing Dynasty* (1934; reprint, New York, 1966), 47, 109–11. A memorial dated YZ 3/7/25 (September 1, 1725) records an imperial edict concerning the installation of the dragon god in the Yuanmingyuan: another, dated QL 18/4/27 (May 29, 1753) records the emperor's order to reduce the number of Daoist priests stationed at the Buddha tower (*fo-lou*) in the Yuanmingyuan: see Zhongguo diyi lishi dang'anguan, *Yuanmingyuan: Qingdai dang'an shiliao* (Shanghai, 1991 [hereafter *Yuanmingyuan*]), 1:11, 71; *Qinding gongzhong xianxing zeli*, 1.94b–96b, edict dated DG 12/8/3 (August 28, 1832); memorial dated JQ 1/11/23 (December 21, 1796) [Archives 446-5-55/325], QL 6/9/19 (October 28, 1741) [446-5-55/35]. See Zhaolian, *Xiaoting xulu* (1909; reprint, Beijing, 1980), 500 on an earthgod shrine under the gallery of the Imperial Clan Court which was "very *ling* (efficacious)"; also memorial dated XF 8/2/20 (April 3, 1858), in *Yuanmingyuan*, 2:546–48 on the installation of an earth-god shrine.

13. Memorial dated QL 18/4/27 (May 29, 1753) in *Yuanmingyuan*, 1:71–72; the same edict is reported with some variations in 2:1016, which summarizes the 1839 edict.

14. Prayer in Archives 467-4-85/112; the Chinese text is undated but the Manchu text has the date cited here.

15. Bilingual prayer in Archives 467-4-85/112; although neither the Chinese nor the Manchu version has a precise date, both stipulate the Shunzhi reign. On the development of the cult of Zaojun, see Robert L. Chard, "Master of the Family: History and Development of the Chinese Cult to the Stove" (Ph.D. diss., University of California, Berkeley, 1990). According to Po Sung-nien and David Johnson, *Domesticated Deities and Auspicious Emblems* (Berkeley, 1992), 78–79, wells were traditionally covered on New Year's eve and opened on the second day of the New Year.

16. Quoted in Susan S. Landesman, "Mirror Divination: Shamanistic and Non-Shamanistic Divinations," *Central and Inner Asian Studies* 6 (1992): 20.

17. Bilingual texts of prayers at the Fengxiandian, in Archives 467-4-85/112 dated KX 57 (1718), YZ 1 (1723) and YZ 2 (1724). See Landesman, "Mirror Divination"; He Ling, "Xibozu 'samange' chutan," *Xinjiang shehui kexue* 6 (1987): 107, for a shamanic song that refers to the "protecting the heart mirror" worn by the shaman.

18. Compare the New Year record in *Shengzu Ren huangdi shilu*, 1:544; *Shizong Xian huangdi shilu*, 1:779; *Gaozong Chun huangdi shilu*, 12:327 and 19:602–3; *Renzong Rui huangdi shilu*, 5:839–40; *Xuanzong Cheng huangdi shilu*, 7:846; *Wenzong Xian huangdi shilu*, 1:682–83; *Muzong Yi huangdi shilu*, 7:789; *Dezong Jing huangdi shilu*, 3:856 and 4:731. The rites at the *tangzi* were not performed by the emperor during a regency.

19. Arlington and Lewisohn, *Old Peking*, 132; Zhang Naiwei, *Qing gong shuwen*, 960–61; E. T. Williams, "The State Religion of China During the Manchu Dynasty," *Journal, North China Branch of the Royal Asiatic Society* 44 (1913): 38.

20. On worshiping the household god, see Manchu memorial dated QL 50/12/14 (January 13, 1786) [Archives 446-5-55/281]; Wan Yi, "Qingdai gongsu"; spring and autumn equinoxes in 1748 documents, 467-4-85/2338; Guangxu-period documents on Qingming and the 7/15 rituals in 467-4-85/2300; the release of 20,000 lanterns for 7/15 is found in a 1778 document in 557-5-66-4/3778.

21. Discussions of the revised ritual schedules for the New Year occur for the Xianfeng and Tongzhi emperors' funerals: see memorials dated XF 11/10/25 (November 27, 1861) [Archives 446-5-55/570], TZ 13/12/11 (January 18, 1875) [446-5-55/610].

22. Schedule in Archives 467-4-85/2302; Zhang Naiwei, *Qing gong shuwen*, 946.

23. Memorials dated QL 58 (1793) [Archives 446-5-55/3]; JQ 2/11/27 (January 13, 1798) [446-5-55/328], DG 3/11/25 (December 26, 1823), DG 4/11/25 (January 13, 1825), DG 5/11/27 (January 5, 1826), DG 8/11/29 (January 4, 1829), DG 9/11/29 (January 23, 1830), DG 10/11/28 (January 11, 1831) [467-4-85/2298]; TZ 1/11/24 (January 13, 1863) [446-5-55/574], GX 1/11/14 (January 10, 1876) [446-5-55/614].

24. Memorial of QL 1/11/21 (December 13, 1736) [Archives 446-5-55/7]; Zhang Naiwei, *Qing gong shuwen*, 718, 683–86; memorial dated JQ 3/7/18 (August 29, 1798) [446-5-55/330]; Arlington and Lewisohn, *Old Peking*, 138.

25. Ritual schedule for GX 11, 12 (1885, 1886), Archives 467-4-85/2303.

26. Wang Jiapeng, "Zhongzhengdian yu Qing gong Zang zhuan fojiao," *Gugong bowuyuan yuankan* 3 (1991): 58–71. See memorial of XF 11/2/7 (March 17, 1861) [Archives 446-5-55/568] on the installation of copies of the heart sutra, with dharani, into the Buddha hall of the "inner palace," perhaps the Cininggong.

27. Manchu-language memorial dated XF 4/2/5 (March 3, 1854) [Archives 557-5-66-3/0912]; Zhang Naiwei, *Qing gong shuwen*, 944–47; Arlington and Lewisohn, *Old Peking*, 81, 300.

28. See identical documents on the 1/6 and 1/8 rite for 1736 (Archives 446-5-55/3), 1798 (446-5-55/328), 1800 (446-5-55/336), and 1845 (446-5-55/579). On sutra recitations, see documents for 1801 and 1876 in 446-5-55/340, 446-5-55/614; memorials dated JQ 4/12/25 (January 19, 1800) and JQ 4/12/27 (January 21, 1800) [446-5-55/336]; TZ 13/12/14 (January 21, 1875) [446-5-55/610]; GX 1/12/16 (January 12, 1876) [446-5-55/614].

29. Memorial dated QL 1/4/3 (May 13, 1736) [Archives 446-5-55/4]; JQ 3/7/18 (August 29, 1798) [446-5-55/330]; Arlington and Lewisohn, *Old Peking*, 243, 123, 209–10, 205.

30. On Daoist rites, see the bilingual memorial dated QL 1/7/22 (August 28, 1736) [Archives 446-5-55/6] and memorial dated QL 25/7/8 (August 18, 1760) [446-5-55/1], JQ 2/7/19 (September 9, 1797) [446-5-55/327], JQ 3/7/18 (August 29, 1798) [446-5-55/330]. On Buddhist sutra recitations, see Chinese and Manchu-language memorials dated JQ 1/7/22 (August 24, 1796) [446-5-55/324], JQ 1/8/17 (September 17, 1796) [446-5-55/324], JQ 2/8/18 (October 7, 1797) [446-5-55/327], JQ 3/7/18 (August 29, 1798) [446-5-55/330], JQ 3/8/16 (September 25, 1798) [446-5-55/330, JQ 4/10/10 (November 7, 1799) [446-5-55/335], and JQ 5/10/10 (November 26, 1800) [446-5-55/339].

31. Chinese and Manchu-language memorials dated JQ 4/10/10 (November 7, 1799) [Archives 446-5-55/335]; JQ 25/8/16 (September 22, 1820) [446-5-55/430] and DG 1/8/14 (September 9, 1821) [446-5-55/434]; note that the same number of lamas were used, at the same cost.

32. Memorials for 1848, 1849, 1850 in Archives 467-4-85/2298.

33. On the Yanshousi, see Malone, *History of the Peking Summer Palaces*, 109–11. On sutra recitations for his mother's birthdays, see an undated memorial from Yongrong, Sebusheng, and Barjur in Archives 446-5-55/1; on the birthday presents, see Teresa Tse Bartholomew, "Sino-Tibetan Art of the Qianlong Period from the Asian Art Museum of San Francisco," *Orientations* 22, no. 6 (1991): 41–42. On the Qianlong emperor's seventieth birthday presentations, see memorial dated QL 46/2/18 (March 12, 1781) [446-5-55/2], which states that further donations, received since the birthday, contributed to a total of over 331,000 taels of silver.

34. Evelyn S. Rawski, "Qing Imperial Marriage and Problems of Rulership," in *Marriage and Inequality in Chinese Society*, ed. Rubie S. Watson and Patricia B. Ebrey (Berkeley, 1991), 170–203.

35. See J. G. Cormack, *Everyday Customs in China* (London, 1935), 51, 55–56.

36. Document entitled "File of the dahun ritual of Tongzhi 11/9/15" (TZ 11/9/15 dahun li tang), and other documents of similar nature in Archives 467-4-85/2379. See also Rawski, "Qing Imperial Marriage."

37. Memorial dated TZ 11/4/26 (June 1, 1872) [Archives 467-4-85/2379].

38. See the ritual schedule attending Princess Shouzhuang's wedding in 1863 in Archives 467-4-85/2102.

39. See *Qinding Manzhou jishen jitian dianli*, 1.4a–5a; Archives 446-5-55/423, dated JQ 23/12, collects nineteen Manchu-language memorials on the subject of shamanic sacrifice by emperor's sons from KX 17 (1678) on; see also 446-5-55/244, dated QL 44/4/28 (May 7, 1779) and 446-5-55/252, dated QL 46/4 (1781).

40. Memorial dated QL 25/7/14 (September 22, 1760) [Archives 446-5-55/125].

41. Liu Lu, "Qingchu huangshi chengyuan huozang de jiangzheng," *Wenwu* 9 (1993): 69–70; Liu Yi, "Zhao xiling yu Qingdai de hou sangli su gengyi," *Gugong bowuyuan yuankan* 4 (1992): 86–90. On cremations after 1661, see Li Fengmin and Lu Haiying, eds., *Shenjing Zhaoling* (Shenyang, 1994), 50. Further evidence of cremation was found in Nurgaci's consort tomb at the Fuling: see Li Fengmin and Lu Haiying, eds., *Shenyang Fuling* (Shenyang, 1996), 53–54.

42. Xu Guangyuan, "Cong Xiaozhuang sangyi kan Kangxi pojiu wushi jingshen," *Gugong bowuyuan yuankan* 4 (1994): 88–89.

43. Evelyn S. Rawski, "The Imperial Way of Death," in *Death Ritual in Late Imperial and Modern China*, ed. James L. Watson and Evelyn S. Rawski (Berkeley, 1988), 228–53.

44. Zhang Fengrong and Yang Huilan, "Minghuang zhijin duoluojingbei," *Zijincheng* 1 (1992): 27–28; my thanks to Professor Chün-fang Yü for her opinion on the nature of the dharani.

45. On Cixi's grave clothes, see Yu Shanpu, "Cixi de sanjian shouyi," *Zijincheng* 5 (1992): 38. Chen Baorong, *Qing Xiling zong heng* (Shijiazhuang, 1987), 223; see Yu Shanpu, *Qing Dongling duguan* (Shijiazhuang, 1985), 170–73 on the dharani coverlet found in Cixi's tomb, a photograph of which appears in Zhongguo diyi lishi dang'anguan, *Qingdai di wang ling qin* (Beijing, 1982), pl. 49 on 80. Wan Yi et al., eds., *Qingdai gongting shenghuo* (Hong Kong, 1985), pl. 407 on 262, show a dharani coverlet with a red background, and pieces of a dharani coverlet are in the Prince Guo textiles held at the Nelson-Atkins Museum in Kansas City, Missouri: see Lindsay Hughes, "The Kuo Ch'in-wang Textiles," *Gazette des Beaux-Arts* (February 1945), 66–68. The custom of wrapping the corpse in dharani coverlets seems to have become ac-

cepted among many Manchus during the late Qing: see Takeda Masao, *Man Kan reizoku* (Dairen, 1935), 2:3–4.

46. In Archives 549-4-93/255.

47. See, for example, a memorial dated XF 10/13/25 (May 15, 1860) [Archives 446-5-55/565], reporting on the coffin of Princess Shou'an that carries the inscriptions.

48. On the writing of dharani on the lacquered coffin, see memorial dated QL 31/6/9 (July 15, 1766) [Archives 557-5-66-4/3778]; memorial dated QL 1/1/21 (March 3, 1736) [446-5-55/3]; Wei Kaibi, *Yonghegong manlu* (Henan, 1985), 2–6. For variations on the color of the coffin, see Wan Yi et al., eds., *Qingdai gongting shenghuo*, 262, caption to pl. 407. M. L. C. Bogan, *Manchu Customs and Superstitions* (Tientsin, 1928), 74 notes that ordinary Manchus also observed this custom.

49. J. J. M. Amiot, *Mémoires concernant l'histoire, les sciences, les arts, les moeurs, les usages, etc. des chinois par les missionaires de Pé-kin* (Paris, 1780), 356.

50. Yu Shanpu, *Qing Dongling*, 109, 113; Chen Baorong, *Qing Xiling*, 226–27, 233. Lists of the specific items to be burned at a given rite are found in Archives 446-5-55/568 (on the Xianfeng emperor's funeral); 446-5-55/610 (on the Tongzhi emperor's funeral); 446-5-55/738 (on the Guangxu emperor's funeral).

51. Memorials dated QL 1/7/24 (August 30, 1736) [Archives 446-5-55/6], QL 1/9/3 (October 7, 1736) [Archives 446-5-55/7].

52. Memorials dated XF 11/8/22 (September 26, 1861), XF 11/8/24 (September 28, 1861), XF 11/10/13 (November 15, 1861) [Archives 446-5-55/569]; XF 11/10/11 (November 13, 1861) [446-5-55/570].

53. Memorials dated GX 34/11/10 (December 3, 1908), GX 34/12/5 (December 27, 1908), GX 34/12/23 (January 14, 1908), GX 34/12/28 (January 19, 1908) [Archives 446-5-55/738]; GX 34/12/5 (December 27, 1908) [467-4-85/2332]; in 446-5-55/738. Information on Empress Dowager Ci'an's funerary rites is found in 467-4-85/2330; on Empress Dowager Cixi's funerary rites, in 446-5-55/738.

54. Memorials dated TZ 13/12/17 (January 24, 1875) [Archives 446-5-55/610]; GX 34/11/13 (December 6, 1908) [446-5-55/738]; Arlington and Lewisohn, *Old Peking*, 123.

55. *Gaozong Chun huangdi shilu*, 1:652 (death of Xi *pin*, QL 2/1/2); 1:720 (death of Ji *fei*, QL 2/4/7); 2:374 (death of Jin *pin*, QL 4/3/16); 3:420 (death of Shouqi *huanggui taifei*, QL 8/4/1); 8:150–52 (death of Jing *pin*, QL 23/6/6), 8:867–68 (death of Li *guiren*, QL 25/4/25, discussed in archival records but absent from the *shilu*); 10:657 (death of Xian *fei*, QL 32/5/21); 10:900 (death of Wenhui *huanggui taifei*, QL 33/3/14); 16:376 (death of Yu *huanggui taifei*, QL 49/12/17).

56. *Gaozong Chun huangdi shilu*, 18:880, QL 57/5/21 (July 9, 1792); 12:861, QL 38/12/20 (January 31, 1774).

57. Memorial dated QL 40/1/29 (February 28, 1775) [Archives 446-5-55/220]. Information on the funerary rites for other consorts appears in memorials dated QL 1/7/29 (September 4, 1736) [446-5-55/6], QL 5/10/17 (December 5, 1740) [446-5-55/30], QL 40/2/19 (March 20, 1775) [446-5-55/220], GX 3/10/26 (November 30, 1877) and GX 3/11/12 (December 16, 1877) [467-4-85/2299].

58. *Gaozong Chun huangdi shilu*, 9:709 (death of Xin *fei*, QL 29/4/28, May 28, 1764); 13:852–53 (death of Shu *fei*, QL 42/5/30, July 4, 1777).

59. Dan Shi, *Yige Qing gong taijian de zaoyu* (Beijing, 1989), 90; Wang Zuoxian, "Manzu sangyi," *Zijincheng* 51 (1989): 24–25.

60. J. J. M. de Groot, *The Religious System of China* (1892–1910; reprint, Taipei, 1969), 3:1290; documents in Archives 446-5-55/278, 446-5-55/132, 446-5-55/220, 446-5-55/2299; Xu Guangyuan, Mai zangguo sanci de huanghou," *Zijincheng* 49 (1988): 34–5.

61. *Gaozong Chun huangdi shilu*, 2:879–91, vs. documents dated QL 5/10/17 (December 5, 1740) [Archives 446-5-55/30]. Also 8:867–68, 9:22–33, vs. memorials dated QL 25/4/28 (June 11, 1760) [446-5-55/124] and QL 26/2/6 (March 12, 1761) [446-5-55/128] for the death and funerary rites of Li *guiren*.

62. *Gaozong Chun huangdi shilu*, 1:548–56; memorial dated QL 1/8/8 (September 12, 1736) [Archives 446-5-55/6].

63. See memorials dated QL 25/4/28 (June 11, 1760) [Archives 446-5-55/124], QL 26/8/27 (September 25, 1761) [446-5-55/132], XF 10/intercalary 3/12 (May 2, 1860) [446-5-55/565], XF 11/1/7 (February 16, 1861) [446-5-55/568], GX 11/4/21 (June 3, 1885) [467-4-85/2298].

64. The record in *Shengzu Ren huangdi shilu*, 1:1195–1206 (KX 20/3/30) is laconic; see *Kangxi qijuzhu*, KX 20/3/28, KX 20/3/30, and KX 20/4/2.

65. *Gaozong Chun huangdi shilu*, 10:30–31, 55–65 (QL 30/3/8) on death of Hongzhan; 11:596, 601–02 (QL 35/7/9, 35/7/13) on death of Hongzhou.

66. *Gaozong Chun huangdi shilu*, 5:956–67 (QL 15/3/15); 5:968–79 (QL 3/15/16 to 3/15/20).

67. Memorial dated QL 59/7/6 (August 1, 1794) and QL 59/7/17 (August 10, 1794) [Archives 446-5-55/316]. On funerals of consorts, see earlier sections, and memorials dated QL 1/11/6 (December 7, 1736) [446-5-55/8] on the funeral of Xian *fei;* JQ 4/9/9 (October 7, 1799) and JQ 4/9/11 (October 9, 1799) [446-5-55/334] on the funeral of Fulungga (Xun) *guifei*. Memorials dated JQ 6/7/18 (August 26, 1801) and JQ 6/7/24 (September 1, 1801) [446-5-55/342] show that the emperor provided his brother Yonglin, Prince Qing, with money and a storage place for his wife's coffin; another, dated QL 31/6/9 (July 15, 1766) [557-5-66-4/3778] describes the Zhangyisi's management of the funeral of the emperor's fifth son, Yongqi.

68. Takeda, *Man Kan reizoku*, 2:3–4; also Bogan, *Manchu Customs*, 69; Zhaolian, *Xiaoting xulu*, 2:384.

69. Cen Dali, "Qingdai Manzu de sangzang xisu," *Gugong bowuyuan*

yuankan 4 (1992): 91–94; Takeda, *Man Kan reizoku* 1:60–61; J. G. Cormack, *Everyday Customs in China*, 4th ed. (London, 1935), 97.

70. Rawski, "Imperial Way of Death."

71. Archives 467-4-85/2298, 467-4-85/2303; on the eastern and western Buddha halls, see Zhang Naiwei, *Qing gong shuwen*, 703–6, 738, 768–70, 796. Luo Wenhua, "Kangxi shenpai," *Zijincheng* 4 (1991): 19.

72. Zhang Naiwei, *Qing gong shuwen*, 586, 796.

73. Memorial dated QL 1/1/21 (March 3, 1736) [Archives 446-5-55/3]; XF 11/12/21 (January 20, 1862), XF 11/12/28 (January 27, 1862) [446-5-55/570]; TZ 1/10/6 (November 27, 1862) [446-5-55/574]; TZ 13/12/24 (January 31, 1875) [446-5-55/610].

74. See the rituals linked with the movement of the tablets in a memorial dated JQ 25/9/22 (October 28, 1820) [Archives 446-5-55/431].

75. Memorial dated JQ 25/9/22 (October 28, 1820) [Archives 446-5-55/431] on the funerary rites for the Jiaqing emperor, includes the precedents for the Qianlong emperor's rites of JQ 4/3/15 (April 19, 1799). For the Tongzhi decision, see memorial dated TZ 2/10/16 (November 26, 1863) [446-5-55/576]; on the Tongzhi funerary rites, see documents in 495-14-1/53. See Zhang Naiwei, *Qing gong shuwen*, 738, on the lighting of incense in the Yuqing palace on 2/7, the deathday of the Jiaqing emperor's first empress, Xiaoshu.

76. Archives 467-4-85/2303; Zhang Naiwei, *Qing gong shuwen*, 703–6, 738, 768–70.

77. Documents on deathday observances in Archives 467-4-85/1017, 467-4-85/2299, 467-4-85/2300.

78. Manchu-language memorial dated QL 1/31/15 (April 25, 1736) [Archives 446-5-55/4].

79. For example, in 1871 he did not so observe the birthday of his great-grandfather, the Jiaqing emperor: *Muzong Yi huangdi shilu*, 7:250–52 nor did he so honor his grandmother (7:39–40). See 7:143 and 7:194 for Zaichun's observances on the birthdays of the Xianfeng and Daoguang emperors.

80. *Muzong Yi huangdi shilu*. 7:143 for TZ 10/6/9 (July 26, 1871); document from the Tongzhi reign, Archives 467-4-85/2299; document from the Guangxu reign, 467-4-85/2300. Zhang Shiyun, "Qianlong shengmu de jinzhi fata," *Lishi dang'an* 3 (1993): back cover.

81. On the Yongling and Zhaozu, the focal ancestor, see de Groot, *Religious System*, 3:1354–56; Li Fengmin, "Yipi Nuerhachi, Huangtaiji yiwu de laili," *Liaoning daxue xuebao* 3 (1991): 47–49, also his "Shengjing simiao shouzang de Qing Taizu, Taizong yiwu," *Zijincheng* 6 (1992): 14–16.

82. Yu Shanpu, *Qing Dongling*, 72–74; Chen Baorong, *Qing Xiling*, 228; "Shang yinian yung" dated Xuantong reign (hereafter XT) 1/2/5 (February 24, 1909) [Archives 467-4-85/2105]. Li Fengmin, "Yipi Nuerhachi," 49; Jin Jishui and Zhou Shachen, *Wang fu shenghuo shilu* (Beijing, 1988), 10.

83. Edict and record of Cixi's worship in Archives 467-4-85/2299.

84. On deathday observances see memorial dated TZ 1/7/17 (August 12,

1862) and other undated documents [Archives 467-4-85/2299], documents of the Guangxu reign in 467-4-85/2300; Zhang Naiwei, *Qing gong shuwen*, 738, 696; memorial dated DG 25/7/14 (August 16, 1845) [467-4-85/2298].

85. See Rawski, "Imperial Way of Death"; Ann Paludan, "The Chinese Spirit Road," *Orientations* 21, no. 3 (1990): 56; Paula Swart and Barry Till, "Nurhachi and Abahai: Their Palace and Mausolea: The Manchu Adoption and Adaptation of Chinese Architecture," *Arts of Asia* (1988): 149–57. Yang Zhen, "Shunzhi qinbu lingdi yu Yongzheng lingpi lingqu," *Gugong bowuyuan yuankan* 4(1992): 78–85 cites the common myths concerning the choice of the cemetery sites by the Shunzhi and Yongzheng emperors.

86. De Groot, *Religious System*; Chen Baorong, *Qing Xiling*; Yu Shanpu, *Qing Dongling*.

87. Memorial dated JQ 5/10/28 (December 14, 1809) [Archives 446-5-55/339]; memorial dated QL 59/6/20 (July 16, 1794) [446-5-55/316].

88. De Groot, *Religious System*, 3:1165. On Manchu princes' tombs in Liaoyang, see Giovanni Stary, "Die mandschurischen Prinzengräber in Liaoyang, 1988," *Central Asiatic Journal* 33 (1989): 108–17.

89. Li Fengmin, Lu Haiying, and Fu Bo, eds., *Xinjing Yongling* (Shenyang, 1996), 22, 38–39; Wang Peihuan, "Fuling yu Ming Qing huangling de bijiao yanjiu," *Qingshi yanjiu* 2 (1995): 81–86; Li Fengmin and Lu Haiying, eds., *Shenyang Fuling*, 49, 51–57, 61; Li Fengmin and Lu Haiying, eds., *Shengjing Zhaoling* (Shenyang, 1994), 56–65. Yu Shanpu, *Qing Dongling*, 208; Archives 446-5-55/540; *Kangxi qijuzhu* 1:419 on Longxi's death.

90. Feng Qili, "Yixian Shenshizhuang de Dundu qinwang fen," *Manzu yanjiu* 4 (1990): 46; Chen Baorong, *Qing Xiling*, 219–20; E. Fonssagrives, *Si-ling: Etudes sur les tombeaux de l'ouest de la dynastie des Ts'ing* (Paris, 1907), 121–23, 128–29, 132–34. On other princes' tombs near Xiling, see 115–18, 119, 124–27, 130–31, 135–37 in this work.

91. De Groot, *Religious System*, 3:1165; Archives 446-5-55/316, memorial dated QL 59/6/20 (July 16, 1794). There are similar reports on the funerary arrangements for Hongli's seventeenth son, Yonglin [446-5-55/429, memorials dated JQ 25/3/9 to 3/22 (April 21 to May 2, 1820)], and his grandson Mianhui [446-5-55/324, memorial dated JQ 1/8/8 (September 8, 1796)]. One report on a funeral for a consort that was conducted during the Allied Expeditionary invasion of the capital city, is included in *Yuanmingyuan*, 1:570–71, memorial dated XF 10/9/26 (November 8, 1860).

92. Yu Shanpu, *Qing Dongling*, 191.

93. Yu Shanpu, *Qing Dongling*, 122–23; Chen Baorong, *Qing Xiling*, 173.

94. For a listing of the coffins in each imperial tomb, see the lists of emperors and empresses appended to *Qingdai di wang lingqin*. Chen Baorong, *Qing Xiling*, 149–50, 172; Yu Shanpu, *Qing Dongling*, 157–73.

95. Yu Shanpu, *Qing Dongling*, 54–58; de Groot, *Religious System*, 3:1290.

96. Xu Guangyu, "Jingling shuang fei yuanqin," *Zijincheng* 42 (1987): 37; Yu Shanpu, *Qing Dongling*, 76–82.

97. Chen Baorong, *Qing Xiling,* 113–18, 149–52, 171–74; Yu Shanpu, *Qing Dongling,* 121–49, 174–79.

98. Xu Guangyuan, "Jingmin huangguifei yu kong quan," *Zijincheng* 56 (1990): 44–45; Shang Hongying, "Wangye yuanqin," *Zijincheng* 3 (1994): 31.

99. Bai Xinliang, "Qianlong jiating mian mianguan," *Zijincheng* 54 (1989): 3–4; Yu Shanpu, *Qing Dongling,* 205–7, 207–8. The death of the fourteenth son, Yongge, is reported in a Manchu-language memorial dated QL 25/3/9 (April 23, 1760) [Archives 446-5-55/123].

100. Xu Guangyuan, "Mai zangguo sanci de huanghou"; Yu Shanpu, *Qing Dongling,* 207–8.

101. Xu Guangyuan, "Jingmin huangguifei"; Xu Guangyuan, "Mai zangguo sanci de huanghou."

102. See de Groot, *Religious System,* 3:1184–86; Ann Paludan, *The Imperial Ming Tombs* (New Haven, 1981), 216–18 describes the sacrifice on Qingming 1901 at the western cemetery.

103. See memorials concerning the funeral of the Daoguang emperor in Archives 446-5-55/540.

104. Memorials dated GX 1/9/23 (October 21, 1875) [Archives 446-5-55/613], XT 1/8/8 (September 21, 1909) [446-5-55/742], and XT 1/9/21 (November 3, 1909) [446-5-55/742].

CONCLUSION

1. Kenneth Pomeranz, "Water to Iron, Widows to Warlords: The Handan Rain Shrine in Modern Chinese History," *Late Imperial China* 12, no. 1 (1991): 62–99.

2. Prasenjit Duara, *Rescuing History from the Nation: Questioning Narratives of Modern China* (Chicago, 1995), ch. 2.

3. James Millward, "A Uyghur Muslim in Qianlong's Court: The Meanings of the Fragrant Concubine," *Journal of Asian Studies* 53, no. 2 (1994): 427–58. See also Evelyn S. Rawski, "Re-envisioning the Qing: The Significance of the Qing Period in Chinese History," *Journal of Asian Studies* 55, no. 4 (1996): 829–50.

4. See chapter 4.

5. Thomas J. Barfield, *The Perilous Frontier: Nomadic Empires and China* (Oxford, 1989).

6. On the theme of Qing impact, see Rawski, "Re-envisioning the Qing," 836, 840–41.

7. Badarongga, "Manzhouyu yu Dawoeryu de guanxi," *Qingyu yanjiu* 2 (1993): 35–38; Rawski, "Re-envisioning the Qing," 836; Walther Heissig, *Die Pekinger lamaistischen Blockdrucke in mongolischer Sprache; Materialen zur mongolischen Literaturegeschichte* (Wiesbaden, 1954). Of course there was also extremely fruitful interaction between the cultures of the periphery and Han Chinese culture: see Lü Minghui, "Qingdai beifang geminzu yu

zhongyuan Hanzu de wenhua jiaoliu ji qi gongxian," *Qingshi yanjiu* 6 (1988): 122–40.

8. The economic changes in the northeast are described in Dawoerzu jianshi bianxiezu, *Dawoerzu jianshi* (Huhehaote, 1987), Ewenkezu jianshi bianxiezu, *Ewenkezu jianshi* (Huhehaote, 1983); Elunchunzu jianshi bianxiezu, *Elunchunzu jianshi* (Huhehaote, 1983); on Mongolia, see M. Sanjdorj, *Manchu Chinese Colonial Rule in Northern Mongolia*, trans. and ed. Urgunge Onon (New York, 1980).

Bibliography

ARCHIVAL SOURCES

Below are listed the titles and call numbers of the catalogs from which archival documents were quoted in the notes. All these sources are held in the First Historical Archives, Beijing.

Gongzhong dang'an 宮中檔案 549-4-9.
Gongzhong gexiang dangbu dengji 宮中各項檔簿登記 (account book records of various palace matters). Five catalogues under this title, numbered 155-4-16-1 through 155-4-16-5.
Gongzhong zajian 宮中雜件 (miscellaneous palace affairs archives) 467-4-85.
Libu anjuan 禮部安卷 (Board of Rites archives) 495-14-1.
Neiwufu dang'an 內務府檔案 (Imperial Household Department archives) 557-5-66-1 through 557-5-66-5.
Neiwufu zou'an 內務府奏案 (Imperial Household Department palace memorial archives) 446-5-55.
Neiwufu zouxiao dang 內務府奏消檔 (Imperial Household Department account registers) 396-5-5.
Zongrenfu dang'an 宗人府檔案 (Imperial Clan Court archives) 550-6-9-1 through 550-6-9-3.
Zongrenfu tang yinku dang'an 宗人府堂銀庫檔案 (Imperial Clan Court bullion vaults archives) 510-6-6-1.

PRIMARY SOURCES

Aixin juelo zongpu 愛新覺羅宗譜 (Genealogy of the Aixin Gioro). Edited by Jin Songqiao 金松喬 et al. 8 vols. Fengtian, 1937–38 (cited in notes as *AJZP*).
Baqi Manzhou shizu tongpu 八旗滿洲氏族通譜 (Collected genealogies of the Eight Banner Manchu clans). Edited by Hongzhou 弘畫, Ortai 鄂爾泰, et al. 1744. Reprint, Shenyang: Liao Shen shushe, 1989 (cited in notes as *BMST*).

(Qinding) Baqi tongzhi 欽定八旗通志 (Imperially commissioned general history of the eight banners). Edited by Ortai 鄂爾泰 et al. 8 vols. 1739. Reprint, Changchun: Dongbei shifandaxue chubanshe, 1986 (cited in notes as *BQTZ*).

(Qinding) Baqi tongzhi xubian 欽定八旗通志續編 (Imperially commissioned sequel to the geneal history of the eight banners). Edited by Tiebao 鐵保 et al. 60 vols. 1799. Reprint, Taipei: Xuesheng shuju, 1968 (cited in notes as *BQTZXB*).

Da Ming huidian 大明會典 (Collected regulations of the Ming dynasty). Edited by Shen Shixing 申時行 et al. 5 vols. 1587 edition. Reprint, Taipei: Dongnan shu bao she, 1964.

Da Qing shilu 大清實錄 (The veritable records of the Qing dynasty). Reprinted in 60 vols. under the title *Qing shilu* 清實錄 (Beijing: Zhonghua shuju, 1986). This work is cited by its individual reign titles, for example *Dezong Jing huangdi shilu* 德宗景皇帝實錄, and the volume and page number of the 1986 modern edition (cited in notes as *DQSL*).

Da Qing qijuzhu 大清起居注 (The diaries of rest and repose of the Qing dynasty). The portions that have been cited are listed separately under their compilers, below.

(Qinding) Da Qing huidian 欽定大清會典 (Imperially commissioned collected regulations of the Qing dynasty). 1899. Reprint, Taipei: Xinwen feng chuban gongsi, 1976 (cited in notes as *DQHD*).

(Qinding) Da Qing huidian shili 欽定大清會典事例 (Imperially commissioned collected regulations and precedents of the Qing dynasty). 19 vols. Guangxu edition, reprinted with *DQHD* in 1976 (cited in notes as *DQHDSL*).

(Qinding) Da Qing huidian tu 欽定大清會典圖 (Imperially commissioned regulations and illustrations of the Qing dynasty). 4 vols. Guangxu edition, reprinted with *DQHD* in 1976 (cited in notes as *DQHDT*).

(Yuzhi) Da Qing tongli 御製大清通禮 (Collected rituals of the Qing dynasty by imperial order). Edited by Laiboo 來保 et al. 50 *juan*. 1759 edition held by the Library of Congress. A subsequent revised edition, *Qinding da Qing tongli* 欽定大清通禮 (Imperially commissioned rituals of the Qing dynasty), edited by Mukedengge 穆克登額 et al. 54 *juan*. 1824 (cited in notes as *DQTL*).

Da Qing yudie 大清玉牒 (Qing imperial genealogy). Ms. Periodically revised throughout the dynasty, this imperial genealogy is held in the Shenyang Palace Museum and the First Historical Archives, Beijing. A microfilm copy in Chinese with some portions in Manchu is held by the Utah Genealogical Society, Salt Lake City, Utah (cited in notes as *DQYD*).

Guochao gong shi 國朝宮史 (History of the Qing palaces). Edited by Ortai 鄂爾泰 and Zhang Tingyu 張廷玉. 2 vols. 1769. Reprint, Beijing: Beijing guji chubanshe, 1987.

Guoli Gugong bowuyuan 國立故宮博物院. *Gongzhong dang Kangxi chao zouzhe* 宮中檔康熙朝奏摺 (Palace memorials of the Kangxi reign). Vols. 8, 9: *Manwen yuzhe* 滿文諭摺 (Manchu-language edicts and memorials). Shilin: Gugong bowuyuan, 1977.

Huangchao liqi tushi 皇朝禮器圖式 (Illustrated compendium of Qing rituals). Edited by Yinlu 允祿 et al. 1759. Reprinted in *Siku quanshu zhenben liuji* 四庫全書珍本六集, edited by Wang Yunwu 王雲五, vols. 354–68. (Taipei: Taipei shangwu yinshuguan, 1976).

Qinding gongzhong xianxing zeli 欽定宮中現行則例 (Imperially commissioned current palace regulations). Ms 1742. Photoreproduction of 1856 ms with this title in *Jindai Zhongguo shiliao congkan* 近代中國史料叢刊, edited by Shen Yunlong 沈雲龍, vols. 621–24. (Taipei: Wenhai, 1979).

Qinding Guanglusi zeli 欽定光祿司則例 (Imperially commissioned regulations of the Banqueting Department). 90 *juan*. 1839 preface.

Qinding libu zeli 欽定六部則例 (Imperially commissioned regulations of the Board of Rites). 202 *juan*. 1844. Photoreproduction. Taipei: Chengwen, 1966.

Qinding liubu chufen zeli 欽定六部處分則例 (Imperially commissioned regulations on punishments for the Six Boards). 1892. Reprinted in *Jindai Zhongguo shiliao congkan* 近代中國史料叢刊, edited by Shen Yunlong 沈雲龍, vols. 332a, 332b. (Taipei: Wenhai, 1972).

Qinding Manzhou jishen jitian dianli 欽定滿洲祭神祭天典禮 (Imperially commissioned Manchu rituals for sacrificing to deities and to heaven). 1747. Reprinted in *Jindai Zhongguo shiliao congkan* 近代中國史料叢刊, edited by Shen Yunlong 沈雲龍, vol. 371, (Taipei: Wenhai, 1969).

Qinding wang gong chufen zeli 欽定王公處分則例 (Imperially commissioned regulations on the punishment of princes and other nobles). 4 *juan*. n.d.

Qinding zongguan Neiwufu tang xianxing zeli 欽定總管內務府堂現行則例 (Imperially commissioned regulations on the office of the Ministers of the Imperial Household Department). 4 *juan*. 1884 preface.

Qinding zongrenfu zeli 欽定宗人府則例 (Imperially commissioned regulations of the Imperial Clan Court). 31 *juan*. 1840 preface. Also in an 1898 and 1908 edition.

Qinggui 慶桂 et al., eds. *Guochao gongshi xubian* 國朝宮史續編 (Sequel to the Qing history of the palace). 5 vols. Reprint, Taipei: Taiwan xuesheng shuju, 1965.

"Qing Neiwufu zang jingcheng quantu" 清內務府藏京城全圖 (Map of the capital city held in the Qing Imperial Household Department). 1940.

Taichangsi zeli 太常司則例 (Regulations of the Department of Sacrificial Worship). 133 *juan*. Daoguang edition.

Uksun i wang gung sai gungge faššan be iletulere ulabun (Biographies of meritorious princes in the imperial lineage). 7 *juan*. Harvard-Yenching Treasure Room.

Xu Zhixiang 徐致祥 et al., eds. *Guoli gugong bowuyuan zhen zang Qingdai qijuzhu: Guangxu chao* 國立故宮博物院珍藏清代起居注: 光緒朝 (Diaries of rest and repose housed in the National Palace Museum: the Guangxu reign). 80 vols. Taipei: Lianhebao, Wenhua jijin hui, Guoxue wenxianguan, 1987.

Zhaolian 昭棟. *Xiaotingzalu* 嘯亭雜錄 (Random notes from the Whistling Pavilion), *Xiaoting xulu* 嘯亭續錄 (More notes from the Whistling Pavilion). 1909. Reprint, Beijing: Xinhua shudian, 1980.

Zhongguo diyi lishi dang'anguan 中國第一歷史檔案館. *Kangxi qijuzhu* 康熙起居注 (Diaries of rest and repose of the Kangxi reign). 3 vols. Beijing: Zhonghua shuju, 1984.

―――. *Yuanmingyuan: Qingdai dang'an shiliao* 圓明園: 清代檔案史料 (Yuanmingyuan: historical materials from the Qing archives). 2 vols. Shanghai: Guji chubanshe, 1991.

Qinding zongguan neiwufu xianxing zeli 欽定總管內務府現行則例 (Imperially commissioned current regulations of the Ministers of the Imperial Household Department). 4 *juan*. Editions of 1871, 1884, 1908. Edition of 7 *juan*. Peking: Guoli Beiping gugong bowuyuan, wenxianguan, 1937 (cited in notes as *ZNXZ*).

Zongguan neiwufu xianxing tiaoli Guangchusi 總管內務府現行條例光儲司 (Current regulations of the Ministers of the Imperial Household Department for the Department of the Privy Purse). Reprint. *Jindai Zhongguo shiliao congkan*. 近代中國史料叢刊, edited by Shen Yunlong 沈雲龍, vols. 852–54 (Taipei: Wenhai, 1972).

Zongshi wang gong shizhi zhangjing juezhi xici quanbiao 宗室王公世職章京爵秩襲次全表 (Charts of hereditary noble titles for imperial mainline princes and nobles). Edited by Mou Qiwen 牟其汶. 10 *juan*. Preface dated Guangxu 32 (1906).

SECONDARY LITERATURE

Ahmad, Zahiruddin. *Sino-Tibetan Relations in the Seventeenth Century*. Rome: Istituto italiano per il medio ed estremo oriente, 1970.

Aisin-Gioro Pu Yi. *From Emperor to Citizen*. Translated by W. J. F. Jenner. 1964. Reprint, New York: Oxford University Press, 1987.

Aixinjuelo Yingsheng 愛新覺羅瀛生. "Tantan Manyu de jingyu" 談談滿語的京語 (Chats on the capital version of the Manchu language). *Manyu yanjiu* 滿語研究 1 (1987): 2–15, 73; 2 (1988): 25–34; 1 (1989): 4–20; 2 (1990): 22–36; 2 (1991): 3–15; 2 (1992): 1–17; 2 (1993): 25–34, 24; 1 (1994): 15–23, 36; 1 (1995): 13–20.

Akamatsu Chijo 赤松智城. "Manshū hatanin no ie-matsuri" 滿洲旗人の家祭 (The family rituals of Manchu bannermen). *Minzokugaku kenkyū* 民族學研究 1, no. 2 (1935): 223–31.

Akamatsu Chijo and Akiba Takashi 秋葉隆. *Manmō no minzoku to shūkyō* 滿蒙の民族と宗教 (The Manchu and Mongol people and their religion). Kyoto: Osaka yagō shoten, 1941.

Akiba Takashi 秋葉隆. "Sama no fusai to daisen no fujutsu — Manshū fuzokutō sa hōkoku" 薩瑪の巫祭と大仙の巫術――滿洲巫蹈查報告 (The shaman's sacrifice and the shamanic arts of the *daxian*—an investigatory report on Manchu shamanic dances). *Minzokugaku kenkyū* 民族學研究 1, no. 2 (1935): 237–57.

Alekseev, N. A. "Shamanism among the Turkic Peoples of Siberia: Shamans and Their Religious Practices." In *Shamanism: Soviet Studies of Traditional*

Religion in Siberia and Central Asia, edited by Marjorie M. Balzer, 49–109. Armonk, N.Y.: M.E. Sharpe, 1990.

Allen, Sarah. "Drought, Human Sacrifice and the Mandate of Heaven in a Lost Text from the *Shang Shu.*" *Bulletin, School of Oriental and African Studies, London University* 47 (1984): 523–39.

Anderson, Benedict. *Imagined Communities: Reflections on the Origin and Spread of Nationalism.* Revised ed. London: Verso, 1991.

Appadurai, Arjun. *The Social Life of Things: Commodities in Cultural Perspective.* New York: Cambridge University Press, 1986.

Arlington, L.C., and William Lewisohn. *In Search of Old Peking.* 1935. Reprint. New York: Paragon, 1967.

Atkinson, Jane M. *The Art and Politics of Wana Shamanship.* Berkeley: University of California Press, 1989.

———. "Shamanisms Today." *Annual Review of Anthropology* 21 (1992): 307–30.

Ayscough, Florence. "Notes on the Symbolism of the Purple Forbidden City." *Journal, North China Branch of the Royal Asiatic Society,* n.s., 52 (1921): 51–78.

Aziz, Barbara N. "Reincarnation Reconsidered—Or the Reincarnate Lama as Shaman." In *Spirit Possession in the Nepal Himalayas,* edited by John T. Hitchcock and Rex L. Jones, 343–60. New Delhi: Vikas Publishing House, 1976.

Badarongga 巴達榮嘎. "Manzhouyu yu Dawoeryu de guanxi" 滿洲語與達斡爾的關係 (The relationship between Manchu and Daur). *Manyu yanjiu* 滿語研究 2 (1993): 35–38.

Bai Fengqi 白風岐. "Qiantan Ming Qing shiqi Liaoning Mengguzu de jingji" 淺談明清時期遼寧蒙古族的經濟 (A brief discussion of the economy of Mongols in Liaoning during the Ming and Qing periods). *Manzu yanjiu* 滿族研究 4 (1991): 79–88.

———. "Qingdai dui Mengguzu de zhengce shulüe" 清代對蒙古族的政策述略 (A brief summary of Qing policies regarding the Mongols). *Heilongjiang minzu congkan* 黑龍江民族叢刊 3 (1991): 79–84.

Bai Hongxi 白洪希. "Qing tangzi tanze" 清堂子探賾 (Exploring the mysteries of the Qing tangzi sacrifices). *Manzu yanjiu* 滿族研究 3 (1995): 61–63.

Bai Jie 白杰 and Zhang Ping 張萍. "Jiaqing cusi yu Daoguang jiwei zhi zhenxiang" 嘉慶猝死與道光繼位之眞相 (The truth about Jiaqing's sudden death and Daoguang's accession). *Qingshi yanjiu* 清史研究 3 (1994): 97–100.

Bai Xinliang 白新良. "Lun Qianlong mimi jianchu" 論乾隆秘密建儲 (Regarding the Qianlong emperor's secret testament). *Gugong bowuyuan yuankan* 故宮博物院院刊 2 (1989): 3–10.

———. "Qianlong jiating mian mianguan" 乾隆家庭面面觀 (Aspects of Qianlong's family). *Zijincheng* 紫禁城 54 (1989): 3–4.

———. *Qianlong zhuan* 乾隆傳 (Biography of Qianlong). Shenyang: Liaoning jiaoyu chubanshe, 1990.

Bao Chengguan 寶成關. *Yixin Cixi zhengzheng ji* 奕訢慈禧政爭記 (The record of the political struggle between Yixin and Cixi). Changchun: Jilin wenshi chubanshe, 1980.

Bao Guiqin 包桂芹, ed. *Qingdai Menggu guanshi zhuan* 清代蒙古官使傳 (Biographies of Qing Mongol officials). Beijing: Minzu chubanshe, 1995.

Bao Qunli 包群立. "Cong tifa zhidu kan Qingchao de minzu zhengce" 從剃髮制度看清朝的民族政策 (A look at the ethnic policy of the Qing dynasty from the perspective of the regulations concerning the shaving of foreheads). *Nei Menggu minzu shiyuan xuebao (zhexue, shehuixue)* 內蒙古民族師院學報 (哲學, 社會學) 3 (1991): 66–70, 87.

Barfield, Thomas J. *The Perilous Frontier: Nomadic Empires and China.* Oxford: Basil Blackwell, 1989.

Bartholomew, Teresa Tse. "Sino-Tibetan Art of the Qianlong Period from the Asian Art Museum of San Francisco." *Orientations* 22, no. 6 (1991): 34–45.

———. "The Walters Art Gallery 1764 Jade *Qing* Lithophone and Related Pieces." *The Journal of the Walters Art Gallery* 49–50 (1991–1992): 131–39.

———. "Three Thangkas from Chengde." In *Tibetan Studies: Proceedings of the Fifth Seminar of the International Association of Tibetan Studies, Narita, 1989,* 353–59. Narita: Naritasan shinshoji, 1992.

———. "The Legacy of Chinggis Khan." *Orientations* 26, no. 6 (1995): 46–52.

Bartlett, Beatrice S. *Monarchs and Ministers: The Grand Council in Mid-Ch'ing China, 1723–1820.* Berkeley: University of California Press, 1991.

Basilov, V. "Shamanism in Central Asia." In *The Realm of the Extra-Human: Agents and Audiences,* edited by Agehananda Bharati, 149–57. The Hague: Mouton, 1976.

Bawden, C. R. *The Jebtsundamba Khutukhtus of Urga: Text, Translation and Notes.* Wiesbaden: Harrassowitz, 1961.

———. *The Modern History of Mongolia.* London: Weidenfeld and Nicolson, 1968.

Beckwith, Christopher I. *The Tibetan Empire in Central Asia: A History of the Struggle for Great Power among Tibetans, Turks, Arabs, and Chinese during the Early Middle Ages.* Princeton: Princeton University Press, 1987.

Béguin, Gilles. "Mongolian Art Treasures from the 17th–19th Centuries." *Oriental Art* 39, no. 4 (1993–94): 14–21.

Berger, Patricia. "'A Buddha from Former Times': Zanabazar and the Mongol Renaissance." *Orientations* 26, no. 6 (1995): 53–59.

———. "After Xanadu." In *Mongolia: The Legacy of Chinggis Khan,* edited by Patricia Berger and Terese Tse Bartholomew, 50–75. San Francisco: Asian Art Museum of San Francisco, 1995.

Beurdeley, Cécile, and Michel Beurdeley. *Giuseppe Castiglione: A Jesuit Painter at the Court of the Chinese Emperors,* translated by Michael Bullock. Rutland: Charles E. Tuttle, 1971.

Bills, Sheila C. "Bronze Sculptures of the Early Ming (1403–1450)." *Arts of Asia* 24, no. 5 (1994): 73–87.

Blodget, Henry. "The Worship of Heaven and Earth by the Emperor of China." *Journal, American Oriental Society* 20 (1899): 58–69.

Bo Yang 柏楊. *Zhongguo diwang huanghou qinwang gongzhu shixi lu* 中國帝王皇后親王公主世系錄 (The descent lines of China's emperors, empresses, princes and princesses). Beijing: Zhongguo youyi chuban gongsi, 1986.

Boettcher, Cheryl M. "In Search of Manchu Bibliography." Master's thesis, University of Illinois, 1989.

Bogan, M. L. C. *Manchu Customs and Superstitions*. Tientsin: China Booksellers, 1928.

Bolz, Judith M. *A Survey of Taoist Literature, Tenth to Seventeenth Centuries*. Berkeley: Institute of East Asian Studies, University of California, 1987.

Bouvet, Joachim. *The History of Cang-Hy the Present Emperor of China*. London: F. Coggan, 1699.

Bredon, Juliet. *Peking: A Historical and Intimate Description of Its Chief Places of Interest*. Shanghai: Kelly and Walsh, 1922.

Brunnert, H. S., and V. V. Hagelstrom. *Present-Day Political Organization of China*. Translated by A. Beltchenko and E. E. Moran. Foochow: n.p., 1911.

Cai Shiying 蔡世英. *Qing mo quanjian Li Lianying* 清末權監李蓮英 (The powerful late Qing eunuch Li Lianying). Hebei: Hebei renmin chubanshe, 1986.

Cai Zhichun 蔡志純. "Menggu lama guizu xingcheng chutan" 蒙古喇嘛貴族形成初探 (An inquiry into the formation of the Mongol Lamaist nobility). *Minzu yanjiu* 民族研究 1 (1987): 50–56.

Cammann, Schuyler V. R. *China's Dragon Robes*. New York: Ronald Press, 1952.

Cannadine, David, and Simon Price, eds. *Rituals of Royalty: Power and Ceremony in Traditional Societies*. Cambridge: Cambridge University Press, 1987.

Cao Lijuan 曹麗娟. "Hanjun bazu jisi ge wu bianzhe—jianlun Man Han minzu jian wenhua de ronghe" 漢軍八族祭祀歌舞辨折——兼論滿漢民族間文化的融合 (Analysis of *Hanjun* ritual song and dance: the merger of Manchu and Han Chinese popular culture). *Manzu yanjiu* 滿族研究 1 (1993): 86–90.

Cao Zhenqing 曹振卿. "Puyi rumu Wang Jiao shi" 溥儀乳母焦氏 (Puyi's wet-nurse, Mrs. Wang). *Zijincheng* 紫禁城 48 (1988): 40.

Cen Dali 岑大利 "Qingdai Manzu de sangzang xisu" 清代滿族的喪葬習俗 (Manchu funerary customs during the Qing dynasty). *Gugong bowuyuan yuankan* 故宮博物院院刊 4 (1992): 91–94.

Chaffee, John. "The Marriage of Sung Imperial Clanswomen." In *Marriage and Inequality in Chinese Society*, edited by Rubie S. Watson and Patricia B. Ebrey, 133–69. Berkeley: University of California Press, 1991.

Chan, Hok-lam. "'Ta Chin' (Great Golden): the origin and changing interpretations of the Jurchen State Name." *T'oung Pao* 77, nos. 4–5 (1991): 253–99.

Chandra, Lokesh. *Buddhist Iconography*. New Delhi: D. K. Fine Arts Press, 1988.

Chang, Te-ch'ang. "The Economic Role of the Imperial Household in the Ch'ing Dynasty." *Journal of Asian Studies* 31, no. 2 (1972): 243–73.

Changbaishanren 長白山人. "Qingdai baozuo" 清代寶座 (Qing thrones). In *Suoji Qinggong* 瑣記清宮, edited by Wei Jiangong 魏建功 et al., 159–64. Beijing: Zijincheng chubanshe, 1990.

Chang Jiang 常江 and Li Li 李理. *Qing gong shiwei* 清宮侍衛 (The imperial guards in the Qing palace). Shenyang: Liaoning daxue chubanshe, 1993.

Chang Lin-sheng. "Introduction to the Historical Development of Qing Dynasty Painted Enamelware." *National Palace Museum Bulletin* 25, nos. 4–5 (1990): 1–22.

———. "Qing Dynasty Imperial Enamelled Glassware." *Arts of Asia* 21, no. 3 (1991): 95–109.

Chard, Robert L. "Master of the Family: History and Development of the Chinese Cult to the Stove." Ph.D. diss., University of California, Berkeley, 1990.

Chase, Hanson. "The Status of the Manchu Language in the Early Qing." Ph.D. diss., University of Washington, Seattle, 1979.

Chatterjee, Partha. *The Nation and Its Fragments: Colonial and Post-Colonial Histories*. Princeton: Princeton University Press, 1993.

Chayet, Anne. *Les Temples de Rehe et leurs modèles tibétains*. Paris: Editions Recherche sur les civilisations, 1985.

Chen, Chieh-hsien. "Introduction to the Manchu Text Version of the Ch'ing Emperors' Ch'i-chü-chu (Notes on the Emperors' Daily Activities)." *Central Asiatic Journal* 17, nos. 2–4 (1973): 111–27.

———. "A Study of the Manchu Posthumous Titles of the Ch'ing Emperors." *Central Asiatic Journal* 26, nos. 3–4 (1982): 187–92.

———. *Manchu Archival Materials*. Taipei: Linking Publishing, 1988.

Chen Baorong 陳寶蓉. *Qing Xiling zong heng* 清西陵縱橫 (An examination of the Qing western tombs). Shijiazhuang: Hebei renmin chubanshe, 1987.

Chen Guoguang 陳國光. "Xi Menggu fojiao jingji de xingshuai" 西蒙古佛教經濟的興衰 (The rise and fall of the Buddhist economy of the Western Mongols). *Xinjiang shehui kexue* 新疆社會科學 4 (1987): 103–11.

Chen Huixue 陳會學. "Manzhou shizu shenhua yanjiu zongshu" 滿洲始祖神話研究縱述 (A survey of the research on Manchu legends about the founding ancestor). *Heihe xuekan* 黑河學刊 1 (1991): 83–93.

Chen Jinling 陳金陵. "Jianlun Qingdai huangquan yu shiwei" 簡論清代皇權與侍衛 (On the imperial prerogative and the Qing imperial guards). In *Qingshi luncong 1992* 清史論叢, 61–68. Shenyang: Liaoning renmin chubanshe, 1993.

Chen Keji 陳可冀 et al. *Cixi Guangxu yifang xuanyi* 慈禧光緒醫方選議 (Selected discussions of medical aspects of Cixi and Guangxu). Beijing: Zhonghua shuju, 1986.

Chen Qingying 陳慶英. "Si zhi jiushi Banchan dashi yi ji tamen de lingta" 四至九世班單喇嘛大師以及他們的靈塔 (The fourth to ninth Panchen lamas and their stupas). *Qinghai shehui kexue* 青海社會科學 3 (1989): 89–97.

———. "Guan yu Beijing Xiangshan Zangzuren de quanwen ji shiji jizai" 關于北京香山藏族人的傳聞及史籍記載 (Stories and historical records about the Tibetans living in the Western Hills). *Zhongguo Zangxue* 中國藏學 4 (1990): 104–15.

Chen Xiaoqiang 陳小强. "Cong Menggu lama Neijituoyin yishi de huodong kan Manzhou Qing zheng quan dui Zang zhuan Fojiao de fuzhi he xianzhi" 從蒙古喇嘛內齊陀音一世的活動看滿洲清政權對藏傳佛教的扶植和限制 (Evaluating the Qing government's support and restraint of Tibetan Buddhism, from the perspective of the activities of the Mongol lama Neijitoyin). *Qinghai minzu xueyuan xuebao* 青海民族學院學報 4 (1991): 39–44, 38.

Chen Yuan 陳垣. "Yong, Qian jian feng Tianzhujiao zhi zongshi" 雍乾間奉天主教之宗室 (Imperial clansmen who accepted Christianity in the Yongzheng and Qianlong reigns). *Furen xuezhi* 輔仁學誌 3, no. 2 (1931): 1–35.

Chen Yufeng 陳玉峰. "Dongbei huangzhuang shengchan guanxi de yanbian" 東北皇莊生產關係的演變 (Changes in the production relations of imperial estates in the northeast). *Shixue jikan* 史學集刊 2 (1988): 27–32.

Chen Yuning 陳育寧 and Tang Xiaofang 湯曉芳. "Qingdai lamajiao zai Mengguzu diqu de tequan ji qi shuailuo" 清代喇嘛教在蒙古族地區的特權及其衰落 (The special prerogatives and decline of Tibetan Buddhism in the Mongol areas during the Qing) *Qinghai shehui kexue* 青海社會科學 5 (1988): 98–102.

Chengde shi wenwuju 承德市文物局 and Renmin daxue, Qingshi yanjiu suo 人民大學, 清史研究所, *Chengde Bishu shanzhuang* 承德避暑山莊 (The Bishu shanzhuang in Chengde). Beijing: Wenwu chubanshe, 1980.

Chevenix-Trench, Charles P. *A History of Horsemanship*. New York: Doubleday, 1970.

Chia, Ning. "The Li-fan Yuan in the Early Ch'ing Dynasty." Ph.D. diss., Johns Hopkins University, 1992.

———. "The Lifanyuan and the Inner Asian Rituals in the Early Qing (1644–1795)." *Late Imperial China* 14, no. 1 (1993): 60–92.

Chiodo, Elizabetta. "The Book of the Offerings to the Holy Činggis Qagan: A Mongolian Ritual Text." *Zentralasiatische Studien* 22 (1989–91): 190–220.

Chow, Kai-wing. *The Rise of Confucian Ritualism in Late Imperial China: Ethics, Classics, and Lineage Discourse*. Stanford: Stanford University Press, 1994.

———. "Narrating Nation, Race, and Culture: Imagining the Hanzu Identity in Modern China." Presented at the conference, "Narratives, Art, and Ritual: Imagining and Constructing Nationhood in Modern East Asia," University of Illinois at Champaign-Urbana, November 15–17, 1996.

Chuang, Chi-fa. "The Emperor's New Pets: Naming Castiglione's 'Ten Champion Dogs.'" Translated by Mark Elliott. *National Palace Museum Bulletin* 23, no. 1 (1988): 1–13.

Chung, Sue Fawn. "The Much Maligned Empress Dowager: A Revisionist Study of the Empress Dowager Tz'u-Hsi in the Period 1898 to 1900." Ph.D. diss., University of California, 1975.

Clark, Walter E. *Two Lamaistic Pantheons*. New York: Paragon, 1965.

Clarke, John. "A Group of Sino-Mongolian Metalwork in the Tibetan Style." *Orientations* 23, no. 5 (1992): 65–75.

Cohen, Alvin P. "Coercing the Rain Deities in Ancient China." *History of Religions* 17, nos. 3–4 (1978): 244–65.

Cormack, J. G. *Everyday Customs in China*. 4th edition. Edinburgh: Moray Press, 1935.

Crossley, Pamela K. "The Tong in Two Worlds: Cultural Identities in Liaodong and Nurgan during the 13th–17th Centuries." *Ch'ing-shih wen-t'i* 4, no. 9 (1983): 21–46.

———. "An Introduction to the Qing Foundation Myth." *Late Imperial China* 6, no. 2 (1985): 13–36.

———. "*Manzhou yuanliu kao* and the Formalization of the Manchu Heritage." *Journal of Asian Studies* 46, no. 4 (1987): 761–90.

———. "The Qianlong Retrospect on the Chinese-martial (hanjun) Banners." *Late Imperial China* 10, no. 1 (1989): 63–107.

———. *Orphan Warriors: Three Manchu Generations and the End of the Qing World*. Princeton: Princeton University Press, 1990.

———. "Thinking About Ethnicity in Early Modern China." *Late Imperial China* 1 (1990): 1–34.

———. "Review Article: The Rulerships of China." *American Historical Review* 97, no. 5 (1992): 1468–83.

———. "Manchu Education." In *Education and Society in Late Imperial China, 1600–1900*, edited by Benjamin A. Elman and Alexander Woodside, 340–78. Berkeley: University of California Press, 1994.

———. *The Manchus*. Oxford: Basil Blackwell, 1997.

———. *A Translucent Mirror: History and Identity in the Transformations of Qing Imperial Ideology*. Berkeley: University of California Press, forthcoming.

Crossley, Pamela K., and Evelyn S. Rawski. "A Profile of the Manchu Language in Ch'ing History." *Harvard Journal of Asiatic Studies* 53, no. 1 (1993): 63–102.

Cui Guobi 崔國璧. "Lun Kangxi dui Heilongjiang liuyu de shibian zhengce" 論康熙對黑龍江流域的實邊政策 (Kangxi's border policy on the Heilongjiang drainage). *Heihe xuekan* 黑河學刊 3 (1991): 114–20, 40.

Cui Xiji 崔羲季 and Cui Xiongquan 崔雄權. "Cong Chaoxianzu zhuan shuo kan Nuerhachi zuxian de faxiang di" 從朝鮮族傳說看努爾哈赤祖先的發祥地 (Examining Nurgaci's regional origins from Korean accounts). *Manzu yanjiu* 滿族研究 2 (1993): 18–24.

Dai Yi 戴逸. "Qianlong de jiating beiju ji youguan de zhengzhi fengbo" 乾隆的家庭悲劇及有關的政治風波 (A domestic tragedy for the Qianlong emperor and its political repercussions). *Qingshi yanjiu tongxun* 清史研究通訊 1 (1986): 1–6.

———. "Qianlongdi he Beijing de chengshi jianshe" 乾隆帝和北京的城市建設 (The Qianlong emperor and the establishment of Peking). In *Qingshi yanjiu ji* 清史研究集, Zhongguo renmin daxue Qingshi yanjiu suo 中國人民大學,清史研究所, 6: 1–37. Beijing: Guangming ribao chubanshe, 1988.

Dan Shi 丹石. *Yige Qing gong taijian de zaoyu* 一個清宮太監的遭遇 (The hard lot of a Qing palace eunuch). Beijing: Taisheng chubanshe, 1989.

Dawoerzu jianshi bianxie zu 達斡爾族簡史編寫組, *Dawoerzu jianshi* 達斡爾族簡史 (A short history of the Daur). Huhehaote: Nei Menggu renmin chubanshe, 1986.

Dawson, Christopher. *Mission to Asia*. Toronto: University of Toronto Press, 1980.

de Groot, J. J. M. *The Religious System of China*. 6 vols. 1892–1910. Reprint. Taipei: Chengwen, 1969.

de Harlez, Charles. "La Religion nationale des Tartares orientaux, Mandchous et Mongols, comparée à la religion des anciens Chinois." *Memoires couronnés et autres mémoires,* no. 40. Brussels: Royal Academy of Sciences, Letters, and Fine Arts, 1887.

Diao Shuren 刁書仁. "Lüe lun Qianlong chao jingqi sula de yizhu" 略論乾隆朝京旗蘇拉的移駐 (On the change in residence of *sula* in the capital garrison during the Qing). *Beifang wenwu* 北方文物 2 (1994): 65–68.

Dickinson, Gary, and Linda Wrigglesworth. *Imperial Wardrobe*. London: Bamboo Publications, 1990.

di Cosmo, Nicola. "Manchu Rites and Ceremonies at the Qing Court: A Study based on the *Manjusai wecere metere kooli bithe,* The Code of Sacrifices and Rituals of the Manchus." In *State Ritual in China,* edited by Joseph McDermott. Cambridge: Cambridge University Press, forthcoming.

Ding Yizhuang 定宜庄. "Shilun Qingdai de Man Han tonghun" 試論清代的滿漢通婚 (Banner-commoner intermarriage in the Qing). Presented at the Association of Asian Studies Annual Meeting, Chicago, March 14, 1997.

Dong Baocai 董寶才 and Zhang Xiaochang 張孝昌. "Boerjijite Xiaozhuang—Qing jiechu nü zhengzhijia" 博爾濟吉特孝庄——清杰出女政治家 (The Borjigit empress Xiaozhuang—an outstanding Qing female politician). *Zhongyang minzu xueyuan xuebao* 中央民族學院學報 3 (1989): 8–11.

Dong Jianzhong 董建中. "Qing Qianlong chao wang gong dachen guan yuan jingong wenti chutan" 清乾隆朝王公大臣官員進貢問題初探 (A preliminary inquiry into the tribute offered by princes, high officials, and officials during the Qianlong reign). *Qingshi yanjiu* 清史研究 1 (1996): 40–66.

Dong Shouyi 董守義. *Gong qinwang Yixin dazhuan* 恭親王奕訢大傳 (Biography of Yixin, Prince Gong). Shenyang: Liaoning renmin chubanshe, 1989.

Dong Wanlun 董萬崙. "Lun Manzu san xiannü shenhua de xingcheng yu jiazhi" 論滿族三仙女神話的形成與價值 (On the formation and value of Manchu legends about the three immortal maidens). *Minzu yanjiu* 民族研究 3 (1992): 32–39.

———. "Jiu Manzhou dang ji Qing shizu zhuanshuo yanjiu" 舊滿洲檔記清始祖傳說研究 (Research on the legend of the Qing first ancestor from the old Manchu archives). *Gugong xueshu jikan* 故宮學術季刊 11, no. 1 (1993): 79–89.

Dray-Novey, Alison Jean. "Policing Imperial Peking: The Ch'ing Gendarmerie 1650–1850." Ph.D. diss., Harvard University, 1981.

Drompp, Michael R. "Supernumerary Sovereigns: Superfluity and Mutability in the Elite Power Structure of the Early Türks (Tu-jue)." In *Rulers from the Steppe: State Formation on the Eurasian Periphery*, edited by Gary Seaman and Daniel Marks, 2: 92–115. Los Angeles: Ethnographics Press, 1991.

Duara, Prasenjit. "Superscribing Symbols: The Myth of Guandi, Chinese God of War." *Journal of Asian Studies* 47, no. 4 (1988): 778–95.

———. *Rescuing History from the Nation: Questioning Narratives of Modern China*. Chicago: University of Chicago Press, 1995.

Du Jiaji 杜家驥. "Dui Qingdai Yizheng wang dachen huiyi de mouxie kaocha" 對清代議政王大臣會議的某些考察 (Inquiries into the character of the Deliberative Council of the Qing). *Qingshi luncong* 清史論叢 7 (1986): 115–24.

———. "Cong Qingdai de gongzhong jisi he tangzi jisi kan samanjiao" 從清代的宮中祭祀和堂子祭祀看薩滿教 (Perspectives on shamanism from palace and *tangzi* rites in the Qing dynasty). *Manzu yanjiu* 滿族研究 1 (1990): 45–49.

———. "Qingdai de huangzi jiaoyu" 清代的皇子教育 (The education of imperial sons in the Qing). *Gugong bowuyuan yuankan* 故宮博物院院刊 2 (1990): 88–92, 51.

———. "Yongzheng di jiwei qian de fengqi ji xiangguan wenti kaozhe" 雍正帝繼位前的封旗及相關問題考折 (Analysis of the banner assignment and related issues concerning Yongzheng before his accession). *Zhongguoshi yanjiu* 中國史研究 4 (1990): 84–89.

———. "Qingdai zongshi fenfengzhi shulun" 清代宗室分封制述論 (On the investiture of the Qing mainline). *Shehui kexue jikan* 社會科學輯刊 4 (1991): 90–95.

———. "Qianlong zhi nü jia Kongfu ji xiangguan wenti zhi kaobian" 乾隆之女嫁孔府及相關問題之考辨 (An examination of the marriage of Qianlong's daughter into the Kong family and related issues). *Lishi dang'an* 歷史檔案 3 (1992): 98–101.

Du Jianye et al., eds. *Yonghegong: Palace of Harmony*. Hong Kong: Art Blooming Publishing, n.d.

Eisenberg, Andrew. "Retired Emperorship in Medieval China: the Northern Wei." *T'oung Pao* 77, nos. 1–3 (1991): 49–87.

Eliade, Mircea. *Shamanism: Archaic Techniques of Ecstacy*. Translated by Willard R. Trask. Princeton: Princeton University Press, 1964.

Elias, Norbert. *The Court Society*. Translated by Edmund Jephcott. New York: Pantheon Books, 1983.

Elliott, Mark C. "Resident Aliens: The Manchu Experience in China, 1644–1760." Ph.D. diss., University of California, Berkeley, 1993.

Elunchunzu jianshi bianxie zu 鄂倫春族簡史編寫組, *Elunchunzu jianshi* 鄂倫春族簡史 (A short history of the Oroqen). Huhehaote: Nei Menggu renmin chubanshe, 1983.

Ewenkezu jianshi bienxie zu 鄂溫克族簡史編寫組, *Ewenkezu jianshi* 鄂溫克族簡史 (A short history of the Ewenk). Huhehaote: Nei Menggu renmin chubanshe, 1983.

Fairbank, John K. *Trade and Diplomacy on the China Coast: The Opening of the Treaty Ports, 1842–1854.* Cambridge, Mass.: Harvard University Press, 1953.

Fang, Chao-ying. "A Technique for Estimating the Numerical Strength of the Early Manchu Military Forces." *Harvard Journal of Asiatic Studies* 13, no. 1 (1950): 192–214.

Fang Yujin 方裕謹. "Qing di zai zheng yue chuyi zhe yitian" 清帝載正月初一這一天 (The Qing emperor on New Year's day). *Zijincheng* 紫禁城 5 (1981): 37.

Farquhar, David. "The Origins of the Manchus' Mongolian Policy." In *The Chinese World Order: Traditional China's Foreign Relations*, edited by John K. Fairbank, 198–205. Cambridge, Mass.: Harvard University Press, 1968.

———. "Mongolian vs. Chinese Elements in the Early Manchu State." *Ch'ing-shih wen-t'i* 1, no. 6 (1971): 11–23.

———. "Emperor as Bodhisattva in the Governance of the Qing Empire." *Harvard Journal of Asiatic Studies* 38 (1978): 5–34.

Feng Erkang 馮爾康. "Kangxi chao de chuwei zhi zheng he Yinzhen de shengli" 康熙朝的儲位之爭和胤禛的勝利 (The succession struggle during the Kangxi reign and Yinzhen's victory). *Gugong bowuyuan yuankan* 故宮博物院院刊 3 (1981): 12–24.

———. *Yongzheng zhuan* 雍正傳 (Biography of Yongzheng). Beijing: Renmin chubanshe, 1985.

———. *Qing shi shiliaoxue chugao* 清史史料學初稿 (Draft historiography of Qing history). Tianjin: Nankai daxue chubanshe, 1986.

Feng Qili 馮其利. "Yixian Shenshizhuang de Chundu qinwang fen" 易縣神石莊的淳度親王墳 (The grave of Prince Chun in Shenshizhuang, Yi county). *Manzu yanjiu* 滿族研究 4 (1990): 46.

Feng Zuozhe 馮佐哲. "Qing gong ji 'Zao'" 清宮祭皂 (The Qing court worships the kitchen god). *Zijincheng* 紫禁城 11 (1982): 28.

Finlay, John R. "Chinese Embroidered Mandarin Squares from the Schuyler V. R. Cammann Collection." *Orientations* 25, no. 4 (1994): 57–63.

Fletcher, Joseph. "The heyday of the Ch'ing order in Mongolia, Sinkiang and Tibet." In *The Cambridge History of China: Late Ch'ing 1800–1911, Part 1*, edited by John K. Fairbank, 351–408. Cambridge: Cambridge University Press, 1978.

Fong, Wen C. "Imperial Patronage of the Arts Under the Ch'ing." In *Possessing the Past: Treasures from the National Palace Museum, Taipei*, edited by Wen C. Fong and James C. Y. Watt, 555–63. New York: Metropolitan Museum of Art, 1996.

Fonssagrives, E. *Si-ling: Etudes sur les tombeaux de l'ouest de la dynastie des Ts'ing.* Paris: Ernest Leroux, 1907.

Forêt, Philippe C. "Making an Imperial Landscape in Chengde, Jehol: The Manchu Landscape Enterprise." Ph.D. diss., University of Chicago, 1992.

Foulk, T. Griffith, and Robert H. Sharf. "On the Ritual Use of Ch'an Portraiture in Medieval China." *Cahiers d'Extrême-Asie* 7 (1993): 149–219.

Franke, Herbert. *From Tribal Chieftain to Universal Emperor and God: The*

Legitimation of the Yuan Dynasty. Munich: Verlag der Baerischen Akademie der Wissenschaften, 1978.

———. "The Forest Peoples of Manchuria: Kitans and Jurchens." In *The Cambridge History of Early Inner Asia*, edited by Denis Sinor. Cambridge: Cambridge University Press, 1990.

———. "The Jin dynasty." In *The Cambridge History of China: Alien Regimes and Border States, 907–1368*, edited by Herbert Franke and Denis Twitchett, 215–320. Cambridge: Cambridge University Press, 1994.

Fu Kedong 傅英仁. "Baqi Manzhou de jishen lisu" 八旗滿洲的祭神禮俗 (Religious customs of the Manchu bannermen). *Manzu yanjiu* 滿族研究 3 (1989): 20–26.

———. "Cong neizuoling he guanling tandao Qingdai xinzheku ren" 從內佐領和管領談到清代辛者庫人 (Qing state slaves: from the inner companies and the *guanling*). *Qingshi tongxun* 清史通訊 3 (1986): 8–13.

Fu Yingren 傅英仁, ed. *Manzu shenhua gushi* 滿族神話故事 (Manchu legendary stories). Harbin: Beifang wenyi chubanshe, 1985.

Fu Yuguang 富育光. "Samanjiao tian qiong guannian chu kao" 薩滿教天穹觀念初考 (A preliminary examination of the concept of heaven). *Heilongjiang minzu congkan* 黑龍江民族叢刊 3 (1987): 35–42.

———. "Qing gong tangzi jisi biankao" 清宮堂子祭祀辨考 (Investigation of sacrifices in the Qing *tangzi*). *Shehui kexue zhanxian* 社會科學戰線 4 (1988): 204–10.

———. *Samanjiao yu shenhua* 薩滿教與神話 (Shamanism and legends). Shenyang: Liaoning daxue chubanshe, 1990.

Fu Yuguang and Meng Huiying 孟慧英. *Manzu samanjiao yanjiu* 滿族薩滿教研究 (Research on Manchu shamanism). Beijing: Beijing daxue chubanshe, 1991.

Gao Bingzhong 高丙忠. "Dongbei zhutun Manzu de xueyuan zuzhi—cong shizu dao jiazu zai dao jiahu de yanbian" 東北駐屯滿族的血緣組織——從氏族到家族再到家戶的演變 (The consanguineal organization of Manchus garrisoned in the northeast—the transition from clan to family to household). *Manzu yanjiu* 滿族研究 1 (1996): 16–24.

Geertz, Clifford. "Centers, Kings, and Charisma: Reflections on the Symbolics of Power." In *Rites of Power: Symbolism, Ritual, and Politics Since the Middle Ages*, edited by Sean Wilentz, 13–38. Philadelphia: University of Pennsylvania Press, 1985.

Gegengaoxing 葛根高姓. "Shilun Qingdai Mengguzu wenhua de tezheng" 試論清代蒙古族文化的特征 (On the characteristics of Qing Mongol culture). *Nei Menggu shehui kexue* 內蒙古社會科學 4 (1991): 83–90.

Gellner, Ernest. *Nations and Nationalism.* Ithaca: Cornell University Press, 1983.

Gernet, Jacques. *China and the Christian Impact: A Conflict of Cultures.* Translated by Janet Lloyd. Cambridge: Cambridge University Press, 1985.

Greiner, Peter. "Das Hofzeremoniell der Mandschu-Dynastie." In *Palastmuseum Peking: Schätze aus der Verbotenen Stadt*, edited by Lothar Ledderose, 56–69. Frankfurt: Ernst Auflag, 1985.

Greissler, Margareta T. J. "The Last Dynastic Funeral: Ritual Sequence at the Demise of the Empress Dowager Cixi." *Oriens Extremus* 34, nos. 1–2 (1991): 7–35.

Grupper, Samuel. "The Manchu Imperial Cult of the Early Qing Dynasty: Texts and Studies on the Tantric Sanctuary of Mahākāla at Mukden." Ph.D. diss., Indiana University, 1979.

———. "Manchu Patronage and Tibetan Buddhism during the First Half of the Qing Dynasty: A Review Article." *Journal of the Tibet Society* 4 (1984): 47–75.

Guan Jialu 關嘉錄 and Tong Yonggong 佟永功. "Cong 'Xiang hongqi dang' kan Yongzheng di zhengzhi qiwu" 從 '鑲紅旗檔' 看雍正帝整飭旗務 (The Yongzheng emperor's control of banner affairs as seen from the Bordered Red Banner archives). In *Ming Qing dang'an yu lishi yanjiu: Zhongguo diyi lishi dang'anguan liushi zhou nian lunwenji* 明清檔案與歷史研究: 中國第一歷史檔案館六十年周年論文集 (The Ming-Qing archives and historical research: collected essays commemorating the sixtieth anniversary of the First Historical Archives of China), 2: 669–80. Beijing: Zhonghua shuju, 1988.

———. "Cong 'Sanxing dang' kan Qingdai Jilin guanzhuang" 從三姓檔看清代吉林官莊 (The Yongzheng emperor's control of banner affairs as seen from the Sanxing archives). *Lishi dang'an* 歷史檔案 2 (1991): 80–86.

Guan Wenfa 關文發. *Jiaqing di* 喜慶帝 (The Jiaqing emperor). Changchun: Jilin wenshi chubanshe, 1993.

Guan Xiaolian 關孝廉. "Lun 'Manwen laodang'" 論滿文老檔 (On the Manchu archives). *Manzu yanjiu* 滿族研究 1 (1988): 52–58.

Guoli gugong bowuyuan 國立故宮博物院. *Qingdai dihou xiang* 清代帝后像 (Portraits of the Qing emperors and empresses). Peking: Gugong bowuyuan, 1931.

———. *Wenxian congbian* 文獻叢編 (Collected documents). 1930. Reprint, Taipei: Guofeng chubanshe, 1964.

———, ed. *Qing gong Zangzhuan Fojiao wenwu* 清宮藏傳佛教文物 (Cultural relics of Tibetan Buddhism collected in the Qing palace). Hong Kong: Forbidden City Press, 1992.

Gui Fu 珪夫 and He Shimin 何世敏. "Nuerhachi de zongjiao zhengce yu qi baye" 努爾哈赤的宗教政策與其霸業 (Nurgaci's religious policies and the hegemonic enterprise). *Nei Menggu shida xuebao (zhexue shehui kexue ban)* 內蒙古師大學報 (哲學社會科學版) 1 (1990): 84–89.

Guo Chengkang 郭成康. "Qingchu Menggu baqi kaoshi" 清初蒙古八旗考釋 (An examination of the Mongol banners in early Qing). *Minzu yanjiu* 民族研究 3 (1986): 51–58.

Guo Chengkang et al. *Qianlong huangdi quanzhuan* 乾隆皇帝全傳 (A complete biography of the Qianlong emperor). Beijing: Xueyuan chubanshe, 1994.

Guo Fuxiang 郭福祥. "Qianlong yu Qingdai yinzhi" 乾隆與清代印制 (Qianlong and the Qing seal system). *Zijincheng* 紫禁城 1 (1992): 14–15.

———. "Qingdai di hou shifa yu gugong bowuyuan zang Qingdai di hou shice shibao" 清代帝后諡法與故宮博物院藏清代帝后諡冊諡寶 (The death-naming practice of the Qing emperors and empresses, and the Qing mortuary tablets and seals held in the Palace Museum). *Gugong bowuyuan yuankan* 故宮博物院院刊 4 (1994): 69–87.

Guo Shuyun 郭淑云. "'Manzhou jishen jitian dianli' lunzhe" 滿洲祭神祭天典禮論折 (An analysis of the Manchu shamanic code). *Shehui kexue jikan* 社會科學輯刊 5 (1992): 79–85.

Guo Songyi 郭松義. "Lun Ming Qing shiqi de Guan Yu chongbai" 論明清時期的關羽崇拜 (On the worship of Guan Yu in Ming and Qing times). *Zhongguoshi yanjiu* 中國史研究 3 (1990): 127–39.

Haboush, JaHyun Kim. *A Heritage of Kings: One Man's Monarchy in the Confucian World*. New York: Columbia University Press, 1988.

Hanguanquejia 韓官卻加. "Jian tan Qingchao qianqi Qinghai Menggu de tongzhi" 簡談清朝前期對青海蒙古的統治 (A brief discussion of the control of Mongols in Qinghai during the early Qing). *Qinghai minzu xueyuan xuebao (shehui kexue ban)* 青海民族學院學報 (社會科學版) 3 (1988): 33–36.

Harrell, Stevan, Susan Naquin, and Deyuan Ju. "Lineage Genealogy: The Genealogical Records of the Qing Imperial Lineage." *Late Imperial China* 6, no. 2 (1985): 37–47.

He Ling 賀靈. "Yili xin Manying de zujian ji gongliu qitun" 伊犁新滿營的組建及鞏留族屯 (The founding of the new Manchu garrison at Ili and the strengthening of the banner colony system). *Manzu yanjiu* 滿族研究 3 (1991): 22–25.

He Ling and Tong Keli 佟克力. "Samange" 薩滿歌 (Shamanic songs). *Manzu wenhua* 滿族文化 13 (1990): 26–37.

Headland, Isaac Taylor. *Court Life in China: The Capital, Its Officials and People*. New York: Fleming H. Revell, 1909.

Hedin, Sven. *Jehol: City of Emperors*. Translated by E. G. Nash. London: Kegan Paul, Trench, Trubner, 1932.

Heeren, J. J. "Father Bouvet's Picture of Emperor K'ang Hsi (With Appendices)." *Asia Major*, 1st s., 7 (1932): 556–72.

Heissig, Walther. *Die Pekinger lamaistischen Blockdrucke in mongolischer Sprache; Materialen zur mongolischen Literaturgeschichte*. Wiesbaden: Harrassowitz, 1954.

———. *The Religions of Mongolia*. Translated by Geoffrey Samuel. Berkeley: University of California Press, 1970.

Hemmi Baiei 逸見梅榮 and Nakano Hanshirō 仲野半四郎. *Manmō no ramakyō bijutsu* 滿蒙の喇嘛教美術 (Manchu and Mongol Tibetan Buddhist art). 2 vols. Tokyo: Hōzōkan, 1943.

Hevia, James L. "Emperors, Lamas, and Rituals: Political Implications in Qing Imperial Ceremonies." *Journal of the International Association of Buddhist Studies* 16, no. 2 (1993): 243–78.

———. "Sovereignty and Subject: Constructing Relations of Power in Qing Imperial Ritual." In *Body, Subjectivity, and Power in China*, edited by Angela Zito and Tani Barlow, 181–200. Chicago: University of Chicago Press, 1994.

————. *Cherishing Men from Afar: Qing Guest Ritual and the Macartney Embassy of 1793.* Durham: Duke University Press, 1995.

Ho, Ping-ti. *The Ladder of Success in Imperial China: Aspects of Social Mobility, 1368–1911.* New York: Columbia University Press, 1962.

————. "The Significance of the Ch'ing Period in Chinese History." *Journal of Asian Studies* 26, no. 2 (1967): 189–95.

Holmgren, Jennifer. "Marriage, Kinship, and Succession under the Ch'i-tan Rulers of the Liao Dynasty." *T'oung Pao* 72 (1986): 44–91.

————. "Political Organization of Non-Han States in China: The Role of Imperial Princes in Wei, Liao, and Yüan." *Journal of Oriental Studies* 25, no. 1 (1987): 4–5.

————. "A Question of Strength: Military Capability and Princess-Bestowal in Imperial China's Foreign Relations (Han to Ch'ing)." *Monumenta Serica* 39 (1990–91): 31–85.

————. "Imperial Marriage in the Native Chinese and Non-Han State, Han to Ming." In *Marriage and Inequality in Chinese Society*, edited by Rubie S. Watson and Patricia B. Ebrey, 58–96. Berkeley: University of California Press, 1991.

Hosoya Yoshio 細谷良夫. "Shinchō ni okeru hakki seido no sui-i" 清朝における八旗制の推移 (Transition in the Qing eight banner system). *Tōyō gakuhō* 東洋學方 51, no. 1 (1968): 1–43.

————, ed. *Chūgoku tōhokubu ni okeru Shinchō no shiseki* 中國東北部における清朝の史跡 (Historical landmarks of the Qing dynasty in China's northeast). Tokyo: Toyo Bunko, 1991.

Hou Renzhi 候仁之, ed. *Beijing lishi dituji* 北京歷史地圖集 (Historical atlas of Beijing). Beijing: Beijing chubanshe, 1985.

Hou Renzhi and Jin Tao 金濤. *Beijing shi hua* 北京市話 (Historical talks about Peking). Shanghai: Shanghai renmin chubanshe, 1980.

Hou Shouchang 候壽昌. "Kangxi muxi kao" 康熙母系考 (Kangxi's maternal relations). *Lishi dang'an* 歷史檔案 4 (1982): 100–105.

Hsu, James. "Shijiu shiji Beijing neicheng jiedaotu" 十九世紀北京內城街道圖 (Map of the streets of Peking's inner city in the nineteenth century). N.d.

Hu Desheng 胡德生. "Qianlong lujiaoyi" 乾隆鹿角椅 (Qianlong's antler chair). *Wenwu* 文物 7 (1986): 84–85.

Hu Ji 胡戟, Li Xiaocong 李孝聰, and Rong Xinjiang 榮新江. *Tulufan* 吐魯番 (Turfan). Shaanxi: Sanqin chubanshe, 1987.

Hu Qisong 胡啓松. "Qingdai zaoqi zongshi renkou shouming qiantan" 清代早期宗室人口壽命淺探 (A study of the longevity of the Qing imperial family during the early Qing). *Lishi dang'an* 歷史檔案 2 (1993): 86–89.

Hu Rubo 胡汝波. "Mulan weichang yu weichang diming" 木蘭圍場與圍場地名 (On the Mulan hunting ground and its name). *Diming zhishi* 地名知識 4 (1991): 32–33.

Huang, Pei. *Autocracy at Work: A Study of the Yongzheng Period, 1723–1735.* Bloomington: Indiana University Press, 1974.

————黃培. "Qingchu de Manzhou guizu (1583–1795)—Niuhulu zu" 清初的滿洲貴族 (1583–1795)——鈕祜祿族 (The early Manchu aristocracy:

the Niohuru clan, 1583–1795). In *Lao Zhenyi xiansheng bazhi rong qing lunwen ji* 勞眞一先生八秩榮慶論文集 (Collected essays commemorating Professor Lao Zhenyi's eightieth birthday), edited by Lao Zhenyi xiansheng bazhi rong qing lunwenji weiyuan hui, 629–64. Taipei: Shangwu yinshuguan, 1986.

Huang, Ray. *1587: A Year of No Significance*. New Haven: Yale University Press, 1981.

Huang Chongwen 黃崇文. "Xumifushou zhi miao de jianli ji qi lishi yiyi" 須彌福壽之廟的建立及其歷史意義 (The Xumifushou temple and its historical significance). *Xizang yanjiu* 西藏研究 3 (1989): 80–83.

Huang Haitao 黃海濤 and Wan Yi 萬依. *Qingdai gongting yinyue* 清代宮廷音樂 (Qing court music). Hong Kong: Zhonghua shuju, 1985.

Hucker, Charles. *The Traditional Chinese State in Ming Times (1368–1644)*. Tucson: University of Arizona Press, 1961.

Hughes, Lindsay. "The Kuo Ch'in-wang Textiles." *Gazette des Beaux-Arts* (February 1945): 66–68.

Hummel, Arthur W., ed. *Eminent Chinese of the Ch'ing Period (1644–1912)*. 2 vols. Washington, D.C.: U.S. Government Printing Office, 1943 (cited in notes as *ECCP*).

Humphrey, Caroline. "Shamanic Practices and the State in Northern Asia: Views from the Center and Periphery." In *Shamanism, History, and the State*, edited by Nicholas Thomas and Caroline Humphrey, 191–228. Ann Arbor: University of Michigan Press, 1984.

Hyer, Paul. "An Historical Sketch of Köke-Khota City Capital of Inner Mongolia." *Central Asiatic Journal*, 26, nos. 1–2 (1982): 56–77.

Im, Kaye Soon. "The Rise and Decline of the Eight Banner Garrisons in the Ch'ing Period (1644–1911): A Study of the Kuang-chou, Hang-chou, and Ching-chou Garrisons." Ph.D. diss., University of Illinois, 1981.

Imanishi Shunju 今西春秋. "Gotai Shinbunkan kaidai" 五體清文鑑譯解題 (Synopsis of the five-language Manchu dictionary). In *Gotai Shinbunkan yakkai* 五體清文鑑譯解 (Annotated translation of the five-language Manchu dictionary), edited by Tamura Jitsuzō 田村實造 et al., 17–29. Kyoto: Kyoto daigaku bungaku bu, 1966.

Inoue Ichii 井上以智爲. "Shintei samankyō no saishin ni tsuite" 清廷薩滿教の祭神に就て (Shamanic rites in the Qing court). *Tōyōshi kenkyū* 東洋史研究 8, no. 1 (1943): 39–40.

———. "Shinchō kyūtei samankyō shiden ni tsuite" 清朝宮廷薩滿教祠殿に就て (Shamanic sanctuaries in the Qing palace). In *Haneda hakase shōju kinen Tōyōshi ronsō* 羽田博士頌壽記念東洋史論叢 (Collected essays on Oriental history, in honor of Professor Haneda), edited by Haneda hakase shōju kinen kai, 75–94. Kyoto: Tōyōshi kenkyūkai, 1950.

Ishibashi, Takao. "The Formation of the Power of Early Ch'ing Emperors." *Memoirs of the Research Department of the Tōyō Bunkō* 48 (1990): 1–15.

Ishibashi Ushio 石橋丑雄. *Peipin no samankyō ni tsuite* 北平の薩滿教に就て (On Beiping's shamanism). Tokyo: Gaimusho bunka jibu, 1934.

———. *Tentan* 天壇 (The altar of heaven). Tokyo: Yamamoto shoten, 1958.

Ishihama Yumiko 石濱裕美子. "Gushi Han ōke no Chibetto ōken sōshitsu katei ni kansuru ichi kōsatsu—Ropusan Danjin no 'hanran' saikō" グシハン王家のチベット王權喪失過程に關する一考察——ロブサンダンヅンの反亂再考 (The process by which the Guši khan family lost its royal authority over Tibet: a reconsideration of the rebellion of Blo bzang bstan 'dzin). *Tōyō gakuhō* 東洋學報 69, nos. 3–4 (1988): 151–71.

———. "Jūhachi seiki shotō ni okeru Chibetto bukkyōkai no seijiteki tachiba ni tsuite" 十八世紀初頭におけるチベット佛教會の政治的立場について (On the political stance of Tibetan Buddhism in the early eighteenth century). *Tōhō gakuhō* 東方學報 77 (1989): 129–43.

———. "On the Dissemination of the Belief in the Dalai Lama as a Manifestation of the Bodhisattva Avalokitesvara." *Acta Asiatica* 64 (1993): 38–56.

Jagchid, Sechin. "Chinese Buddhism and Taoism during the Mongolian Rule of China." *Mongolian Studies* 6 (1980): 61.

———. "Mongolian-Manchu Intermarriage in the Ch'ing Period." *Zentralasiatische Studien* 19 (1986): 68–87.

———. "Chinggis Khan in Mongolian Folklore." In *Essays in Mongolian Studies*. Provo: David M. Kennedy Center for International Studies, Brigham Young University, 1988.

Jan, Yün-hua. "Chinese Buddhism in Ta-tu: The New Situation and New Problems." In *Yüan Thought: Chinese Thought and Religion Under the Mongols*, edited by Hok-lam Chan and William Theodore de Bary, 375–417. New York: Columbia University Press, 1982.

Ji Yonghai 季永海. "Qingdai cihao kaoyi" 清代賜號考譯 (On the titles conferred during the Qing). *Manyu yanjiu* 滿族研究 2 (1993): 69–78.

Jiang Tao 姜濤. "Qingdai jingshi daolu he huangdi chuxun de yudao" 清代京師道路和皇帝出巡的御道 (The roads of the capital in the Qing and imperial routes). *Beifang wenwu* 北方文物 2 (1991): 72–77.

Jiang Xiangshun 姜相順. "Qing Taizong de Chongde wugong hou fei ji qita" 清太宗的崇德五宮后妃及其他 (Taizong's five Chongde palace consorts and others). *Gugong bowuyuan yuankan* 故宮博物院院刊 4 (1987): 67–71.

———. "Qing chu gongting de saman jisi" 清初宮廷的薩滿祭祀 (Shamanic sacrifices at the early Qing court). *Beifang wenwu* 北方文物 2 (1988): 72–75.

———. "Cong Manzu de wenhua xisu kan Shenyang gugong de menshen he bianlian" 從滿族的文化習俗看沈陽故宮的門神和匾聯 (Looking at the Shenyang Museum's door gods and placards from the perspective of Manchu cultural customs). *Manzu yanjiu* 滿族研究 4 (1990): 40–45.

———. "Qianlong di dongxun Shengjing yu Qingninggong jishen" 乾隆帝東巡盛京于清寧宮祭神 (The sacrifices to the deities made by the Qianlong emperor during his eastern tour). *Manzu yanjiu* 滿族研究 2 (1991): 40–47.

———. "Qing gong samanjisi ji qi lishi yanbian" 清宮薩滿祭祀及其歷史演變 (Shamanic rites in the Qing palace and their historical evolution). *Qingshi yanjiu* 清史研究 1 (1994): 71–78.

———. "Kangxi di wannian lichu zhi mi" 康熙帝晚年立儲之謎 (On the

puzzle that the Kangxi emperor set up an heir in his late years). *Manzu yanjiu* 滿族研究 1 (1995): 40–45.

———. "Lun Qing gong saman" 論清宮薩滿 (On Qing court shamans). *Shenyang gugong bowuyuan yuankan* 瀋陽故宮博物院院刊 1 (1995): 62–66.

Jin Baochen 金寶忱. "Samanjiao zhong de shengtiao chongbai" 薩滿教中的繩條崇拜 (Veneration of the rope in shamanism). *Heilongjiang minzu congkan* 黑龍江民族叢刊 1 (1989): 57–59.

Jin Baosen 金寶森. "Qiantan Qianlong dui fazhan Manwen de gongxian" 淺談乾隆對發展滿文的貢獻 (A brief discussion of the Qianlong emperor's contribution to the development of Manchu). *Qingshi yanjiu* 清史研究 1 (1992): 78–80.

Jin Jishui 金寄水 and Zhou Shachen 周沙塵. *Wang fu shenghuo shilu* 王府生活實錄 (Veritable records of life in the princely establishments). Beijing: Zhongguo qingnian chubanshe, 1988.

Jin Qizong 金啓孮. "Jing qi de Manzu" 京旗的滿族 (The Manchus in the metropolitan banners). *Manzu yanjiu* 滿族研究 3 (1988): 63–66; 4 (1988): 58–64; 1 (1989): 58–63; 2 (1989): 66–80.

Jochim, Christian. "The Imperial Audience Ceremonies of the Ch'ing Dynasty." *Society for the Study of Chinese Religions*, no. 7 (1979): 88–103.

Ju Deyuan 菊德源. "Qingchao huangzu zongpu yu huangzu renkou chutan" 清朝皇族宗譜與皇族人口初探 (Investigations into the Qing imperial genealogy and the population of imperial clansmen). In *Ming Qing dang'an yu lishi yanjiu: Zhongguo diyi lishi dang'anguan liushi zhounian jinian lunwenji* 明清檔案與歷史研究, 中國第一歷史檔案館六十周年紀念論文集 (Ming-Qing archives and historical research: Collected essays commemorating the sixtieth anniversary of the First Historical Archives of China), 1: 408–40. Beijing: Zhonghua shudian, 1988.

———. "Qing gongting huajia Lang Shining nianpu" 清宮廷畫家郎世寧年譜 (Chronicle of the Qing court painter Giuseppe Castiglione). *Gugong bowuyuan yuankan* 故宮博物院院刊 2 (1988): 27–71.

Kahn, Harold. "The Politics of Filiality: Justification for Imperial Action in Eighteenth-Century China." *Journal of Asian Studies* 26, no. 2 (1967): 197–203.

———. *Monarchy in the Emperor's Eyes: Image and Reality in the Qianlong Reign*. Cambridge, Mass.: Harvard University Press, 1971.

Kane, Daniel. *The Sino-Jurchen Vocabulary of the Bureau of Interpreters*. Bloomington: Research Institute for Inner Asian Studies, Indiana University, 1989.

Karmay, Heather. *Early Sino-Tibetan Art*. Warminster, England: Aris and Phillips, 1975.

Katō Naoto. "Lobjang Danjin's Rebellion of 1723; with a Focus on the Eve of the Rebellion." *Acta Asiatica* 64 (1993): 57–80.

Kendall, Laurel. *Shamans, Housewives, and Other Restless Spirits*. Honolulu: University of Hawaii Press, 1985.

Kertzer, David. *Ritual, Politics, and Power*. New Haven: Yale University Press, 1988.

Kessler, Lawrence D. *K'ang-hsi and the Consolidation of Ch'ing Rule, 1661–1684.* Chicago: University of Chicago Press, 1976.

Keswick, Maggie. *The Chinese Garden.* New York: Rizzoli, 1980.

Khan, Almaz. "Chinggis Khan: From Imperial Ancestor to Ethnic Hero." In *Cultural Encounters on China's Ethnic Frontiers,* edited by Stevan Harrell, 248–77. Seattle: University of Washington Press, 1994.

Khazanov, Anatoly M. "The Spread of World Religions in Medieval Nomadic Societies of the Eurasian Steppes." In *Nomadic Diplomacy, Destruction and Religion from the Pacific to the Adriatic,* edited by Michael Gervers and Wayne Schlepp. Toronto: Joint Centre for Asia Pacific Studies, 1994.

Khordarkovsky, Michael. *Where Two Worlds Met: The Russian State and the Kalmyk Nomads, 1600–1771.* Ithaca: Cornell University Press, 1992.

Kohara, Hironobu. "The Qianlong Emperor's Skill in the Connoisseurship of Chinese Painting." In *The Elegant Brush: Chinese Painting Under the Qianlong Emperor, 1735–1795,* edited by Ju-hsi Chou and Claudia Brown, 56–73. Phoenix: Arizona State University, 1985.

Kun Shi. "Ny Dan the Manchu Shamaness." In *Religions of China in Practice,* edited by Donald S. Lopez, Jr., 223–28. Princeton: Princeton University Press, 1996.

Kwong, Luke. *A Mosaic of the Hundred Days: Personalities, Politics, and Ideas of 1898.* Cambridge, Mass.: Council on East Asian Studies, Harvard University, 1984.

Lai Huimin 賴惠敏. "Qingdai Neiwufu dang'an ziliao jian jie" 清代內務府檔案資料簡介 (A brief introduction to the Qing Imperial Household Department archival materials). *Jindai Zhongguoshi yanjiu tongxun* 近代中國史研究通訊 12 (1991): 155–57.

————. "Qingdai huangzu de jingji shenghuo" 清代皇族的經濟生活 (The economic life of the Qing imperial clan). *Zhongyang yanjiuyuan, Jindaishi yanjiusuo jikan* 中央研究院所, 近代史研究所集刊 24, no. 2 (1995): 473–516.

Lam, Joseph S. C. "Creativity Within Bounds: State Sacrificial Songs from the Ming Dynasty (1368–1644 A.D.)." Ph.D. diss., Harvard University, 1987.

Landesman, Susan S. "Mirror Divination: Shamanistic and Non-Shamanistic Divinations." *Central and Inner Asian Studies* 6 (1992): 16–33.

Langlois, John D., Jr. Introduction to *China Under Mongol Rule,* edited by John D. Langlois, Jr., 3–22. Princeton: Princeton University Press, 1981.

Lattimore, Owen. *The Mongols of Manchuria: Their Tribal Divisions, Geographical Distribution, Historical Relations with Manchus and Chinese and Present Political Problems.* New York: John Day, 1934.

Lauf, Detlaf Ingo. *Tibetan Sacred Art: The Heritage of Tantra.* Berkeley: Shambhala, 1976.

Lee, James, Cameron Campbell, and Wang Feng. "The Last Emperors: An Introduction to the Demography of the Qing (1644–1911) Imperial Lineage." In *Old and New Methods in Historical Demography,* edited by David S. Rehen and Roger Schofield, 361–82. Oxford: Clarendon Press, 1993.

Lee, James, Wang Feng, and Cameron Campbell. "Infant and Child Mortality among the Qing Nobility: Implications for Two Types of Positive Check." *Population Studies* 48 (1994): 395–411.

Lentz, Thomas, and Glenn D. Lowry, eds. *Timur and the Princely Vision: Persian Art and Culture in the Fifteenth Century.* Washington, D.C.: Smithsonian Institution Press, 1989.

Lessing, Ferdinand D. *Yung-Ho-Kung: An Iconography of the Lamaist Cathedral in Peking with Notes on Lamaist Mythology and Cult.* 1942. Reprint, Taipei: Huyoushe, wenhua shiye, 1993.

Lettres édifiantes et curieuses concernant l'Asie, l'Afrique et l'Amérique, avec quelques relations nouvelles des missions et des notes géographiques et historiques. Edited by M. A. Aimé-Martin. Vols. 3 and 4. Paris: Société du Panthéon littéraire, 1843.

Levin, M. G., and L. P. Potapov, eds., *The Peoples of Siberia.* Translated and edited by Stephen Dunn. 1965, Chicago: University of Chicago Press, 1964.

Lha-ma bkras-Shis 拉毛扎西 "Qinghai lamajiao siyuan jingji de goucheng yinsu chutan" 青海喇嘛教寺院經濟的構成因素初探 (A preliminary investigation of the structural elements in the economy of Qinghai Tibetan Buddhist monasteries). *Qinghai shehui kexue* 青海社會科學 6 (1988): 98–103.

Li, Gertraude Roth. "The Rise of the Early Manchu State: A Portrait Drawn from Manchu Sources to 1936." Ph.D. diss., Harvard University, 1975.

Li De 李德. "Manzu wudao tangai" 滿族舞蹈譯概 (A general discussion of Manchu dance). *Manzu yanjiu* 滿族研究 1 (1995): 66–74.

Li Fengmin 李風民. "Heshi gongzhu Mukushi de hunpei wenti" 和碩公主穆庫什的婚配問題 (The marriage issue of Princess Mukushi). *Gugong bowuyuan yuankan* 故宮博物院院刊 2 (1984): 26.

———. "Yipi Nuerhachi, Huangtaiji yiwu de laili" 一批努爾哈赤, 皇太極遺物的來歷 (The history of the death mementos of Nurgaci and Hongtaiji). *Liaoning daxue xuebao* 遼寧大學學報 3 (1991): 47–49.

———. "Shengjing simiao shouzang de Qing Taizu, Taizong yiwu" 盛京寺廟收藏的清太祖, 太宗遺物 (The mementos of Taizu and Taizong stored in Shengjing temples). *Zijincheng* 紫禁城 73 (1992): 14–16.

Li Fengmin and Lu Haiying 陸海英. "Qingchao kaiguo di yi ducheng—Hetu ala" 清朝開國第一都城——赫圖阿拉 (The first capital of the nascent Qing state—Hetu Ala). *Zijincheng* 紫禁城 81 (1994): 10–12.

———, eds. *Shengjing Zhaoling* 盛京昭陵 (The Zhao mausoleum at Shengjing). Shenyang: Shenyang chubanshe, 1994.

———. *Gugong zaqu* 故宮雜趣 (Points of interest in the former palace). Shenyang: Dongbei daxue chubanshe, 1996.

———. *Shenyang Fuling* 沈陽福陵 (The Fu mausoleum at Shenyang). Shenyang: Dongbei daxue chubanshe, 1996.

Li Fengmin, Lu Haiying, and Fu Bo 傅波, eds. *Xingjing Yongling* 興京永陵 (The Yong mausoleum at Xingjing). Shenyang: Dongbei daxue chubanshe, 1996.

Li Fengzhen 李風珍. "Qingdai Xizang lama chaogong gaishu: jian pingli chaxun de Xizang chaogong shi waijiao he maoyi guanxi de miulun" 清代西藏喇嘛朝貢概述: 兼評理查遜的西藏朝貢是外交和貿易關係的謬論 (A general description of the tribute brought by Tibetan lamas in the Qing; and an evaluation as to whether Tibetan tribute was foreign relations or trade). *Zhongguo Zangxue* 中國藏學 1 (1991): 70–81.

Li Guoliang 李國梁. "Bishushanzhuang yushan zatan" 避暑山莊御膳雜談 (Discussion of food at Bishu shanzhuang). *Gugong bowuyuan yuankan* 故宮博物院院刊 1 (1988): 83–85.

Li Jichang 李繼昌. "Nanyuan jiugong Deshousi—Qingdai zhongyang yu Xizang difang guanxi shishang de yichu zhongyao yiji" 南苑舊宮德壽寺——清代中央與西藏地方關係史上的一處重要遺跡 (The Deshou temple in the old Nanyuan palace: a major artifact of the Qing center's historical relationship with Tibet). *Wenshi zhishi* 文史知識 8 (1990): 112–14.

Li Li 李理. "Lun Qingchu yizhang zhi zhi de yanbian" 論清初儀仗之制的演變 (On the changes in the regalia system in early Qing). *Liaoning daxue xuebao* 遼寧大學學報 5 (1992): 42–46.

Li Lin 李林. "Qingdai huangdi de nanxun yu dongxun" 清代皇帝的南巡與東巡 (The imperial tours of the south and east during the Qing). *Qingshi yanjiu* 清史研究 1 (1991): 29–32.

Li Luhua 李陸華. "Lun Qing ruguan qianhou Manzu wenhua de xingcheng yu yanbian" 論清入關前後滿族文化的形成與演變 (The formation and evolution of Manchu culture around 1644). *Beifang wenwu* 北方文物 4 (1995): 84–87.

Li Pengnian 李鵬年. "Guangxu di dahun bciban haoyong gaishu" 光緒帝大婚備辦耗用概述 (A general study of the expenditures on the Guangxu emperor's wedding). *Gugong bowuyuan yuankan* 故宮博物院院刊 2 (1983): 80–86.

———. *Qingdai zhongyang guojia jiguan gaishu* 清代中央國家機關概述 (Central government organs during the Qing). Harbin: Heilongjiang renmin chubanshe, 1983.

Li Qiao 李喬. "Qingdai Beijing neiwai cheng shehui shenghuo xisu zhi yi" 清代北京內外城社會生活習俗之異 (Differences in social living customs in the inner and outer cities of Peking during the Qing). *Ming Qing shi yuekan* 明清史月刊 12 (1987): 33–35.

Li Shangying 李尙英. "Jiaqing qinzheng" 嘉慶親政 (Jiaqing takes personal charge of government). *Gugong bowuyuan yuankan* 故宮博物院院刊 2 (1992): 40–42.

Li Shu 李書. "Qingdai Heilongjiang jiangjun yamen de jianzhi yu yan'ge" 清代黑龍江將軍衙門的建置與沿革 (The establishment and evolution of the Heilongjiang military governor's office in the Qing). *Manyu yanjiu* 滿語研究 1 (1991): 120–31, 83.

Li Shutian 李澍田 and Yin Yushan 尹郁山. "Ula Manzu hala xintan" 烏拉滿族哈拉新探 (A new inquiry into the clan names of the Ula Manchus). *Qingshi yanjiu* 清史研究 3 (1992): 8–16, 23.

Li Tongqing 李同慶. "Cong Bishushanzhuang he waibamiao de jianzhu tese kan Qing wangchao de minzu zhengce" 從避暑山莊和外八廟的建築特色看清王朝的民族政策 (Qing ethnic policies from the perspective of the architectural features of the Bishu shanzhuang and the outer eight temples). *Zhongyang minzu xueyuan xuebao* 中央民族學院學報 4 (1988): 37–39.

Li Xianqing 李憲慶 and Zhang Shaoxiang 張紹祥. "Qing Shizong xiaoruo zhuwang qizhu shili de douzheng" 清世宗消弱諸王旗主勢力的斗爭 (The struggle whereby Yongzheng weakened the power of the banner princes) In *K'ang Yong Qian sandi pingyi* 康雍乾三帝評議 (An evaluation of the Kangxi, Yongzheng, and Qianlong emperors), edited by Zuo Buqing 左步光, 304–15. Beijing: Zijincheng chubanshe, 1986.

Li Yanguang 李燕光 and Li Lin 李林. "Qingdai de wangzhuang" 清代的王莊 (Princely estates during the Qing). *Manzu yanjiu* 滿族研究 1 (1988):46–51.

Li Yanping 李艷平. "Manzu yinshi wenhua" 滿族飲食文化 (Manchu cuisine). *Manyu yanjiu* 滿語研究 2 (1994): 78–82.

Li Yinghua 李英華. "Qingdai guanfu zhidu de tedian" 清代冠服制度的特點 (The special features of the Qing dress code). *Gugong bowuyuan yuankan* 故宮博物院院刊 1 (1990): 63–66.

Li Zhitan 李之檀. "'Da Zang jing' zang, Manwen ban xiancun gugong" 大藏經藏, 滿文版現存故宮 (The Manchu edition of the Tripitaka has been preserved in the Palace Museum). *Wenxian* 文獻 4 (1991): 286–87.

Liang Bing 梁冰. *Chengjisi han ling yu Oerduosi* 成吉思汗陵與鄂爾多斯 (Chinggis Khan's tomb and the Ordos). Huhehaote: Nei Menggu renmin chubanshe, 1988.

Liang Qizi 梁其姿. "Ming Qing yufang tianhua cuoshi zhi yanbian" 明清預防天花措施之演變 (Changes in measures to prevent smallpox in the Ming and Qing). In *Tao Xisheng xiansheng jiu zhi rongqing zhu shou lunwen ji Guoshi yilun* 陶希聖先生九秩榮慶祝壽論文集國史譯論 (Essays on Chinese history, celebrating Professor Tao Xisheng's ninetieth birthday), edited by Tao Xisheng xiansheng jiuzhi rongqing zhu shou weiyuanhui, 239–53. Taipei: Shihuo chubanshe, 1987.

Liang Xizhe 梁希哲. *Yongzheng di* 雍正帝 (Emperor Yongzheng). Changchun: Jilin wenshi chubanshe, 1993.

Liao Ning 遼寧 and Tong Yonggong 佟永功. "Qianlong huangdi yu Manyu diming" 乾隆皇帝與滿語地名 (The Qianlong emperor and Manchu place-names). *Diming congkan* 地名叢刊 6 (1987): 33–34.

Lin Qian 林乾. "Lun Kangxi shiqi de pengdang ji qi dui Qingchu zhengzhi de yingxiang" 論康熙時期的朋黨及其對清初政治的影響 (Factions in the Kangxi reign and their influence on early Qing politics). *Songliao xuekan* 松遼學刊 1 (1984): 33–39.

Lin Yongkuang 林永匡 and Wang Xi 王熹. "Qingdai huangshi yu nianli suigong" 清代皇室與年例歲貢 (The Qing imperial family and annual tribute). *Gugong bowuyuan yuankan* 故宮博物院院刊 4 (1990): 72–79.

Lindner, Rudi. "Nomadism, Horses, and Huns." *Past and Present* 92 (1981): 3–19.

———. "What was a nomadic tribe?" *Comparative Studies in Society and History* 24 (1982): 689–711.

Lipman, Jonathan N. "Hyphenated Chinese: Sino-Muslim Identity in Modern China." In *Remapping China: Fissures in Historical Terrain*, edited by Gail Hershatter, Emily Honig, Jonathan N. Lipman, and Randall Stross, 97–112. Stanford: Stanford University Press, 1996.

Liu, Ts'un-yan, and Judith Berling. "The 'Three Teachings' in the Mongol-Yüan Period." In *Yüan Thought: Chinese Thought and Religion Under the Mongols*, edited by Hok-lam Chan and William Theodore de Bary, 479–512. New York: Columbia University Press, 1982.

Liu Guilin 劉桂林. "Xiaoxian huanghou zhi si ji sangzang yubo" 孝賢皇后之死及喪葬余波 (The repercussions of Empress Xiaoxian's death and funeral). *Gugong bowuyuan yuankan* 故宮博物院院刊 4 (1981): 24–28.

Liu Housheng 劉厚生. "Changbaishan yu Manzu de zuxian chongbai" 長白山與滿族的祖先崇拜 (Changbaishan and the ancestor worship of the Manchus). *Qingshi yanjiu* 清史研究 3 (1996): 93–96.

Liu Housheng and Chen Siling 陳思玲. "'Qinding Manzhou jishen jitian dianli' pingzhe" 欽定滿洲祭神祭天典禮評折 (An evaluation of the imperially commissioned Manchu shamanic code). *Qingshi yanjiu* 清史研究 1 (1994): 66–70.

Liu Jiaju 劉家駒. "Kangxi huangdi younian suoshou jiaoyu ji qi yingxiang" 康熙皇帝幼年所受教育及其影響 (The education of the young Kangxi emperor and its influence). *Dongwu wenshi xuebao* 東吳文史學報 9 (1991): 83–102.

Liu Liang-yu. "Chinese Painted and Cloisonné Enamel: Introduction, The Imperial Workshops." Translated by Mary Man-li Loh. *Arts of Asia* 8, no. 6 (1978): 83–85.

Liu Lu 劉潞. "Qingchu huangshi chengyuan huozang de jianzheng" 清初皇室成員火葬的見証 (Proof of cremation of members of the imperial family in early Qing). *Wenwu* 文物 9 (1983): 69–70.

———. "Qing Taizu, Taizong shi Man Meng hunyin kao" 清太祖, 太宗時滿蒙婚姻考 (An investigation of Manchu-Mongol marriage during the Taizu and Taizong reigns). *Gugong bowuyuan yuankan* 故宮博物院院刊 3 (1995): 67–91.

———. "Kunning gong wei Qing di dongfang yuanyin lun" 坤寧宮爲清帝洞房原因論 (Reasons why the Kunning palace was the sleeping place of the Qing emperors). *Gugong bowuyuan yuankan* 故宮博物院院刊 3 (1996): 72–77.

Liu Shizhe 劉世哲. "Nuerhachi shiqi de zongshi fanzui yu chufa" 努爾哈赤時期的宗室犯罪與處罰 (Crimes committed by imperial agnates and their punishment in Nurgaci's time). *Beifang wenwu* 北方文物 1 (1992): 69–76.

———. "Qing Taizong shiqi zongshi fanzui de liangxing yuanze he chufa" 清太宗時期宗室犯罪的量刑原則和處罰 (Regulations and punishments during the Hongtaiji reign for crimes of kinsmen). *Minzu yanjiu* 民族研究 5 (1993): 84–96.

Liu Wennuo 劉文娜 and Deng Qing 鄧慶. "Qingdai qianqi de lubu yizhi" 清代前期的鹵簿儀制 (The regalia system in early Qing). In *Qingdai gongshi tanwei* 清代宮史探微 (Explorations of Qing palace history), edited by Qingdai gongshi yanjiu hui, 98–105. Beijing: Zijincheng chubanshe, 1991.

Liu Xiaomeng 劉小萌. "Manzu zhaoxing shiqi suo shou Menggu wenhua de yingxiang" 滿族肇興時期所受蒙古文化的影響 (The Mongol cultural influences absorbed by the Manchus in their formative stage). *Shehui kexue zhanxian* 社會科學戰線 6 (1994): 169–75.

———. "Cong fang qiwenshu kan Qingdai Beijing chengzhong de qimin jiaochan" 從房契文書看清代北京城中的旗民交產 (Examining the exchange of property of bannermen in Qing Beijing, from housing contracts). *Lishi dang'an* 歷史檔案 3 (1996): 83–90.

Liu Yi 劉毅. "Qingchao de huangwei queli fangshi he zechu biaozhun" 清朝的皇位確立方式和擇儲標準 (Qing modes of verification of the imperial position and selection of an heir). *Nankai xuebao* 南開學報 3 (1992): 51–56, 80.

———. "Cong lamajiao bihua kan Xizang yu Ming Qing zhongyang zhengfu de guanxi" 從喇嘛教壁畫看西藏與明清中央政府的關係 (Relations between Tibet and the Ming and Qing central governments, as seen from the Tibetan Buddhist wall murals). *Lishi da guanyuan* 歷史大觀園 5 (1993): 8–11.

Liu Ziyang 劉子揚 and Zhang Li 張莉. "Manwen laodang 'Taizong chao' zongxi" 滿文老檔太宗朝綜析 (Analysis of the old Manchu records of Hongtaiji's reign). *Manyu yanjiu* 滿語研究 2 (1995): 59–69, 77.

Lowry, J. "Tibet, Nepal, or China? An Early Group of Dated *Tangkas*." *Oriental Art*, n.s. 19 (1973): 306–15.

Lü Minghui 盧明輝. "Qingdai Beifang geminzu yu zhongyuan Hanzu de wenhua jiaoliu ji qi gongxian" 清代北方各民族與中原漢族的文化交流及其貢獻 (The cultural mix and contributions of the northern ethnic minorities and the Han people of the North China plain in the Qing). *Qingshi yanjiu ji* 清史研究集 6 (1988): 122–40.

Lu Qi 魯琪 and Liu Jingyi 劉精義. "Qingdai taijian Enjizhuang yingdi" 清代太監恩濟庄塋地 (A eunuch cemetery in the Qing). *Gugong bowuyuan yuankan* 故宮博物院院刊 3 (1979): 51–58.

Luo Chongliang 羅崇良. "Cong dang'an cailiao kan Qianlong nianjian taijian de chutao" 從檔案材料看乾隆年間太監的出逃 (The flight of eunuchs during the Qianlong reign as seen from archival materials). *Qingshi yanjiu tongxun* 清史研究通訊 4 (1986): 21–24.

Luo Lida 羅麗達. "Yongzheng chunian de huangzi jiaodu" 雍正初年的皇子教讀 (The education of imperial sons in the early Yongzheng reign). *Qingshi yanjiu* 清史研究 2 (1993): 93–94.

———. "Yunsi zuji yu Xiyang daifu de yibian" 允禩足蔟與西洋大夫的一編 (A Manchu document concerning Yinsi's foot ailment and the Western doctor). *Lishi dang'an* 歷史檔案 3 (1993): 129–30.

Luo Qi 羅綺. "Manzu shenhua de minzu tedian" 滿族神話的民族特點 (Characteristics of Manchu legends). *Manzu yanjiu* 滿族研究 1 (1993): 76–85.

Luo Wenhua 羅文華. "Kangxi shenpai" 康熙神牌 (Kangxi's spirit tablet). *Zijincheng* 紫禁城 65 (1991): 19.

Ma Dongyu 馬東玉. "Qingliu pai yu Guangxu jitong" 清流派與光緒繼統

(The Qingliu faction and the Guangxu succession). *Zijincheng* 紫禁城 2 (1994): 38–39.

Ma Lin 馬林. "Qianlong chunian Zhunheer bu shouci ru Zang aocha shimo" 乾隆初年准喝爾部首次入藏熬茶始末 (The Zunghar chieftain first entered Tibet in the early Qianlong reign pursuing tea) *Xizang yanjiu* 四藏研究 1 (1988): 62–69.

———. "Cong liyi zhi zheng kan zhu Zang dachen tong Dalai lama ji Xizang difang zhengfu shezheng de guanxi" 從禮儀之爭看駐藏大臣同大賴喇嘛及西藏地方政府攝政的關係 (Relations between the high officials stationed in Tibet with the Dalai lama and the regent of the Tibetan local government, as seen from the ritual struggles). *Qinghai shehui kexue* 青海社會科學 6 (1989): 95–101.

Ma Ruheng 馬汝珩 and Zhao Yuntian 趙云田. "Qingdai bianjiang minzu zhengci jianlun" 清代邊疆民族政策簡論 (A brief survey of Qing policy on border peoples). *Qingshi yanjiu* 清史研究 2 (1991): 1–11.

Macartney, G. M. *An Embassy to China; Being the journal kept by Lord Macartney during his embassy to the Emperor Ch'ien-lung, 1793–1794.* Edited by J. L. Cranmer-Byng. London: Longmans, 1962.

Mackerras, Colin. *The Rise of the Peking Opera, 1770–1870: Social Aspects of the Theatre in Manchu China.* Oxford: Clarendon Press, 1972.

Malone, Carroll Brown. *History of the Peking Summer Palaces under the Ch'ing Dynasty.* 1934. Reprint. New York: Paragon, 1966.

Mancall, Mark. *Russia and China: Their Diplomatic Relations to 1728.* Cambridge, Mass.: Harvard University Press, 1971.

Manz, Beatrice F. *The Rise and Rule of Tamerlane.* Cambridge: Cambridge University Press, 1989.

Mao Xianmin 毛憲民. "Yongzheng di zhongshi gongzhong fanghuo cuoshi" 雍正帝重視宮中防火措施 (The Yongzheng emperor emphasized fire prevention measures in the palace). *Zijincheng* 紫禁城 6 (1990): 40–42.

Markbreiter, Stephen. "The Imperial Palace of Peking." *Arts of Asia* 8, no. 6 (1978): 66–77; 9, no. 6 (1979): 103–15.

Martin, Dan. "Bonpo Canons and Jesuit Cannons: On Sectarian Factors Involved in the Ch'ien-lung Emperor's Second Goldstream Expedition of 1771–1776 Based Primarily on Some Tibetan Sources." *The Tibet Journal* 15, no. 2 (1990): 3–28.

Matsumura Jun 松村潤. "Syurugachi kō" シュルガチ考 (On Šurgaci). In *Nairaku Ajia, Nishi Ajia no shakai to bunka* 內陸アジア。西アジアの社會と文化, edited by Mori Masao 護雅夫, 275–302. Tokyo: Yamakawa shuppan-sha, 1983.

Meech, S. E. "The Imperial Worship at the Altar of Heaven." *The Chinese Recorder* 47, no. 2 (1916): 112–17.

Meng Huiying 孟慧英. *Manzu minjian wenhua lunji* 滿族民間文化論集 (Essays on Manchu popular culture). Shenyang: Jilin renmin chubanshe, 1990.

Meng Lin 蒙林. "'Manwen laodang' yu Menggushi yanjiu" '滿文老檔' 與蒙

古史研究 (The old Manchu archives and research on Mongol history). *Nei Menggu shehui kexue* 內蒙古社會科學 4 (1987): 85–86.

———. "Qing Taizu shiqi de Man Meng guanxi" 清太祖時期的滿蒙關係 (Manchu-Mongol relations during the time of Qing Taizu). *Nei Menggu shida xuebao (Hanwen zhexue shehui kexue ban)* 內蒙古師大學報 (漢文哲學社會科學版) 1 (1989): 77–81.

Meng Sen 孟森. *Qingdai shi* 清代史 (Qing history). Taipei: Zhengzhong shuju, 1962.

Meng Yunsheng 孟允升. "Beijing de Menggu wangfu" 北京的蒙古王府 (Peking's Mongol princely establishments). *Manzu yanjiu* 滿族研究 3 (1989): 51–55.

Meng Zhaoxin 孟昭信. "Guanyu Nanshufang de shishe shijian wenti" 關于南書房的始設時間問題 (Issues concerning Kangxi's campaign against Galdan). *Shixue jikan* 史學集刊 3 (1988): 33–35.

Meng Zhaozhen 孟兆禎. *Bishushanzhuang yuanlin yishu* 避暑山莊園林藝術 (The garden arts of the Bishu shanshuang). Beijing: Zijincheng chubanshe, 1985.

Menzies, Nicholas K. *Forest and Land Management in Imperial China*. New York: St. Martin's Press, 1994.

Meyer, Jeffrey F. *The Dragons of Tiananmen: Beijing as a Sacred City*. Columbia: University of South Carolina Press, 1991.

Michael, Franz. *The Origin of Manchu Rule in China: Frontier and Bureaucracy as Interacting Forces in the Chinese Empire*. 1942. Reprint. New York: Octagon Books, 1979.

Miller, Robert J. *Monasteries and Culture Change in Inner Mongolia*. Wiesbaden: Harrassowitz, 1959.

Millward, James A. "Beyond the Pass: Commerce, Ethnicity, and the Qing Empire in Xinjiang, 1759–1864." Ph.D. diss., Stanford University, 1993.

———. "A Uyghur Muslim in Qianlong's Court: The Meanings of the Fragrant Concubine." *Journal of Asian Studies* 53, no. 2 (1994): 427–58.

Minzu wenti wu zhong congshu, Liaoning sheng bianji weiyuan hui 民族問題五種叢書, 遼寧省編輯委員會, *Manzu shehui lishi diaocha* 滿族社會歷史調查 (Historical survey of Manchu society). Shenyang: Liaoning renmin chubanshe, 1985.

Mitamura Taisuke 三田村泰助. "Manshū syamanizumu no saishi to shukushi" 滿洲シャマニズムの祭祀と祝詞 (The rituals and prayers of Manchu shamanism). In *Ishihama sensei koki kinen Tōyōgaku ronshū* 石濱先生古稀記念東洋學論集 (Collected works on Oriental history commemorating Professor Ishihama's seventieth birthday), ed. Ishihama sensei koki kinen kai, 536–50. Osaka: Kansai daigaku, 1958.

Miyawaki, Junko. "The Qalqa Mongols and the Oyirad in the Seventeenth Century." *Journal of Asian History* 18 (1984): 136–73.

Mo Zhuang. "Report from China: Pearl Robe Discovered in Tomb." *Oriental Art* 31, no. 4 (1985–86): 452–53.

Moses, Larry W. *The Political Role of Mongol Buddhism*. Bloomington: Asian Studies Research Institute, 1977.

Mu Sou 木叟. "Naibobo he nai chapu" 奶餑餑和奶茶鋪(Milk biscuits and biscuit shops). *Zijincheng* 紫禁城 39 (1987): 27.

Muercha 穆爾察 and Zhan Kun 占堃. "Manzu de 'mama koudai' ji 'kaisuo' xisu de tantao" 滿族的 '媽媽口袋' 及 '開鎖' 習俗的探討 (An inquiry into the Manchu customs of the 'mama bag' and 'opening the key'). *Manzu yanjiu* 滿族研究 1 (1989): 77–79.

Murata Jirō 村田治郎. "Dōshi (Shin kūshitsu syamanizumu sono ichi)" 堂子 (清宮室シャマニズムその一) (The *tangzi*; shamanism in the Qing palace, 1). *Manmō* 滿蒙 16, no. 1 (1935): 95–110.

———. "Shin-nei-kū to Kon-nei-kū (Shin kūshitsu syamanizumu sono ni)" 清寧宮と坤寧宮 (清宮室シャマニズムその二) (The Qingning palace and the Kunning palace: shamanism in the Qing palace, 2). *Manmō* 滿蒙 16, no. 2 (1935): 22–31.

———. "Shin-nei-kū no saiki (Shin kūshitsu syamanizumu sono san)" 清寧宮の祭器 (清宮室シャマニズムその三) (The sacrificial implements in the Qingning palace: shamanism in the Qing palace, 3). *Manmō* 滿蒙 16, no. 3 (1935): 61–72.

Naitō Torajirō 內藤虎次郎. *Naitō Kōnan zenshū* 內藤胡南全書. Vol. 6. To-kyo: Chikuma shobō, 1972.

Naquin, Susan. *Millenarian Rebellion in China: The Eight Trigrams Uprising of 1813*. New Haven: Yale University Press, 1976.

——— and Chün-fang Yü, eds. *Pilgrims and Sacred Sites in China*. Berkeley: University of California Press, 1992.

National Palace Museum, *Catalogue of a Special Exhibition of Hindustan Jade in the National Palace Museum*. Taipei: National Palace Museum, 1983.

———. *Special Exhibition of Ch'ing Dynasty Enamelled Porcelains of the Imperial Ateliers*. Taipei: National Palace Museum, 1992.

Nie Chongzheng 聶崇正. "Tan Qingdai 'Ziguangge gongchenxiang'" 談清代 '紫光閣功臣像' (Qing paintings of meritorious officials in the Ziguangge). *Wenwu* 文物 1 (1990): 65–69.

Ning Changying 寧昶英. "Lun Manzu de sheliu xisu" 論滿族的射柳習俗 (On the Manchu custom of shooting at willow branches). *Manzu wenhua* 滿族文化 16 (1992): 66–68.

———. "Man Han quanxi ji qi xingcheng" 滿漢全席及其形成 (Manchu and Chinese cuisine and their formation). *Beifang minzu* 北方民族 1 (1992): 104–6.

Norman, Jerry. *A Concise Manchu-English Lexicon*. Seattle: University of Washington Press, 1978.

Nowak, Margaret, and Stephen Durrant. *The Tale of the Nišan Shamaness: A Manchu Folk Epic*. Seattle: University of Washington Press, 1977.

Ogawa, K. *Photographs of Palace Buildings of Peking, compiled by the Imperial Museum of Tokyo*. 2 vols. Tokyo: Imperial Museum, 1906.

Okada, Hidehiro. "Jesuit Influence in Emperor K'ang-hsi's Manchu Letters." In *Proceedings of the XXVIII Permanent International Altaistic Conference: Venice, 8–14 July 1985*, edited by Giovanni Stary, 165–71. Wiesbaden: Harrassowitz, 1989.

————. "Origin of the Čahar Mongols." *Mongolian Studies* 14 (1991): 155–79.

Oxnam, Robert B. *Ruling from Horseback: Manchu Politics in the Oboi Regency, 1661–1669.* Chicago: University of Chicago Press, 1975.

Oyama Hikoichi 大山彦一. "Samankyō to Manshūzoku no kazoku seido" 薩滿教と滿洲族の家族制度 (Shamanism and the Manchu peoples' family system). *Minzokugaku kenkyū* 民族學研究 7, no. 2 (1941): 157–86.

Pal, Pratapaditya. "An Early Ming Embroidered Masterpiece." *Christie's International Magazine* (May–June 1994): 62–63.

Paludan, Ann. "The Chinese Spirit Road." *Orientations* 19, no. 9 (1988): 55–65; 20, no. 4 (1989): 64–73; 21, no. 3 (1990): 56–66.

Pang, Tatjana A., and Giovanni Stary. "On the Discovery of a Manchu Epic." *Central Asiatic Journal* 38, no. 1 (1994): 58–70.

Park, Nancy E. "Corruption and Its Recompense: Bribes, Bureaucracy, and the Law in Late Imperial China." Ph.D. diss., Harvard University, 1993.

Parker, Geoffrey. *The Military Revolution: Military Innovation and the Rise of the West, 1500–1800.* Cambridge: Cambridge University Press, 1988.

Petech, L. *China and Tibet in the Early XVIIIth Century: History of the Establishment of Chinese Protectorate in Tibet.* Leiden: E. J. Brill, 1972.

————. *Aristocracy and Government in Tibet, 1728–1959.* Rome: Istituto italiano per il medio ed estremo oriente, 1973.

Po Song-nien and David Johnson. *Domesticated Deities and Auspicious Emblems.* Berkeley: Popular Culture Project, 1992.

Podzneyev, Aleksei M. *Mongolia and the Mongols.* 1892. Translated by John Roger Shaw and Dale Plank. Bloomington: Indiana University, 1971.

Pomeranz, Kenneth. "Water to Iron, Widows to Warlords: The Handan Rain Shrine in Modern Chinese History." *Late Imperial China* 12, no. 1 (1991): 62–99.

Poppe, Nicholas, Leon Hurvitz, and Hidehiro Okada. *Catalogue of the Manchu-Mongol Section of the Tōyō Bunkō.* Tokyo: Tōyō Bunkō, 1964.

Portal, Jane. "Later Chinese Cloisonné." *Orientations* 23, no. 11 (1992): 72–77.

Pozzi, Alessandra. "A journey to the original places of Manchu people." *Zentralasiatische Studien* 20 (1987): 208–18.

Puren 溥任. "Wan Qing fengwang fenfu" 晚清封王分府 (Princely investiture and the establishment of separate households in the late Qing). *Zijincheng* 紫禁城 52 (1989): 40–41.

Pu Wencheng 蒲文成. "Qinghai de Mengguzu de siyuan" 青海的蒙古族的寺院 (Mongol temples in Qinghai). *Qinghai shehui kexue* 青海社會科學 6 (1989): 102–109.

————. "Zang zhuan Fojiao zhu pai zai Qinghai de zaoqi zhuanbo ji qi gaizong" 藏傳佛教諸派在青海的早期傳播及其改宗 (The early propagation and reform of Tibetan Buddhist sects in Qinghai). *Xizang yanjiu* 西藏研究 2 (1990): 107–12, 125.

Qi Feng 琦楓. "Jiaotai dian" 交泰殿 (The Jiaotai hall). *Zijincheng* 紫禁城 6 (1981): 6–8.

Qian Shifu 錢實甫. *Qingji xinshe zhiguan nianbiao* 清季新設職官年表

(Chronological tables of officials in new posts in the Qing). Beijing: Zhonghua shuju, 1977.

———. *Qingji zhongyao zhiguan nianbiao* 清季重要職官年表 (Chronological table of officials in major posts in the Qing). Beijing: Zhonghua shuju, 1977.

———. *Qingdai zhiguan nianbiao* 清代職官年表 (Chronological tables of Qing officials). 4 vols. Beijing: Zhonghua shuju, 1980.

Qian Zongfan 錢宗范. *Qianlong* 乾隆 (The Qianlong emperor). Nanning: Guangxi renmin chubanshe, 1986.

Qiao Zhizhong 喬治忠. "Hou Jin Manwen dangce de chansheng ji qi shixue yiyi" 後金滿文檔冊的產生及其史學意義 (The production of the Later Jin Manchu-language archive and its historical significance). *Shehui kexue zhanxian* 社會科學戰線 3 (1994): 155–60.

Qin Guojing 秦國經. "Qingdai gongting de jingwei zhidu" 清代宮廷的警衛制度 (The Qing court's security guard system). *Gugong bowuyuan yuankan* 故宮博物院院刊 4 (1990): 64–71.

Qin Yongzhang 秦永章 and Li Li 李麗. "'Huang Qing zhigong tu' yu Qing chu Qinghai shaoshu minzu fushi xisu" '皇清職貢圖' 與清初青海少數民族服飾習俗 (The 'Huang Qing zhigong tu' and the dress and customs of the Qinghai minorities in the early Qing). *Qinghai minzu xueyuan xuebao* 青海民族學院學報 3 (1991): 35–39.

Ratchnevsky, Paul. *Genghis Khan: His Life and Legacy.* Translated by Thomas Haining. Oxford: Basil Blackwell, 1991.

Rawski, Evelyn S. "The Imperial Way of Death: Ming and Ch'ing Emperors and Death Ritual." In *Death Ritual in Late Imperial and Modern China*, edited by James L. Watson and Evelyn S. Rawski, 228–53. Berkeley: University of California Press, 1988.

———. "Qing Imperial Marriage and Problems of Rulership." In *Marriage and Inequality in Chinese Society*, edited by Rubie S. Watson and Patricia B. Ebrey, 170–203. Berkeley: University of California Press, 1991.

———. "The Creation of an Emperor in Eighteenth-Century China." In *Harmony and Counterpoint: Ritual Music in Chinese Context*, edited by Bell Yung, Evelyn S. Rawski, and Rubie S. Watson, 150–74. Stanford: Stanford University Press, 1996.

———. "Re-envisioning the Qing: The Significance of the Qing Period in Chinese History." *Journal of Asian Studies* 55, no. 4 (1996): 829–50.

Ripa, M. *Memoirs of Father Ripa during thirteen years' residence at the Court of Peking*. Selected and translated from the Italian by Fortunato Prandi. London: John Murray, 1844.

Rockhill, W. W. "The Dalai Lamas of Lhasa and Their Relations with the Manchu Emperors of China." *T'oung Pao*, 2d s., 11 (1910): 1–104.

Rogers, Howard. "Court Painting under the Qianlong Emperor." In *The Elegant Brush: Chinese Painting under the Qianlong Emperor, 1735–1795*, edited by Ju-hsi Chou and Claudia Brown, 303–17. Phoenix: Arizona State University, 1985.

————. "For Love of God: Castiglione at the Qing Imperial Court." In *The Elegant Brush: Chinese Painting Under the Qianlong Emperor, 1735–1795*, edited by Ju-hsi Chou and Claudia Brown, 141–60. Phoenix: Arizona State University, 1985.

Rosenzweig, Daphne Lange. "Court Painters of the K'ang-hsi Period." Ph.D. diss., Columbia University, 1973.

————. "Painters at the Early Qing Court: The Socioeconomic Background." *Monumenta Serica* 31 (1974–75): 475–87.

Rossabi, Morris. *China and Inner Asia from 1368 to the Present Day*. New York: Pica Press, 1975.

————. *The Jurchens in the Yüan and Ming*. Ithaca: Cornell China-Japan Program, 1982.

————. *Khubilai Khan: His Life and Times*. Berkeley: University of California Press, 1988.

Ruegg, D. Seyfort. "*Mchod yon, yon mchod* and *mchod gnas/yon gnas*: On the Historiography and Semantics of a Tibetan Religio-Social and Religio-Political Concept." In *Tibetan History and Language: Studies Dedicated to Uray Geza on His Seventieth Birthday*, edited by Ernst Steinkellner, 441–53. Vienna: Arbetskreis für Tibetische und Buddhistische Studien, Universität Wien, 1991.

Ruo Jing 若菁. "Qianlong di chiyu huangzi xianxi qishe" 乾隆帝飭諭皇子嫻習騎射 (The Qianlong emperor admonishes the imperial sons to be adept at mounted archery). In *Qing gong yishi* 清宮軼事 (Anecdotes of the Qing palace), edited by Zheng Yimei 鄭逸梅 et al., 57–59. Beijing: Zijincheng chubanshe, 1985.

Rupen, Robert A. "The City of Urga in the Manchu Period." *Studia Altaica: Festschrift für Nikolaus Poppe zum 60. Geburtstag am 8. August 1957*, 157–69. Wiesbaden: Harrassowitz, 1957.

Sacks, Karen. *Sisters and Wives: The Past and Future of Sexual Equality*. Westport: Greenwood Press, 1979.

Samuel, Geoffrey. *Civilized Shamans: Buddhism in Tibetan Societies*. Washington, D.C.: Smithsonian Institution Press, 1993.

Sanjdorj, M. *Manchu Chinese Colonial Rule in Northern Mongolia*. Translated and edited by Urgunge Onon. New York: St. Martin's Press, 1980.

Sangren, Steven. "Female Gender in Chinese Religious Symbols: Kuan Yin, Ma Tsu, and The 'Eternal Mother.'" *Signs* 9 (1983): 4–25.

————. *History and Magical Power in a Chinese Community*. Stanford: Stanford University Press, 1987.

Scott, James C. *Domination and the Arts of Resistance: Hidden Transcripts*. New Haven: Yale University Press, 1990.

Serruys, Henry. "The Čahar Population During the Ch'ing." *Journal of Asian History* 12 (1978): 58–79.

Shan Shiyuan 單士元. "Guanyu Qing gong de xiunü he gongnü" 關于清宮的秀女和宮女 (The Qing palace's recruitment of brides and maidservants). *Gugong bowuyuan yuankan* 故宮博物院院刊 2 (1960): 97–103.

————. "Gongting jianzhu qiao jiang—Yang Shilei" 宮廷建築巧匠——樣

式雷(A clever artisanal palace architect: Yang Shilei). In *Yuanmingyuan ziliao ji* 圓明園資料集 (Collected materials on the Yuanmingyuan), edited by Shu Mu 舒牧, Shen Wei 申偉, and He Naixian 賀乃賢, 95–101. Beijing: Shumu wenxian chubanshe, 1984.

———. "Gugong Nansansuo kao" 故宮南三所考 (On the palace's "Southern Three Residences"). *Gugong bowuyuan yuankan* 故宮博物院院刊 3 (1988): 20–22.

Shang Hongkui 商鴻逵. "Qing 'xiaozhuang Wen huanghou' xiaoji (Qingshi zhaji yize)" 清 '孝庄文皇后' 小記 (清史札記一則) (A note on the Xiao-zhuang Wen empress of the Qing [A reading note on Qing history]). *Qingshi luncong* 清史論叢 2 (1980): 275–77.

———. *Qingshi Manyu cidian* 清史滿語辭典 (Dictionary of Qing historical Manchu). Shanghai: Shanghai guji chubanshe, 1990.

Shang Hongying 尚洪英. "Wangye yuanqin" 王爺園寢 (The prince's tomb). *Zijincheng* 紫禁城 3 (1994): 31.

Shenyang gugong bowuyuan 沈陽故宮博物院, Tie Yuqin 鐵玉欽, et al. *Shengjing huanggong* 盛京皇宮 (The Shengjing imperial palace). Beijing: Zijincheng chubanshe, 1987.

———. *Shenyang gugong bowuyuan wenwu jingpin huicui* 沈陽故宮博物院文物精品薈萃 (The gathering of select gems from the Shenyang Palace Museum collection). Shenyang: Liaoning meishu chubanshe, 1991.

Shi Kekuan 施克寬. *Renzao de disanxing: Zhongguo huan guan mishi* 人造的第三性: 中國宦官秘史 (The manmade third sex: a secret history of China's eunuch officials). Beijing: Baowen tang shudian, 1988.

Shiga, Shūzō. "Family Property and the Law of Inheritance in Traditional China." In *Chinese Family Law and Social Change in Historical and Comparative Perspective*, edited by David C. Buxbaum, 109–50. Seattle: University of Washington Press, 1978.

Shirokogoroff, Sergei M. "General Theory of Shamanism Among the Tungus." *Journal, North China Branch of the Royal Asiatic Society* 54 (1923): 246–49.

———. *Social Organization of the Manchus: A Study of the Manchu Clan Organization*. Shanghai: Royal Asiatic Society, North China Branch, 1924.

———. *Social Organization of the Northern Tungus, with Introductory Chapters Concerning Geographical Distribution and History of These Groups*. Shanghai: Commercial Press, 1929.

Shu Mu 舒牧, Shen Wei 申偉, and He Naixian 賀乃賢, eds. *Yuanmingyuan ziliao ji* 圓明園資料集 (Collected materials on the Yuanmingyuan). Beijing: Shumu wenxian, 1984.

Sirén, Osvald. *The Walls and Gates of Peking*. London: Bodley Head, 1924.

———. *The Imperial Palaces of Peking*. 1926. Reprint. New York: AMS Press, 1976.

———. *Gardens of China*. New York: Ronald Press, 1949.

Smith, Richard J. "Ritual in Qing Culture." In *Orthodoxy in Late Imperial China*, edited by Kwang-ching Liu, 281–310. Berkeley: University of California Press, 1990.

Snellgrove, David L., and Hugh Richardson. *A Cultural History of Tibet*. New York: Praeger, 1968.

Sokol, Stefan. "The Asian Reverse Bow: Reflex and Retroflex Systems." *Arts of Asia* 24, no. 5 (1994): 146–49.

Soullière, Ellen. "Reflections on Chinese Despotism and the Power of the Inner Court." *Asian Profile* 12, no. 2 (1984): 130–45.

———. "The Imperial Marriages of the Ming Dynasty." *Papers on Far Eastern History* 37 (1988): 1–30.

Spence, Jonathan. *Ts'ao Yin and the K'ang-hsi Emperor: Bondservant and Master*. New Haven: Yale University Press, 1966.

———. *Emperor of China: Self-Portrait of K'ang-hsi*. New York: Alfred Knopf, 1974.

———. "Ch'ing." In *Food in Chinese Culture: Anthropological and Historical Perspectives*, edited by K. C. Chang, 259–94. New Haven: Yale University Press, 1977.

Sperling, Elliot. "Early Ming Policy Toward Tibet: An Examination of the Proposition that the Early Ming Emperors Adopted a 'Divide and Rule' Policy Toward Tibet." Ph.D. diss., Indiana University, 1983.

Stary, Giovanni. "Die mandschurischen Prinzengräber in Liaoyang, 1988." *Central Asiatic Journal* 33 (1989): 108–17.

———. "The Meaning of the Word 'Manchu': A New Solution to an Old Problem." *Central Asiatic Journal* 34, nos. 1–2 (1990): 109–19.

———. "'Praying in the Darkness': New Texts for a Little-Known Manchu Shamanic Rite." *Shaman* 1, no. 1 (1993): 15–29.

Stary, Giovanni, Nicola Di Cosmo, Tatiana A. Pang, and Alessandra Pozzi, eds. *On the Tracks of Manchu Culture, 1644–1994: 350 Years After the Conquest of Peking*. Wiesbaden: Harrassowitz, 1995.

Steinhardt, Nancy Shatzman. "Altar to Heaven Complex." In *Chinese Traditional Architecture*, edited by Nancy Shatzman Steinhardt et al., 139–49. New York: China Institute in America, 1984.

———. *Chinese Imperial City Planning*. Honolulu: University of Hawaii Press, 1990.

Struve, Lynn, ed. and trans. *Voices from the Ming Qing Cataclysm: China in Tigers' Jaws*. New Haven: Yale University Press, 1993.

Stuart, Kevin, and Li Xuewei, eds. *Tales from China's Forest Hunters: Oroqen Folktales*. Philadelphia: Department of Asian and Middle Eastern Studies, University of Pennsylvania, 1994.

Stuart, Keven, Li Xuewei, and Shelear, eds. *China's Dagur Minority: Society, Shamanism, and Folklore*. Philadelphia: Department of Asian and Middle Eastern Studies, University of Pennsylvania, 1994.

Su Jianxin 蘇建新. "Qingdai Jilin guozilou ji qi gongpin chutan" 清代吉林果子樓及其貢品初探 (A preliminary inquiry into the 'fruit towers' and tribute from Jilin during the Qing). *Beifang wenwu* 北方文物 3 (1991): 88–92.

Sun Wenfan 孫文范, Feng Shibo 馮士鉢, and Yu Boming 于伯銘. *Daoguang di* 道光帝 (Emperor Daoguang). Changchun: Jilin wenshi chubanshe, 1993.

Sun Wenliang 孫文良. "Lun Qingchu Man Han minzu zhengce de xingcheng" 論清初滿漢民族政策的形成 (The formation of Manchu and Han ethnic policies in early Qing). *Liaoning daxue xuebao* 遼寧大學學報 1 (1991): 89–94.

Sun Wenliang et al, eds. *Manzu da cidian* 滿族大辭典 (Manchu dictionary). Shenyang: Liaoning daxue chubanshe, 1990.

Sun Wenliang and Li Zhiting 李治亭. *Qing Taizong quan zhuan* 清太宗全傳 (Complete biography of Qing Taizong). Changchun: Jilin wenshi chubanshe, 1983. Reissued under the title *Tianzong han: Chongde di* 天聰汗:崇德帝 (Tianzong Khan, Emperor Chongde) (Changchun: Jilin wenshi chubanshe, 1993).

Sun Wenliang, Zhang Jie 張杰, and Zheng Chuanshui 鄭川水. *Qianlong di* 乾隆帝 (Emperor Qianlong). Changchun: Jilin wenshi chubanshe, 1993.

Sun Xiao'en 孫孝恩. *Guangxu pingzhuan* 光緒評傳 (A critical biography of the Guangxu emperor). Shenyang: Liaoning jiaoyu chubanshe, 1985.

Swart, Paula, and Barry Till. "Nurhachi and Abahai: Their Palace and Mausolea: The Manchu Adoption and Adaptation of Chinese Architecture." *Arts of Asia* (1988): 149–57.

Symons, Van Jay. *Ch'ing Ginseng Management: Ch'ing Monopolies in Microcosm.* Tempe: Center for Asian Studies, Arizona State University, 1981.

Takeda Masao 武田昌雄. *Man Kan reizoku* 滿漢禮俗 (Ritual customs of the Manchus and Han Chinese). Dairen: Kinhōdō shoten, 1935.

Tambiah, S. J. *World Conqueror and World Renouncer: A Study of Buddhism and Polity in Thailand Against a Historical Background.* Cambridge: Cambridge University Press, 1976.

Tang Bangzhi 唐邦治. *Qing huangshi sipu* 清皇室四譜 (Four records of the Qing imperial family). In *Jindai Zhongguo shiliao congkan* 近代中國史料叢刊 (Collection of modern Chinese historical materials), edited by Shen Yunlong 沈雲龍, vol. 71. Taipei: Wenhai, 1967.

Tang Yinian 唐益年. *Qing gong taijian* 清宮太監 (Qing palace eunuchs). Shenyang: Liaoning daxue chubanshe, 1993.

Tao, Jing-shen. *The Jurchen in Twelfth-Century China.* Seattle: University of Washington Press, 1976.

Tao Lifan 陶立璠. "Qingdai gongting de saman jisi" 清代宮廷的薩滿祭祀 (The shamanic sacrifices in the Qing court). *Xibei minzu yanjiu* 西北民族研究 1 (1992): 221–32.

Teng Shaozhen 騰紹箴. *Nuerhachi pingzhuan* 努爾哈赤評傳 (A critical biography of Nurgaci). Shenyang: Liaoning renmin chubanshe, 1985.

———. "Nüzhen shehui fazhan pingshu" 女眞社會發展評述 (On the social development of the Jurchen). *Heilongjiang minzu congkan* 黑龍江民族叢刊 2 (1988): 62–68, 107.

———. *Qingdai baqi zidi* 清代八旗子弟 (The Qing bannermen). Beijing: Huaqiao chubanshe, 1989.

Tian Jiaqing. *Classic Chinese Furniture of the Qing Dynasty.* Translated by Lark E. Mason, Jr., and Juliet Yung-yi Chou. Hong Kong: Philip Wilson Publishers, 1996.

Tong Jiajiang 佟佳江. "Qingdai Menggu guizu juezhi suoyi" 清代蒙古貴族爵職瑣議 (Discussion of Mongol noble titles during the Qing). *Minzu yanjiu* 民族研究 1 (1987): 63–70.

Tong Yonggong 佟永功 and Guan Jialu 關嘉錄. "Shengjing shang sanqi baoyi zuoling shulüe" 盛京上三旗包衣佐領述略 (A brief discussion of the upper three banner bondservant companies in Shengjing). *Lishi dang'an* 歷史檔案 3 (1992): 93–97.

———. "Qianlong chao Shengjing zongguan neiwufu de sheli" 乾隆朝盛京總官內務府的設立 (The establishment of the Imperial Household Department in Shengjing in the Qianlong reign). *Gugong bowuyuan yuankan* 故宮博物院院刊 2 (1994): 19–23.

———. "Qianlong chao 'Qinding xin Qingyu' tanxi" 乾隆朝欽定新清語探析 (An analysis of the 'Imperially commissioned new Manchu' of the Qianlong reign). *Manyu yanjiu* 滿語研究 2 (1995): 66–70.

Tong Yüe 佟悅. "Qing Shengjing taimiao kaoshu" 清盛京太廟考述 (On the Qing Temple of the Ancestors in Shengjing). *Gugong bowuyuan yuankan* 故宮博物院院刊 3 (1987): 24–29.

Tong Yüe and Lü Jihong 呂霽虹. *Qing gong huangzi* 清宮皇子 (Qing imperial sons). Shenyang: Liaoning daxue chubanshe, 1993.

Torbert, Preston M. *The Ch'ing Imperial Household Department: A Study of Its Organization and Principal Functions, 1662–1796.* Cambridge, Mass.: Council on East Asian Studies, Harvard University, 1977.

Tsang, Ka Bo. "The Dragon in Chinese Art." *Arts of Asia* 18, no. 1 (1988): 60–67.

———. "Portraits of Meritorious Officials: Eight Examples from the First Set Commissioned by the Qianlong Emperor," *Arts asiatique* 47 (1992): 69–88.

Tucci, Giuseppe. *The Religions of Tibet.* Translated by Geoffrey Samuel. Berkeley: University of California Press, 1980.

Tuguan Luosang queji nima 土觀洛桑郤吉尼瑪. *Zhangjia guoshi Ruobidorji zhuan* 章嘉國師若必多吉傳 (Biography of the lCang skya khutukhtu Rol pa'i rdo rje).Translated by Chen Qingying 陳慶英 and Ma Lianlong. 馬連龍. Beijing: Minzu chubanshe, 1988.

Tun, Li-ch'en. *Annual Customs and Festivals of Peking.* Translated by Derk Bodde. 2d edition. Hong Kong: Hong Kong University Press, 1987.

Twitchett, Denis, and Klaus-Peter Tietze. "The Liao." In *The Cambridge History of China: Alien Regimes and Border States, 907–1368,* edited by Herbert Franke and Denis Twitchett, 6: 45–153. Cambridge: Cambridge University Press, 1994.

Ueno Saneyoshi 上野實義. "Dōshi saishi kō" 堂子祭祀考 (On the *tangzi* rites). In *Shigaku kenkyū kinen ronsō* 史學研究記念論叢. Compiled by Hiroshima bunrika daigaku, Shigakka kyōshitsu 廣島文理科大學, 史學科教室, 337–38. Hiroshima: Yanagihara shoten, 1950.

Uitzinger, Ellen. "Emperorship in China." In *De Verboden Stad: Hofculture van de Chinese keizers (1644–1911),* edited by J. R. ten Model and E. Uitzinger, 71–91. Rotterdam: Museum Boymans-van Beuningen, 1990.

Vasilevič, G. M. "The Acquisition of Shamanistic Ability Among the Evenki

(Tungus)." In *Popular Beliefs and Folklore Tradition in Siberia,* edited by V. Dioszegi, 339–49. Bloomington: Indiana University Press, 1968.

Vollmer, John. *In the Presence of the Dragon Throne: Qing Dynasty Costume (1644–1911) in the Royal Ontario Museum.* Toronto: Royal Ontario Museum, 1977.

von Staël-Holstein, A. "The Emperor Ch'ien-lung and the larger *Shūramgasūtra.*" *Harvard Journal of Asiatic Studies* 1, no. 1 (1936): 136–46.

Waddell, L. Austine. *Tibetan Buddhism with Its Mystic Cults, Symbolism, and Mythology.* Originally published in 1895 as *The Buddhism of Tibet, or Lamaism.* New York: Barnes and Noble, 1972.

Wadley, Stephen. "Altaic Influences on Beijing Dialect: The Manchu Case." *Journal of the American Oriental Society* 116, no. 1 (1996): 99–104.

Wakeman, Frederic, Jr. "The Canton Trade and the Opium War." In *The Cambridge History of China: Late Ch'ing 1800–1911, Part 1,* edited by John K. Fairbank, 204–5. Cambridge: Cambridge University Press, 1978.

———. *The Great Enterprise: The Manchu Reconstruction of Imperial Order in Seventeenth-Century China.* 2 vols. Berkeley: University of California Press, 1975.

Waley-Cohen, Joanna. *Exile in Mid-Qing China: Banishment to Xinjiang, 1758–1820.* New Haven: Yale University Press, 1991.

Wan Yi 萬依. "Qianlong shiqi de yuanyou" 乾隆時期的園囿 (Gardens and animal enclosures in the Qianlong reign). *Gugong bowuyuan yuankan* 故宮博物院院刊 2 (1984): 13–20.

———. "Cong Cixi shengzi kan Qing gong louxi" 從慈禧生子看清宮陋習 (The vulgar customs of the Qing palace, as seen in the pregnancy and childbirth of Cixi). In *Xitaihou* 西太后 (The empress dowager of the west [i.e., Cixi]), edited by Yu Bingkun 俞炳坤 et al., 63–70. Beijing: Zijincheng chubanshe, 1985.

———. "Qingdai gongsu yu jingshi minsu" 清代宮俗與京師民俗 (Qing court customs and the popular customs of the capital city). In *Zhongguo gudu yanjiu* 中國古都研究 (Research on China's ancient capitals), edited by Zhongguo gudu xuehui 中國古都學會, 75–82. Hangzhou: Zhejiang renmin chubanshe, 1986.

Wan Yi and Huang Haitao. 黃海濤. *Qingdai gongting yinyue* 清代宮廷音樂 (Qing court music). Hong Kong: Zhonghua shuju, 1985.

Wan Yi et al., eds. *Qingdai gongting shenghuo* 清代宮廷生活 (Court life in the Qing dynasty). Hong Kong: Commercial Press, 1985.

Wang, Xiangyun. "Tibetan Buddhism at the Court of Qing: The Life and Work of lCang-skya Rol-pa'i-rdo-rje (1717–1786)." Ph.D. diss., Harvard University, 1995.

Wang Chonglu 王充閭. "Nuerhachi qiandu tanze" 努爾哈赤遷都探賾 (An exploration of Nurgaci's changes of capitals). *Manzu yanjiu* 滿族研究 3 (1994): 19–24.

Wang Daocheng 王道成. "Cixi de jiazu, jiating, he rugong zhi chu de shenfen" 慈禧的家族, 家庭和入宮初的身分 (Cixi's family and her status when she first entered the palace). *Qingshi yanjiuji* 清史研究集 3 (1984): 187–220.

———. "Beihai yu Qianlong" 北海與乾隆 (Beihai and the Qianlong emperor). *Qingshi yanjiu* 清史研究 2 (1992): 75–77.

Wang Dongfang 王冬芳. "Zaoqi Manzu funü zai jiating zhong de diwei" 早期滿族婦女在家庭中的地位 (The status of Manchu women in their families in the early period). *Liaoning daxue xuebao* 遼寧大學學報 5 (1994): 64–68, 60.

Wang Gesheng 王革生. "Qingdai dongbei 'wangzhuang'" 清代東北王莊 (Qing princely estates in the northeast). *Manzu yanjiu* 滿族研究 1 (1989): 25–27.

Wang Guangyao 王光堯. "Qingdai hou fei shengqin yu Qing gong kefang" 清代后妃省親與清宮客房 (The reunions of Qing consorts with their natal families and guest quarters in the palace). *Zijincheng* 紫禁城 2 (1991): 14.

Wang Honggang. 王宏剛. "Manzu samanjiao de sanzhong xingtai ji qi yanbian" 滿族薩滿教的三種形態及其演變 (Three forms of Manchu shamanism and their evolution). *Shehui kexue zhanxian* 社會科學戰線 1 (1988): 187–93.

Wang Honggang and Fu Yuguang 富育光, "Saman shen'gu tanwei" 薩滿神鼓探微 (Exploration of the shamanic drum). *Beifang wenwu* 北方文物 1 (1992): 48–51.

Wang Huo 王火. "Qingdai baqi zhong Gaoliren mingzi de yuyan he minsu tezheng" 清代八旗中高麗人名字的語言和民俗特征 (The speech and customs of the Koreans in the banners during the Qing). *Manzu yanjiu* 滿族研究 2 (1995): 43–49.

Wang Jiapeng 王家鵬. "Zhangjia hutuketu xiang xiaokao: jiantan Qianlong huangdi yu Zhangjia Guoshi de guanxi" 章嘉呼圖克圖像小考: 兼談乾隆皇帝與章嘉國師的關係 (A brief investigation of the lCang skya khutukhtu: on the relationship of the Qianlong emperor and the lCang skya national preceptor). *Gugong bowuyuan yuankan* 故宮博物院院刊 4 (1987): 48, 88–93.

———. "Gugong yuhuage tan yuan" 故宮雨花閣探源 (On the origins of the Yuhua pavilion in the palace). *Gugong bowuyuan yuankan* 故宮博物院院刊 1 (1990): 50–62.

———. "Minzu tuanjie de lishi huajuan—liushi Banchan huaxiang" 民族團結的歷史畫卷——六世班禪畫像 (Historical paintings of ethnic unity: the paintings of the sixth Panchen lama). *Zijincheng* 紫禁城 2 (1990): 11–13.

———. "Zhongzhengdian yu Qinggong Zang zhuan Fojiao" 中正殿與清宮藏傳佛教 (The Zhongzheng hall and the Tibetan Buddhist faith in the Qing palace). *Gugong bowuyuan yuankan* 故宮博物院院刊 3 (1991): 58–71.

———. "Qianlong yu Manzu lama siyuan" 乾隆與滿族喇嘛寺院 (Qianlong and Manchu Tibetan Buddhist temples). *Gugong bowuyuan yuankan* 故宮博物院院刊 1 (1995): 58–65.

Wang Laiyin 王萊茵. *Gugong jiu wen yi hua* 故宮舊聞軼話 (Old anecdotes about the palace). Tianjin: Renmin chubanshe, 1986.

———. "Hexiao gongzhu—Qianlong di de zhangshang mingzhu" 和孝公主——乾隆帝的掌上明珠 (Princess Hexiao: the bright pearl held by the Qianlong emperor). In *Qing gong jie mi* 清宮揭秘 (Secrets of the Qing palace), edited by Zheng Yimei 鄭逸梅 et al., 112–15. Hong Kong: Nanyue chubanshe, 1987,

Wang Lizhen 汪麗珍. "Guanyu Manzu de niao wenhua" 關于滿族的鳥文化 (The bird culture of the Manchus). *Zhongyang minzu xueyuan xuebao* 中央民族學院學報 2 (1993): 62–66, 79.

Wang Lu 王璐 and Tian Fang 天放. "Chengde waibamiao yu Xizang de guanxi" 承德外八廟與西藏的關係 (The eight outer temples of Chengde and relations with Tibet). *Zhongyang minzu xueyuan xuebao* 中央民族學院學報 4 (1988): 34–36.

Wang Peihuan 王佩環. *Qing gong hou fei* 清宮后妃 (Consorts in the Qing palace). Shenyang: Liaoning daxue chubanshe, 1993.

———. "Fuling yu Ming Qing huangling de bijiao yanjiu" 福陵與明清皇陵的比較研究 (Comparisons between the Fuling and Ming and Qing imperial mausolea). *Qingshi yanjiu* 清史研究 2 (1995): 81–86.

Wang Shuqing 王樹卿. "Qingdai hou fei zhidu zhong de jige wenti"清代后妃制度中的几個問題 (Several issues in the Qing consort system). *Gugong bowuyuan yuankan* 故宮博物院院刊 1 (1980): 38–46.

———. "Qingdai huanghou de celi" 清代皇后的冊立 (Investiture of Qing empresses). *Gugong bowuyuan yuankan* 故宮博物院院刊 3 (1980): 40–48.

———. "Qingdai de huangquan douzheng" 清代的皇權斗爭 (Struggle over the imperial prerogative in the Qing). *Gugong bowuyuan yuankan* 故宮博物院院刊 4 (1981): 65–73.

———. "Qingdai gongzhu" 清代公主 (Qing princesses). *Gugong bowuyuan yuankan* 故宮博物院院刊 3 (1982): 31–38.

———. "Qingdai gongzhong shanshi" 清代宮中膳食 (Food in the Qing palace). *Gugong bowuyuan yuankan* 故宮博物院院刊 3 (1983): 57–64.

———. "Qingchao taijian zhidu" 清朝太監制度 (The Qing eunuch system). *Gugong bowuyuan yuankan* 故宮博物院院刊 3 (1984): 58.

Wang Shuyun 王淑云. *Qingdai beixun yudao he saiwai xinggong* 清代北巡御道和塞外行宮 (The temporary palaces of the Qing on the northern route outside the passes). Beijing: Zhongguo huanjing kexue chubanshe, 1989.

Wang Sizhi 王思治. "Huangtaiji siwei yu zhu da beile de maodun" 皇太極嗣位與諸大貝勒的矛盾 (The accession of Hongtaiji and the contradictions among the great *beile*). *Lishi dang'an* 歷史檔案 3 (1984): 79–84.

———. "Huangtaiji yanjiu zhong de jige wenti" 皇太極研究的几個問題 (Several issues in research on Hongtaiji). *Shehui kexue zhanxian* 社會科學戰線 3 (1984): 134–42.

Wang Yao. "The Cult of Mahākāla and a Temple in Beijing." *Journal of Chinese Religions* 22 (1994): 117–26.

Wang Zhizhang 王芷章. *Qing Shengpingshu zhilüe* 清昇平署志略 (Brief study of the Qing Court Theatrical Bureau). 1937. Reprint. Taipei: Xinwenfeng chuban gongsi, 1981.

Wang Zhonghan 王鍾翰. "Guanyu Manzu xingcheng zhong de jige wenti" 關于滿族形成中的几個問題 (Several problems regarding the formation of the Manchu people). In *Manzushi yanjiu ji* 滿族研究集 (Collected researches on Manchu history), 1–16. Beijing: Zhongguo shehui kexueyuan chubanshe, 1988.

——. "'Guoyu qishe' yu Manzu de fazhan" 國語騎射與滿族的發展 (Skill in Manchu and mounted archery and the development of the Manchu people). In *Manzu shi yanjiu ji* 滿族史研究集, 195–208. Beijing: Zhongguo shehui kexue chubanshe, 1988.

——. "Qingdai baqi zhong de Man Han minzu chengfen wenti" 清代八族中的滿漢民族成分問題 (Several issues concerning the roles of Manchus and Han Chinese in the Qing banners). *Minzu yanjiu* 民族研究 3 (1990): 36–46, 4 (1990): 57–66.

Wang Zilin 王子林. "Qingdai gong shi" 清代弓矢 (Qing-era bows and arrows). *Gugong bowuyuan yuankan* 故宮博物院院刊 1 (1994): 86–96.

Wang Zuoxian 王佐賢. "Manzu sangyi" 滿族喪儀 (Manchu funeral rituals). *Zijincheng* 紫禁城 51 (1989): 24–25.

Watson, Rubie S. "Afterword: Marriage and Gender Inequality." In *Marriage and Inequality in Chinese Society*, edited by Rubie S. Watson and Patricia B. Ebrey, 347–68. Berkeley: University of California Press, 1991.

Watt, James C. Y. "The Antique-Elegant." In *Possessing the Past: Treasures from the National Palace Museum, Taipei*, edited by Wen C. Fong and James C. Y. Watt, 503–53. New York: Metropolitan Museum of Art, 1996.

Wechsler, Howard J. *Offerings of Jade and Silk: Ritual and Symbol in the Legitimation of the T'ang Dynasty*. New Haven: Yale University Press, 1985.

Wei Dong 畏冬. "'Huang Qing zhigongtu' chuangzhi shimo" 皇清職貢圖創製始末 (On the creation of the "Foreign Envoys Bearing Tribute"). *Zijincheng* 紫禁城 72 (1992): 8–12.

Wei Kaizhao 魏開肇, *Yonghegong man lu* 雍和宮漫錄 (Informal records of the Yonghegong). Henan: Renmin chubanshe, 1985.

Wei Qingyuan 韋慶遠. *Ming Qing shi bianzhe* 明清史辨折 (Analysis of Ming and Qing history). Beijing: Zhongguo shehui kexue chubanshe, 1989.

Wei Qingyuan, Wu Qiyan 吳奇衍, and Lu Su 魯素, *Qingdai nübi zhidu* 清代奴婢制度 (The Qing slave system). Beijing: Renmin daxue chubanshe, 1982.

Weiers, Michael. "Zum Verhältnis des Ch'ing-staats zur Lamaistischen Kirche in der Frühen Yung-cheng Zeit." *Zentralasiatische Studien* 21 (1988): 115–31.

Weiner, Annette B. *Inalienable Possessions: The Paradox of Keeping-While-Giving*. Berkeley: University of California Press, 1992.

Wilentz, Sean. *Rites of Power: Symbolism, Ritual and Politics Since the Middle Ages*. Philadelphia: University of Pennsylvania Press, 1985.

Williams, Brackette F. "A CLASS ACT: Anthropology and the Race to Nation Across Ethnic Terrain." *Annual Review of Anthropology* 18 (1989): 401–44.

Williams, E. T. "The State Religion of China During the Manchu Dynasty." *Journal, North China Branch of the Royal Asiatic Society*, n.s., 44 (1913): 11–45.

————. "Worshipping Imperial Ancestors in Peking." *Journal, North China Branch of the Royal Asiatic Society*, n.s., 70 (1939): 46–65.

Wills, John E., Jr. "Museums and Sites in North China." In *Ming and Qing Historical Studies in the People's Republic of China*, edited by Frederic Wakeman, Jr., 13–14. Berkeley: University of California Press, 1980.

Wittfogel, Karl A., and Feng Chia-sheng. "History of Chinese Society: Liao (907–1125)." *Transactions of the American Philosophical Society*, n.s., 36 (1946).

Wolf, Margery. *Women and the Family in Rural Taiwan*. Stanford: Stanford University Press, 1972.

Wright, Arthur F. *Buddhism in Chinese History*. Stanford: Stanford University Press, 1959.

Wright, Mary C. *The Last Stand of Chinese Conservatism: The T'ung-chih Restoration, 1862–1874*. Stanford: Stanford University Press, 1957.

Wu, Silas H. L. *Communication and Imperial Control in China: Evolution of the Palace Memorial System, 1693–1735*. Cambridge, Mass.: Harvard University Press, 1970.

————. "Emperors at work: The daily schedules of the K'ang-hsi and Yung-cheng Emperors, 1661–1735." *Tsing Hua Journal of Chinese Studies*, n.s., 8, nos. 1–2 (1970): 210–27.

————. *Passage to Power: K'ang-hsi and His Heir Apparent, 1661–1722*. Cambridge, Mass.: Harvard University Press, 1979.

Wubing'an 烏丙安. "Saman shijie de 'zhen shen'—saman" 薩滿世界的眞神——薩滿 (The true god of the shamanic world—the shaman). *Manzu yanjiu* 滿族研究 1 (1989): 65–76.

Wu Changyuan 吳長元. *Chen Yuan shilüe* 宸垣識略 (Briefings on the imperial city). 1788. Reprint. Beijing: Guji chubanshe, 1981.

Wu Fengpei 吳豐培 and Zeng Guoqing 曾國慶. *Qingchao zhu Zang dachen zhidu de jianli yu yange* 清朝駐藏大臣制度的建立與沿革 (The establishment and evolution of the Qing system of stationing commissioners in Tibet). Beijing: Zangxue chubanshe, 1989.

Wu Fengpei and Zeng Guoqing, eds. *Qingdai zhu Zang dachen zhuanlüe* 清代駐藏大臣傳略 (Brief biographies of high Qing officials stationed in Tibet). Lhasa: Xizang renmin chubanshe, 1988.

Wu Hung. "Emperor's Masquerade—'Costume Portraits' of Yongzheng and Qianlong." *Orientations* 26, no. 7 (1995): 25–41.

————. *The Double Screen: Medium and Representation in Chinese Painting*. Chicago: University of Chicago Press, 1996.

————. "Beyond Stereotypes: The Twelve Beauties in Qing Court Art and the 'Dream of the Red Chamber.'" In *Writing Women in Late Imperial China*, edited by Ellen Widmer and Kang-i Sun Chang, 306–65. Stanford: Stanford University Press, 1997.

Wu Xingyao 吳興堯. "Shilun Manzu de dengji zhidu" 試論滿族的等級制度 (On the Manchu ranking system). *Heilongjiang minzu congkan* 黑龍江民族叢刊 4 (1991): 50–53.

Wu Xuejuan 吳雪娟. "Tan Qingdai Manwen dang'an zhong de gongwen taoyu" 談清代滿文檔案中的公文套語 (Forms and formulae of official documents in the Qing Manchu-language archives). *Manyu yanjiu* 滿語研究 1 (1992): 119–24, 89.

Wu Yang 吳洋. "Qingdai 'Eluosi zuoling' kaolüe" 清代俄羅斯佐領考略 (The Russian company in the Qing). *Lishi yanjiu* 歷史研究 5 (1985): 83–84.

Wu Yuanfeng 吳元豐 and Zhao Zhiqiang 趙志強. "Xibozu you Keerqin Mengguqi bianru Manzhou baqi shimo" 錫伯族由科爾沁蒙古旗編入滿洲八旗始末 (An account of how the Xibo were moved from the Khorchin Mongol to the Manchu banners). *Minzu yanjiu* 民族研究 5 (1985): 60–66.

Wuyunbilege 烏云畢力格. "Heshite han ting de jianli guocheng" 和碩特汗廷的建立過程 (The process by which the Khosot khan court was established). *Nei Menggu shehui kexue* 內蒙古社會科學 4 (1988): 70–74.

Wu Yuqing 吳玉清. "Yongzheng yu Yi qinwang Yunxiang" 雍正與怡親王允祥 (The Yongzheng emperor and Prince Yi, Yinxiang). *Qingshi yanjiu* 清史研究 1 (1993): 99–103.

Wu Yuqing and Wu Yongxing 吳永興, eds. *Qing chao ba da qinwang* 清朝八大親王 (The eight great first-degree princes of the Qing dynasty). Beijing: Xueyuan chubanshe, 1991.

Wu Zhaoqing 吳兆清. "Qingdai zaobanchu de jigou he jiangyi" 清代造辦處的機構和匠役 (The structure of the Qing palace workshops and the artisans). *Lishi dang'an* 歷史檔案 4 (1991): 79–85, 89.

———. "Qing Neiwufu huojidang" 清內務府活計檔 (The Qing Imperial Household Department's employment archives). *Wenwu* 文物 3 (1991): 89–96, 55.

Wu Zhengge 吳正格. *Man Han quanxi* 滿漢全席 (The Manchu-Chinese combined cuisine). Tianjin: Tianjin kexue jishu chubanshe, 1986.

———. *Manzu shisu yu Qing gong yushan* 滿族食俗與清宮御膳 (Manchu cuisine and the Qing palace cuisine). Shenyang: Liaoning kexue jishu chubanshe, 1988.

Wylie, Turrell. "Reincarnation: A Political Innovation in Tibetan Buddhism." In *Proceedings of the Csoma de Körös Memorial Symposium Held at Mátrafüred, Hungary, 24–30 September 1976*, edited by Louis Ligeti, 579–86. Budapest: Akádemiao Kiadó, 1978.

———. "Lama tribute in the Ming dynasty." In *Tibetan Studies in Honour of Hugh Richardson: Proceedings of the International Seminar on Tibetan Studies, Oxford, 1979*, edited by Michael Aris and Aung San Suu Kyi, 335–40. Warminster: Aris and Phillips, 1980.

Xiaoshi 蕭奭. *Yongxian lu* 永憲錄 (Records of Yongxian). 1722. Reprint. Beijing: Zhonghua shuju, 1959.

Xie Jingfang 謝景芳. "Baqi Hanjun de mingcheng ji hanyi yange kaoshi" 八旗漢軍的名稱及含義沿革考釋 (The evolution of names and meaning of the term "Hanjun" in the eight banners). *Beifang wenwu* 北方文物 3 (1991): 84–88.

Xing Li 邢莉. "Lamajiao de Mengguhua" 喇嘛教的蒙古化 (The Mongolization of Tibetan Buddhism). *Heilongjiang minzu congkan* 黑龍江民族叢刊 4 (1993): 91–96.

Xizang wenguan hui, wenwu pucha dui 西藏文管會, 文物普查隊. "Dazhaosi zang Yongle nianjian wenwu" 大昭寺藏永樂年間文物 (The Dazhao temple holds an artifact of the Yongle period). *Wenwu* 文物 11 (1985): 66–71.

Xu Guangyuan 徐廣源. "Jingling shuang fei yuanqin" 景陵雙妃園寢 (The tombs of the two consorts at the Jingling). *Zijincheng* 紫禁城 42 (1987): 37.

———. "Mai zangguo sanci de huanghou" 埋葬過三次的皇后 (The empress who was buried three times). *Zijincheng* 紫禁城 49 (1988): 34–35.

———. "Jingmin huangguifei yu kong quan" 敬敏皇貴妃與空券 (Consort Jingmin and the empty marker). *Zijincheng* 紫禁城 56 (1990): 44–45.

———. "Cong Xiaozhuang sangyi kan Kangxi pojiu wushi jingshen" 從孝莊喪儀看康熙破舊務實精神 (How the Kangxi emperor destroyed the old dealings with spirits, seen from the perspective of Empress Xiaozhuang's funerary rites). *Gugong bowuyuan yuankan* 故宮博物院院刊 4 (1994): 88–89.

Xu Ke 徐珂. *Qing bai leichao* 清稗類鈔 (Anecdotal sources on the Qing). 1917. Reprint. Taipei: Commercial Press, 1966.

Xu Kun 許鯤. "Qingchu huangshi yu douzhen fangzhi" 清初皇室與痘疹防治 (The imperial family and smallpox prevention in early Qing). *Gugong bowuyuan yuankan* 故宮博物院院刊 3 (1994): 91–96, 90.

Xu Liting 徐立亭. *Xianfeng, Tongzhi di* 咸豐, 同治帝 (Emperors Xianfeng and Tongzhi). Changchun: Jilin wenshi chubanshe, 1993.

Xu Qixian 徐啓憲. "Qingdai huangdi de yongshan" 清代皇帝的用膳 (The meals of the Qing emperors). *Zijincheng* 紫禁城 4 (1980): 10–11.

———. "Qingdai baoxi lüetan" 清代寶璽略談 (A brief discussion of Qing imperial seals). *Gugong bowuyuan yuankan* 故宮博物院院刊 3 (1995): 62–66.

Xu Shiyan 徐世彥 and Li Dongshan 李東山. *Da taijian An Dehai zhi si* 大太監安德海之死 (The death of the chief eunuch An Dehai). Jilin: Jilin renmin chubanshe, 1986.

Xu Shuming 許淑明. "Qing qianqi Heilongjiang diqu de sanzuo xincheng — Aihun, Moergen he Qiqiheer" 清前期黑龍江地區的三座新城——愛琿, 墨爾根和齊齊和爾 (The three new garrisons on the Heilongjiang drainage in early Qing: Aigun, Mergen, and Qiqihar). *Qingshi yanjiu tongxun* 清史研究通訊 3 (1988): 17–22.

———. "Qingdai qianqi Heilongjiang xiayu diqu de minzu ji xingzheng guanli" 清代前期黑龍江下淤地區的民族及行政管理 (The extension of administrative control over peoples living along the lower reaches of the Heilongjiang in early Qing). *Zhongguo bianjiang shidi yanjiu* 中國邊疆史地研究 1 (1991): 89–93.

Xu Xiaoguang 徐曉光 and Zhou Jian 周健. "Qingchao zhengfu dui lamajiao li fa chutan" 清朝政府對喇嘛教立法初探 (The establishment of laws regarding Tibetan Buddhism by the Qing government). *Nei Menggu shehui kexue* 內蒙古社會科學 1 (1988): 55–59.

Xu Yang 徐揚. "Huangtaiji xide chuan'guoxi" 皇太極喜得傳國璽 (Hongtaiji joyfully obtains the seal that transmits state legitimacy). *Manzu yanjiu* 滿族研究 3 (1993): 11–12.

Xu Yilin 許以林. "Fengxiandian" 奉先殿 (The hall of the ancestors). *Gugong bowuyuan yuankan* 故宮博物院院刊 1 (1989): 70–76, 48.

Yan Chongnian 閻崇年. *Nuerhachi zhuan* 努爾哈赤傳 (Biography of Nurgaci). Beijing: Beijing chubanshe, 1983.

———. "Kangxi jiao zi" 康熙教子 (Kangxi teaches his sons). In *Qing gong yishi* 清宮軼事, edited by Zheng Yimei 鄭逸梅 et al., 10–13. Beijing: Zijincheng, 1985.

———. "Hou Jin ducheng Fei Ala boyi" 後金都城佛阿拉駁議 (Debates on the Later Jin capital, Fei Ala). *Qingshi yanjiu tongxun* 清史研究通訊 1 (1988): 30–33.

———. "Qingchu sijing yu ducheng sanqian" 清初四京與都城三遷 (The four early Qing capitals and the three moves of the capital). In his *Yanbuji* 燕步集 (Collected writings), 365–93. Beijing: Beijing Yanshan chubanshe, 1989.

———. "Manzhou shen'gan sishen kaoyuan" 滿洲神杆祀神考源 (On the origins of the worship of the Manchu spirit pole). *Lishi dang'an* 歷史檔案 3 (1993): 81–85.

———. "Qingdai gongting yu saman wenhua" 清代宮廷與薩滿文化 (The Qing court and shamanic culture). *Gugong bowuyuan yuankan* 故宮博物院院刊 2 (1993): 55–64.

———. *Tianming han* 天命汗 (Tianming khan). Changchun: Jilin wenshi chubanshe, 1993.

———. "Kangxi huangdi yu Mulan weichang" 康熙皇帝與木蘭圍場 (The Kangxi emperor and the Mulan hunting grounds). *Gugong bowuyuan yuankan* 故宮博物院院刊 2 (1994): 3–13.

Yan Ziyou 晏子有. "Qingchao zongshi fengjue zhidu chutan" 清朝宗室封爵制度初探 (A preliminary discussion of the investiture system of the Qing main descent line). *Hebei xuekan* 河北學刊 5 (1991): 67–74.

Yang, Boda. "A Brief Account of Qing Dynasty Glass." In *The Robert H. Clague Collection, Chinese Glass of the Qing Dynasty, 1644–1911*, edited by Claudia Brown and Donald Rabiner, 71–86. Phoenix: Phoenix Art Museum, 1987.

———. "The Characteristics and Status of Guangdong Handicrafts as Seen from Eighteenth Century Tributes from Guangdong in the Collection of the Former Qing Palace." In *Tributes from Guangdong to the Qing Court*, edited by the Palace Museum, Beijing, and the Art Gallery, the Chinese University of Hong Kong, 39–67. Hong Kong: The Chinese University of Hong Kong, 1987.

———. "Castiglione at the Qing Court—An Important Artistic Contribution." *Orientations* 19, no. 11 (1988): 44–51.

———. "'Qianlong shejian youhua guaping' shukao" 乾隆射箭油畫掛屏述考 (On the hanging oil screen painting of the Qianlong emperor shooting with bow and arrow). *Gugong bowuyuan yuankan* 故宮博物院院刊 1 (1991): 26–38.

Yang, Xin. "Court Painting in the Yongzheng and Qianlong Periods of the Qing Dynasty." In *The Elegant Brush: Chinese Painting Under the Qianlong Emperor, 1735–1795*, edited by Ju-hsi Chou and Claudia Brown, 343–57. Phoenix: Arizona State University, 1985.

Yang Daye 楊大業. "Qinggong Huizu yuyi Zhao Shiying he Liu Yuduo" 清宮回族御醫趙士英和劉裕鐸 (The Muslim physicians Zhao Shiying and Liu Yuduo at the Qing court). *Lishi dang'an* 歷史檔案 4 (1995): 126.

Yang Hongbo 楊洪波. "Qingchu Manzhou guizu jituan neizheng yu huangquan jiaqiang" 清初滿洲貴族集團內爭與皇權加強 (The internal strife among the Manchu nobility in early Qing and the strengthening of the imperial prerogative). *Manzu yanjiu* 滿族研究 2 (1988): 26–31.

Yang Naiji 楊乃濟. "Qianlong Jingcheng quantu kaolüe" 乾隆京城全圖考略 (A brief investigation of the Qianlong-era map of Peking). *Gugong bowuyuan yuankan* 故宮博物院院刊 3 (1984): 8–24.

———. "Qingdi de rumu yu baomu" 清帝的乳母與保母 (The wet-nurses and nurses of the Qing emperors). *Yandu* 燕都 6 (1987): 39–40.

Yang Qiqiao 楊啓樵. "Kangxi yizhao yu Yongzheng cuanwei" 康熙遺詔與雍正篡位 (The Kangxi will and Yongzheng's usurpation). In *Qingshi luncong 1992* 清史論叢, 131–34. Shenyang: Liaoning renmin chubanshe, 1993.

Yang Xuechen 楊學琛. "Qingdai de wang gong zhuangyuan" 清代的王公莊園 (The Qing princely estates). *Shehui kexue jikan* 社會科學輯刊 1 (1980): 81–88; 2 (1980): 75–84.

Yang Xuechen and Zhou Yuanlian 周元廉. *Qingdai baqi wang gong guizu xing shuai shi* 清代八旗王公貴族興衰史 (History of the rise and fall of the Eight Banner nobility of the Qing dynasty). Shenyang: Liaoning renmin chubanshe, 1986.

Yang Zhen 楊珍. "Kangxi wan nian de mimi jianchu jihua" 康熙晚年的秘密建儲計劃 (The plan for a secret succession in the late Kangxi reign). *Gugong bowuyuan yuankan* 故宮博物院院刊 1 (1991): 11–20.

———. "Shunzhi qin bu lingdi yu Yongzheng ling pi lingqu" 順治親卜陵地與雍正另辟陵區 (The Shunzhi emperor personally practiced divination for his mausoleum and Yongzheng opens up a separate cemetery). *Gugong bowuyuan yuankan* 故宮博物院院刊 4 (1992): 78–85.

———. "Yongzheng shazi bianyi" 雍正殺子辨疑 (Evaluating the statement that Yongzheng killed a son). *Qingshi yanjiu* 清史研究 3 (1992): 41–46.

———. "Yunti chujun diwei wenti yanjiu" 允禵儲君地位問題研究 (Research on the problems concerning Yinti's struggle for the succession). In *Qingshi luncong 1992* 清史論叢, 107–22. Shenyang: Liaoning renmin chubanshe, 1993.

———. "Dong'e fei de laili ji qi Dong'e fei zhi si" 董鄂妃的來歷及其董鄂妃之死 (The Dong'e consort's history and her death). *Gugong bowuyuan yuankan* 故宮博物院院刊 1 (1994): 66–73.

———. "Sumalagu yu Kangxi di" 蘇麻喇姑與康熙帝 (Sumalagu and the Kangxi emperor). *Gugong bowuyuan yuankan* 故宮博物院院刊 1 (1995): 34–41.

Yang Zhengguang 楊爭光. *Zhongguo zuihou yige da taijian* 中國最後一個 大太監 (China's last chief eunuch). Beijing: Chunzhong chubanshe, 1990.

Ye Zhiru 葉志如. "Kang, Yong, Qian shiqi xinzheku ren de chengfen ji renshen guanxi" 康雍乾時期辛者庫人的成分及人身關係 (The status and personal relations of *sinjeku* in the Kangxi, Yongzheng, and Qianlong reigns). *Minzu yanjiu* 民族研究 1 (1984): 34–46.

———. "Qianlong shi neifu diandangye gaishu" 乾隆時內府典當業概述 (The pawnshops of the Imperial Household Department in the Qianlong reign). *Lishi dang'an* 歷史檔案 2 (1985): 92–98.

———. "Cong huangshi wangfu nüpu xiaren diwei kan Qingdai shehui de fuxiu moluo" 從皇室王府奴僕下人地位看清代社會的腐朽沒洛 (Examining the rotten decline of Qing society from the personal status of slaves of the princely households). *Gugong bowuyuan yuankan* 故宮博物院院刊 1 (1988): 21–28.

Yee, Cordell D. K. "Traditional Chinese Cartography and the Myth of Westernization." In *The History of Cartography*, edited by J. B. Harley and David Woodward, vol. 2, book 2, 71–95. Chicago: University of Chicago Press, 1994.

Yü, Chün-fang. "Chung-feng Ming-pen and Ch'an Buddhism in the Yüan." In *Yüan Thought: Chinese Thought and Religion Under the Mongols*, edited by Hok-lam Chan and William Theodore de Bary, 419–77. New York: Columbia University Press, 1982.

Yu Bingkun 俞炳坤. "Cixi rugong shijian, shenfen he fenghao" 慈禧入宮時 間, 身份和封號 (When Cixi entered the palace, her background, and her title). In *Xitaihou* 西太后, edited by Yu Bingkun et al., 55–62. Beijing: Zijincheng chubanshe, 1985.

Yu Shanpu 于善浦. *Qing Dongling daguan* 清東陵大觀 (Survey of the Qing eastern cemetery). Shijiazhuang: Hebei renmin chubanshe, 1985.

———. "Cixi de sanjian shouyi" 慈禧的三件壽衣 (Three of Cixi's grave garments). *Zijincheng* 紫禁城 5 (1992): 38.

———. "Daoguang hou fei yuan nü duo" 道光后妃怨女多 (The Daoguang emperor had lots of complaints about his consorts). *Zijincheng* 紫禁城 1 (1994): 18–20.

Yu Zhuoyun, ed. *Palaces of the Forbidden City*. Translated by Ng Mau-sang et al. New York: Viking Press, 1984.

Yuan Hongqi 苑洪琪. "Qing gongting guonian yili" 清宮廷過年儀禮 (The New Year rites at the Qing court). *Yandu* 燕都 1 (1989): 29–30.

———. "Qianlong shiqi de gongting jieqing huodong" 乾隆時期的宮廷節 慶活動 (Celebratory activities at court during the Qianlong period). *Gugong bowuyuan yuankan* 故宮博物院院刊 3 (1991): 26, 81–87.

———. "Qing Qianlong di de changshou yu shanshi" 清乾隆帝的長壽與膳 食 (The Qing emperor Qianlong's longevity and his diet). *Lishi dang'an* 歷 史檔案 4 (1993): 134–35.

Yuan Shenpo 袁燊坡, "Qingdai kouwai xinggong de youlai yu Chengde Bishu shanzhuang de fazhan guocheng" 清代口外行宮的由來與承德避署山 莊的發展過程 (The origins of the summer sojourn outside the pass and the development of the summer villa). *Qingshi luncong* 清史論叢 2 (1980): 286–319.

Zeng Jiabao 曾嘉寶. "Ji feng gong, shu wei ji: Qing Gaozong shiquan wugong de tuxiang jilu—gong chen xiang yu zhantu" 紀豐功, 述偉績: 清高宗十全武功的圖像記錄——功臣像與戰圖 (Record meritorious deeds, relate glorious achievements: on paintings of Qing Gaozong's ten great victories—paintings of meritorious officials and battle scenes). *Gugong wenwu yuekan* 故宮文物月刊 93 (1990): 38–65.

Zhang Bofeng 章伯鋒. *Qingdai gedi jiangjun dutong dachen deng nianbiao* 清代各地將軍都統大臣等年表 (Chronology of those filling the lieutenant generalship and other positions in localities during the Qing). Beijing: Zhonghua shuju, 1977.

Zhang Dexin 張德信. "Mingdai zongshi renkou fenglu ji qi dui shehui jingji de yingxiang" 明代宗室人口俸祿及其對社會經濟的影響 (The population and stipends of the Ming imperial lineage and its influence on the society and economy). *Ming Qing shi yuekan* 明清史月刊 4 (1988): 25–30.

Zhang Deze 張德澤, ed. *Qingdai guojia jiguan kaolüe* 清代國家機關考略 (Brief investigation of state organs during the Qing). Beijing: Renmin daxue chubanshe, 1984.

Zhang Fengrong 張鳳榮 and Yang Huilan 楊惠蘭. "Minghuang zhijin tuolojingbei" 明黃織金陀羅經被 (The yellow and gold embroidered dharani shroud). *Zijincheng* 紫禁城 1 (1992): 27–28.

Zhang Hong 張虹. "Qianlong chao 'Qinding xin Manyu'" 乾隆朝欽定新清語 ('The imperially commissioned new Qing language' of the Qianlong reign). Translated by Cheng Dakun 程大鯤. *Manyu yanjiu* 滿語研究 2 (1993): 79–84, 55, 2 (1994): 68–77, 50; 2 (1995): 51–58.

Zhang Jie 張杰. "Qingchu zhaofu xin Manzhou shulüe" 清初招撫新滿洲述略 (A brief discussion of the pacification of the new Manchus in early Qing times). *Qingshi yanjiu* 清史研究 1 (1994): 23–30.

———. "Qingdai Manzu yuyan wenzi zai dongbei de xingfei yu yingxiang" 清代滿族語言文字在東北的興廢與影響 (The rise, fall, and influence of Manchu writing in the northeast during the Qing). *Beifang wenwu* 北方文物 1 (1995): 63–68.

Zhang Jinfan 張晉藩 and Guo Chengkang 郭成康. *Qing ruguan qian guojia falü zhidu shi* 清入關前國家法律制度史 (The Qing legal system's history before 1644). Shenyang: Liaoning renmin chubanshe, 1988.

Zhang Naiwei 章乃煒. *Qing gong shuwen* 清宮述聞 (Jottings on the Qing palaces). 1937. Reprint. Beijing: Guji chubanshe, 1988. 1st and 2d editions combined. Beijing: Zijincheng chubanshe, 1990.

Zhang Qixiang 張琦翔. "Qianlong di" 潛龍邸 (Future emperors' princely mansions). *Zijincheng* 紫禁城 9 (1981): 22–24.

Zhang Shiyun 張世蕓. "Tongzhi dahun liyi" 同治大婚禮儀 (The wedding rites of the Tongzhi emperor). *Gugong bowuyuan yuankan* 故宮博物院院刊 1 (1992): 41–43.

———. "Qianlong shengmu de jinzhi fata" 乾隆生母的金質髮塔 (The gold

hair stupa of Qianlong's mother). *Lishi dang'an* 歷史檔案 3 (1993): back cover.

―――. "Yipin yuxi miwen" 懿嬪遇喜秘聞 (Consort Yi and the confidential intelligence about her pregnancy). *Lishi dang'an* 歷史檔案 1 (1994): 131–32.

Zhang Wei 張威. "Qingdai Manzu funü de shenghuo" 清代滿族婦女的生活 (The life of Manchu women in the Qing). *Zhongguo dianji yu wenhua* 中國典籍與文化 3 (1994): 76–80.

Zhang Weiguang 張維光. "Mingchao zhengfu zai Hehuang diqu de Zang zhuan Fojiao zhengce shulun" 明朝政府在河湟地區的藏傳佛教政策述略 (Discussion of the Ming government policy on Tibetan Buddhism in the region where the Yellow River bends). *Qinghai shehui kexue* 青海社會科學 2 (1989): 93–96.

Zhang Yongjiang 張永江. "Qingdai baqi Menggu guanxue" 清代八旗蒙古官學 (The official Mongol schools for the Qing banners). *Minzu yanjiu* 民族研究 6 (1990): 96–102.

Zhang Yufen 張玉芬. "Qianlong jianchu shimo" 乾隆建儲始末 (On Qianlong's designation of an heir). *Liaoning shifan daxue xuebao (sheke ban)* 遼寧師範大學學報 (社科版) 2 (1988): 77–82.

―――. "Daoguang jiwei, xuanchu ji" 道光繼位, 選儲記 (The Daoguang succession and selection of an heir). *Zijincheng* 紫禁城 2 (1994): 40–41.

Zhang Yuxin 張羽新. "Qingdai Beijing de Weiwuerzu" 清代北京的維吾爾族 (Uighurs in Peking in the Qing). *Xinjiang shehui kexue* 新疆社會科學 4 (1984): 92–97.

―――. "Nuerhachi dui Mengguzu de zhengce" 努爾哈赤對蒙古族的政策 (Nurgaci's policies toward the Mongols). *Manzu yanjiu* 滿族研究 2 (1988): 21–25.

―――. *Qing zhengfu yu lamajiao* 清政府與喇嘛教 (The Qing government and Tibetan Buddhism). Xuchang: Xizang renmin chubanshe, 1988.

―――. *Qingdai si da huofo* 清代四大活佛 (The four great living Buddhas in the Qing period). Beijing: Renmin daxue chubanshe, 1989.

Zhao, Qiguang. "Dragon: The Symbol of China." *Oriental Art*, n.s., 37, no. 2 (1991): 72–80.

Zhao Kai 趙凱. "Qingdai qigu zuoling kaobian—jianlun youguan Qingdai baoyi de ruogan wenti" 清代旗鼓佐領考辨: 兼論有關清代包衣的若干問題 (On the officer in charge of the flags and drums during the Qing: and on several related issues concerning Qing bondservants). *Gugong bowuyuan yuankan* 故宮博物院院刊 1 (1988): 3–11, 20.

Zhao Shu 趙書. "Yuanmingyuan baqi yingfang shulüe" 圓明園八旗營房述略 (A brief survey of the banner garrison at Yuanmingyuan). *Manzu yanjiu* 滿族研究 4 (1994): 32–35.

Zhao Yi 趙毅. "Mingdai zongshi renkou yu zonglu wenti" 明代宗室人口與宗祿問題 (Issues concerning the Ming imperial clan's population and stipends). *Ming Qing shi yuekan* 明清史月刊 11 (1986): 24–30.

Zhao Yuntian 趙雲田. "Qingdai de 'beizhi efu' zhidu" 清代的備指額駙制度

(The institution for selecting imperial sons-in-law in the Qing). *Gugong bowuyuan yuankan* 故宮博物院院刊 4 (1984): 28–37, 96.

———. *Ming Qing gongting mishi* 明清宮廷秘史 (Secret history of the Ming and Qing courts). Shijiazhuang: Hebei renmin chubanshe, 1985.

———. "Guan yu Qianlong chao neifu chaoben 'Lifanyuan zeli'" 關于乾隆朝內府抄本理藩院則例 (On the Imperial Household Department's ms copy of the Qianlong regulations of the Lifanyuan). *Xibei shidi* 西北史地 2 (1988): 122–25.

———. "'Menggu lüli' he 'Lifanyuan zeli'" 蒙古律例和理藩院則例 (The Mongol law code and the "Regulations for the Court of Colonial Affairs"). *Qingshi yanjiu* 清史研究 3 (1995): 106–10.

Zhao Zhiqiang 趙志强. "Yongzheng chao Junji dachen kaobu" 雍正朝軍機大臣考補 (How grand councillors were examined and replaced during the Yongzheng reign). *Lishi dang'an* 歷史檔案 3 (1991): 93–104.

Zhazha 扎扎. "Shishu Labulengsi yu Qingchao zhongyang zhengfu de guanxi" 試述拉卜楞寺與清朝中央政府的關係 (On Labrang monastery and its relations with the Qing central government). *Xizang yanjiu* 西藏研究 4 (1991): 123–28.

Zheng Lianzhang 鄭連章. *Zijincheng cheng chi* 紫禁城城池 (The walls and moats of the Forbidden City). Beijing: Zijincheng chubanshe, 1986.

Zhongguo diyi lishi dang'anguan 中國第一歷史檔案館. *Qingdai di wang lingqin* 清代帝王陵寢 (The imperial and princely tombs of the Qing dynasty). Beijing: Dang'anguan chubanshe, 1982.

———. "Qingmo bufen baqi dutong luli" 清末部分八旗都統履歷 (Antecedents of some eight banner lieutenant generals in the late Qing). *Lishi dang'an* 歷史檔案 4 (1989): 36–45.

Zhou Suqin 周蘇琴. "Qingdai Shunzhi, Kangxi liangdi zuichu de qingong" 清代順治, 康熙兩帝最初的寢宮 (The earliest sleeping quarters of the Shunzhi and Kangxi emperors). *Gugong bowuyuan yuankan* 故宮博物院院刊 3 (1995): 45–49.

Zhou Xuan 周軒. "Qingdai zongshi juelo liufang renwu shulüe" 清代宗室覺羅流放人物述略 (A brief survey of the Qing imperial kinsmen who were banished). *Gugong bowuyuan yuankan* 故宮博物院院刊 1 (1994): 56–65.

Zhou Yuanlian 周遠廉. "Guanyu shiliu shiji sishi–bashi niandai chu Jianzhou Nüzhen he zaoqi Manzu shehui xingzhi wenti" 關于十六世紀四十–八十年代初建洲女眞和早期滿族社會性質問題 (On the Jianzhou Jurchen and the characteristics of early Manchu society during the 1540s to 1580s). *Qingshi luncong* 清史論叢 1 (1979): 158–76.

———. *Qingchao kaiguoshi yanjiu* 清朝開國史研究 (Studies of the founding of the Qing dynasty). Shenyang: Liaoning renmin chubanshe, 1980.

———. *Qingchao xingqi shi* 清朝興起史 (History of the rise of the Qing dynasty). Changchun: Jilin wenshi chubanshe, 1986.

Zhou Yuanlian and Zhao Shiyu 趙世瑜. *Huangfu shezheng wang Doergun quanzhuan* 皇父攝政王多爾袞全傳 (Biography of Regent Father Dorgon). Changchun: Jilin wenshi chubanshe, 1986.

Zhou Zhifu 周志輔, ed. *Qing Shengpingshu cundang shili manchao* 清昇平署存檔事例漫抄 (Informal draft of surviving archival precedents of the Qing Court Theatrical Bureau). 1933. Reprinted in *Jindai Zhongguo shiliao congkan, Jili ju xiqu congshu, di sizhong* 近代中國史料叢刊, 幾禮居戲曲叢書, 第四種 (Taipei: Wenhai chubanshe, 1971).

Zhu Jiajin 朱家溍. "Gugong suo zang Ming Qing liangdai you guan Xizang de wenwu" 故宮所藏明清兩代有關西藏的文物 (Documents concerning Ming and Qing relations with Tibet stored in the Palace Museum). *Wenwu* 文物 7 (1959): 14–19.

———. "Castiglione's *Tieluo* Paintings." *Orientations* 19, no. 11 (1988): 80–83.

———. "Yongzheng Lacquerware." *Orientations* 19, no. 3 (1988): 28–39.

Zhu Jinfu 朱金甫. "Lun Kangxi shiqi de nanshufang" 論康熙時期的南書房 (On the southern study during the Kangxi era). *Gugong bowuyuan yuankan* 故宮博物院院刊 2 (1990): 27–38.

Zhu Qiqian 朱啓鈐. "Yang Shilei shijia kao" 樣式雷世家考 (On the Yang Shilei hereditary line). In *Yuanmingyuan ziliao ji* 圓明園資料集, edited by Shu Mu 舒牧 et al., 102–104. Beijing: Shumu wenxian chubanshe, 1984.

Zito, Angela. "Grand Sacrifice as Text/Performance: Writing and Ritual in Eighteenth-Century China." Ph.D. diss., University of Chicago, 1989.

———. "The Imperial Birthday: Ritual Encounters Between the Panchen Lama and the Qianlong Emperor in 1780." Presented to the "Conference on State and Ritual in East Asia," organized by the Committee for European/North American Scholarly Cooperation in East Asian Studies, Paris, June 28–July 1, 1995.

Zuo Buqing 左步青. *Kang Yong Qian sandi pingyi* 康雍乾三帝評議 (A critical appraisal of the Kangxi, Yongzheng, and Qianlong emperors). Beijing: Zijincheng chubanshe, 1986.

———. "Qianlong de chuzheng" 乾隆的初政 (The early rule of the Qianlong emperor). *Gugong bowuyuan yuankan* 故宮博物院院刊 4 (1987): 49–59.

———. "Manzhou guizu de shangwu jingshen ji qi minmie" 滿洲貴族的尚武精神及其泯滅 (The martial spirit of the Manchu aristocracy and its extinction). *Gugong bowuyuan yuankan* 故宮博物院院刊 3 (1989): 32–37.

Zuo Shu'e 左書諤. *Cixi taihou* 慈禧太后 (Empress dowager Cixi). Changchun: Jilin wenshi chubanshe, 1993.

Zuo Yunpeng 左雲鵬. "Qingdai qixia nüpu de diwei ji qi bianhua" 清代旗下奴僕的地位及其變化 (The status of banner slaves and its alterations in the Qing). *Shaanxi shi daxuebao* 陝西師大學報 1 (1980): 42–51.

Glossary-Index

Chinese characters are not included below for well-known place names, reign names, titles in the bibliography, and personal names of officials who have biographies in Arthur W. Hummel's *Eminent Chinese of the Ch'ing Period*. M. = Manchu; Mo. = Mongol; T. = Tibetan; italic page numbers indicate illustrations.